BASIC DOCUMENTS ON INTERNATIONAL LAW
AND THE ENVIRONMENT

Basic Documents on International Law and The Environment

P. W. BIRNIE and A. E. BOYLE

CLARENDON PRESS · OXFORD
1995

Oxford University Press, Walton Street, Oxford OX2 6DP
Oxford New York
Athens Auckland Bangkok Bombay
Calcutta Cape Town Dar es Salaam Delhi
Florence Hong Kong Istanbul Karachi
Kuala Lumpur Madras Madrid Melbourne
Mexico City Nairobi Paris Singapore
Taipei Tokyo Toronto
and associated companies in
Berlin Ibadan

Oxford is a trade mark of Oxford University Press

Published in the United States
by Oxford University Press Inc., New York

British Library Cataloguing in Publication Data
Data available

Library of Congress Cataloging in Publication Data
Basic documents on international law and the environment / [collected
by] P.W. Birnie and A.E. Boyle.
p.   cm.
1. Environmental law, International—Sources   2. Environmental
protection—International cooperation.   I. Birnie, Patricia W.
II. Boyle, Alan E.
K3583.B375   1995
341.7'62—dc20   95-20278

ISBN 0–19–876320–4. —ISBN 0–19–876321–2 (pbk)

Typeset by Best-set Typesetter Ltd., Hong Kong
Printed in Great Britain
on acid-free paper by
Biddles Ltd., Guildford and King's Lym

CONTENTS

PREFACE

This collection of treaties and other documents is primarily intended for student use in courses on international environmental law, and not as a comprehensive work of reference. Its contents have been selected for their importance as precedents in the development of international environmental law, or in the case of some of the newer instruments, because they are likely to be of significance in the future. Views will of course differ on what should or should not be included in any selection of this kind. We have concentrated on instruments which are of global scope, but a small number of regional agreements dealing with matters not otherwise regulated globally are also included. We have also tried to reflect the work of the 1992 UN Conference on Environment and Development, and subsequent developments, including the creation of a Commission on Sustainable Development and the restructuring of the Global Environmental Facility. As not all of the instruments reprinted here are treaties and not all of the treaties are in force at the time of writing, readers will have to judge for themselves their current status in international law. They must, of course, be read in conjunction with existing and developing customary international law if a complete picture of international law relating to protection of the environment is to be obtained. For this purpose reference should be made to the same authors' earlier work: *International Law and the Environment* (Oxford University Press, 1992).

Our thanks are due to many people who have provided information and assistance. In particular, we are grateful to Mete Erdem and Johanne Picard for research assistance, to Susan Laroux and Annette Graham for typing the manuscript, to Jon Prater of the Tarlton Law Library of the University of Texas at Austin, to the IUCN Environmental Law Centre, the Foreign Office, and Dr. Gerhard Loibl for information on the status of conventions, and to John Whelan of OUP for his support.

P. W. Birnie
A. E. Boyle
March, 1995.

ABBREVIATIONS

AFDI = Annuaire Français de Droit International
AJIL = American Journal of International Law
Am UJILP = American University Journal of International Law and Policy
Boston Coll. Env. Aff. LR = Boston College Environmental Affairs Law Review
Cal WILJ = California Western Journal of International Law
Case Western Reserve JIL = Case Western Reserve Journal of International Law
CLP = Current Legal Problems
Colorado JIELP = Colorado Journal of International Environmental Law and Policy
CYIL = Canadian Yearbook of International Law
Ecol LQ = Ecology Law Quarterly
EPL = Environmental Policy and Law
ETS = European Treaty Series
Germ YIL = German Yearbook of International Law
Hague YBIL = Hague Yearbook of International Law
Harv ILJ = Harvard International Law Journal
ICLQ = International and Comparative Law Quarterly
ILM = International Legal Materials
JMLC = Journal of Maritime Law and Commerce
LMCLQ = Lloyds Maritime and Commercial Law Quarterly
LNTS = League of Nations Treaty Series
Nat Res J = Natural Resources Journal
Neths YIL = Netherlands Yearbook of International Law
ODIL = Ocean Development and International Law
Proc ASIL = Proceedings of the American Society of International Law
RECIEL = Review of European Community and International Environmental Law
UKTS = United Kingdom Treaty Series
UNTS = United Nations Treaty Series
UST = United States Treaties
Yale JIL = Yale Journal of International Law
YIEL = Yearbook of International Environmental Law
ZAÖRV = Zeitschrift für Ausländisches und Öffentliches Recht und Völkerrecht

1. CODIFICATION AND DEVELOPMENT OF INTERNATIONAL ENVIRONMENTAL LAW

Declaration of the UN Conference on the Human Environment, Stockholm, 5–16 June 1972

The first UN Conference held specifically to consider problems of the environment met at Stockholm in 1972. It was attended by 113 states and adopted a Declaration and an Action Plan. General Assembly resolution 2398 (XXIII) 1968 convening the Conference noted that there was 'an urgent need for intensified action at national and international level to limit and, where possible, to eliminate the impairment of the human environment.' The preparatory committee established by UNGA Resolution 2581 (XXIV) 1969 decided that the Declaration should be 'a document of basic principles calling mankind's urgent attention to the many varied and interrelated problems of the environment, and to draw attention to the rights and obligations of man and state and the international community in regard thereto,' UN Doc. A/CONF. 48/PC/6, para 27 (1970). The Declaration thus fulfils an important inspirational purpose, and is not primarily a legalistic document, nor is it prima facie binding on states. But it does represent in UN practice a formalization used only when principles of special importance are being laid down and 'the general tone is one of a strong sense of dedication to the idea of trying to establish the basic rules of international environmental law' (Sohn, 1973). In that sense, it can be compared to the Universal Declaration of Human Rights adopted by the UN in 1948. However, few of the principles are expressed in the obligatory 'shall' form; most use 'should' or 'must', and there is evident reluctance to couch all principles in the form of clear duties of states. Thus, only a handful are of special legal significance. Principle 1 has had some very limited influence on the protection of environmental rights, mainly in national law, but was completely reformulated in Principle 1 of the 1992 Rio Declaration on Environment and Development (q.v.) Principle 7 is reflected in the subsequent development of the law of the sea, and particularly in Part XII of the 1982 UN Convention on the Law of the Sea. Principle 21 was thought to represent international law at the time of adoption, and has subsequently been referred to as such in UNGA Resolution 2996 (XXVII) 1972 and in a number of multilateral environmental treaties. It constitutes a basic principle of contemporary international environmental law and reappears in modified form in the 1992 Rio Declaration. Principle 22 has had limited effect, mainly in national law, and is reiterated in the 1992 Rio Declaration. No agreement could be reached on the proposed inclusion of an article dealing with notification and consultation in cases of transboundary risk from proposed activities, and this was instead the subject of UNGA Resolution 2995 (XXVII) 1972.

The full Report of the Conference together with the much more detailed Action Plan is found in UN Doc. A/CONF. 48/14/REV. 1 (1972). *Reports of the Preparatory Committee* relevant to the Declaration are in the series UN Doc. A/CONF. 48/PC 9, 13 and 17. *The Final Report of the Working Group on the Declaration* is in UN Doc. A/Conf. 48/14/Rev. 1/Annex II. On the Declaration see in particular L. B. Sohn, 'The Stockholm Declaration on the Human Environment', 14 *Harv. ILJ* (1973), 423, and generally, S. C. McCaffrey, G. Handl, H. Taubenfeld, 'Ten Years After Stockholm: International Environmental Law: A Panel', 77 *Proc. ASIL* (1983), 411;

L. K. Caldwell, *International Environmental Policy* (2nd edn., Durham, N. C., 1990), Chs. 2 and 3; P. W. Birnie and A. E. Boyle, *International Law and the Environment* (Oxford, 1992) 39ff.

TEXT

The United Nations Conference on the Human Environment,

Having met at Stockholm from 5 to 16 June 1972,

Having considered the need for a common outlook and for common principles to inspire and guide the peoples of the world in the preservation and enhancement of the human environment,

I

Proclaim that:

1. Man is both creature and moulder of his environment, which gives him physical sustenance and affords him the opportunity for intellectual, moral, social and spiritual growth. In the long and tortuous evolution of the human race on this planet a stage has been reached when, through the rapid acceleration of science and technology, man has acquired the power to transform his environment in countless ways and on an unprecedented scale. Both aspects of man's environment, the natural and the man-made, are essential to his well-being and to the enjoyment of basic human rights—even the right to life itself.

2. The protection and improvement of the human environment is a major issue which affects the well-being of peoples and economic development throughout the world; it is the urgent desire of the peoples of the whole world and the duty of all Governments.

3. Man has constantly to sum up experience and go on discovering, inventing, creating and advancing. In our time, man's capability to transform his surroundings, if used wisely, can bring to all peoples the benefits of development and the opportunity to enhance the quality of life. Wrongly or heedlessly applied, the same power can do incalculable harm to human beings and the human environment. We see around us growing evidence of man-made harm in many regions of the earth: dangerous levels of pollution in water, air, earth and living beings; major and undesirable disturbances to the ecological balance of the biosphere; destruction and depletion of irreplaceable resources; and gross deficiences harmful to the physical, mental and social health of man, in the man-made environment, particularly in the living and working environment.

4. In the developing countries most of the environmental problems are caused by under-development. Millions continue to live far below

the minimum levels required for a decent human existence, deprived of adequate food and clothing, shelter and education, health and sanitation. Therefore, the developing countries must direct their efforts to development, bearing in mind their priorities and the need to safeguard and improve the environment. For the same purpose, the industrialized countries should make efforts to reduce the gap between themselves and the developing countries. In the industrialized countries, environmental problems are generally related to industrialization and technological development.

5. The natural growth of population continuously presents problems on the preservation of the environment, and adequate policies and measures should be adopted, as appropriate, to face these problems. Of all things in the world, people are the most precious. It is the people that propel social progress, create social wealth, develop science and technology and, through their hard work, continuously transform the human environment. Along with social progress and the advance of production, science and technology, the capability of man to improve the environment increases with each passing day.

6. A point has been reached in history when we must shape our actions throughout the world with a more prudent care for their environmental consequences. Through ignorance or indifference we can do massive and irreversible harm to the earthly environment on which our life and well-being depend. Conversely, through fuller knowledge and wiser action, we can achieve for ourselves and our posterity a better life in an environment more in keeping with human needs and hopes. There are broad vistas for the enhancement of environmental quality and the creation of a good life. What is needed is an enthusiastic but calm state of mind and intense but orderly work. For the purpose of attaining freedom in the world of nature, man must use knowledge to build, in collaboration with nature, a better environment. To defend and improve the human environment for present and future generations has become an imperative goal for mankind—a goal to be pursued together with, and in harmony with, the established and fundamental goals of peace and of world-wide economic and social development.

7. To achieve this environmental goal will demand the acceptance of responsibility by citizens and communities and by enterprises and institutions at every level, all sharing equitably in common efforts. Individuals in all walks of life as well as organizations in many fields, by their values and the sum of their actions will shape the world environment of the future. Local and national governments will bear the greatest burden for large-scale environmental policy and action within their jurisdictions. International co-operation is also needed in order to raise resources to support the developing countries in carrying out their responsibilities in this field. A growing class of environmental problems, because they are regional or

global in extent or because they affect the common international realm, will require extensive co-operation among nations and action by international organizations in the common interest. The Conference calls upon Governments and peoples to exert common efforts for the preservation and improvement of the human environment, for the benefit of all the people and for their posterity.

II
Principles

States the common conviction that:

Principle 1

Man has the fundamental right to freedom, equality and adequate conditions of life, in an environment of a quality that permits a life of dignity and well-being, and he bears a solemn responsibility to protect and improve the environment for present and future generations. In this respect, policies promoting or perpetuating *apartheid*, racial segregation, discrimination, colonial and other forms of oppression and foreign domination stand condemned and must be eliminated.

Principle 2

The natural resources of the earth including the air, water, land, flora and fauna and especially representative samples of natural ecosystems must be safeguarded for the benefit of present and future generations through careful planning or management, as appropriate.

Principle 3

The capacity of the earth to produce vital renewable resources must be maintained and, wherever practicable, restored or improved.

Principle 4

Man has a special responsibility to safeguard and wisely manage the heritage of wildlife and its habitat which are now gravely imperilled by a combination of adverse factors. Nature conservation including wildlife must therefore receive importance in planning for economic development.

Principle 5

The non-renewable resources of the earth must be employed in such a way as to guard against the danger of their future exhaustion and to ensure that benefits from such employment are shared by all mankind.

Principle 6

The discharge of toxic substances or of other substances and the release of heat, in such quantities or concentrations as to exceed the capacity of the environment to render them harmless, must be halted in order to ensure that serious or irreversible damage is not inflicted upon ecosystems. The just struggle of the peoples of all countries against pollution should be supported.

Principle 7

States shall take all possible steps to prevent pollution of the seas by substances that are liable to create hazards to human health, to harm living resources and marine life, to damage amenities or to interfere with other legitimate uses of the sea.

Principle 8

Economic and social development is essential for ensuring a favour-able living and working environment for man and for creating condi-tions on earth that are necessary for the improvement of the quality of life.

Principle 9

Environmental deficiencies generated by the conditions of underdevelop-ment and natural disasters pose grave problems and can best be remedied by accelerated development through the transfer of substantial quantities of financial and technological assistance as a supplement to the domestic effort of the developing countries and such timely assistance as may be required.

Principle 10

For the developing countries, stability of prices and adequate earnings for primary commodities and raw material are essential to environmental man-agement since economic factors as well as ecological processes must be taken into account.

Principle 11

The environmental policies of all States should enhance and not adversely affect the present or future development potential of developing countries, nor should they hamper the attainment of better living conditions for all, and appropriate steps should be taken by States and international organiz-ations with a view to reaching agreement on meeting the possible national and international economic consequences resulting from the application of environmental measures.

Principle 12

Resources should be made available to preserve and improve the environment, taking into account the circumstances and particular requirements of developing countries and any costs which may emanate from their incorporating environmental safeguards into their development planning and the need for making available to them, upon their request, additional international technical and financial assistance for this purpose.

Principle 13

In order to achieve a more rational management of resources and thus to improve the environment, States should adopt an integrated and co-ordinated approach to their development planning so as to ensure that development is compatible with the need to protect and improve the human environment for the benefit of their population.

Principle 14

Rational planning constitutes an essential tool for reconciling any conflict between the needs of development and the need to protect and improve the environment.

Principle 15

Planning must be applied to human settlements and urbanization with a view to avoiding adverse effects on the environment and obtaining maximum social, economic and environmental benefits for all. In this respect projects which are designed for colonialist and racist domination must be abandoned.

Principle 16

Demographic policies, which are without prejudice to basic human rights and which are deemed appropriate by Governments concerned, should be applied in those regions where the rate of population growth or excessive population concentrations are likely to have adverse effects on the environment or development, or where low population density may prevent improvement of the human environment and impede development.

Principle 17

Appropriate national institutions must be entrusted with the task of planning, managing or controlling the environmental resources of States with the view to enhancing environmental quality.

Principle 18

Science and technology, as part of their contribution to economic and social development, must be applied to the identification, avoidance and control of environmental risks and the solution of environmental problems and for the common good of mankind.

Principle 19

Education in environmental matters, for the younger generation as well as adults, giving due consideration to the underprivileged, is essential in order to broaden the basis for an enlightened opinion and responsible conduct by individuals, enterprises and communities in protecting and improving the environment in its full human dimension. It is also essential that mass media of communications avoid contributing to the deterioration of the environment, but, on the contrary, disseminate information of an educational nature, on the need to protect and improve the environment in order to enable man to develop in every respect.

Principle 20

Scientific research and development in the context of environmental problems, both national and multinational, must be promoted in all countries, especially the developing countries. In this connexion, the free flow of up-to-date scientific information and transfer of experience must be supported and assisted, to facilitate the solution of environmenal problems; environmental technologies should be made available to developing countries on terms which would encourage their wide dissemination without constituting an economic burden on the developing countries.

Principle 21

States have, in accordance with the Charter of the United Nations and the principles of international law, the sovereign right to exploit their own resources pursuant to their own environmental policies, and the responsibility to ensure that activities within their jurisdiction or control do not cause damage to the environment of other States or of areas beyond the limits of national jurisdiction.

Principle 22

States shall co-operate to develop further the international law regarding liability and compensation for the victims of pollution and other environmental damage caused by activities within the jurisdiction or control of such States to areas beyond their jurisdiction.

Principle 23

Without prejudice to such criteria as may be agreed upon by the international community, or to standards which will have to be determined nationally, it will be essential in all cases to consider the systems of values prevailing in each country, and the extent of the applicability of standards which are valid for the most advanced countries but which may be inappropriate and of unwarranted social cost for the developing countries.

Principle 24

International matters concerning the protection and improvement of the environment should be handled in a co-operative spirit by all countries, big or small, on an equal footing. Co-operation through multilateral or bilateral arrangements or other appropriate means is essential to effectively control, prevent, reduce and eliminate adverse environmental effects resulting from activities conducted in all spheres, in such a way that due account is taken of the sovereignty and interests of all States.

Principle 25

States shall ensure that international organizations play a co-ordinated, efficient and dynamic role for the protection and improvement of the environment.

Principle 26

Man and his environment must be spared the effects of nuclear weapons and all other means of mass destruction. States must strive to reach prompt agreement, in the relevant international organs, on the elimination and complete destruction of such weapons.

Declaration of the UN Conference on Environment and Development, Rio de Janeiro, 3–14 June 1992

Twenty years after the seminal Stockholm Conference, a second major UN conference, this time on environment *and* development, met at Rio in 1992 and adopted a Declaration on Environment and Development, a programme of action (Agenda 21), the Conventions on Biological Diversity (q.v.), and Climate Change (q.v.), and a Non-Binding Statement of Consensus on Forest Principles. UNGA Resolution 44/228 (1989), which convened the Conference, included within its mandate the further development of international environmental law and an examination of the feasibility of elaborating 'general rights and obligations of states, as appropriate, in the field of the environment, and taking into account existing legal instruments.' The text reproduced here was subsequently endorsed by the General Assembly in Resolution 47/190 (1992). Resolution 47/191 (1992) (q.v.), which establishes the Commission on Sustainable Development, requires it to promote incorporation of the principles of the Declaration in the implementation of Agenda 21. Resolution 48/190 (1993) also urges governments to promote dissemination of these principles in the public and private sectors and requests the Secretary-General to ensure that the UN system incorporates them in its 'programmes and processes'.

Like the Stockholm Declaration, the Rio Declaration is not formally binding, but its adoption by a consensus of 176 states, after a prolonged negotiating process, and its normative character, make it a particularly important example of the use of soft law instruments in the process of codification and development of international law. Although, in the preamble, the Stockholm Declaration is reaffirmed, in certain respects some of the earlier Stockholm Principles have been modified (Principle 21) or weakened (Principle 1). But the Rio Declaration also introduces important new principles, including precautionary action, environmental impact assessment, the polluter pays principle, and public participation, which had not previously secured such widespread support, but which have gradually become more widely evidenced in treaties and state practice. Moreover, the inclusion of principles dealing with notification of emergencies and prior notification and consultation in cases of transboundary risk reflect the development of customary law since 1972. The Declaration as a whole thus goes significantly beyond what could be achieved at Stockholm and can be seen in part as a codification of existing and emerging principles of international law concerning the environment. The document as finally drafted nevertheless represents a delicate balance between proposals from developed states for a more overtly ecological 'Earth Charter', affirming global principles for promoting the integration of environment and development, and the concerns of developing states that their developmental priorities and 'differentiated responsibility' should be recognised in a more anthropocentric document. On adoption of the Declaration the United States of America made an interpretative statement expressing reservations to Principles 3, 7, 12 and 23, UN Doc. A/CONF. 151/26, Vol. IV., para 16.

For *Reports of the Preparatory Committee*, see UN Doc. A/CONF. 151/PC/L. 31, Annex (1991); A/CONF. 151/PC/78 (1991); A/CONF.151/PC/WG. III.2 (1991); A/CONF. 151/PC/WG III/L5, L6, L8/Rev. 1 (1991), and L.20–L.28 (1992). For the text of the accompanying Agenda 21, see *Report of the UN Conference on Environment and Development*, UN Doc. A/CONF. 151/26/REV. 1, Vols. I–III (1992).

On the Declaration, see P. Sand, 'International Law on the Agenda of the UN

Conference on Environment and Development', 3 *Colorado J. of IELP* (1992) 1; *id*, 'UNCED and the Development of International Environmental Law', 3 *YBIEL* (1992) 3; H. Mann, 'The Rio Declaration', *Proc. ASIL* (1992) 405; and generally, G. Handl, 'Environmental Security and Global Change: The Challenge to International Law', 1 *YBIEL* (1990) 3; P. M. Dupuy, 'Soft Law and the International Law of the Environment', 12 *Mich. JIL* (1991) 420; S. Johnson (ed.), *The Earth Summit* (London, 1991); Sir G. Palmer, New Ways to Make International Environmental Law, 86 *AJIL* (1992) 259; M. Pallemaerts, in P. Sands (ed.), *The Greening of International Law* (London, 1994), Ch. 1; A. Adede, 'International Environmental Law from Stockholm to Rio—An Overview of Past Lessons and Future Challenges', 22 *EPL* (1992) 88; G. Biggs, H. Mann, and L. Kimball, 'Issues Relating to the 1992 Brazil Conference on the Environment', 86 *Proc. ASIL* (1992) 401; M. Jahnke, 'UNCED—Rio Conference on Environment and Development', 22 *EPL* (1992) 204; R. Panjabi, 'Idealism and Self Interest in International Environmental Law: The Rio Dilemma', 23 *Cal. WILJ* (1992) 177; various authors, 'United Nations Conference on Environment and Development', 4 *Col. JIELP* (1993) 1–215.

TEXT

Preamble

The United Nations Conference on Environment and Development,

Having met at Rio de Janeiro from 3 to 14 June 1992,

Reaffirming the Declaration of the United Nations Conference on the Human Environment, adopted at Stockholm on 16 June 1972, and seeking to build upon it,

With the goal of establishing a new and equitable global partnership through the creation of new levels of cooperation among States, key sectors of societies and people,

Working towards international agreements which respect the interests of all and protect the integrity of the global environmental and developmental system,

Recognizing the integral and interdependent nature of the Earth, our home,

Proclaims that:

Principle 1

Human beings are at the centre of concerns for sustainable development. They are entitled to a healthy and productive life in harmony with nature.

Principle 2

States have, in accordance with the Charter of the United Nations and the principles of international law, the sovereign right to exploit their own resources pursuant to their own environmental and developmental policies, and the responsibility to ensure that activities within their jurisdiction or control do not cause damage to the environment of other States or of areas beyond the limits of national jurisdiction.

Principle 3

The right to development must be fulfilled so as to equitably meet developmental and environmental needs of present and future generations.

Principle 4

In order to achieve sustainable development, environmental protection shall constitute an integral part of the development process and cannot be considered in isolation from it.

Principle 5

All States and all people shall cooperate in the essential task of eradicating poverty as an indispensable requirement for sustainable development, in order to decrease the disparities in standards of living and better meet the needs of the majority of the people of the world.

Principle 6

The special situation and needs of developing countries, particularly the least developed and those most environmentally vulnerable, shall be given special priority. International actions in the field of environment and development should also address the interests and needs of all countries.

Principle 7

States shall cooperate in a spirit of global partnership to conserve, protect and restore the health and integrity of the Earth's ecosystem. In view of the different contributions to global environmental degradation, States have common but differentiated responsibilities. The developed countries acknowledge the responsibility that they bear in the international pursuit of sustainable development in view of the pressures their societies place on the global environment and of the technologies and financial resources they command.

Principle 8

To achieve sustainable development and a higher quality of life for all people, States should reduce and eliminate unsustainable patterns of production and consumption and promote appropriate demographic policies.

Principle 9

States should cooperate to strengthen endogenous capacity-building for sustainable development by improving scientific understanding through exchanges of scientific and technological knowledge, and by enhancing the development, adaptation, diffusion and transfer of technologies, including new and innovative technologies.

Principle 10

Environmental issues are best handled with the participation of all concerned citizens, at the relevant level. At the national level, each individual
shall have appropriate access to information concerning the environment
that is held by public authorities, including information on hazardous
materials and activities in their communities, and the opportunity to participate in decision-making processes. States shall facilitate and encourage
public awareness and participation by making information widely available.
Effective access to judicial and administrative proceedings, including redress and remedy, shall be provided.

Principle 11

States shall enact effective environmental legislation. Environmental standards, management objectives and priorities should reflect the environmental and developmental context to which they apply. Standards applied by
some countries may be inappropriate and of unwarranted economic and
social cost to other countries, in particular developing countries.

Principle 12

States should cooperate to promote a supportive and open international
economic system that would lead to economic growth and sustainable
development in all countries, to better address the problems of environmental degradation. Trade policy measures for environmental purposes
should not constitute a means of arbitrary or unjustifiable discrimination or
a disguised restriction on international trade. Unilateral actions to deal
with environmental challenges outside the jurisdiction of the importing
country should be avoided. Environmental measures addressing transboundary or global environmental problems should, as far as possible, be based
on an international consensus.

Principle 13

States shall develop national law regarding liability and compensation for
the victims of pollution and other environmental damage. States shall also
cooperate in an expeditious and more determined manner to develop
further international law regarding liability and compensation for adverse
effects of environmental damage caused by activities within their jurisdiction or control to areas beyond their jurisdiction.

Principle 14

States should effectively cooperate to discourage or prevent the re-
location and transfer to other States of any activities and substances that
cause severe environmental degradation or are found to be harmful to
human health.

Principle 15

In order to protect the environment, the precautionary approach shall be widely applied by States according to their capabilities. Where there are threats of serious or irreversible damage, lack of full scientific certainty shall not be used as a reason for postponing cost-effective measures to prevent environmental degradation.

Principle 16

National authorities should endeavour to promote the internalization of environmental costs and the use of economic instruments, taking into account the approach that the polluter should, in principle, bear the cost of pollution, with due regard to the public interest and without distorting international trade and investment.

Principle 17

Environmental impact assessment, as a national instrument, shall be undertaken for proposed activities that are likely to have a significant adverse impact on the environment and are subject to a decision of a competent national authority.

Principle 18

States shall immediately notify other States of any natural disasters or other emergencies that are likely to produce sudden harmful effects on the environment of those States. Every effort shall be made by the international community to help States so afflicted.

Principle 19

States shall provide prior and timely notification and relevant information to potentially affected States on activities that may have a significant adverse transboundary environmental effect and shall consult with those States at an early stage and in good faith.

Principle 20

Women have a vital role in environmental management and development. Their full participation is therefore essential to achieve sustainable development.

Principle 21

The creativity, ideals and courage of the youth of the world should be mobilized to forge a global partnership in order to achieve sustainable development and ensure a better future for all.

Principle 22

Indigenous people and their communities, and other local communities, have a vital role in environmental management and development because of their knowledge and traditional practices. States should recognize and duly support their identity, culture and interests and enable their effective participation in the achievement of sustainable development.

Principle 23

The environment and natural resources of people under oppression, domination and occupation shall be protected.

Principle 24

Warfare is inherently destructive of sustainable development. States shall therefore respect international law providing protection for the environment in times of armed conflict and cooperate in its further development, as necessary.

Principle 25

Peace, development and environmental protection are interdependent and indivisible.

Principle 26

States shall resolve all their environmental disputes peacefully and by appropriate means in accordance with the Charter of the United Nations.

Principle 27

States and people shall cooperate in good faith and in a spirit of partnership in the fulfilment of the principles embodied in this Declaration and in the further development of international law in the field of sustainable development.

World Charter for Nature, 28 October 1982

The World Charter is an example of the use of 'soft law' principles, the status of which can only be assessed by monitoring their adoption into national and international practice. Following the 1972 Stockholm Conference, the International Union for Conservation of Nature (IUCN) perceived the need for general recognition at the international level of principles against which human management of nature and natural resources could be evaluated. A draft Charter was prepared by an international group of experts following a proposal made by Zaire and adopted at the IUCN Twelfth General Assembly in September 1975. In 1980, again on the initiative of Zaire, the UN General Assembly sought the views of Member States on the draft Charter. The proposal proved controversial though it was strongly supported by a meeting of the Non-aligned States held in 1980 and by the Council of Ministers of the Organisation of African Unity in 1981. Fifty States responded to the General Assembly's request, including Australia, Canada, France, Japan, and the Soviet Union, but not the United States of America. On 28 October 1982 the Charter was adopted by General Assembly Resolution 37/7, *repr.* 22 *ILM* (1983) 455; 37 UNGAOR Supp. No. 51, (1982), at 17, by a majority of 111 votes to 1 (USA) with 18 abstentions, which included the eight signatories of the Treaty for Amazonian Co-operation (17 *ILM* (1978), 1045), who stressed their permanent sovereignty over their natural resources.

The Charter is addressed to individuals as well as States. Though formulated in mandatory terms, the generality of its provisions suggests that some articles constitute little more than policy guidelines. Nevertheless, Article 14 requires that the principles set forth in the Charter 'shall be reflected in the law and practice of each State, as well as at the international level', and Article 24 states that 'each person has a duty to act in accordance with the provisions of the present Charter; acting individually, and in association with others or through participating in the political process, each person shall strive to ensure that the objectives and requirements of the present Charter are met'. Moreover the Charter's 'General Principles' and Articles 10–12 and 21–3 must now be read in the light of developments in international law, including adoption of the Rio Declaration (q.v.) and the Convention on Biological Diversity (q.v.). A report on preparation of the Charter is found in *Consideration and Adoption of the Revised Draft World Charter for Nature: Report of the Secretary-General,* 37/UN GAOR, UN Doc. A/398 (1982). On the Charter, see in particular W. Burhenne and W. Irwin, *The World Charter for Nature: A Background Paper* (Berlin, 1983); La 'Charte de la Nature', M. Rémond-Gouillous, 2 *Rev. jurid. de l'env.* (1982) 120–4: H.W. Wood, 'The UN World Charter for Nature', 12 *Ecol. LQ* (1985) 981ff; P. W. Birnie and A. E. Boyle, *International Law and the Environment* (Oxford, 1992), 431ff; L. Caldwell, *International Environmental Policy* (2nd edn., Durham N. C., 1990), 90–93.

TEXT

The General Assembly,

Reaffirming the fundamental purposes of the United Nations, in particular the maintenance of international peace and security, the development of friendly relations among nations and the achievement of international co-operation in solving international problems of an economic, social, cultural, technical, intellectual or humanitarian character,

Aware that:

(a) Mankind is a part of nature and life depends on the uninterrupted functioning of natural systems which ensure the supply of energy and nutrients,

(b) Civilization is rooted in nature, which has shaped human culture and influenced all artistic and scientific achievement, and living in harmony with nature gives man the best opportunities for the development of his creativity, and for rest and recreation,

Convinced that:

(a) Every form of life is unique, warranting respect regardless of its worth to man, and, to accord other organisms such recognition, man must be guided by a moral code of action,

(b) Man can alter nature and exhaust natural resources by his action or its consequences and, therefore, must fully recognize the urgency of maintaining the stability and quality of nature and of conserving natural resources,

Persuaded that:

(a) Lasting benefits from nature depend upon the maintenance of essential ecological processes and life support systems, and upon the diversity of life forms, which are jeopardized through excessive exploitation and habitat destruction by man,

(b) The degradation of natural systems owing to excessive consumption and misuse of natural resources, as well as to failure to establish an appropriate economic order among peoples and among States, leads to the breakdown of the economic, social and political framework of civilization,

(c) Competition for scarce resources creates conflicts, whereas the conservation of nature and natural resources contributes to justice and the maintenance of peace and cannot be achieved until mankind learns to live in peace and to forsake war and armaments,

Reaffirming that man must acquire the knowledge to maintain and enhance his ability to use natural resources in a manner which ensures the preservation of the species and ecosystems for the benefit of present and future generations,

Firmly convinced of the need for appropriate measures, at the national and international, individual and collective, and private and public levels, to protect nature and promote international co-operation in this field,

Adopts, to these ends, the present World Charter for Nature, which proclaims the following principles of conservation by which all human conduct affecting nature is to be guided and judged.

I. General Principles

1. Nature shall be respected and its essential processes shall not be impaired.

2. The genetic viability on the earth shall not be compromised, the population levels of all life forms, wild and domesticated, must be at least sufficient for their survival, and to this end necessary habitats shall be safeguarded.

3. All areas of the earth, both land and sea, shall be subject to these principles of conservation, special protection shall be given to unique areas, to representative samples of all the different types of ecosystems and to the habitats of rare or endangered species.

4. Ecosystems and organisms, as well as the land, marine and atmospheric resources that are utilized by man, shall be managed to achieve and maintain optimum sustainable productvity, but not in such a way as to endanger the integrity of those other ecosystems or species with which they coexist.

5. Nature shall be secured against degradation caused by warfare or other hostile activities.

II. Functions

6. In the decision-making process it shall be recognized that man's needs can be met only by ensuring the proper functioning of natural systems and by respecting the principles set forth in the present Charter.

7. In the planning and implementation of social and economic development activities, due account shall be taken of the fact that the conservation of nature is an integral part of those activities.

8. In formulating long-term plans for economic development, population growth and the improvement of standards of living, due account shall be taken of the long-term capacity of natural systems to ensure the subsistence and settlement of the populations concerned, recognizing that this capacity may be enhanced through science and technology.

9. The allocation of areas of the earth to various uses shall be planned, and due account shall be taken of the physical constraints, the biological productivity and diversity and the natural beauty of the areas concerned.

10. Natural resources shall not be wasted, but used with a restraint

appropriate to the principles set forth in the present Charter, in accordance with the following rules:

  (a) Living resources shall not be utilized in excess of their natural capacity for regeneration;
  (b) The productivity of soils shall be maintained or enhanced through measures which safeguard their long-term fertility and the process of organic de-composition, and prevent erosion and all other forms of degradation;
  (c) Resources, including water, which are not consumed as they are used shall be reused or recycled;
  (d) Non-renewable resources which are consumed as they are used shall be exploited with restraint, taking into account their abundance, the rational possibilities of converting them for consumption, and the compatibility of their exploitation with the functioning of natural systems.

11. Activities which might have an impact on nature shall be controlled, and the best available technologies that minimize significant risks to nature or other adverse effects shall be used, in particular:

  (a) Activities which are likely to cause irreversible damage to nature shall be avoided;
  (b) Activities which are likely to pose a significant risk to nature shall be preceded by an exhaustive examination; their proponents shall demonstrate that expected benefits outweigh potential damage to nature, and where potential adverse effects are not fully understood, the activities should not proceed;
  (c) Activities which may disturb nature shall be preceded by assessment of their consequences, and environmental impact studies of development projects shall be conducted sufficiently in advance, and if they are to be undertaken, such activities shall be planned and carried out so as to minimize potential adverse effects;
  (d) Agriculture, grazing, forestry and fisheries practices shall be adapted to the natural characteristics and constraints of given areas;
  (e) Areas degraded by human activities shall be rehabilitated for purposes in accord with their natural potential and compatible with the well-being of affected populations.

12. Discharge of pollutants into natural systems shall be avoided and:

  (a) Where this is not feasible, such pollutants shall be treated at the source, using the best practicable means available;
  (b) Special precautions shall be taken to prevent discharge of radio-active or toxic wastes.

13. Measure intended to prevent, control or limit natural disasters, infes-

tations and diseases shall be specifically directed to the causes of these scourges and shall avoid adverse side-effects on nature.

III. Implementation

14. The principles set forth in the present Charter shall be reflected in the law and practice of each State, as well as at the international level.

15. Knowledge of nature shall be broadly disseminated by all possible means, particularly by ecological education as an integral part of general education.

16. All planning shall include, among its essential elements, the formulation of strategies for the conservation of nature, the establishment of inventories of ecosystems and assessments of the effects on nature of proposed policies and activities; all of these elements shall be disclosed to the public by appropriate means in time to permit effective consultation and participation.

17. Funds, programmes and administrative structures necessary to achieve the objective of the conservation of nature shall be provided.

18. Constant efforts shall be made to increase knowledge of nature by scientific research and to disseminate such knowledge unimpeded by restrictions of any kind.

19. The status of natural processes, ecosystems and species shall be closely monitored to enable early detection of degradation or threat, ensure timely intervention and facilitate the evaluation of conservation policies and methods.

20. Military activities damaging to nature shall be avoided.

21. States and, to the extent they are able, other public authorities, international organizations, individuals, groups and corporations shall:

(a) Co-operate in the task of conserving nature through common activities and other relevant actions, including information exchange and consultations;

(b) Establish standards for products and manufacturing processes that may have adverse effects on nature, as well as agreed methodologies for assessing these effects;

(c) Implement the applicable international legal provisions for the conservation of nature and the protection of the environment;

(d) Ensure that activities within their jurisdictions or control do not cause damage to the natural systems located within other States or in the areas beyond the limits of national jurisdiction;

(e) Safeguard and conserve nature in areas beyond national jurisdiction.

22. Taking fully into account the sovereignty of States over their natural resources, each State shall give effect to the provisions of the present

Charter through its competent organs and in co-operation with other States.

23. All persons, in accordance with their national legislation, shall have the opportunity to participate, individually or with others, in the formulation of decisions of direct concern to their environment, and shall have access to means of redress when their environment has suffered damage or degradation.

24. Each person has a duty to act in accordance with the provisions of the present Charter; acting individually, in association with others or through participation in the political process, each person shall strive to ensure that the objectives and requirements of the present Charter are met.

UNEP Principles on Conservation and Harmonious Utilization of Natural Resources Shared by Two or More States, 19 May 1978

A succession of UN General Assembly resolutions has recognized the need for states to exercise their sovereignty over shared natural resources with due regard for other states and to co-operate in their use. Following recommendations of the 1972 Stockholm Conference on the Human Environment, UNGA Resolution 3129 (XXVIII) 1973, called for adequate international standards for the conservation and utilization of natural resources common to two or more states to be established, and affirmed that there should be co-operation between states on the basis of information exchange and prior consultation. It called for UNEP to report on implementation of the resolution. Article 3 of the Charter of Economic Rights and Duties of States, UNGA Resolution 3281 (XXIX) 1974, sets out the same principle more fully: 'In the exploitation of natural resources shared by two or more countries, each state must cooperate on the basis of a system of information and prior consultation in order to achieve optimum use of such resources without causing damage to the legitimate interests of others.' These resolutions formed the basis for the adoption by the UN Environment Programme's Governing Council of the Principles on Conservation and Harmonious Utilization of Natural Resources Shared by Two or More States. However, several states, including Brazil, Mexico, Colombia, and Spain, were either unable to join in the consensus, or expressed reservations. Moreover, the language of the document explicitly avoids the implication that there are existing legal obligations and disavows any intention to incorporate new principles into the body of general international law. The General Assembly was reluctant to give the Principles its full endorsement, and, in Resolution 34/186 (1979), merely 'took note' of them, including the explanatory statement that they were 'without prejudice to the binding nature of those rules already recognized as such in international law', but it did call on states to use them as 'guidelines and recommendations' in the formulation of bilateral and multilateral conventions. This use of principles which are expressed in a non-binding form and in very general terms stems from the controversy and opposition that earlier UN resolutions on the subject had aroused, and does indicate that they cannot necessarily be regarded as settled law nor as enjoying the support of all states. In this sense, they are at best an example of the 'soft law' form favoured by UNEP when a binding treaty would be inappropriate or unattainable. Nevertheless, that in many important respects the Principles do reflect international law and the practice of a significant number of states can be observed in the 1992 Rio Convention on Biological Diversity (q.v.), in the Rio Declaration on Environment and Development (q.v.), and in the ILC's Draft Articles on Non-Navigational Uses of International Watercourses (q.v.). UNEP's Principles also adopt a well-established principle of international law in relying on equitable utilization as the basis of co-operation. Continued opposition to the concept of 'shared natural resources', however, has led to the removal of all reference to it in the work of the ILC on international watercourses. Moreover, the most notable omission from the Principles and from the UN resolutions concerns their failure to define which resources should be treated as shared, although the Executive Director's Report, UNEP/GC/44 (1975), para 86, indicates that at least the following should be included: river systems, enclosed and semi-enclosed seas, air sheds, mountain chains, forests, conservation areas, and migratory species.

For consideration of the draft principles, see *Report of the Governing Council of the UNEP*, 6th Session, UNEP/GC.1/L.6/Add. 5 (1978); *Reports of the Intergovernmental*

Working Group of Experts on Natural Resources Shared by Two or More States, 1st Session, UNEP/GC/74; 2nd Session, UNEP/IG.3/3; 3rd Session, UNEP/IG.7/3; 4th Session, UNEP/IG.10/2; 5th Session, UNEP/IG.12/2 (1978), repr. 17 *ILM* (1978), 1094; and *Report of the Executive Director*, UNEP/GC/44/Corr. 1 and 2 and Add. 1 (1975). See generally, P. Sand, 'Environmental Law in the UN Environment Programme', in R. J. Dupuy (ed.) *The Future of International Law of the Environment* (Dordrecht, 1984), 51; A. Adede, 'Utilization of Shared Natural Resources: Towards a Code of Conduct', 5 *EPL* (1979) 66; P. W. Birnie and A. E. Boyle, *International Law and the Environment* (Oxford, 1992), Ch. 3.

TEXT

Explanatory Note

The draft principles of conduct in this note further referred to as 'the principles', have been drawn up for the guidance of States in the field of the environment with respect to the conservation and harmonious utilization of natural resources shared by two or more States. The principles refer to such conduct of individual States as is considered conducive to the attainment of the said objective in a manner which does not adversely affect the environment. Moreover, the principles aim to encourage States sharing a natural resource to co-operate in the field of the environment.

An attempt has been made to avoid language which might create the impression of intending to refer to, as the case may be, either a specific legal obligation under international law, or to the absence of such obligation.

The language used throughout does not seek to prejudice whether or to what extent the conduct envisaged in the principles is already prescribed by existing rules of general international law. Neither does the formulation intend to express an opinion as to whether or to what extent and in what manner the principles—as far as they do not reflect already existing rules of general international law—should be incorporated in the body of general international law.

Draft

Principle 1

It is necessary for States to co-operate in the field of the environment concerning the conservation and harmonious utilization of natural resources shared by two or more States. Accordingly, it is necessary that, consistent with the concept of equitable utilization of shared natural resources, States co-operate with a view to controlling, preventing, reducing or eliminating adverse environmental effects which may result from the utilization of such resources. Such co-operation is to take place on an equal footing and taking into account the sovereignty, rights and interests of the States concerned.

Principle 2

In order to ensure effective international co-operation in the field of the environment concerning the conservation and harmonious utilization of natural resources shared by two or more States, States sharing such natural resources should endeavour to conclude bilateral or multilateral agreements between or among themselves in order to secure specific regulation of their conduct in this respect, applying as necessary the present principles in a legally binding manner, or should endeavour to enter into other arrangements, as appropriate, for this purpose. In entering into such agreements or arrangements, States should consider the establishment of institutional structures, such as joint international commissions, for consultations on environmental problems relating to the protection and use of shared natural resources.

Principle 3

1. States have, in accordance with the Charter of the United Nations and the principles of international law, the sovereign right to exploit their own resources pursuant to their own environmental policies, and the responsibility to ensure that activities within their jurisdiction or control do not cause damage to the environment of other States or of areas beyond the limits of national jurisdiction.

2. The principles set forth in paragraph 1, as well as the other principles contained in this document, apply to shared natural resources.

3. Accordingly, it is necessary for each State to avoid to the maximum extent possible and to reduce to the minimum extent possible the adverse environmental effects beyond its jurisdiction of the utilization of a shared natural resource so as to protect the environment, in particular when such utilization might:

(a) cause damage to the environment which could have repercussions on the utilization of the resource by another sharing State;
(b) threaten the conservation of a shared renewable resource;
(c) endanger the health of the population of another State.

Without prejudice to the generality of the above principle, it should be interpreted, taking into account, where appropriate, the practical capabilities of States sharing the natural resource.

Principle 4

States should make environmental assessments before engaging in any activity with respect to a shared natural resource which may create a risk of significantly[1] affecting the environment of another State or States sharing that resource.

Principle 5

States sharing a natural resource should, to the extent practicable, ex-

[1] See definition.

change information and engage in consultations on a regular basis on its environmental aspects.

Principle 6

1. It is necessary for every State sharing a natural resource with one or more other States:

    (a) to notify in advance the other State or States of the pertinent details of plans to initiate, or make a change in, the conservation or utilization of the resource which can reasonably be expected to affect significantly[1] the environment in the territory of the other State or States; and

    (b) upon request of the other State or States, to enter into consultations concerning the above-mentioned plans; and

    (c) to provide, upon request to that effect by the other State or States, specific additional pertinent information concerning such plans; and

    (d) if there has been no advance notification as envisaged in sub-paragraph (a) above, to enter into consultations about such plans upon request of the other State or States.

2. In cases where the transmission of certain information is prevented by national legislation or international conventions, the State or States withholding such information shall nevertheless, on the basis, in particular, of the principle of good faith and in the spirit of good neighbourliness, co-operate with the other interested State or States with the aim of finding a satisfactory solution.

Principle 7

Exchange of information, notification, consultations and other forms of co-operation regarding shared natural resources are carried out on the basis of the principle of good faith and in the spirit of good neighbourliness and in such a way as to avoid any unreasonable delays either in the forms of co-operation or in carrying out development or conservation projects.

Principle 8

When it would be useful to clarify environmental problems relating to a shared natural resource, States should engage in joint scientific studies and assessments, with a view to facilitating the finding of appropriate and satisfactory solutions to such problems on the basis of agreed data.

Principle 9

1. States have a duty urgently to inform other States which may be affected:

    (a) Of any emergency situation arising from the utilization of a shared

---

[1] See definition.

natural resource which might cause sudden harmful effects on their environment;

(b) Of any sudden grave natural events related to a shared natural resource which may affect the environment of such States.

2. States should also, when appropriate, inform the competent international organizations of any such situation or event.

3. States concerned should co-operate, in particular by means of agreed contingency plans, when appropriate, and mutual assistance, in order to avert grave situations, and to eliminate, reduce or correct, as far as possible, the effects of such situations or events.

Principle 10

States sharing a natural resource should, when appropriate, consider the possibility of jointly seeking the services of any competent international organization in clarifying the environmental problems relating to the conservation or utilization of such natural resource.

Principle 11

1. The relevant provisions of the Charter of the United Nations and of the Declaration of Principles of International Law concerning Friendly Relations and Co-operation among States in accordance with the Charter of the United Nations apply to the settlement of environmental disputes arising out of the conservation or utilization of shared natural resources.

2. In case negotiations or other non-binding means have failed to settle a dispute within a reasonable time, it is necessary for States to submit the dispute to an appropriate settlement procedure which is mutually agreed by them, preferably in advance. The procedure should be speedy, effective and binding.

3. It is necessary for the States parties to such a dispute to refrain from any action which may aggravate the situation with respect to the environment to the extent of creating an obstacle to the amicable settlement of the dispute.

Principle 12

1. States are responsible for the fulfillment of their international obligations in the field of the environment concerning the conservation and utilization of shared natural resources. They are subject to liability in accordance with applicable international law for environmental damage resulting from violations of these obligations caused to areas beyond their jurisdiction.

2. States should co-operate to develop further international law regarding liability and compensation for the victims of environmental damage arising

out of the utilization of a shared natural resource and caused to areas beyond their jurisdiction.

Principle 13

It is necessary for States, when considering, under their domestic environment policy, the permissibility of domestic activities, to take into account the potential adverse environmental effects arising out of the utilization of shared natural resources, without discrimination as to whether the effects would occur within their jurisdiction or outside it.

Principle 14

States should endeavour, in accordance with their legal systems and, where appropriate, on a basis agreed by them, to provide persons in other States who have been or may be adversely affected by environmental damage resulting from the utilization of shared natural resources with equivalent access to and treatment in the same administrative and judicial proceedings, and make available to them the same remedies as are available to persons within their own jurisdictions who have been or may be similarly affected.

Principle 15

The present principles should be interpreted and applied in such a way as to enhance and not to affect adversely development and the interests of all countries, and in particular of the developing countries.

Definition

In the present text, the expression 'significantly affect' refers to any appreciable effects on a shared natural resource and excludes '*de minimis*' effects.

UNEP Goals and Principles of Environmental Impact Assessment, 17 June 1987

UNEP's Goals and Principles of Environmental Impact Assessment are another example of the use of soft law principles whose significance can only be measured by reference to their reception in national and international practice. At the time of their adoption, the few precedents for a requirement of environmental impact assessment in international law were found mainly in marine pollution and international watercourse treaties and dealt only with the assessment of transboundary effects. UNEP's principles were novel in their broader purpose of promoting the integration of environmental and natural resources issues in the planning of activities likely to have significant effects, whether on the domestic or the international environment. Apart from the growing trend in national environmental law to require such assessments, the influence of the UNEP Principles is most apparent in Principle 17 of the 1992 Rio Declaration on Environment and Development (q.v.), in the 1992 Biological Diversity Convention (q.v.), in the 1985 ASEAN Agreement on the Conservation of Nature and Natural Resources, and in the practice of the World Bank. UNEP's formulation now compares unfavourably, however, with the more detailed and onerous provisions of the 1991 Espoo Convention on Environmental Impact Assessment in a Transboundary Context (q.v.), and with the 1991 Protocol to the Antarctic Treaty on Environmental Protection (q.v.).

The Governing Council of UNEP adopted the Guidelines in Resolution GC14/25; they were 'endorsed' by UNGA Resolution 42/184 (1987). For background papers, see *Reports of the UNEP Working Group of Experts on Environmental Law*, 1983– (UNEP/WG.107/–); and see J. Bonine, 'Environmental Impact Assessment', 17 *EPL* (1987) 5; W. Irwin, 'Impact Assessment', 13 *EPL* (1984), 51. See generally N. Robinson, 'International Trends in Environmental Impact Assessment', 19 *Boston Coll. Env. Aff. LR* (1992) 591.

TEXT

Environmental Impact Assessment (EIA)

EIA means an examination, analysis and assessment of planned activities with a view to ensuring environmentally sound and sustainable development.

The EIA goals and principles set out below are necessarily general in nature and may be further refined when fulfilling EIA tasks at the national, regional and international levels.

Goals

1. To establish that before decisions are taken by the competent authority or authorities to undertake or to authorize activities that are likely to significantly affect the environment, the environmental effects of those activities should be taken fully into account.

2. To promote the implementation of appropriate procedures in all countries consistent with national laws and decision-making processes, through which the foregoing goal may be realized.

3. To encourage the development of reciprocal procedures for information exchange, notification and consultation between States when proposed activities are likely to have significant transboundary effects on the environment of those States.

Principles

Principle 1

States (including their competent authorities) should not undertake or authorize activities without prior consideration, at an early stage, of their environmental effects. Where the extent, nature or location of a proposed activity is such that it is likely to significantly affect the environment, a comprehensive environmental impact assessment should be undertaken in accordance with the following principles.

Principle 2

The criteria and procedures for determining whether an activity is likely to significantly affect the environment and is therefore subject to an EIA, should be defined clearly by legislation, regulation, or other means, so that subject activities can be quickly and surely identified, and EIA can be applied as the activity is being planned.[1]

Principle 3

In the EIA process the relevant significant environmental issues should be

---

[1] For instance, this principle may be implemented through a variety of mechanisms, including:

   (a) Lists of categories of activities that by their nature are, or are not, likely to have significant effects;
   (b) Lists of areas that are of special importance or sensitivity (such as national parks or wetland areas), so that any activity affecting such areas is likely to have significant effects;
   (c) Lists of categories of resources (such as water, tropical rain forests, etc.), or environmental problems (such as increased soil erosion, desertification, deforestation) which are of special concern, so that any diminution of such resources or exacerbation of such problems is likely to be 'significant';
   (d) An 'initial environmental evaluation', a quick and informal assessment of the proposed activity to determine whether its effects are likely to be significant;
   (e) Criteria to guide determinations whether the effects of a proposed activity are likely to be significant.

If a listing system is used, it is recommended that States reserve the discretion to require the preparation of an EIA on an *ad hoc* basis, to ensure that they have the flexibility needed to respond to unanticipated cases.

identified and studied. Where appropriate, all efforts should be made to identify these issues at an early stage in the process.

Principle 4

An EIA should include, at a minimum:

(a) A description of the proposed activity;
(b) A description of the potentially affected environment, including specific information necessary for identifying and assessing the environmental effects of the proposed activity;
(c) A description of practical alternatives, as appropriate;
(d) An assessment of the likely or potential environmental impacts of the proposed activity and alternatives, including the direct, indirect, cumulative, short-term and long-term effects;
(e) An identification and description of measures available to mitigate adverse environmental impacts of the proposed activity and alternatives, and an assessment of those measures;
(f) An indication of gaps in knowledge and uncertainties which may be encountered in compiling the required information;
(g) An indication of whether the environment of any other State or areas beyond national jurisdiction is likely to be affected by the proposed activity or alternatives;
(h) A brief, non-technical summary of the information provided under the above headings.

Principle 5

The environmental effects in an EIA should be assessed with a degree of detail commensurate with their likely environmental significance.

Principle 6

The information provided as part of EIA should be examined impartially prior to the decision.

Principle 7

Before a decision is made on an activity, government agencies, members of the public, experts in relevant disciplines and interested groups should be allowed appropriate opportunity to comment on the EIA.

Principle 8

A decision as to whether a proposed activity should be authorized or undertaken should not be taken until an appropriate period has elapsed to consider comments pursuant to principles 7 and 12.

Principle 9

The decision on any proposed activity subject to an EIA should be in writing, state the reasons therefore, and include the provisions, if any, to prevent, reduce or mitigate damage to the environment.

This decision should be made available to interested persons or groups.

Principle 10

Where it is justified, following a decision on an activity which has been subject to an EIA, the activity and its effects on the environment or the provisions (pursuant to principle 9) of the decision on this activity should be subject to appropriate supervision.

Principle 11

States should endeavour to conclude bilateral, regional or multilateral arrangements, as appropriate, so as to provide, on the basis of reciprocity, notification, exchange of information, and agreed-upon consultation on the potential environmental effects of activities under their control or jurisdiction which are likely to significantly affect other States or areas beyond national jurisdiction.

Principle 12

When information provided as part of an EIA indicates that the environment within another State is likely to be significantly affected by a proposed activity, the State in which the activity is being planned should, to the extent possible:

    (a) Notify the potentially affected State of the proposed activity;
    (b) Transmit to the potentially affected State any relevant information from the EIA, the transmission of which is not prohibited by national laws or regulations; and
    (c) When it is agreed between the States concerned, enter into timely consultations.

Principle 13

Appropriate measures should be established to ensure implementation of EIA procedures.

Convention on Environmental Impact Assessment in a Transboundary
Context, Espoo, 25 February 1991

This is the first convention to lay down detailed rules, procedures, and practices for
transboundary environmental impact assessment, although articles requiring such
assessments can be found in earlier treaties, including the 1982 UNCLOS (q.v.), the
1983 Convention for the Protection and Development of the Marine Environment
of the Wider Caribbean Region *repr.* 22 *ILM* (1983) 221 and the 1986 Convention
for the Protection of the Natural Resources and Environment of the South Pacific
Region *repr.* 26 *ILM* (1987) 38. Prior environmental impact assessment is also
included in OECD Council Recommendations on transfrontier pollution *repr.*
OECD and the Environment (Paris, 1986), in UNEP's Principles of Shared Natural
Resources, 1978 (q.v.), in its Conclusions on Offshore Mining and Drilling, 1981,
and in its Goals and Principles of Environmental Impact Assessment, 1987 (q.v.).
An increasing number of national legal systems also make provision for such
assessments, irrespective of whether the effects are domestic or transboundary. The
Espoo Convention applies to a range of proposed activities that are 'likely to cause
significant adverse transboundary impact.' It requires each party to establish an
environmental impact assessment procedure that permits public participation and
the preparation of appropriate documentation. Other states likely to be affected
must be notified and given the opportunity to enter into consultations and make
representations on the assessment, which must be taken into account in any final
decision on the proposed activity. For negotiating history, see *Reports of the Working
Group on Environmental Impact Assessment.* The text of the Convention is in UN Doc.
E/ECE/1250; Misc 15 (1991), Cm. 1645; 30 *ILM* (1991) 802. For parties, reservations, and declarations, see UN, *Multilateral Treaties Deposited with the Secretary General,*
UN Doc. ST/LEG/SER.E/(current year). The Convention is open to UN ECE
member states and the EC. It was signed by 29 states and the EC in 1991–3 and had
8 parties on 1 January 1995, but was not in force.

TEXT

The Parties of this Convention,

Aware of the interrelationship between economic activities and their
environmental consequences,

Affirming the need to ensure environmentally sound and sustainable
development,

Determined to enhance international co-operation in assessing environmental impact in particular in a transboundary context,

Mindful of the need and importance to develop anticipatory policies
and of preventing, mitigating and monitoring significant adverse
environmental impact in general and more specifically in a transboundary
context.

Recalling the relevant provisions of the Charter of the United Nations,
the Declaration of the Stockholm Conference on the Human Environment, the Final Act of the Conference on Security and Co-operation in

Europe (CSCE) and the Concluding Documents of the Madrid and Vienna Meetings of Representatives of the Participating States of the CSCE,

Commending the ongoing activities of States to ensure that, through their national legal and administrative provisions and their national policies, environmental impact assessment is carried out.

Conscious of the need to give explicit consideration to environmental factors at an early stage in the decision-making process by applying environmental impact assessment, at all appropriate administrative levels, as a necessary tool to improve the quality of information presented to decision makers so that environmentally sound decisions can be made paying careful attention to minimizing significant adverse impact, particularly in a transboundary context.

Mindful of the efforts of international organizations to promote the use of environmental impact assessment both at national and international levels, and taking into account work on environmental impact assessment carried out under the auspices of the United Nations Economic Commission for Europe, in particular results achieved by the Seminar on Environmental Impact Assessment (September 1987, Warsaw, Poland) as well as noting the Goals and Principles on environmental impact assessment adopted by the Governing Council of the United Nations Environment Programme, and the Ministerial Declaration on Sustainable Development (May 1990, Bergen, Norway),

Have agreed as follows,

Article 1
Definitions

For the purposes of this Convention,

  (i) 'Parties' means, unless the text otherwise indicates, the Contracting Parties to this Convention;
 (ii) 'Party of origin' means the Contracting Party or Parties to this Convention under whose jurisdiction a proposed activity is envisaged to take place;
(iii) 'Affected Party' means the Contracting Party or Parties to this Convention likely to be affected by the transboundary impact of a proposed activity;
 (iv) 'Concerned Parties' means the Party of origin and the affected Party of an environmental impact assessment pursuant to this Convention;
  (v) 'Proposed activity' means any activity or any major change to an activity subject to a decision of a competent authority in accordance with an applicable national procedure;
 (vi) 'Environmental impact assessment' means a national procedure for evaluating the likely impact of a proposed activity on the environment;

(vii) 'Impact' means any effect caused by a proposed activity on the environment including human health and safety, flora, fauna, soil, air, water, climate, landscape and historical monuments or other physical structures or the interaction among those factors; it also includes effects on cultural heritage or socio-economic conditions resulting from alterations to those factors;

(viii) 'Transboundary impact' means any impact, not exclusively of a global nature, within an area under the jurisdiction of a Party caused by a proposed activity the physical origin of which is situated wholly or in part within the area under the jurisdiction of another Party;

(ix) 'Competent authority' means the national authority or authorities designated by a Party as responsible for performing the tasks covered by this Convention and/or the authority or authorities entrusted by a Party with decision-making powers regarding a proposed activity;

(x) 'The Public' means one or more natural or legal persons.

Article 2
General Provisions

1. The Parties shall, either individually or jointly, take all appropriate and effective measures to prevent, reduce and control significant adverse transboundary environmental impact from proposed activities.

2. Each Party shall take the necessary legal, administrative or other measures to implement the provisions of the Convention, including, with respect to proposed activities listed in Appendix I that are likely to cause significant adverse transboundary impact, the establishment of an environmental impact assessment procedure that permits public participation and preparation of the environmental impact assessment documentation described in Appendix II.

3. The Party of origin shall ensure that in accordance with the provisions of this Convention an environmental impact assessment is undertaken prior to a decision to authorize or undertake a proposed activity listed in Appendix I that is likely to cause a significant adverse transboundary impact.

4. The Party of origin shall, consistent with the provisions of this Convention, ensure that affected Parties are notified of a proposed activity listed in Appendix I that is likely to cause a significant adverse transboundary impact.

5. Concerned Parties shall, at the initiative of any such Party, enter into discussions on whether one or more proposed activities not listed in Appendix I is or are likely to cause a significant adverse transboundary impact and thus should be treated as if it or they were so listed. Where those Parties so agree, the activity or activities shall be thus treated. General guidance for

identifying criteria to determine significant adverse impact is set forth in Appendix III.

6. The Party of origin shall provide, in accordance with the provisions of this Convention, an opportunity to the public in the areas likely to be affected to participate in relevant environmental impact assessment procedures regarding proposed activities and shall ensure that the opportunity provided to the public of the affected Party is equivalent to that provided to the public of the Party of origin.

7. Environmental impact assessments as required by this Convention shall, as a minimum requirement, be undertaken at the project level of the proposed activity. To the extent appropriate, the Parties shall endeavour to apply the principles of environmental impact assessment to policies, plans and programmes.

8. The provisions of this Convention shall not affect the right of Parties to implement national laws, regulations, administrative provisions or accepted legal practices protecting information the supply of which would be prejudicial to industrial and commercial secrecy or national security.

9. The provisions of this Convention shall not affect the right of particular Parties to implement, by bilateral or multilateral agreement where appropriate, more stringent measures than those of this Convention.

10. The provisions of this Convention shall not prejudice any obligations of the Parties under international law with regard to activities having or likely to have a transboundary impact.

Article 3
Notification

1. For a proposed activity listed in Appendix I that is likely to cause a significant adverse transboundary impact, the Party of origin shall, for the purposes of ensuring adequate and effective consultations under Article 5, notify any Party which it considers may be an affected Party as early as possible and no later than when informing its own public about that proposed activity.

2. This notification shall contain, *inter alia,*

    (a) Information on the proposed activity, including any available information on its possible transboundary impact;

    (b) The nature of the possible decision; and

    (c) An indication of a reasonable time within which a response under paragraph 3 of this Article is required, taking into account the nature of the proposed activity; and may include the information set out in paragraph 5 of this Article.

3. The affected Party shall respond to the Party of origin within the time specified in the notification, acknowledging receipt of the notification, and

shall indicate whether it intends to participte in the environmental impact assessment procedure.

4. If the affected Party indicates that it does not intend to participate in the environmental impact assessment procedure, or if it does not respond within the time specified in the notification, the provisions in paragraphs 5, 6, 7 and 8 of this Article and in Articles 4 to 7 will not apply. In such circumstances the right of a Party of origin to determine whether to carry out an environmental impact assessment on the basis of its national law and practice is not prejudiced.

5. Upon receipt of a response from the affected Party indicating its desire to participate in the environmental impact assessment procedure, the Party of origin shall, if it has not already done so, provide to the affected Party:

(a) Relevant information regarding the environmental impact assessment procedure, including an indication of the time schedule for transmittal of comments; and

(b) Relevant information on the proposed activity and its possible significant adverse transboundary impact.

6. An affected Party shall, at the request of the Party of origin, provide the latter with reasonably obtainable information relating to the potentially affected environment under the jurisdiction of the affected Party, where such information is necessary for the preparation of the environmental impact assessment documentation. The information shall be furnished promptly and, as appropriate, through a joint body where one exists.

7. When a Party considers that it would be affected by a significant adverse transboundary impact of a proposed activity listed in Appendix I, and when no notification has taken place in accordance with paragraph 1 of this Article, the concerned Parties shall, at the request of the affected Party, exchange sufficient information for the purposes of holding discussions on whether there is likely to be a significant adverse transboundary impact. If those Parties agree that there is likely to be a significant adverse transboundary impact, the provisions of this Conventon shall apply accordingly. If those Parties cannot agree whether there is likely to be a significant adverse transboundary impact, any such Party may submit that question to an inquiry commission in accordance with the provisions of Appendix IV to advise on the likelihood of significant adverse transboundary impact, unless they agree on another method of settling this question.

8. The concerned Parties shall ensure that the public of the affected Party in the areas likely to be affected be informed of, and be provided with possibilities for making comments or objections on, the proposed activity, and for the transmittal of these comments or objections to the competent authority of the Party of origin, either directly to this authority or, where appropriate, through the Party of origin.

Article 4
Preparation of The Environmental Impact Assessment Documentation

1. The environmental impact assessment documentation to be submitted to the competent authority of the Party of origin shall contain, as a minimum, the information described in Appendix II.

2. The Party of origin shall furnish the affected Party, as appropriate through a joint body where one exists, with the environmental impact assessment documentation. The concerned Parties shall arrange for distribution of the documentation to the authorities and the public of the affected Party in the area likely to be affected and for the submission of comments to the competent authority of the Party of origin, either directly to this authority or, where appropriate, through the Party of origin within a reasonable time before the final decision is taken on the proposed activity.

Article 5
Consultations on the Basis of The Environmental Impact
Assessment Documentation

The Party of origin shall, after completion of the environmental impact assessment documentation, without undue delay enter into consultations with the affected Party concerning, *inter alia*, the potential transboundary impact of the proposed activity and measures to reduce or eliminate its impact. Consultations may relate to:

  (a) Possible alternatives to the proposed activity, including the no-action alternative and possible measures to mitigate significant adverse transboundary impact and to monitor the effects of such measures at the expense of the Party of origin;
  (b) Other forms of possible mutual assistance in reducing any significant adverse transboundary impact of the proposed activity, and
  (c) Any other appropriate matters relating to the proposed activity.

The Parties shall agree, at the commencement of such consultations, on a reasonable time-frame for the duration of the consultation period. Any such consultations may be conducted through an appropriate joint body, where one exists.

Article 6
Final Decision

1. The Parties shall ensure that, in the final decision on the proposed activity, due account is taken of the outcome of the environment impact assessment, including the environmental impact assessment documentation, as well as the comments thereon received pursuant to Article 3,

paragraph 8 and Article 4, paragraph 2, and the outcome of the consultations as referred to in Article 5.

2. The Party of origin shall provide to the affected Party the final decision on the proposed activity along with the reasons and considerations on which it was based.

3. If additional information on the significant transboundary impact of a proposed activity, which was not available at the time a decision was made with respect to that activity and which could have materially affected the decision, becomes available to a concerned Party before work on that activity commences, that Party shall immediately inform the other concerned Party or Parties. If one of the concerned Parties so requests, consultations shall be held as to whether the decision needs to be revised.

Article 7
Post-project Analysis

1. The concerned Parties, at the request of any such Party, shall determine whether, and if so to what extent, a post-project analysis shall be carried out, taking into account the likely significant adverse transboundary impact of the activity for which an environmental impact assessment has been undertaken pursuant to this Convention. Any post-project analysis undertaken shall include, in particular, the surveillance of the activity and the determination of any adverse transboundary impact. Such surveillance and determination may be undertaken with a view to achieving the objectives listed in Appendix V.

2. When, as a result of post-project analysis, the Party of origin or the affected Party has reasonable grounds for concluding that there is a significant adverse transboundary impact or factors have been discovered which may result in such an impact, it shall immediately inform the other Party. The concerned Parties shall then consult on necessary measures to reduce or eliminate the impact.

Article 8
Bilateral and Multilateral Co-operation

The Parties may continue existing or enter into new bilateral or multilateral agreements or other arrangements in order to implement their obligations under this Convention. Such agreements or other arrangements may be based on the elements listed in Appendix VI.

Article 9
Research Programmes

The Parties shall give special consideration to the setting up, or intensification of, specific research programmes aimed at:

(a) Improving existing qualitative and quantitative methods for assessing the impacts of proposed activities;

(b) Achieving a better understanding of cause-effect relationships and their role in integrated environmental management;

(c) Analysing and monitoring the efficient implementation of decisions on proposed activities with the intention of minimizing or preventing impacts;

(d) Developing methods to stimulate creative approaches in the search for environmentally sound alternatives to proposed activities, production and consumption patterns;

(e) Developing methodologies for the application of the principles of environmental impact assessment at the macro-economic level.

The results of the programmes listed above shall be exchanged by the Parties.

Article 10
Status of the Appendices

The Appendices attached to this Convention form an integral part of the Convention.

Article 11
Meeting of Parties

1. The Parties shall meet, so far as possible, in connection with the annual sessions of the Senior Advisers to ECE Governments on Environmental and Water Problems. The first meeting of the Parties shall be convened not later than one year after the date of the entry into force of this Convention.

Thereafter, meetings of the Parties shall be held at such other times as may be deemed necessary by a meeting of the Parties, or at the written request of any Party; provided that, within six months of the request being communicated to them by the secretariat, it is supported by at least one third of the Parties.

2. The Parties shall keep under continuous review the implementation of this Convention, and, with this purpose in mind, shall:

(a) Review the policies and methodological approaches to environmental impact assessment by the Parties with a view to further improving environmental impact assessment procedures in a transboundary context;

(b) Exchange information regarding experience gained in concluding and implementing bilateral and multilateral agreements or other arrangements regarding the use of environmental impact assessment in a transboundary context to which one or more of the Parties are party;

(c) Seek, where appropriate, the services of competent international bodies and scientific committees in methodological and technical aspects pertinent to the achievement of the purposes of this Convention;

(d) At their first meeting, consider and by consensus adopt rules of procedure for their meetings;

(e) Consider and, where necessary, adopt proposals for amendments to this Convention;

(f) Consider and undertake any additional action that may be required for the achievement of the purposes of this Convention.

Article 12
Right to Vote

1. Each Party to this Convention shall have one vote.

2. Except as provided for in paragraph 1 of this Article, regional economic integration organizations, in matters within their competence, shall exercise their right to vote with a number of votes equal to the number of their member States which are Parties to this Convention. Such organizations shall not exercise their right to vote if their member States exercise theirs, and vice versa.

Article 13
Secretariat

The Executive Secretary of the Economic Commission for Europe shall carry out the following secretariat functions:

(a) The convening and preparing of meetings of the Parties;

(b) The transmission of reports and other information received in accordance with the provisions of this Convention to the Parties, and

(c) The performance of other functions as may be provided for in this Convention or as may be determined by the Parties.

Article 14
Amendments to the Convention

1. Any Party may propose amendments to this Convention.

2. Proposed amendments shall be submitted in writing to the secretariat, which shall communicate them to all Parties. The proposed amendments shall be discussed at the next meeting of the Parties, provided these proposals have been circulated by the secretariat to the Parties at least ninety days in advance.

3. The Parties shall make every effort to reach agreement on any proposed amendment to this Convention by consensus. If all efforts at consensus have been exhausted, and no agreement reached, the amendment shall as a last resort be adopted by a three-fourths majority vote of the Parties present and voting at the meeting.

4. Amendments to this Convention adopted in accordance with paragraph 3 of this Article shall be submitted by the Depositary to all Parties for ratification, approval or acceptance. They shall enter into force for parties having ratified, approved or accepted them on the ninetieth day after the receipt by the Depositary of notification of their ratification, approval or acceptance by at least three fourths of these Parties. Thereafter they shall enter into force for any other Party on the ninetieth day after that Party deposits its instrument of ratification, approval or acceptance of the amendments.

5. For the purpose of this Article, 'Parties present and voting' means Parties present and casting an affirmative or negative vote.

6. The voting procedure set forth in paragraph 3 of this Article is not intended to constitute a precedent for future agreements negotiated within the Economic Commission for Europe.

Article 15
Settlement of Disputes

1. If a dispute arises between two or more Parties about the interpretation or application of this Convention, they shall seek a solution by negotiation or by any other method of dispute settlement acceptable to the parties to the dispute.

2. When signing, ratifying, accepting, approving or acceding to this Convention, or at any time thereafter, a Party may declare in writing to the Depositary that for a dispute not resolved in accordance with paragraph 1 of this Article, it accepts one or both of the following means of dispute settlement as compulsory in relation to any Party accepting the same obligation:

(a) Submission of the dispute to the International Court of Justice;
(b) Arbitration in accordance with the procedure set out in Appendix VII.

3. If the parties to the dispute have accepted both means of dispute settlement referred to in paragraph 2 of this Article, the dispute may be submitted only to the International Court of Justice, unless the parties agree otherwise.

Article 16
Signature

This Convention shall be open for signature at Espoo (Finland) from 25 February to 1 March 1991 and thereafter at United Nations Headquarters in New York until 2 September 1991 by States members of the Economic Commission for Europe as well as States having consultative status with the Economic Commission for Europe pursuant to paragraph 8 of the Economic and Social Council resolution 36 (IV) of 28 March 1947, and by regional economic integration organizations constituted by sovereign States members of the Economic Commission for Europe to which their member States have transferred competence in respect of matters governed by this Convention, including the competence to enter into treaties in respect of these matters.

Article 17
Ratification, Acceptance, Approval and Accession

1. This Convention shall be subject to ratification, acceptance or approval by signatory States and regional economic integration organizations.

2. This Convention shall be open for accession as from 3 September 1991 by the States and organizations referred to in Article 16.

3. The instruments of ratification, acceptance, approval or accession shall be deposited with the Secretary-General of the United Nations, who shall perform the functions of Depositary.

4. Any organization referred to in Article 16 which becomes a Party to this Convention without any of its member States being a Party shall be bound by all the obligations under this Convention. In the case of such organizations, one or more of whose member States is a Party to this Convention, the organization and its member States shall decide on their respective responsibilities for the performance of their obligations under this Convention. In such cases, the organization and the member States shall not be entitled to exercise rights under this Convention concurrently.

5. In their instruments of ratification, acceptance, approval or accession, the regional economic integration organizations referred to in Article 16 shall declare the extent of their competence with respect to the matters governed by this Convention. These organizations shall also inform the Depositary of any relevant modification to the extent of their competence.

Article 18
Entry into Force

1. This Convention shall enter into force on the nineteenth day after the date of deposit of the sixteenth instrument of ratification, acceptance, approval or accession.

2. For the purposes of paragraph 1 of this Article, any instrument deposited by a regional economic integration organization shall not be counted as additional to those deposited by States members of such an organization.

3. For each State or organization referred to in Article 16 which ratifies, accepts or approves this Convention or accedes thereto after the deposit of the sixteenth instrument of ratification, acceptance, approval or accession, this Convention shall enter into force on the ninetieth day after the date of

deposit by such State or organization of its instrument of ratification, acceptance, approval or accession.

Article 19
Withdrawal

At any time after four years from the date on which this Convention has come into force with respect to a Party, that Party may withdraw from this Convention by giving written notification to the Depositary. Any such withdrawal shall take effect on the nineteenth day after the date of its receipt by the Depositary. Any such withdrawal shall not affect the application of Articles 3 to 6 of this Convention to a proposed activity in respect of which a notification has been made pursuant to Article 3, paragraph 1, or a request has been made pursuant to Article 3, paragraph 7, before such withdrawal took effect.

Article 20
Authentic Texts

The original of this Convention, of which the English, French and Russian texts are equally authentic, shall be deposited with the Secretary-General of the United Nations.

IN WITNESS WHEREOF the undersigned, being duly authorized thereto, have signed this Convention.

DONE at Espoo (Finland), this twenty-fifth day of February one thousand nine hundred and ninety-one.

Appendix I
List of Activities

1. Crude oil refineries (excluding undertakings manufacturing only lubricants from crude oil) and installations for the gasification and liquefaction of 500 tonnes or more of coal or bituminous shale per day.

2. Thermal power stations and other combustion installations with a heat output of 300 megawatts or more and nuclear power stations and other nuclear reactors (except research installations for the production and conversion of fissionable and fertile materials, whose maximum power does not exceed 1 kilowatt continuous thermal load).

3. Installations solely designed for the production or enrichment of nuclear fuels, for the reprocessing of irradiated nuclear fuels or for the storage, disposal and processing of radioactive waste.

4. Major installations for the initial smelting of cast-iron and steel and for the production of non-ferrous metals.

5. Installations for the extraction of asbestos and for the processing and transformation of asbestos and products containing asbestos: for asbestos-

cement products, with an annual production of more than 20,000 tonnes finished product, for friction material, with an annual production of more than 50 tonnes finished product, and for other asbestos utilization of more than 200 tonnes per year.

6. Integrated chemical installations.

7. Construction of motorways, express roads[1] and lines for long-distance railway traffic and of airports with a basic runway length of 2,100 metres or more.

8. Large-diameter oil and gas pipelines.

9. Trading ports and also inland waterways and ports for inland-waterway traffic which permit the passage of vessels of over 1,350 tonnes.

10. Waste-disposal installations for the incineration, chemical treatment or landfill of toxic and dangerous wastes.

11. Large dams and reservoirs.

12. Groundwater abstraction activities in cases where the annual volume of water to be abstracted amounts to 10 million cubic metres or more.

13. Pulp and paper manufacturing of 200 air-dried metric tonnes or more per day.

14. Major mining, on-site extraction and processing of metal ores or coal.

15. Offshore hydrocarbon production.

16. Major storage facilities for petroleum, petrochemical and chemical products.

17. Deforestation of large areas.

Appendix II
Content of the Environmental Impact Assessment Documentation

Information to be included in the environmental impact assessment documentation shall, as a minimum, contain, in accordance with Article 4:

---

[1] For the purposes of this Convention:
— 'Motorway' means a road specially designed and built for motor traffic, which does not serve properties bordering on it, and which:

   (a) Is provided, except at special points or temporarily, with separate carriageways for the two directions of traffic, separated from each other by a dividing strip not intended for traffic or, exceptionally, by other means.
   (b) Does not cross at level with any road, railway or tramway track, or footpath, and
   (c) Is specially sign-posted as a motorway.

— 'Express road' means a road reserved for motor traffic accessible only from interchanges or controlled junctions and on which, in particular, stopping and parking are prohibited on the running carriageway(s).

(a) A description of the proposed activity and its purpose,
(b) A description, where appropriate, of reasonable alternatives (for example, locational or technological) to the proposed activity and also the no-action alternative,
(c) A description of the environment likely to be significantly affected by the proposed activity and its alternatives,
(d) A description of the potential environmental impact of the proposed activity and its alternatives and an estimation of its significance,
(e) A description of mitigation measures to keep adverse environmental impact to a minimum,
(f) An explicit indication of predictive methods and underlying assumptions as well as the relevant environmental data used,
(g) An identification of gaps in knowledge and uncertainties encountered in compiling the required information,
(h) Where appropriate, an outline for monitoring and management programmes and any plans for post-project analysis, and
(i) A non-technical summary including a visual presentation as appropriate (maps, graphs, etc.).

Appendix III
General Criteria to Assist in the Determination of the Environmental Significance of Activities Not Listed in Appendix I

1. In considering proposed activities to which Article 2, paragraph 5, applies, the concerned Parties may consider whether the activity is likely to have a significant adverse transboundary impact in particular by virtue of one or more of the following criteria:

(a) *Size*: proposed activities which are large for the type of the activity,
(b) *Location*: proposed activities which are located in or close to an area of special environmental sensitivity or importance (such as wetlands designated under the Ramsar Convention, national parks, nature reserves, sites of special scientific interest, or sites of archaeological, cultural or historical importance), also, proposed activities in locations where the characteristics of proposed development would be likely to have significant effects on the population,
(c) *Effects*: proposed activities with particularly complex and potentially adverse effects, including those giving rise to serious effects on humans or on valued species or organisms, those which threaten the existing or potential use of an affected area and those causing additional loading which cannot be sustained by the carrying capacity of the environment.

2. The concerned Parties shall consider for this purpose proposed activities which are located close to an international frontier as well as more remote proposed activities which could give rise to significant transboundary effects far removed from the site of development.

Appendix IV
Inquiry Procedure

1. The requesting Party or Parties shall notify the secretariat that it or they submits(s) the question of whether a proposed activity listed in Appendix I is likely to have a significant adverse transboundary impact to an inquiry commission established in accordance with the provisions of this Appendix. This notification shall state the subject-matter of the inquiry. The secretariat shall notify immediately all Parties to this Convention of this submission.

2. The inquiry commission shall consist of three members. Both the requesting party and the other party to the inquiry procedure shall appoint a scientific or technical expert, and the two experts so appointed shall designate by common agreement the third expert, who shall be the president of the inquiry commission. The latter shall not be a national of one of the parties to the inquiry procedure, or have his or her usual place of residence in the territory of one of these parties, nor be employed by any of them, nor have dealt with the matter in any other capacity.

3. If the president of the inquiry commission has not been designated within two months of the appointment of the second expert, the Executive Secretary of the Economic Commission for Europe shall, at the request of either party, designate the president within a further two-month period.

4. If one of the parties to the inquiry procedure does not appoint an expert within one month of its receipt of the notification by the secretariat, the other party may inform the Executive Secretary of the Economic Commission for Europe, who shall designate the president of the inquiry commission within a further two-month period. Upon designation, the president of the inquiry commission shall request the party which has not appointed an expert to do so within one month. After such a period, the president shall inform the Executive Secretary of the Economic Commission for Europe, who shall make this appointment within a further two-month period.

5. The inquiry commission shall adopt its own rules of procedure.

6. The inquiry commission may take all appropriate measures in order to carry out its functions.

7. The parties to the inquiry procedure shall facilitate the work of the inquiry commission and, in particular, using all means at their disposal, shall:

   (a) Provide it with all relevant documents, facilities and information, and

   (b) Enable it, where necessary, to call witnesses or experts and receive their evidence.

8. The parties and the experts shall protect the confidentiality of any information they receive in confidence during the work of the inquiry commission.

9. If one of the parties to the inquiry procedure does not appear before the inquiry commission or fails to present its case, the other party may request the inquiry commission to continue the proceedings and to complete its work. Absence of a party or failure of a party to present its case shall not constitute a bar to the continuation and completion of the work of the inquiry commission.

10. Unless the inquiry commission determines otherwise because of the particular circumstances of the matter, the expenses of the inquiry commission, including the remuneration of its members, shall be borne by the parties to the inquiry procedure in equal shares. The inquiry commission shall keep a record of all its expenses, and shall furnish a final statement thereof to the parties.

11. Any Party having an interest of a factual nature in the subject-matter of the inquiry procedure, and which may be affected by an opinion in the matter, may intervene in the proceedings with the consent of the inquiry commission.

12. The decisions of the inquiry commission on matters of procedure shall be taken by majority vote of its members. The final opinion of the inquiry commission shall reflect the view of the majority of its members and shall include any dissenting view.

13. The inquiry commission shall present its final opinion within two months of the date on which it was established unless it finds it necessary to extend this time limit for a period which should not exceed two months.

14. The final opinion of the inquiry commission shall be based on accepted scientific principles. The final opinion shall be transmitted by the inquiry commission to the parties to the inquiry procedure and to the secretariat.

Appendix V
Post-project Analysis

Objectives include:

   (a) Monitoring compliance with the conditions as set out in the authorization or approval of the activity and the effectiveness of mitigation measures,

(b) Review of an impact for proper management and in order to cope with uncertainties,

(c) Verification of past predictions in order to transfer experience to future activities of the same type.

Appendix VI
Elements for Bilateral and Multilateral Co-operation

1. Concerned Parties may set up, where appropriate, institutional arrangements or enlarge the mandate of existing institutional arrangements within the framework of bilateral and multilateral agreements in order to give full effect to this Convention.

2. Bilateral and multilateral agreements or other arrangements may include:

(a) Any additional requirements for the implementation of this Convention, taking into account the specific conditions of the subregion concerned,

(b) Institutional, administrative and other arrangements, to be made on a reciprocal and equivalent basis,

(c) Harmonization of their policies and measures for the protection of the environment in order to attain the greatest possible similarity in standards and methods related to the implementation of environmental impact assessment,

(d) Developing, improving, and/or harmonizing methods for the identification, measurement, prediction and assessment of impacts, and for post-project analysis,

(e) Developing and/or improving methods and programmes for the collection, analysis, storage and timely dissemination of comparable data regarding environmental quality in order to provide input into environmental impact assessment,

(f) The establishment of threshold levels and more specified criteria for defining the significance of transboundary impact related to the location, nature or size of proposed activities, for which environmental impact assessment in accordance with the provisions of this Convention shall be applied, and the establishment of critical loads of transboundary pollution,

(g) Undertaking, where appropriate, joint environmental impact assessment, development of joint monitoring programmes, intercalibration of monitoring devices and harmonization of methodologies with a view to rendering the data and information obtained compatible.

Appendix VII
Arbitration

1. The claimant Party or Parties shall notify the secretariat that the Parties have agreed to submit the dispute to arbitration pursuant to Article 15, paragraph 2, of this Convention. The notification shall state the subject-matter of arbitration and include, in particular, the Articles of this Convention, the interpretation or application of which are at issue. The secretariat shall forward the information received to all Parties to this Convention.

2. The arbitral tribunal shall consist of three members. Both the claimant Party or Parties and the other Party or Parties to the dispute shall appoint an arbitrator, and the two arbitrators so appointed shall designate by common agreement the third arbitrator, who shall be the president of the arbitral tribunal. The latter shall not be a national of one of the parties to the dispute, nor have his or her usual place of residence in the territory of one of these parties, nor be employed by any of them, nor have dealt with the case in any other capacity.

3. If the president of the arbitral tribunal has not been designated within two months of the appointment of the second arbitrator, the Executive Secretary of the Economic Commission for Europe shall, at the request of either party to the dispute, designate the president within a further two-month period.

4. If one of the parties to the dispute does not appoint an arbitrator within two months of the receipt of the request, the other party may inform the Executive Secretary of the Economic Commission for Europe, who shall designate the president of the arbitral tribunal within a further two-month period. Upon designation, the president of the arbitral tribunal shall request the party which has not appointed an arbitrator to do so within two months. After such a period, the president shall inform the Executive Secretary of the Economic Commission for Europe, who shall make this appointment within a further two-month period.

5. The arbitral tribunal shall render its decision in accordance with international law and in accordance with the provisions of this Convention.

6. Any arbitral tribunal constituted under the provisions set out herein shall draw up its own rules or procedure.

7. The decisions of the arbitral tribunal, both on procedure and on substance, shall be taken by majority vote of its members.

8. The tribunal may take all appropriate measures in order to establish the facts.

9. The parties to the dispute shall facilitate the work of the arbitral tribunal and, in particular, using all means at their disposal, shall:

(a) Provide it with all relevant documents, facilities and information, and

(b) Enable it, where necessary, to call witnesses or experts and receive their evidence.

10. The parties and the arbitrators shall protect the confidentiality of any information they receive in confidence during the proceedings of the arbitral tribunal.

11. The arbitral tribunal may, at the request of one of the parties, recommend interim measures of protection.

12. If one of the parties to the dispute does not appear before the arbitral tribunal or fails to defend its case, the other party may request the tribunal to continue the proceedings and to render its final decision. Absence of a party or failure of a party to defend its case shall not constitute a bar to the proceedings. Before rendering its final decision, the arbitral tribunal must satisfy itself that the claim is well founded in fact and law.

13. The arbitral tribunal may hear and determine counter-claims arising directly out of the subject-matter of the dispute.

14. Unless the arbitral tribunal determines otherwise because of the particular circumstances of the case, the expenses of the tribunal, including the remuneration of its members, shall be borne by the parties to the dispute in equal shares. The tribunal shall keep a record of all its expenses, and shall furnish a final statement thereof to the parties.

15. Any Party to this Convention having an interest of a legal nature in the subject-matter of the dispute, and which may be affected by a decision in the case, may intervene in the proceedings with the consent of the tribunal.

16. The arbitral tribunal shall render its award within five months of the date on which it is established unless it finds it necessary to extend the time limit for a period which should not exceed five months.

17. The award of the arbitral tribunal shall be accompanied by a statement of reasons. It shall be final and binding upon all parties to the dispute. The award will be transmitted by the arbitral tribunal to the parties to the dispute and to the secretariat. The secretariat will forward the information received to all Parties to this Convention.

18. Any dispute which may arise between the parties concerning the interpretation or execution of the award may be submitted by either party to the arbitral tribunal which made the award or, if the latter cannot be seized thereof, to another tribunal constituted for this purpose in the same manner as the first.

Convention on the Transboundary Effects of Industrial Accidents,
Helsinki, 17 March 1992

This Convention is the first treaty to set out comprehensive principles for the prevention of, preparedness for, and response to, the effects of industrial accidents capable of causing transboundary effects. It applies only to accidents or activities involving hazardous substances and includes provisions on accident prevention, consultation, emergency preparedness and response, public information and participation, and mutual assistance. Some of these provisions undoubtedly draw upon 'international law and custom, in particular the principles of good neighbourliness, reciprocity, non-discrimination and good faith' (preamble). Earlier examples of attempts to codify and develop international law with regard to accidents are the International Convention on Oil Pollution Preparedness, Response and Co-operation, 1990, *repr.* 30 *ILM* (1991) 735; the Convention on Early Notification of a Nuclear Accident, 1986 (q.v.); and the Convention on Assistance in the Case of a Nuclear Accident or Radiological Emergency, 1986, *repr.* 25 *ILM* (1986) 1377. There are thirteen annexes (not reproduced) to the Convention, *repr.* 31 *ILM* (1992) 1333 and UN Doc. E/ECE/1268. Participation is open to the European Community and all member states of the UN Economic Commission for Europe. For parties, reservations, and declarations see UN, *Multilateral Treaties Deposited with the Secretary-General,* UN Doc. ST/LEG/SER.E/ (current year). Twenty-six states and the EC signed the Convention in 1992. Negotiation of the Convention was initiated in 1989 by the Sofia Meeting of the CSCE on the Protection of the Environment. For background information, see ECE/ENVWA/R. 54. On 1 January 1995 it had six parties, but was not in force.

TEXT

Preamble

The Parties to this Convention,

Mindful of the special importance, in the interest of present and future generations, of protecting human beings and the environment against the effects of industrial accidents,

Recognizing the importance and urgency of preventing serious adverse effects of industrial accidents on human beings and the environment, and of promoting all measures that stimulate the rational, economic and efficient use of preventive, preparedness and response measures to enable environmentally sound and sustainable economic development,

Taking into account the fact that the effects of industrial accidents may make themselves felt across borders, and require cooperation among States,

Affirming the need to promote active international cooperation among the States concerned before, during and after an accident, to enhance appropriate policies and to reinforce and coordinate action at all appropriate levels for promoting the prevention of, preparedness for and response to the transboundary effects of industrial accidents,

Noting the importance and usefulness of bilateral and multilateral arrangements for the prevention of, preparedness for and response to the effects of industrial accidents,

Conscious of the role played in this respect by the United Nations Economic Commission for Europe (ECE) and recalling, *inter alia*, the ECE Code of Conduct on Accidental Pollution of Transboundary Inland Waters and the Convention on Environmental Impact Assessment in a Transboundary Context,

Having regard to the relevant provisions of the Final Act of the Conference on Security and Cooperation in Europe (CSCE), the Concluding Document of the Vienna Meeting of Representatives of the Participating States of the CSCE, and the outcome of the Sofia Meeting on the Protection of the Environment of the CSCE, as well as to pertinent activities and mechanisms in the United Nations Environment Programme (UNEP), in particular the APELL programme, in the International Labour Organisation (ILO), in particular the Code of Practice on the Prevention of Major Industrial Accidents, and in other relevant international organizations,

Considering the pertinent provisions of the Declaration of the United Nations Conference on the Human Environment, and in particular principle 21, according to which States have, in accordance with the Charter of the United Nations and the principles of international law, the sovereign right to exploit their own resources pursuant to their own environmental policies, and the responsibility to ensure that activities within their jurisdiction or control do not cause damage to the environment of other States or of areas beyond the limits of national jurisdiction,

Taking account of the polluter-pays principle as a general principle of international environmental law,

Underlining the principles of international law and custom, in particular the principles of good-neighbourliness, reciprocity, non-discrimination and good faith,

Have agreed as follows:

Article 1
Definitions

For the purposes of this Convention,

  (a) 'Industrial accident' means an event resulting from an uncontrolled development in the course of any activity involving hazardous substances either:
  (i) In an installation, for example during manufacture, use, storage, handling, or disposal; or
  (ii) During transportation in so far as it is covered by paragraph 2(d) of Article 2;

(b) 'Hazardous activity' means any activity in which one or more hazardous substances are present or may be present in quantities at or in excess of the threshold quantities listed in Annex I hereto, and which is capable of causing transboundary effects;

(c) 'Effects' means any direct or indirect, immediate or delayed adverse consequences caused by an industrial accident on, *inter alia*:
  (i) Human beings, flora and fauna;
  (ii) Soil, water, air and landscape;
  (iii) The interaction between the factors in (i) and (ii);
  (iv) Material assets and cultural heritage, including historical monuments;

(d) 'Transboundary effects' means serious effects within the jurisdiction of a Party as a result of an industrial accident occurring within the jurisdiction of another Party;

(e) 'Operator' means any natural or legal person, including public authorities, in charge of an activity, e.g. supervising, planning to carry out or carrying out an activity;

(f) 'Party' means, unless the text otherwise indicates, a Contracting Party to this Convention;

(g) 'Party of origin' means any Party or Parties under whose jurisdiction an industrial accident occurs or is capable of occurring;

(h) 'Affected Party' means any Party or Parties affected or capable of being affected by transboundary effects of an industrial accident;

(i) 'Parties concerned' means any Party of origin and any affected Party;

(j) 'The public' means one or more natural or legal persons.

Article 2
Scope

1. This Convention shall apply to the prevention of, preparedness for and response to industrial accidents capable of causing transboundary effects, including the effects of such accidents caused by natural disasters, and to international cooperation concerning mutual assistance, research and development, exchange of information and exchange of technology in the area of prevention of, preparedness for and response to industrial accidents.

2. This Convention shall not apply to:

(a) Nuclear accidents or radiological emergencies;
(b) Accidents at military installations;
(c) Dam failures, with the exception of the effects of industrial accidents caused by such failures;
(d) Land-based transport accidents with the exception of:
  (i) Emergency response to such accidents;
  (ii) Transportation on the site of the hazardous activity;

(e) Accidental release of genetically modified organisms;

(f) Accidents caused by activities in the marine environment, including seabed exploration or exploitation;

(g) Spills of oil or other harmful substances at sea.

Article 3
General Provisions

1. The Parties shall, taking into account efforts already made at national and international levels, take appropriate measures and cooperate within the framework of this Convention, to protect human beings and the environment against industrial accidents by preventing such accidents as far as possible, by reducing their frequency and severity and by mitigating their effects. To this end, preventive, preparedness and response measures, including restoration measures, shall be applied.

2. The Parties shall, by means of exchange of information, consultation and other cooperative measures and without undue delay, develop and implement policies and strategies for reducing the risks of industrial accidents and improving preventive, preparedness and response measures, including restoration measures, taking into account, in order to avoid unnecessary duplication, efforts already made at national and international levels.

3. The Parties shall ensure that the operator is obliged to take all measures necessary for the safe performance of the hazardous activity and for the prevention of industrial accidents.

4. To implement the provisions of this Convention, the Parties shall take appropriate legislative, regulatory, administrative and financial measures for the prevention of, preparedness for and response to industrial accidents.

5. The provisions of this Convention shall not prejudice any obligations of the Parties under international law with regard to industrial accidents and hazardous activities.

Article 4
Identification, Consultation and Advice

1. For the purpose of undertaking preventive measures and setting up preparedness measures, the Party of origin shall take measures, as appropriate, to identify hazardous activities within its jurisdiction and to ensure that affected Parties are notified of any such proposed or existing activity.

2. Parties concerned shall, at the initiative of any such Party, enter into discussions on the identification of those hazardous activities that are, reasonably, capable of causing transboundary effects. If the Parties concerned do not agree on whether an activity is such a hazardous activity, any

such Party may, unless the Parties concerned agree on another method of resolving the question, submit that question to an inquiry commission in accordance with the provisions of Annex II hereto for advice,

3. The Parties shall, with respect to proposed or existing hazardous activities, apply the procedures set out in Annex III hereto.

4. When a hazardous activity is subject to an environmental impact assessment in accordance with the Convention on Environmental Impact Assessment in a Transboundary Context and that assessment includes an evaluation of the transboundary effects of industrial accidents from the hazardous activity which is performed in conformity with the terms of this Convention, the final decision taken for the purposes of the Convention on Environmental Impact Assessment in a Transboundary Context shall fulfil the relevant requirements of this Convention.

Article 5
Voluntary Extension

Parties concerned should, at the initiative of any of them, enter into discussions on whether to treat an activity not covered by Annex I as a hazardous activity. Upon mutual agreement, they may use an advisory mechanism of their choice, or an inquiry commission in accordance with Annex II, to advise them. Where the Parties concerned so agree, this Convention, or any part thereof, shall apply to the activity in question as if it were a hazardous activity.

Article 6
Prevention

1. The Parties shall take appropriate measures for the prevention of industrial accidents, including measures to induce action by operators to reduce the risk of industrial accidents. Such measures may include, but are not limited to those referred to in Annex IV hereto.

2. With regard to any hazardous activity, the Party of origin shall require the operator to demonstrate the safe performance of the hazardous activity by the provision of information such as basic details of the process, including but not limited to, analysis and evaluation as detailed in Annex V hereto.

Article 7
Decision-making on Siting

Within the framework of its legal system, the Party of origin shall, with the objective of minimizing the risk to the population and the environment of all affected Parties, seek the establishment of policies on the siting of new hazardous activities and on significant modifications to existing hazardous activities. Within the framework of their legal systems, the affected Parties shall seek the establishment of policies on significant developments in areas which could be affected by transboundary effects of an industrial accident arising out of a hazardous activity so as to minimize the risks involved. In elaborating and establishing these policies, the Parties should consider the matters set out in Annex V, paragraph 2, subparagraphs (1) to (8), and Annex VI hereto.

Article 8
Emergency Preparedness

1. The Parties shall take appropriate measures to establish and maintain adequate emergency preparedness to respond to industrial accidents. The Parties shall ensure that preparedness measures are taken to mitigate transboundary effects of such accidents, on-site duties being undertaken by operators. These measures may include, but are not limited to those referred to in Annex VII hereto. In particular, the Parties concerned shall inform each other of their contingency plans.

2. The Party of origin shall ensure for hazardous activities the preparation and implementation of on-site contingency plans, including suitable measures for response and other measures to prevent and minimize transboundary effects. The Party of origin shall provide to the other Parties concerned the elements it has for the elaboration of contingency plans.

3. Each Party shall ensure for hazardous activities the preparation and implementation of off-site contingency plans covering measures to be taken within its territory to prevent and minimize transboundary effects. In preparing these plans, account shall be taken of the conclusions of analysis and evaluation, in particular the matters set out in Annex V, paragraph 2, subparagraphs (1) to (5). Parties concerned shall endeavour to make such plans compatible. Where appropriate, joint off-site contingency plans shall be drawn up in order to facilitate the adoption of adequate response measures.

4. Contingency plans should be reviewed regularly, or when circumstances so require, taking into account the experience gained in dealing with actual emergencies.

Article 9
Information to, and Participation of the Public

1. The Parties shall ensure that adequate information is given to the public in the areas capable of being affected by an industrial accident arising out of a hazardous activity. This information shall be transmitted through such channels as the Parties deem appropriate, shall include the elements contained in Annex VIII hereto and should take into account matters set out in Annex V, paragraph 2, subparagraphs (1) to (4) and (9).

2. The Party of origin shall, in accordance with the provisions of this

Convention and whenever possible and appropriate, give the public in the areas capable of being affected an opportunity to participate in relevant procedures with the aim of making known its views and concerns on prevention and preparedness measures, and shall ensure that the opportunity given to the public of the affected Party is equivalent to that given to the public of the Party of origin.

3. The Parties shall, in accordance with their legal systems and, if desired, on a reciprocal basis provide natural or legal persons who are being or are capable of being adversely affected by the transboundary effects of an industrial accident in the territory of a Party, with access to, and treatment in the relevant administrative and judicial proceedings, including the possibilities of starting a legal action and appealing a decision affecting their rights, equivalent to those available to persons within their own jurisdiction.

Article 10
Industrial Accident Notification Systems

1. The Parties shall, with the aim of obtaining and transmitting industrial accident notifications containing information needed to counteract transboundary effects, provide for the establishment and operation of compatible and efficient industrial accident notification systems at appropriate levels.

2. In the event of an industrial accident, or imminent threat thereof, which causes or is capable of causing transboundary effects, the Party of origin shall ensure that affected Parties are, without delay, notified at appropriate levels through the industrial accident notification systems. Such notification shall include the elements contained in Annex IX hereto.

3. The Parties concerned shall ensure that, in the event of an industrial accident or imminent threat thereof, the contingency plans prepared in accordance with Article 8 are activated as soon as possible and to the extent appropriate to the circumstances.

Article 11
Response

1. The Parties shall ensure that, in the event of an industrial accident, or imminent threat thereof, adequate response measures are taken, as soon as possible and using the most efficient practices, to contain and minimize effects.

2. In the event of an industrial accident, or imminent threat thereof, which causes or is capable of causing transboundary effects, the Parties concerned shall ensure that the effects are assessed—where appropriate, jointly for the purpose of taking adequate response measures.The Parties concerned shall endeavour to coordinate their response measures.

Article 12
Mutual Assistance

1. If a Party needs assistance in the event of an industrial accident, it may ask for assistance from other Parties, indicating the scope and type of assistance required. A Party to whom a request for assistance is directed shall promptly decide and inform the requesting Party whether it is in a position to render the assistance required and indicate the scope and terms of the assistance that might be rendered.

2. The Parties concerned shall cooperate to facilitate the prompt provision of assistance agreed to under paragraph 1 of this Article, including, where appropriate, action to minimize the consequences and effects of the industrial accident, and to provide general assistance. Where Parties do not have bilateral or multilateral agreements which cover their arrangements for providing mutual assistance, the assistance shall be rendered in accordance with Annex X hereto, unless the Parties agree otherwise.

Article 13
Responsibility and Liability

The Parties shall support appropriate international efforts to elaborate rules, criteria and procedures in the field of responsibility and liability.

Article 14
Research and Development

The Parties shall, as appropriate, initiate and cooperate in the conduct of research into, and in the development of methods and technologies for the prevention of, preparedness for and response to industrial accidents. For these purposes, the Parties shall encourage and actively promote scientific and technological cooperation, including research into less hazardous processes aimed at limiting accident hazards and preventing and limiting the consequences of industrial accidents.

Article 15
Exchange of Information

The Parties shall, at the multilateral or bilateral level, exchange reasonably obtainable information, including the elements contained in Annex XI hereto.

Article 16
Exchange of Technology

1. The Parties shall, consistent with their laws, regulations and practices, facilitate the exchange of technology for the prevention of, preparedness for and response to the effects of industrial accidents, particularly through the promotion of:

(a) Exchange of available technology on various financial bases;
(b) Direct industrial contacts and cooperation;
(c) Exchange of information and experience;
(d) Provision of technical assistance.

2. In promoting the activities specified in paragraph 1, subparagraphs (a) to (d) of this Article, the Parties shall create favourable conditions by facilitating contacts and cooperation among appropriate organizations and individuals in both the private and the public sectors that are capable of providing technology, design and engineering services, equipment or finance.

Article 17
Competent Authorities and Points of Contact

1. Each Party shall designate or establish one or more competent authorities for the purposes of this Convention.

2. Without prejudice to other arrangements at the bilateral or multilateral level, each Party shall designate or establish one point of contact for the purpose of industrial accident notifications pursuant to Article 10, and one point of contact for the purpose of mutual assistance pursuant to Article 12. These points of contact should preferably be the same.

3. Each Party shall, within three months of the date of entry into force of this Convention for that Party, inform the other Parties, through the secretariat referred to in Article 20, which body or bodies it has designated as its point(s) of contact and as its competent authority or authorities.

4. Each Party shall, within one month of the date of decision, inform the other Parties, through the secretariat, of any changes regarding the designation(s) it has made under paragraph 3 of this Article.

5. Each Party shall keep its point of contact and industrial accident notification systems pursuant to Article 10 operational at all times.

6. Each Party shall keep its point of contact and the authorities responsible for making and receiving requests for, and accepting offers of assistance pursuant to Article 12 operational at all times.

Article 18
Conference of the Parties

1. The representatives of the Parties shall constitute the Conference of the Parties of this Convention and hold their meetings on a regular basis. The first meeting of the Conference of the Parties shall be convened not later than one year after the date of the entry into force of this Convention. Thereafter, a meeting of the Conference of the Parties shall be held at least once a year or at the written request of any Party, provided that, within six

months of the request being communicated to them by the secretariat, it is supported by at least one third of the Parties.

2. The Conference of the Parties shall:

(a) Review the implementation of this Convention;

(b) Carry out advisory functions aimed at strengthening the ability of Parties to prevent, prepare for and respond to the transboundary effects of industrial accidents, and at facilitating the provision of technical assistance and advice at the request of Parties faced with industrial accidents;

(c) Establish, as appropriate, working groups and other appropriate mechanisms to consider matters related to the implementation and development of this Convention and, to this end, to prepare appropriate studies and other documentation and submit recommendations for consideration by the Conference of the Parties;

(d) Fulfil such other functions as may be appropriate under the provisions of this Convention;

(e) At its first meeting, consider and, by consensus, adopt rules of procedure for its meetings.

3. The Conference of the Parties, in discharging its functions, shall, when it deems appropriate, also cooperate with other relevant international organizations.

4. The Conference of the Parties shall, at its first meeting, establish a programme of work, in particular with regard to the items contained in Annex XII hereto. The Conference of the Parties shall also decide on the method of work, including the use of national centres and cooperation with relevant international organizations and the establishment of a system with a view to facilitating the implementation of this Convention, in particular for mutual assistance in the event of an industrial accident, and building upon pertinent existing activities within relevant international organizations. As part of the programme of work, the Conference of the Parties shall review existing national, regional and international centres, and other bodies and programmes aimed at coordinating information and efforts in the prevention of, preparedness for and response to industrial accidents, with a view to determining what additional international institutions or centres may be needed to carry out the tasks listed in Annex XII.

5. The Conference of the Parties shall, at its first meeting, commence consideration of procedures to create more favourable conditions for the exchange of technology for the prevention of, preparedness for and response to the effects of industrial accidents.

6. The Conference of the Parties shall adopt guidelines and criteria to facilitate the identification of hazardous activities for the purposes of this Convention.

Article 19
Right to Vote

1. Except as provided for in paragraph 2 of this Article, each Party to this Convention shall have one vote.

2. Regional economic integration organizations as defined in Article 27 shall, in matters within their competence, exercise their right to vote with a number of votes equal to the number of their member States which are Parties to this Convention. Such organizations shall not exercise their right to vote if their member States exercise theirs, and vice versa.

Article 20
Secretariat

The Executive Secretary of the Economic Commission for Europe shall carry out the following secretariat functions:

 (a) Convene and prepare meetings of the Parties;
 (b) Transmit to the Parties reports and other information received in accordance with the provisions of this Convention;
 (c) Such other functions as may be determined by the Parties.

Article 21
Settlement of Disputes

1. If a dispute arises between two or more Parties about the interpretation or application of this Convention, they shall seek a solution by negotiation or by any other method of dispute settlement acceptable to the parties to the dispute.

2. When signing, ratifying, accepting, approving or acceding to this Convention, or at any time thereafter, a Party may declare in writing to the Depositary that, for a dispute not resolved in accordance with paragraph 1 of this Article, it accepts one or both of the following means of dispute settlement as compulsory in relation to any Party accepting the same obligation:

 (a) Submission of the dispute to the International Court of Justice;
 (b) Arbitration in accordance with the procedure set out in Annex XIII hereto.

3. If the parties to the dispute have accepted both means of dispute settlement referred to in paragraph 2 of this Article, the dispute may be submitted only to the International Court of Justice, unless the parties to the dispute agree otherwise.

Article 22
Limitations on the Supply of Information

1. The provisions of this Convention shall not affect the rights or the

obligations of Parties in accordance with their national laws, regulations, administrative provisions or accepted legal practices and applicable international regulations to protect information related to personal data, industrial and commercial secrecy, including intellectual property, or national security.

2. If a Party nevertheless decides to supply such protected information to another Party, the Party receiving such protected information shall respect the confidentiality of the information received and the conditions under which it is supplied, and shall only use that information for the purposes for which it was supplied.

Article 23
Implementation

The Parties shall report periodically on the implementation of this Convention.

Article 24
Bilateral and Multilateral Agreements

1. The Parties may, in order to implement their obligations under this Convention, continue existing or enter into new bilateral or multilateral agreements or other arrangements.

2. The provisions of this Convention shall not affect the right of Parties to take, by bilateral or multilateral agreement where appropriate, more stringent measures than those required by this Convention.

Article 25
Status of Annexes

The Annexes to this Convention form an integral part of the Convention.

Article 26
Amendments to the Convention

1. Any Party may propose amendments to this Convention.

2. The text of any proposed amendment to this Convention shall be submitted in writing to the Executive Secretary of the Economic Commission for Europe, who shall circulate it to all Parties. The Conference of the Parties shall discuss proposed amendments at its next annual meeting, provided that such proposals have been circulated to the Parties by the Executive Secretary of the Economic Commission for Europe at least ninety days in advance.

3. For amendments to this Convention—other than those to Annex I, for which the procedure is described in paragraph 4 of this Article:

(a) Amendments shall be adopted by consensus of the Parties present at the meeting and shall be submitted by the Depositary to all Parties for ratification, acceptance or approval;

(b) Instruments of ratification, acceptance or approval of amendments shall be deposited with the Depositary. Amendments adopted in accordance with this Article shall enter into force for Parties that have accepted them on the ninetieth day following the day of receipt by the Depositary of the sixteenth instrument of ratification, acceptance or approval;

(c) Thereafter, amendments shall enter into force for any other Party on the ninetieth day after that Party deposits its instruments of ratification, acceptance or approval of the amendments.

4. For amendments to Annex I:

(a) The Parties shall make every effort to reach agreement by consensus. If all efforts at consensus have been exhausted and no agreement reached, the amendments shall, as a last resort, be adopted by a nine-tenths majority vote of the Parties present and voting at the meeting. If adopted by the Conference of the Parties, the amendments shall be communicated to the Parties and recommended for approval;

(b) On the expiry of twelve months from the date of their communication by the Executive Secretary of the Economic Commission for Europe, the amendments to Annex I shall become effective for those Parties to this Convention which have not submitted a notification in accordance with the provisions of paragraph 4(c) of this Article, provided that at least sixteen Parties have not submitted such a notification;

(c) Any Party that is unable to approve an amendment to Annex I of this Convention shall so notify the Executive Secretary of the Economic Commission for Europe in writing within twelve months from the date of the communication of the adoption. The Executive Secretary shall without delay notify all Parties of any such notification received. A Party may at any time substitute an acceptance for its previous notification and the amendment to Annex I shall thereupon enter into force for that Party.

(d) For the purpose of this paragraph 'Parties present and voting' means Parties present and casting an affirmative or negative vote.

Article 27
Signature

This Convention shall be open for signature at Helsinki from 17 to 18 March 1992 inclusive, and thereafter at United Nations Headquarters in New York until 18 September 1992, by States members of the Economic Commission for Europe, as well as States having consultative status with the

Economic Commission for Europe pursuant to paragraph 8 of Economic and Social Council resolution 36 (IV) of 28 March 1947, and by regional economic integration organizations constituted by sovereign States members of the Economic Commission for Europe to which their member States have transferred competence in respect of matters governed by this Convention, including the competence to enter into treaties in respect of these matters.

Article 28
Depositary

The Secretary-General of the United Nations shall act as the Depositary of this Convention.

Article 29
Ratification, Acceptance, Approval and Accession

1. This Convention shall be subject to ratification, acceptance or approval by the signatory States and regional economic integration organizations referred to in Article 27.

2. This Convention shall be open for accession by the States and organizations referred to in Article 27.

3. Any organization referred to in Article 27 which becomes Party to this Convention without any of its member States being a Party shall be bound by all the obligations under this Convention. In the case of such organizations, one or more of whose member States is a Party to this Convention, the organization and its member States shall decide on their respective responsibilities for the performance of their obligations under this Convention. In such cases, the organization and the member States shall not be entitled to exercise rights under this Convention concurrently.

4. In their instruments of ratification, acceptance, approval or accession, the regional economic integration organizations referred to in Article 27 shall declare the extent of their competence with respect to the matters governed by this Convention. These organizations shall also inform the Depositary of any substantial modification to the extent of their competence.

Article 30
Entry into Force

1. This Convention shall enter into force on the ninetieth day after the date of deposit of the sixteenth instrument of ratification, acceptance, approval or accession.

2. For the purposes of paragraph 1 of this Article, any instrument deposited by an organization referred to in Article 27 shall not be counted as additional to those deposited by States members of such an organization.

3. For each State or organization referred to in Article 27 which ratifies, accepts or approves this Convention or accedes thereto after the deposit of the sixteenth instrument of ratification, acceptance, approval or accession, this Convention shall enter into force on the ninetieth day after the date of deposit by such State or organization of its instrument of ratification, acceptance, approval or accession.

Article 31
Withdrawal

1. At any time after three years from the date on which this Convention has come into force with respect to a Party, that Party may withdraw from this Convention by giving written notification to the Depositary. Any such withdrawal shall take effect on the ninetieth day after the date of the receipt of the notification by the Depositary.

2. Any such withdrawal shall not affect the application of Article 4 to an activity in respect of which a notification has been made pursuant to Article 4, paragraph 1, or a request for discussions has been made pursuant to Article 4, paragraph 2.

Article 32
Authentic Texts

The original of this Convention, of which the English, French and Russian texts are equally authentic, shall be deposited with the Secretary-General of the United Nations.

IN WITNESS WHEREOF the undersigned, being duly authorized thereto, have signed this Convention.

DONE at Helsinki, this seventeenth day of March one thousand nine hundred and ninety-two.

2. LIABILITY FOR ENVIRONMENTAL DAMAGE

Convention on Third Party Liability in the Field of Nuclear Energy,
Paris, 29 July 1960, with Supplementary Convention, Brussels,
31 January 1963

The Paris Convention is a regional treaty, adopted by OECD in 1960, which harmonizes national laws on liability for nuclear accidents within Western Europe. It creates a common scheme for loss distribution among the victims, and channels absolute but limited liability to the operator of the nuclear installation. A global Convention on Civil Liability for Nuclear Damage (not reproduced here) was adopted at Vienna by the International Atomic Energy Agency in 1963, and is modelled closely on the Paris Convention, to which it is now linked by a Joint Protocol Relating to Application (not reproduced here) adopted in 1988 following the Chernobyl disaster. The Paris Convention must also be read in conjunction with the Brussels Supplementary Convention of 1963, which creates a system of state funded compensation to meet losses in excess of the operator's limited liability. Up to a prescribed limit these are met by the state of installation; in more serious cases they are spread equitably across the community of Western European nuclear states.

The Paris Convention entered into force on 1 April 1968 subject to amendments adopted in 1964. It is reproduced in 956 *UNTS* 251; *UKTS* 69 (1968), Cmnd. 3755; 55 *AJIL* (1961) 1082. 1982 amendments are *repr. UKTS* 6 (1989), Cm. 589, in force 7 October 1988. The amended text is reproduced here. Reservations are permitted within the terms of Article 18. The Convention had fourteen parties in 1995. There is an explanatory memorandum in 8 *European Yearbook* (1960) 225. The Brussels Supplementary Convention entered into force on 4 December 1974 subject to amendments adopted in 1964. It is reproduced in 1041 *UNTS* 358; 2 *ILM* (1963) 685; *UKTS* 44 (1975) Cmnd. 5948. 1982 amendments are *repr. UKTS* 117 (1992) Cm. 1832, in force 1 August 1991. The Supplementary Convention had eleven parties in 1995. 1988 Joint Protocol *repr.* 42 *Nuclear Law Bulletin* (1988) 56, ten parties 1995. The 1963 Vienna Convention, *repr.* Misc. 9 (1964), Cmnd. 2333 and 2 *ILM* (1963) 727, fourteen parties in 1995; negotiations for its reform began in 1990 and were still in progress in 1995. For additional treaties on nuclear liability see IAEA, *International Conventions on Civil Liability for Nuclear Damage* (Vienna, 1976).

Generally, see G. Arrangio-Ruiz, 'Some International Legal Problems of the Civil Uses of Nuclear Energy', 107 *Recueil des Cours* (1962) 582ff; P. W. Birnie and A. E. Boyle, *International Law and the Environment*, (Oxford, 1992) 371ff; IAEA, *Nuclear Law for a Developing World* (Vienna, 1969); R. Fornassier, 'Une Expérience de Solidarité Internationale: La Convention Complémentaire . . .', 8 *AFDI* (1962), 762; OECD, *Nuclear Accidents: Liabilities and Guarantees* (Paris, 1993); G. Doeker and T. Gehring, 'Private or International Liability for Transnational Environmental Damage—The Precedent of Conventional Liability Regimes', 2 *JEL* (1990) 1; O. Von Busekist, 'A Bridge Between Two Conventions on Civil Liability for Nuclear Damage: the Joint Protocol . . .', 43 *Nuclear Law Bulletin* (1989) 10.

TEXT OF THE PARIS CONVENTION

The Governments of the Federal Republic of Germany, the Republic of Austria, the Kingdom of Belgium, the Kingdom of Denmark, Spain, the French Republic, the Kingdom of Greece, the Italian Republic, the Grand Duchy of Luxembourg, the Kingdom of Norway, the Kingdom of the Netherlands, the Portuguese Republic, the United Kingdom of Great Britain and Northern Ireland, the Kingdom of Sweden, the Swiss Confederation and the Turkish Republic;

Considering that the European Nuclear Energy Agency, established within the framework of the Organization for European Economic Co-operation (hereinafter referred to as the 'Organization'), is charged with encouraging the elaboration and harmonization of legislation relating to nuclear energy in participating countries, in particular with regard to third party liability and insurance against atomic risks;

Desirous of ensuring adequate and equitable compensation for persons who suffer damage caused by nuclear incidents whilst taking the necessary steps to ensure that the development of the production and uses of nuclear energy for peaceful purposes is not thereby hindered;

Convinced of the need for unifying the basic rules applying in the various countries to the liability incurred for such damage, whilst leaving these countries free to take, on a national basis, any additional measures which they deem appropriate, including the application of the provisions of this Convention to damage caused by incidents due to ionizing radiations not covered therein;

Have Agreed as follows:

Article 1

(a) For the purposes of this Convention:

    (i) 'A nuclear incident' means any occurrence or succession of occurrences having the same origin which causes damage, provided that such occurrence or succession of occurrences, or any of the damage caused, arises out of or results from the radioactive properties, or a combination of radioactive properties with toxic, explosive, or other hazardous properties of nuclear fuel or radioactive products or waste or with any of them.

    (ii) 'Nuclear installation' means reactors other than those comprised in any means of transport; factories for the manufacture or processing of nuclear substances; factories for the separation of isotopes of nuclear fuel; factories for the reprocessing of irradiated nuclear fuel; facilities for the storage of nuclear substances other than storage incidental to the carriage of such substances; and such other installations in which there are nuclear fuel or radioactive products or waste as the Steering Committee of the European Nuclear Energy Agency (hereinafter referred to as the 'Steering Committee') shall from time to time determine.

(iii) 'Nuclear fuel' means fissionable material in the form of uranium metal, alloy, or chemical compound (including natural uranium), plutonium metal, alloy, or chemical compound, and such other fissionable material as the Steering Committee shall from time to time determine.

(iv) 'Radioactive products or waste' means any radioactive material produced in or made radioactive by exposure to the radiation incidental to the process of producing or utilizing nuclear fuel, but does not include (1) nuclear fuel, or (2) radioisotopes outside a nuclear installation which are used or intended to be used for any industrial, commercial, agricultural, medical or scientific purpose.

(v) 'Nuclear substances' means nuclear fuel (other than natural uranium and other than depleted uranium) and radioactive products or waste.

(vi) 'Operator' in relation to a nuclear installation means the person designated or recognized by the competent public authority as the operator of that installation.

(b) The Steering Committee may, if in its view the small extent of the risks involved so warrants, exclude any nuclear installation, nuclear fuel, or nuclear substances from the application of this Convention.

Article 2

This Convention does not apply to nuclear incidents occurring in the territory of non-Contracting States or to damage suffered in such territory, unless otherwise provided by the legislation of the Contracting Party in whose territory the nuclear installation of the operator liable is situated, and except in regard to rights referred to in Article 6(e).

Article 3

(a) The operator of a nuclear installation shall be liable, in accordance with this Convention, for:

(i) damage to or loss of life of any person; and

(ii) damage to or loss of any property other than

(1) the nuclear installation itself and any property on the site of that installation which is used or to be used in connection with that installation;

(2) in the cases within Article 4, the means of transport upon which

the nuclear substances involved were at the time of the nuclear incident, upon proof that such damage or loss (hereinafter referred to as 'damage') was caused by a nuclear incident involving either nuclear fuel or radioactive products or waste in, or nuclear substances coming from such installation, except as otherwise provided for in Article 4.

(b) Where the damage or loss is caused jointly by a nuclear incident and by an incident other than a nuclear incident, that part of the damage or loss which is caused by such other incident shall, to the extent that it is not reasonably separable from the damage or loss caused by the nuclear incident, be considered to be damage caused by the nuclear incident. Where the damage or loss is caused jointly by a nuclear incident and by an emission of ionizing radiation not covered by this Convention, nothing in this Convention shall limit or otherwise affect the liability of any person in connection with that emission of ionizing radiation.

(c) Any Contracting Party may by legislation provide that the liability of the operator of a nuclear installation situated in its territory shall include liability for damage which arises out of or results from ionizing radiations emitted by any source or radiation inside that installation, other than those referred to in paragraph (a) of this Article.

Article 4

In the case of carriage of nuclear substances, including storage incidental thereto, without prejudice to Article 2:

(a) The operator of a nuclear installation shall be liable, in accordance with this Convention, for damage upon proof that it was caused by a nuclear incident outside that installation and involving nuclear substances in the course of carriage therefrom, only if the incident occurs:

  (i) before liability with regard to nuclear incidents involving the nuclear substances has been assumed, pursuant to the express terms of a contract in writing, by the operator of another nuclear installation;

 (ii) in the absence of such express terms, before the operator of another nuclear installation has taken charge of the nuclear substances; or

(iii) where the nuclear substances are intended to be used in a reactor comprised in a means of transport, before the person duly authorized to operate that reactor has taken charge of the nuclear substances; but

 (iv) where the nuclear substances have been sent to a person within the territory of a non-Contracting State, before they have been unloaded from the means of transport by which they have arrived in the territory of that non-Contracting State.

(b) The operator of a nuclear installation shall be liable, in accordance with this Convention, for damage upon proof that it was caused by a nuclear incident outside that installation and involving nuclear substances in the course of carriage thereto, only if the incident occurs:

   (i) after liability with regard to nuclear incidents involving the nuclear substances has been assumed by him, pursuant to the express terms of a contract in writing, from the operator of another nuclear installation;

   (ii) in the absence of such express terms, after he has taken charge of the nuclear substances; or

   (iii) after he has taken charge of the nuclear substances from a person operating a reactor comprised in a means of transport; but

   (iv) where the nuclear substances have, with the written consent of the operator, been sent from a person within the territory of a non-Contracting State, after they have been loaded on the means of transport by which they are to be carried from the territory of that State.

(c) The operator liable in accordance with this Convention shall provide the carrier with a certificate issued by or on behalf of the insurer or other financial guarantor furnishing the security required pursuant to Article 10. The certificate shall state the name and address of that operator and the amount, type and duration of the security, and these statements may not be disputed by the person by whom or on whose behalf the certificate was issued. The certificate shall also indicate the nuclear substances and the carriage in respect of which the security applies and shall include a statement by the competent public authority that the person named is an operator within the meaning of this Convention.

(d) A Contracting Party may provide by legislation that, under such terms as may be contained therein and upon fulfilment of the requirements of Article 10(a), a carrier may, at his request and with the consent of an operator of a nuclear installation situated in its territory, by decision of the competent public authority, be liable in accordance with this Convention in place of that operator. In such case for all the purposes of this Convention the carrier shall be considered, in respect of nuclear incidents occurring in the course of carriage of nuclear substances, as an operator of a nuclear installation on the territory of the Contracting Party whose legislation so provides.

Article 5

(a) If the nuclear fuel or radioactive products or waste involved in a nuclear incident have been in more than one nuclear installation and are in a nuclear installation at the time damage is caused, no operator of any nuclear installation in which they have previously been shall be liable for the damage.

(b) Where, however, damage is caused by a nuclear incident occurring in a nuclear installation and involving only nuclear substances stored therein incidentally to their carriage, the operator of the nuclear installation shall not be liable where another operator or person is liable pursuant to Article 4.

(c) If the nuclear fuel or radioactive products or waste involved in a nuclear incident have been in more than one nuclear installation and are not in a nuclear installation at the time damage is caused, no operator other than the operator of the last nuclear installation in which they were before the damage was caused or an operator who has subsequently taken them in charge shall be liable for the damage.

(d) If damage gives rise to liability of more than one operator in accordance with this Convention, the liability of these operators shall be joint and several: provided that where such liability arises as a result of damage caused by a nuclear incident involving nuclear substances in the course of carriage in one and the same means of transport, or, in the case of storage incidental to the carriage, in one and the same nuclear installation, the maximum total amount for which such operators shall be liable shall be the highest amount established with respect to any of them pursuant to Article 7 and provided that in no case shall any one operator be required, in respect of a nuclear incident, to pay more than the amount established with respect to him pursuant to Article 7.

Article 6

(a) The right to compensation for damage caused by a nuclear incident may be exercised only against an operator liable for the damage in accordance with this Convention, or, if a direct right of action against the insurer or other financial guarantor furnishing the security required pursuant to Article 10 is given by national law, against the insurer or other financial guarantor.

(b) Except as otherwise provided in this Article, no other person shall be liable for damage caused by a nuclear incident, but this provision shall not affect the application of any international agreement in the field of transport in force or open for signature, ratification or accession at the date of this Convention.

(c)   (i) Nothing in this Convention shall affect the liability:

        (1) of any individual for damage caused by a nuclear incident for which the operator, by virtue of Article 3(a)(ii)(1) and (2) or Article 9, is not liable under this Convention and which results from an act or omission of that individual done with intent to cause damage;

        (2) of a person duly authorized to operate a reactor comprised in a means of transport for damage caused by a nuclear incident

when an operator is not liable for such damage pursuant to Article 4(a)(iii) or (b)(iii).

(ii) The operator shall incur no liability outside this Convention for damage caused by a nuclear incident except where use has not been made of the right provided for in Article 7(c), and then only to the extent that national legislation or the legislation of the Contracting Party in whose territory the nuclear installation of the operator liable is situated has made specific provisions concerning damage to the means of transport.

(d) Any person who has paid compensation in respect of damage caused by a nuclear incident under any international agreement referred to in paragraph (b) of this Article or under any legislation of a non-Contracting State shall, up to the amount which he has paid, acquire by subrogation the rights under this Convention of the person suffering damage whom he has so compensated.

(e) Any person who has his principal place of business in the territory of a Contracting Party or who is the servant of such a person and who has paid compensation in respect of damage caused by a nuclear incident occurring in the territory of a non-Contracting State or in respect of damage suffered in such territory shall, up to the amount which he has paid, acquire the rights which the person so compensated would have had against the operator but for the provisions of Article 2.

(f) The operator shall have a right of recourse only:

(i) if the damage caused by a nuclear incident results from an act or omission done with intent to cause damage, against the individual acting or omitting to act with such intent;

(ii) if and to the extent that it is so provided expressly by contract.

(g) If the operator has a right of recourse to any extent pursuant to paragraph (f) of this Article against any person, that person shall not, to that extent, have a right against the operator under paragraphs (d) or (e) of this Article.

(h) Where provisions of national or public health insurance, social security, workmen's compensation or occupational disease compensation systems include compensation for damage caused by a nuclear incident, rights of beneficiaries of such systems and rights of recourse by virtue of such systems shall be determined by the law of the Contracting Party or by the regulations of the inter-governmental organization which has established such systems.

Article 7

(a) The aggregate of compensation required to be paid in respect of damage caused by a nuclear incident shall not exceed the maximum liability established in accordance with this Article.

(b) The maximum liability of the operator in respect of damage caused by a nuclear incident shall be 15,000,000 European Monetary Agreement units of account as defined at the date of this Convention (hereinafter referred to as 'units of account'): provided that any Contracting Party, taking into account the possibilities for the operator of obtaining the insurance or other financial security required pursuant to Article 10 may establish by legislation a greater or less amount, but in no event less than 5,000,000 units of account. The sums mentioned above may be converted into national currency in round figures.

(c) Any Contracting Party may by legislation provide that the exception in Article 3(a)(ii)(2) shall not apply: provided that in no case shall the inclusion of damage to the means of transport result in reducing the liability of the operator in respect of other damage to an amount less than 5,000,000 units of account.

(d) The amount of liability of operators of nuclear installations in the territory of a Contracting Party established in accordance with paragraph (b) of this Article as well as the provisions of any legislation of a Contracting Party pursuant to paragraph (c) of this Article shall apply to the liability of such operators wherever the nuclear incident occurs.

(e) A Contracting Party may subject the transit of nuclear substances through its territory to the condition that the maximum amount of liability of the foreign operator concerned be increased, if it considers that such amount does not adequately cover the risks of a nuclear incident in the course of the transit: provided that the maximum amount thus increased shall not exceed the maximum amount of liability of operators of nuclear installations situated in its territory.

(f) The provisions of paragraph (e) of this Article shall not apply:
  (i)   to carriage by sea where, under international law, there is a right of entry in cases of urgent distress into the ports of such Contracting Party or a right of innocent passage through its territory; or
  (ii) to carriage by air where, by agreement or under international law there is a right to fly over or land on the territory of such Contracting Party.

(g) Any interest and costs awarded by a court in actions for compensation under this Convention shall not be considered to be compensation for the purposes of this Convention and shall be payable by the operator in addition to any sum for which he is liable in accordance with this Article.

Article 8

(a) The right of compensation under this Convention shall be extinguished if an action is not brought within ten years from the date of the nuclear incident. National legislation may, however, establish a period longer than ten years if measures have been taken by the Contracting Party in whose territory the nuclear installation of the operator liable is situated to cover the liability of that operator in respect of any actions for compensation begun after the expiry of the period of ten years and during such longer period: provided that such extension of the extinction period shall in no case affect the right of compensation under this Convention of any person who has brought an action in respect of loss of life or personal injury against the operator before the expiry of the period of ten years.

(b) In the case of damage caused by a nuclear incident involving nuclear fuel or radioactive products or waste which, at the time of the incident have been stolen, lost, jettisoned or abandoned and have not yet been recovered, the period established pursuant to paragraph (a) of this Article shall be computed from the date of that nuclear incident, but the period shall in no case exceed twenty years from the date of the theft, loss, jettison or abandonment.

(c) National legislation may establish a period of not less than two years for the extinction of the right or as a period of limitation either from the date at which the person suffering damage has knowledge or from the date at which he ought reasonably to have known of both the damage and the operator liable: provided that the period established pursuant to paragraphs (a) and (b) of this Article shall not be exceeded.

(d) Where the provisions of Article 13(c)(ii) are applicable, the right of compensation shall not, however, be extinguished if, within the time provided for in paragraph (a) of this Article,

(i) prior to the determination by the Tribunal referred to in Article 17, an action has been brought before any of the courts from which the Tribunal can choose; if the Tribunal determines that the competent court is a court other than that before which such action has already been brought, it may fix a date by which such action has to be brought before the competent court so determined; or

(ii) a request has been made to a Contracting Party concerned to initiate a determination by the Tribunal of the competent court pursuant to Article 13(c)(ii) and an action is brought subsequent to such determination within such time as may be fixed by the Tribunal.

(e) Unless national law provides to the contrary, any person suffering damage caused by a nuclear incident who has brought an action for compensation within the period provided for in this Article may amend his claim in respect of any aggravation of the damage after the expiry of such period provided that final judgment has not been entered by the competent court.

Article 9

The operator shall not be liable for damage caused by a nuclear incident directly due to an act of armed conflict, hostilities, civil war, insurrection or, except in so far as the legislation of the Contracting Party in whose territory his nuclear installation is situated may provide to the contrary, a grave natural disaster of an exceptional character.

Article 10

(a) To cover the liability under this Convention, the operator shall be required to have and maintain insurance or other financial security of the amount established pursuant to Article 7 and of such type and terms as the competent public authority shall specify.

(b) No insurer or other financial guarantor shall suspend or cancel the insurance or other financial security provided for in paragraph (a) of this Article without giving notice in writing of at least two months to the competent public authority or in so far as such insurance or other financial security relates to the carriage of nuclear substances, during the period of the carriage in question.

(c) The sums provided as insurance, reinsurance or other financial security may be drawn upon only for compensation for damage caused by a nuclear incident.

Article 11

The nature, form and extent of the compensation within the limits of this Convention, as well as the equitable distribution thereof, shall be governed by national law.

Article 12

Compensation payable under this Convention, insurance and reinsurance premiums, sums provided as insurance, reinsurance, or other financial security required pursuant to Article 10, and interest and costs referred to in Article 7(g), shall be freely transferable between the monetary areas of the Contracting Parties.

Article 13

(a) Except as otherwise provided in this Article, jurisdiction over actions under Articles 3, 4, 6(a) and 6(e) shall lie only with the courts of the Contracting Party in whose territory the nuclear incident occurred.

(b) Where a nuclear incident occurs outside the territory of the Contracting Parties, or where the place of the nuclear incident cannot be determined with certainty, jurisdiction over such actions shall lie with the courts of the Contracting Party in whose territory the nuclear installation of the operator liable is situated.

(c) Where jurisdiction would lie with the courts of more than one Contracting Party by virtue of paragraphs (a) or (b) of this Article, jurisdiction shall lie,

(i) if the nuclear incident occurred partly ourside the territory of any Contracting Party and partly in the territory of a single Contracting Party, with the courts of that Contracting Party; and

(ii) in any other case, with the courts of the Contracting Party determined, at the request of a Contracting Party concerned, by the Tribunal referred to in Article 17 as being the most closely related to the case in question.

(d) Judgments entered by the competent court under this Article after trial, or by default, shall, when they have become enforceable under the law applied by that court, become enforceable in the territory of any of the other Contracting Parties as soon as the formalities required by the Contracting Party concerned have been complied with. The merits of the case shall not be the subject of further proceedings. The foregoing provisions shall not apply to interim judgments.

(e) If an action is brought against a Contracting Party under this Convention, such Contracting Party may not, except in respect of measures of execution, invoke any jurisdictional immunities before the court competent in accordance with this Article.

Article 14

(a) This Convention shall be applied without any discrimination based upon nationality, domicile, or residence.

(b) 'National law' and 'national legislation' mean the national law or the national legislation of the court having jurisdiction under this Convention over claims arising out of a nuclear incident, and that law or legislation shall apply to all matters both substantive and procedural not specifically governed by this Convention.

(c) That law and legislation shall be applied without any discrimination based upon nationality, domicile, or residence.

Article 15

(a) Any Contracting Party may take such measures as it deems necessary to provide for an increase in the amount of compensation specified in this Convention.

(b) In so far as compensation for damage involves public funds and is in excess of the 5,000,000 units of account referred to in Article 7, any such measure in whatever form may be applied under conditions which may derogate from the provisions of this Convention.

Article 16

Decisions taken by the Steering Committee under Article 1(a)(iii), 1(a)(iii) and 1(b) shall be adopted by mutual agreement of the members representing the Contracting Parties.

Article 17

Any dispute arising between two or more Contracting Parties concerning the interpretation or application of this Convention shall be examined by the Steering Committee and in the absence of friendly settlement shall, upon the request of a Contracting Party concerned, be submitted to the Tribunal established by the Convention of 20 December 1957 on the Establishment of a Security Control in the Field of Nuclear Energy.

Article 18

(a) Reservations to one or more of the provisions of this Convention may be made at any time prior to ratification of or accession to this Convention or prior to the time of notification under Article 23 in respect of any territory or territories mentioned in the notification, and shall be admissible only if the terms of these reservations have been expressly accepted by the Signatories.

(b) Such acceptance shall not be required from a Signatory which has not itself ratified this Convention within a period of twelve months after the date of notification to it of such reservation by the Secretary-General of the Organization in accordance with Article 24.

(c) Any reservation admitted in accordance with this Article may be withdrawn at any time by notification addressed to the Secretary-General of the Organization.

Article 19

(a) This Convention shall be ratified. Instruments of ratification shall be deposited with the Secretary-General of the Organization.

(b) This Convention shall come into force upon the deposit of instruments of ratification by not less than five of the Signatories. For each Signatory ratifying thereafter, this Convention shall come into force upon the deposit of its instrument of ratification.

Article 20

Amendments to this Convention shall be adopted by mutual agreement of all the Contracting Parties. They shall come into force when ratified or confirmed by two-thirds of the Contracting Parties. For each Contracting Party ratifying or confirming thereafter, they shall come into force at the date of such ratification or confirmation.

Article 21

(a) The Government of any Member or Associate country of the Organization which is not Signatory to this Convention may accede thereto by notification addressed to the Secretary-General of the Organization.

(b) The Government of any other country which is not a Signatory to this

Convention may accede thereto by notification addressed to the Secretary-General of the Organization and with the unanimous assent of the Contracting Parties. Such accession shall take effect from the date of such assent.

Article 22

(a) This Convention shall remain in effect for a period of ten years as from the date of its coming into force. Any Contracting Party may, by giving twelve months' notice to the Secretary-General of the Organization, terminate the application of this Convention to itself at the end of the period of ten years.

(b) This Convention shall, after the period of ten years, remain in force for a period of five years for such Contracting Parties as have not terminated its application in accordance with paragraph (a) of this Article, and thereafter for successive periods of five years for such Contracting Parties as have not terminated its application at the end of one of such periods of five years by giving twelve months' notice to that effect to the Secretary-General of the Organization.

(c) A conference shall be convened by the Secretary-General of the Organization in order to consider revisions to this Convention after a period of five years as from the date of its coming into force or, at any other time, at the request of a Contracting Party, within six months from the date of such request.

Article 23

(a) This Convention shall apply to the metropolitan territories of the Contracting Parties.

(b) Any Signatory or Contracting Party may, at the time of signature or ratification of or accession to this Convention or at any later time, notify the Secretary-General of the Organization that this Convention shall apply to those of its territories, including the territories for whose international relations it is responsible, to which this Convention is not applicable in accordance with paragraph (a) of this Article and which are mentioned in the notification. Any such notification may in respect of any territory or territories mentioned therein be withdrawn by giving twelve months' notice to that effect to the Secretary-General of the Organization.

(c) Any territories of a Contracting Party, including the territories for whose international relations it is responsible, to which this Convention does not apply shall be regarded for the purposes of this Convention as being a territory of a non-Contracting State.

Article 24

The Secretary-General of the Organization shall give notice to all Signatories and acceding Governments of the receipt of any instrument of ratification, accession, withdrawal, notification under Article 23, and decisions of the Steering Committee under Article 1(a)(ii), 1(a)(iii) and 1(b). He shall also notify them of the date on which this Convention comes into force, the text of any amendment thereto, and of the date on which such amendment comes into force, and any reservation made in accordance with Article 18.

Annex I

The following reservations were accepted either at the time of signature of the Convention or at the time of signature of the Additional Protocol:

1. *Article 6(b) and (c) and (d):*
   Reservation by the Government of the Federal Republic of Germany, the Government of the Republic of Austria and the Government of the Kingdom of Greece.
   Reservation of the right to provide, by national law, that persons other than the operator may continue to be liable for damage caused by a nuclear incident on condition that these persons are fully covered in respect of their liability, including defence against unjustified actions, by insurance or other financial security obtained by the operator or out of State funds.

2. *Article 6(b) and (d):*
   Reservation by the Government of the Republic of Austria, the Government of the Kingdom of Greece, the Government of the Kingdom of Norway and the Government of the Kingdom of Sweden.
   Reservation of the right to consider their national legislation which includes provisions equivalent to those included in the international agreements referred to in Article 6(b) as being international agreements within the meaning of Article 6(b) and (d).

3. *Article 8(a):*
   Reservation by the Government of the Federal Republic of Germany and the Government of the Republic of Austria.
   Reservation of the right to establish, in respect of nuclear incidents occurring in the Federal Republic of Germany and in the Republic of Austria respectively, a period longer than ten years if measures have been taken to cover the liability of the operator in respect of any actions for compensation begun after the expiry of the period of ten years and during such longer period.

4. *Article 9:*
   Reservation by the Government of the Federal Republic of Germany and the Government of the Republic of Austria.

Reservation of the right to provide, in respect of nuclear incidents occurring in the Federal Republic of Germany and in the Republic of Austria respectively, that the operator shall be liable for damage caused by a nuclear incident directly due to an act of armed conflict, hostilities, civil war, insurrection or a grave natural disaster of an exceptional character.

5. *Article 19:*
   Reservation by the Government of the Federal Republic of Germany, the Government of the Republic of Austria, and the Government of the Kingdom of Greece.
Reservation of the right to consider ratification of this Convention as constituting an obligation under international law to enact national legislation on third party liability in the field of nuclear energy in accordance with the provisions of this Convention.

Annex II

This Convention shall not be interpreted as depriving a Contracting Party, on whose territory damage was caused by a nuclear incident occurring in the territory of another Contracting Party, of any recourse which might be available to it under international law.

TEXT OF THE BRUSSELS SUPPLEMENTARY CONVENTION

The Governments of the Federal Republic of Germany, the Republic of Austria, the Kingdom of Belgium, the Kingdom of Denmark, Spain, the French Republic, the Italian Republic, the Grand Duchy of Luxembourg, the Kingdom of Norway, the Kingdom of the Netherlands, the United Kingdom of Great Britain and Northern Ireland, the Kingdom of Sweden and the Swiss Confederation;

Being Parties to the Convention of 29 July 1960 on Third Party Liability in the Field of Nuclear Energy, concluded within the framework of the Organization for European Economic Co-operation, now the Organization for Economic Co-operation and Development and as modified by the Additional Protocol concluded in Paris on 28 January 1964 (hereinafter referred to as the 'Paris Convention');

Desirous of supplementing the measures provided in that Convention with a view to increasing the amount of compensation for damage which might result from the use of nuclear energy for peaceful purposes;

Have Agreed as follows:

Article 1

The system instituted by this Convention is supplementary to that of the Paris Convention, shall be subject to the provisions of the Paris Convention, and shall be applied in accordance with the following Articles.

Article 2

(a) The system of this Convention shall apply to damage caused by nuclear incidents, other than those occurring entirely in the territory of a State which is not a Party to this Covention:

   (i) for which an operator of a nuclear installation, used for peaceful purposes, situated in the territory of a Contracting Party to this Convention (hereinafter referred to as a 'Contracting Party'), and which appears on the list established and kept up to date in accordance with the terms of Article 13, is liable under the Paris Convention, and
  (ii) suffered
      (1) in the territory of a Contracting Party; or
      (2) on or over the high seas on board a ship or aircraft registered in the territory of a Contracting Party; or
      (3) on or over the high seas by a national of a Contracting Party, provided that, in the case of damage to a ship or an aircraft, the ship or aircraft is registered in the territory of a Contracting Party;

provided that the courts of a Contracting Party have jurisdiction pursuant to the Paris Convention.

(b) Any Signatory or acceding Government may, at the time of signature of, or accession to, this Convention or on the deposit of its instrument of ratification, declare that, for the purposes of the application of paragraph (a)(ii) of this Article, individuals or certain categories thereof, considered under its law as having their habitual residence in its territory, are assimilated to its own nationals.

(c) In this Article, the expression 'a national of a Contracting Party' shall include a Contracting Party or any of its constituent sub-divisions, or a partnership, or any public or private body whether corporate or not established in the territory of a Contracting Party.

Article 3

(a) Under the conditions established by this Convention, the Contracting Parties undertake that compensation in respect of the damage referred to in Article 2 shall be provided up to the amount of 120 million units of account per incident.

(b) Such compensation shall be provided:

   (i) up to an amount of at least 5 million units of account, out of funds provided by insurance or other financial security, such amount to be established by the legislation of the Contracting Party in whose territory the nuclear installation of the operator liable is situated;

  (ii) between this amount and 70 million units of account, out of public funds to be made available by the Contracting Party in whose territory the nuclear installation is situated;

 (iii) between 70 million and 120 million units of account, out of public funds to be made available by the Contracting Parties according to the formula for contributions specified in Article 12.

(c) For this purpose, each Contracting Party shall either:

   (i) establish the maximum liability of the operator, pursuant to Article 7 of the Paris Convention, at 120 million units of account, and provide that such liability shall be covered by all the funds referred to in paragraph (b) of this Article; or

  (ii) establish the maximum liability of the operator at an amount at least equal to that established pursuant to paragraph (b)(i) of this Article and provide that, in excess of such amount and up to 120 million units of account, the public funds referred to in paragraph (b)(ii) and (iii) of this Article shall be made available by some means other than as cover for the liability of the operator, provided that the rules of substance and procedure laid down in this Convention are not thereby affected.

(d) The obligation of the operator to pay compensation, interest or costs out of public funds made available pursuant to paragraphs (b)(ii) and (iii), and (f) of this Article shall only be enforceable against the operator as and when such funds are in fact made available.

(e) The Contracting Parties, in carrying out this Convention, undertake not to make use of the right provided for in Article 15(b) of the Paris Convention to apply special conditions:

   (i) in respect of compensation for damage provided out of the funds referred to in paragraph (b)(i) of this Article;

  (ii) other than those laid down in this Convention in respect of compensation for damage provided out of the public funds referred to in paragraph (b)(ii) and (iii) of this Article.

(f) The interest and costs referred to in Article 7(g) of the Paris Convention are payable in addition to the amounts referred to in paragraph (b) of this Article and shall be borne in so far as they are awarded in respect of compensation payable out of the funds referred to in:

    (i) paragraph (b)(i) of this Article, by the operator liable;

   (ii) paragraph (b)(ii) of this Article, by the Contracting Party in whose territory the nuclear installation of that operator is situated;

  (iii) paragraph (b)(iii) of this Article, by the Contracting Parties together.

(g) For the purposes of this Convention, 'unit of account' means the unit of account of the European Monetary Agreement as defined at the date of the Paris Convention.

Article 4

(a) If a nuclear incident causes damage which gives rise to liability of more than one operator, the aggregate liability provided for in Article 5(d) of the Paris Convention shall not, to the extent that public funds have to be made available pursuant to Article 3(b)(ii) and (iii), exceed 120 million units of account.

(b) The total amount of the public funds made available pursuant to Article 3(b)(ii) and (iii) shall not, in such event, exceed the difference between 120 million units of account and the sum of the amounts established with respect to such operators pursuant to Article 3(b)(i) or, in the case of an operator whose nuclear installation is situated in the territory of a State which is not a Party to this Convention, the amount established pursuant to Article 7 of the Paris Convention. If more than one Contracting Party is required to make available public funds pursuant to Article 3(b)(ii), such funds shall be made available by them in proportion to the number of nuclear installations situated in their respective territories, which are involved in the nuclear incident and of which the operators are liable.

Article 5

(a) Where the operator liable has a right of recourse pursuant to Article 6(f) of the Paris Convention, the Contracting Party in whose territory the nuclear installation of that operator is situated shall take such legislative measures as are necessary to enable both that Contracting Party and the other Contracting Parties to benefit from this recourse to the extent that public funds have been made available pursuant to Article 3(b)(ii) and (iii), and (f).

(b) Such legislation may provide for the recovery of public funds made available pursuant to Article 3(b)(ii) and (iii), and (f) from such operator if the damage results from fault on his part.

Article 6

In calculating the public funds to be made available pursuant to this Convention, account shall be taken only of those rights to compensation exercised within ten years from the date of the nuclear incident. In the case of damage caused by a nuclear incident involving nuclear fuel or radioactive products or waste which, at the time of the incident have been stolen, lost, jettisoned, or abandoned and have not yet been recovered, such period shall not in any case exceed 20 years from the date of the theft, loss, jettison or abandonment. It shall also be extended in the cases and under the conditions laid down in Article 8(d) of the Paris Convention. Amendments made to claims after the expiry of this period, under the conditions laid down in Article 8(e) of the Paris Convention, shall also be taken into account.

Article 7

Where a Contracting Party makes use of the right provided for in Article 8(c) of the Paris Convention, the period which it establishes shall be a period of prescription of three years either from the date at which the person suffering damage has knowledge or from the date at which he ought reasonably to have known of both the damage and the operator liable.

Article 8

Any person who is entitled to benefit from the provisions of this Convention shall have the right to full compensation in accordance with national law for damage suffered, provided that, where the amount of damage exceeds or is likely to exceed:

  (i) 120 million units of account; or
  (ii) if there is aggregate liability under Article 5(d) of the Paris Convention and a higher sum results therefrom, such higher sum, any Contracting Party may establish equitable criteria for apportionment. Such criteria shall be applied whatever the origin of the funds and, subject to the provisions of Article 2, without discrimination based on the nationality, domicile or residence of the person suffering the damage.

Article 9

(a) The system of disbursements by which the public funds required under Article 3(b)(ii) and (iii), and (f) are to be made available shall be that of the Contracting Party whose courts have jurisdiction.

(b) Each Contracting Party shall ensure that persons suffering damage may enforce their rights to compensation without having to bring separate proceedings according to the origin of the funds provided for such compensation.

(c) No Contracting Party shall be required to make available the public funds referred to in Article 3(b)(ii) and (iii) so long as any of the funds referred to in Article 3(b)(i) remain available.

Article 10

(a) The Contracting Party whose courts have jurisdiction shall be required to inform the other Contracting Parties of a nuclear incident and its circumstances as soon as it appears that the damage caused by such incident exceeds, or is likely to exceed, 70 million units of account. The Contracting Parties shall, without delay, make all the necessary arrangements to settle the procedure for their relations in this connection.

(b) Only the Contracting Party whose courts have jurisdiction shall be entitled to request the other Contracting Parties to make available the public funds required under Article 3(b)(ii) and (f) and shall have exclusive competence to disburse such funds.

(c) Such Contracting Party shall, when the occasion arises, exercise the right of recourse provided for in Article 5 on behalf of the other Contracting Parties who have made available public funds pursuant to Article 3(b)(iii) and (f).

(d) Settlements effected in respect of the payment of compensation out of the public funds referred to in Article 3(b)(ii) and (iii) in accordance with the conditions established by national legislation shall be recognized by the other Contracting Parties, and judgments entered by the competent courts in respect of such compensation shall become enforceable in the territory of the other Contracting Parties in accordance with the provisions of Article 13(d) of the Paris Convention.

Article 11

(a) If the courts having jurisdiction are those of a Contracting Party other than the Contracting Party in whose territory the nuclear installation of the operator liable is situated, the public funds required under Article 3(b)(ii) and (f) shall be made available by the first-named Contracting Party. The Contracting Party in whose territory the nuclear installation of the operator liable is situated shall reimburse to the other Contracting Party the sums paid. These two Contracting Parties shall agree on the procedure for reimbursement.

(b) In adopting all legislative, regulatory or administrative provisions, after the nuclear incident has occurred, concerning the nature, form and extent of the compensation, the procedure for making available the public funds required under Article 3(b)(ii) and, if necessary, the criteria for the apportionment of such funds, the Contracting Party whose courts have jurisdiction shall consult the Contracting Party in whose territory the nuclear installation of the operator liable is situated. It shall further take all measures necessary to enable the latter to intervene in proceedings and to participate in any settlement concerning compensation.

Article 12

(a) The Formula for contributions according to which the Contracting Parties shall make available the public funds referred to in Article 3(b)(iii) shall be determined as follows:

  (i) as to 50 per cent, on the basis of the ratio between the gross national product at current prices of each Contracting Party and the total of the gross national products at current prices of all Contracting Parties as shown by the official statistics published by the Organization for Economic Co-operation and Development for the year preceding the year in which the nuclear incident occurs;

  (ii) as to 50 per cent, on the basis of the ratio between the thermal power of the reactors situated in the territory of each Contracting Party and the total thermal power of the reactors situated in the territories of all the Contracting Parties. This calculation shall be made on the basis of the thermal power of the reactors shown at the date of the nuclear incident in the list referred to in Article 2(a)(i): provided that a reactor shall only be taken into consideration for the purposes of this calculation as from the date when it first reaches criticality.

(b) For the purposes of this Convention, 'thermal power' means

  (i) before the issue of a final operating licence, the planned thermal power;

  (ii) after the issue of such licence, the thermal power authorized by the competent national authorities.

Article 13

(a) Each Contracting Party shall ensure that all nuclear installations used for peaceful purposes situated in its territory, and falling within the definition in Article 1 of the Paris Convention, appear in the list referred to in Article 2(a)(i).

(b) For this purpose, each Signatory or acceding Government shall, on the deposit of its instrument of ratification or accession, communicate to the Belgian Government full particulars of such installations.

(c) Such particulars shall indicate:

  (i) in the case of installations not yet completed, the expected date on which the risk of a nuclear incident will exist;

  (ii) and further, in the case of reactors, the expected date on which they will first reach criticality, and also their thermal power.

(d) Each Contracting Party shall also communicate to the Belgian Government the exact date of the existence of the risk of a nuclear incident and, in the case of reactors, the date on which they first reached criticality.

(e) Each Contracting Party shall also communicate to the Belgian Government all modifications to be made to the list. Where such modifications include the addition of a nuclear installation, the communication must be made at least three months before the expected date on which the risk of a nuclear incident will exist.

(f) If a Contracting Party is of the opinion that the particulars, or any modification to be made to the list, communicated by another Contracting Party do not comply with the provisions of Article 2(a)(i) and of this Article, it may raise objections thereto only by addressing them to the Belgian Government within three months from the date on which it has received notice pursuant to paragraph (h) of this Article.

(g) If a Contracting Party is of the opinion that a communication required in accordance with this Article has not been made within the time prescribed in this Article, it may raise objections only by addressing them to the Belgian Government within three months from the date on which it knew of the facts which, in its opinion, ought to have been communicated.

(h) The Belgian Government shall give notice as soon as possible to each Contracting Party of the communications and objections which it has received pursuant to this Article.

(i) The list referred to in Article 2(a)(i) shall consist of all the particulars and modifications referred to in paragraphs (b), (c), (d) and (e) of this Article, it being understood that objections submitted pursuant to paragraphs (f) and (g) of this Article shall have effect retrospective to the date on which they were raised, if they are sustained.

(j) The Belgian Government shall supply any Contracting Party on demand with an up-to-date statement of the nuclear installations covered by this Convention and the details supplied in respect of them pursuant to this Article.

Article 14

(a) Except in so far as this Convention otherwise provides, each Contracting Party may exercise the powers vested in it by virtue of the Paris Convention, and any provisions made thereunder may be invoked against the other Contracting Parties in order that the public funds referred to in Article 3(b)(ii) and (iii) be made available.

(b) Any such provisions made by a Contracting Party pursuant to Articles 2, 7(c) and 9 of the Paris Convention as a result of which the public funds referred to in Article 3(b)(ii) and (iii) are required to be made available may not be invoked against any other Contracting Party unless it has consented thereto.

(c) Nothing in this Convention shall prevent a Contracting Party from making provisions outside the scope of the Paris Convention and of this Convention, provided that such provisions shall not involve any further obligation on the part of the other Contracting Parties in so far as their public funds are concerned.

Article 15

(a) Any Contracting Party may conclude an agreement with a State which is not a Party to this Convention concerning compensation out of public funds for damage caused by a nuclear incident.

(b) To the extent that the conditions for payment of compensation under any such agreement are not more favourable than those which result from the measures adopted by the Contracting Party concerned for the application of the Paris Convention and of this Convention, the amount of damage caused by a nuclear incident covered by this Convention and for which compensation is payable by virtue of such an agreement may be taken into consideration, where the proviso to Article 8 applies, in calculating the total amount of damage caused by that incident.

(c) The provisions of paragraphs (a) and (b) of this Article shall in no case affect the obligations under Article 3(b)(ii) and (iii) of those Contracting Parties which have not given their consent to such agreement.

(d) Any Contracting Party intending to conclude such an agreement shall notify the other Contracting Parties of its intention. Agreements concluded shall be notified to the Belgian Government.

Article 16

(a) The Contracting Parties shall consult each other upon all problems of common interest raised by the application of this Convention and of the Paris Convention, especially Articles 20 and 22(c) of the latter Convention.

(b) They shall consult each other on the desirability of revising this Convention after a period of five years from the date of its coming into force, and at any other time upon the request of a Contracting Party.

Article 17

Any dispute arising between two or more Contracting Parties concerning the interpretation or application of this Convention shall, upon the request of a Contracting Party concerned, be submitted to the European Nuclear Energy Tribunal established by the Convention of 20 December 1957 on the Establishment of a Security Control in the Field of Nuclear Energy.

Article 18

(a) Reservations to one or more of the provisions of this Convention may be made at any time prior to ratification of this Convention if the terms of these reservations have been expressly accepted by all Signatories or, at the time of accession or of the application of the provisions of Articles 21 and 24, if the terms of these reservations have been expressly accepted by all Signatories and acceding Governments.

(b) Such acceptance shall not be required from a Signatory which has not itself ratified this Convention within a period of twelve months after the date of notification to it of such reservation by the Belgian Government in accordance with Article 25.

(c) Any reservation accepted in accordance with the provisions of paragraph (a) of this Article may be withdrawn at any time by notification addressed to the Belgian Government.

Article 19

No State may become or continue to be a Contracting Party to this Convention unless it is a Contracting Party to the Paris Convention.

Article 20

(a) The Annex to this Convention shall form an integral part thereof.

(b) This Convention shall be ratified. Instruments of ratification shall be deposited with the Belgian Government.

(c) This Convention shall come into force three months after the deposit of the sixth instrument of ratification.

(d) For each Signatory ratifying this Convention after the deposit of the sixth instrument of ratification, it shall come into force three months after the date of the deposit of its instrument of ratification.

Article 21

Amendments to this Convention shall be adopted by agreement among all the Contracting Parties. They shall come into force on the date when all Contracting Parties have ratified or confirmed them.

Article 22

(a) After the coming into force of this Convention, any Contracting Party to the Paris Convention which has not signed this Convention may request accession to this Convention by notification addressed to the Belgian Government.

(b) Such accession shall require the unanimous assent of the Contracting Parties.

(c) Once such assent has been given, the Contracting Party to the Paris Convention requesting accession shall deposit its instrument of accession with the Belgian Government.

(d) The accession shall take effect three months from the date of deposit of the instrument of accession.

Article 23

(a) This Convention shall remain in force until the expiry of the Paris Convention.

(b) Any Contracting Party may, by giving twelve months' notice to the Belgian Government, terminate the application of this Convention to itself after the end of the period of ten years specified in Article 22(a) of the Paris Convention. Within six months after receipt of such notice, any other Contracting Party may, by notice to the Belgian Government, terminate the application of this Convention to itself as from the date when it ceases to have effect in respect of the Contracting Party which first gave notice.

(c) The expiry of this Convention or the withdrawal of a Contracting Party shall not terminate the obligations assumed by each Contracting Party under this Convention to pay compensation for damage caused by nuclear incidents occurring before the date of such expiry or withdrawal.

(d) The Contracting Parties shall, in good time, consult each other on what measures should be taken after the expiry of this Convention or the withdrawal of one or more of the Contracting Parties, to provide compensation comparable to that accorded by this Convention for damage caused by nuclear incidents occurring after the date of such expiry or withdrawal and for which the operator of a nuclear installation in operation before such date within the territories of the Contracting Parties is liable.

Article 24

(a) This Convention shall apply to the metropolitan territories of the Contracting Parties.

(b) Any Contracting Party desiring the application of this Convention to one or more of the territories in respect of which, pursuant to Article 23 of the Paris Convention, it has given notification of application of that Convention, shall address a request to the Belgian Government.

(c) The application of this Convention to any such territory shall require the unanimous assent of the Contracting Parties.

(d) Once such assent has been given, the Contracting Party concerned shall address to the Belgian Government a notification which shall take effect as from the date of its receipt.

(c) Such notification may, as regards any territory mentioned therein, be withdrawn by the Contracting Party which has made it by giving 12 months' notice to that effect to the Belgian Government.

(f) If the Paris Convention ceases to apply to any such territory, this Convention shall also cease to apply thereto.

Article 25

The Belgian Government shall notify all Signatories and acceding Governments of the receipt of any instrument of ratification, accession or withdrawal, and shall also notify them of the date on which this Convention comes into force, the text of any amendment thereto and the date on which such amendment comes into force, any reservations made in accordance with Article 18, and all notifications which it has received.

Annex

THE GOVERNMENTS OF THE CONTRACTING PARTIES declare that compensation for damage caused by a nuclear incident not covered by the Supplementary Convention solely by reason of the fact that the relevant nuclear installation, on account of its utilization, is not on the list referred to in Article 2 of the Supplementary Convention (including the case where such installation is considered by one or more but not all of the Governments to be outside the Paris Convention):

- — shall be provided without discrimination among the nationals of the Contracting Parties to the Supplementary Convention; and
- — shall not be limited to less than 120 million units of account.

In addition, if they have not already done so, they shall endeavour to make the rules for compensation of persons suffering damage caused by such incidents as similar as possible to those established in respect of nuclear incidents occurring in connection with nuclear installations covered by the Supplementary Convention.

Convention on Civil Liability for Oil Pollution Damage, London, 27 November 1992 and Convention on the Establishment of an International Fund for Compensation for Oil Pollution Damage, London, 27 November 1992, with Protocols of 1992

These two conventions were adopted by IMO in 1992 to replace earlier treaties with the same title concluded at Brussels on 29 November 1969 and 18 December 1971 respectively. They are notable because they deal with liability for ultrahazardous activities by facilitating direct recourse against the polluter, without involving states. The Liability Convention creates a common scheme of civil liability for oil pollution damage, including environmental damage, caused by oil tankers. This scheme is based on the principle of strict but limited liability, channelled, in this case, to shipowners. The Fund Convention provides for additional compensation funded by industry, in this case primarily the cargo owners.

The 1969 text of the Liability Convention is *repr. UKTS* 106 (1975) Cmnd. 6183; 9 *ILM* (1970) 45; 64 *AJIL* (1970) 481; 973 *UNTS* 3; in force 19 June 1975; 90 parties 24 February 1995; amended by 1976 protocol, *repr.* 16 *ILM* (1977) 617, in force 8 April 1981, 49 parties 24 February 1995. The 1971 text of the Fund Convention is *repr. UKTS* 95 (1978) Cmnd. 7383; 66 *AJIL* (1972) 712; 11, *ILM* (1972) 284; in force 16 October 1978; 65 parties 24 February 1995; amended by 1976 Protocol, *repr.* 16 *ILM* (1977) 621, in force 22 November 1994; 30 parties 24 February 1995. Both conventions were amended by protocols in 1984 which did not enter into force and were replaced by further protocols of amendment, adopted 27 November 1992, *repr.* IMO/LEG/CONF. 9/15 and 16. The 1992 text is reproduced here. The relationship between the 1992 Conventions and earlier texts is referred to in Resolutions 1–5 of the Final Act of the Conference on the Revision of the 1969 Civil Liability Convention and the 1971 Fund Convention, IMO/LEG/ CONF. 9/17 (1992). The 1992 Liability Convention requires ten parties, including four States each with not less than one million units of gross tanker tonnage, before it can enter into force. The 1992 Fund Convention requires eight parties with a liability to contribute in respect of at least 450 million tons of oil before it can enter into force. Both conventions: 6 parties 24 February 1995.

For parties, reservations and declarations see IMO, *Status of Multilateral Conventions and Instruments in Respect of which the IMO or its Secretary-General Performs Depository or other Functions* (current year). For information on the operation of the Fund, see International Oil Pollution Compensation Fund, *Annual Reports*. On the 1969 Convention, see IMCO, *Official Records of the International Legal Conference on Marine Pollution Damage* (London, 1969). See generally D. W. Abecassis and R. L. Jarashow, *Oil Pollution from Ships* (2nd edn., London, 1985), Chs. 10 and 11; P. W. Birnie and A. E. Boyle, *International Law and the Environment* (Oxford, 1992) 292ff; E. D. Brown in W. E. Butler (ed.), *The Law of the Sea and International Shipping* (New York, 1985), 275; M. Jacobsson and N. Trotz, 'The Definition of Pollution Damage in the 1984 Protocols . . . ', 17 *JMLC* (1986) 467; A. Popp, 'Liability and Compensation for Pollution Damage Caused by Ships Revisited', *LMCLQ* (1985) 118; D. J. Wilkinson, 'Moving the Boundaries of Compensable Environmental Damage Caused by Marine Oil Spills: The Effect of Two New International Protocols', 5 *JEL* (1993) 71; N. Gaskell, 'Compensation for Oil Pollution: 1992 Protocols to the Civil Liability Convention and Funds Convention', *Int. J. Marine and Coastal L.* (1993) 286. For industry schemes of compensation see also TOVALOP Agreement, 8 *ILM* (1969) 497 and CRISTAL Agreement, 10 *ILM* (1971) 137.

TEXT OF THE LIABILITY CONVENTION

Article I

For the purposes of this Convention:

1. 'Ship' means any sea-going vessel and sea-borne craft of any type whatsoever constructed or adapted for the carriage of oil in bulk as cargo, provided that a ship capable of carrying oil and other cargoes shall be regarded as a ship only when it is actually carrying oil in bulk as cargo and during any voyage following such carriage unless it is proved that it has no residues of such carriage of oil in bulk aboard.

2. 'Person' means any individual or partnership or any public or private body, whether corporate or not, including a State or any of its constituent sub-divisions.

3. 'Owner' means the person or persons registered as the owner of the ship or, in the absence of registration, the person or persons owning the ship. However in the case of a ship owned by a State and operated by a company which in that State is registered as the ship's operator, 'owner' shall mean such a company.

4. 'State of the ship's registry' means in relation to registered ships the State of registration of the ship, and in relation to unregistered ships the State whose flag the ship is flying.

5. 'Oil' means any persistent hydrocarbon mineral oil such as crude oil, fuel oil, heavy diesel oil and lubricating oil, whether carried on board a ship as cargo or in the bunkers of such a ship.

6. 'Pollution damage' means:

   (a) loss or damage caused outside the ship by contamination resulting from the escape or discharge of oil from the ship, wherever such escape or discharge may occur, provided that compensation for impairment of the environment other than loss of profit from such impairment shall be limited to costs of reasonable measures of reinstatement actually undertaken or to be undertaken;

   (b) the costs of preventive measures and further loss or damage caused by preventive measures.

7. 'Preventive measures' means any reasonable measures taken by any person after an incident has occurred to prevent or minimize pollution damage.

8. 'Incident' means any occurrence, or series of occurrences having the same origin, which causes pollution damage or creates a grave and imminent threat of causing such damage.

9. 'Organization' means the International Maritime Organization.

10. '1969 Liability Convention' means the International Convention on Civil Liability for Oil Pollution Damage, 1969. For States Parties to the

Protocol of 1976 to that Convention, the term shall be deemed to include the 1969 Liability Convention as amended by that Protocol.

Article II

This Convention shall apply exclusively:

(a) to pollution damage caused:
   (i) in the territory, including the territorial sea, of a Contracting State, and
   (ii) in the exclusive economic zone of a Contracting State, established in accordance with international law, or, if a Contracting State has not established such a zone, in an area beyond and adjacent to the territorial sea of that State determined by that State in accordance with international law and extending not more than 200 nautical miles from the baselines from which the breadth of its territorial sea is measured;
(b) to preventive measures, whenever taken to prevent or minimize such damage.

Article III

1. Except as provided in paragraphs 2 and 3 of this Article, the owner of a ship at the time of an incident, or where the incident consists of a series of occurrences at the time of the first such occurrence, shall be liable for any pollution damage caused by the ship as a result of the incident.

2. No liability for pollution damage shall attach to the owner if he proves that the damage:

(a) resulted from an act of war, hostilities, civil war, insurrection or a natural phenomenon of an exceptional, inevitable and irresistible character, or
(b) was wholly caused by an act or omission done with intent to cause damage by a third party, or
(c) was wholly caused by the negligence or other wrongful act of any Government or other authority responsible for the maintenance of lights or other navigational aids in the exercise of that function.

3. If the owner proves that the pollution damage resulted wholly or partially either from an act or omission done with intent to cause damage by the person who suffered the damage or from the negligence of that person, the owner may be exonerated wholly or partially from his liability to such person.

4. No claim for compensation for pollution damage may be made against the owner otherwise than in accordance with this Convention. Subject to paragraph 5 of this Article, no claim for compensation for pollution damage under this Convention or otherwise may be made against:

    (a) the servants or agents of the owner or the members of the crew;

    (b) the pilot or any other person who, without being a member of the crew, performs services for the ship;

    (c) any charterer (howsoever described, including a bareboat charterer), manager or operator of the ship;

    (d) any person performing salvage operations with the consent of the owner or on the instructions of a competent public authority;

    (e) any person taking preventive measures;

    (f) all servants or agents of persons mentioned in sub-paragraphs (c), (d) and (e):

unless the damage resulted from their personal act or omission, committed with the intent to cause such damage, or recklessly and with knowledge that such damage would probably result.

5. Nothing in this Convention shall prejudice any right of recourse of the owner against third parties.

Article IV

When an incident involving two or more ships occurs and pollution damage results therefrom, the owners of all the ships concerned, unless exonerated under Article III, shall be jointly and severally liable for all such damage which is not reasonably separable.

Article V

1. The owner of a ship shall be entitled to limit his liability under this Convention in respect of any one incident to an aggregate amount calculated as follows:

    (a) 3 million units of account for a ship not exceeding 5,000 units of tonnage;

    (b) for a ship with a tonnage in excess thereof, for each additional unit of tonnage, 420 units of account in addition to the amount mentioned in sub-paragraph (a);

provided, however, that this aggregate amount shall not in any event exceed 59.7 million units of account.

2. The owner shall not be entitled to limit his liability under this Convention if it is proved that the pollution damage resulted from his personal act or omission, committed with the intent to cause such damage, or recklessly and with knowledge that such damage would probably result.

3. For the purpose of availing himself of the benefit of limitation provided for in paragraph 1 of this Article the owner shall constitute a fund for the total sum representing the limit of his liability with the Court or other

competent authority of any one of the Contracting States in which action is brought under Article IX or, if no action is brought, with any Court or other competent authority in any one of the Contracting States in which an action can be brought under Article IX. The fund can be constituted either by depositing the sum or by producing a bank guarantee or other guarantee, acceptable under the legislation of the Contracting State where the fund is constituted, and considered to be adequate by the Court or other competent authority.

4. The fund shall be distributed among the claimants in proportion to the amounts of their established claims.

5. If before the fund is distributed the owner or any of his servants or agents or any person providing him insurance or other financial security has as a result of the incident in question, paid compensation for pollution damage, such person shall, up to the amount he has paid, acquire by subrogation the rights which the person so compensated would have enjoyed under this Convention.

6. The right of subrogation provided for in paragraph 5 of this Article may also be exercised by a person other than those mentioned therein in respect of any amount of compensation for pollution damage which he may have paid but only to the extent that such subrogation is permitted under the applicable national law.

7. Where the owner or any other person establishes that he may be compelled to pay at a later date in whole or in part any such amount of compensation, with regard to which such person would have enjoyed a right of subrogation under paragraphs 5 or 6 of this Article, had the compensation been paid before the fund was distributed, the Court or other competent authority of the State where the fund has been constituted may order that a sufficient sum shall be provisionally set aside to enable such person at such later date to enforce his claim against the fund.

8. Claims in respect of expenses reasonably incurred or sacrifices reasonably made by the owner voluntarily to prevent or minimize pollution damage shall rank equally with other claims against the fund.

9. (a) The 'unit of account' referred to in paragraph 1 of this Article is the Special Drawing Right as defined by the International Monetary Fund. The amounts mentioned in paragraph 1 shall be converted into national currency on the basis of the value of that currency by reference to the Special Drawing Right on the date of the constitution of the fund referred to in paragraph 3. The value of the national currency, in terms of the Special Drawing Right, of a Contracting State which is a member of the International Monetary Fund shall be calculated in accordance with the method of valuation applied by the International Monetary Fund in effect on the date in

question for its operations and transactions. The value of the national currency, in terms of the Special Drawing Right, of a Contracting State which is not a member of the International Monetary Fund, shall be calculated in a manner determined by that State.

(b) Nevertheless, a Contracting State which is not a member of the International Monetary Fund and whose law does not permit the application of the provisions of paragraph 9(a) may, at the time of ratification, acceptance, approval of or accession to this Convention or at anytime thereafter, declare that the unit of account referred to in paragraph 9(a) shall be equal to 15 gold francs. The gold franc referred to in this paragraph corresponds to sixty-five and a half milligrammes of gold of millesimal fineness nine hundred. The conversion of the gold franc into the national currency shall be made according to the law of the State concerned.

(c) The calulation mentioned in the last sentence of paragraph 9(a) and the conversion mentioned in paragraph 9(b) shall be made in such manner as to express in the national currency of the Contracting State as far as possible the same real value for the amounts in paragraph 1 as would result from the application of the first three sentences of paragraph 9(a). Contracting States shall communicate to the depositary the manner of calculation pursuant to paragraph 9(a), or the result of the conversion in paragraph 9(b) as the case may be, when depositing an instrument of ratification, acceptance, approval of or accession to this Convention and whenever there is a change in either.

10. For the purpose of this Article the ship's tonnage shall be the gross tonnage calculated in accordance with the tonnage measurement regulations contained in Annex I of the International Convention on Tonnage Measurement of Ships, 1969.

11. The insurer or other person providing financial security shall be entitled to consititute a fund in accordance with this Article on the same conditions and having the same effect as if it were constituted by the owner. Such a fund may be constituted even if, under the provisions of paragraph 2, the owner is not entitled to limit his liability, but its constitution shall in that case not prejudice the rights of any claimant against the owner.

Article VI

1. Where the owner, after an incident, has constituted a fund in accordance with Article V, and is entitled to limit his liability,

(a) no person having a claim for pollution damage arising out of that incident shall be entitled to exercise any right against any other assets of the owner in respect of such claim;

(b) the Court or other competent authority of any Contracting State shall order the release of any ship or other property belonging to the owner which has been arrested in respect of a claim for pollution damage arising out of that incident, and shall similarly release any bail or other security furnished to avoid such arrest.

2. The foregoing shall, however, only apply if the claimant has access to the Court administering the fund and the fund is actually available in respect of his claim.

Article VII

1. The owner of a ship registered in a Contracting State and carrying more than 2,000 tons of oil in bulk as cargo shall be required to maintain insurance or other financial security, such as the guarantee of a bank or a certificate delivered by an international compensation fund, in the sums fixed by applying the limits of liability prescribed in Article V, paragraph 1 to cover his liability for pollution damage under this Convention.

2. A certificate attesting that insurance or other financial security is in force in accordance with the provisions of this Convention shall be issued to each ship after the appropriate authority of a Contracting State has determined that the requirements of paragraph 1 have been complied with. With respect to a ship registered in a Contracting State such certificate shall be issued or certified by the appropriate authority of the State of the ship's registry; with respect to a ship not registered in a Contracting State it may be issued or certified by the appropriate authority of any Contracting State. This certificate shall be in the form of the annexed model and shall contain the following particulars:

(a) name of ship and port of registration;
(b) name and principal place of business of owner;
(c) type of security;
(d) name and principal place of business of insurer or other person giving security and, where appropriate, place of business where the insurance or security is established;
(e) period of validity of certificate which shall not be longer than the period of validity of the insurance or other security.

3. The certificate shall be in the official language or languages of the issuing State. If the language used is neither English nor French, the text shall include a translation into one of these languages.

4. The certificate shall be carried on board the ship and a copy shall be deposited with the authorities who keep the record of the ship's registry or, if the ship is not registered in a Contracting State, with the authorities of the State issuing or certifying the certificate.

5. An insurance or other financial security shall not satisfy the requirements of this Article if it can cease, for reasons other than the expiry

of the period of validity of the insurance or security specified in the certificate under paragraph 2 of this Article, before three months have elapsed from the date on which notice of its termination is given to the authorities referred to in paragraph 4 of this Article, unless the certificate has been surrendered to these authorities or a new certificate has been issued within the said period. The foregoing provisions shall similarly apply to any modification which results in the insurance or security no longer satisfying the requirements of this Article.

6. The State of registry shall, subject to the provisions of this Article, determine the conditions of issue and validity of the certificate.

7. Certificates issued or certified under the authority of a Contracting State in accordance with paragraph 2 shall be accepted by other Contracting States for the purposes of this Convention and shall be regarded by other Contracting States as having the same force as certificates issued or certified by them even if issued or certified in respect of a ship not registered in a Contracting State. A Contracting State may at any time request consultation with the issuing or certifying State should it believe that the insurer or guarantor named in the certificate is not financially capable of meeting the obligations imposed by this Convention.

8. Any claim to compensation for pollution damage may be brought directly against the insurer or other person providing financial security for the owner's liability for pollution damage. In such case the defendant may, even if the owner is not entitled to limit his liability according to Article V, paragraph 2, avail himself of the limits of liability prescribed in Article V, paragraph 1. He may further avail himself of the defences (other than the bankruptcy or winding up of the owner) which the owner himself would have been entitled to invoke. Furthermore, the defendant may avail himself of the defence that the pollution damage resulted from the wilful misconduct of the owner himself, but the defendant shall not avail himself of any other defence which he might have been entitled to invoke in proceedings brought by the owner against him. The defendant shall in any event have the right to require the owner to be joined in the proceedings.

9. Any sums provided by insurance or by other financial security maintained in accordance with paragraph 1 of this Article shall be available exclusively for the satisfaction of claims under this Convention.

10. A Contracting State shall not permit a ship under its flag to which this Article applies to trade unless a certificate has been issued under paragraph 2 or 12 of this Article.

11. Subject to the provisions of this Article, each Contracting State shall ensure, under its national legislation, that insurance or other security to the extent specified in paragraph 1 of this Article is in force in respect of any ship, wherever registered, entering or leaving a port in its territory, or

arriving at or leaving an offshore terminal in its territorial sea, if the ship actually carries more than 2,000 tons of oil in bulk as cargo.

12. If insurance or other financial security is not maintained in respect of a ship owned by a Contracting State, the provisions of this Article relating thereto shall not be applicable to such ship, but the ship shall carry a certificate issued by the appropriate authorities of the State of the ship's registry stating that the ship is owned by that State and that the ship's liability is covered within the limits prescribed by Article V, paragraph 1. Such a certificate shall follow as closely as practicable the model prescribed by paragraph 2 of this Article.

Article VIII

Rights of compensation under this Convention shall be extinguished unless an action is brought thereunder within three years from the date when the damage occurred. However, in no case shall an action be brought after six years from the date of the incident which caused the damage. Where this incident consists of a series of occurrences, the six years' period shall run from the date of the first such occurrence.

Article IX

1. Where an incident has caused pollution damage in the territory, including the territorial sea or an area referred to in Article II, of one or more Contracting States or preventive measures have been taken to prevent or minimize pollution damage in such territory including the territorial sea or area, actions for compensation may only be brought in the Courts of any such Contracting State or States. Reasonable notice of any such action shall be given to the defendant.

2. Each Contracting State shall ensure that its Courts possess the necessary jurisdiction to entertain such actions for compensation.

3. After the fund has been constituted in accordance with Article V the Courts of the State in which the fund is constituted shall be exclusively competent to determine all matters relating to the appointment and distribution of the fund.

Article X

1. Any judgment given by a Court with jurisdiction in accordance with Article IX which is enforceable in the State of origin where it is no longer subject to ordinary forms of review, shall be recognized in any Contracting State, except:

   (a) where the judgment was obtained by fraud; or
   (b) where the defendant was not given reasonable notice and a fair opportunity to present his case.

2. A judgment recognized under paragraph 1 of this Article shall be enforceable in each Contracting State as soon as the formalities required in that State have been complied with. The formalities shall not permit the merits of the case to be re-opened.

Article XI

1. The provisions of this Convention shall not apply to warships or other ships owned or operated by a State and used, for the time being, only on government non-commercial service.

2. With respect to ships owned by a Contracting State and used for commercial purposes, each State shall be subject to suit in the jurisdictions set forth in Article IX and shall waive all defences based on its status as a sovereign State.

Article XII

This Convention shall supersede any International Conventions in force or open for signature, ratification or accession at the date on which the Convention is opened for signature, but only to the extent that such Conventions would be in conflict with it; however, nothing in this Article shall affect the obligations of Contracting States to non-Contracting States arising under such International Conventions.

Article XII bis
Transitional provisions

The following transitional provisions shall apply in the case of a State which at the time of an incident is a Party both to this Convention and to the 1969 Liability Convention:

(a) where an incident has caused pollution damage within the scope of this Convention, liability under this Convention shall be deemed to be discharged if, and to the extent that, it also arises under the 1969 Liability Convention;

(b) where an incident has caused pollution damage within the scope of this Convention, and the State is a Party both to this Convention and to the International Convention on the Establishment of an International Fund for Compensation for Oil Pollution Damage, 1971, liability remaining to be discharged after the application of subparagraph (a) of this Article shall arise under this Convention only to the extent that pollution damage remains uncompensated after application of the said 1971 Convention;

(c) in the application of Article III, paragraph 4, of this Convention the expression 'this Convention' shall be interpreted as referring to this Convention or the 1969 Liability Convention, as appropriate;

(d) in the application of Article V, paragraph 3, of this Convention the total sum of the fund to be constituted shall be reduced by the amount by which liability has been deemed to be discharged in accordance with subparagraph (a) of this Article.

Article XII ter
Final clauses

The final clauses of this Convention shall be Articles 12 to 18 of the Protocol of 1992 to amend the 1969 Liability Convention. References in this Convention to Contracting States shall be taken to mean references to the Contracting States of that Protocol.

TEXT OF 1992 PROTOCOL (ARTICLES 10–18)

Article 10

The model of a certificate annexed to the 1969 Liability Convention is replaced by the model annexed to this Protocol. [NOT REPRODUCED— Eds.]

Article 11

1. The 1969 Liability Convention and this Protocol shall, as between the Parties to this Protocol, be read and interpreted together as one single instrument.

2. Articles I to XII *ter*, including the model certificate, of the 1969 Liability Convention as amended by this Protocol shall be known as the International Convention on Civil Liability for Oil Pollution Damage, 1992 (1992 Liability Convention).

Final Clauses

Article 12
Signature, ratification, acceptance, approval and accession

1. This Protocol shall be open for signature at London from 15 January 1993 to 14 January 1994 by all States.

2. Subject to paragraph 4, any State may become a Party to this Protocol by:

(a) signature subject to ratification, acceptance or approval followed by ratification, acceptance or approval; or
(b) accession.

3. Ratification, acceptance, approval or accession shall be effected by the deposit of a formal instrument to that effect with the Secretary-General of the Organization.

4. Any Contracting State to the International Covention on the Establishment of an International Fund for Compensation for Oil Pollution Damage, 1971, hereinafter referred to as the 1971 Fund Convention, may ratify, accept, approve or accede to this Protocol only if it ratifies, accepts, approves or accedes to the Protocol of 1992 to amend that Convention at the same time, unless it denounces the 1971 Fund Convention to take effect on the date when this Protocol enters into force for that State.

5. A State which is a Party to this Protocol but not a Party to the 1969 Liability Convention shall be bound by the provisions of the 1969 Liability Convention as amended by this Protocol in relation to other States Parties hereto, but shall not be bound by the provisions of the 1969 Liability Convention in relation to States Parties thereto.

6. Any instrument of ratification, acceptance, approval or accession deposited after the entry into force of an amendment to the 1969 Liability Convention as amended by this Protocol shall be deemed to apply to the Convention so amended, as modified by such amendment.

Article 13
Entry into force

1. This Protocol shall enter into force twelve months following the date on which ten States including four States each with not less than one million units of gross tanker tonnage have deposited instruments of ratification, acceptance, approval or accession with the Secretary-General of the Organization.

2. However, any Contracting State to the 1971 Fund Convention may, at the time of the deposit of its instrument of ratification, acceptance, approval or accession in respect of this Protocol, declare that such instrument shall be deemed not to be effective for the purposes of this Article until the end of the six-month period in Article 31 of the Protocol of 1992 to amend the 1971 Fund Convention. A State which is not a Contracting State to the 1971 Fund Convention but which deposits an instrument of ratification, acceptance, approval or accession in respect of the Protocol of 1992 to amend the 1971 Fund Convention may also make a declaration in accordance with this paragraph at the same time.

3. Any State which has made a declaration in accordance with the preceding paragraph may withdraw it at any time by means of a notification addressed to the Secretary-General of the Organization. Any such withdrawal shall take effect on the date the notification is received, provided that such State shall be deemed to have deposited its instrument of ratification, acceptance, approval or accession in respect of this Protocol on that date.

4. For any State which ratifies, accepts, approves or accedes to it after the conditions in paragraph 1 for entry into force have been met, this Protocol

shall enter into force twelve months following the date of deposit by such State of the appropriate instrument.

Article 14
Revision and amendment

1. A Conference for the purpose of revising or amending the 1992 Liability Convention may be convened by the Organization.

2. The Organization shall convene a Conference of Contracting States for the purpose of revising or amending the 1992 Liability Convention at the request of not less than one third of the Contracting States.

Article 15
Amendments of limitation amounts

1. Upon the request of at least one quarter of the Contracting States any proposal to amend the limits of liability laid down in Article V, paragraph 1, of the 1969 Liability Convention as amended by this Protocol shall be circulated by the Secretary-General to all Members of the Organization and to all Contracting States.

2. Any amendment proposed and circulated as above shall be submitted to the Legal Committee of the Organization for consideration at a date at least six months after the date of its circulation.

3. All Contracting States to the 1969 Liability Convention as amended by this Protocol, whether or not Members of the Organization, shall be entitled to participate in the proceedings of the Legal Committee for the consideration and adoption of amendments.

4. Amendments shall be adopted by a two-thirds majority of the Contracting States present and voting in the Legal Committee, expanded as provided for in paragraph 3, on condition that at least one half of the Contracting States shall be present at the time of voting.

5. When acting on a proposal to amend the limits, the Legal Committee shall take into account the experience of incidents and in particular the amount of damage resulting therefrom, changes in the monetary values and the effect of the proposed amendment on the cost of insurance. It shall also take into account the relationship between the limits in Article V, paragraph 1, of the 1969 Liability Convention as amended by this Protocol and those in Article 4, paragraph 4, of the International Convention on the Establishment of an International Fund for Compensation for Oil Pollution Damage, 1992.

6. (a) No amendment of the limits of liability under this Article may be considered before 15 January 1998 nor less than five years from the date of entry into force of a previous amendment under this Article. No amendment under this Article shall be considered before this Protocol has entered into force.

(b) No limit may be increased so as to exceed an amount which corresponds to the limit laid down in the 1969 Liability Convention as amended by this Protocol increased by 6 per cent per year calculated on a compound basis from 15 January 1993.

(c) No limit may be increased so as to exceed an amount which corresponds to the limit laid down in the 1969 Liability Convention as amended by this Protocol multiplied by 3.

7. Any amendment adopted in accordance with paragraph 4 shall be notified by the Organization to all Contracting States. The amendment shall be deemed to have been accepted at the end of a period of eighteen months after the date of notification, unless within that period not less than one quarter of the States that were Contracting States at the time of the adoption of the amendment by the Legal Committee have communicated to the Organization that they do not accept the amendment in which case the amendment is rejected and shall have no effect.

8. An amendment deemed to have been accepted in accordance with paragraph 7 shall enter into force eighteen months after its acceptance.

9. All Contracting States shall be bound by the amendment, unless they denounce this Protocol in accordance with Article 16, paragraphs 1 and 2, at least six months before the amendment enters into force. Such denunciation shall take effect when the amendment enters into force.

10. When an amendment has been adopted by the Legal Committee but the eighteen-month period for its acceptance has not yet expired, a State which becomes a Contracting State during that period shall be bound by the amendment if it enters into force. A State which becomes a Contracting State after that period shall be bound by an amendment which has been accepted in accordance with paragraph 7. In the cases referred to in this paragraph, a State becomes bound by an amendment when that amendment enters into force, or when this Protocol enters into force for that State, if later.

Article 16
Denunciation

1. This Protocol may be denounced by any Party at any time after the date on which it enters into force for that Party.

2. Denunciation shall be effected by the deposit of an instrument with the Secretary-General of the Organization.

3. A denunciation shall take effect twelve months, or such longer period as may be specified in the instrument of denunciation, after its deposit with the Secretary-General of the Organization.

4. As between the Parties to this Protocol, denunciation by any of them of the 1969 Liability Convention in accordance with Article XVI thereof shall not be construed in any way as a denunciation of the 1969 Liability Convention as amended by this Protocol.

5. Denunciation of the Protocol of 1992 to amend the 1971 Fund Convention by a State which remains a Party to the 1971 Fund Convention shall be deemed to be a denunciation of this Protocol. Such denunciation shall take effect on the date on which denunciation of the Protocol of 1992 to amend the 1971 Fund Convention takes effect according to Article 34 of that Protocol.

Article 17
Depositary

1. This Protocol and any amendments accepted under Article 15 shall be deposited with the Secretary-General of the Organization.

2. The Secretary-General of the Organization shall:

   (a) inform all States which have signed or acceded to this Protocol of:
      (i) each new signature or deposit of an instrument together with the date thereof;
      (ii) each declaration and notification under Article 13 and each declaration and communication under Article V, paragraph 9, of the 1992 Liability Convention;
      (iii) the date of entry into force of this Protocol;
      (iv) any proposal to amend limits of liability which has been made in accordance with Article 15, paragraph 1;
      (v) any amendment which has been adopted in accordance with Article 15, paragraph 4;
      (vi) any amendment deemed to have been accepted under Article 15, paragraph 7, together with the date on which that amendment shall enter into force in accordance with paragraphs 8 and 9 of that Article;
      (vii) the deposit of any instrument of denunciation of this Protocol together with the date of the deposit and the date on which it takes effect;
      (viii) any denunciation deemed to have been made under Article 16, paragraph 5;
      (ix) any communication called for by any Article of this Protocol;
   (b) transmit certified true copies of this Protocol to all Signatory States and to all States which accede to this Protocol.

3. As soon as this Protocol enters into force, the text shall be transmitted by the Secretary-General of the Organization to the Secretariat of the United

Nations for registration and publication in accordance with Article 102 of the Charter of the United Nations.

Article 18
Languages

This Protocol is established in a single original in the Arabic, Chinese, English, French, Russian and Spanish languages, each text being equally authentic.

DONE AT LONDON, this twenty-seventh day of November one thousand nine hundred and ninety-two.

IN WITNESS WHEREOF the undersigned, being duly authorized by their respective Governments for that purpose, have signed this Protocol.

TEXT OF FUND CONVENTION

General Provisions

Article 1

For the purposes of this Convention:

1. '1992 Liability Convention' means the International Convention on Civil Liability for Oil Pollution Damage, 1992.

1. *bis.* '1971 Fund Convention' means the International Convention on the Establishment of an International Fund for Compensation for Oil Pollution Damage, 1971. For States Parties to the Protocol of 1976 to that Convention, the term shall be deemed to include the 1971 Fund Convention as amended by that Protocol.

2. 'Ship', 'Person', 'Owner', 'Oil', 'Pollution Damage', 'Preventive Measures', 'Incident', and 'Organization' have the same meaning as in Article 1 of the 1992 Liability Convention.

3. 'Contributing Oil' means crude oil and fuel oil as defined in sub-paragraphs (a) and (b) below:

  (a) 'Crude Oil' means any liquid hydrocarbon mixture occuring naturally in the earth whether or not treated to render it suitable for transportation. It also includes crude oils from which certain distillate fractions have been removed (sometimes referred to as 'topped crudes') or to which certain distillate fractions have been added (sometimes referred to as 'spiked' or 'reconstituted' crudes).

  (b) 'Fuel Oil' means heavy distillates or residues from crude oil or blends of such materials intended for use as a fuel for the production of heat or power of a quality equivalent to the 'American Society for Testing and Materials' Specification for Number Four Fuel Oil (Designation D 396–69), or heavier.

4. 'Unit of account' has the same meaning as in Article V, paragraph 9, of the 1992 Liability Convention.

5. 'Ship's tonnage' has the same meaning as in Article V, paragraph 10, of the 1992 Liability Convention.

6. 'Ton', in relation to oil, means a metric ton.

7. 'Guarantor' means any person providing insurance or other financial security to cover an owner's liability in pursuance of Article VII, paragraph 1, of the 1992 Liability Convention.

8. 'Terminal Installation' means any site for the storage of oil in bulk which is capable of receiving oil from waterborne transportation, including any facility situated offshore and linked to such site.

9. Where an incident consists of a series of occurrences, it shall be treated as having occurred on the date of the first such occurrence.

Article 2

1. An International Fund for compensation for pollution damage, to be named 'The International Oil Pollution Compensation Fund 1992' and hereinafter referred to as 'the Fund', is hereby established with the following aims:

   (a) to provide compensation for pollution damage to the extent that the protection afforded by the 1992 Liability Convention is inadequate;
   (b) to give effect to the related purposes set out in this Convention.

2. The Fund shall in each Contracting State be recognized as a legal person capable under the laws of that State of assuming rights and obligations and of being a party in legal proceedings before the courts of that State. Each Contracting State shall recognize the Director of the Fund (hereinafter referred to as 'The Director') as the legal representative of the Fund.

Article 3

This Convention shall apply exclusively:

   (a) to pollution damage caused:
      (i) in the territory, including the territorial sea, of a Contracting State, and
      (ii) in the exclusive economic zone of a Contracting State, established in accordance with international law, or, if a Contracting State has not established such a zone, in an area beyond and adjacent to the territorial sea of that State determined by that State in accordance with international law and extending not more than 200 nautical miles from the baselines from which the breadth of its territorial sea is measured;
   (b) to preventive measures, wherever taken, to prevent or minimize such damage.

Compensation

Article 4

1. For the purpose of fulfilling its function under Article 2, paragraph 1 (a), the Fund shall pay compensation to any person suffering pollution damage if such person has been unable to obtain full and adequate compensation for the damage under the terms of the 1992 Liability Convention,

(a) because no liability for the damage arises under the 1992 Liability Convention;

(b) because the owner liable for the damage under the 1992 Liability Convention is financially incapable of meeting his obligations in full and any financial security that may be provided under Article VII of that Convention does not cover or is insufficient to satisfy the claims for compensation for the damage; an owner being treated as financially incapable of meeting his obligations and a financial security being treated as insufficient if the person suffering the damage has been unable to obtain full satisfaction of the amount of compensation due under the 1992 Liability Convention after having taken all reasonable steps to pursue the legal remedies available to him;

(c) because the damage exceeds the owner's liability under the 1992 Liability Convention as limited pursuant to Article V, paragraph 1, of that Convention or under the terms of any other international Convention in force or open for signature, ratification or accession at the date of this Convention.

Expenses reasonably incurred or sacrifices reasonably made by the owner voluntarily to prevent or minimize pollution damage shall be treated as pollution damage for the purposes of this Article.

2. The Fund shall incur no obligation under the preceding paragraph if:

(a) it proves that the pollution damage resulted from an act of war, hostilities, civil war or insurrection or was caused by oil which has escaped or been discharged from a warship or other ship owned or operated by a State and used, at the time of the incident, only on Government non-commercial service; or

(b) the claimant cannot prove that the damage resulted from an incident involving one or more ships.

3. If the Fund proves that the pollution damage resulted wholly or partially either from an act or omission done with the intent to cause damage by the person who suffered the damage or from the negligence of that person, the Fund may be exonerated wholly or partially from its obligation to pay compensation to such person. The Fund shall in any event be exonerated to the extent that the shipowner may have been exonerated under Article III, paragraph 3, of the 1992 Liability Convention. However, there shall be no such exoneration of the Fund with regard to preventive measures.

4. (a) Except as otherwise provided in sub-paragraphs (b) and (c) of this paragraph, the aggregate amount of compensation payable by the Fund under this Article shall in respect of any one incident be limited, so that the total sum of that amount and the amount of compensation actually paid under the 1992 Liability Convention

for pollution damage within the scope of application of this Convention as defined in Article 3 shall not exceed 135 million units of account.

(b) Except as otherwise provided in sub-paragraph (c), the aggregate amount of compensation payable by the Fund under this Article for pollution damage resulting from a natural phenomenon of an exceptional, inevitable and irresistible character shall not exceed 135 million units of account.

(c) The maximum amount of compensation referred to in sub-paragraphs (a) and (b) shall be 200 million units of account with respect to any incident occurring during any period when there are three Parties to this Convention in respect of which the combined relevant quantity of contributing oil received by persons in the territories of such Parties, during the preceding calender year, equalled or exceeded 600 million tons.

(d) Interest accrued on a fund constituted in accordance with Article V, paragraph 3, of the 1992 Liability Convention, if any, shall not be taken into account for the computation of the maximum compensation payable by the Fund under this Article.

(e) The amounts mentioned in this Article shall be converted into national currency on the basis of the value of that currency by reference to the Special Drawing Right on the date of the decision of the Assembly of the Fund as to the first date of payment of compensation.

5. Where the amount of established claims against the Fund exceeds the aggregate amount of compensation payable under paragraph 4, the amount available shall be distributed in such a manner that the proportion between any established claim and the amount of compensation actually recovered by the claimant under this Convention shall be the same for all claimants.

6. The Assembly of the Fund may decide that in exceptional cases, compensation in accordance with this Convention can be paid even if the owner of the ship has not constituted a fund in accordance with Article V, paragraph 3, of the 1992 Liability Convention. In such case paragraph 4(e) of this Article applies accordingly.

7. The Fund shall, at the request of a Contracting State, use its good offices as necessary to assist that State to secure promptly such personnel, material and services as are necessary to enable the State to take measures to prevent or mitigate pollution damage arising from an incident in respect of which the Fund may be called upon to pay compensation under this Convention.

8. The Fund may on conditions to be laid down in the Internal Regulations provide credit facilities with a view to the taking of preventive measures

against pollution damage arising from a particular incident in respect of which the Fund may be called upon to pay compensation under this Convention.

Article 5
(deleted)

Article 6

Rights to compensation under Article 4 shall be extinguished unless an action is brought thereunder or a notification has been made pursuant to Article 7, paragraph 6, within three years from the date when the damage occurred. However, in no case shall an action be brought after six years from the date of the incident which caused the damage.

Article 7

1. Subject to the subsequent provisions of this Article, any action against the Fund for compensation under Article 4 of this Convention shall be brought only before a court competent under Article IX of the 1992 Liability Convention in respect of actions against the owner who is or who would, but for the provisions of Article III, paragraph 2, of that Convention, have been liable for pollution damage caused by the relevant incident.

2. Each Contracting State shall ensure that its courts possess the necessary jurisdiction to entertain such actions against the Fund as are referred to in paragraph 1.

3. Where an action for compensation for pollution damage has been brought before a court competent under Article IX of the 1992 Liability Convention against the owner of a ship or his guarantor, such court shall have exclusive jurisdictional competence over any action against the Fund for compensation under the provisions of Article 4 of this Convention in respect of the same damage. However, where an action for compensation for pollution damage under the 1992 Liability Convention has been brought before a court in a State Party to the 1992 Liability Convention but not to this Convention, any action against the Fund under Article 4 of this Convention shall at the option of the claimant be brought either before a court of the State where the Fund has its headquarters or before any court of a State Party to this Convention competent under Article IX of the 1992 Liability Convention.

4. Each Contracting State shall ensure that the Fund shall have the right to intervene as a party to any legal proceedings instituted in accordance with Article IX of the 1992 Liability Convention before a competent court of that State against the owner of a ship or his guarantor.

5. Except as otherwise provided in paragraph 6, the Fund shall not be bound by any judgment or decision in proceedings to which it has not been a party or by any settlement to which it is not a party.

6. Without prejudice to the provisions of paragraph 4, where an action under the 1992 Liability Convention for compensation for pollution damage has been brought against an owner or his guarantor before a competent court in a Contracting State, each party to the proceedings shall be entitled under the national law of that State to notify the Fund of the proceedings. Where such notification has been made in accordance with the formalities required by the law of the court seized and in such time and in such a manner that the Fund has in fact been in a position effectively to intervene as a party to the proceedings, any judgment rendered by the court in such proceedings shall, after it has become final and enforceable in the State where the judgment was given, become binding upon the Fund in the sense that the facts and findings in that judgment may not be disputed by the Fund even if the Fund has not actually intervened in the proceedings.

Article 8

Subject to any decision concerning the distribution referred to in Article 4, paragraph 5, any judgment given against the Fund by a court having jurisdiction in accordance with Article 7, paragraphs 1 and 3, shall, when it has become enforceable in the State of origin and is in that State no longer subject to ordinary forms of review, be recognized and enforceable in each Contracting State on the same conditions as are prescribed in Article X of the 1992 Liability Convention.

Article 9

1. The Fund shall, in respect of any amount of compensation for pollution damage paid by the Fund in accordance with Article 4, paragraph 1, of this Convention, acquire by subrogation the rights that the person so compensated may enjoy under the 1992 Liability Convention against the owner or his guarantor.

2. Nothing in this Convention shall prejudice any right of recourse or subrogation of the Fund against persons other than those referred to in the preceding paragraph. In any event the right of the Fund to subrogation against such person shall not be less favourable than that of an insurer of the person to whom compensation has been paid.

3. Without prejudice to any other rights of subrogation or recourse against the Fund which may exist, a Contracting State or agency thereof which has paid compensation for pollution damage in accordance with provisions of national law shall acquire by subrogation the rights which the person so compensated would have enjoyed under this Convention.

Contributions

Article 10

1. Annual contributions to the Fund shall be made in respect of each Contracting State by any person who, in the calendar year referred to in Article 12, paragraphs 2 (a) or (b), has received in total quantities exceeding 150,000 tons:

   (a) in the ports or terminal installations in the territory of that State contributing oil carried by sea to such ports or terminal installations; and

   (b) in any installations situated in the territory of that Contracting State contributing oil which has been carried by sea and discharged in a port or terminal installation of a non-Contracting State, provided that contributing oil shall only be taken into account by virtue of this sub-paragraph on first receipt in a Contracting State after its discharge in that non-Contracting State.

2. (a) For the purposes of paragraph 1, where the quantity of contributing oil received in the territory of a Contracting State by any person in a calendar year when aggregated with the quantity of contributing oil received in the same Contracting State in that year by any associated person or persons exceeds 150,000 tons, such person shall pay contributions in respect of the actual quantity received by him notwithstanding that that quantity did not exceed 150,000 tons.

   (b) 'Associated person' means any subsidiary or commonly controlled entity. The question whether a person comes within this definition shall be determined by the national law of the State concerned.

Article 11
(deleted)

Article 12

1. With a view to assessing the amount of annual contributions due, if any, and taking account of the necessity to maintain sufficient liquid funds, the Assembly shall for each calendar year make an estimate in the form of a budget of:

   (i) Expenditure
      (a) costs and expenses of the administration of the Fund in the relevant year and any deficit from operations in preceding years;
      (b) payments to be made by the Fund in the relevant year for the satisfaction of claims against the Fund due under Article 4,

including repayment on loans previously taken by the Fund for the satisfaction of such claims, to the extent that the aggregate amount of such claims in respect of any one incident does not exceed four million units of account;

(c) payments to be made by the Fund in the relevant year for the satisfaction of claims against the Fund due under Article 4, including repayments on loans previously taken by the Fund for the satisfaction of such claims, to the extent that the aggregate amount of such claims in respect of any one incident is in excess of four million units of account;

(ii) Income

(a) surplus funds from operations in preceding years, including any interest;

(b) initial contributions to be paid in the course of the year;

(c) annual contributions, if required to balance the budget;

(d) any other income.

2. The Assembly shall decide the total amount of contributions to be levied. On the basis of that decision, the Director shall, in respect of each Contracting State, calculate for each person referred to in Article 10 the amount of his annual contribution:

(a) in so far as the contribution is for the satisfaction of payments referred to in paragraph 1 (i) (a) and (b) on the basis of a fixed sum for each ton of contributing oil received in the relevant State by such persons during the preceding calendar year; and

(b) in so far as the contribution is for the satisfaction of payments referred to in paragraph 1 (i) (c) of this Article on the basis of a fixed sum for each ton of contributing oil received by such person during the calendar year preceding that in which the incident in question occurred, provided that State was a Party to this Convention at the date of the incident.

3. The sums referred to in paragraph 2 above shall be arrived at by dividing the relevant total amount of contributions required by the total amount of contributing oil received in all Contracting States in the relevant year.

4. The annual contribution shall be due on the date to be laid down in the Internal Regulations of the Fund. The Assembly may decide on a different date of payment.

5. The Assembly may decide, under conditions to be laid down in the Financial Regulations of the Fund, to make transfers between funds received in accordance with Article 12.2(a) and funds received in accordance with Article 12.2(b).

Article 13

1. The amount of any contribution due under Article 12 and which is in arrear shall bear interest at a rate which shall be determined in accordance with the Internal Regulations of the Fund, provided that different rates may be fixed for different circumstances.

2. Each Contracting State shall ensure that any obligation to contribute to the Fund arising under this Convention in respect of oil received within the territory of that State is fulfilled and shall take any appropriate measures under its law, including the imposing of such sanctions as it may deem necessary, with a view to the effective execution of any such obligation; provided, however, that such measures shall only be directed against those persons who are under an obligation to contribute to the Fund.

3. Where a person who is liable in accordance with the provisions of Articles 10 and 12 to make contributions to the Fund does not fulfill his obligations in respect of any such contribution or any part thereof and is in arrear, the Director shall take all appropriate action against such person on behalf of the Fund with a view to the recovery of the amount due. However, where the defaulting contributor is manifestly insolvent or the circumstances otherwise so warrant, the Assembly may, upon recommendation of the Director, decide that no action shall be taken or continued against the contributor.

Article 14

1. Each Contracting State may at the time when it deposits its instrument of ratification or accession or at any time thereafter declare that it assumes itself obligations that are incumbent under this Convention on any person who is liable to contribute to the Fund in accordance with Article 10, paragraph 1, in respect of oil received within the territory of that State. Such declaration shall be made in writing and shall specify which obligations are assumed.

2. Where a declaration under paragraph 1 is made prior to the entry into force of this Convention in accordance with Article 40, it shall be deposited with the Secretary-General of the Organization who shall after the entry into force of the Convention communicate the declaration to the Director.

3. A declaration under paragraph 1 which is made after the entry into force of this Convention shall be deposited with the Director.

4. A declaration made in accordance with this Article may be withdrawn by the relevant State giving notice thereof in writing to the Director. Such notification shall take effect three months after the Director's receipt thereof.

5. Any State which is bound by a declaration made under this Article shall, in any proceedings brought against it before a competent court in respect

of any obligation specified in the declaration, waive any immunity that it would otherwise be entitled to invoke.

Article 15

1. Each Contracting State shall ensure that any person who receives contributing oil within its territory in such quantities that he is liable to contribute to the Fund appears on a list to be established and kept up to date by the Director in accordance with the subsequent provisions of this Article.

2. For the purposes set out in paragraph 1, each Contracting State shall communicate, at a time and in the manner to be prescribed in the Internal Regulations, to the Director the name and address of any person who in respect of that State is liable to contribute to the Fund pursuant to Article 10, as well as data on the relevant quantities of contributing oil received by any such person during the preceding calendar year.

3. For the purposes of ascertaining who are, at any given time, the persons liable to contribute to the Fund in accordance with Article 10, paragraph 1, and of establishing, where applicable, the quantities of oil to be taken into account for any such person when determining the amount of his contribution, the list shall be *prima facie* evidence of the facts stated therein.

4. Where a Contracting State does not fulfil its obligations to submit to the Director the communication referred to in paragraph 2 and this results in a financial loss for the Fund, that Contracting State shall be liable to compensate the Fund for such loss. The Assembly shall, on the recommendation of the Director, decide whether such compensation shall be payable by that Contracting State.

Organization and Administration

Article 16

The Fund shall have an Assembly and a Secretariat headed by a Director.

Assembly

Article 17

The Assembly shall consist of all Contracting States to this Convention.

Article 18

The functions of the Assembly shall be:
1. to elect at each regular session its Chairman and two Vice-Chairmen who shall hold office until the next regular session;

2. to determine its own rules of procedure, subject to the provisions of this Convention;

3. to adopt Internal Regulations necessary for the proper functioning of the Fund;

4. to appoint the Director and make provisions for the appointment of such other personnel as may be necessary and determine the terms and conditions of service of the Director and other personnel;

5. to adopt the annual budget and fix the annual contributions;

6. to appoint auditors and approve the accounts of the Fund;

7. to approve settlements of claims against the fund, to take decisions in respect of the distribution among claimants of the available amount of compensation in accordance with Article 4, paragraph 5, and to determine the terms and conditions according to which provisional payments in respect of claims shall be made with a view to ensuring that victims of pollution damage are compensated as promptly as possible;

8. (deleted)

9. to establish any temporary or permanent subsidiary body it may consider to be necessary, to define its terms of reference and to give it the authority needed to perform the functions entrusted to it; when appointing the members of such body, the Assembly shall endeavour to secure an equitable geographical distribution of members and to ensure that the Contracting States, in respect of which the largest quantities of contributing oil are being received, are appropriately represented; the Rules of Procedure of the Assembly may be applied, *mutatis mutandis,* for the work of such subsidiary body;

10. to determine which non-Contracting States and which inter-governmental and international non-governmental organizations shall be admitted to take part, without voting rights, in meetings of the Assembly and subsidiary bodies;

11. to give instructions concerning the administration of the Fund to the Director and subsidiary bodies;

12. (deleted)

13. to supervise the proper execution of the Convention and of its own decisions;

14. to perform such other functions as are allocated to it under the Convention or are otherwise necessary for the proper operation of the Fund.

Article 19

1. Regular sessions of the Assembly shall take place once every calendar year upon convocation by the Director.

2. Extraordinary sessions of the Assembly shall be convened by the Director at the request of at least one-third of the members of the Assembly and may be convened on the Director's own initiative after consultation with the Chairman of the Assembly. The Director shall give members at least thirty days' notice of such sessions.

Article 20

A majority of the members of the Assembly shall constitute a quorum for its meetings.

Articles 21–27
(deleted)

Secretariat

Article 28

1. The Secretariat shall comprise the Director and such staff as the administration of the Fund may require.

2. The Director shall be the legal representative of the Fund.

Article 29

1. The Director shall be the chief administrative officer of the Fund. Subject to the instructions given to him by the Assembly, he shall perform those functions which are assigned to him by this Convention, the Internal Regulations of the Fund and the Assembly.

2. The Director shall in particular:
   (a) appoint the personnel required for the administration of the Fund;
   (b) take all appropriate measures with a view to the proper administration of the Fund's assets;
   (c) collect the contributions due under this Convention while observing in particular the provisions of Article 13, paragraph 3;
   (d) to the extent necessary to deal with claims against the Fund and carry out the other functions of the Fund, employ the services of legal, financial and other experts;
   (e) take all appropriate measures for dealing with claims against the Fund within the limits and on conditions to be laid down in the Internal Regulations, including the final settlement of claims without the prior approval of the Assembly where these Regulations so provide;
   (f) prepare and submit to the Assembly the financial statements and budget estimates for each calendar year;
   (g) prepare, in consultation with the Chairman of the Assembly, and

publish a report on the activities of the Fund during the previous calendar year;

(h) prepare, collect and circulate the papers, documents, agenda, minutes and information that may be required for the work of the Assembly and subsidiary bodies.

Article 30

In the performance of their duties the Director and the staff and experts appointed by him shall not seek or receive instructions from any Government or from any authority external to the Fund. They shall refrain from any action which might reflect on their position as international officials. Each Contracting State on its part undertakes to respect the exclusively international character of the responsibilities of the Director and the staff and experts appointed by him, and not to seek to influence them in the discharge of their duties.

Finances

Article 31

1. Each Contracting State shall bear the salary, travel and other expenses of its own delegation to the Assembly and of its representatives on subsidiary bodies.

2. Any other expenses incurred in the operation of the Fund shall be borne by the Fund.

Voting

Article 32

The following provisions shall apply to voting in the Assembly:

(a) each member shall have one vote;

(b) except as otherwise provided in Article 33, decisions of the Assembly shall be by a majority vote of the members present and voting;

(c) decisions where a three-fourths or a two-thirds majority is required shall be by a three-fourths or two-thirds majority vote, as the case may be, of those present;

(d) for the purpose of this Article the phrase 'members present' means 'members present at the meeting at the time of the vote', and the phrase 'members present and voting' means 'members present and casting an affirmative or negative vote'. Members who abstain from voting shall be considered as not voting.

Article 33

The following decisions of the Assembly shall require a two-thirds majority:

(a) a decision under Article 13, paragraph 3, not to take or continue action against a contributor;
(b) the appointment of the Director under Article 18, paragraph 4;
(c) the establishment of subsidiary bodies, under Article 18, paragraph 9, and matters relating to such establishment.

Article 34

1. The Fund, its assets, income, including contributions, and other property shall enjoy in all Contracting States exemption from all direct taxation.

2. When the Fund makes substantial purchases of movable or immovable property, or has important work carried out which is necessary for the exercise of its official activities and the cost of which includes indirect taxes or sales taxes, the Government of Member States shall take, whenever possible, appropriate measures for the remission or refund of the amount of such duties and taxes.

3. No exemption shall be accorded in the case of duties, taxes or dues which merely constitute payment for public utility services.

4. The Fund shall enjoy exemption from all customs duties, taxes and other related taxes on articles imported or exported by it or on its behalf for its official use. Articles thus imported shall not be transferred either for consideration or gratis on the territory of the country into which they have been imported except on conditions agreed by the Government of that country.

5. Persons contributing to the Fund and victims and owners of ships receiving compensation from the Fund shall be subject to the fiscal legislation of the State where they are taxable, no special exemption or other benefit being conferred on them in this respect.

6. Information relating to individual contributors supplied for the purpose of this Convention shall not be divulged outside the Fund except in so far as it may be strictly necessary to enable the Fund to carry out its functions including the bringing and defending of legal proceedings.

7. Independently of existing or future regulations concerning currency or transfers, Contracting States shall authorize the transfer and payment of any contribution to the Fund and of any compensation paid by the Fund without any restriction.

Transitional Provisions

Article 35

Claims for compensation under Article 4 arising from incidents occuring after the date of entry into force of this Convention may not be brought against the Fund earlier than the one hundred and twentieth day after that date.

Article 36

The Secretary-General of the Organization shall convene the first session of the Assembly. This session shall take place as soon as possible after entry into force of this Convention and, in any case, not more than thirty days after such entry into force.

Article 36 bis

The following transitional provisions shall apply in the period, hereinafter referred to as the transitional period, commencing with the date of entry into force of this Convention and ending with the date on which the denunciations provided for in Article 31 of the 1992 Protocol to amend the 1971 Fund Convention take effect:

(a) In the application of paragraph 1(a) of Article 2 of this Convention, the reference to the 1992 Liability Convention shall include reference to the International Convention on Civil Liability for Oil Pollution Damage, 1969, either in its original version or as amended by the Protocol thereto of 1976 (referred to in this Article as 'the 1969 Liability Convention'), and also the 1971 Fund Convention.

(b) Where an incident has caused pollution damage within the scope of this Convention, the Fund shall pay compensation to any person suffering pollution damage only if, and to the extent that, such person has been unable to obtain full and adequate compensation for the damage under the terms of the 1969 Liability Convention, the 1971 Fund Convention and the 1992 Liability Convention, provided that, in respect of pollution damage within the scope of this Convention in respect of a Party to this Convention but not a Party to the 1971 Fund Convention, the Fund shall pay compensation to any person suffering pollution damage only if, and to the extent that, such person would have been unable to obtain full and adequate compensation had that State been party to each of the above-mentioned Conventions.

(c) In the application of Article 4 of this Convention, the amount to be taken into account in determining the aggregate amount of compensation payable by the Fund shall also include the amount of compensation actually paid under the 1969 Liability Convention, if any, and the amount of compensation actually paid or deemed to have been paid under the 1971 Fund Convention.

(d) Paragraph 1 of Article 9 of this Convention shall also apply to the rights enjoyed under the 1969 Liability Convention.

Article 36 ter

1. Subject to paragraph 4 of this Article, the aggregate amount of the annual contributions payable in respect of contributing oil received in a single Contracting State during a calendar year shall not exceed 27.5% of the total amount of annual contributions pursuant to the 1992 Protocol to amend the 1971 Fund Convention, in respect of that calendar year.

2. If the application of the provisions in paragraphs 2 and 3 of Article 12 would result in the aggregate amount of the contributions payable by contributors in a single Contracting State in respect of a given calendar year exceeding 27.5% of the total annual contributions, the contributions payable by all contributors in that State shall be reduced *pro rata* so that their aggregate contributions equal 27.5% of the total annual contributions to the Fund in respect of that year.

3. If the contributions payable by persons in a given Contracting State shall be reduced pursuant to paragraph 2 of this Article, the contributions payable by persons in all other Contracting States shall be increased *pro rata* so as to ensure that the total amount of contributions payable by all persons liable to contribute to the Fund in respect of the calendar year in question will reach the total amount of contributions decided by the Assembly.

4. The provisions in paragraphs 1 to 3 of this Article shall operate until the total quantity of contributing oil received in all Contracting States in a calendar year has reached 750 million tons or until a period of 5 years after the date of entry into force of the said 1992 Protocol has elapsed, whichever occurs earlier.

Article 36 quater

Notwithstanding the provisions of this Convention, the following provisions shall apply to the administration of the Fund during the period in which both the 1971 Fund Convention and this Convention are in force:

(a) The Secretariat of the Fund, established by the 1971 Fund Convention (hereinafter referred to as 'the 1971 Fund'), headed by the Director, may also function as the Secretariat and the Director of the Fund.

(b) If, in accordance with subparagraph (a), the Secretariat and the Director of the 1971 Fund also perform the function of Secretariat and Director of the Fund, the Fund shall be represented, in cases of conflict of interests between the 1971 Fund and the Fund, by the Chairman of the Assembly of the Fund.

(c) The Director and the staff and experts appointed by him, performing their duties under this Convention and the 1971 Fund Convention, shall not be regarded as contravening the provisions of Article 30 of this Convention in so far as they discharge their duties in accordance with this Article.

(d) The Assembly of the Fund shall endeavour not to take decisions which are incompatible with decisions taken by the Assembly of the 1971 Fund. If differences of opinion with respect to common administrative issues arise, the Assembly of the Fund shall try to reach a consensus with the Assembly of the 1971 Fund, in a spirit of mutual co-operation and with the common aims of both organizations in mind.

(e) The Fund may succeed to the rights, obligations and assets of the 1971 Fund if the Assembly of the 1971 Fund so decides, in accordance with Article 44, paragraph 2, of the 1971 Fund Convention.

(f) The Fund shall reimburse to the 1971 Fund all costs and expenses arising from administrative services performed by the 1971 Fund on behalf of the Fund.

Final clauses

Article 36 quinquies

The final clauses of this Convention shall be Articles 28 to 39 of the Protocol of 1992 to amend the 1971 Fund Convention. References in this Convention to Contracting States shall be taken to mean references to the Contracting States of that Protocol.

TEXT OF 1992 PROTOCOL (ARTICLES 27–39)

Article 27

1. The 1971 Fund Convention and this Protocol shall, as between the Parties to this Protocol, be read and interpreted together as one single instrument.

2. Articles 1 to 36 *quinquies* of the 1971 Fund Convention as amended by this Protocol shall be known as the International Convention on the Establishment of an International Fund for Compensation for Oil Pollution Damage, 1992 (1992 Fund Convention).

Final Clauses

Article 28
Signature, ratification, acceptance, approval and accession

1. This Protocol shall be open for signature at London from 15 January 1993 to 14 January 1994 by any State which has signed the 1992 Liability Convention.

2. Subject to paragraph 4, this Protocol shall be ratified, accepted or approved by States which have signed it.

3. Subject to paragraph 4, this Protocol is open for accession by States which did not sign it.

4. This Protocol may be ratified, accepted, approved or acceded to only by States which have ratified, accepted, approved or acceded to the 1992 Liability Convention.

5. Ratification, acceptance, approval or accession shall be effected by the deposit of a formal instrument to that effect with the Secretary-General of the Organization.

6. A State which is a Party to this Protocol but is not a Party to the 1971 Fund Convention shall be bound by the provisions of the 1971 Fund Convention as amended by this Protocol in relation to other Parties hereto, but shall not be bound by the provisions of the 1971 Fund Convention in relation to Parties thereto.

7. Any instrument of ratification, acceptance, approval or accession deposited after the entry into force of an amendment to the 1971 Fund Convention as amended by this Protocol shall be deemed to apply to the Convention so amended, as modified by such amendment.

Article 29
Information on contributing oil

1. Before this Protocol comes into force for a State, that State shall, when depositing an instrument referred to in Article 28, paragraph 5, and annually thereafter at a date to be determined by the Secretary-General of the Organization, communicate to him the name and address of any person who in respect of that State would be liable to contribute to the Fund pursuant to Article 10 of the 1971 Fund Convention as amended by this Protocol as well as data on the relevant quantities of contributing oil received by any such person in the territory of that State during the preceding calendar year.

2. During the transitional period, the Director shall, for Parties, communicate annually to the Secretary-General of the Organization data on quanti-

ties of contributing oil received by persons liable to contribute to the Fund pursuant to Article 10 of the 1971 Fund Convention as amended by this Protocol.

Article 30
Entry into force

1. This Protocol shall enter into force twelve months following the date on which the following requirements are fulfilled:

   (a) at least eight states have deposited instruments of ratification, acceptance, approval or accession with the Secretary-General of the Organization; and
   (b) the Secretary-General of the Organization has received information in accordance with Article 29 that those persons who would be liable to contribute pursuant to Article 10 of the 1971 Fund Convention as amended by this Protocol have received during the preceding calendar year a total quantity of at least 450 million tons of contributing oil.

2. However, this Protocol shall not enter into force before the 1992 Liability Convention has entered into force.

3. For each State which ratifies, accepts, approves or accedes to this Protocol after the conditions in paragraph 1 for entry into force have been met, the Protocol shall enter into force twelve months following the date of the deposit by such State of the appropriate instrument.

4. Any State may, at the time of the deposit of its instrument of ratification, acceptance, approval or accession in respect of this Protocol declare that such instrument shall not take effect for the purpose of this Article until the end of the six-month period in Article 31.

5. Any State which has made a declaration in accordance with the preceding paragraph may withdraw it at any time by means of a notification addressed to the Secretary-General of the Organization. Any such withdrawal shall take effect on the date the notification is received, and any State making such a withdrawal shall be deemed to have deposited its instrument of ratification, acceptance, approval or accession in respect of this Protocol on that date.

6. Any State which has made a declaration under Article 13, paragraph 2, of the Protocol of 1992 to amend the 1969 Liability Convention shall be deemed to have also made a declaration under paragraph 4 of this Article. Withdrawal of a declaration under the said Article 13, paragraph 2, shall be deemed to constitute withdrawal also under paragraph 5 of this Article.

Article 31
Denunciation of the 1969 and 1971 Conventions

Subject to Article 30, within six months following the date on which the following requirements are fulfilled:

(a) at least eight States have become Parties to this Protocol or have deposited instruments of ratification, acceptance, approval or accession with the Secretary-General of the Organization, whether or not subject to Article 30, paragraph 4, and

(b) the Secretary-General of the Organization has received information in accordance with Article 29 that those persons who are or would be liable to contribute pursuant to Article 10 of the 1971 Fund Convention as amended by this Protocol have received during the preceding calendar year a total quantity of at least 750 million tons of contributing oil;

each Party to this Protocol and each State which has deposited an instrument of ratification, acceptance, approval or accession, whether or not subject to Article 30, paragraph 4, shall, if Party thereto, denounce the 1971 Fund Convention and the 1969 Liability Convention with effect twelve months after the expiry of the above-mentioned six-month period.

Article 32
Revision and amendment

1. A conference for the purpose of revising or amending the 1992 Fund Convention may be convened by the Organization.

2. The Organization shall convene a Conference of Contracting States for the purpose of revising or amending the 1992 Fund Convention at the request of not less than one third of all Contracting States.

Article 33
Amendment of compensation limits

1. Upon the request of at least one quarter of the Contracting States, any proposal to amend the limits of amounts of compensation laid down in Article 4, paragraph 4, of the 1971 Fund Convention as amended by this Protocol shall be circulated by the Secretary-General to all Members of the Organization and to all Contracting States.

2. Any amendment proposed and circulated as above shall be submitted to the Legal Committee of the Organization for consideration at a date at least six months after the date of its circulation.

3. All Contracting States to the 1971 Fund Convention as amended by this Protocol, whether or not Members of the Organization, shall be entitled to

participate in the proceedings of the Legal Committee for the consideration and adoption of amendments.

4. Amendments shall be adopted by a two-thirds majority of the Contracting States present and voting in the Legal Committee, expanded as provided for in paragraph 3, on condition that at least one half of the Contracting States shall be present at the time of voting.

5. When acting on a proposal to amend the limits, the Legal Committee shall take into account the experience of incidents and in particular the amount of damage resulting therefrom and changes in the monetary values. It shall also take into account the relationship between the limits in Article 4, paragraph 4, of the 1971 Fund Convention as amended by this Protocol and those in Article V, paragraph 1, of the International Convention on Civil Liability for Oil Pollution Damage, 1992.

6. (a) No amendment of the limits under this Article may be considered before 15 January 1998 nor less than five years from the date of entry into force of a previous amendment under this Article. No amendment under this Article shall be considered before this Protocol has entered into force.

   (b) No limit may be increased so as to exceed an amount which corresponds to the limit laid down in the 1971 Fund Convention as amended by this Protocol increased by six per cent per year calculated on a compound basis from 15 January 1993.

   (c) No limit may be increased so as to exceed an amount which corresponds to the limit laid down in the 1971 Fund Convention as amended by this Protocol multiplied by three.

7. Any amendment adopted in accordance with paragraph 4 shall be notified by the Organization to all Contracting States. The amendment shall be deemed to have been accepted at the end of a period of eighteen months after the date of notification unless within that period not less than one quarter of the States that were Contracting States at the time of the adoption of the amendment by the Legal Committee have communicated to the Organization that they do not accept the amendment in which case the amendment is rejected and shall have no effect.

8. An amendment deemed to have been accepted in accordance with paragraph 7 shall enter into force eighteen months after its acceptance.

9. All Contracting States shall be bound by the amendment, unless they denounce this Protocol in accordance with Article 34, paragraphs 1 and 2, at least six months before the amendment enters into force. Such denunciation shall take effect when the amendment enters into force.

10. When an amendment has been adopted by the Legal Committee but the eighteen-month period for its acceptance has not yet expired, a State which becomes a Contracting State during that period

shall be bound by the amendment if it enters into force. A State which becomes a Contracting State after that period shall be bound by an amendment which has been accepted in accordance with paragraph 7. In the cases referred to in this paragraph, a State becomes bound by an amendment when that amendment enters into force, or when this Protocol enters into force for that State, if later.

Article 34
Denunciation

1. This Protocol may be denounced by any Party at any time after the date on which it enters into force for that Party.

2. Denunciation shall be effected by the deposit of an instrument with the Secretary-General of the Organization.

3. A denunciation shall take effect twelve months, or such longer period as may be specified in the instrument of denunciation, after its deposit with the Secretary-General of the Organization.

4. Denunciation of the 1992 Liability Convention shall be deemed to be a denunciation of this Protocol. Such denunciation shall take effect on the date on which denunciation of the Protocol of 1992 to amend the 1969 Liability Convention takes effect according to Article 16 of that Protocol.

5. Any Contracting State to this Protocol which has not denounced the 1971 Fund Convention and the 1969 Liability Convention as required by Article 31 shall be deemed to have denounced this Protocol with effect twelve months after the expiry of the six-month period mentioned in that Article. As from the date on which the denunciations provided for in Article 31 take effect, any Party to this Protocol which deposits an instrument of ratification, acceptance, approval or accession to the 1969 Liability Convention shall be deemed to have denounced this Protocol with effect from the date on which such instrument takes effect.

6. As between the Parties to this Protocol, denunciation by any of them of the 1971 Fund Convention in accordance with Article 41 thereof shall not be construed in any way as a denunciation of the 1971 Fund Convention as amended by this Protocol.

7. Notwithstanding a denunciation of this Protocol by a Party pursuant to this Article, any provisions of this Protocol relating to the obligations to make contributions under Article 10 of the 1971 Fund Convention as amended by this Protocol with respect to an incident referred to in Article 12, paragraph 2(b), of that amended Convention and occurring before the denunciation takes effect shall continue to apply.

Article 35
Extraordinary sessions of the Assembly

1. Any Contracting State may, within ninety days after the deposit of an instrument of denunciation the result of which it considers will significantly increase the level of contributions for the remaining Contracting States, request the Director to convene an extraordinary session of the Assembly. The Director shall convene the Assembly to meet not later than sixty days after receipt of the request.

2. The Director may convene, on his own initiative, an extraordinary session of the Assembly to meet within sixty days after the deposit of any instrument of denunciation, if he considers that such denunciation will result in a significant increase in the level of contributions of the remaining Contracting States.

3. If the Assembly at an extraordinary session convened in accordance with paragraph 1 or 2 decides that the denunciation will result in a significant increase in the level of contributions for the remaining Contracting States, any such State may, not later than one hundred and twenty days before the date on which the denunciation takes effect, denounce this Protocol with effect from the same date.

Article 36
Termination

1. This Protocol shall cease to be in force on the date when the number of Contracting States falls below three.

2. States which are bound by this Protocol on the day before the date it ceases to be in force shall enable the Fund to exercise its functions as described under Article 37 of this Protocol and shall, for that purpose only, remain bound by this Protocol.

Article 37
Winding up of the Fund

1. If this Protocol ceases to be in force, the Fund shall nevertheless:

   (a) meet its obligations in respect of any incident occurring before the Protocol ceased to be in force;
   (b) be entitled to exercise its rights to contributions to the extent that these contributions are necessary to meet the obligations under subparagraph (a), including expenses for the administration of the Fund necessary for this purpose.

2. The Assembly shall take all appropriate measures to complete the winding up of the Fund including the distribution in an equitable manner

of any remaining assets among those persons who have contributed to the Fund.

3. For the purposes of this Article the Fund shall remain a legal person.

Article 38
Depositary

1. This Protocol and any amendments accepted under Article 33 shall be deposited with the Secretary-General of the Organization.

2. The Secretary-General of the Organization shall:

  (a) inform all States which have signed or acceded to this Protocol of:
- (i) each new signature or deposit of an instrument together with the date thereof;
- (ii) each declaration and notification under Article 30 including declarations and withdrawals deemed to have been made in accordance with that Article;
- (iii) the date of entry into force of this Protocol;
- (iv) the date by which denunciations provided for in Article 31 are required to be made;
- (v) any proposal to amend limits of amounts of compensation which has been made in accordance with Article 33, paragraph 1;
- (vi) any amendment which has been adopted in accordance with Article 33, paragraph 4;
- (vii) any amendment deemed to have been accepted under Article 33, paragraph 7, together with the date on which that amendment shall enter into force in accordance with paragraphs 8 and 9 of that Article;
- (viii) the deposit of an instrument of denunciation of this Protocol together with the date of the deposit and the date on which it takes effect;
- (ix) any denunciation deemed to have been made under Article 34, paragraph 5;
- (x) any communication called for by any Article in this Protocol;

  (b) transmit certified true copies of this Protocol to all Signatory States and to all States which accede to the Protocol.

3. As soon as this Protocol enters into force, the text shall be transmitted by the Secretary-General of the Organization to the Secretariat of the United Nations for registration and publication in accordance with Article 102 of the Charter of the United Nations.

Article 39
Languages

This Protocol is established in a single original in the Arabic, Chinese, English, French, Russian and Spanish languages, each text being equally authentic.

DONE AT LONDON this twenty-seventh day of November one thousand nine hundred and ninety-two.

Convention on Civil Liability for Damage Resulting from Activities Dangerous to the Environment, Lugano, 21 June 1993

This is a Council of Europe Convention which makes provision for harmonization of national laws on environmental liability in member states, in accordance with Principle 13 of the 1992 Rio Declaration on Environment and Development (q.v.). It imposes a common scheme of strict liability for dangerous activities or dangerous substances on the operator of the activity in question, or in the case of permanently deposited waste, on the operator of the site. Unlike earlier liability conventions, liability is not limited in amount, but recovery is similarly assured by compulsory insurance or other financial security. 'Damage' is widely defined and includes impairment of the environment, which may include the cost of reasonable preventative measures, reinstatement, and loss of profit. Jurisdiction is based on the provisions of the 1968 Brussels Convention on Jurisdiction and Enforcement of Judgments in Civil and Commercial Matters, *OJEC* L 304/77. Although not yet widely ratified, the Liability Convention provides an illustrative example of the elements required for regional harmonization of environmental liability.

The Convention had no parties in 1994. It requires three ratifications to enter into force in accordance with article 32. Reservations may only be made in the terms of Article 35. Text *repr.* 32 *ILM* (1993) 1228; 4 *YIEL* (1993) 691; *ETS* 150. For Commentary see Council of Europe, *Explanatory Report*, (1992), *CDCJ* (92) 50, Addendum. See also D. Wilkinson, 'The Council of Europe Convention on Civil Liability for Damage Resulting from Activities Dangerous to the Environment: A Comparative Review', *European Environmental LR* (1993) 130ff; A. Bianchi, 'The Harmonization of Laws on Liability for Environmental Damage in Europe', 6 *JEL* (1994) 21.

TEXT

The member States of the Council of Europe, the other States and the European Economic Community signatory hereto,

Considering that the aim of the Council of Europe is to achieve a greater unity between its members;

Noting that one of the objectives of the Council of Europe is to contribute to the quality of life of human beings, in particular by promoting a natural, healthy and agreeable environment;

Considering the wish of the Council of Europe to co-operate with other States in the field of nature conservation and protection of the environment;

Realising that man, the environment and property are exposed to specific dangers caused by certain activities;

Considering that emissions released in one country may cause damage in another country and that, therefore, the problems of adequate compensation for such damage are also of an international nature;

Having regard to the desirability of providing for strict liability in this field taking into account the 'Polluter Pays' Principle;

Mindful of the work which has already been carried out at an international level, in particular to prevent damage and to deal with damage caused by nuclear substances and the carriage of dangerous goods;

Having noted Principle 13 of the 1992 Rio Declaration on Environment and Development, according to which 'States shall develop national law regarding liability and compensation for the victims of pollution and other environmental damage; they shall also co-operate in an expeditious and more determined manner to develop further international law regarding liability and compensation for adverse effects of environmental damage caused by activities within their jurisdiction or control to areas beyond their jurisdiction';

Recognising the need to adopt further measures to deal with grave and imminent threats of damage from dangerous activities and to facilitate the burden of proof for persons requesting compensation for such damage,

Have agreed as follows:

Chapter I—General provisions

Article 1—*Object and purpose*

This Convention aims at ensuring adequate compensation for damage resulting from activities dangerous to the environment and also provides for means of prevention and reinstatement.

Article 2—*Definitions*

For the purpose of this Convention:

1. 'Dangerous activity' means one or more of the following activities provided that it is performed professionally, including activities conducted by public authorities:

   (a) the production, handling, storage, use or discharge of one or more dangerous substances or any operation of a similar nature dealing with such substances;

   (b) the production, culturing, handling, storage, use, destruction, disposal, release or any other operation dealing with one or more:
   — genetically modified organisms which as a result of the properties of the organism, the genetic modification and the conditions under which the operation is exercised, pose a significant risk for man, the environment or property;
   — micro-organisms which as a result of their properties and the conditions under which the operation is exercised pose a significant risk for man, the environment or property, such

as those micro-organisms which are pathogenic or which produce toxins;

(c) the operation of an installation or site for the incineration, treatment, handling or recycling of waste, such as those installations or
sites specified in Annex II, provided that the quantities involved pose
a significant risk for man, the environment or property;

(d) the operation of a site for the permanent deposit of waste.

2. 'Dangerous substance' means:

(a) substances or preparations which have properties which constitute a
significant risk for man, the environment or property. A substance
or preparation which is explosive, oxidizing, extremely flammable,
highly flammable, flammable, very toxic, toxic, harmful, corrosive,
irritant, sensitizing, carcinogenic, mutagenic, toxic for reproduction
or dangerous for the environment within the meaning of Annex I,
Part A to this Convention shall in any event be deemed to constitute
such a risk;

(b) substances specified in Annex I, Part B to this Convention. Without
prejudice to the application of sub-paragraph a above, Annex I, Part
B may restrict the specification of dangerous substances to certain
quantities or concentrations, certain risks or certain situations.

3. 'Genetically modified organism' means any organism in which the
genetic material has been altered in a way which does not occur naturally
by mating and/or natural recombination.

However, the following genetically modified organisms are not covered by
the Convention:

— organisms obtained by mutagenesis on condition that the genetic
modification does not involve the use of genetically modified organisms as recipient organisms; and

— plants obtained by cell fusion (including protoplast fusion) if the
resulting plant can also be produced by traditional breeding
methods and on condition that the genetic modification does not
involve the use of genetically modified organisms as parental organisms.

'Organism' refers to any biological entity capable of replication or of
transferring genetic material.

4. 'Micro-organism' means any microbiological entity, cellular or non-
cellular, capable of replication or of transferring genetic material.

5. 'Operator' means the person who exercises the control of a dangerous
activity.

6. 'Person' means any individual or partnership or any body governed by public or private law, whether corporate or not, including a State or any of its constituent subdivisions.

7. 'Damage' means:

(a) loss of life or personal injury;
(b) loss of or damage to property other than to the installation itself or property held under the control of the operator, at the site of the dangerous activity;
(c) loss or damage by impairment of the environment in so far as this is not considered to be damage within the meaning of sub-paragraphs a or b above provided that compensation for impairment of the environment, other than for loss of profit from such impairment, shall be limited to the costs of measures of reinstatement actually undertaken or to be undertaken;
(d) the costs of preventive measures and any loss or damage caused by preventive measures,

to the extent that the loss or damage referred to in sub-paragraphs a to c of this paragraph arises out of or results from the hazardous properties of the dangerous substances, genetically modified organisms or micro-organisms or arises or results from waste.

8. 'Measures of reinstatement' means any reasonable measures aiming to reinstate or restore damaged or destroyed components of the environment, or to introduce, where reasonable, the equivalent of these components into the environment. Internal law may indicate who will be entitled to take such measures.

9. 'Preventive measures' means any reasonable measures taken by any person, after an incident has occurred to prevent or minimise loss or damage as referred to in paragraph 7, sub-paragraphs a to c of this Article.

10. 'Environment' includes:

— natural resources both abiotic and biotic, such as air, water, soil, fauna and flora and the interaction between the same factors;
— property which forms part of the cultural heritage; and
— the characteristic aspects of the landscape.

11. 'Incident' means any sudden occurrence or continuous occurrence or any series of occurrences having the same origin, which causes damage or creates a grave and imminent threat of causing damage.

Article 3—Geographical scope

Without prejudice to the provisions of Chapter III, this Convention shall apply:

(a) when the incident occurs in the territory of a Party, as determined in accordance with Article 34, regardless of where the damage is suffered;

(b) when the incident occurs outside the territory referred to in sub-paragraph a above and the conflict of laws rules lead to the application of the law in force for the territory referred to in sub-paragraph a above.

Article 4—Exceptions

1. This Convention shall not apply to damage arising from carriage; carriage includes the period from the beginning of the process of loading until the end of the process of unloading. However, the Convention shall apply to carriage by pipeline, as well as to carriage performed entirely in an installation or on a site inaccessible to the public where it is accessory to other activities and is an integral part thereof.

2. This Convention shall not apply to damage caused by a nuclear substance:

(a) arising from a nuclear incident the liability of which is regulated either by the Paris Convention of 29 July 1960 on third party liability in the field of nuclear energy, and its Additional Protocol of 28 January 1964, or the Vienna Convention of 21 May 1963 on civil liability for nuclear damage; or

(b) if liability for such damage is regulated by a specific internal law, provided that such law is as favourable, with regard to compensation for damage, as any of the instruments referred to under sub-paragraph a above.

3. This Convention shall not apply to the extent that it is incompatible with the rules of the applicable law relating to workmen's compensation or social security schemes.

Chapter II—Liability

Article 5—Transitional provisions

1. The provisions of this chapter shall apply to incidents occurring after the entry into force of the Convention in respect of a Party. When the incident consists of a continuous occurrence or a series of occurrences having the same origin and part of these occurrences took place before the entry into force of this Convention, this chapter shall only apply to damage caused by occurrences or part of a continuous occurrence taking place after the entry into force.

2. In respect of damage caused by waste deposited at a site for the permanent deposit of waste the provisions of this chapter shall apply to

damage which becomes known after the entry into force of the Convention in respect of the Party on the territory of which the site is situated. However this chapter shall not apply if:

(a) the site was closed in accordance with the provisions of internal law before the entry into force of the Convention;

(b) the operator proves, in the case where the operation of the site continues after that entry into force of the Convention, that the damage was caused solely by waste deposited there before that entry into force.

Article 6—Liability in respect of substances, organisms and certain waste installations or sites

1. The operator in respect of a dangerous activity mentioned under Article 2, paragraph 1, sub-paragraphs a to c shall be liable for the damage caused by the activity as a result of incidents at the time or during the period when he was exercising the control of that activity.

2. If an incident consists of a continuous occurrence, all operators successively exercising the control of the dangerous activity during that occurrence shall be jointly and severally liable. However, the operator who proves that the occurrence during the period when he was exercising the control of the dangerous activity caused only a part of the damage shall be liable for that part of the damage only.

3. If an incident consists of a series of occurrences having the same origin, the operators at the time of any such occurrence shall be jointly and severally liable. However, the operator who proves that the occurrence at the time when he was exercising the control of the dangerous activity caused only a part of the damage shall be liable for that part of the damage only.

4. If the damage resulting from a dangerous activity becomes known after all such dangerous activity in the installation or on the site has ceased, the last operator of this activity shall be liable for that damage unless he or the person who suffered damage proves that all or part of the damage resulted from an incident which occurred at a time before he became the operator. If it is so proved, the provisions of paragraphs 1 to 3 of this Article shall apply.

5. Nothing in this Convention shall prejudice any right of recourse of the operator against any third party.

Article 7—Liability in respect of sites for the permanent deposit of waste

1. The operator of a site for the permanent deposit of waste at the time when damage caused by waste deposited at that site becomes known, shall be liable for this damage. Should the damage caused by waste deposited

before the closure of such a site become known after that closure, the last operator shall be liable.

2. Liability under this Article shall apply to the exclusion of any liability of the operator under Article 6, irrespective of the nature of the waste.

3. Liability under this Article shall apply to the exclusion of any liability of the operator under Article 6 if the same operator conducts another dangerous activity on the site for the permanent deposit of waste.

However, if this operator or the person who has suffered damage proves that only a part of the damage was caused by the activity concerning the permanent deposit of waste, this Article shall only apply to that part of the damage.

4. Nothing in this Convention shall prejudice any right of recourse of the operator against any third party.

Article 8—Exemptions

The operator shall not be liable under this Convention for damage which he proves:

(a) was caused by an act of war, hostilities, civil war, insurrection or a natural phenomenon of an exceptional, inevitable and irresistible character;

(b) was caused by an act done with the intent to cause damage by a third party, despite safety measures appropriate to the type of dangerous activity in question;

(c) resulted necessarily from compliance with a specific order or compulsory measure of a public authority;

(d) was caused by pollution at tolerable levels under local relevant circumstances; or

(e) was caused by a dangerous activity undertaken lawfully in the interests of the person who suffered the damage, whereby it was reasonable towards this person to expose him to the risks of the dangerous activity.

Article 9—Fault of the person who suffered the damage

If the person who suffered the damage or a person for whom he is responsible under internal law, has, by his own fault, contributed to the damage, the compensation may be reduced or disallowed having regard to all the circumstances.

Article 10—Causality

When considering evidence of the causal link between the incident and the damage or, in the context of a dangerous activity as defined in Article 2, paragraph 1, sub-paragraph d, between the activity and the damage, the court shall take due account of the increased danger of causing such damage inherent in the dangerous activity.

Article 11—Plurality of installations or sites

When damage results from incidents which have occurred in several installations or on several sites where dangerous activities are conducted or from dangerous activities under Article 2, paragraph 1, sub-paragraph d, the operators of the installations or sites concerned shall be jointly and severally liable for all such damage. However, the operator who proves that only part of the damage was caused by an incident in the installation or on the site where he conducts the dangerous activity or by a dangerous activity under Article 2, paragraph 1, sub-paragraph d, shall be liable for that part of the damage only.

Article 12—Compulsory financial security scheme

Each Party shall ensure that where appropriate, taking due account of the risks of the activity, operators conducting a dangerous activity on its territory be required to participate in a financial security scheme or to have and maintain a financial guarantee up to a certain limit, of such type and terms as specified by internal law, to cover the liability under this Convention.

Chapter III—Access to information

Article 13—Definition of public authorities

For the purpose of this Chapter 'public authorities' means any public administration of a Party at national, regional or local level with responsibilities, and possessing information relating to the environment, with the exception of bodies acting in a judicial or legislative capacity.

Article 14—Access to information held by public authorities

1. Any person shall, at his request and without his having to prove an interest, have access to information relating to the environment held by public authorities.
The Parties shall define the practical arrangements under which such information is effectively made available.

2. The right of access may be restricted under internal law where it affects:

— the confidentiality of the proceedings of public authorities, international relations and national defence;
— public security;
— matters which are or have been *sub judice*, or under enquiry (including disciplinary enquiries), or which are the subject of preliminary investigation proceedings;
— commercial and industrial confidentiality, including intellectual property;

— the confidentiality of personal data and/or files;
— material supplied by a third party without that party being under a legal obligation to do so; or
— material, the disclosure of which would make it more likely that the environment to which that material related would be damaged.

Information held by public authorities shall be supplied in part where it is possible to separate out information on items concerning the interests referred to above.

3. A request for information may be refused where it would involve the supply of unfinished documents or data or internal communications, or where the request is manifestly unreasonable or formulated in too general a manner.

4. A public authority shall respond to a person requesting information as soon as possible and at the latest within two months. The reasons for a refusal to provide the information requested must be given.

5. A person who considers that his request for information has been unreasonably refused or ignored, or has been inadequately answered by a public authority, may seek a judicial or administrative review of the decision, in accordance with the relevant internal legal system.

6. The Parties may make a charge for supplying the information, but such a charge may not exceed a reasonable cost.

Article 15—Access to information held by bodies with public responsibilities for the environment

On the same terms and conditions as those set out in Article 14 any person shall have access to information relating to the environment held by bodies with public responsibilities for the environment and under the control of a public authority. Access shall be given via the competent public administration or directly by the bodies themselves.

Article 16—Access to specific information held by operators

1. The person who suffered the damage may, at any time, request the court to order an operator to provide him with specific information, in so far as this is necessary to establish the existence of a claim for compensation under this Convention.

2. Where, under this Convention, a claim for compensation is made to an operator, whether or not in the framework of judicial proceedings, this operator may request the court to order another operator to provide him with specific information, in so far as this is necessary to establish the extent of his possible obligation to compensate the person who has suffered the damage, or of his own right to compensation from the other operator.

3. The operator shall be required to provide information under paragraphs 1 and 2 of this Article concerning the elements which are available to him and dealing essentially with the particulars of the equipment, the machinery used, the kind and concentration of the dangerous substances or waste as well as the nature of genetically modified organisms or micro-organisms.

4. These measures shall not affect measures of investigation which may legally be ordered under internal law.

5. The court may refuse a request which places a disproportionate burden on the operator, taking into account all the interests involved.

6. In addition to the restrictions under Article 14, paragraph 2 of this Convention, which shall apply *mutatis mutandis*, the operator may refuse to provide information where such information would incriminate him.

7. Any reasonable charge shall be paid by the person requesting the information. The operator may require an appropriate guarantee for such payment. However a court, when allowing a claim for compensation, may establish that this charge shall be borne by the operator, except to the extent that the request resulted in unnecessary costs.

Chapter IV—Actions for compensation and other claims

Article 17—Limitation periods

1. Actions for compensation under this Convention shall be subject to a limitation period of three years from the date on which the claimant knew or ought reasonably to have known of the damage and of the identity of the operator. The laws of the Parties regulating suspension or interruption of limitation periods shall apply to the limitation period prescribed in this paragraph.

2. However, in no case shall actions be brought after thirty years from the date of the incident which caused the damage. Where the incident consists of a continuous occurrence the thirty years' period shall run from the end of that occurrence. Where the incident consists of a series of occurrences having the same origin the thirty years' period shall run from the date of the last of such occurrences. In respect of a site for the permanent deposit of waste the thirty years' period shall at the latest run from the date on which the site was closed in accordance with the provisions of internal law.

Article 18—Requests by organisations

1. Any association or foundation which according to its statutes aims at the protection of the environment and which complies with any further con-

ditions of internal law of the Party where the request is submitted may, at any time, request:

- (a) the prohibition of a dangerous activity which is unlawful and poses a grave threat of damage to the environment;
- (b) that the operator be ordered to take measures to prevent an incident or damage;
- (c) that the operator be ordered to take measures, after an incident, to prevent damage; or
- (d) that the operator be ordered to take measures of reinstatement.

2. Internal law may stipulate cases where the request is inadmissible.

3. Internal law may specify the body, whether administrative or judicial, before which the request referred to in paragraph 1 above should be made. In all cases provision shall be made for a right of review.

4. Before deciding upon a request mentioned under paragraph 1 above the requested body may, in view of the general interests involved, hear the competent public authorities.

5. When the internal law of a Party requires that the association or foundation has its registered seat or the effective centre of its activities in its territory, the Party may declare at any time, by means of a notification addressed to the Secretary General of the Council of Europe, that, on the basis of reciprocity, an association or foundation having its seat or centre of activities in the territory of another Party and complying in that other Party with the other conditions mentioned in paragraph 1 above shall have the right to submit requests in accordance with paragraphs 1 to 3 above. The declaration will become effective on the first day of the month following the expiration of a period of three months after the date of its reception by the Secretary General.

Article 19—Jurisdiction

1. Actions for compensation under this Convention may only be brought within a Party at the court of the place:

- (a) where the damage was suffered;
- (b) where the dangerous activity was conducted; or
- (c) where the defendant has his habitual residence.

2. Requests for access to specific information held by operators under Article 16, paragraphs 1 and 2 may only be submitted within a Party at the court of the place:

- (a) where the dangerous activity is conducted; or
- (b) where the operator who may be required to provide the information has his habitual residence.

3. Requests by organisations under Article 18, paragraph 1, sub-paragraph a may only be submitted within a Party at the court or, if internal law so

provides, at a competent administrative authority of the place where the dangerous activity is or will be conducted.

4. Requests by organisations under Article 18, paragraph 1, sub-paragraphs b, c and d may only be submitted within a Party at the court or, if internal law so provides, at a competent administrative authority:

(a) of the place where the dangerous activity is or will be conducted; or

(b) of the place where the measures are to be taken.

Article 20—Notification

The court shall stay the proceedings so long as it is not shown that the defendant has been able to receive the document instituting the proceedings or an equivalent document in sufficient time to enable him to arrange for his defence, or that all necessary steps have been taken to this end.

Article 21—Lis pendens

1. Where proceedings involving the same cause of action and between the same parties are brought in the courts of different Parties, any court other than the court first seised shall of its own motion stay its proceedings until such time as the jurisdiction of the court first seised is established.

2. Where the jurisdiction of the court first seised is established, any court other than the court first seised shall decline jurisdiction in favour of that court.

Article 22—Related actions

1. Where related actions are brought in the courts of different Parties, any court other than the court first seised may, while the actions are pending at first instance, stay its proceedings.

2. A court other than the court first seised may also, on the application of one of the parties, decline jurisdiction if the law of that court permits the consolidation of related actions and the court first seised has jurisdiction over both actions.

3. For the purposes of this Article, actions are deemed to be related where they are so closely connected that it is expedient to hear and determine them together to avoid the risk of irreconcilable judgments resulting from separate proceedings.

Article 23—Recognition and enforcement

1. Any decision given by a court with jurisdiction in accordance with Article 19 above where it is no longer subject to ordinary forms of review, shall be recognised in any Party, unless:

(a) such recognition is contrary to public policy in the Party in which recognition is sought;

(b) it was given in default of appearance and the defendant was not duly served with the document which instituted the proceedings or with an equivalent document in sufficient time to enable him to arrange for his defence;

(c) the decision is irreconcilable with a decision given in a dispute between the same parties in the Party in which recognition is sought; or

(d) the decision is irreconcilable with an earlier decision given in another State involving the same cause of action and between the same parties, provided that this latter decision fulfils the conditions necessary for its recognition in the Party addressed.

2. A decision recognised under paragraph 1 above which is enforceable in the Party of origin shall be enforceable in each Party as soon as the formalities required by that Party have been completed. The formalities shall not permit the merits of the case to be re-opened.

Article 24—Other treaties relating to jurisdiction, recognition and enforcement

Whenever two or more Parties are bound by a treaty establishing rules of jurisdiction or providing for recognition and enforcement in a Party of decisions given in another Party, the provisions of that treaty shall replace the corresponding provisions of Articles 19 to 23.

Chapter V—Relation between this Convention and other provisions

Article 25—Relation between this Convention and other provisions

1. Nothing in this Convention shall be construed as limiting or derogating from any of the rights of the persons who have suffered the damage or as limiting the provisions concerning the protection or reinstatement of the environment which may be provided under the laws of any Party or under any other treaty to which it is a Party.

2. In their mutual relations, Parties which are members of the European Economic Community shall apply Community rules and shall therefore not apply the rules arising from this Convention except in so far as there is no Community rule governing the particular subject concerned.

Chapter VI—The Standing Committee

Article 26—The Standing Committee

1. For the purposes of this Convention, a Standing Committee is hereby set up.

2. Each Party may be represented on the Standing Committee by one or more delegates.

3. Each delegation shall have one vote. However, within the areas of its competence the European Economic Community shall exercise its right to vote in the Standing Committee with a number of votes equal to the number of its member States which are Parties to this Convention. It shall not exercise its right to vote in cases where the member States exercise theirs and conversely. As long as no member State of the European Economic Community is a Party, the Community as a Party shall have one vote.

4. Any State referred to in Article 32 or invited to accede to the Convention in accordance with the provisions of Article 33 which is not a Party to this Convention may be represented on the Standing Committee by an observer. If the European Economic Community is not a Party it may be represented on the Standing Committee by an observer.

5. Unless, at least one month before the meeting, a Party has informed the Secretary General of its objection, the Standing Committee may invite the following to attend as observers at all its meetings or one or part of a meeting:

— any State not referred to in paragraph 4 above;
— any international or national, governmental or non-governmental body technically qualified in the fields covered by this Convention.

6. The Standing Committee may seek the advice of experts in order to discharge its functions.

7. The Standing Committee shall be convened by the Secretary General of the Council of Europe. It shall meet whenever one-third of the Parties or the Committee of Ministers of the Council of Europe so request.

8. One-third of the Parties shall constitute a quorum for holding a meeting of the Standing Committee.

9. Decisions may only be taken in the Standing Committee if at least one-half of the Parties are present.

10. Subject to Articles 27 and 29 to 31 the decisions of the Standing Committee shall be taken by a majority of the members present.

11. Subject to the provisions of this Convention the Standing Committee shall draw up its own rules of procedure.

Article 27—Functions of the Standing Committee

The Standing Committee shall keep under review problems relating to this Convention. It may, in particular:

(a) consider any question of a general nature referred to it concerning interpretation or implementation of the Convention. The Standing Committee's conclusions concerning implementation of the Convention may take the form of a recommendation; recommendations shall be adopted by a three-quarters majority of the votes cast;

(b) propose any necessary amendments to the Convention including its Annexes and examine those proposed in accordance with Articles 29 to 31.

Article 28—Reports of the Standing Committee

After each meeting, the Standing Committee shall forward to the Parties and the Committee of Ministers of the Council of Europe a report on its discussions and any decisions taken.

Chapter VII—Amendments to the Convention

Article 29—Amendments to the Articles

1. Any amendment to the Articles of this Convention proposed by a Party or the Standing Committee shall be communicated to the Secretary General of the Council of Europe and forwarded by him at least two months before the meeting of the Standing Committee to the member States of the Council of Europe, to the European Economic Community, to any Signatory, to any Party, to any State invited to sign this Convention in accordance with the provisions of Article 32 and to any State invited to accede to it in accordance with the provisions of Article 33.

2. Any amendment proposed in accordance with the provisions of the preceding paragraph shall be examined by the Standing Committee which:

(a) for amendments to Articles 1 to 25 shall submit the text adopted by a three-quarters majority of the votes cast to the Parties for acceptance;

(b) for amendments to Articles 26 to 37 shall submit the text adopted by a three-quarters majority of the votes cast to the Committee of Ministers for approval. After its approval, this text shall be forwarded to the Parties for acceptance.

3. Any amendment to Articles 1 to 25 shall enter into force, in respect of those Parties which have accepted it, on the first day of the month following the expiration of a period of one month after the date on which three Parties, including at least two member States of the Council of Europe, have informed the Secretary General that they have accepted it.

In respect of any Party which subsequently accepts it, the amendment shall enter into force on the first day of the month following the expiration of a period of one month after the date on which that Party has informed the Secretary General of its acceptance.

4. Any amendment to Articles 26 to 37 shall enter into force on the first day of the month following the expiration of a period of one month after

the date on which all Parties have informed the Secretary General that they have accepted it.

Article 30—Amendments to the Annexes

1. Any amendment to the Annexes of this Convention proposed by a Party or the Standing Committee shall be communicated to the Secretary General of the Council of Europe and forwarded by him at least two months before the meeting of the Standing Committee to the member States of the Council of Europe, to the European Economic Community, to any Signatory, to any Party, to any State invited to sign this Convention in accordance with the provisions of Article 32 and to any State invited to accede to it in accordance with the provisions of Article 33.

2. Any amendment proposed in accordance with the provisions of the preceding paragraph or, where appropriate, of Article 31 shall be examined by the Standing Committee, which may adopt it by a three-quarters majority of the votes cast. The text adopted shall be forwarded to the Parties.

3. On the first day of the month following the expiration of a period of eighteen months after its adoption by the Standing Committee, unless more than one-third of the Parties have notified objections, any amendment shall enter into force for those Parties which have not notified objections.

Article 31—Tacit amendments to Annex I, Parts A and B

1. Whenever the European Economic Community adopts an amendment to one of the Annexes to the Directives referred to in Annex I, Parts A and B of this Convention, the Secretary General shall communicate it to all the Parties not later than four months after its publication in the *Official Journal of the European Communities.*

2. Within a time limit of six months after this communication, any Party may request that the amendment be submitted to the Standing Committee, in which case the procedure under Article 30, paragraphs 2 and 3, shall be followed. If no Party requests the submission of the amendment to the Standing Committee, the provisions of paragraph 3 below shall apply.

3. On the first day of the month following the expiration of a period of eighteen months after the communication of the amendment to all Parties, and unless more than one-third of the Parties have notified objections, the amendment shall enter into force for those Parties which have not notified objections.

However, the entry into force of the amendment shall be postponed to the date fixed for the Member States of the European Economic Community for the compliance of their domestic law with the directive, if this date is later than that resulting from the time limit stated in the first part of this paragraph.

Chapter VIII—Final clauses

Article 32—Signature, ratification and entry into force

1. This Convention shall be open for signature by the member States of the Council of Europe, the non-member States which have participated in its elaboration and by the European Economic Community.

2. This Convention is subject to ratification, acceptance or approval. Instruments of ratification, acceptance or approval shall be deposited with the Secretary General of the Council of Europe.

3. This Convention shall enter into force on the first day of the month following the expiration of a period of three months after the date on which three States, including at least two member States of the Council of Europe, have expressed their consent to be bound by the Convention in accordance with the provisions of paragraph 2 of the present Article.

4. In respect of any Signatory which subsequently expresses its consent to be bound by it, the Convention shall enter into force on the first day of the month following the expiration of a period of three months after the date of the deposit of its instrument of ratification, acceptance or approval.

Article 33—Non-member States

1. After the entry into force of this Convention, the Committee of Ministers of the Council of Europe may, on its own initiative or following a proposal from the Standing Committee and after consultation of the Parties, invite any non-member State of the Council of Europe to accede to this Convention by a decision taken by the majority provided for in Article 20, sub-paragraph d of the Statute of the Council of Europe, and by the unanimous vote of the representatives of the Contracting States entitled to sit on the Committee of Ministers.

2. In respect of any acceding State, the Convention shall enter into force on the first day of the month following the expiration of a period of three months after the date of deposit of the instrument of accession with the Secretary General of the Council of Europe.

Article 34—Territories

1. Any Signatory may, at the time of signature or when depositing its instrument of ratification, acceptance or approval, specify the territory or territories to which this Convention shall apply. Any other State may formulate the same declaration when depositing its instrument of accession.

2. Any Party may, at any later date, by a declaration addressed to the Secretary General of the Council of Europe, extend the application of this Convention to any other territory specified in the declaration and for whose international relations it is responsible or on whose behalf it is authorised to give undertakings. In respect of such territory the Conven-

tion shall enter into force on the first day of the month following the expiration of a period of three months after the date of receipt of such declaration by the Secretary General.

3. Any declaration made under the two preceding paragraphs may, in respect of any territory specified in such declaration, be withdrawn by a notification addressed to the Secretary General. The withdrawal shall become effective on the first day of the month following the expiration of a period of three months after the date of receipt of such notification by the Secretary General.

Article 35—Reservations

1. Any Signatory may declare, at the time of signature or when depositing its instrument of ratification, acceptance or approval, that it reserves the right:

   (a) to apply Article 3, sub-paragraph a, to damage suffered in the territory of the States which are not Parties to this Convention only on the basis of reciprocity;
   (b) to provide in its internal law that, without prejudice to Article 8, the operator shall not be liable if he proves that in the case of damage caused by a dangerous activity mentioned under Article 2, paragraph 1, sub-paragraphs a and b, the state of scientific and technical knowledge at the time of the incident was not such as to enable the existence of the dangerous properties of the substance or the significant risk involved in the operation dealing with the organism to be discovered;
   (c) not to apply Article 18.

Any other State may formulate the same reservations when depositing its instrument of accession.

2. Any Signatory or any other State which makes use of a reservation shall notify the Secretary General of the Council of Europe of the relevant contents of its internal law.

3. Any Party which extends the application of this Convention to a territory mentioned in the declaration referred to in Article 34, paragraph 2, may, in respect of the territory concerned, make a reservation in accordance with the provisions of the preceding paragraphs.

4. No reservation shall be made to the provisions of this Convention, except those mentioned in this Article.

5. Any Party which has made one of the reservations mentioned in this Article may withdraw it by means of a declaration addressed to the Secretary General of the Council of Europe. The withdrawal shall become effective on the first day of the month following the expiration of a period of one month after the date of its receipt by the Secretary General.

Article 36—Denunciation

1. Any Party may at any time denounce this Convention by means of a notification addressed to the Secretary General of the Council of Europe.

2. Such denunciation shall become effective on the first day of the month following the expiration of a period of three months after the date of receipt of notification by the Secretary General.

Article 37—Notifications

The Secretary General of the Council of Europe shall notify the member States of the Council, any Signatory, any Party and any other State which has been invited to accede to this Convention of:

    (a)   any signature;
    (b)   the deposit of any insturment of ratification, acceptance, approval or accession;
    (c)   any date of entry into force of this Convention in accordance with Articles 32 or 33;
    (d)   any amendment adopted in accordance with Articles 29, 30 or 31, and the date on which such an amendment enters into force;
    (e)   any declaration made under the provisions of Articles 18 or 34;
    (f)   any reservation and withdrawal of reservation made in pursuance of the provisions of Article 35;
    (g)   any other act, notification or communication relating to this Convention.

In witness whereof the undersigned, being duly authorised thereto, have signed this Convention.

Done at Lugano, this 21st day of June 1993, in English and French, both texts being equally authentic, in a single copy which shall be deposited in the archives of the Council of Europe. The Secretary General of the Council of Europe shall transmit certified copies to each member State of the Council of Europe, to the non-member States which have participated in the elaboration of this Convention, to the European Economic Community and to any State invited to accede to this Convention.

Annex I Dangerous substances

*A Criteria and methods to be applied to categories of dangerous substances
(Article 2, paragraph 2, sub-paragraph a)*

The properties referred to in Article 2, paragraph 2, sub-paragraph a, shall be determined by the criteria and methods referred to in or annexed to:

— the Council Directive of the European Communities 67/548/EEC of 27 June 1967 (OJEC No. L196/1) on the approximation of the laws, regulations and administrative provisions relating to the classification, packaging and labelling of dangerous substances
  • as amended, for the seventh time, in the Council Directive of the European Communities 92/32/EEC of 30 April 1992 (OJEC No. L154/1), and
  • as adapted to technical progress, for the sixteenth time, by Commission Directive of the European Communities 92/37/EEC of 30 April 1992 (OJEC No. L154/30),
— the Council Directive of the European Communities 88/379/EEC of the 7 June 1988 (OJEC No. L187/14) on the approximation of the laws, regulations and administrative provisions of the member States relating to the classification, packaging and labelling of dangerous preparations as adapted to technical progress by the Directive of the Commission of the European Communities 90/492/EEC of 5 October 1990 (OJEC No. L275/35).

B List of dangerous substances (Article 2, paragraph 2, sub-paragraph b)

The substances referred to in Article 2, paragraph 2, sub-paragraph b, shall be those listed in Annex I of the Council Directive of the European Communities 67/548/EEC of 27 June 1967 (OJEC No. 196/1), on the approximation of the laws regulations and administrative provisions relating to the classification packaging and labelling of dangerous substances as adapted to technical progress, for the sixteenth time, by Commission Directive of the European Communities 92/37/EEC of 30 April 1992 (OJEC No. L154/30).

Annex II Installations or sites for the incineration, treatment, handling or recycling of waste (See Article 2, paragraph 1, sub-paragraph c)

1. Installations or sites for the partial or complete disposal of solid, liquid or gaseous wastes by incineration on land or at sea.

2. Installations or sites for thermal degradation of solid, gaseous or liquid wastes under reduced oxygen supply.

3. Installations or sites for high temperature degradation or thermal degasification of solid, gaseous or liquid wastes.

4. Installations or sites for thermal recovery of compounds from solid or liquid wastes.

5. Installations or sites for chemical, physical or biological treatment of wastes for recycling or disposal.

6. Installations or sites for blending or mix prior to submission to the operation of a site for permanent deposit.

7. Installations or sites for repacking prior to submission to the operation of a site for permanent deposit.

8. Installations or sites for handling and treatment of solid, liquid or gaseous wastes for re-use or recycling such as:

  — solvent reclamation/regeneration;
  — recycling/reclamation of organic substances (not used as solvents) and inorganic materials;
  — regeneration of acid and bases;
  — recovery of components used for pollution abatement;
  — recovery of components from catalysts;
  — waste oil re-refining or other re-uses of waste oil;
  — recovery of components from discarded cars.

9. Installations or sites for storage of materials intended for submission to any operation in this Annex or to the operation of a site for the permanent deposit of waste, temporary storage excluded, pending collection, on the site where it is produced.

3. MARINE ENVIRONMENT

United Nations Convention on the Law of the Sea (Part XII), adopted
Montego Bay, 10 December 1982

The Third United Nations Conference on the Law of the Sea was convened in 1973
in accordance with General Assembly resolution 3067 (XXVIII) for the purpose of
concluding a comprehensive treaty 'dealing with all matters relating to the law of
the sea ... bearing in mind that the problems of ocean space are closely interrelated and need to be considered as a whole'. The Convention also establishes a
Law of the Sea Tribunal with extensive jurisdiction over disputes, and an International Seabed Authority to regulate mineral exploitation of the deep seabed.
Over 150 nations took part in the negotiations, which proceeded by consensus until
1982, when the text which was finally adopted by vote was opposed by the United
States of America, Israel, Turkey, and Venezuela. Seventeen other states, mainly
European, abstained. The full text is found in UN, *Official Text of the United Nations
Convention on the Law of the Sea* (1983); *repr.* in 21 *ILM* (1982) 1261. The Conven-
tion entered into force on 16 November 1994. The initial sixty ratifications were,
with the exception of Iceland, all developing states. No reservations are permitted.
For signatories, parties, and declarations, see: UN, *Multilateral Treaties Deposited with
the Secretary-General,* UN Doc ST/LEG/SER.E/ (current year); UN, *Law of the Sea
Bulletin* (New York, 1983–). An Agreement Relating to the implementation of part
XI of the 1982 UN Convention on the Law of the Sea, adopted by UNGA Res. 48/
263 in 1994, is intended to facilitate more widespread ratification or accession,
especially by developed states, *repr.* 33 *ILM* (1994) 1311.

Generally on the law of the sea, see: D. P. O'Connell, *The International Law of the
Sea* (Oxford, 1984, 2 vols.); R. R. Churchill and A. V. Lowe, *The Law of the Sea* (2nd
edn., Manchester, 1988); J. Van Dyke, D. Zaelke, and G. Hewison, *Freedom of the Seas
in the 21st Century* (Washington, 1993); R. J. Dupuy and D. Vignes (eds.), *A Handbook on the New Law of the Sea,* 2 vols. (Dordrecht, 1991).

Part XII of the 1982 Convention, which is reproduced here, deals with protection
of the marine environment and provides a framework of general rules intended to
accommodate existing and additional conventions on regional or sectoral issues
such as pollution from dumping or ships. It provides evidence of rules which have
become widely accepted in many respects, and represents a significant contribution
to the codification and development of international law relating to the marine
environment. For the drafting history of Part XII, see M. Nordquist (ed.), *United
Nations Convention on the Law of the Sea: A Commentary,* Volume IV (Dordrecht, 1991),
and for preparatory material see *Third United Conference on the Law of the Sea: Official
Records,* 17 vols. (1975–1984).

On the Convention's significance for the law relating to the marine environment
see in particular: UN Secretary General, *Report on the Protection and Preservation of the
Marine Environment,* UN Doc. A/44/461 (1989); UN, *Report of the UNCED* (New
York, 1993), Vol. 1, Agenda 21, Ch. 17, which refers to 'International Law, as
reflected in the provisions of the United Nations Convention on the Law of the Sea';
P. W. Birnie and A. E. Boyle, *International Law and the Environment* (Oxford, 1992),
Chs. 7 and 8; D. M. Johnston (ed.), *The Environmental Law of the Sea* (Berlin, 1981);
F. Gold and J. McConnell, 'The Modern Law of the Sea: Framework for the

Protection and Preservation of the Marine Environment', 23 *Case Western Reserve JIL* (1991) 83; R. McGonigle, 'Developing Sustainability and the Emerging Norms of International Environmental Law: the Case of Land-based Marine Pollution Control', 28 *CYIL* (1990), 169; M. A. Stephenson, 'Vessel Source Pollution Under the Law of the Sea Convention—an Analysis of the Prescriptive Standards', 17 *U Queensland LJ* (1992) 117; R. Lotilla, 'The Efficacy of Anti-Pollution Legislation Provisions of the 1982 Law of the Sea Convention: a View from S. E. Asia', 41 *ICLQ* (1992) 137; D. Dzidzorm and B. Tsamenyi, 'Enhancing International Control of Vessel Source Oil Pollution under the Law of the Sea Convention 1982: A Reassessment', 10 *U Tasmania LR* (1991) 269; D. Bodansky, 'protecting the Marine Environment from Vessel-Source Pollution: UNCLOS III and Beyond', 18 *Ecol LQ* (1991) 719.

For national legislation and tables of claims to territorial sea, contiguous zones, and exclusive economic or fishery zones, see: K. R. Simmonds (ed.), *New Directions in the Law of the Sea* (New York/Looseleaf, 1986–); UN, *Law of the Sea Bulletin* (New York, 1983–); UN, *The Law of the Sea: National Claims to Maritime Jurisdiction* (New York, 1992); UN, *The Law of the Sea: National Legislation on the EEZ* (New York, 1993); UN, *National Legislation and Treaties Relating to the Law of the Sea*, ST/LEG/SER.B/19 (New York, 1980).

TEXT OF UNCLOS PART XII—PROTECTION AND PRESERVATION OF THE MARINE ENVIRONMENT

Section 1. General Provisions

Article 192
General obligation

States have the obligation to protect and preserve the marine environment.

Article 193
Sovereign right of States to exploit their natural resources

States have the sovereign right to exploit their natural resources pursuant to their environmental policies and in accordance with their duty to protect and preserve the marine environment.

Article 194
Measures to prevent, reduce and control pollution of the marine environment

1. States shall take, individually or jointly as appropriate, all measures consistent with this Convention that are necessary to prevent, reduce and control pollution of the marine environment from any source, using for this purpose the best practicable means at their disposal and in accordance with their capabilities, and they shall endeavour to harmonize their policies in this connection.

2. States shall take all measures necessary to ensure that activities under their jurisdiction or control are so conducted as not to cause damage by pollution to other States and their environment, and that pollution arising

from incidents or activities under their jurisdiction or control does not spread beyond the areas where they exercise sovereign rights in accordance with this Convention.

3. The measures taken pursuant to this Part shall deal with all sources of pollution of the marine environment. These measures shall include, *inter alia*, those designed to minimize to the fullest possible extent:

   (a) the release of toxic, harmful or noxious substances, especially those which are persistent, from land-based sources, from or through the atmosphere or by dumping;

   (b) pollution from vessels, in particular measures for preventing accidents and dealing with emergencies, ensuring the safety of operations at sea, preventing intentional and unintentional discharges, and regulating the design, construction, equipment, operation and manning of vessels;

   (c) pollution from installations and devices used in exploration or exploitation of the natural resources of the sea-bed and subsoil, in particular measures for preventing accidents and dealing with emergencies, ensuring the safety of operations at sea, and regulating the design, construction, equipment, operation and manning of such installations or devices;

   (d) pollution from other installations and devices operating in the marine environment, in particular measures for preventing accidents and dealing with emergencies, ensuring the safety of operations at sea, and regulating the design, construction, equipment, operation and manning of such installations or devices.

4. In taking measures to prevent, reduce or control pollution of the marine environment, States shall refrain from unjustifiable interference with activities carried out by other States in the exercise of their rights and in pursuance of their duties in conformity with this Convention.

5. The measures taken in accordance with this Part shall include those necessary to protect and preserve rare or fragile ecosystems as well as the habitat of depleted, threatened or endangered species and other forms of marine life.

Article 195
Duty not to transfer damage or hazards or transform one type of pollution into another

In taking measures to prevent, reduce and control pollution of the marine environment, States shall act so as not to transfer, directly or indirectly, damage or hazards from one area to another or transform one type of pollution into another.

Article 196
Use of technologies or introduction of alien or new species

1. States shall take all measures necessary to prevent, reduce and control pollution of the marine environment resulting from the use of technologies under their jurisdiction or control, or the intentional or accidental introduction of species, alien or new, to a particular part of the marine environment, which may cause significant and harmful changes thereto.

2. This article does not affect the application of this Convention regarding the prevention, reduction and control of pollution of the marine environment.

Section 2. Global and Regional Co-operation

Article 197
Co-operation on a global or regional basis

States shall co-operate on a global basis and, as appropriate, on a regional basis, directly or through competent international organizations, in formulating and elaborating international rules, standards and recommended practices and procedures consistent with this Convention, for the protection and preservation of the marine environment, taking into account characteristic regional features.

Article 198
Notification of imminent or actual damage

When a State becomes aware of cases in which the marine environment is in imminent danger of being damaged or has been damaged by pollution, it shall immediately notify other States it deems likely to be affected by such damage, as well as the competent international organizations.

Article 199
Contingency plans against pollution

In the cases referred to in article 198, States in the area affected, in accordance with their capabilities, and the competent international organizations shall co-operate, to the extent possible, in eliminating the effects of pollution and preventing or minimizing the damage. To this end, States shall jointly develop and promote contingency plans for responding to pollution incidents in the marine environment.

Article 200
Studies, research programmes and exchange of information and data

States shall co-operate, directly or through competent international organizations, for the purpose of promoting studies, undertaking programmes of scientific research and encouraging the exchange of information and data acquired about pollution of the marine environment. They shall endeavour to participate actively in regional and global programmes to acquire knowledge for the assessment of the nature and extent of pollution, exposure to it, and its pathways, risks and remedies.

Article 201
Scientific criteria for regulations

In the light of the information and data acquired pursuant to article 200, States shall co-operate, directly or through competent international organizations, in establishing appropriate scientific criteria for the formulation and elaboration of rules, standards and recommended practices and procedures for the prevention, reduction and control of pollution of the marine environment.

Section 3. Technical Assistance

Article 202
Scientific and technical assistance to developing States

States shall, directly or through competent international organizations:

(a) promote programmes of scientific, educational, technical and other assistance to developing States for the protection and preservation of the marine environment and the prevention, reduction and control of marine pollution. Such assistance shall include, *inter alia*:
  (i) training of their scientific and technical personnel;
  (ii) facilitating their participation in relevant international programmes;
  (iii) supplying them with necessary equipment and facilities;
  (iv) enhancing their capacity to manufacture such equipment;
  (v) advice on and developing facilities for research, monitoring, educational and other programmes;
(b) provide appropriate assistance, especially to developing States, for the minimization of the effects of major incidents which may cause serious pollution of the marine environment;
(c) provide appropriate assistance, especially to developing States, concerning the preparation of environmental assessments.

Article 203
Preferential treatment for developing States

Developing States shall, for the purposes of prevention, reduction and control of pollution of the marine environment or minimization of its effects, be granted preference by international organizations in:

(a) the allocation of appropriate funds and technical assistance; and

(b) the utilization of their specialized services.

Section 4. Monitoring and Environmental Assessment

Article 204
Monitoring of the risks or effects of pollution

1. States shall, consistent with the rights of other States, endeavour, as far as practicable, directly or through the competent international organizations, to observe, measure, evaluate and analyse, by recognized scientific methods, the risks or effects of pollution of the marine environment.

2. In particular, States shall keep under surveillance the effects of any activities which they permit or in which they engage in order to determine whether these activities are likely to pollute the marine environment.

Article 205
Publication of reports

States shall publish reports of the results obtained pursuant to article 204 or provide such reports at appropriate intervals to the competent international organizations, which should make them available to all States.

Article 206
Assessment of potential effects of activities

When States have reasonable grounds for believing that planned activities under their jurisdiction or control may cause substantial pollution of or significant and harmful changes to the marine environment, they shall, as far as practicable, assess the potential effects of such activities on the marine environment and shall communicate reports of the results of such assessments in the manner provided in article 205.

Sections 5. International Rules and National Legislation to Prevent, Reduce and Control Pollution of the Marine Environment

Article 207
Pollution from land-based sources

1. States shall adopt laws and regulations to prevent, reduce and control pollution of the marine environment from land-based sources, including rivers, estuaries, pipelines and outfall structures, taking into account internationally agreed rules, standards and recommended practices and procedures.

2. States shall take other measures as may be necessary to prevent, reduce and control such pollution.

3. States shall endeavour to harmonize their policies in this connection at the appropriate regional level.

4. States, acting especially through competent international organizations or diplomatic conference, shall endeavour to establish global and regional rules, standards and recommended practices and procedures to prevent, reduce and control pollution of the marine environment from land-based sources, taking into account characteristic regional features, the economic capacity of developing States and their need for economic development. Such rules, standards and recommended practices and procedures shall be re-examined from time to time as necessary.

5. Laws, regulations, measures, rules, standards and recommended practices and procedures referred to in paragraphs 1, 2 and 4 shall include those designed to minimize, to the fullest extent possible, the release of toxic, harmful or noxious substances, especially those which are persistent, into the marine environment.

Article 208
Pollution from sea-bed activities subject to national jurisdiction

1. Coastal States shall adopt laws and regulations to prevent, reduce and control pollution of the marine environment arising from or in connection with seabed activities subject to their jurisdiction and from artificial islands, installations and structures under their jurisdiction, pursuant to articles 60 and 80.

2. States shall take other measures as may be necessary to prevent, reduce and control such pollution.

3. Such laws, regulations and measures shall be no less effective than international rules, standards and recommended practices and procedures.

4. States shall endeavour to harmonize their policies in this connection at the appropriate regional level.

5. States, acting especially through competent international organizations or diplomatic conference, shall establish global and regional rules, standards and recommended practices and procedures to prevent, reduce and control pollution of the marine environment referred to in paragraph 1. Such rules, standards and recommended practices and procedures shall be re-examined from time to time as necessary.

Article 209
Pollution from activities in the Area

1. International rules, regulations and procedures shall be established in accordance with Part XI to prevent, reduce and control pollution of the

marine environment from activities in the Area. Such rules, regulations and procedures shall be re-examined from time to time as necessary.

2. Subject to the relevant provisions of this section, States shall adopt laws and regulations to prevent, reduce and control pollution of the marine environment from activities in the Area undertaken by vessels, installations, structures and other devices flying their flag or of their registry or operating under their authority, as the case may be. The requirements of such laws and regulations shall be no less effective than the international rules, regulations and procedures referred to in paragraph 1.

Article 210
Pollution by dumping

1. States shall adopt laws and regulations to prevent, reduce and control pollution of the marine environment by dumping.

2. States shall take other measures as may be necessary to prevent, reduce and control such pollution.

3. Such laws, regulations and measures shall ensure that dumping is not carried out without the permission of the competent authorities of States.

4. States, acting especially through competent international organizations or diplomatic conference, shall endeavour to establish global and regional rules, standards and recommended practices and procedures to prevent, reduce and control such pollution. Such rules, standards and recommended practices and procedures shall be re-examined from time to time as necessary.

5. Dumping within the territorial sea and the exclusive economic zone or onto the continental shelf shall not be carried out without the express prior approval of the coastal State, which has the right to permit, regulate and control such dumping after due consideration of the matter with other States which by reason of their geographical situation may be adversely affected thereby.

6. National laws, regulations and measures shall be no less effective in preventing, reducing and controlling such pollution than the global rules and standards.

Article 211
Pollution from vessels

1. States, acting through the competent international organization or general diplomatic conference, shall establish international rules and standards to prevent, reduce and control pollution of the marine environment from vessels and promote the adoption, in the same manner, wherever appropriate, of routeing systems designed to minimize the threat of accidents which might cause pollution of the marine environment, including the coastline, and pollution damage to the related interests of coastal

States. Such rules and standards shall, in the same manner, be re-examined from time to time as necessary.

2. States shall adopt laws and regulations for the prevention, reduction and control of pollution of the marine environment from vessels flying their flag or of their registry. Such laws and regulations shall at least have the same effect as that of generally accepted international rules and standards established through the competent international organization or general diplomatic conference.

3. States which establish particular requirements for the prevention, reduction and control of pollution of the marine environment as a condition for the entry of foreign vessels into their ports or internal waters or for a call at their off-shore terminals shall give due publicity to such requirements and shall communicate them to the competent international organization. Whenever such requirements are established in identical form by two or more coastal States in an endeavour to harmonize policy, the communication shall indicate which States are participating in such co-operative arrangements. Every State shall require the master of a vessel flying its flag or of its registry, when navigating within the territorial sea of a State participating in such co-operative arrangements, to furnish, upon the request of that State, information as to whether it is proceeding to a State of the same region participating in such co-operative arrangements and, if so, to indicate whether it complies with the port entry requirements of that State. This article is without prejudice to the continued exercise by a vessel of its right of innocent passage or to the application of article 25, paragraph 2.

4. Coastal States may, in the exercise of their sovereignty within their territorial sea, adopt laws and regulations for the prevention, reduction and control of marine pollution from foreign vessels, including vessels exercising the right of innocent passage. Such laws and regulations shall, in accordance with Part II, section 3, not hamper innocent passage of foreign vessels.

5. Coastal States, for the purpose of enforcement as provided for in section 6, may in respect of their exclusive economic zones adopt laws and regulations for the prevention, reduction and control of pollution from vessels conforming to and giving effect to generally accepted international rules and standards established through the competent international organization or general diplomatic conference.

6. (a) Where the international rules and standards referred to in paragraph 1 are inadequate to meet special circumstances and coastal States have reasonable grounds for believing that a particular, clearly defined area of their respective exclusive economic zones is an area where the adoption of special mandatory measures for the prevention of pollution from vessels is required for recognized technical

reasons in relation to its oceanographical and ecological conditions, as well as its utilization or the protection of its resources and the particular character of its traffic, the coastal States, after appropriate consultations through the competent international organization with any other States concerned, may, for that area, direct a communication to that organization, submitting scientific and technical evidence in support and information on necessary reception facilities. Within 12 months after receiving such a communication, the organization shall determine whether the conditions in that area correspond to the requirements set out above. If the organization so determines, the coastal States may, for that area, adopt laws and regulations for the prevention, reduction and control of pollution from vessels implementing such international rules and standards or navigational practices as are made applicable, through the organization, for special areas. These laws and regulations shall not become applicable to foreign vessels until 15 months after the submission of the communication to the organization.

(b) The coastal States shall publish the limits of any such particular, clearly defined area.

(c) If the coastal States intend to adopt additional laws and regulations fot the same area for the prevention, reduction and control of pollution from vessels, they shall, when submitting the aforesaid communication, at the same time notify the organization thereof. Such additional laws and regulations may relate to discharges or navigational practices but shall not require foreign vessels to observe design, construction, manning or equipment standards other than generally accepted international rules and standards; they shall become applicable to foreign vessels 15 months after the submission of the communication to the organization, provided that the organization agrees within 12 months after the submission of the communication.

7. The international rules and standards referred to in this article should include *inter alia* those relating to prompt notification to coastal States, whose coastline or related interests may be affected by incidents, including maritime casualties, which involve discharges or probability of discharges.

Article 212
Pollution from or through the atmosphere

1. States shall adopt laws and regulations to prevent, reduce and control pollution of the marine environment from or through the atmosphere, applicable to the air space under their sovereignty and to vessels flying their flag or vessels or aircraft of their registry, taking into account internationally agreed rules, standards and recommended practices and procedures and the safety of air navigation.

2. States shall take other measures as may be necessary to prevent, reduce and control such pollution.

3. States, acting especially through competent international organizations or diplomatic conference, shall endeavour to establish global and regional rules, standards and recommended practices and procedures to prevent, reduce and control such pollution.

Section 6. Enforcement

Article 213
Enforcement with respect to pollution from land-based sources

States shall enforce their laws and regulations adopted in accordance with article 207 and shall adopt laws and regulations and take other measures necessary to implement applicable international rules and standards established through competent international organizations or diplomatic conference to prevent, reduce and control pollution of the marine environment from land-based sources.

Article 214
Enforcement with respect to pollution from sea-bed activities

States shall enforce their laws and regulations adopted in accordance with article 208 and shall adopt laws and regulations and take other measures necessary to implement applicable international rules and standards established through competent international organizations or diplomatic conference to prevent, reduce and control pollution of the marine environment arising from or in connection with sea-bed activities subject to their jurisdiction and from artificial islands, installations and structures under their jurisdiction, pursuant to articles 60 and 80.

Article 215
Enforcement with respect to pollution from activities in the Area

Enforcement of international rules, regulations and procedures, established in accordance with Part XI to prevent, reduce and control pollution of the marine environment from activities in the Area shall be governed by that Part.

Article 216
Enforcement with respect to pollution by dumping

1. Laws and regulations adopted in accordance with this Convention and applicable international rules and standards established through competent international organizations or diplomatic conference for the prevention, reduction and control of pollution of the marine environment by dumping shall be enforced:

(a) by the coastal State with regard to dumping within its territorial sea or its exclusive economic zone or onto its continental shelf;

(b) by the flag State with regard to vessels flying its flag or vessels or aircraft of its registry;

(c) by any State with regard to acts of loading of wastes or other matter occurring within its territory or at its off-shore terminals.

2. No State shall be obliged by virtue of this article to institute proceedings when another State has already instituted proceedings in accordance with this article.

Article 217
Enforcement by flag States

1. States shall ensure compliance by vessels flying their flag or of their registry with applicable international rules and standards, established through the competent international organization or general diplomatic conference, and with their laws and regulations adopted in accordance with this Convention for the prevention, reduction and control of pollution of the marine environment from vessels and shall accordingly adopt laws and regulations and take other measures necessary for their implementation. Flag States shall provide for the effective enforcement of such rules, standards, laws and regulations, irrespective of where a violation occurs.

2. States shall, in particular, take appropriate measures in order to ensure that vessels flying their flag or of their registry are prohibited from sailing, until they can proceed to sea in compliance with the requirements of the international rules and standards referred to in paragraph 1, including requirements in respect of design, construction, equipment and manning of vessels.

3. States shall ensure that vessels flying their flag or of their registry carry on board certificates required by and issued pursuant to international rules and standards referred to in paragraph 1. States shall ensure that vessels flying their flag are periodically inspected in order to verify that such certificates are in conformity with the actual condition of the vessels. These certificates shall be accepted by other States as evidence of the condition of the vessels and shall be regarded as having the same force as certificates issued by them, unless there are clear grounds for believing that the condition of the vessel does not correspond substantially with the particulars of the certificates.

4. If a vessel commits a violation of rules and standards established through the competent international organization or general diplomatic conference, the flag State, without prejudice to articles 218, 220 and 228, shall provide for immediate investigation and where appropriate institute proceedings in respect of the alleged violation irrespective of where the

violation occurred or where the pollution caused by such violation has occurred or has been spotted.

5. Flag States conducting an investigation of the violation may request the assistance of any other State whose co-operation could be useful in clarifying the circumstances of the case. States shall endeavour to meet appropriate requests of flag States.

6. States shall, at the written request of any State, investigate any violation alleged to have been committed by vessels flying their flag. If satisfied that sufficient evidence is available to enable proceedings to be brought in respect of the alleged violation, flag States shall without delay institute such proceedings in accordance with their laws.

7. Flag States shall promptly inform the requesting State and the competent international organization of the action taken and its outcome. Such information shall be available to all States.

8. Penalties provided for by the laws and regulations of States for vessels flying their flag shall be adequate in severity to discourage violations wherever they occur.

Article 218
Enforcement by port States

1. When a vessel is voluntarily within a port or at an off-shore terminal of a State, that State may undertake investigations and, where the evidence so warrants, institute proceedings in respect of any discharge from that vessel outside the internal waters, territorial sea or exclusive economic zone of that State in violation of applicable international rules and standards established through the competent international organization or general diplomatic conference.

2. No proceedings pursuant to paragraph 1 shall be instituted in respect of a discharge violation in the internal waters, territorial sea or exclusive economic zone of another State unless requested by that State, the flag State, or a State damaged or threatened by the discharge violation, or unless the violation has caused or is likely to cause pollution in the internal waters, territorial sea or exclusive economic zone of the State instituting the proceedings.

3. When a vessel is voluntarily within a port or at an off-shore terminal of a State, that State shall, as far as practicable, comply with requests from any State for investigation of a discharge violation referred to in paragraph 1, believed to have occurred in, caused, or threatened damage to the internal waters, territorial sea or exclusive economic zone of the requesting State. It shall likewise, as far as practicable, comply with requests from the flag State for investigation of such a violation, irrespective of where the violation occurred.

4. The records of the investigation carried out by a port State pursuant to this article shall be transmitted upon request to the flag State or to the coastal State. Any proceedings instituted by the port State on the basis of such an investigation may, subject to section 7, be suspended at the request of the coastal State when the violation has occurred within its internal waters, territorial sea or exclusive economic zone. The evidence and records of the case, together with any bond or other financial security posted with the authorities of the port State, shall in that event be transmitted to the coastal State. Such transmittal shall preclude the continuation of proceedings in the port State.

Article 219
Measures relating to seaworthiness of vessels to avoid pollution

Subject to section 7, States which, upon request or on their own initiative, have ascertained that a vessel within one of their ports or at one of their offshore terminals is in violation of applicable international rules and standards relating to seaworthiness of vessels and thereby threatens damage to the marine environment shall, as far as practicable, take administrative measures to prevent the vessel from sailing. Such States may permit the vessel to proceed only to the nearest appropriate repair yard and, upon removal of the causes of the violation, shall permit the vessel to continue immediately.

Article 220
Enforcement by coastal States

1. When a vessel is voluntarily within a port or at an off-shore terminal of a State, that State may, subject to section 7, institute proceedings in respect of any violation of its laws and regulations adopted in accordance with this Convention or applicable international rules and standards for the prevention, reduction and control of pollution from vessels when the violation has occurred within the territorial sea or the exclusive economic zone of that State.

2. Where there are clear grounds for believing that a vessel navigating in the territorial sea of a State has, during its passage therein, violated laws and regulations of that State adopted in accordance with this Convention or applicable international rules and standards for the prevention, reduction and control of pollution from vessels, that State, without prejudice to the application of the relevant provisions of Part II, section 3, may undertake physical inspection of the vessel relating to the violation and may, where the evidence so warrants, institute proceedings, including detention of the vessel, in accordance with its laws, subject to the provisions of section 7.

3. Where there are clear grounds for believing that a vessel navigating in the exclusive economic zone or the territorial sea of a State has, in the exclusive economic zone, committed a violation of applicable international

rules and standards for the prevention, reduction and control of pollution from vessels or laws and regulations of that State conforming and giving effect to such rules and standards, that State may require the vessel to give information regarding its identity and port of registry, its last and its next port of call and other relevant information required to establish whether a violation has occurred.

4. States shall adopt laws and regulations and take other measures so that vessels flying their flag comply with requests for information pursuant to paragraph 3.

5. Where there are clear grounds for believing that a vessel navigating in the exclusive economic zone or the territorial sea of a State has, in the exclusive economic zone, committed a violation referred to in paragraph 3 resulting in a substantial discharge causing or threatening significant pollution of the marine environment, that State may undertake physical inspection of the vessel for matters relating to the violation if the vessel has refused to give information or if the information supplied by the vessel is manifestly at variance with the evident factual situation and if the circumstances of the case justify such inspection.

6. Where there is clear objective evidence that a vessel navigating in the exclusive economic zone or the territorial sea of a State has, in the exclusive economic zone, committed a violation referred to in paragraph 3 resulting in a discharge causing major damage or threat of major damage to the coastline or related interests of the coastal State, or to any resources of its territorial sea or exclusive economic zone, that State may, subject to section 7, provided that the evidence so warrants, institute proceedings, including detention of the vessel, in accordance with its laws.

7. Notwithstanding the provisions of paragraph 6, whenever appropriate procedures have been established, either through the competent international organization or as otherwise agreed, whereby compliance with requirements for bonding or other appropriate financial security has been assured, the coastal State if bound by such procedures shall allow the vessel to proceed.

8. The provisions of paragraphs 3, 4, 5, 6 and 7 also apply in respect of national laws and regulations adopted pursuant to article 211, paragraph 6.

Article 221
Measures to avoid pollution arising from maritime casualties

1. Nothing in this Part shall prejudice the right of States, pursuant to international law, both customary and conventional, to take and enforce measures beyond the territorial sea proportionate to the actual or threatened damage to protect their coastline or related interests, including fishing, from pollution or threat of pollution following upon a maritime casualty or acts relating to such a casualty, which may reasonably be expected to result in major harmful consequences.

2. For the purposes of this article, 'maritime casualty' means a collision of vessels, stranding or other incident of navigation, or other occurrence on board a vessel or external to it resulting in material damage or imminent threat of material damage to a vessel or cargo.

Article 222
Enforcement with respect to pollution from or through the atmosphere

States shall enforce, within the air space under their sovereignty or with regard to vessels flying their flag or vessels or aircraft of their registry, their laws and regulations adopted in accordance with article 212, paragraph 1, and with other provisions of this Convention and shall adopt laws and regulations and take other measures necessary to implement applicable international rules and standards established through competent international organizations or diplomatic conference to prevent, reduce and control pollution of the marine environment from or through the atmosphere, in conformity with all relevant international rules and standards concerning the safety of air navigation.

Section 7. Safeguards

Article 223
Measures to facilitate proceedings

In proceedings instituted pursuant to this Part, States shall take measures to facilitate the hearing of witnesses and the admission of evidence submitted by authorities of another State, or by the competent international organization, and shall facilitate the attendance at such proceedings of official representatives of the competent international organization, the flag State and any State affected by pollution arising out of any violation. The official representatives attending such proceedings shall have such rights and duties as may be provided under national laws and regulations or international law.

Article 224
Exercise of powers of enforcement

The powers of enforcement against foreign vessels under this Part may only be exercised by officials or by warships, military aircraft, or other ships or aircraft clearly marked and identifiable as being on government service and authorized to that effect.

Article 225
Duty to avoid adverse consequences in the exercise of the powers of enforcement

In the exercise under this Convention of their powers of enforcement against foreign vessels, States shall not endanger the safety of navigation or otherwise create any hazard to a vessel, or bring it to an unsafe port or anchorage, or expose the marine environment to an unreasonable risk.

Article 226
Investigation of foreign vessels

1. (a) States shall not delay a foreign vessel longer than is essential for purposes of the investigations provided for in articles 216, 218 and 220. Any physical inspection of a foreign vessel shall be limited to an examination of such certificates, records or other documents as the vessel is required to carry by generally accepted international rules and standards or of any similar documents which it is carrying; further physical inspection of the vessel may be undertaken only after such an examination and only when:
    (i) there are clear grounds for believing that the condition of the vessel or its equipment does not correspond substantially with the particulars of those documents;
    (ii) the contents of such documents are not sufficient to confirm or verify a suspected violation; or
    (iii) the vessel is not carrying valid certificates and records.
   (b) If the investigation indicates a violation of applicable laws and regulations or international rules and standards for the protection and preservation of the marine environment, release shall be made promptly subject to reasonable procedures such as bonding or other appropriate financial security.
   (c) Without prejudice to applicable international rules and standards relating to the seaworthiness of vessels, the release of a vessel may, whenever it would present an unreasonable threat of damage to the marine environment, be refused or made conditional upon proceeding to the nearest appropriate repair yard. Where release has been refused or made conditional, the flag State of the vessel must be promptly notified, and may seek release of the vessel in accordance with Part XV.

2. States shall co-operate to develop procedures for the avoidance of unnecessary physical inspection of vessels at sea.

Article 227
Non-discrimination with respect to foreign vessels

In exercising their rights and performing their duties under this Part, States shall not discriminate in form or in fact against vessels of any other State.

Article 228
Suspension and restrictions on institution of proceedings

1. Proceedings to impose penalties in respect of any violation of applicable laws and regulations or international rules and standards relating to the

prevention, reduction and control of pollution from vessels committed by a foreign vessel beyond the territorial sea of the State instituting proceedings shall be suspended upon the taking of proceedings to impose penalties in respect of corresponding charges by the flag State within six months of the date on which proceedings were first instituted, unless those proceedings relate to a case of major damage to the coastal State or the flag State in question has repeatedly disregarded its obligation to enforce effectively the applicable international rules and standards in respect of violations committed by its vessels. The flag State shall in due course make available to the State previously instituting proceedings a full dossier of the case and the records of the proceedings, whenever the flag State has requested the suspension of proceedings in accordance with this article. When proceedings instituted by the flag State have been brought to a conclusion, the suspended proceedings shall be terminated. Upon payment of costs incurred in respect of such proceedings, any bond posted or other financial security provided in connection with the suspended proceedings shall be released by the coastal State.

2. Proceedings to impose penalties on foreign vessels shall not be instituted after the expiry of three years from the date on which the violation was committed, and shall not be taken by any State in the event of proceedings having been instituted by another State subject to the provisions set out in paragraph 1.

3. The provisions of this article are without prejudice to the right of the flag State to take any measures, including proceedings to impose penalties, according to its laws irrespective of prior proceedings by another State.

Article 229
Institution of civil proceedings

Nothing in this Convention affects the institution of civil proceedings in respect of any claim for loss or damage resulting from pollution of the marine environment.

Article 230
Monetary penalties and the observance of recognized rights of the accused

1. Monetary penalties only may be imposed with respect to violations of national laws and regulations or applicable international rules and standards for the prevention, reduction and control of pollution of the marine environment, committed by foreign vessels beyond the territorial sea.

2. Monetary penalties only may be imposed with respect to violations of national laws and regulations or applicable international rules and standards for the prevention, reduction and control of pollution of the marine environment, committed by foreign vessels in the territorial sea,

except in the case of a wilful and serious act of pollution in the territorial sea.

3. In the conduct of proceedings in respect of such violations committed by a foreign vessel which may result in the imposition of penalties, recognized rights of the accused shall be observed.

Article 231
Notification to the flag State and other States concerned

States shall promptly notify the flag State and any other State concerned of any measures taken pursuant to section 6 against foreign vessels, and shall submit to the flag State all official reports concerning such measures. However, with respect to violations committed in the territorial sea, the foregoing obligations of the coastal State apply only to such measures as are taken in proceedings. The diplomatic agents or consular officers and where possible the maritime authority of the flag State, shall be immediately informed of any such measures taken pursuant to section 6 against foreign vessels.

Article 232
Liability of States arising from enforcement measures

States shall be liable for damage or loss attributable to them arising from measures taken pursuant to section 6 when such measures are unlawful or exceed those reasonably required in the light of available information. States shall provide for recourse in their courts for actions in respect of such damage or loss.

Article 233
Safeguards with respect to straits used for international navigation

Nothing in sections 5, 6 and 7 affects the legal régime of straits used for international navigation. However, if a foreign ship other than those referred to in section 10 has committed a violation of the laws and regulations referred to in article 42, paragraph 1(a) and (b), causing or threatening major damage to the marine environment of the straits, the States bordering the straits may take appropriate enforcement measures and if so shall respect *mutatis mutandis* the provisions of this section.

Section 8. Ice-covered Areas

Article 234
Ice-covered areas

Coastal States have the right to adopt and enforce non-discriminatory laws and regulations for the prevention, reduction and control of marine pollution from vessels in ice-covered areas within the limits of the exclusive economic zone, where particularly severe climatic conditions and the presence of ice covering such areas for most of the year create obstructions or exceptional hazards to navigation, and pollution of the marine environment could cause major harm to or irreversible disturbance of the ecological balance. Such laws and regulations shall have due regard to navigation and the protection and preservation of the marine environment based on the best available scientific evidence.

Section 9. Responsibility and Liability

Article 235
Responsibility and liability

1. States are responsible for the fulfilment of their international obligations concerning the protection and preservation of the marine environment. They shall be liable in accordance with international law.

2. States shall ensure that recourse is available in accordance with their legal systems for prompt and adequate compensation or other relief in respect of damage caused by pollution of the marine environment by natural or juridical persons under their jurisdiction.

3. With the objective of assuring prompt and adequate compensation in respect of all damage caused by pollution of the marine environment, States shall co-operate in the implementation of existing international law and the further development of international law relating to responsibility and liability for the assessment of and compensation for damage and the settlement of related disputes, as well as, where appropriate, development of criteria and procedures for payment of adequate compensation, such as compulsory insurance or compensation funds.

Section 10. Sovereign Immunity

Article 236
Sovereign immunity

The provisions of this Convention regarding the protection and preservation of the marine environment do not apply to any warship, naval auxiliary, other vessels or aircraft owned or operated by a State and used, for the time being, only on government non-commercial service. However, each State shall ensure, by the adoption of appropriate measures not impairing operations or operational capabilities of such vessels or aircraft owned or operated by it, that such vessels or aircraft act in a manner consistent, so far as is reasonable and practicable, with this Convention.

Section 11. Obligations Under Other Conventions on the Protection
and Preservation of the Marine Environment

Article 237
Obligations under other conventions on the protection and preservation of the
marine environment

1. The provisions of this Part are without prejudice to the specific obligations assumed by States under special conventions and agreements concluded previously which relate to the protection and preservation of the marine environment and to agreements which may be concluded in furtherance of the general principles set forth in this Convention.

2. Specific obligations assumed by States under special conventions, with respect to the protection and preservation of the marine environment, should be carried out in a manner consistent with the general principles and objectives of this Convention.

Convention for the Prevention of Marine Pollution by Dumping of
Wastes and Other Matter, adopted London, Mexico City, Moscow,
Washington, 29 December 1972

This is a global convention whose purpose is to regulate the dumping of wastes at
sea. Draft articles prepared for the 1972 UN Conference on the Human Environment were referred to an intergovernmental conference in which over ninety states
took part. The convention entered into force on 30 August 1975 and by 1994 had
seventy-two parties, including both developed and developing states, industrialized
states with an interest in dumping, and island states opposed to this method of waste
disposal. It should be read in conjunction with Articles 194, 210, and 216 of the
1982 UN Convention on the Law of the Sea; see UN, *The Law of the Sea: Pollution by
Dumping* (New York, 1985). There are also important regional treaties or protocols
covering dumping in the North Sea and North East Atlantic, the Baltic, the Mediterranean, and the South Pacific. The 1972 text of the Convention is found in *UKTS*
43 (1976) Cmnd. 6486; 26 *UST* 2403, TIAS 8165; 11 *ILM* (1972) 1294; 1046 *UNTS*
120. Important amendments to Annexes I and II of the convention were adopted
on 12 November 1993 by the Sixteenth Consultative Meeting of Contracting Parties
through resolutions LC.49(16), LC.50(16), and LC.51(16). The amendments entered into force on 20 February 1994 except for those parties which had submitted
a declaration of non-acceptance pursuant to Article XV(2) of the Convention. The
revised annexes are reproduced here. The effect of these is to prohibit all dumping
of radioactive waste, to phase out the dumping of industrial waste, and to ban
incineration of waste at sea. Amendments to Articles 11, 14, and 15 adopted in
1978 have not entered into force and are not reproduced. Annexes I and II were
also amended in 1979 and 1989, and Annex III in 1990. For documentation on
developments in the Convention see UN, *Law of the Sea: Annual Review of Ocean
Affairs*, 1985–. The operation of the Convention is assessed in *UN Conference on
Environment and Development*, Prepcom, UN Doc. A/Conf. 151/PC/31 (1991). For
the text of annexes, amendments, and other material related to the Convention see
IMO, *The London Dumping Convention: The First Decade and Beyond* (London, 1991)
and documentation of the Consultative Meetings of the Contracting Parties, issued
by IMO. For parties, reservations and declarations see IMO, *Status of Multilateral
Conventions and Instruments in Respect of which the IMO or its Secretary-General Performs
Depository or other Functions* (current year). On dumping in international law, see
R. R. Churchill and A. V. Lowe, *The Law of the Sea* (2nd. edn., Manchester, 1988),
268ff; D. M. Johnston (ed.), *The Environmental Law of the Sea* (Berlin, 1981), 217ff;
P. W. Birnie and A. E. Boyle, *International Law and the Environment* (Oxford, 1992),
320ff.

TEXT

The Contracting Parties to the Convention,

Recognizing that the marine environment and the living organisms which
it supports are of vital importance to humanity, and all people have an
interest in assuring that it is so managed that its quality and resources are
not impaired;

Recognizing that the capacity of the sea to assimilate wastes and render them harmless, and its ability to regenerate natural resources, is not unlimited;

Recognizing that States have, in accordance with the Charter of the United Nations and the principles of international law, the sovereign right to exploit their own resources pursuant to their own environmental policies, and the responsibility to ensure that activities within their jurisdiction or control do not cause damage to the environment of other States or of areas beyond the limits of national jurisdiction;

Recalling Resolution 2749 (XXV) of the General Assembly of the United Nations on the principles governing the sea-bed and the ocean floor and the subsoil thereof, beyond the limits of national jurisdiction;

Noting that marine pollution originates in many sources, such as dumping and discharges through the atmosphere, rivers, estuaries, outfalls and pipelines, and that it is important that States use the best practicable means to prevent such pollution and develop products and processes which will reduce the amount of harmful wastes to be disposed of;

Being convinced that international action to control the pollution of the sea by dumping can and must be taken without delay but that this action should not preclude discussion of measures to control other sources of marine pollution as soon as possible; and

Wishing to improve protection of the marine environment by encouraging States with a common interest in particular geographical areas to enter into appropriate agreements supplementary to this Convention;

Have Agreed as follows:

Article I

Contracting Parties shall individually and collectively promote the effective control of all sources of pollution of the marine environment, and pledge themselves especially to take all practicable steps to prevent the pollution of the sea by the dumping of waste and other matter that is liable to create hazards to human health, to harm living resources and marine life, to damage amenities or to interfere with other legitimate uses of the sea.

Article II

Contracting Parties shall, as provided for in the following Articles, take effective measures individually, according to their scientific, technical and economic capabilities, and collectively, to prevent marine pollution caused by dumping and shall harmonize their policies in this regard.

Article III

For the purposes of this Convention:
1. (a) 'Dumping' means:
       (i) any deliberate disposal at sea of wastes or other matter from vessels, aircraft, platforms or other man-made structures at sea;

    (ii) any deliberate disposal at sea of vessels, aircraft, platforms or other man-made structures at sea.

(b) 'Dumping' does not include:

   (i) the disposal at sea of wastes, or other matter incidental to, or derived from the normal operations of vessels, aircraft, platforms, or other man-made structures at sea and their equipment, other than wastes or other matter transported by or to vessels, aircraft, platforms or other man-made structures at sea, operating for the purpose of disposal of such matter or derived from the treatment of such wastes or other matter on such vessels, aircraft, platforms or structures;

   (ii) placement of matter for a purpose other than the mere disposal thereof, provided that such placement is not contrary to the aims of this Convention.

(c) The disposal of wastes or other matter directly arising from, or related to the exploration, exploitation and associated off-shore processing of sea-bed mineral resources will not be covered by the provisions of this Convention.

2. 'Vessels and aircraft' means waterborne or airborne craft of any type whatsoever. This expression includes air cushioned craft and floating craft, whether self-propelled or not.

3. 'Sea' means all marine waters other than the internal waters of States.

4. 'Wastes or other matter' means material and substance of any kind, form or description.

5. 'Special permit' means permission granted specifically on application in advance and in accordance with Annex II and Annex III.

6. 'General permit' means permission granted in advance and in accordance with Annex III.

7. 'The Organization' means the Organization designated by the Contracting Parties in accordance with Article XIV(2).

Article IV

1. In accordance with the provisions of this Convention Contracting Parties shall prohibit the dumping of any wastes or other matter in whatever form or condition except as otherwise specified below:

(a) the dumping of wastes or other matter listed in Annex I is prohibited;

(b) the dumping of wastes or other matter listed in Annex II requires a prior special permit;

(c) the dumping of all other wastes or matter requires a prior general permit.

2. Any permit shall be issued only after careful consideration of all the factors set forth in Annex III, including prior studies of the characteristics of the dumping site, as set forth in Sections B and C of that Annex.

3. No provision of this Convention is to be interpreted as preventing a Contracting Party from prohibiting, insofar as that Party is concerned, the dumping of wastes or other matter not mentioned in Annex I. That Party shall notify such measures to the Organization.

Article V

1. The provisions of Article IV shall not apply when it is necessary to secure the safety of human life or of vessels, aircraft, platforms or other man-made structures at sea in cases of *force majeure* caused by stress of weather, or in any case which constitutes a danger to human life or a real threat to vessels, aircraft, platforms or other man-made structures at sea, if dumping appears to be the only way of averting the threat and if there is every probability that the damage consequent upon such dumping will be less than would otherwise occur. Such dumping shall be so conducted as to minimize the likelihood of damage to human or marine life and shall be reported forthwith to the Organization.

2. A Contracting Party may issue a special permit as an exception to Article IV(1)(a), in emergencies, posing unacceptable risk relating to human health and admitting no other feasible solution. Before doing so the Party shall consult any other country or countries that are likely to be affected and the Organization which, after consulting other Parties, and international organizations as appropriate, shall, in accordance with Article XIV promptly recommend to the Party the most appropriate procedures to adopt. The Party shall follow these recommendations to the maximum extent feasible consistent with the time within which action must be taken and with the general obligation to avoid damage to the marine environment and shall inform the Organization of the action it takes. The Parties pledge themselves to assist one another in such situations.

3. Any Contracting Party may waive its rights under paragraph (2) at the time of or subsequent to ratification of, or accession to this Convention.

Article VI

1. Each Contracting Party shall designate an appropriate authority or authorities to:

   (a) issue special permits which shall be required prior to, and for, the dumping of matter listed in Annex II and in the circumstances provided for in Article V(2);
   (b) issue general permits which shall be required prior to, and for, the dumping of all other matter;

(c) keep records of the nature and quantities of all matter permitted to be dumped and the location, time and method of dumping;
(d) monitor individually, or in collaboration with other Parties and competent international organizations, the condition of the seas for the purposes of this Convention.

2. The appropriate authority or authorities of a Contracting Party shall issue prior special or general permits in accordance with paragraph (1) in respect of matter intended for dumping:

(a) loaded in its territory;
(b) loaded by a vessel or aircraft registered in its territory or flying its flag, when the loading occurs in the territory of a State not party to this Convention.

3. In issuing permits under sub-paragraphs (1)(a) and (b) above, the appropriate authority or authorities shall comply with Annex III, together with such additional criteria, measures and requirements as they may consider relevant.

4. Each Contracting Party, directly or through a Secretariat established under a regional agreement, shall report to the Organization, and where appropriate to other Parties, the information specified in sub-paragraphs (c) and (d) of paragraph (1) above, and the criteria, measures and requirements it adopts in accordance with paragraph (3) above. The procedure to be followed and the nature of such reports shall be agreed by the Parties in consultation.

Article VII

1. Each Contracting Party shall apply the measures required to implement the present Convention to all:

(a) vessels and aircraft registered in its territory or flying its flag;
(b) vessels and aircraft loading in its territory or territorial seas matter which is to be dumped;
(c) vessels and aircraft and fixed or floating platforms under its jurisdiction believed to be engaged in dumping.

2. Each Party shall take in its territory appropriate measures to prevent and punish conduct in contravention of the provisions of this Convention.

3. The Parties agree to co-operate in the development of procedures for the effective application of this Convention particularly on the high seas, including procedures for the reporting of vessels and aircraft observed dumping in contravention of the Convention.

4. This Convention shall not apply to those vessels and aircraft entitled to sovereign immunity under international law. However, each Party shall

ensure by the adoption of appropriate measures that such vessels and aircraft owned or operated by it act in a manner consistent with the object and purpose of this Convention, and shall inform the Organization accordingly.

5. Nothing in this Convention shall affect the right of each Party to adopt other measures, in accordance with the principles of international law, to prevent dumping at sea.

Article VIII

In order to further the objectives of this Convention, the Contracting Parties with common interests to protect in the marine environment in a given geographical area shall endeavour, taking into account characteristic regional features, to enter into regional agreements consistent with this Convention for the prevention of pollution, especially by dumping. The Contracting Parties to the present Convention shall endeavour to act consistently with the objectives and provisions of such regional agreements, which shall be notified to them by the Organization. Contracting Parties shall seek to co-operate with the Parties to regional agreements in order to develop harmonized procedures to be followed by Contracting Parties to the different conventions concerned. Special attention shall be given to co-operation in the field of monitoring and scientific research.

Article IX

The Contracting Parties shall promote, through collaboration within the Organization and other international bodies, support for those Parties which request it for:

(a) the training of scientific and technical personnel;
(b) the supply of necessary equipment and facilities for research and monitoring;
(c) the disposal and treatment of waste and other measures to prevent or mitigate pollution caused by dumping;

preferably within the countries concerned, so furthering the aims and purposes of this Convention.

Article X

In accordance with the principles of international law regarding State responsibility for damage to the environment of other States or to any other area of the environment, caused by dumping of wastes and other matter of all kinds, the Contracting Parties undertake to develop procedures for the assessment of liability and the settlement of disputes regarding dumping.

Article XI

The Contracting Parties shall at their first consultative meeting consider procedures for the settlement of disputes concerning the interpretation and application of this Convention.

Article XII

The Contracting Parties pledge themselves to promote, within the competent specialized agencies and other international bodies, measures to protect the marine environment against pollution caused by:

(a) hydrocarbons, including oil, and their wastes;
(b) other noxious or hazardous matter transported by vessels for purposes other than dumping;
(c) wastes generated in the course of operation of vessels, aircraft, platforms and other man-made structures at sea;
(d) radio-active pollutants from all sources, including vessels;
(e) agents of chemical and biological warfare;
(f) wastes or other matter directly arising from, or related to the exploration, exploitation and associated off-shore processing or sea-bed mineral resources.

The Parties will also promote, within the appropriate international organization, the codification of signals to be used by vessels engaged in dumping.

Article XIII

Nothing in this Convention shall prejudice the codification and development of the law of the sea by the United Nations Conference on the Law of the Sea convened pursuant to Resolution 2750 C(XXV) of the General Assembly of the United Nations nor the present or future claims and legal views of any State concerning the law of the sea and the nature and extent of coastal and flag State jurisdiction. The Contracting Parties agree to consult at a meeting to be convened by the Organization after the Law of the Sea Conference, and in any case not later than 1976, with a view to defining the nature and extent of the right and the responsibility of a coastal State to apply the Convention in a zone adjacent to its coast.

Article XIV

1. The Government of the United Kingdom of Great Britain and Northern Ireland as a depositary shall call a meeting of the Contracting Parties not later than three months after the entry into force of this Convention to decide on organizational matters.

2. The Contracting Parties shall designate a component Organization existing at the time of that meeting to be responsible for Secretariat duties in

relation to this Convention. Any Party to this Convention not being a member of this Organization shall make an appropriate contribution to the expenses incurred by the Organization in performing these duties.

3. The Secretariat duties of the Organization shall include:

(a) the convening of consultative meetings of the Contracting Parties not less frequently than once every two years and of special meetings of the Parties at any time on the request of two-thirds of the Parties;

(b) preparing and assisting, in consultation with the Contracting Parties and appropriate International Organizations, in the development and implementation of procedures referred to in sub-paragraph (4)(e) of this Article;

(c) considering enquiries by, and information from the Contracting Parties, consulting with them and with the appropriate International Organizations, and providing recommendations to the Parties on questions related to, but not specifically covered by the Convention;

(d) conveying to the Parties concerned all notifications received by the Organization in accordance with Article IV(3), V(1) and (2), VI(4), XV, XX and XXI.

Prior to the designation of the Organization these functions shall, as necessary, be performed by the depositary, who for this purpose shall be the Government of the United Kingdom of Great Britain and Northern Ireland.

4. Consultative or special meetings of the Contracting Parties shall keep under continuing review the implementation of this Convention and may, *inter alia*:

(a) review and adopt amendments to this Convention and its Annexes in accordance with Article XV;

(b) invite the appropriate scientific body or bodies to collaborate with and to advise the Parties or the Organization on any scientific or technical aspect relevant to this Convention, including particularly the content of the Annexes;

(c) receive and consider reports made pursuant to Article VI(4);

(d) promote co-operation with and between regional organizations concerned with the prevention of marine pollution;

(e) develop or adopt, in consultation with appropriate International Organizations, procedures referred to in Article V(2), including basic criteria for determining exceptional and emergency situations, and procedures for consultative advice and the safe disposal of matter in such circumstances, including the designation of appropriate dumping areas, and recommend accordingly;

(f) consider any additional action that may be required.

5. The Contracting Parties at their first consultative meeting shall establish rules of procedure as necessary.

Article XV

1. (a) At meetings of the Contracting Parties called in accordance with Article XIV amendments to this Convention may be adopted by a two-thirds majority of those present. An amendment shall enter into force for the Parties which have accepted it on the sixtieth day after two-thirds of the Parties shall have deposited an instrument of acceptance of the amendment with the Organization. Thereafter the amendment shall enter into force for any other Party 30 days after that Party deposits its instrument of acceptance of the amendment.

   (b) The Organization shall inform all Contracting Parties of any request made for a special meeting under Article XIV and of any amendments adopted at meetings of the Parties and of the date on which each such amendment enters into force for each Party.

2. Amendments to the Annexes will be based on scientific or technical considerations. Amendments to the Annexes approved by a two-thirds majority of those present at a meeting called in accordance with Article XIV shall enter into force for each Contracting Party immediately on notification of its acceptance to the Organization and 100 days after approval by the meeting for all other Parties except for those which before the end of the 100 days make a declaration that they are not able to accept the amendment at that time. Parties should endeavour to signify their acceptance of an amendment to the Organization as soon as possible after approval at a meeting. A Party may at any time substitute an acceptance for a previous declaration of objection and the amendment previously objected to shall thereupon enter into force for that Party.

3. An acceptance or declaration of objection under this Article shall be made by the deposit of an instrument with the Organization. The Organization shall notify all Contracting Parties of the receipt of such instruments.

4. Prior to the designation of the Organization, the Secretarial functions herein attributed to it, shall be performed temporarily by the Government of the United Kingdom of Great Britain and Northern Ireland, as one of the depositaries of this Convention.

Article XVI

This Convention shall be open for signature by any State at London, Mexico City, Moscow and Washington from 29 December 1972 until 31 December 1973.

Article XVII

This Convention shall be subject to ratification. The instruments of ratification shall be deposited with the Governments of Mexico, the Union of

Soviet Socialist Republics, the United Kingdom of Great Britain and Northern Ireland, and the United States of America.

Article XVIII

After 31 December 1973, this Convention shall be open for accession by any State. The instruments of accession shall be deposited with the Governments of Mexico, the Union of Soviet Socialist Republics, the United Kingdom of Great Britain and Northern Ireland, and the United States of America.

Article XIX

1. This Convention shall enter into force on the thirtieth day following the date of deposit of the fifteenth instrument of ratification or accession.
2. For each Contracting Party ratifying or acceding to the Convention after the deposit of the fifteenth instrument of ratification or accession, the Convention shall enter into force on the thirtieth day after deposit by such Party of its instrument of ratification or accession.

Article XX

The depositaries shall inform Contracting Parties:

    (a) of signatures to this Convention and of the deposit of instruments of ratification, accession or withdrawal, in accordance with Articles XVI, XVII, XVIII and XXI, and

    (b) of the date on which this Convention will enter into force, in accordance with Article XIX.

Article XXI

Any Contracting Party may withdraw from this Convention by giving six months' notice in writing to a depositary, which shall promptly inform all Parties of such notice.

Article XXII

The original of this Convention of which the English, French, Russian and Spanish texts are equally authentic, shall be deposited with the Governments of Mexico, the Union of Soviet Socialist Republics, the United Kingdom of Great Britain and Northern Ireland and the United States of America who shall send certified copies thereof to all States.

Annex I[1]

1. Organohalogen compounds.
2. Mercury and mercury compounds.

[1] Amendments of 1993 are indicated in italics.

3. Cadmium and cadmium compounds.

4. Persistent plastics and other persistent synthetic materials, for example, netting and ropes, which may float or may remain in suspension in the sea in such a manner as to interfere materially with fishing, navigation or other legitimate uses of the sea.

5. Crude oil and its wastes, refined petroleum products, petroleum, distillate residues, and any mixtures containing any of these, taken on board for the purpose of dumping.

6. *Radioactive wastes or other radioactive matter.*

7. Materials in whatever form (e.g. solids, liquids, semi-liquids, gases or in a living state) produced for biological and chemical warfare.

8. *With the exception of paragraph 6 above,* the preceding paragraphs of this Annex do not apply to substances which are rapidly rendered harmless by physical, chemical or biological processes in the sea provided they do not:

    (i) make edible marine organisms unpalatable, or
    (ii) endanger human health or that of domestic animals.

The consultative procedure provided for under Article XIV should be followed by a Party if there is doubt about the harmlessness of the substance.

9. *Except for industrial waste as defined in paragraph 11 below,* this Annex does not apply to wastes or other materials (e.g. sewage sludge and dredged *material*) containing the matters referred to in paragraphs 1–5 above as trace contaminants. Such wastes shall be subject to the provisions of Annexes II and III as appropriate.

Paragraph 6 does not apply to wastes or other materials (e.g. sewage sludge and dredged material) containing de minimis (exempt) levels of radioactivity as defined by the IAEA and adopted by the Contracting Parties. Unless otherwise prohibited by Annex I, such wastes shall be subject to the provisions of Annexes II and III as appropriate.

10. (a) *Incineration at sea of industrial waste, as defined in paragraph 11 below, and sewage sludge is prohibited.*
     (b) *The incineration at sea of any other wastes or other matter requires the issue of a special permit.*
     (c) *In the issue of special permits for incineration at sea Contracting Parties shall apply regulations as are developed under this Convention.*[1]
     (d) *For the purpose of this Annex:*

---

[1] Addendum to Annex I, containing Regulations for the Control of Incineration at Sea, adopted by the Third Consultative Meeting of Contracting Parties in 1978 is not reproduced hereunder.

(i) *'Marine incineration facility' means a vessel, platform, or other man-made structure operating for the purpose of incineration at sea.*

(ii) *'Incineration at sea' means the deliberate combustion of wastes or other matter on marine incineration facilities for the purpose of their thermal destruction. Activities incidental to the normal operation of vessels, platforms or other man-made structures are excluded from the scope of this definition.*

11. *Industrial waste as from 1 January 1996.*
For the purposes of this Annex:
'Industrial waste' means waste materials generated by manufacturing or processing operations and does not apply to:

(a) *dredged material;*

(b) *sewage sludge;*

(c) *fish waste, or organic materials resulting from industrial fish processing operations;*

(d) *vessels and platforms or other man-made structures at sea, provided that material capable of creating floating debris or otherwise contributing to pollution of the marine environment has been removed to the maximum extent;*

(e) *uncontaminated inert geological materials the chemical constituents of which are unlikely to be released into the marine environment;*

(f) *uncontaminated organic materials of natural origin.*

Dumping of wastes and other matter specified in subparagraphs (a)–(f) above shall be subject to all other provisions of Annex I, and to the provisions of Annexes II and III.
This paragraph shall not apply to the radioactive wastes or any other radioactive matter referred to in paragraph 6 of this Annex.

12. *Within 25 years from the date on which the amendment to paragraph 6 enters into force and at each 25 year interval thereafter, the Contracting Parties shall complete a scientific study relating to all radioactive wastes and other radioactive matter other than high level wastes or matter, taking into account such other factors as the Contracting Parties consider appropriate, and shall review the position of such substances on Annex I in accordance with the procedures set forth in Article XV.*

Annex II[1]

The following substances and materials requiring special care are listed for the purposes of Article VI(1)(a).

---

[1] Amendments of 1993 are indicated in italics.

A Wastes containing significant amounts of the matters listed below:

arsenic
beryllium
chromium
copper
lead   }   and their compounds
nickel
vanadium
zinc
organosilicon compounds
cyanides
fluorides
pesticides and their by-products not covered in Annex I.

B Containers, scrap metal and other bulky wastes liable to sink to the sea bottom which may present a serious obstacle to fishing or navigation.

C In the issue of special permits for the incineration of substances and materials listed in this Annex, the Contracting Parties shall apply the Regulations for the Control of Incineration of Wastes and Other Matter at Sea set forth in the Addendum to Annex I and take full account of the Technical Guidelines on the Control of Incineration of Wastes and Other Matter at Sea adopted by the Contracting Parties in consultation, to the extent specified in these Regulations and Guidelines.

D *Materials* which, though of a non-toxic nature, may become harmful due to the quantities in which they are dumped, or which are liable to seriously reduce amenities.

Annex III

Provisions to be considered in establishing criteria governing the issue of permits for the dumping of matter at sea, taking into account Article IV(2), include:

A—Characteristics and Composition of the Matter

1. Total amount and average composition of matter dumped (e.g. per year).

2. Form, e.g. solid, sludge, liquid, or gaseous.

3. Properties: physical (e.g. solubility and density), chemical and biochemical (e.g. oxygen demand, nutrients) and biological (e.g. presence of viruses, bacteria, yeasts, parasites).

4. Toxicity.

5. Persistence: physical, chemical and biological.

6. Accumulation and biotransformation in biological materials or sediments.

7. Susceptibility to physical, chemical and biochemical changes and inter-action in the aquatic environment with other dissolved organic and inor-ganic materials.

8. Probability of production of taints or other changes reducing market-ability of resources (fish, shellfish, etc.)

9. In issuing a permit for dumping, Contracting Parties should consider whether an adequate scientific basis exists concerning characteristics and composition of the matter to be dumped to assess the impact of the matter on marine life and on human health.[1]

B—Characteristics of Dumping Site and Method of Deposit

1. Location (e.g. co-ordinates of the dumping area, depth and distance from the coast), location in relation to other areas (e.g. amenity areas, spawning, nursery and fishing areas and exploitable resources).

2. Rate of disposal per specific period (e.g. quantity per day, per week, per month).

3. Methods of packaging and containment, if any.

4. Initial dilution achieved by proposed method of release.

5. Dispersal characteristics (e.g. effects of currents, tides and wind on horizontal transport and vertical mixing).

6. Water characteristics (e.g. temperature, pH, salinity, stratification, oxy-gen indices of pollution—dissolved oxygen (DO), chemical oxygen de-mand (COD), biochemical oxygen demand (BOD)—nitrogen present in organic and mineral form including ammonia, suspended matter, other nutrients and productivity).

7. Bottom characteristics (e.g. topography, geochemical and geological characteristics and biological productivity).

8. Existence and effects of other dumpings which have been made in the dumping area (e.g. heavy metal background reading and organic carbon content).

9. In issuing a permit for dumping, Contracting Parties should consider whether an adequate scientific basis exists for assessing the consequences of such dumping, as outlined in this Annex, taking into account seasonal variations.

---

[1] Additional paragraph adopted in 1989 by the Twelfth Consultative Meeting. The amend-ment entered into force on 19 May 1992.

C—General Considerations and Conditions

1. Possible effects on amenities (e.g. presence of floating or stranded material, turbidity, objectionable odour, discolouration and foaming).

2. Possible effects on marine life, fish and shellfish culture, fish stocks and fisheries, seaweed harvesting and culture.

3. Possible effects on other uses of the sea (e.g. impairment of water quality for industrial use, underwater corrosion of structures, interference with ship operations from floating materials, interferences with fishing or navigation through deposit of waste or solid objects on the sea floor and protection of areas of special importance for scientific or conservation purposes).

4. The practical availability of alternative land-based methods of treatment, disposal or elimination, or of treatment to render the matter less harmful for dumping at sea.

Convention for the Prevention of Pollution from Ships, as Modified by Protocol of 1978, adopted London, 17 February 1978

This convention, known as MARPOL 1973/78, regulates pollution of the sea from ships, and for most maritime states it has replaced the earlier 1954 Convention for the Prevention of Pollution of the Sea by Oil. Parties must apply the Convention not only to their own vessels but also to violations within their jurisdiction. The initial text adopted by IMO in 1973 was amended before entering into force by a protocol adopted in 1978, which is reproduced here, and which entered into force on 2 October 1983. There are five annexes (not reproduced) which contain regulations governing different types of pollutant. Only Annex IV (on sewage) was not yet in force at 1 January 1995. For the full text of the annexes and amendments together with unified interpretations see IMO, *MARPOL 73/78 Consolidated Edition 1991* (London, 1992). Annex I was further amended in 1992 by IMO resolutions MEPC. 51(32) and MEPC. 52(32), *repr.* 4 *YIEL* (1993) 814, in force 6 July 1993. For parties, reservations, and declarations, see IMO, *States of Multilateral Conventions and Instruments in Respect of which the IMO or its Secretary-General Performs Depository or other Functions* (current year). The 1978 Protocol and Annexes I and II had ninety-three parties on 1 January 1995, representing ninety-two per cent of world tonnage, but participation in the other Annexes varies.

The MARPOL Convention and its Annexes also provide the main source for the international rules and standards for pollution from ships referred to in Articles 194, 211, 218, and 220 of the 1982 UN Convention on the Law of the Sea; under these Articles 'international rules and standards' must not only be applied by flag states but may also be enforced against foreign vessels by port states and, within the exclusive economic zone, by coastal states. On the law relating to pollution from ships see D. W. Abecassis and R. L. Jarashow, *Oil Pollution from Ships* (2nd edn., London, 1984); P. W. Birnie and A. E. Boyle, *International Law and the Environment* (Oxford, 1992), Ch. 7; R. R. Churchill and A. V. Lowe, *The Law of the Sea* (2nd edn., Manchester, 1988), 248ff; D. Bodansky, 'Protecting the Marine Environment from Vessel-Source Pollution: UNCLOS III and Beyond', 18 *Ecol. L.Q.* (1991), 719; G. Peet, 'The MARPOL Convention: Implementation and Effectiveness', 7 *Int J Estuarine and Coastal L* (1992) 277. For a history of the negotiation of MARPOL see: D. McGonigle and M. Zacher, *Pollution, Politics and International Law* (London, 1979). On the status of MARPOL and other IMO and ILO Conventions as 'generally accepted international rules and standards' see A. Soons (ed.), *Implementation of the Law of the Sea Convention through International Institutions* (Honolulu, 1990), 187ff and 405ff. The impact of the Convention on marine pollution is reviewed in A. Couper and E. Gold, *The Marine Environment and Sustainable Development: Law Policy and Science* (Honolulu, 1993), 306ff.

TEXT

The Parties to the Convention,

Being conscious of the need to preserve the human environment in general and the marine environment in particular,

Recognizing that deliberate, negligent or accidental release of oil and other harmful substances from ships constitutes a serious source of pollution,

Recognizing also the importance of the International Convention for the Prevention of Pollution of the Sea by Oil, 1954, as being the first multilateral instrument to be concluded with the prime objective of protecting the environment, and appreciating the significant contribution which that Convention has made in preserving the seas and coastal environment from pollution,

Desiring to achieve the complete elimination of intentional pollution of the marine environment by oil and other harmful substances and the minimization of accidental discharge of such substances,

Considering that this object may best be achieved by establishing rules not limited to oil pollution having a universal purport,

Have agreed as follows:

Article 1
General obligations under the Convention

(1) The Parties to the Convention undertake to give effect to the provisions of the present Convention and those Annexes thereto by which they are bound, in order to prevent the pollution of the marine environment by the discharge of harmful substances or effluents containing such substances in contravention of the Convention.

(2) Unless expressly provided otherwise, a reference to the present Convention constitutes at the same time a reference to its Protocols and to the Annexes.

Article 2
Definitions

For the purposes of the present Convention, unless expressly provided otherwise:

(1) 'Regulation' means the regulations contained in the Annexes to the present Convention.

(2) 'Harmful substance' means any substance which, if introduced into the sea, is liable to create hazards to human health, to harm living resources and marine life, to damage amenities or to interfere with other legitimate uses of the sea, and includes any substance subject to control by the present Convention.

(3) (a) 'Discharge', in relation to harmful substances or effluents containing such substances, means any release howsoever caused from a ship and includes any escape, disposal, spilling, leaking, pumping, emitting or emptying;

(b) 'Discharge' does not include:

(i) dumping within the meaning of the Convention on the Prevention of Marine Pollution by Dumping of Wastes and Other Matter, done at London on 13 November 1972; or

   (ii) release of harmful substances directly arising from the exploration, exploitation and associated offshore processing of sea-
bed mineral resources; or

   (iii) release of harmful substances for purposes of legitimate
scientific research into pollution abatement or control.

(4) 'Ship' means a vessel of any type whatsoever operating in the marine
environment and includes hydrofoil boats, air-cushion vehicles, sub-
mersibles, floating craft and fixed or floating platforms.

(5) 'Administration' means the Government of the State under whose
authority the ship is operating. With respect to a ship entitled to fly a flag
of any State, the Administration is the Government of that State. With
respect to fixed or floating platforms engaged in exploration and exploitation of the sea-bed and subsoil thereof adjacent to the coast over which
the coastal State exercises sovereign rights for the purposes of exploration
and exploitation of their natural resources, the Administration is the
Government of the coastal State concerned.

(6) 'Incident' means an event involving the actual or probable discharge
into the sea of a harmful substance, or effluents containing such a
substance.

(7) 'Organization' means the Inter-Governmental Maritime Consultative
Organization.[1]

Article 3
Application

(1) The present Convention shall apply to:

   (a) ships entitled to fly the flag of a Party to the Convention; and
   (b) ships not entitled to fly the flag of a Party but which operate under
the authority of a Party.

(2) Nothing in the present article shall be construed as derogating from or
extending the sovereign rights of the Parties under international law over
the sea-bed and subsoil thereof adjacent to their coasts for the purposes of
exploration and exploitation of their natural resources.

(3) The present Convention shall not apply to any warship, naval auxiliary
or other ship owned or operated by a State and used, for the time being,
only on government non-commercial service. However, each Party shall
ensure by the adoption of appropriate measures not impairing the operations or operational capabilities of such ships owned or operated by it, that
such ships act in a manner consistent, so far as is reasonable and practicable, with the present Convention.

---

[1] The name of the Organization was changed to 'International Maritime Organization' by
virtue of amendments to the Organization's Convention which entered into force on 22 May
1982.

Article 4
Violation

(1) Any violation of the requirements of the present Convention shall be prohibited and sanctions shall be established therefor under the law of the Administration of the ship concerned wherever the violation occurs. If the Administration is informed of such a violation and is satisfied that sufficient evidence is available to enable proceedings to be brought in respect of the alleged violation, it shall cause such proceedings to be taken as soon as possible, in accordance with its law.

(2) Any violation of the requirements of the present Convention within the jurisdiction of any Party to the Convention shall be prohibited and sanctions shall be established therefor under the law of that Party. Whenever such a violation occurs, that Party shall either:

    (a) cause proceedings to be taken in accordance with its law; or
    (b) furnish to the Administration of the ship such information and
        evidence as may be in its possession that a violation has occurred.

(3) Where information or evidence with respect to any violation of the present Convention by a ship is furnished to the Administration of that ship, the Administration shall promptly inform the Party which has furnished the information or evidence, and the Organization, of the action taken.

(4) The penalties specified under the law of a Party pursuant to the present article shall be adequate in severity to discourage violations of the present Convention and shall be equally severe irrespective of where the violations occur.

Article 5
Certificates and special rules on inspection of ships

(1) Subject to the provisions of paragraph (2) of the present article a certificate issued under the authority of a Party to the Convention in accordance with the provisions of the regulations shall be accepted by the other Parties and regarded for all purposes covered by the present Convention as having the same validity as a certificate issued by them.

(2) A ship required to hold a certificate in accordance with the provisions of the regulations is subject, while in the ports or offshore terminals under the jurisdiction of a Party, to inspection by officers duly authorized by that Party. Any such inspection shall be limited to verifying that there is on board a valid certificate, unless there are clear grounds for believing that the condition of the ship or its equipment does not correspond substantially with the particulars of that certificate. In that case, or if the ship does not carry a valid certificate, the Party carrying out the inspection shall take

such steps as will ensure that the ship shall not sail until it can proceed to sea without presenting an unreasonable threat of harm to the marine environment. That Party may, however, grant such a ship permission to leave the port or offshore terminal for the purpose of proceeding to the nearest appropriate repair yard available.

(3) If a Party denies a foreign ship entry to the ports or offshore terminals under its jurisdiction or takes any action against such a ship for the reason that the ship does not comply with the provisions of the present Convention, the Party shall immediately inform the consul or diplomatic representative of the Party whose flag the ship is entitled to fly, or if this is not possible, the Administration of the ship concerned. Before denying entry or taking such action the Party may request consultation with the Administration of the ship concerned. Information shall also be given to the Administration when a ship does not carry a valid certificate in accordance with the provisions of the regulations.

(4) With respect to the ships of non-Parties to the Convention, Parties shall apply the requirements of the present Convention as may be necessary to ensure that no more favourable treatment is given to such ships.

Article 6
Detection of violations and enforcement of the Convention

(1) Parties to the Convention shall co-operate in the detection of violations and the enforcement of the provisions of the present Convention, using all appropriate and practicable measures of detection and environmental monitoring, adequate procedures for reporting and accumulation of evidence.

(2) A ship to which the present Convention applies may, in any port or offshore terminal of a Party, be subject to inspection by officers appointed or authorized by that Party for the purpose of verifying whether the ship has discharged any harmful substances in violation of the provisions of the regulations. If an inspection indicates a violation of the Convention, a report shall be forwarded to the Administration for any appropriate action.

(3) Any Party shall furnish to the Administration evidence, if any, that the ship has discharged harmful substances or effluents containing such substances in violation of the provisions of the regulations. If it is practicable to do so, the competent authority of the former Party shall notify the master of the ship of the alleged violation.

(4) Upon receiving such evidence, the Administration so informed shall investigate the matter, and may request the other Party to furnish further or better evidence of the alleged contravention. If the Administration is satisfied that sufficient evidence is available to enable proceedings to be

brought in respect of the alleged violation, it shall cause such proceedings to be taken in accordance with its law as soon as possible. The Administration shall promptly inform the Party which has reported the alleged violation, as well as the Organization, of the action taken.

(5) A Party may also inspect a ship to which the present Convention applies when it enters the ports or offshore terminals under its jurisdiction, if a request for an investigation is received from any Party together with sufficient evidence that the ship has discharged harmful substances or effluents containing such substances in any place. The report of such investigation shall be sent to the Party requesting it and to the Administration so that the appropriate action may be taken under the present Convention.

Article 7
Undue delay to ships

(1) All possible efforts shall be made to avoid a ship being unduly detained or delayed under articles 4, 5 or 6 of the present Convention.

(2) When a ship is unduly detained or delayed under articles 4, 5 or 6 of the present Convention, it shall be entitled to compensation for any loss or damage suffered.

Article 8
Reports on incidents involving harmful substances

(1) A report of an incident shall be made without delay to the fullest extent possible in accordance with the provisions of Protocol I to the present Convention.

(2) Each Party to the Convention shall:

   (a) make all arrangements necessary for an appropriate officer or agency to receive and process all reports on incidents; and
   (b) notify the Organization with complete details of such arrangements for circulation to other Parties and Member States of the Organization.

(3) Whenever a Party receives a report under the provisions of the present article, that Party shall relay the report without delay to:

   (a) the Administration of the ship involved; and
   (b) any other State which may be affected.

(4) Each Party to the Convention undertakes to issue instructions to its maritime inspection vessels and aircraft and to other appropriate services to report to its authorities any incident referred to in Protocol I to the present Convention. That Party shall, if it considers it appropriate, report accordingly to the Organization and to any other Party concerned.

Article 9
Other treaties and interpretation

(1) Upon its entry into force, the present Convention supersedes the International Convention for the Prevention of Pollution of the Sea by Oil, 1954, as amended, as between Parties to that Convention.

(2) Nothing in the present Convention shall prejudice the codification and development of the law of the sea by the United Nations Conference on the Law of the Sea convened pursuant to resolution 2750 C(XXV) of the General Assembly of the United Nations nor the present or future claims and legal views of any State concerning the law of the sea and the nature and extent of coastal and flag State jurisdiction.

(3) The term 'jurisdiction' in the present Convention shall be construed in the light of international law in force at the time of application or interpretation of the present Convention.

Article 10
Settlement of disputes

Any dispute between two or more Parties to the Convention concerning the interpretation or application of the present Convention shall, if settlement by negotiation between the Parties involved has not been possible, and if these Parties do not otherwise agree, be submitted upon request of any of them to arbitration as set out in Protocol II to the present Convention.

Article 11
Communication of information

(1) The Parties to the Convention undertake to communicate to the Organization:

  (a) the text of laws, orders, decrees and regulations and other instruments which have been promulgated on the various matters within the scope of the present Convention;
  (b) a list of nominated surveyors or recognized organizations which are authorized to act on their behalf in the administration of matters relating to the design, construction, equipment and operation of ships carrying harmful substances in accordance with the provisions of the regulations for circulation to the Parties for information of their officers. The Administration shall therefore notify the Organization of the specific responsibilities and conditions of the authority delegated to nominate surveyors or recognized organizations;
  (c) a sufficient number of specimens of their certificates issued under the provisions of the regulations;
  (d) a list of reception facilities including their location, capacity and available facilities and other characteristics;

(e) official reports or summaries of official reports in so far as they show the results of the application of the present Convention; and

(f) an annual statistical report, in a form standardized by the Organization, of penalties actually imposed for infringement of the present Convention.

(2) The Organization shall notify Parties of receipt of any communications under the present article and circulate to all Parties any information communicated to it under subparagraphs (1)(b) to (f) of the present article.

Article 12
Casualties to ships

(1) Each Administration undertakes to conduct an investigation of any casualty occurring to any of its ships subject to the provisions of the regulations if such casualty has produced a major deleterious effect upon the marine environment.

(2) Each Party to the Convention undertakes to supply the Organization with information concerning the findings of such investigation, when it judges that such information may assist in determining what changes in the present Convention might be desirable.

Article 13
Signature, ratification, acceptance, approval and accession

(1) The present Convention shall remain open for signature at the Headquarters of the Organization from 15 January 1974 until 31 December 1974 and shall thereafter remain open for accession. States may become Parties to the present Convention by:

(a) signature without reservation as to ratification, acceptance or approval; or

(b) signature subject to ratification, acceptance or approval, followed by ratification, acceptance or approval; or

(c) accession.

(2) Ratification, acceptance, approval or accession shall be effected by the deposit of an instrument to that effect with the Secretary-General of the Organization.

(3) The Secretary-General of the Organization shall inform all States which have signed the present Convention or acceded to it of any signature or of the deposit of any new instrument of ratification, acceptance, approval or accession and the date of its deposit.

Article 14
Optional annexes

(1) A State may at the time of signing, ratifying, accepting, approving or acceding to the present Convention declare that it does not accept any one

or all of Annexes III, IV and V (hereinafter referred to as 'Optional Annexes') of the present Convention. Subject to the above, Parties to the Convention shall be bound by any Annex in its entirety.

(2) A State which has declared that it is not bound by an Optional Annex may at any time accept such Annex by depositing with the Organization an instrument of the kind referred to in article 13(2).

(3) A State which makes a declaration under paragraph (1) of the present article in respect of an Optional Annex and which has not subsequently accepted that Annex in accordance with paragraph (2) of the present article shall not be under any obligation nor entitled to claim any privileges under the present Convention in respect of matters related to such Annex and all references to Parties in the present Convention shall not include that State in so far as matters related to such Annex are concerned.

(4) The Organization shall inform the States which have signed or acceded to the present Convention of any declaration under the present article as well as the receipt of any instrument deposited in accordance with the provisions of paragraph (2) of the present article.

Article 15
Entry in force

(1) The present Convention shall enter into force 12 months after the date on which not less than 15 States, the combined merchant fleets of which constitute not less than 50 per cent of the gross tonnage of the world's merchant shipping, have become parties to it in accordance with article 13.

(2) An Optional Annex shall enter into force 12 months after the date on which the conditions stipulated in paragraph (1) of the present article have been satisfied in relation to that Annex.

(3) The Organization shall inform the States which have signed the present Convention or acceded to it of the date on which it enters into force and of the date on which an Optional Annex enters into force in accordance with paragraph (2) of the present article.

(4) For States which have deposited an instrument of ratification, acceptance, approval or accession in respect of the present Convention or any Optional Annex after the requirements for entry into force thereof have been met but prior to the date of entry into force, the ratification, acceptance, approval or accession shall take effect on the date of entry into force of the Convention or such Annex or three months after the date of deposit of the instrument whichever is the later date.

(5) For States which have deposited an instrument of ratification, acceptance, approval or accession after the date on which the Convention or an Optional Annex entered into force, the Convention or the Optional Annex

shall become effective three months after the date of deposit of the instrument.

(6) After the date on which all the conditions required under article 16 to bring an amendment to the present Convention or an Optional Annex into force have been fulfilled, any instrument of ratification, acceptance, approval or accession deposited shall apply to the Convention or Annex as amended.

Article 16
Amendments

(1) The present Convention may be amended by any of the procedures specified in the following paragraphs.

(2) Amendments after consideration by the Organization:

(a) any amendment proposed by a Party to the Convention shall be submitted to the Organization and circulated by its Secretary-General to all Members of the Organization and all Parties at least six months prior to its consideration;

(b) any amendment proposed and circulated as above shall be submitted to an appropriate body by the Organization for consideration;

(c) Parties to the Convention, whether or not Members of the Organization, shall be entitled to participate in the proceedings of the appropriate body;

(d) amendments shall be adopted by a two-thirds majority of only the Parties to the Convention present and voting;

(e) if adopted in accordance with subparagraph (d) above, amendments shall be communicated by the Secretary-General of the Organization to all the Parties to the Convention for acceptance;

(f) an amendment shall be deemed to have been accepted in the following circumstances:

(i) an amendment to an article of the Convention shall be deemed to have been accepted on the date on which it is accepted by two-thirds of the Parties, the combined merchant fleets of which constitute not less than 50 per cent of the gross tonnage of the world's merchant fleet;

(ii) an amendment to an Annex to the Convention shall be deemed to have been accepted in accordance with the procedure specified in subparagraph (f)(iii) unless the appropriate body, at the time of its adoption, determines that the amendment shall be deemed to have been accepted on the date on which it is accepted by two-thirds of the Parties, the combined merchant fleets of which constitute not less than 50 per cent of the gross tonnage of the world's merchant fleet. Nevertheless, at any time before the entry into force of an amendment to an Annex to the Convention, a Party may notify the Secretary-General of the Organization that its express approval will be necessary before the amendment enters into force for it. The latter shall bring such notification and the date of its receipt to the notice of Parties;

(iii) an amendment to an appendix to an Annex to the Convention shall be deemed to have been accepted at the end of a period to be determined by the appropriate body at the time of its adoption, which period shall be not less than ten months, unless within that period an objection is communicated to the Organization by not less than one third of the Parties or by the Parties the combined merchant fleets of which constitute not less than 50 per cent of the gross tonnage of the world's merchant fleet whichever condition is fulfilled;

(iv) an amendment to Protocol I to the Convention shall be subject to the same procedures as for the amendments to the Annexes to the Convention, as provided for in subparagraphs (f)(ii) or (f)(iii) above;

(v) an amendment to Protocol II to the Convention shall be subject to the same procedures as for the amendments to an article of the Convention, as provided for in subparagraph (f)(i) above;

(g) the amendment shall enter into force under the following conditions:

(i) in the case of an amendment to an article of the Convention, to Protocol II, or to Protocol I or to an Annex to the Convention not under the procedure specified in subparagraph (f)(iii), the amendment accepted in conformity with the foregoing provisions shall enter into force six months after the date of its acceptance with respect to the Parties which have declared that they have accepted it;

(ii) in the case of an amendment to Protocol I, to an appendix to an Annex or to an Annex to the Convention under the procedure specified in subparagraph (f)(iii), the amendment deemed to have been accepted in accordance with the foregoing conditions shall enter into force six months after its acceptance for all the Parties with the exception of those which, before that date, have made a declaration that they do not accept it or a declaration under subparagraph (f)(ii), that their express approval is necessary.

(3) Amendment by a Conference:

(a) Upon the request of a Party, concurred in by at least one-third of the Parties, the Organization shall convene a Conference of Parties to the Convention to consider amendments to the present Convention.

(b) Every amendment adopted by such a Conference by a two-thirds majority of those present and voting of the Parties shall be communicated by the Secretary-General of the Organization to all Contracting Parties for their acceptance.

(c) Unless the Conference decides otherwise, the amendment shall be deemed to have been accepted and to have entered into force in accordance with the procedures specified for that purpose in paragraph (2)(f) and (g) above.

(4) (a) In the case of an amendment to an Optional Annex, a reference in the present article to a 'Party to the Convention' shall be deemed to mean a reference to a Party bound by that Annex.

(b) Any Party which has declined to accept an amendment to an Annex shall be treated as a non-Party only for the purpose of application of that amendment.

(5) The adoption and entry into force of a new annex shall be subject to the same procedures as for the adoption and entry into force of an amendment to an article of the Convention.

(6) Unless expressly provided otherwise, any amendment to the present Convention made under this article, which relates to the structure of a ship, shall apply only to ships for which the building contract is placed, or in the absence of a building contract, the keel of which is laid, on or after the date on which the amendment comes into force.

(7) Any amendment to a Protocol or to an Annex shall relate to the substance of that Protocol or Annex and shall be consistent with the articles of the present Convention.

(8) The Secretary-General of the Organization shall inform all Parties of any amendments which enter into force under the present article, together with the date on which each such amendment enters into force.

(9) Any declaration of acceptance or of objection to an amendment under the present article shall be notified in writing to the Secretary-General of the Organization. The latter shall bring such notification and the date of its receipt to the notice of the Parties to the Convention.

Article 17
Promotion of technical co-operation

The Parties to the Convention shall promote, in consultation with the Organization and other international bodies, with assistance and coordination by the Executive Director of the United Nations Environment Programme, support for those Parties which request technical assistance for:

(a) the training of scientific and technical personnel;

(b) the supply of necessary equipment and facilities for reception and monitoring;

(c) the facilitation of other measures and arrangements to prevent or mitigate pollution of the marine environment by ships; and

(d) the encouragement of research;

preferably within the countries concerned, so furthering the aims and purposes of the present Convention.

Article 18
Denunciation

(1) The present Convention or any Optional Annex may be denounced by any Parties to the Convention at any time after the expiry of five years from the date on which the Convention or such Annex enters into force for that Party.

(2) Denunciation shall be effected by notification in writing to the Secretary-General of the Organization who shall inform all the other Parties of any such notification received and of the date of its receipt as well as the date on which such denunciation takes effect.

(3) A denunciation shall take effect 12 months after receipt of the notification of denunciation by the Secretary-General of the Organization or after the expiry of any other longer period which may be indicated in the notification.

Article 19
Deposit and registration

(1) The present Convention shall be deposited with the Secretary-General of the Organization who shall transmit certified true copies thereof to all States which have signed the present Convention or acceded to it.

(2) As soon as the present Convention enters into force, the text shall be transmitted by the Secretary-General of the Organization to the Secretary-General of the United Nations for registration and publication, in accordance with Article 102 of the Charter of the United Nations.

Article 20
Languages

The present Convention is established in a single copy in the English, French, Russian and Spanish languages, each text being equally authentic. Official translations in the Arabic, German, Italian and Japanese languages shall be prepared and deposited with the signed original.

DONE AT LONDON this second day of November, one thousand nine hundred and seventy-three.

[ANNEXES OMITTED]

TEXT OF PROTOCOL I

Provisions concerning Reports on Incidents Involving Harmful Substances (in accordance with Article 8 of the Convention)

Article I
Duty to report

(1) The master or other person having charge of any ship involved in an incident referred to in article II of this Protocol shall report the particulars of such incident without delay and to the fullest extent possible in accordance with the provisions of this Protocol.

(2) In the event of the ship referred to in paragraph (1) of this article being abandoned, or in the event of a report from such a ship being incomplete or unobtainable, the owner, charterer, manager or operator of the ship, or their agent shall, to the fullest extent possible, assume the obligations placed upon the master under the provisions of this Protocol.

Article II
When to make reports

(1) The report shall be made when an incident involves:

  (a) a discharge or probable discharge of oil, or noxious liquid substances carried in bulk, resulting from damage to the ship or its equipment, or for the purpose of securing the safety of a ship or saving life at sea; or
  (b) a discharge or probable discharge of harmful substances in packaged form, including those in freight containers, portable tanks, road and rail vehicles and shipborne barges; or
  (c) a discharge during the operation of the ship of oil or noxious liquid substances in excess of the quantity or instantaneous rate permitted under the present Convention.

(2) For the purposes of this Protocol:

  (a) 'Oil' referred to in subparagraph 1(a) of this article means oil as defined in regulation 1(1) of Annex I of the Convention.
  (b) 'Noxious liquid substances' referred to in subparagraph 1(a) of this article means noxious liquid substances as defined in regulation 1(6) of Annex II of the Convention.
  (c) 'Harmful substances' in packaged form referred to in subparagraph 1(b) of this article means substances which are identified as marine pollutants in the International Maritime Dangerous Goods Code (IMDG Code).

Article III
Contents of report

Reports shall in any case include:

   (a) identity of ships involved;
   (b) time, type and location of incident;
   (c) quantity and type of harmful substance involved;
   (d) assistance and salvage measures.

Article IV
Supplementary report

Any person who is obliged under the provisions of this Protocol to send a report shall, when possible:

   (a) supplement the initial report, as necessary, and provide information concerning further developments; and
   (b) comply as fully as possible with requests from affected States for additional information.

Article V
Reporting procedures

(1) Reports shall be made by the fastest telecommunications channels available with the highest possible priority to the nearest coastal State.

(2) In order to implement the provisions of this Protocol, Parties to the present Convention shall issue, or cause to be issued, regulations or instructions on the procedures to be followed in reporting incidents involving harmful substances, based on guidelines developed by the Organization.

[PROTOCOL NO. 2 OMITTED]

Convention Relating to Intervention on the High Seas in Cases of Oil Pollution Casualties, adopted Brussels, 29 November 1969

This treaty provides for coastal states to take measures of self-protection beyond the territorial sea against foreign shipping casualties which are causing or threatening to cause oil pollution damage. It can be regarded as illustrating the principle of necessity as a justification in international law for otherwise wrongful conduct. It entered into force on 6 May 1975 and in 1995 had sixty-five parties. For parties, reservations, and declarations, see IMO, *States of Multilateral Conventions and Instruments in Respect of which the IMO or its Secretary-General Performs Depository or Other Functions* (current year). A Protocol adopted on 2 November 1973 extends the Convention to substances other than oil and entered into force on 30 March 1983. Article 221 of the 1982 UNCLOS and Article 9 of the 1989 Convention on Salvage respectively assume the existence of a right of coastal state intervention under customary and conventional international law or under generally recognised principles of law, but in terms significantly broader than permitted by the 1969 Convention. For negotiating history of the Convention, see IMCO, *Official Records of the International Legal Conference on Marine Pollution Damage.* (London, 1973) and generally see: E. D. Brown, 'The Lessons of the Torrey Canyon', 21 *CLP* (1968) 113; S. P. Jagota, 'State Responsibility: Circumstances Precluding Wrongfulness', 16 *Neths. YIL* (1985) 249; P. W. Birnie and A. E. Boyle, *International Law and the Environment*, (Oxford, 1992), 285ff; D. W. Abecassis and R. L. Jarashow, *Oil Pollution from Ships* (2nd edn., London, 1984).

TEXT

The States Parties to the Present Convention,

Conscious of the need to protect the interests of their peoples against the grave consequences of a maritime casualty resulting in danger of oil pollution of sea and coastlines,

Convinced that under these circumstances measures of an exceptional character to protect such interests might be necessary on the high seas and that these measures do not affect the principle of freedom of the high seas,

Have Agreed as follows:

Article I

1. Parties to the present Convention may take such measures on the high seas as may be necessary to prevent, mitigate or eliminate grave and imminent danger to their coastline or related interests from pollution or threat of pollution of the sea by oil, following upon a maritime casualty or acts related to such a casualty, which may reasonably be expected to result in major harmful consequences.

2. However, no measures shall be taken under the present Convention against any warship or other ship owned or operated by a State and used, for the time being, only on government non-commercial service.

Article II

For the purposes of the present Convention:

1. 'Maritime casualty' means a collision of ships, stranding or other incident of navigation, or other occurrence on board a ship or external to it resulting in material damage or imminent threat of material damage to a ship or cargo;

2. 'Ship' means:

(a) any sea-going vessel of any type whatsoever, and
(b) any floating craft, with the exception of an installation or device engaged in the exploration and exploitation of the resources of the sea-bed and the ocean floor and the subsoil thereof;

3. 'Oil' means crude oil, fuel oil, diesel oil and lubricating oil;

4. 'Related interests' means the interests of a coastal State directly affected or threatened by the maritime casualty, such as:

(a) maritime coastal, port or estuarine activities, including fisheries activities, constituting an essential means of livelihood of the persons concerned;
(b) tourist attractions of the area concerned;
(c) the health of the coastal population and the well-being of the area concerned, including conservation of living marine resources and of wildlife;

5. 'Organization' means the Inter-Governmental Maritime Consultative Organization.[1]

Article III

When a coastal State is exercising the right to take measures in accordance with Article I, the following provisions shall apply:

(a) before taking any measures, a coastal State shall proceed to consultation with other States affected by the maritime casualty, particularly with the flag State or States;
(b) the coastal State shall notify without delay the proposed measures to any persons physical or corporate known to the coastal State, or made known to it during the consultations, to have interests which can reasonably be expected to be affected by those measures. The coastal State shall take into account any views they may submit;
(c) before any measure is taken, the coastal State may proceed to a consultation with independent experts, whose names shall be chosen from a list maintained by the Organization;

[1] Now the International Maritime Organization.

(d) in cases of extreme urgency requiring measures to be taken immediately, the coastal State may take measures rendered necessary by the urgency of the situation, without prior notification or consultation or without continuing consultations already begun;

(e) a coastal State shall, before taking such measures and during their course, use its best endeavours to avoid any risk to human life, and to afford persons in distress any assistance of which they may stand in need, and in appropriate cases to facilitate the repatriation of ships' crews, and to raise no obstacle thereto;

(f) measures which have been taken in application of Article I shall be notified without delay to the States and to the known physical or corporate persons concerned, as well as to the Secretary-General of the Organization.

Article IV

1. Under the supervision of the Organization, there shall be set up and maintained the list of experts contemplated by Article III of the present Convention, and the Organization shall make necessary and appropriate regulations in connexion therewith, including the determination of the required qualifications.

2. Nominations to the list may be made by Member States of the Organization and by Parties to this Convention. The experts shall be paid on the basis of services rendered by the States utilizing those services.

Article V

1. Measures taken by the coastal State in accordance with Article I shall be proportionate to the damage actual or threatened to it.

2. Such measures shall not go beyond what is reasonably necessary to achieve the end mentioned in Article I and shall cease as soon as that end has been achieved; they shall not unnecessarily interfere with the rights and interests of the flag State, third States and of any persons, physical or corporate, concerned.

3. In considering whether the measures are proportionate to the damage, account shall be taken of:

(a) the extent and probability of imminent damage if those measures are not taken; and

(b) the likelihood of those measures being effective; and

(c) the extent of the damage which may be caused by such measures.

Article VI

Any Party which has taken measures in contravention of the provisions of the present Convention causing damage to others, shall be obliged to pay compensation to the extent of the damage caused by measures which exceed those reasonably necessary to achieve the end mentioned in Article I.

Article VII

Except as specifically provided, nothing in the present Convention shall prejudice any otherwise applicable right, duty, privilege or immunity or deprive any of the Parties or any interested physical or corporate person of any remedy otherwise applicable.

Article VIII

1. Any controversy between the Parties as to whether measures taken under Article I were in contravention of the provisions of the present Convention, to whether compensation is obliged to be paid under Article VI, and to the amount of such compensation shall, if settlement by negotiation between the Parties involved or between the Party which took the measures and the physical or corporate claimants has not been possible, and if the Parties do not otherwise agree, be submitted upon request of any of the Parties concerned to conciliation or, if conciliation does not succeed, to arbitration, as set out in the Annex to the present Convention.

2. The Party which took the measures shall not be entitled to refuse a request for conciliation or arbitration under provisions of the preceding paragraph solely on the grounds that any remedies under municipal law in its own courts have not been exhausted.

Article IX

1. The present Convention shall remain open for signature until 31 December 1970 and shall thereafter remain open for accession.

2. States Members of the United Nations or any of the Specialized Agencies or of the International Atomic Energy Agency or Parties to the Statute of the International Court of Justice may become Parties to this Convention by:

  (a) signature without reservation as to ratification, acceptance or approval;
  (b) signature subject to ratification, acceptance or approval followed by ratification, acceptance or approval; or
  (c) accession.

Article X

1. Ratification, acceptance, approval or accession shall be effected by the deposit of a formal instrument to that effect with the Secretary-General of the Organization.

2. Any instrument of ratification, acceptance, approval or accession deposited after the entry into force of an amendment to the present Convention with respect to all existing Parties or after the completion of all measures required for the entry into force of the amendment with respect to those Parties shall be deemed to apply to the Convention as modified by the amendment.

Article XI

1. The present Convention shall enter into force on the ninetieth day following the date on which Governments of fifteen States have either signed it without reservation as to ratification, acceptance, or approval or have deposited instruments of ratification, acceptance, approval or accession with the Secretary-General of the Organization.

2. For each State which subsequently ratifies, accepts, approves or accedes to it the present Convention shall come into force on the ninetieth day after deposit by such State of the appropriate instrument.

Article XII

1. The present Convention may be denounced by any Party at any time after the date on which the Convention comes into force for that State.

2. Denunciation shall be effected by the deposit of an instrument with the Secretary-General of the Organization.

3. A denunciation shall take effect one year, or such longer period as may be specified in the instrument of denunciation, after its deposit with the Secretary-General of the Organization.

Article XIII

1. The United Nations where it is the administering authority for a territory, or any State Party to the present Convention responsible for the international relations of a territory, shall as soon as possible consult with the appropriate authorities of such territories or take such other measures as may be appropriate, in order to extend the present Convention to that territory and may at any time by notification in writing to the Secretary-General of the Organization declare that the present Convention shall extend to such territory.

2. The present Convention shall, from the date of receipt of the notification or from such other date as may be specified in the notification, extend to the territory named therein.

3. The United Nations, or any Party which has made a declaration under paragraph 1 of this Article may at any time after the date on which the Convention has been so extended to any territory declare by notification in writing to the Secretary-General of the Organization that the present Con-

vention shall cease to extend to any such territory named in the notification.

4. The present Convention shall cease to extend to any territory mentioned in such notification one year, or such longer period as may be specified therein, after the date of receipt of the notification by the Secretary-General of the Organization.

Article XIV

1. A Conference for the purpose of revising or amending the present Convention may be convened by the Organization.

2. The Organization shall convene a Conference of the States Parties to the present Convention for revising or amending the present Convention at the request of not less than one-third of the Parties.

Article XV

1. The present Convention shall be deposited with the Secretary-General of the Organization.

2. The Secretary-General of the Organization shall:

  (a) inform all States which have signed or acceded to the Convention of:
    (i) each new signature or deposit of instrument together with the date thereof;
    (ii) the deposit of any instrument of denunciation of this Convention together with the date of the deposit;
    (iii) the extension of the present Convention to any territory under paragraph 1 of Article XIII and of the termination of any such extension under the provisions of paragraph 4 of that Article stating in each case the date on which the present Convention has been or will cease to be so extended;
  (b) transmit certified true copies of the present Convention to all Signatory States and to all States which accede to the present Convention.

Article XVI

As soon as the present Convention comes into force, the text shall be transmitted by the Secretary-General of the Organization to the Secretariat of the United Nations for registration and publication in accordance with Article 102 of the Charter of the United Nations.

Article XVII

The present Convention is established in a single copy in the English and French languages, both texts being equally authentic. Official translations in the Russian and Spanish languages shall be prepared and deposited with the signed original.

DONE at Brussels this twenty-ninth day of November 1969.

[ANNEX OMITTED]

4. PROTECTION OF THE ATMOSPHERE

Convention for the Protection of the Ozone Layer, Vienna, 22 March 1985, and Protocol on Substances that Deplete the Ozone Layer, Montreal, 16 September 1987

Apart from the institutions it establishes, the Ozone Convention is largely an empty framework, requiring further action by the parties, who proved unable in 1985 to agree on proposals for more specific measures to control ozone depletion of the upper atmosphere. Nevertheless, it is an important precedent with wider significance in environmental law. First, it is explicitly concerned with the global environment and its definition of 'adverse effects' both recognises the impact of ozone depletion on climate change, and adopts an ecosystem approach in terms which suggest that the natural environment has a value independent of its immediate utility to humans. Secondly, it is one of the first treaties to provide for preventive action in advance of firm proof of actual harm, and in that sense is indicative of the emergence of the 'precautionary approach' subsequently endorsed in the 1992 Rio Declaration on Environment and Development.

The Montreal Protocol is a more substantial agreement than the Convention and sets an important precedent for the special treatment of developing states, the position of non-parties, the amendment of control measures, and institutional supervision. The influence of its example on later treaties is apparent.

The full text of the Ozone Convention, including annexes, is published in *UKTS* 1 (1990), Cm. 910; 26 *ILM* (1987) 1529. It entered into force on 22 September 1988, and on 1 January 1995 had 148 parties. No reservations are permitted. The Montreal Protocol is published in *UKTS* 19 (1990), Cm. 997; 26 *ILM* (1987) 1550; 17 *EPL* (1987) 256. It entered into force on 1 January 1989, and on 1 January 1995 had 145 parties. Amendments were adopted at London in 1990, *repr.* in *UKTS* 4 (1993), Cm. 2132; 30 *ILM* (1991) 541; (in force 10 August 1992; ninety-three parties on 1 October 1994); and in Copenhagen, 1992, *repr.* in 32 *ILM* (1993) 874 (in force 1 June 1994; thirty-four parties on 1 October 1994). Adjustments regarding controlled substances entered into force on 7 March 1991 and 22 September 1993 *repr.* in 30 *ILM* (1991) 539 and 32 *ILM* (1993) 874. Annex D, in force 27 May 1992 is *repr.* in *UKTS* 14 (1993), Cm. 2231. The text reproduced here contains amendments and adjustments adopted in 1990 and 1992.

For signatories, parties, and declarations to the Convention and the Protocol see: UN, *Multilateral Treaties Deposited with the Secretary-General,* UN Doc. ST/LEG/ SER.E/ (current year). The negotiating history of the Convention is found in UNEP, *Reports of the Ad Hoc Working Group on the Ozone Convention* (1981–85), and of the Protocol in UNEP, *Reports of the Ad Hoc Working Group of Legal and Technical Experts* (1986–87). UNEP, *Handbook for the Montreal Protocol on Substances that Deplete the Ozone Layer* (Nairobi, 1991) includes agreed definitions, revisions, decisions by the Parties, and other relevant material. See also *Reports of Meetings of the Parties to the Montreal Protocol* (1989–) and of the *Ad Hoc Working Group of Legal Experts on Non-Compliance* (1989–). Decisions of the 4th, 5th, and 6th Meetings of the Parties are in UN Docs. UNEP/OzL/Pro. 4, 5, and 6, noted 3 *YBIEL* (1992) 226; 4 *YBIEL* (1993) 139 and 867; 25 *EPL* (1995) 21 and 81. See generally R. Benedick, *Ozone Diplomacy* (Cambridge, Mass., 1991); P. Lawrence, 'International Legal Regulation for the Protection of the Ozone Layer: Some Problems of Implementation', 2 *JEL*

(1990) 17; P. W. Birnie and A. E. Boyle, *International Law and the Environment* (Oxford, 1992) 404ff.

TEXT OF THE CONVENTION

Preamble

The Parties to this Convention,

Aware of the potentially harmful impact on human health and the environment through modification of the ozone layer,

Recalling the pertinent provisions of the Declaration of the United Nations Conference on the Human Environment, and in particular principle 21, which provides that 'States have, in accordance with the Charter of the United Nations and the principles of international law, the sovereign right to exploit their own resources pursuant to their own environmental polices, and the responsibility to ensure that activities within their jurisdiction or control do not cause damage to the environment of other States or of areas beyond the limits of national jurisdiction',

Taking into acount the circumstances and particular requirements of developing countries,

Mindful of the work and studies proceeding within both international and national organizations and, in particular, of the World Plan of Action on the Ozone Layer of the United Nations Environment Programme,

Mindful also of the precautionary measures for the protection of the ozone layer which have already been taken at the national and international levels,

Aware that measures to protect the ozone layer from modifications due to human activities require international co-operation and action, and should be based on relevant scientific and technical considerations,

Aware also of the need for further research and systematic observations to further develop scientific knowledge of the ozone layer and possible adverse effects resulting from its modification,

Determined to protect human health and the environment against adverse effects resulting from modifications of the ozone layer,

Have agreed as follows:

Article 1
Definitions

For the purposes of this Convention:

1. 'The ozone layer' means the layer of atmospheric ozone above the planetary boundary layer.

2. 'Adverse effects' means changes in the physical environment or biota,

including changes in climate, which have significant deleterious effects on human health or on the composition, resilience and productivity of natural and managed ecosystems, or on materials useful to mankind.

3. 'Alternative technologies or equipment' means technologies or equipment the use of which makes it possible to reduce or effectively eliminate emissions of substances which have or are likely to have adverse effects on the ozone layer.

4. 'Alternative substances' means substances which reduce, eliminate or avoid adverse effects on the ozone layer.

5. 'Parties' means, unless the text otherwise indicates, Parties to this Convention.

6. 'Regional economic integration organization' means an organization constituted by sovereign States of a given region which has competence in respect of matters governed by this Convention or its protocols and has been duly authorized, in accordance with its internal procedures, to sign, ratify, accept, approve or accede to the instruments concerned.

7. 'Protocols' means protocols to this Convention.

Article 2
General Obligations

1. The Parties shall take appropriate measures in accordance with the provisions of this Convention and of those protocols in force to which they are party to protect human health and the environment against adverse effects resulting or likely to result from human activities which modify or are likely to modify the ozone layer.

2. To this end the Parties shall, in accordance with the means at their disposal and their capabilities:

(a) Co-operate by means of systematic observations, research and information exchange in order to better understand and assess the effects of human activities on the ozone layer and the effects on human health and the environment from modification of the ozone layer;

(b) Adopt appropriate legislative or administrative measures and co-operate in harmonizing appropriate polices to control, limit, reduce or prevent human activities under their jurisdiction or control should it be found that these activities have or are likely to have adverse effects resulting from modification or likely modification of the ozone layer;

(c) Co-operate in the formulation of agreed measures, procedures and standards for the implementation of this Convention, with a view to the adoption of protocols and annexes;

(d) Co-operate with competent international bodies to implement effectively this Convention and protocols to which they are party.

3. The provisions of this Convention shall in no way affect the right of Parties to adopt, in accordance with international law, domestic measures additional to those referred to in paragraphs 1 and 2 above, nor shall they affect additional domestic measures already taken by a Party, provided that these measures are not incompatible with their obligations under this Convention.

4. The application of this article shall be based on relevant scientific and technical considerations.

Article 3
Research and Systematic Observations

1. The Parties undertake, as appropriate, to initiate and co-operate in, directly or through competent international bodies, the conduct of research and scientific assessments on:

(a) The physical and chemical processes that may affect the ozone layer;
(b) The human health and other biological effects deriving from any modifications of the ozone layer, particularly those resulting from changes in ultra-violet solar radiation having biological effects (UV–B);
(c) Climatic effects deriving from any modifications of the ozone layer;
(d) Effects deriving from any modifications of the ozone layer and any consequent change in UV–B radiation on natural and synthetic materials useful to mankind;
(e) Substances, practices, processes and activities that may affect the ozone layer, and their cumulative effects;
(f) Alternative substances and technologies;
(g) Related socio-economic matters;

and as further elaborated in annexes I and II.

2. The Parties undertake to promote or establish, as appropriate, directly or through competent international bodies and taking fully into account national legislation and relevant ongoing activities at both the national and international levels, joint or complementary programmes for systematic observation of the state of the ozone layer and other relevant parameters, as elaborated in annex I.

3. The Parties undertake to co-operate, directly or through competent international bodies, in ensuring the collection, validation and transmission of research and observational data through appropriate world data centres in a regular and timely fashion.

Article 4
Co-operation in the Legal, Scientific and Technical Fields

1. The Parties shall facilitate and encourage the exchange of scientific, technical, socio-economic, commercial and legal information relevant to

this Convention as further elaborated in annex II. Such information shall be supplied to bodies agreed upon by the Parties. Any such body receiving information regarded as confidential by the supplying Party shall ensure that such information is not disclosed and shall aggregate it to protect its confidentiality before it is made available to all Parties.

2. The Parties shall co-operate, consistent with their national laws, regulations and practices and taking into account in particular the needs of the developing countries, in promoting, directly or through competent international bodies, the development and transfer of technology and knowledge. Such co-operation shall be carried out particularly through:

(a) Facilitation of the acquisition of alternative technologies by other Parties;
(b) Provision of information on alternative technologies and equipment, and supply of special manuals or guides to them;
(c) The supply of necessary equipment and facilities for research and systematic observations;
(d) Appropriate training of scientific and technical personnel.

Article 5
Transmission of Information

The Parties shall transmit, through the secretariat, to the Conference of the Parties established under article 6 information on the measures adopted by them in implementation of this Convention and of protocols to which they are party in such form and at such intervals as the meetings of the parties to the relevant instruments may determine.

Article 6
Conference of the Parties

1. A Conference of the Parties is hereby established. The first meeting of the Conference of the Parties shall be convened by the secretariat designated on an interim basis under article 7 not later than one year after entry into force of this Convention. Thereafter, ordinary meetings of the Conference of the Parties shall be held at regular intervals to be determined by the Conference at its first meeting.

2. Extraordinary meetings of the Conference of the Parties shall be held at such other times as may be deemed necessary by the Conference, or at the written request of any Party, provided that, within six months of the request being communicated to them by the secretariat, it is supported by at least one-third of the Parties.

3. The Conference of the Parties shall by consensus agree upon and adopt rules of procedure and financial rules for itself and for any subsidiary bodies it may establish, as well as financial provisions governing the functioning of the secretariat.

4. The Conference of the Parties shall keep under continuous review the implementation of this Convention, and, in addition, shall:

(a) Establish the form and the intervals for transmitting the information to be submitted in accordance with article 5 and consider such information as well as reports submitted by any subsidiary body;

(b) Review the scientific information on the ozone layer, on its possible modification and on possible effects of any such modification;

(c) Promote, in accordance with article 2, the harmonization of appropriate policies, strategies and measures for minimizing the release of substances causing or likely to cause modification of the ozone layer, and make recommendations on any other measures relating to this Convention;

(d) Adopt, in accordance with articles 3 and 4, programmes for research, systematic observations, scientific and technological co-operation, the exchange of information and the transfer of technology and knowledge;

(e) Consider and adopt, as required, in accordance with articles 9 and 10, amendments to this Convention and its annexes;

(f) Consider amendments to any protocol, as well as to any annexes thereto, and, if so decided, recommend their adoption to the parties to the protocol concerned;

(g) Consider and adopt, as required, in accordance with article 10, additional annexes to this Convention;

(h) Consider and adopt, as required, protocols in accordance with article 8;

(i) Establish such subsidiary bodies as are deemed necessary for the implementation of this Convention;

(j) Seek where appropriate the services of competent international bodies and scientific committees, in particular the World Meteorological Organization and the World Health Organization, as well as the Co-ordinating Committee on the Ozone Layer, in scientific research, systematic observations and other activities pertinent to the objectives of this Convention, and make use as appropriate of information from these bodies and committees;

(k) Consider and undertake any additional action that may be required for the achievement of the purposes of this Convention.

5. The United Nations, its specialized agencies and the International Atomic Energy Agency, as well as any State not party to this Convention, may be represented at meetings of the Conference of the Parties by observers. Any body or agency, whether national or international, governmental or non-governmental, qualified in fields relating to the protection of the ozone layer which has informed the secretariat of its wish to be represented at a meeting of the Conference of the Parties as an observer may be

admitted unless at least one-third of the Parties present object. The admission and participation of observers shall be subject to the rules of procedure adopted by the Conference of the Parties.

Article 7
Secretariat

1. The functions of the secretariat shall be:

   (a) To arrange for and service meetings provided for in articles 6, 8, 9 and 10;
   (b) To prepare and transmit reports based upon information received in accordance with articles 4 and 5, as well as upon information derived from meetings of subsidiary bodies established under article 6;
   (c) To perform the functions assigned to it by any protocol;
   (d) To prepare reports on its activities carried out in implementation of its functions under this Convention and present them to the Conference of the Parties;
   (e) To ensure the necessary co-ordination with other relevant international bodies, and in particular to enter into such administrative and contractural arrangements as may be required for the effective discharge of its functions;
   (f) To perform such other functions as may be determined by the Conference of the Parties.

2. The secretariat functions will be carried out on an interim basis by the United Nations Environment Programme until the completion of the first ordinary meeting of the Conference of the Parties held pursuant to article 6. At its first ordinary meeting, the Conference of the Parties shall designate the secretariat from amongst those existing competent international organizations which have signified their willingness to carry out the secretariat functions under this Convention.

Article 8
Adoption of Protocols

1. The Conference of the Parties may at a meeting adopt protocols pursuant to article 2.

2. The text of any proposed protocol shall be communicated to the Parties by the secretariat at least six months before such a meeting.

Article 9
Amendment of the Convention or Protocols

1. Any Party may propose amendments to this Convention or to any protocol. Such amendments shall take due account, *inter alia*, of relevant scientific and technical considerations.

2. Amendments to this Convention shall be adopted at a meeting of the Conference of the Parties. Amendments to any protocol shall be adopted at a meeting of the Parties to the protocol in question. The text of any proposed amendment to this Convention or to any protocol, except as may otherwise be provided in such protocol, shall be communicated to the Parties by the secretariat at least six months before the meeting at which it is proposed for adoption. The secretariat shall also communicate proposed amendments to the signatories to this Convention for information.

3. The Parties shall make every effort to reach agreement on any proposed amendment to this Convention by consensus. If all efforts at consensus have been exhausted, and no agreement reached, the amendment shall as a last resort be adopted by a three-fourths majority vote of the Parties present and voting at the meeting, and shall be submitted by the Depositary to all Parties for ratification, approval or acceptance.

4. The procedure mentioned in paragraph 3 above shall apply to amendments to any protocol, except that a two-thirds majority of the parties to that protocol present and voting at the meeting shall suffice for their adoption.

5. Ratification, approval or acceptance of amendments shall be notified to the Depositary in writing. Amendments adopted in accordance with paragraphs 3 or 4 above shall enter into force between parties having accepted them on the ninetieth day after the receipt by the Depositary of notification of their ratification, approval or acceptance by at least three-fourths of the Parties to this Convention or by at least two-thirds of the parties to the protocol concerned, except as may otherwise be provided in such protocol. Thereafter the amendments shall enter into force for any other Party on the ninetieth day after that Party deposits its instrument of ratification, approval or acceptance of the amendments.

6. For the purposes of this article, 'Parties present and voting' means Parties present and casting an affirmative or negative vote.

Article 10
Adoption and Amendment of Annexes

1. The annexes to this Convention or to any protocol shall form an integral part of this Convention or of such protocol, as the case may be, and, unless expressly provided otherwise, a reference to this Convention or its protocols constitutes at the same time a reference to any annexes thereto. Such annexes shall be restricted to scientific, technical and administrative matters.

2. Except as may be otherwise provided in any protocol with respect to its annexes, the following procedure shall apply to the proposal, adoption and entry into force of additional annexes to this Convention or of annexes to a protocol:

(a) Annexes to this Convention shall be proposed and adopted according to the procedure laid down in article 9, paragraphs 2 and 3, while annexes to any protocol shall be proposed and adopted according to the procedure laid down in article 9, paragraphs 2 and 4;

(b) Any party that is unable to approve an additional annex to this Convention or an annex to any protocol to which it is party shall so notify the Depositary, in writing, within six months from the date of the communication of the adoption by the Depositary. The Depositary shall without delay notify all Parties of any such notification received. A Party may at any time substitute an acceptance for a previous declaration of objection and the annexes shall thereupon enter into force for that Party;

(c) On the expiry of six months from the date of the circulation of the communication by the Depositary, the annex shall become effective for all Parties to this Convention or to any protocol concerned which have not submitted a notification in accordance with the provision of subparagraph (b) above.

3. The proposal, adoption and entry into force of amendments to annexes to this Convention or to any protocol shall be subject to the same procedure as for the proposal, adoption and entry into force of annexes to the Convention or annexes to a protocol. Annexes and amendments thereto shall take due account, *inter alia*, of relevant scientific and technical considerations.

4. If an additional annex or an amendment to an annex involves an amendment to this Convention or to any protocol, the additional annex or amended annex shall not enter into force until such time as the amendment to this Convention or to the protocol concerned enters into force.

Article 11
Settlement of Disputes

1. In the event of a dispute between Parties concerning the interpretation or application of this Convention, the parties concerned shall seek solution by negotiation.

2. If the parties concerned cannot reach agreement by negotiation, they may jointly seek the good offices of, or request mediation by, a third party.

3. When ratifying, accepting, approving or acceding to this Convention, or at any time thereafter, a State or regional economic integration organization may declare in writing to the Depositary that for a dispute not resolved in accordance with paragraph 1 or paragraph 2 above, it accepts one or both of the following means of dispute settlement as compulsory:

(a) Arbitration in accordance with procedures to be adopted by the Conference of the Parties at its first ordinary meeting;

(b) Submission of the dispute to the International Court of Justice.

4. If the parties have not, in accordance with paragraph 3 above, accepted the same or any procedure, the dispute shall be submitted to conciliation in accordance with paragraph 5 below unless the parties otherwise agree.

5. A conciliation commission shall be created upon the request of one of the parties to the dispute. The commission shall be composed of an equal number of members appointed by each party concerned and a chairman chosen jointly by the members appointed by each party. The commission shall render a final and recommendatory award, which the parties shall consider in good faith.

6. The provisions of this article shall apply with respect to any protocol except as otherwise provided in the protocol concerned.

Article 12
Signature

This Convention shall be open for signature by States and by regional economic integration organizations at the Federal Ministry for Foreign Affairs of the Republic of Austria in Vienna from 22 March 1985 to 21 September 1985, and at United Nations Headquarters in New York from 22 September 1985 to 21 March 1986.

Article 13
Ratifications, Acceptance or Approval

1. This Convention and any protocol shall be subject to ratification, acceptance or approval by States and by regional economic integration organizations. Instruments of ratification, acceptance or approval shall be deposited with the Depositary.

2. Any organization referred to in paragraph 1 above which becomes a Party to this Convention or any protocol without any of its member States being a Party shall be bound by all the obligations under the Convention or the protocol, as the case may be. In the case of such organizations, one or more of whose member States is a Party to the Convention or relevant protocol, the organization and its member States shall decide on their respective responsibilities for the performance of their obligation under the Convention or protocol, as the case may be. In such cases, the organization and the member States shall not be entitled to exercise rights under the Convention or relevant protocol concurrently.

3. In their instruments of ratification, acceptance or approval, the organizations referred to in paragraph 1 above shall declare the extent of their competence with respect to the matters governed by the Convention or the relevant protocol. These organizations shall also inform the Depositary of any substantial modification in the extent of their competence.

Article 14
Accession

1. This Convention and any protocol shall be open for accession by States and by regional economic integration organizations from the date on which the Convention or the protocol concerned is closed for signature. The instruments of accession shall be deposited with the Depositary.

2. In their instruments of accession, the organizations referred to in paragraph 1 above shall declare the extent of their competence with respect to the matters governed by the Convention or the relevant protocol. These organizations shall also inform the Depositary of any substantial modification in the extent of their competence.

3. The provisions of article 13, paragraph 2, shall apply to regional economic integration organizations which accede to this Convention or any protocol.

Article 15
Right to Vote

1. Each party to this Convention or to any protocol shall have one vote.

2. Except as provided for in paragraph 1 above, regional economic integration organizations, in matters within their competence, shall exercise their right to vote with a number of votes equal to the number of their member States which are Parties to the Convention or the relevant protocol. Such organizations shall not exercise their right to vote if their member States exercise theirs, and vice versa.

Article 16
Relationship between the Convention and its Protocols

1. A State or a regional economic integration organization may not become a party to a protocol unless it is, or becomes at the same time, a Party to the Convention.

2. Decisions concerning any protocol shall be taken only by the parties to the protocol concerned.

Article 17
Entry into Force

1. This Convention shall enter into force on the ninetieth day after the date of deposit of the twentieth instrument of ratification, acceptance, approval or accession.

2. Any protocol, except as otherwise provided in such protocol, shall enter into force on the ninetieth day after the date of deposit of the eleventh instrument of ratification, acceptance or approval of such protocol or accession thereto.

3. For each Party which ratifies, accepts or approves this Convention or accedes thereto after the deposit of the twentieth instrument of ratification, acceptance, approval or accession, it shall enter into force on the ninetieth day after the date of deposit by such Party of its instrument of ratification, acceptance, approval or accession.

4. Any protocol, except as otherwise provided in such protocol, shall enter into force for a party that ratifies, accepts or approves that protocol or accedes thereto after its entry into force pursuant to paragraph 2 above, on the ninetieth day after the date on which that party deposits its instrument of ratification, acceptance, approval or accession, or on the date on which the Convention enters into force for that Party, whichever shall be the later.

5. For the purposes of paragraphs 1 and 2 above, any instrument deposited by a regional economic integration organization shall not be counted as additional to those deposited by member States of such organization.

Article 18
Reservations

No reservations may be made to this Convention.

Article 19
Withdrawal

1. At any time after four years from the date on which this Convention has entered into force for a Party, that Party may withdraw from this Convention by giving written notification to the Depositary.

2. Except as may be provided in any protocol, at any time after four years from the date on which such protocol has entered into force for a party, that party may withdraw from the protocol by giving written notification to the Depositary.

3. Any such withdrawal shall take effect upon expiry of one year after the date of its receipt by the Depositary, or on such later date as may be specified in the notification of the withdrawal.

4. Any Party which withdraws from this Convention shall be considered as also having withdrawn from any protocol to which it is party.

Article 20
Depositary

1. The Secretary-General of the United Nations shall assume the functions of depositary of this Convention and any protocols.

2. The Depositary shall inform the Parties, in particular, of:

    (a) The signature of this Convention and of any protocol, and the deposit of instruments of ratification, acceptance, approval or accession in accordance with articles 13 and 14;

(b) The date on which the Convention and any protocol will come into force in accordance with article 17;

(c) Notifications of withdrawal made in accordance with article 19;

(d) Amendments adopted with respect to the Convention and any protocol, their acceptance by the parties and their date of entry into force in accordance with article 9;

(e) All communications relating to the adoption and approval of annexes and to the amendment of annexes in accordance with article 10;

(f) Notifications by regional economic integration organizations of the extent of their competence with respect to matters governed by this Convention and any protocols, and of any modifications thereof;

(g) Declarations made in accordance with article 11, paragraph 3.

Article 21
Authentic Texts

The original of this Convention, of which the Arabic, Chinese, English, French, Russian and Spanish texts are equally authentic, shall be deposited with the Secretary-General of the United Nations.

In witness whereof the undersigned, being duly authorized to that effect, have signed this Convention.

DONE at Vienna on the 22nd day of March 1985.

TEXT OF THE MONTREAL PROTOCOL

The Parties to this Protocol,

Being Parties to the Vienna Convention for the protection of the ozone layer,

Mindful of their obligations under that Convention to take appropriate measures to protect human health and the environment against adverse effects resulting or likely to result from human activities which modify or are likely to modify the ozone layer,

Recognizing that world-wide emissions of certain substances can significantly deplete and otherwise modify the ozone layer in a manner that is likely to result in adverse effects on human health and the environment,

Conscious of the potential climatic effects of emissions of these substances,

Aware that measures taken to protect the ozone layer from depletion should be based on relevant scientific knowledge, taking into account technical and economic considerations,

Determined to protect the ozone layer by taking precautionary measures to control equitably total global emissions of substances that deplete it, with the ultimate objective of their elimination on the basis of developments in scientific knowledge, taking into account technical and economic considerations and bearing in mind the developmental needs of developing countries,

Acknowledging that special provision is required to meet the needs of developing countries, including the provision of additional financial resources and access to relevant technologies, bearing in mind that the magnitude of funds necessary is predictable, and the funds can be expected to make a substantial difference in the world's ability to address the scientifically established problem of ozone depletion and its harmful effects,

Noting the precautionary measures for controlling emissions of certain chlorofluorocarbons that have already been taken at national and regional levels,

Considering the importance of promoting international cooperation in the research, development and transfer of alternative technologies relating to the control and reduction of emissions of substances that deplete the ozone layer, bearing in mind in particular the needs of developing countries,

Have agreed as follows:

Article 1
Definitions

For the purposes of this Protocol:

1. 'Convention' means the Vienna Convention for the protection of the ozone layer, adopted on 22 March 1985.

2. 'Parties' means, unless the text otherwise indicates, Parties to this Protocol.

3. 'Secretariat' means the secretariat of the Convention.

4. 'Controlled substance' means a substance in Annex A, Annex B, Annex C or Annex E to this Protocol, whether existing alone or in a mixture. It includes the isomers of any such substance, except as specified in the relevant Annex, but excludes any controlled substance or mixture which is in a manufactured product other than a container used for the transportation or storage of that substance.

5. 'Production' means the amount of controlled substances produced, minus the amount destroyed by technologies to be approved by the Parties and minus the amount entirely used as feedstock in the manufacture of other chemicals. The amount recycled and reused is not to be considered as 'production'.

6. 'Consumption' means production plus imports minus exports of controlled substances.

7. 'Calculated levels' of production, imports, exports and consumption means levels determined in accordance with Article 3.

8. 'Industrial rationalization' means the transfer of all or a portion of the calculated level of production of one Party to another, for the purpose of achieving economic efficiencies or responding to anticipated shortfalls in supply as a result of plant closures.

Article 2
Control measures

[Paragraphs 1–4 have been transferred to other Articles or deleted]

5. Any Party may, for any one or more control periods, transfer to another Party any portion of its calculated level of production set out in Articles 2A to 2E and Article 2H, provided that the total combined calculated levels of production of the Parties concerned for any group of controlled substances do not exceed the production limits set out in those Articles for that group. Such transfer of production shall be notified to the Secretariat by each of the Parties concerned, stating the terms of such transfer and the period for which it is to apply.

5. *bis.* Any Party not operating under paragraph 1 of Article 5 may, for one or more control periods, transfer to another such Party any portion of its calculated level of consumption set out in Article 2F, provided that the calculated level of consumption of controlled substances in Group I of Annex A of the Party transferring the portion of its calculated level of consumption did not exceed 0.25 kilograms per capita in 1989 and that the total combined calculated levels of consumption of the Parties concerned

do not exceed the consumption limits set out in Article 2F. Such transfer of consumption shall be notified to the Secretariat by each of the Parties concerned, stating the terms of such transfer and the period for which it is to apply.

6. Any Party not operating under Article 5, that has facilities for the production of Annex A or Annex B controlled substances under construction, or contracted for, prior to 16 September 1987, and provided for in national legislation prior to 1 January 1987, may add the production from such facilities to its 1986 production of such substances for the purposes of determining its calculated level of production for 1986, provided that such facilities are completed by 31 December 1990 and that such production does not raise that Party's annual calculated level of consumption of the controlled substances above 0.5 kilograms per capita.

7. Any transfer of production pursuant to paragraph 5 or any addition of production pursuant to paragraph 6 shall be notified to the secretariat, no later than the time of the transfer or addition.

8. (a) Any Parties which are Member States of a regional economic integration organisation as defined in Article 1(6) of the Convention may agree that they shall jointly fulfil their obligations respecting consumption under this Article and Articles 2A to 2E provided that their total combined calculated level of consumption does not exceed the levels required by this Article and Articles 2A to 2H.

   (b) The Parties to any such agreement shall inform the secretariat of the terms of the agreement before the date of the reduction in consumption with which the agreement is concerned.

   (c) Such agreement will become operative only if all Member States of the regional economic integration organisation and the organisation concerned are Parties to the Protocol and have notified the secretariat of their manner of implementation.

9. (a) Based on the assessment made pursuant to Article 6, the Parties may decide whether:

      (i) adjustments to the ozone-depleting potentials specified in Annex A, Annex B, Annex C and/or Annex E should be made and, if so, what the adjustments should be; and

      (ii) further adjustments and reductions of production or consumption of the controlled substances should be undertaken and, if so, what the scope, amount and timing of any such adjustment and reductions should be.

   (b) Proposals for such adjustments shall be communicated to the Parties by the secretariat at least six months before the meeting of the Parties at which they are proposed for adoption.

   (c) In taking such decisions, the Parties shall make every effort to reach agreement by consensus. If all efforts at consensus have been exhausted, and no agreement reached, such decisions shall, as a last resort, be adopted by a two-thirds majority vote of the Parties present and voting representing a majority of the Parties operating under Article 5(1) present and voting and a majority of the Parties not so operating present and voting.

(d) The decisions, which shall be binding on all Parties, shall forthwith be communicated to the Parties by the Depositary. Unless otherwise provided in the decisions, they shall enter into force on the expiry of six months from the date of the circulation of the communication by the Depositary.

10. Based on the assessment made pursuant to Article 6 of this Protocol and in accordance with the procedure set out in Article 9 of the Convention, the Parties may decide:

(i) whether any substances, and if so which, should be added to or removed from any annex to this Protocol; and

(ii) the mechanism, scope and timing of the control measures that should apply to those substances.

11. Notwithstanding the provisions contained in this Article and Articles 2A to 2H, Parties may take more stringent measures than those required by this Article and Articles 2A to 2H.

Article 2A
CFCs

1. Each Party shall ensure that for the 12-month period commencing on the first day of the seventh month following the date of the entry into force of this Protocol, and in each 12-month period thereafter, its calculated level of consumption of the controlled substances in Group I of Annex A does not exceed its calculated level of consumption in 1986. By the end of the same period, each Party producing one or more of these substances shall ensure that its calculated level of production of the substances does not exceed its calculated level of production in 1986, except that such level may have increased by no more than 10% based on the 1986 level. Such increase shall be permitted only so as to satisfy the basic domestic needs of the Parties operating under Article 5 and for the purposes of industrial rationalization between Parties.

2. Each Party shall ensure that for the period from 1 July 1991 to 31 December 1992 its calculated levels of consumption and production of the controlled substances in Group I of Annex A do not exceed 150% of its calculated levels of production and consumption of those substances in 1986; with effect from 1 January 1993, the 12-month control period for these controlled substances shall run from 1 Jaunary to 31 December each year.

3. Each Party shall ensure that for the 12-month period commencing on 1 January 1994, and in each 12-month period thereafter, its calculated level of consumption of the controlled substances in Group I of Annex A does not exceed, annually, twenty-five per cent of its calculated level of consumption in 1986. Each Party producing one or more of these substances shall, for the same periods, ensure that its calculated level of production of the substances does not exceed, annually, twenty-five per cent of its calculated level of production in 1986. However, in order to satisfy the basic domestic needs of the Parties operating under paragraph 1 of Article 5, its calculated level of production may exceed that limit by up to ten per cent of its calculated level of production in 1986.

4. Each Party shall ensure that for the 12-month period commencing on 1 January 1996, and in each 12-month period thereafter, its calculated level of consumption of the controlled substances in Group I of Annex A does not exceed zero. Each Party producing one or more of these substances shall, for the same periods, ensure that its calculated level of production of the substances does not exceed zero. However, in order to satisfy the basic domestic needs of the Parties operating under paragraph 1 of Article 5, its calculated level of production may exceed that limit by up to fifteen per cent of its calculated level of production in 1986. This paragraph will apply save to the extent that the Parties decide to permit the level of production or consumption that is necessary to satisfy uses agreed by them to be essential.

Article 2B
Halons

1. Each Party shall ensure that for the 12-month period commencing on 1 January 1992, and in each 12-month period thereafter, its calculated level of consumption of the controlled substances in Group II of Annex A does not exceed, annually, its calculated level of consumption in 1986. Each Party producing one or more of these substances shall, for the same periods, ensure that its calculated level of production of the substances does not exceed, annually, its calculated level of production in 1986. However, in order to satisfy the basic domestic needs of the Parties operating under Article 5(1), its calculated level of production may exceed that limit by up to 10% of its calculated level of production in 1986.

2. Each Party shall ensure that for the 12-month period commencing on 1 January 1994, and in each 12-month period thereafter; its calculated level of consumption of the controlled substances in Group II of Annex A does not exceed zero. Each Party producing one or more of these substances shall, for the same periods, ensure that its calculated level of production of the substances does not exceed zero. However, in order to satisfy the basic

domestic needs of the Parties operating under paragraph 1 of Article 5, its calculated level of production may exceed that limit by up to fifteen per cent of its calculated level of production in 1986. This paragraph will apply save to the extent that the Parties decide to permit the level of production or consumption that is necessary to satisfy uses agreed by them to be essential.

Article 2C
Other Fully Halogenated CFCs

1. Each Party shall ensure that for the 12-month period commencing on 1 January 1993, its calculated level of consumption of the controlled substances in Group I of Annex B does not exceed, annually, eighty per cent of its calculated level of consumption in 1989. Each Party producing one or more of these substances shall, for the same period, ensure that its calculated level of production of the substances does not exceed, annually, eighty per cent of its calculated level of production in 1989. However, in order to satisfy the basic domestic needs of the Parties operating under paragraph 1 of Article 5, its calculated level of production may exceed that limit by up to ten per cent of its calculated level of production in 1989.

2. Each Party shall ensure that for the 12-month period commencing on 1 January 1994, and in each 12-month period thereafter, its calculated level of consumption of the controlled substances in Group I of Annex B does not exceed, annually, twenty-five per cent of its calculated level of consumption in 1989. Each Party producing one or more of these substances shall, for the same periods, ensure that its calculated level of production of the substances does not exceed, annually, twenty-five per cent of its calculated level of production in 1989. However, in order to satisfy the basic domestic needs of the Parties operating under paragraph 1 of Article 5, its calculated level of production may exceed that limit by up to ten per cent of its calculated level of production in 1989.

3. Each Party shall ensure that for the 12-month period commencing on 1 January 1996, and in each 12-month period thereafter, its calculated level of consumption of the controlled substances in Group I of Annex B does not exceed zero. Each Party producing one or more of these substances shall, for the same periods, ensure that its calculated level of production of the substances does not exceed zero. However, in order to satisfy the basic domestic needs of the Parties operating under paragraph 1 of Article 5, its calculated level of production may exceed that limit by up to fifteen per cent of its calculated level of production in 1989. This paragraph will apply save to the extent that the Parties decide to permit the level of production or consumption that is necessary to satisfy uses agreed by them to be essential.

Article 2D
Carbon Tetrachloride

1. Each Party shall ensure that for the 12-month period commencing on 1 January 1995, its calculated level of consumption of the controlled substances in Group II of Annex B does not exceed, annually, fifteen per cent of its calculated level of consumption in 1989. Each Party producing the substance shall, for the same period, ensure that its calculated level of production of the substance does not exceed, annually, fifteen per cent of its calculated level of production in 1989. However, in order to satisfy the basic domestic needs of the Parties operating under paragraph 1 of Article 5, its calculated level of production may exceed that limit by up to ten per cent of its calculated level of production in 1989.

2. Each Party shall ensure that for the 12-month period commencing on 1 January 1996, and in each 12-month period thereafter, its calculated level of consumption of the controlled substance in Group II of Annex B does not exceed zero. Each Party producing the substance shall, for the same periods, ensure that its calculated level of production of the substance does not exceed zero. However, in order to satisfy the basic domestic needs of the Parties operating under paragraph 1 of Article 5, its calculated level of production may exceed that limit by up to fifteen per cent of its calculated level of production in 1989. This paragraph will apply save to the extent that the Parties decide to permit the level of production or consumption that is necessary to satisfy uses agreed by them to be essential.

Article 2E
1, 1, 1—Trichloroethane (Methyl Chloroform)

1. Each Party shall ensure that for the 12-month period commencing on 1 January 1993, its calculated level of consumption of the controlled substance in Group III of Annex B does not exceed, annually, its calculated level of consumption in 1989. Each Party producing the substance shall, for the same period, ensure that its calculated level of production of the substance does not exceed, annually, its calculated level of production in 1989. However, in order to satisfy the basic domestic needs of the Parties operating under paragraph 1 of Article 5, its calculated level of production may exceed that limit by up to ten per cent of its calculated level of production in 1989.

2. Each Party shall ensure that for the 12-month period commencing on 1 January 1994, and in each 12-month period thereafter, its calculated level of consumption of the controlled substance in Group III of Annex B does not exceed, annually, fifty per cent of its calculated level of consumption in 1989. Each Party producing the substance shall, for the same periods, ensure that its calculated level of production of the substance does not

exceed, annually, fifty per cent of its calculated level of production in 1989. However, in order to satisfy the basic domestic needs of the Parties operating under paragraph 1 of Article 5, its calculated level of production may exceed that limit by up to ten per cent of its calculated level of production in 1989.

3. Each Party shall ensure that for the 12-month period commencing on 1 January 1996, and in each 12-month period thereafter, its calculated level of consumption of the controlled substance in Group III of Annex B does not exceed zero. Each Party producing the substance shall, for the same periods, ensure that its calculated level of production of the substance does not exceed zero. However, in order to satisfy the basic domestic needs of the Parties operating under paragraph 1 of Article 5, its calculated level of production may exceed that limit by up to fifteen per cent of its calculated level of production for 1989. This paragraph will apply save to the extent that the Parties decide to permit the level of production or consumption that is necessary to satisfy uses agreed by them to be essential.

Article 2F
Hydrochlorofluorocarbons

1. Each Party shall ensure that for the 12-month period commencing on 1 January 1996, and in each 12-month period thereafter, its calculated level of consumption of the controlled substances in Group I of Annex C does not exceed, annually, the sum of:

   (a) Three point one per cent of its calculated level of consumption in 1989 of the controlled substances in Group I of Annex A; and

   (b) Its calculated level of consumption in 1989 of the controlled substances in Group I of Annex C.

2. Each Party shall ensure that for the 12-month period commencing on 1 January 2004, and in each 12-month period thereafter, its calculated level of consumption of the controlled substances in Group I of Annex C does not exceed, annually, sixty-five per cent of the sum referred to in paragraph 1 of this Article.

3. Each Party shall ensure that for the 12-month period commencing on 1 January 2010, and in each 12-month period thereafter, its calculated level of consumption of the controlled substances in Group I of Annex C does not exceed, annually, thirty-five per cent of the sum referred to in paragraph 1 of this Article.

4. Each Party shall ensure that for the 12-month period commencing on 1 January 2015, and in each 12-month period thereafter, its calculated level of consumption of the controlled substances in Group I of Annex C does not exceed, annually, ten per cent of the sum referred to in paragraph 1 of this Article.

5. Each Party shall ensure that for the 12-month period commencing on 1 January 2020, and in each 12-month period thereafter, its calculated level of consumption of the controlled substances in Group I of Annex C does not exceed, annually, zero point five per cent of the sum referred to in paragraph 1 of this Article.

6. Each Party shall ensure that for the 12-month period commencing on 1 January 2030, and in each 12-month period thereafter, its calculated level of consumption of the controlled substances in Group I of Annex C does not exceed zero.

7. As of 1 January 1996, each Party shall endeavour to ensure that:

(a) The use of controlled substances in Group I of Annex C is limited to those applications where other more environmentally suitable alternative substances or technologies are not available;

(b) The use of controlled substances in Group I of Annex C is not outside the areas of application currently met by controlled substances in Annexes A, B and C, except in rare cases for the protection of human life or human health; and

(c) Controlled substances in Group I of Annex C are selected for use in a manner that minimizes ozone depletion, in addition to meeting other environmental, safety and economic considerations.

Article 2G
Hydrobromofluorocarbons

Each Party shall ensure that for the 12-month period commencing on 1 January 1996, and in each 12-month period thereafter, its calculated level of consumption of the controlled substances in Group II of Annex C does not exceed zero. Each Party producing the substances shall, for the same periods, ensure that its calculated level of production of the substances does not exceed zero. This paragraph will apply save to the extent that the Parties decide to permit the level of production or consumption that is necessary to satisfy uses agreed by them to be essential.

Article 2H
Methyl Bromide

Each Party shall ensure that for the 12-month period commencing on 1 January 1995, and in each 12-month period thereafter, its calculated level of consumption of the controlled substance in Annex E does not exceed, annually, its calculated level of consumption in 1991. Each Party producing the substance shall, for the same periods, ensure that its calculated level of production of the substance does not exceed, annually, its calculated level of production in 1991. However, in order to satisfy the basic domestic needs of the Parties operating under paragraph 1 of Article 5, its calculated level of production may exceed that limit by up to ten per cent of its calculated level of production in 1991. The calculated levels of consumption and production under this Article shall not include the amounts used by the Party for quarantine and pre-shipment applications.

Article 3
Calculation of control levels

For the purposes of Articles 2, 2A to 2H and 5, each Party shall, for each group of substances in Annex A or Annex B, determine its calculated levels of:

  (a) production by:
      (i) multiplying its annual production of each controlled substance by the ozone-depleting potential specified in respect of it in Annex A, Annex B, Annex C or Annex E; and
      (ii) adding together, for each such group, the resulting figures;
  (b) imports and exports, respectively, by following, *mutatis mutandis*, the procedure set out in subparagraph (a); and
  (c) consumption by adding together its calculated levels of production and imports and subtracting its calculated level of exports as determined in accordance with subparagraphs (a) and (b). However, beginning on 1 January 1993, any export of controlled substances to non-parties shall not be subtracted in calculating the consumption level of the exporting Party.

Article 4
Control of trade with non-parties

1. As of 1 January 1990, each Party shall ban the import of the controlled substances in Annex A from any State not party to this Protocol.

1. *bis.* Within one year of the date of the entry into force of this paragraph, each Party shall ban the import of the controlled substances in Annex B from any State not party to this Protocol.

1. *ter.* Within one year of the date of entry into force of this paragraph, each Party shall ban the import of any controlled substances in Group II of Annex C from any State not party to this Protocol.

2. As of 1 January 1993, each Party shall ban the export of any controlled substances in Annex A to any State not party to this Protocol.

2. *bis.* Commencing one year after the date of entry into force of this paragraph, each Party shall ban the export of any controlled substances in Annex B to any State not party to this Protocol.

2. *ter.* Commencing one year after the date of entry into force of this paragraph, each Party shall ban the export of any controlled substances in Group II of Annex C to any State not party to this Protocol.

3. By 1 January 1992, the Parties shall, following the procedures in Article 10 of the Convention, elaborate in an annex a list of products containing controlled substances in Annex A. Parties that have not objected to the annex in accordance with those procedures shall ban, within one year of the annex having become effective, the import of those products from any State not party to this Protocol.

3. *bis.* Within three years of the date of the entry into force of this paragraph, the Parties shall, following the procedures in Article 10 of the Convention, elaborate in an annex a list of products containing controlled substances in Annex B. Parties that have not objected to the annex in accordance with those procedures shall ban, within one year of the annex having become effective, the import of those products from any State not party to this Protocol.

3. *ter.* Within three years of the date of entry into force of this paragraph, the Parties shall, following the procedures in Article 10 of the Convention, elaborate in an annex a list of products containing controlled substances in Group II of Annex C. Parties that have not objected to the annex in accordance with those procedures shall ban, within one year of the annex having become effective, the import of those products from any State not party to this Protocol.

4. By 1 January 1994, the Parties shall determine the feasibility of banning or restricting, from States not party to this Protocol, the import of products produced with, but not containing, controlled substances in Annex A. If determined feasible, the Parties shall, following the procedures in Article 10 of the Convention, elaborate in an annex a list of such products. Parties that have not objected to the annex in accordance with those procedures shall ban, within one year of the annex having become effective, the import of those products from any State not party to this Protocol.

4. *bis.* Within five years of the date of the entry into force of this paragraph, the Parties shall determine the feasibility of banning or restricting, from States not party to this Protocol, the import of products produced with, but not containing, controlled substances in Annex B. If determined feasible, the Parties shall, following the procedures in Article 10 of the Convention, elaborate in an annex a list of such products. Parties that have not objected to the annex in accordance with those procedures shall ban or restrict, within one year of the annex having become effective, the import of those products from any State not party to this Protocol.

4. *ter.* Within five years of the date of entry into force of this paragraph, the Parties shall determine feasibility of banning or restricting, from States not party to this Protocol, the import of products produced with, but not containing, controlled substances in Group II of Annex C. If determined feasible, the Parties shall, following the procedures in Article 10 of the Convention, elaborate in an annex a list of such products. Parties that have

not objected to the annex in accordance with those procedures shall ban or restrict, within one year of the annex having become effective, the import of those products from any State not party to this Protocol.

5. Each Party undertakes to the fullest practicable extent to discourage the export to any State not party to this Protocol of technology for producing and for utilizing controlled substances in Annexes A and B and Group II of Annex C.

6. Each Party shall refrain from providing new subsidies, aid, credits, guarantees or insurance programmes for the export to States not party to this Protocol of products, equipment, plants or technology that would facilitate the production of controlled substances in Annexes A and B and Group II of Annex C.

7. Paragraphs 5 and 6 shall not apply to products, equipment, plants or technology that improve the containment, recovery, recycling or destruction of controlled substances, promote the development of alternative substances, or otherwise contribute to the reduction of emissions of controlled substances in Annexes A and B and Group II of Annex C.

8. Notwithstanding the provisions of this Article, imports and exports referred to in paragraphs 1 to 4 *ter* of this Article, may be permitted from, or to, any State not party to this Protocol, if that State is determined by a meeting of the Parties to be in full compliance with Article 2, Article 2A to 2E, Article 2G, and this Article and have submitted data to that effect as specified in Article 7.

9. For the purposes of this Article, the term 'State not party to this Protocol' shall include, with respect to a particular controlled substance, a State or regional economic integration organization that has not agreed to be bound by the control measures in effect for that substance.

10. By 1 January 1996, the Parties shall consider whether to amend this Protocol in order to extend the measures in this Article to trade in controlled substances in Group I of Annex C and in Annex E with States not party to the Protocol.

Article 5
Special situation of developing countries

1. Any Party that is a developing country and whose annual calculated level of consumption of the controlled substances in Annex A is less than 0.3 kilograms per capita on the date of the entry into force of the Protocol for it, or any time thereafter until 1 January 1999, shall, in order to meet its basic domestic need, be entitled to delay for 10 years its compliance with the control measures set out in Articles 2A to 2E, provided that any further amendments to the adjustments or Amendments adopted at the Second Meeting of the Parties in London, 29 June 1990, shall apply to the Parties operating under this paragraph after the review provided for in paragraph

8 of this Article has taken place and shall be based on the conclusions of that review.

1. *bis.* The Parties shall, taking into account the review referred to in paragraph 8 of this Article, the assessments made pursuant to Article 6 and any other relevant information, decide by 1 January 1996, through the procedure set forth in paragraph 9 of Article 2:

    (a) With respect to paragraphs 1 to 6 of Article 2F, what base year, initial levels, control schedules and phase-out date for consumption of the controlled substances in Group I of Annex C will apply to Parties operating under paragraph 1 of this Article;

    (b) With respect to Article 2G, what phase-out date for production and consumption of the controlled substances in Group II of Annex C will apply to Parties operating under paragraph 1 of this Article; and

    (c) With respect to Article 2H, what base year, initial levels and control schedules for consumption and production of the controlled substance in Annex E will apply to Parties operating under paragraph 1 of this Article.

2. However, any Party operating under paragraph 1 of this Article shall exceed neither an annual calculated level of consumption of the controlled substances in Annex A of 0.3 kilograms per capita nor an annual calculated level of consumption of the controlled substances of Annex B of 0.2 kilograms per capita.

3. When implementing the control measures set out in Articles 2A to 2E, any Party operating under paragraph 1 of this Article shall be entitled to use:

    (a) for controlled substances under Annex A, either the average of its annual calculated level of consumption for the period 1995 to 1997 inclusive or a calculated level of consumption of 0.3 kilograms per capita, whichever is the lower, as the basis for determining its compliance with the control measures:

    (b) for controlled substances under Annex B, the average of its annual calculated level of consumption for the period 1998 to 2000 inclusive or a calculated level of consumption of 0.2 kilograms per capita, whichever is the lower, as the basis for determining its compliance with the control measures.

4. If a Party operating under paragraph 1 of this Article, at any time before the control measures obligations in Articles 2A to 2H become applicable to it, finds itself unable to obtain an adequate supply of controlled substances, it may notify this to the Secretariat. The Secretariat shall forthwith transmit a copy of such notification to the Parties, which shall consider the matter at their next meeting, and decide upon appropriate action to be taken.

5. Developing the capacity to fulfil the obligations of the Parties operating under paragraph 1 of this Article to comply with the control measures set

out in Articles 2A to 2E, and any control measures in Articles 2F to 2H that are decided pursuant to paragraph 1. *bis* of this Article, and their implementation by those same Parties will depend upon the effective implementation of the financial cooperation as provided by Article 10 and transfer of technology as provided by Article 10A.

6. Any Party operating under paragraph 1 of this Article may, at any time, notify the Secretariat in writing that, having taken all practicable steps it is unable to implement any or all of the obligations laid down in Articles 2A to 2E, or any or all obligations in Articles 2F to 2H that are decided pursuant to paragraph 1. *bis* of this Article, due to the inadequate implementation of Articles 10 and 10A. The Secretariat shall forthwith transmit a copy of the notification to the Parties, which shall consider the matter at their next meeting, giving due recognition to paragraph 5 of this Article and shall decide upon appropriate action to be taken.

7. During the period between notification and the meeting of the Parties at which the appropriate action referred to in paragraph 6 above is to be decided, or for a further period if the meeting of the Parties so decides, the non-compliance procedures referred to in Article 8 shall not be invoked against the notifying Party.

8. A meeting of the Parties shall review, not later than 1995, the situation of the Parties operating under paragraph 1 of this Article, including the effective implementation of financial cooperation and transfer of technology to them, and adopt such revisions that may be deemed necessary regarding the schedule of control measures applicable to those Parties.

9. Decisions of the Parties referred to in paragraphs 4, 6 and 7 of this Article shall be taken according to the same procedure applied to decision-making under Article 10.

Article 6
Assessment and review of control measures

Beginning in 1990, and at least every four years thereafter, the Parties shall assess the control measures provided for in Article 2, Articles 2A to 2H, on the basis of available scientific, environmental, technical and economic information. At least one year before each assessment, the Parties shall convene appropriate panels of experts qualified in the fields mentioned and determine the composition and terms of reference of any such panels. Within one year of being convened, the panels will report their conclusions, through the secretariat, to the Parties.

Article 7
Reporting of data

1. Each Party shall provide to the Secretariat, within three months of becoming a Party, statistical data on its production, imports and exports of

each of the controlled substances in Annex A for the year 1986, or the best possible estimates of such data where actual data are not available.

2. Each Party shall provide to the Secretariat statistical data on its production, imports and exports of each of the controlled substances

— in Annexes B and C, for the year 1989;
— in Annex E, for the year 1991,

or the best possible estimates of such data where actual data are not available, not later than three months after the date when the provisions set out in the Protocol with regard to the substances in Annexes B, C and E respectively enter into force for that Party.

3. Each Party shall provide to the Secretariat statistical data on its annual production (as defined in paragraph 5 of Article 1) of each of the controlled substances listed in Annexes A, B, C and E and, separately, for each substance,

— Amounts used for feedstocks,
— Amounts destroyed by technologies approved by the Parties, and
— Imports from and exports to Parties and non-Parties respectively,

for the year during which provisions concerning the substances in Annexes A, B, C and E respectively entered into force for that Party and for each year thereafter. Data shall be forwarded not later than nine months after the end of the year to which the data relate.

3. *bis.* Each Party shall provide to the Secretariat separate statistical data of its annual imports and exports of each of the controlled substances listed in Group II of Annex A and Group I of Annex C that have been recycled.

4. For Parties operating under the provisions of Article 2(8)(a), the requirements in paragraphs 1, 2 and 3 and 3. *bis* of this Article in respect of statistical data on imports and exports shall be satisfied if the regional economic integration organization concerned provides data on imports and exports between the organization and States that are not members of that organization.

Article 8
Non-compliance

The Parties, at their first meeting, shall consider and approve procedures and institutional mechanisms for determining non-compliance with the provisions of this Protocol and for treatment of Parties found to be in non-compliance.

Article 9
Research, development, public awareness and exchange of information

1. The Parties shall cooperate, consistent with their national laws, regulations and practices and taking into account in particular the needs of

developing countries, in promoting, directly or through competent international bodies, research, development and exchange of information on:

(a) best technologies for improving the containment, recovery, recycling or destruction of controlled substances or otherwise reducing their emissions;

(b) possible alternatives to controlled substances, to products containing such substances, and to products manufactured with them; and

(c) costs and benefits of relevant control strategies.

2. The Parties, individually, jointly or through competent international bodies, shall cooperate in promoting public awareness of the environmental effects of the emissions of controlled substances and other substances that deplete the ozone layer.

3. Within two years of the entry into force of this Protocol and every two years thereafter, each Party shall submit to the Secretariat a summary of the activities it has conducted pursuant to this Article.

Article 10
Financial Mechanism

1. The Parties shall establish a mechanism for the purposes of providing financial and technical cooperation, including the transfer of technologies, to Parties operating under Article 5(1) of this Protocol to enable their compliance with the control measures set out in Articles 2A to 2E, and any control measures in Articles 2F to 2H that are decided pursuant to paragraph 1. *bis* of Article 5 of the Protocol. The mechanism, contributions to which shall be additional to other financial transfers to Parties operating under that paragraph, shall meet all agreed incremental costs of such Parties in order to enable their compliance with the control measures of the Protocol. An indicative list of the categories of incremental costs shall be decided by the meeting of the Parties.

2. The mechanism established under paragraph 1 shall include a Multilateral Fund. It may also include other means of multilateral, regional and bilateral cooperation.

3. The Multilateral Fund shall:

(a) meet, on a grant or concessional basis as appropriate, and according to criteria to be decided upon by the Parties, the agreed incremental costs;

(b) finance clearing-house functions to:

(i) assist Parties operating under Article 5(1), through country-specific studies and other technical cooperation, to identify their needs for cooperation;

(ii) facilitate technical cooperation to meet these identified needs;

     (iii) distribute, as provided for in Article 9, information and relevant materials, and hold workshops, training sessions, and other related activities, for the benefit of Parties that are developing countries; and

     (iv) facilitate and monitor other multilateral, regional and bilateral cooperation available to Parties that are developing countries;

  (c) finance the secretarial services of the Multilateral Fund and related support costs.

4. The Multilateral Fund shall operate under the authority of the Parties who shall decide on its overall policies.

5. The Parties shall establish an Executive Committee to develop and monitor the implementation of specific operational policies, guidelines and administrative arrangements, including the disbursement of resources, for the purpose of achieving the objectives of the Multilateral Fund. The Executive Committee shall discharge its tasks and responsibilities, specified in its terms of reference as agreed by the Parties, with the cooperation and assistance of the International Bank for Reconstruction and Development (World Bank), the United Nations Environment Programme, the United Nations Development Programme or other appropriate agencies depending on their respective areas of expertise. The members of the Executive Committee, which shall be selected on the basis of a balanced representation of the Parties operating under Article 5(1) and of the Parties not so operating, shall be endorsed by the Parties.

6. The Multilateral Fund shall be financed by contributions from Parties not operating under Article 5(1) in convertible currency or, in certain circumstances, in kind and/or in national currency, on the basis of the United Nations scale of assessments. Contributions by other Parties shall be encouraged. Bilateral and, in particular cases agreed by a decision of the Parties, regional cooperation may, up to a percentage and consistent with any criteria to be specified by decision of the Parties, be considered as a contribution to the Multilateral Fund, provided that such cooperation, as a minimum:

  (a) strictly relates to compliance with the provisions of this Protocol;

  (b) provides additional resources; and

  (c) meets agreed incremental costs.

7. The Parties shall decide upon the programme budget of the Multilateral Fund for each fiscal period and upon the percentage of contributions of the individual Parties thereto.

8. Resources under the Multilateral Fund shall be disbursed with the concurrence of the beneficiary Party.

9. Decisions by the Parties under this Article shall be taken by consensus whenever possible. If all efforts at consensus have been exhausted and no

agreement reached, decisions shall be adopted by a two-thirds majority vote of the Parties present and voting, representing a majority of the Parties operating under Article 5(1) present and voting and a majority of the Parties not so operating present and voting.

10. The financial mechanism set out in this Article is without prejudice to any future arrangements that may be developed with respect to other environmental issues.

Article 10A
Transfer of Technology

Each Party shall take every practicable step, consistent with the programmes supported by the financial mechanism, to ensure:

(a) that the best available, environmentally safe substitutes and related technologies are expeditiously transferred to Parties operating under Article 5(1); and

(b) that the transfers referred to in subparagraph (a) occur under fair and most favourable conditions.

Article 11
Meetings of the Parties

1. The Parties shall hold meetings at regular intervals. The Secretariat shall convene the first meeting of the Parties not later than one year after the date of the entry into force of this Protocol and in conjunction with a meeting of the Conference of the Parties to the Convention, if a meeting of the latter is scheduled within that period.

2. Subsequent ordinary meetings of the Parties shall be held, unless the Parties otherwise decide, in conjunction with meetings of the Conference of the Parties to the Convention. Extraordinary meetings of the Parties shall be held at such other times as may be deemed necessary by a meeting of the Parties, or at the written request of any Party, provided that, within six months of such a request being communicated to them by the Secretariat, it is supported by at least one-third of the Parties.

3. The Parties, at their first meeting, shall:

(a) adopt by consensus rules of procedure for their meetings;
(b) adopt by consensus the financial rules referred to in Article 13(2);
(c) establish the panels and determine the terms of reference referred to in Article 6;
(d) consider and approve the procedures and institutional mechanisms specified in Article 8; and
(e) begin preparation of workplans pursuant to Article 10(3).

4. The functions of the meetings of the Parties shall be to:

(a) review the implementation of this Protocol;

(b) decide on any adjustments or reductions referred to in Article 2(9);

(c) decide on any addition to, insertion in or removal from any annex of substances and on related control measures in accordance with Article 2(10);

(d) establish, where necessary, guidelines or procedures for reporting of information as provided for in Article 7 and Article 9(3);

(e) review requests for technical assistance submitted pursuant to Article 10(2);

(f) review reports prepared by the Secretariat pursuant to Article 12(c);

(g) assess, in accordance with Article 6, the control measures;

(h) consider and adopt, as required, proposals for amendment of this Protocol or any annex and for any new annex;

(i) consider and adopt the budget for implementing this Protocol; and

(j) consider and undertake any additional action that may be required for the achievement of the purposes of this Protocol.

5. The United Nations, its specialized agencies and the International Atomic Energy Agency, as well as any State not party to this Protocol, may be represented at meetings of the Parties as observers. Any body or agency, whether national or international, governmental or non-governmental, qualified in fields relating to the protection of the ozone layer which has informed the Secretariat of its wish to be represented at a meeting of the Parties as an observer may be admitted unless at least one-third of the Parties present object. The admission and participation of observers shall be subject to the rules of procedure adopted by the Parties.

Article 12
Secretariat

For the purposes of this Protocol, the Secretariat shall:

(a) arrange for and service meetings of the Parties as provided for in Article 11;

(b) receive and make available, upon request by a Party, data provided pursuant to Article 7;

(c) prepare and distribute regularly to the Parties reports based on information received pursuant to Articles 7 and 9;

(d) notify the Parties of any request for technical assistance received pursuant to Article 10 so as to facilitate the provision of such assistance;

(e) encourage non-parties to attend the meetings of the Parties as observers and to act in accordance with the provisions of this Protocol;

(f) provide, as appropriate, the information and requests referred to in subparagraphs (c) and (d) to such non-party observers; and

(g) perform such other functions for the achievement of the purposes of this Protocol as may be assigned to it by the Parties.

Article 13
Financial Provisions

1. The funds required for the operation of this Protocol, including those for the functioning of the Secretariat related to this Protocol, shall be charged exclusively against contributions from the Parties.

2. The Parties, at their first meeting, shall adopt by consensus financial rules for the operation of this Protocol.

Article 14
Relationship of this Protocol to the Convention

Except as otherwise provided in this Protocol, the provisions of the Convention relating to its protocols shall apply to this Protocol.

Article 15
Signature

This Protocol shall be open for signature by States and by regional economic integration organizations in Montreal on 16 September 1987, in Ottawa from 17 September 1987 to 16 January 1988, and at United Nations Headquarters in New York from 17 January 1988 to 15 September 1988.

Article 16
Entry into force

1. This Protocol shall enter into force on 1 January 1989, provided that at least 11 instruments of ratification, acceptance, approval of the Protocol or accession thereto have been deposited by States or regional economic integration organizations representing at least two-thirds of 1986 estimated global consumption of the controlled substances, and the provisions of Article 17(1) of the Convention have been fulfilled. In the event that these conditions have not been fulfilled by that date, the Protocol shall enter into force on the 90th day following the date on which the conditions have been fulfilled.

2. For the purposes of paragraph 1, any such instrument deposited by a regional economic integration organization shall not be counted as additional to those deposited by member States of such organization.

3. After the entry into force of this Protocol, any State or regional economic integration organization shall become a Party to it on the 90th day following the date of deposit of its instrument of ratification, acceptance, approval or accession.

Article 17
Parties joining after entry into force

Subject to Article 5, any State or regional economic integration organization which becomes a Party to this Protocol after the date of its entry into force, shall fulfil forthwith the sum of the obligations under Article 2, as well as under Articles 2A to 2H, and Article 4, that apply at that date to the States and regional economic integration organizations that became Parties on the date the Protocol entered into force.

Article 18
Reservations

No reservations may be made to this Protocol.

Article 19
Withdrawal

Any Party may withdraw from this Protocol by giving written notification to the Depositary at any time after four years of assuming the obligations specified in Article 2A(1). Any such withdrawal shall take effect upon expiry of one year after the date of its receipt by the Depositary, or on such later date as may be specified in the notification of the withdrawal.

Article 20
Authentic texts

The original of this Protocol, of which the Arabic, Chinese, English, French, Russian and Spanish texts are equally authentic, shall be deposited with the Secretary-General of the United Nations.

In witness whereof the undersigned, being duly authorised to that effect, have signed this Protocol.

DONE at Montreal this sixteenth day of September, one thousand nine hundred and eighty-seven.

[ANNEXES A–E LIST CONTROLLED SUBSTANCES AND ARE NOT REPRODUCED]

[OF ANNEXES I–XV, ONLY ANNEXES IV AND V ARE REPRODUCED]

Annex IV
Non-compliance Procedure

The following procedure has been formulated pursuant to Article 8 of the Montreal Protocol. It shall apply without prejudice to the operation of the settlement of disputes procedure laid down in Article 11 of the Vienna Convention.

1. If one or more Parties have reservations regarding another Party's implementation of its obligations under the Protocol, those concerns may be

addressed in writing to the Secretariat. Such a submission shall be supported by corroborating information.

2. The Secretariat shall, within two weeks of its receiving a submission, send a copy of that submission to the Party whose implementation of a particular provision of the Protocol is at issue. Any reply and information in support thereof are to be submitted to the Secretariat and to the Parties involved within three months of the date of the despatch or such longer period as the circumstances of any particular case may require. The Secretariat shall then transmit the submission, the reply and the information provided by the Parties to the Implementation Committee referred to in paragraph 5, which shall consider the matter as soon as practicable.

3. Where the Secretariat, during the course of preparing its report, becomes aware of possible non-compliance by any Party with its obligations under the Protocol, it may request the Party concerned to furnish necessary information about the matter. If there is no response from the Party concerned within three months or such longer period as the circumstances of the matter may require or the matter is not resolved through administrative action or though diplomatic contacts, the Secretariat shall include the matter in its report to the Meeting of the Parties pursuant to Article 12(c) of the Protocol and inform the Implementation Committee accordingly.

4. Where a Party concludes that, despite having made its best, bona fide efforts, it is unable to comply fully with its obligations under the Protocol, it may address to the Secretariat a submission in writing, explaining, in particular, the specific circumstances that it considers to be the cause of its non-compliance. The Secretariat shall transmit such submission to the Implementation Committee which shall consider it as soon as practicable.

5. An Implementation Committee is hereby established. It shall consist of 10 Parties elected by the meeting of the Parties for two years, based on equitable geographical distribution. Outgoing Parties may be re-elected for one immediate consecutive term. The Committee shall elect its own President and Vice-President. Each shall serve for one year at a time. The Vice-President shall, in addition, serve as the rapporteur of the Committee.

6. The Implementation Committee shall, unless it decides otherwise, meet twice a year. The Secretariat shall arrange for and service its meetings.

7. The functions of the Implementation Committee shall be:

  (a) To receive, consider and report on any submission in accordance with paragraphs 1, 2 and 4;
  (b) To receive, consider and report on any information or observations forwarded by the Secretariat in connection with the preparation of the reports referred to in Article 12(c) of the Protocol and on any other information received and forwarded by the Secretariat concerning compliance with the provisions of the Protocol.

(c) To request, where it considers necessary, through the Secretariat, further information on matters under its consideration;

(d) To undertake, upon the invitation of the Party concerned, information-gathering in the territory of that Party for fulfilling the functions of the Committee;

(e) To maintain, in particular for the purposes of drawing up its recommendations, an exchange of information with the Executive Committee of the Multilateral Fund related to the provision of financial and technical cooperation, including the transfer of technologies to Parties operating under Article 5, paragraph 1, of the Protocol.

8. The Implementation Committee shall consider the submissions, information and observations referred to in paragraph 7 with a view to securing an amicable solution of the matter on the basis of respect for the provisions of the Protocol.

9. The Implementation Committee shall report to the Meeting of the Parties, including any recommendations it considers appropriate. The report shall be made available to the Parties not later than six weeks before their meeting. After receiving a report by the Committee the Parties may, taking into consideration the circumstances of the matter, decide upon and call for steps to bring about full compliance with the Protocol, including measures to assist the Parties' compliance with the Protocol, and to further the Protocol's objectives.

10. Where a Party that is not a member of the Implementation Committee is identified in a submission under paragraph 1, or itself makes such a submission, it shall be entitled to participate in the consideration by the Committee of that submission.

11. No Party, whether or not a member of the Implementation Committee, involved in a matter under consideration by the Implementation Committee, shall take part in the elaboration and adoption of recommendations on that matter to be included in the report of the Committee.

12. The Parties involved in a matter referred to in paragraphs 1, 3 or 4 shall inform, through the Secretariat, the Meeting of the Parties of the results of proceedings taken under Article 11 of the Convention regarding possible non-compliance, about implementation of those results and about implementation of any decision of the Parties pursuant to paragraph 9.

13. The Meeting of the Parties may, pending completion of proceedings initiated under Article 11 of the Convention, issue an interim call and/or recommendations.

14. The Meeting of the Parties may request the Implementation Committee to make recommendations to assist the Meeting's consideration of matters of possible non-compliance.

15. The members of the Implementation Committee and any Party involved in its deliberations shall protect the confidentiality of information they receive in confidence.

16. The report, which shall not contain any information received in confidence, shall be made available to any person upon request. All information exchanged by or with the Committee that is related to any recommendation by the Committee to the Meeting of the Parties shall be made available by the Secretariat to any Party upon its request; that Party shall ensure the confidentiality of the information it has received in confidence.

Annex V
Indicative List of Measures that might be taken by a Meeting of the Parties in respect of Non-compliance with the Protocol

A. Appropriate assistance, including assistance for the collection and reporting of data, technical assistance, technology transfer and financial assistance, information transfer and training.

B. Issuing cautions.

C. Suspension, in accordance with the applicable rules of international law concerning the suspension of the operation of a treaty, of specific rights and privileges under the Protocol, whether or not subject to time limits, including those concerned with industrial rationalization, production, consumption, trade, transfer of technology, financial mechanism and institutional arrangements.

UN General Assembly Resolution 43/53 (1988): Protection of Global
Climate for Present and Future Generations of Mankind

The importance of this resolution lies in its declaration that global climate change
is the 'common concern of mankind', thereby acknowledging what had merely
been implicit in the Ozone Convention, namely that the earth's atmosphere has a
legal status distinct from concepts of sovereign airspace, common property or
common heritage. The same terminology is used in the Climate Change Convention and the Biological Diversity Convention, and was adopted after use of the term
'common heritage' encountered opposition. The more limited legal implications of
'common concern' are that it recognises a common legal interest in matters which,
like human rights, might otherwise fall within the reserved domain of domestic
jurisdiction, but it also entails acceptance by developed states of shared obligations
of international solidarity towards developing countries for the purpose of assisting
them to achieve common environmental goals. The resolution was adopted without
a vote on 6 December 1988. See further R. Churchill and D. Freestone (eds.),
International Law and Global Climate Change (London, 1991), 1ff; J. Brunée, 'Common Interest—Echoes from an Empty Shell', 49 *ZAÖRV* (1989) 791; F. Kirgis,
'Standing to Challenge Human Endeavours that Could Change the Climate', 84
AJIL (1990) 525; UNEP, *Report of the Meeting of the Group of Legal Experts to Examine
the Concept of the Common Concern of Mankind in Relation to Global Environmental Issues*
(1990).

TEXT

The General Assembly,

Welcoming with appreciation the initiative taken by the Government of
Malta in proposing for consideration by the Assembly the item entitled
'Conservation of climate as part of the common heritage of mankind',

Concerned that certain human activities could change global climate patterns, threatening present and future generations with potentially severe
economic and social consequences,

Noting with concern that the emerging evidence indicates that continued
growth in atmospheric concentrations of 'greenhouse' gases could produce global warming with an eventual rise in sea levels, the effects of which
could be disastrous for mankind if timely steps are not taken at all levels,

Recognizing the need for additional research and scientific studies into all
sources and causes of climate change,

Concerned also that emissions of certain substances are depleting the
ozone layer and thereby exposing the earth's surface to increased ultra-
violet radiation, which may pose a threat to, *inter alia,* human health,
agricultural productivity and animal and marine life, and reaffirming in
this context the appeal, contained in its resolution 42/182 of 11 December
1987, to all States that have not yet done so to consider becoming
parties to the Vienna Convention for the Protection of the Ozone Layer,

adopted on 22 March 1985, and the Montreal Protocol on Substances that Deplete the Ozone Layer, adopted on 16 September 1987, as soon as possible,

Recalling its resolutions 42/186 and 42/187 of 11 December 1987 on the Environmental Perspective to the Year 2000 and Beyond and on the report of the World Commission on Environment and Development, respectively,

Convinced that changes in climate have an impact on development,

Aware that a considerable amount of valuable work, particularly at the scientific level and in the legal field, has already been initiated on climate change, in particular by the United Nations Environment Programme, the World Meteorological Organization and the International Council of Scientific Unions and under the auspices of individual States,

Welcoming the convening in 1990 of a second World Climate Conference,

Recalling also the conclusions of the meeting held at Villach, Austria, in 1985, which *inter alia*, recommended a programme on climate change to be promoted by Governments and the scientific community with the collaboration of the World Meteorological Organization, the United Nations Environment Programme and the International Council of Scientific Unions,

Convinced that climate change affects humanity as a whole and should be confronted within a global framework so as to take into account the vital interests of all mankind,

1. *Recognizes* that climate change is a common concern of mankind, since climate is an essential condition which sustains life on earth;

2. *Determines* that necessary and timely action should be taken to deal with climate change within a global framework;

3. *Reaffirms* its resolution 42/184 of 11 December 1987, in which, *inter alia*, it agreed with the Governing Council of the United Nations Environment Programme that the Programme should attach importance to the problem of global climate change and that the Executive Director of the United Nations Environment Programme should ensure that the Programme cooperates closely with the World Meteorological Organization and the International Council of Scientific Unions and maintains an active, influential role in the World Climate Programme;

4. *Considers* that activities in support of the World Climate Programme, approved by the Congress and Executive Council of the World Meteorological Organization and elaborated in the system-wide medium-term environment programme for the period 1990–1995, which was approved by the Governing Council of the United Nations Environment Programme, be accorded high priority by the relevant organs and programmes of the United Nations system;

5. *Endorses* the action of the World Meteorological Organization and the United Nations Environment Programme in jointly establishing an Intergovernmental Panel on Climate Change to provide internationally co-ordinated scientific assessments of the magnitude, timing and potential environmental and socio-economic impact of climate change and realistic response strategies, and expresses appreciation for the work already initiated by the Panel;

6. *Urges* Governments, intergovernmental and non-governmental organizations and scientific institutions to treat climate change as a priority issue, to undertake and promote specific, co-operative action-oriented programmes and research so as to increase understanding on all sources and causes of climate change, including its regional aspects and specific time-frames as well as the cause and effect relationship of human activities and climate, and to contribute, as appropriate, with human and financial resources to efforts to protect the global climate;

7. *Calls upon* all relevant organizations and programmes of the United Nations system to support the work of the Intergovernmental Panel on Climate Change;

8. *Encourages* the convening of conferences on climate change, particularly on global warming, at the national, regional and global levels in order to make the international community better aware of the importance of dealing effectively and in a timely manner with all aspects of climate change resulting from certain human activities;

9. *Calls upon* Governments and intergovernmental organizations to collaborate in making every effort to prevent detrimental effects on climate and activities which affect the ecological balance, and also calls upon non-governmental organizations, industry and other productive sectors to play their due role;

10. *Requests* the Secretary-General of the World Meteorological Organization and the Executive Director of the United Nations Environment Programme, through the Intergovernmental Panel on Climate Change, immediately to initiate action leading, as soon as possible, to a comprehensive review and recommendations with respect to:

  (a) The state of knowledge of the science of climate and climatic change;
  (b) Programmes and studies on the social and economic impact of climate change, including global warming;
  (c) Possible response strategies to delay, limit or mitigate the impact of adverse climate change;
  (d) The identification and possible strengthening of relevant existing international legal instruments having a bearing on climate;
  (e) Elements for inclusion in a possible future international convention on climate;

11. *Also requests* the Secretary-General to bring the present resolution to the attention of all Governments, as well as intergovernmental organizations, non-governmental organizations in consultative status with the Economic and Social Council and well-established scientific institutions with expertise in matters concerning climate;

12. *Further requests* the Secretary-General to report to the General Assembly at its forty-fourth session on the implementation of the present resolution;

13. *Decides* to include this question in the provisional agenda of its forty-fourth session, without prejudice to the application of the principle of biennialization.

Framework Convention on Climate Change, New York, 9 May 1992

This convention was opened for signature at the UN Conference on Environment and Development held at Rio in 1992 and entered into force on 21 March 1994. It seeks to establish a framework for elaboration of further measures to address the causes of climate change and is an important example of the principles of common but differentiated responsibility and of precautionary action endorsed in the Rio Declaration on Environment and Development. The Convention follows the precedent set by UNGA Resolution 43/53 (q.v.) and acknowledges climate change and its adverse effects as a common concern of humankind. No reservations are permitted. For signatories, ratifications and declarations made on signature see UN, *Multilateral Treaties Deposited with the Secretary-General*, UN Doc. ST/LEG/SER.E/ (current year). On 1 June 1995 there were 122 parties, including the United States of America, the European Union, Australia, Canada, China, the Marshall Islands, the Maldives, the Seychelles, and Mauritius.

For background studies see Intergovernmental Panel on Climate Change (IPCC), *First Assessment Report* (1990) and IPCC, Working Group III, *Report on Legal and Institutional Mechanisms* (1990), *repr.* in R. Churchill and D. Freestone, *International Law and Global Climate Change* (London, 1991), 280. For documentation and commentary on the negotiating history of the Convention, see *Report of the Chairman of the Intergovernmental Negotiating Committee for a Framework Convention on Climate Change*, UN Doc. A/CONF. 151/8 (1992); I. M. Mintzer and J. A. Leonard, *Negotiating Climate Change*, (Cambridge, 1994) and D. Bodansky, 'The UN Framework Convention on Climate Change: A Commentary', 18 *Yale JIL* (1993) 451. Preparatory work for the first meeting of the parties, held at Berlin in 1995, is in *Reports of the Intergovernmental Negotiating Committee*, UN Doc. A/AC.237/– and 24 *EPL* (1994) 299. The INC's mandate is defined in UNGA Resolutions 44/207 (1989); 45/212 (1990); 46/169 (1991); and 47/195 (1992). See also UNEP Governing Council, Decisions 14/20 of 18 June 1987, 15/36 of 25 May 1989, SS.II/3 of 3 August 1990; Declaration of the Hague on the Atmosphere, 1989; the Langkawi Declaration on the Environment, 1989; the Noordwijk Declaration on Atmospheric Pollution and Climate Change, 1989; and the Statement of the Meeting of Legal and Policy Experts, Ottawa, 1989, all *repr.* in Churchill and Freestone, *Global Climate Change*, 253ff. A regional Convention on Climate Change was concluded at Guatemala City, 29 October 1993, *repr.* 4 *YIEL* (1993), doc. 8.

See generally R. Churchill and D. Freestone (eds.), *International Law and Global Climate Change* (London, 1991); S. Barrett, *Convention on Climate Change: Economic Aspects of Negotiations* (OECD, 1992); V. P. Nanda (ed.), *World Climate Change: The Role of International Law and Institutions* (Boulder, 1983); *id*, 'Global Warming and International Environmental Law—a Preliminary Inquiry', 30 *Harv. ILJ* (1989) 375; D. Zaelke and J. Cameron, 'Global Warming and Climate Change: An Overview of the International Legal Process', 5 *Am. UJILP* (1990) 249.

TEXT

The Parties to this Convention,

Acknowledging that change in the Earth's climate and its adverse effects are a common concern of humankind,

Concerned that human activities have been substantially increasing the atmospheric concentrations of greenhouse gases, that these increases enhance the natural greenhouse effect, and that this will result on average in an additional warming of the Earth's surface and atmosphere and may adversely affect natural ecosystems and humankind,

Noting that the largest share of historical and current global emissions of greenhouse gases has originated in developed countries, that per capita emissions in developing countries are still relatively low and that the share of global emissions originating in developing countries will grow to meet their social and development needs,

Aware of the role and importance in terrestrial and marine ecosystems of sinks and reservoirs of greenhouse gases,

Noting that there are many uncertainties in predictions of climate change, particularly with regard to the timing, magnitude and regional patterns thereof,

Acknowledging that the global nature of climate change calls for the widest possible cooperation by all countries and their participation in an effective and appropriate international response, in accordance with their common but differentiated responsibilities and respective capabilities and their social and economic conditions,

Recalling the pertinent provisions of the Declaration of the United Nations Conference on the Human Environment, adopted at Stockholm on 16 June 1972,

Recalling also that States have, in accordance with the Charter of the United Nations and the principles of international law, the sovereign right to exploit their own resources pursuant to their own environmental and developmental policies, and the responsibility to ensure that activities within their jurisdiction or control do not cause damage to the environment of other States or of areas beyond the limits of national jurisdiction,

Reaffirming the principle of sovereignty of States in international cooperation to address climate change,

Recognizing that States should enact effective environmental legislation, that environmental standards, management objectives and priorities should reflect the environmental and developmental context to which they apply, and that standards applied by some countries may be inappropriate and of unwarranted economic and social cost to other countries, in particular developing countries,

Recalling the provisions of General Assembly resolution 44/228 of 22 December 1989 on the United Nations Conference on Environment and Development, and resolutions 43/53 of 6 December 1988, 44/207 of 22 December 1989, 45/212 of 21 December 1990 and 46/169 of 19 December 1991 on protection of global climate for present and future generations of mankind,

Recalling also the provisions of General Assembly resolution 44/206 of

22 December 1989 on the possible adverse effects of sea-level rise on islands and coastal areas, particularly low-lying coastal areas and the pertinent provisions of General Assembly resolution 44/172 of 19 December 1989 on the implementation of the Plan of Action to Combat Desertification,

Recalling further the Vienna Convention for the Protection of the Ozone Layer, 1985, and the Montreal Protocol on Substances that Deplete the Ozone Layer, 1987, as adjusted and amended on 29 June 1990,

Noting the Ministerial Declaration of the Second World Climate Conference adopted on 7 November 1990,

Conscious of the valuable analytical work being conducted by many States on climate change and of the important contributions of the World Meteorological Organization, the United Nations Environment Programme and other organs, organizations and bodies of the United Nations system, as well as other international and intergovernmental bodies, to the exchange of results of scientific research and the coordination of research,

Recognizing that steps required to understand and address climate change will be environmentally, socially and economically most effective if they are based on relevant scientific, technical and economic considerations and continually re-evaluated in the light of new findings in these areas,

Recognizing that various actions to address climate change can be justified economically in their own right and can also help in solving other environmental problems,

Recognizing also the need for developed countries to take immediate action in a flexible manner on the basis of clear priorities, as a first step towards comprehensive response strategies at the global, national and, where agreed, regional levels that take into account all greenhouse gases, with due consideration of their relative contributions to the enhancement of the greenhouse effect,

Recognizing further that low-lying and other small island countries, countries with low-lying coastal, arid and semi-arid areas or areas liable to floods, drought and desertification, and developing countries with fragile mountainous ecosystems are particularly vulnerable to the adverse effects of climate change,

Recognizing the special difficulties of those countries, especially developing countries, whose economies are particularly dependent on fossil fuel production, use and exportation, as a consequence of action taken on limiting greenhouse gas emissions,

Affirming that responses to climate change should be coordinated with social and economic development in an integrated manner with a view to avoiding adverse impacts on the latter, taking into full account the legitimate priority needs of developing countries for the achievement of sustained economic growth and the eradication of poverty,

Recognizing that all countries, especially developing countries, need access to resources required to achieve sustainable social and economic development and that, in order for developing countries to progress towards that goal, their energy consumption will need to grow taking into account the possibilities for achieving greater energy efficiency and for controlling greenhouse gas emissions in general, including through the application of new technologies on terms which make such an application economically and socially beneficial,

Determined to protect the climate system for present and future generations,

Have agreed as follows:

Article 1
Definitions[1]

For the purposes of this Convention:

1. 'Adverse effects of climate change' means changes in the physical environment or biota resulting from climate change which have significant deleterious effects on the composition, resilience or productivity of natural and managed ecosystems or on the operation of socio-economic systems or on human health and welfare.

2. 'Climate change' means a change of climate which is attributed directly or indirectly to human activity that alters the composition of the global atmosphere and which is in addition to natural climate variability observed over comparable time periods.

3. 'Climate system' means the totality of the atmosphere, hydrosphere, biosphere and geosphere and their interactions.

4. 'Emissions' means the release of greenhouse gases and/or their precursors into the atmosphere over a specified area and period of time.

5. 'Greenhouse gases' means those gaseous constituents of the atmosphere, both natural and anthropogenic, that absorb and re-emit infra-red radiation.

6. 'Regional economic integration organization' means an organization constituted by sovereign States of a given region which has competence in respect of matters governed by this Convention or its protocols and has been duly authorized, in accordance with its internal procedures, to sign, ratify, accept, approve or accede to the instruments concerned.

7. 'Reservoir' means a component or components of the climate system where a greenhouse gas or a precursor of a greenhouse gas is stored.

8. 'Sink' means any process, activity or mechanism which removes a greenhouse gas, an aerosol or a precursor of a greenhouse gas from the atmosphere.

---

[1] Titles of articles are included solely to assist the reader.

9. 'Source' means any process or activity which releases a greenhouse gas, an aerosol or a precursor of a greenhouse gas into the atmosphere.

Article 2
Objective

The ultimate objective of this Convention and any related legal instruments that the Conference of the Parties may adopt is to achieve, in accordance with the relevant provisions of the Convention, stabilization of greenhouse gas concentrations in the atmosphere at a level that would prevent danger-ous anthropogenic interference with the climate system. Such a level should be achieved within a time frame sufficient to allow ecosystems to adapt naturally to climate change, to ensure that food production is not threatened and to enable economic development to proceed in a sustain-able manner.

Article 3
Principles

In their actions to achieve the objective of the Convention and to im-plement its provisions, the Parties shall be guided, *inter alia*, by the following:

1. The Parties should protect the climate system for the benefit of present and future generations of humankind, on the basis of equity and in accord-ance with their common but differentiated responsibilities and respective capabilities. Accordingly, the developed country Parties should take the lead in combating climate change and the adverse effects thereof.

2. The specific needs and special circumstances of developing country Parties, especially those that are particularly vulnerable to the adverse effects of climate change, and of those Parties, especially developing country Parties, that would have to bear a disproportionate or abnormal burden under the Convention, should be given full consideration.

3. The Parties should take precautionary measures to anticipate, prevent or minimize the causes of climate change and mitigate its adverse effects. Where there are threats of serious or irreversible damage, lack of full scientific certainty should not be used as a reason for postponing such measures, taking into account that policies and measures to deal with climate change should be cost-effective so as to ensure global benefits at the lowest possible cost. To achieve this, such policies and measures should take into account different socio-economic contexts, be comprehensive, cover all relevant sources, sinks and reservoirs of greenhouse gases and adaptation, and comprise all economic sectors. Efforts to address climate change may be carried out cooperatively by interested Parties.

4. The Parties have a right to, and should, promote sustainable develop-ment. Policies and measures to protect the climate system against human-

induced change should be appropriate for the specific conditions of each Party and should be integrated with national development programmes, taking into account that economic development is essential for adopting measures to address climate change.

5. The Parties should cooperate to promote a supportive and open international economic system that would lead to sustainable economic growth and development in all Parties, particularly developing country Parties, thus enabling them better to address the problems of climate change. Measures taken to combat climate change, including unilateral ones, should not constitute a means of arbitrary or unjustifiable discrimination or a disguised restriction on international trade.

Article 4
Commitments

1. All Parties, taking into account their common but differentiated responsibilities and their specific national and regional development priorities, objectives and circumstances, shall:

    (a) Develop, periodically update, publish and make available to the Conference of the Parties, in accordance with Article 12, national inventories of anthropogenic emissions by sources and removals by sinks of all greenhouse gases not controlled by the Montreal Protocol, using comparable methodologies to be agreed upon by the Conference of the Parties;

    (b) Formulate, implement, publish and regularly update national and, where appropriate, regional programmes containing measures to mitigate climate change by addressing anthropogenic emissions by sources and removals by sinks of all greenhouse gases not controlled by the Montreal Protocol, and measures to facilitate adequate adaptation to climate change;

    (c) Promote and cooperate in the development, application and diffusion, including transfer, of technologies, practices and processes that control, reduce or prevent anthropogenic emissions of greenhouse gases not controlled by the Montreal Protocol in all relevant sectors, including the energy, transport, industry, agriculture, forestry and waste management sectors;

    (d) Promote sustainable management, and promote and cooperate in the conservation and enhancement, as appropriate, of sinks and reservoirs of all greenhouse gases not controlled by the Montreal Protocol, including biomass, forests and oceans as well as other terrestrial, coastal and marine ecosystems;

    (e) Cooperate in preparing for adaptation to the impacts of climate change; develop and elaborate appropriate and integrated plans for coastal zone management, water resources and agriculture, and for the protection and rehabilitation of areas, particularly in Africa, affected by drought and desertification, as well as floods;

(f) Take climate change considerations into account, to the extent feasible, in their relevant social, economic and environmental policies and actions, and employ appropriate methods, for example impact assessments, formulated and determined nationally, with a view to minimizing adverse effects on the economy, on public health and on the quality of the environment, of projects or measures undertaken by them to mitigate or adapt to climate change;

(g) Promote and cooperate in scientific, technological, technical, socio-economic and other research, systematic observation and development of data archives related to the climate system and intended to further the understanding and to reduce or eliminate the remaining uncertainties regarding the causes, effects, magnitude and timing of climate change and the economic and social consequences of various response strategies;

(h) Promote and cooperate in the full, open and prompt exchange of relevant scientific, technological, technical, socio-economic and legal information related to the climate system and climate change, and to the economic and social consequences of various response strategies;

(i) Promote and cooperate in education, training and public awareness related to climate change and encourage the widest participation in this process, including that of non-governmental organizations; and

(j) Communicate to the Conference of the Parties information related to implementation, in accordance with Article 12.

2. The developed country Parties and other Parties included in Annex I commit themselves specifically as provided for in the following:

(a) Each of these Parties shall adopt national[1] policies and take corresponding measures on the mitigation of climate change, by limiting its anthropogenic emissions of greenhouse gases and protecting and enhancing its greenhouse gas sinks and reservoirs. These policies and measures will demonstrate that developed countries are taking the lead in modifying longer-term trends in anthropogenic emissions consistent with the objective of the Convention, recognizing that the return by the end of the present decade to earlier levels of anthropogenic emissions of carbon dioxide and other greenhouse gases not controlled by the Montreal Protocol would contribute to such modification, and taking into account the differences in these

---

[1] This includes policies and measures adopted by regional economic integration organizations.

Parties' starting points and approaches, economic structures and resource bases, the need to maintain strong and sustainable economic growth, available technologies and other individual circumstances, as well as the need for equitable and appropriate contributions by each of these Parties to the global effort regarding that objective. These Parties may implement such policies and measures jointly with other Parties and may assist other Parties in contributing to the achievement of the objective of the Convention and, in particular, that of this subparagraph;

(b) In order to promote progress to this end, each of these Parties shall communicate, within six months of the entry into force of the Convention for it and periodically thereafter, and in accordance with Article 12, detailed information on its policies and measures referred to in subparagraph (a) above, as well as on its resulting projected anthropogenic emissions by sources and removals by sinks of greenhouse gases not controlled by the Montreal Protocol for the period referred to in subparagraph (a), with the aim of returning individually or jointly to their 1990 levels these anthropogenic emissions of carbon dioxide and other greenhouse gases not controlled by the Montreal Protocol. This information will be reviewed by the Conference of the Parties, at its first session and periodically thereafter, in accordance with Article 7;

(c) Calculations of emissions by sources and removals by sinks of greenhouse gases for the purposes of subparagraph (b) above should take into account the best available scientific knowledge, including of the effective capacity of sinks and the respective contributions of such gases to climate change. The Conference of the Parties shall consider and agree on methodologies for these calculations at its first session and review them regularly thereafter;

(d) The Conference of the Parties shall, at its first session, review the adequacy of subparagraphs (a) and (b) above. Such review shall be carried out in the light of the best available scientific information and assessment on climate change and its impacts, as well as relevant technical, social and economic information. Based on this review, the Conference of the Parties shall take appropriate action, which may include the adoption of amendments to the commitments in subparagraphs (a) and (b) above. The Conference of the Parties, at its first session, shall also take decisions regarding criteria for joint implementation as indicated in subparagraph (a) above. A second review of subparagraphs (a) and (b) shall take place not later than 31 December 1998, and thereafter at regular intervals determined by the Conference of the Parties, until the objective of the Convention is met;

(e) Each of these Parties shall:

     (i) Coordinate as appropriate with other such Parties, relevant eco-
nomic and administrative instruments developed to achieve the
objective of the Convention; and

    (ii) Identify and periodically review its own policies and practices
which encourage activities that lead to greater levels of
anthropogenic emissions of greenhouse gases not controlled by
the Montreal Protocol than would otherwise occur;

 (f) The Conference of the Parties shall review, not later than 31 December 1998, available information with a view to taking decisions regarding such amendments to the lists in Annexes I and II as may be
appropriate, with the approval of the Party concerned;

(g) Any Party not included in Annex I may, in its instrument of ratification, acceptance, approval or accession, or at any time thereafter,
notify the Depositary that it intends to be bound by subparagraphs
(a) and (b) above. The Depositary shall inform the other signatories
and Parties of any such notification.

3. The developed country Parties and other developed Parties included in
Annex II shall provide new and additional financial resources to meet the
agreed full costs incurred by developing country Parties in complying with
their obligations under Article 12, paragraph 1. They shall also provide
such financial resources, including for the transfer of technology, needed
by the developing country Parties to meet the agreed full incremental costs
of implementing measures that are covered by paragraph 1 of this Article
and that are agreed between a developing country Party and the international entity or entities referred to in Article 11, in accordance with that
Article. The implementation of these commitments shall take into account
the need for adequacy and predictability in the flow of funds and the
importance of appropriate burden sharing among the developed country
Parties.

4. The developed country Parties and other developed Parties included in
Annex II shall also assist the developing country Parties that are particularly
vulnerable to the adverse effects of climate change in meeting costs of
adaptation to those adverse effects.

5. The developed country Parties and other developed Parties included
in Annex II shall take all practicable steps to promote, facilitate and
finance, as appropriate, the transfer of, or access to, environmentally
sound technologies and know-how to other Parties, particularly developing
country Parties, to enable them to implement the provisions of the
Convention. In this process, the developed country Parties shall support
the development and enhancement of endogenous capacities and technologies of developing country Parties. Other Parties and organizations in
a position to do so may also assist in facilitating the transfer of such
technologies.

6. In the implementation of their commitments under paragraph 2 above, a certain degree of flexibility shall be allowed by the Conference of the Parties to the Parties included in Annex I undergoing the process of transition to a market economy, in order to enhance the ability of these Parties to address climate change, including with regard to the historical level of anthropogenic emissions of greenhouse gases not controlled by the Montreal Protocol chosen as a reference.

7. The extent to which developing country Parties will effectively implement their commitments under the Convention will depend on the effective implementation by developed country Parties of their commitments under the Convention related to financial resources and transfer of technology and will take fully into account that economic and social development and poverty eradication are the first and overriding priorities of the developing country Parties.

8. In the implementation of the commitments in this Article, the Parties shall give full consideration to what actions are necessary under the Convention, including actions related to funding, insurance and the transfer of technology, to meet the specific needs and concerns of developing country Parties arising from the adverse effects of climate change and/or the impact of the implementation of response measures, especially on:

(a) Small island countries;
(b) Countries with low-lying coastal areas;
(c) Countries with arid and semi-arid areas, forested areas and areas liable to forest decay;
(d) Countries with areas prone to natural disasters;
(e) Countries with areas liable to drought and desertification;
(f) Countries with areas of high urban atmospheric pollution;
(g) Countries with areas with fragile ecosystems, including mountainous ecosystems;
(h) Countries whose economies are highly dependent on income generated from the production, processing and export, and/or on consumption of fossil fuels and associated energy-intensive products; and
(i) Land-locked and transit countries.

Further, the Conference of the Parties may take actions, as appropriate, with respect to this paragraph.

9. The Parties shall take full account of the specific needs and special situations of the least developed countries in their actions with regard to funding and transfer of technology.

10. The Parties shall, in accordance with Article 10, take into consideration in the implementation of the commitments of the Convention the situation of Parties, particularly developing country Parties, with economies

that are vulnerable to the adverse effects of the implementation of measures to respond to climate change. This applies notably to Parties with economies that are highly dependent on income generated from the production, processing and export, and/or consumption of fossil fuels and associated energy-intensive products and/or the use of fossil fuels for which such Parties have serious difficulties in switching to alternatives.

Article 5
Research and Systematic Observation

In carrying out their commitments under Article 4, paragraph 1(g), the Parties shall:

(a) Support and further develop, as appropriate, international and intergovernmental programmes and networks or organizations aimed at defining, conducting, assessing and financing research, data collection and systematic observation, taking into account the need to minimize duplication of effort;

(b) Support international and intergovernmental efforts to strengthen systematic observation and national scientific and technical research capacities and capabilities, particularly in developing countries, and to promote access to, and the exchange of, data and analyses thereof obtained from areas beyond national jurisdiction; and

(c) Take into account the particular concerns and needs of developing countries and cooperate in improving their endogenous capacities and capabilities to participate in the efforts referred to in subparagraphs (a) and (b) above.

Article 6
Education, Training and Public Awareness

In carrying out their commitments under Article 4, paragraph 1(i), the Parties shall:

(a) Promote and facilitate at the national and, as appropriate, subregional and regional levels, and in accordance with national laws and regulations, and within their respective capacities:

   (i) The development and implementation of educational and public awareness programmes on climate change and its effects;

   (ii) Public access to information on climate change and its effects;

   (iii) Public participation in addressing climate change and its effects and developing adequate responses; and

   (iv) Training of scientific, technical and managerial personnel.

(b) Cooperate in and promote, at the international level, and, where appropriate, using existing bodies:

   (i) The development and exchange of educational and public awareness material on climate change and its effects; and

(ii) The development and implementation of education and training programmes, including the strengthening of national institutions and the exchange or secondment of personnel to train experts in this field, in particular for developing countries.

Article 7
Conference of the Parties

1. A Conference of the Parties is hereby established.

2. The Conference of the Parties, as the supreme body of this Convention, shall keep under regular review the implementation of the Convention and any related legal instruments that the Conference of the Parties may adopt, and shall make, within its mandate, the decisions necessary to promote the effective implementation of the Convention. To this end, it shall:

(a) Periodically examine the obligations of the Parties and the institutional arrangements under the Convention, in the light of the objective of the Convention, the experience gained in its implementation and the evolution of scientific and technological knowledge;

(b) Promote and facilitate the exchange of information on measures adopted by the Parties to address climate change and its effects, taking into account the differing circumstances, responsibilities and capabilities of the Parties and their respective commitments under the Convention;

(c) Facilitate, at the request of two or more Parties, the coordination of measures adopted by them to address climate change and its effects, taking into account the differing circumstances, responsibilities and capabilities of the Parties and their respective commitments under the Convention;

(d) Promote and guide, in accordance with the objective and provisions of the Convention, the development and periodic refinement of comparable methodologies, to be agreed on by the Conference of the Parties, *inter alia*, for preparing inventories of greenhouse gas emissions by sources and removals by sinks, and for evaluating the effectiveness of measures to limit the emissions and enhance the removals of these gases;

(e) Assess, on the basis of all information made available to it in accordance with the provisions of the Convention, the implementation of the Convention by the Parties, the overall effects of the measures taken pursuant to the Convention, in particular environmental, economic and social effects as well as their cumulative impacts and the extent to which progress towards the objective of the Convention is being achieved;

(f) Consider and adopt regular reports on the implementation of the Convention and ensure their publication;

(g) Make recommendations on any matters necessary for the implementation of the Convention;

(h) Seek to mobilize financial resources in accordance with Article 4, paragraphs 3, 4 and 5, and Article 11;

(i) Establish such subsidiary bodies as are deemed necessary for the implementation of the Convention;

(j) Review reports submitted by its subsidiary bodies and provide guidance to them;

(k) Agree upon and adopt, by consensus, rules of procedure and financial rules for itself and for any subsidiary bodies;

(l) Seek and utilize, where appropriate, the services and cooperation of, and information provided by, competent international organizations and intergovernmental and non-governmental bodies; and

(m) Exercise such other functions as are required for the achievement of the objective of the Convention as well as all other functions assigned to it under the Convention.

3. The Conference of the Parties shall, at its first session, adopt its own rules of procedure as well as those of the subsidiary bodies established by the Convention, which shall include decision-making procedures for matters not already covered by decision-making procedures stipulated in the Convention. Such procedures may include specified majorities required for the adoption of particular decisions.

4. The first session of the Conference of the Parties shall be convened by the interim secretariat referred to in Article 21 and shall take place not later than one year after the date of entry into force of the Convention. Thereafter, ordinary sessions of the Conference of the Parties shall be held every year unless otherwise decided by the Conference of the Parties.

5. Extraordinary sessions of the Conference of the Parties shall be held at such other times as may be deemed necessary by the Conference, or at the written request of any Party, provided that, within six months of the request being communicated to the Parties by the secretariat, it is supported by at least one-third of the Parties.

6. The United Nations, its specialized agencies and the International Atomic Energy Agency, as well as any State member thereof or observers thereto not Party to the Convention, may be represented at sessions of the Conference of the Parties as observers. Any body or agency, whether national or international, governmental or non-governmental, which is qualified in matters covered by the Convention, and which has informed the secretariat of its wish to be represented at a session of the Conference of the Parties as an observer, may be so admitted unless at least one-third of the Parties present object. The admission and participation of observers

shall be subject to the rules of procedure adopted by the Conference of the Parties.

Article 8
Secretariat

1. A secretariat is hereby established.
2. The functions of the secretariat shall be:

   (a) To make arrangements for sessions of the Conference of the Parties and its subsidiary bodies established under the Convention and to provide them with services as required;
   (b) To compile and transmit reports submitted to it;
   (c) To facilitate assistance to the Parties, particularly developing country Parties, on request, in the compilation and communication of information required in accordance with the provisions of the Convention;
   (d) To prepare reports on its activities and present them to the Conference of the Parties;
   (e) To ensure the necessary coordination with the secretariats of other relevant international bodies;
   (f) To enter, under the overall guidance of the Conference of the Parties, into such administrative and contractual arrangements as may be required for the effective discharge of its functions; and
   (g) To perform the other secretariat functions specified in the Convention and in any of its protocols and such other functions as may be determined by the Conference of the Parties.

3. The Conference of the Parties, at its first session, shall designate a permanent secretariat and make arrangements for its functioning.

Article 9
Subsidiary body for scientific and technological advice

1. A subsidiary body for scientific and technological advice is hereby established to provide the Conference of the Parties and, as appropriate, its other subsidiary bodies with timely information and advice on scientific and technological matters relating to the Convention. This body shall be open to participation by all Parties and shall be multidisciplinary. It shall comprise government representatives competent in the relevant field of expertise. It shall report regularly to the Conference of the Parties on all aspects of its work.

2. Under the guidance of the Conference of the Parties, and drawing upon existing competent international bodies, this body shall:

   (a) Provide assessments of the state of scientific knowledge relating to climate change and its effects;

(b) Prepare scientific assessments on the effects of measures taken in the implementation of the Convention;

(c) Identify innovative, efficient and state-of-the-art technologies and know-how and advise on the ways and means of promoting development and/or transferring such technologies;

(d) Provide advice on scientific programmes, international cooperation in research and development related to climate change, as well as on ways and means of supporting endogenous capacity-building in developing countries; and

(e) Respond to scientific, technological and methodological questions that the Conference of the Parties and its subsidiary bodies may put to the body.

3. The functions and terms of reference of this body may be further elaborated by the Conference of the Parties.

Article 10
Subsidiary body for implementation

1. A subsidiary body for implementation is hereby established to assist the Conference of the Parties in the assessment and review of the effective implementation of the Convention. This body shall be open to participation by all Parties and comprise government representatives who are experts on matters related to climate change. It shall report regularly to the Conference of the Parties on all aspects of its work.

2. Under the guidance of the Conference of the Parties, this body shall:

(a) Consider the information communicated in accordance with Article 12, paragraph 1, to assess the overall aggregated effect of the steps taken by the Parties in the light of the latest scientific assessments concerning climate change;

(b) Consider the information communicated in accordance with Article 12, paragraph 2, in order to assist the Conference of the Parties in carrying out the reviews required by Article 4, paragraph 2(d); and

(c) Assist the Conference of the Parties, as appropriate, in the preparation and implementation of its decisions.

Article 11
Financial mechanism

1. A mechanism for the provision of financial resources on a grant or concessional basis, including for the transfer of technology, is hereby defined. It shall function under the guidance of and be accountable to the Conference of the Parties, which shall decide on its policies, programme priorities and eligibility criteria related to this Convention. Its operation shall be entrusted to one or more existing international entities.

2. The financial mechanism shall have an equitable and balanced representation of all Parties within a transparent system of governance.

3. The Conference of the Parties and the entity or entities entrusted with the operation of the financial mechanism shall agree upon arrangements to give effect to the above paragraphs, which shall include the following:

(a) Modalities to ensure that the funded projects to address climate change are in conformity with the policies, programme priorities and eligibility criteria established by the Conference of the Parties;

(b) Modalities by which a particular funding decision may be reconsidered in light of these policies, programme priorities and eligibility criteria;

(c) Provision by the entity or entities of regular reports to the Conference of the Parties on its funding operations, which is consistent with the requirement for accountability set out in paragraph 1 above; and

(d) Determination in a predictable and identifiable manner of the amount of funding necessary and available for the implementation of this Convention and the conditions under which that amount shall be periodically reviewed.

4. The Conference of the Parties shall make arrangements to implement the above mentioned provisions at its first session, reviewing and taking into account the interim arrangements referred to in Article 21, paragraph 3, and shall decide whether these interim arrangements shall be maintained. Within four years thereafter, the Conference of the Parties shall review the financial mechanism and take appropriate measures.

5. The developed country Parties may also provide and developing country Parties avail themselves of, financial resources related to the implementation of the Convention through bilateral, regional and other multilateral channels.

Article 12
Communication of information related to implementation

1. In accordance with Article 4, paragraph 1, each Party shall communicate to the Conference of the Parties, through the secretariat, the following elements of information:

(a) A national inventory of anthropogenic emissions by sources and removals by sinks of all greenhouse gases not controlled by the Montreal Protocol, to the extent its capacities permit, using comparable methodologies to be promoted and agreed upon by the Conference of the Parties;

(b) A general description of steps taken or envisaged by the Party to implement the Convention; and

(c) Any other information that the Party considers relevant to the achievement of the objective of the Convention and suitable for inclusion in its communication, including, if feasible, material relevant for calculations of global emission trends.

2. Each developed country Party and each other Party included in Annex I shall incorporate in its communication the following elements of information:

(a) A detailed description of the policies and measures that it has adopted to implement its commitment under Article 4, paragraphs 2(a) and 2(b); and

(b) A specific estimate of the effects that the policies and measures referred to in subparagraph (a) immediately above will have on anthropogenic emissions by its sources and removals by its sinks of greenhouse gases during the period referred to in Article 4, paragraph 2(a).

3. In addition, each developed country Party and each other developed Party included in Annex II shall incorporate details of measures taken in accordance with Article 4, paragraphs 3, 4 and 5.

4. Developing country Parties may, on a voluntary basis, propose projects for financing, including specific technologies, materials, equipment, techniques or practices that would be needed to implement such projects, along with, if possible, an estimate of all incremental costs, of the reductions of emissions and increments of removals of greenhouse gases, as well as an estimate of the consequent benefits.

5. Each developed country Party and each other Party included in Annex I shall make its initial communication within six months of the entry into force of the Convention for that Party. Each Party not so listed shall make its initial communication within three years of the entry into force of the Convention for that Party, or of the availability of financial resources in accordance with Article 4, paragraph 3. Parties that are least developed countries may make their initial communication at their discretion. The frequency of subsequent communications by all Parties shall be determined by the Conference of the Parties, taking into account the differentiated timetable set by this paragraph.

6. Information communicated by Parties under this Article shall be transmitted by the secretariat as soon as possible to the Conference of the Parties and to any subsidiary bodies concerned. If necessary, the procedures for the communication of information may be further considered by the Conference of the Parties.

7. From its first session, the Conference of the Parties shall arrange for the provision to developing country Parties of technical and financial support, on request, in compiling and communicating information under this

Article, as well as in identifying the technical and financial needs associated with proposed projects and response measures under Article 4. Such support may be provided by other Parties, by competent international organizations and by the secretariat, as appropriate.

8. Any group of Parties may, subject to guidelines adopted by the Conference of the Parties, and to prior notification to the Conference of the Parties, make a joint communication in fulfilment of their obligations under this Article, provided that such a communication includes information on the fulfilment by each of these Parties of its individual obligations under the Convention.

9. Information received by the secretariat that is designated by a Party as confidential, in accordance with criteria to be established by the Conference of the Parties, shall be aggregated by the secretariat to protect its confidentiality before being made available to any of the bodies involved in the communication and review of information.

10. Subject to paragraph 9 above, and without prejudice to the ability of any Party to make public its communication at any time, the secretariat shall make communications by Parties under this Article publicly available at the time they are submitted to the Conference of the Parties.

Article 13
Resolution of questions regarding implementation

The Conference of the Parties shall, at its first session, consider the establishment of a multilateral consultative process, available to Parties on their request, for the resolution of questions regarding the implementation of the Convention.

Article 14
Settlement of disputes

1. In the event of a dispute between any two or more Parties concerning the interpretation or application of the Convention, the Parties concerned shall seek a settlement of the dispute through negotiation or any other peaceful means of their own choice.

2. When ratifying, accepting, approving or acceding to the Convention, or at any time thereafter, a Party which is not a regional economic integration organization may declare in a written instrument submitted to the Depositary that, in respect of any dispute concerning the interpretation or application of the Convention, it recognizes as compulsory *ipso facto* and without special agreement, in relation to any Party accepting the same obligation:

   (a) Submission of the dispute to the International Court of Justice, and/or
   (b) Arbitration in accordance with procedures to be adopted by the

Conference of the Parties as soon as practicable, in an annex on arbitration.

A Party which is a regional economic integration organization may make a declaration with like effect in relation to arbitration in accordance with the procedures referred to in subparagraph (b) above.

3. A declaration made under paragraph 2 above shall remain in force until it expires in accordance with its terms or until three months after written notice of its revocation has been deposited with the Depositary.

4. A new declaration, a notice of revocation or the expiry of a declaration shall not in any way affect proceedings pending before the International Court of Justice or the arbitral tribunal, unless the parties to the dispute otherwise agree.

5. Subject to the operation of paragraph 2 above, if after twelve months following notification by one Party to another that a dispute exists between them, the Parties concerned have not been able to settle their dispute through the means mentioned in paragraph 1 above, the dispute shall be submitted, at the request of any of the parties to the dispute, to conciliation.

6. A conciliation commission shall be created upon the request of one of the parties to the dispute. The commission shall be composed of an equal number of members appointed by each party concerned and a chairman chosen jointly by the members appointed by each party. The commission shall render a recommendatory award, which the parties shall consider in good faith.

7. Additional procedures relating to conciliation shall be adopted by the Conference of the Parties, as soon as practicable, in an annex on conciliation.

8. The provisions of this Article shall apply to any related legal instrument which the Conference of the Parties may adopt, unless the instrument provides otherwise.

Article 15
Amendments to the Convention

1. Any Party may propose amendments to the Convention.

2. Amendments to the Convention shall be adopted at an ordinary session of the Conference of the Parties. The text of any proposed amendment to the Convention shall be communicated to the Parties by the secretariat at least six months before the meeting at which it is proposed for adoption. The secretariat shall also communicate proposed amendments to the signatories to the Convention and, for information, to the Depositary.

3. The Parties shall make every effort to reach agreement on any proposed amendment to the Convention by consensus. If all efforts at consensus have

been exhausted, and no agreement reached, the amendment shall as a last resort be adopted by a three-fourths majority vote of the Parties present and voting at the meeting. The adopted amendment shall be communicated by the secretariat to the Depositary, who shall circulate it to all Parties for their acceptance.

4. Instruments of acceptance in respect of an amendment shall be deposited with the Depositary. An amendment adopted in accordance with paragraph 3 above shall enter into force for those Parties having accepted it on the ninetieth day after the date of receipt by the Depositary of an instrument of acceptance by at least three-fourths of the Parties to the Convention.

5. The amendment shall enter into force for any other Party on the ninetieth day after the date on which that Party deposits with the Depositary its instrument of acceptance of the said amendment.

6. For the purposes of this Article, 'Parties present and voting' means Parties present and casting an affirmative or negative vote.

Article 16
Adoption and amendment of Annexes to the Convention

1. Annexes to the Convention shall form an integral part thereof and, unless otherwise expressly provided, a reference to the Convention constitutes at the same time a reference to any annexes thereto. Without prejudice to the provisions of Article 14, paragraphs 2(b) and 7, such annexes shall be restricted to lists, forms and any other material of a descriptive nature that is of a scientific, technical, procedural or administrative character.

2. Annexes to the Convention shall be proposed and adopted in accordance with the procedure set forth in Article 15, paragraphs 2, 3, and 4.

3. An annex that has been adopted in accordance with paragraph 2 above shall enter into force for all Parties to the Convention six months after the date of the communication by the Depositary to such Parties of the adoption of the annex, except for those Parties that have notified the Depositary, in writing, within that period of their non-acceptance of the annex. The annex shall enter into force for Parties which withdraw their notification of non-acceptance on the ninetieth day after the date on which withdrawal of such notification has been received by the Depositary.

4. The proposal, adoption and entry into force of amendments to annexes to the Convention shall be subject to the same procedure as that for the proposal, adoption and entry into force of annexes to the Convention in accordance with paragraphs 2 and 3 above.

5. If the adoption of an annex or an amendment to an annex involves an amendment to the Convention, that annex or amendment to an annex

shall not enter into force until such time as the amendment to the Convention enters into force.

Article 17
Protocols

1. The Conference of the Parties may, at any ordinary session, adopt protocols to the Convention.

2. The text of any proposed protocol shall be communicated to the Parties by the secretariat at least six months before such a session.

3. The requirements for the entry into force of any protocol shall be established by that instrument.

4. Only Parties to the Convention may be Parties to a protocol.

5. Decisions under any protocol shall be taken only by the Parties to the protocol concerned.

Article 18
Right to vote

1. Each Party to the Convention shall have one vote, except as provided for in paragraph 2 below.

2. Regional economic integration organizations, in matters within their competence, shall exercise their right to vote with a number of votes equal to the number of their member States that are Parties to the Convention. Such an organization shall not exercise its right to vote if any of its member States exercises its right, and vice versa.

Article 19
Depositary

The Secretary-General of the United Nations shall be the Depositary of the Convention and of protocols adopted in accordance with Article 17.

Article 20
Signature

This Convention shall be open for signature by States Members of the United Nations or of any of its specialized agencies or that are Parties to the Statute of the International Court of Justice and by regional economic integration organizations at Rio de Janeiro, during the United Nations Conference on Environment and Development, and thereafter at United Nations Headquarters in New York from 20 June 1992 to 19 June 1993.

Article 21
Interim arrangements

1. The secretariat functions referred to in Article 8 will be carried out on an interim basis by the secretariat established by the General Assembly of

the United Nations in its resolution 45/212 of 21 December 1990, until the completion of the first session of the Conference of the Parties.

2. The head of the interim secretariat referred to in paragraph 1 above will cooperate closely with the Intergovernmental Panel on Climate Change to ensure that the Panel can respond to the need for objective scientific and technical advice. Other relevant scientific bodies could also be consulted.

3. The Global Environment Facility of the United Nations Development Programme, the United Nations Environment Programme and the International Bank for Reconstruction and Development shall be the international entity entrusted with the operation of the financial mechanism referred to in Article 11 on an interim basis. In this connection, the Global Environment Facility should be appropriately restructured and its membership made universal to enable it to fulfil the requirements of Article 11.

Article 22
Ratification, acceptance, approval or accession

1. The Convention shall be subject to ratification, acceptance, approval or accession by States and by regional economic integration organizations. It shall be open for accession from the day after the date on which the Convention is closed for signature. Instruments of ratification, acceptance, approval or accession shall be deposited with the Depositary.

2. Any regional economic integration organization which becomes a Party to the Convention without any of its member States being a Party shall be bound by all the obligations under the Convention. In the case of such organizations, one or more of whose member States is a Party to the Convention, the organization and its member States shall decide on their respective responsibilities for the performance of their obligations under the Convention. In such cases, the organization and the member States shall not be entitled to exercise rights under the Convention concurrently.

3. In their instruments of ratification, acceptance, approval or accession, regional economic integration organizations shall declare the extent of their competence with respect to the matters governed by the Convention. These organizations shall also inform the Depositary, who shall in turn inform the Parties, of any substantial modification in the extent of their competence.

Article 23
Entry into force

1. The Convention shall enter into force on the ninetieth day after the date of deposit of the fiftieth instrument of ratification, acceptance, approval or accession.

2. For each State or regional economic integration organization that ratifies, accepts or approves the Convention or accedes thereto after the

deposit of the fiftieth instrument of ratification, acceptance, approval or accession, the Convention shall enter into force on the ninetieth day after the date of deposit by such State or regional economic integration organization of its instrument of ratification, acceptance, approval or accession.

3. For the purposes of paragraphs 1 to 2 above, any instrument deposited by a regional economic integration organization shall not be counted as additional to those deposited by States members of the organization.

Article 24
Reservations

No reservations may be made to the Convention.

Article 25
Withdrawal

1. At any time after three years from the date on which the Convention has entered into force for a Party, that Party may withdraw from the Convention by giving written notification to the Depositary.

2. Any such withdrawal shall take effect upon expiry of one year from the date of receipt by the Depositary of the notification of withdrawal, or on such later date as may be specified in the notification of withdrawal.

3. Any Party that withdraws from the Convention shall be considered as also having withdrawn from any protocol to which it is a Party.

Article 26
Authentic texts

The original of this Convention, of which the Arabic, Chinese, English, French, Russian and Spanish texts are equally authentic, shall be deposited with the Secretary-General of the United Nations.

Annex I

Australia
Austria
Belarus[1]
Belgium
Bulgaria[1]
Canada
Czechoslovakia[1]
Denmark
European Community
Estonia[1]
Finland
France
Germany
Greece
Hungary[1]
Iceland
Ireland
Italy
Japan
Latvia[1]
Lithuania[1]
Luxembourg
Netherlands
New Zealand
Norway
Poland[1]
Portugal
Romania[1]
Russian Federation[1]
Spain
Sweden
Switzerland
Turkey
Ukraine[1]
United Kingdom of Great Britain and Northern Ireland
United States of America

[1] Countries that are undergoing the process of transition to a market economy.

Annex II

Australia
Austria
Belgium
Canada
Denmark
European Community
Finland
France
Germany
Greece
Iceland
Ireland
Italy
Japan
Luxembourg
Netherlands
New Zealand
Norway
Portugal
Spain
Sweden
Switzerland
Turkey
United Kingdom of Great Britain and Northern Ireland
United States of America

Convention on Long-range Transboundary Air Pollution, Geneva, 13
November 1979, and Protocol on Further Reduction of Sulphur
Emissions, Oslo, 14 June 1994

This is not a global convention, but it is the most significant regional agreement on
the regulation of long-range transboundary air pollution. Participation is open to
all member states of the UN Economic Commission for Europe, so it is applicable
to most of the industrialized Northern hemisphere. Parties include the United
States of America, Canada, and the former USSR. It entered into force on 16 March
1983 and had thirty-nine parties on 1 January 1995. The Convention does not deal
with liability for historic or prospective damage to the environment, but it does
reflect the desire of the states concerned to negotiate an equitable solution to acid
rain disputes and other forms of transboundary air pollution. It thus provides a legal
and institutional framework for taking further measures, negotiated through the
UN ECE and adopted in the following protocols:

— Protocol on Long-term Financing of a Cooperative Programme for Monitor-
ing and Evaluation of the Long-Range Transmission of Air Pollutants in
Europe (EMEP), Geneva, 28 September 1984, repr. 27 ILM (1988) 701; UKTS
75 (1988), Cm. 521; UN Doc. ECE/EB.AIR/11. In force 28 January 1988.
Thirty-five parties on 1 January 1994.
— Protocol on the Reduction of Sulphur Emissions or their Transboundary
Fluxes, Helsinki, 8 July 1985 repr. 27 ILM (1988) 707; UN Doc. ECE/EB.AIR/
12. In force 2 September, 1987. Twenty-one parties, 1995.
— Protocol Concerning the Control of Emissions of Nitrogen Oxides or Their
Transboundary Fluxes, Sofia, 31 October 1988. Repr. 28 ILM (1989) 212; 18
EPL 228; UKTS 1 (1992), Cm. 1787. In force 14 February 1991. Twenty-five
parties, 1 January 1995.
— Protocol Concerning the Control of Emissions of Volatile Organic Com-
pounds or Their Transboundary Fluxes, Geneva, 18 November 1991. Repr. 31
ILM (1992) 573; UN Doc. ECE/EB.AIR/30. Not in force. Eleven parties,
1995.
— Protocol on Further Reduction of Sulphur Emissions, Oslo, 14 June 1994.
Repr. 33 ILM (1994) 1542. Not in force.

Only the 1994 Oslo Protocol is reproduced here. This protocol is notable for
setting precise emission limits and a timetable for reductions in Annex II, while
committing parties to ensuring 'in the long term' that depositions do not exceed
'critical loads' specified in Annex I.

For declarations, reservations and current parties to the Convention and
protocols, see: UN, Multilateral Treaties Deposited with the Secretary-General, UN DOC.
ST/LEG/SER.E/(current year). Further development of the Convention and its
protocols is reported in UN Doc. ECE/EB.AIR/ Reports of the Executive Body of the
Convention on Long-Range Transboundary Air Pollution. On the negotiation of the
1979 Convention see E.M. Chossudovsky, East-West Diplomacy for Environment in the
United Nations (UNITAR, 1990). See generally: C. Flinterman, B. Kwiatkowska, and
J. Lammers (eds.), Transboundary Air Pollution (Dordrecht, 1986); M. Pallemaerts,
'International Legal Aspects of Long-Range Transboundary Air Pollution', Hague
YBIL (1988) 189; G. Handl, 'Bi-national Uses of Transboundary Air Resources: The
International Entitlement Issue Reconsidered', 26 Nat. Res. J (1986) 405; A.
Fraenkel, 'The Convention on Long-Range Transboundary Air Pollution: Meeting
the Challenge of International Co-operation', 30 Harv. ILJ (1989) 447; A.

Rosencranz, 'The ECE Convention on Long Range Transboundary Air Pollution', 75 *AJIL* (1981) 975; P. W. Birnie and A. E. Boyle, *International Law and the Environment* (Oxford, 1992), 397.

TEXT

The Parties to the present Convention,

Determined to promote relations and co-operation in the field of environmental protection,

Aware of the significance of the activities of the United Nations Economic Commission for Europe in strengthening such relations and co-operation, particularly in the field of air pollution including long-range transport of air pollutants,

Recognizing the contribution of the Economic Commission for Europe to the multilateral implementation of the pertinent provisions of the Final Act of the Conference on Security and Co-operation in Europe,

Cognizant of the references in the chapter on environment of the Final Act of the Conference on Security and Co-operation in Europe calling for co-operation to control air pollution and its effects, including long-range transport of air pollutants, and to the development through international co-operation of an extensive programme for the monitoring and evaluation of long-range transport of air pollutants, starting with sulphur dioxide and with possible extension to other pollutants,

Considering the pertinent provisions of the Declaration of the United Nations Conference on the Human Environment, and in particular principle 21, which expresses the common conviction that States have, in accordance with the Charter of the United Nations and the principles of international law, the sovereign right to exploit their own resources pursuant to their own environmental policies, and the responsibility to ensure that activities within their jurisdiction or control do not cause damage to the environment of other States or of areas beyond the limits of national jurisdiction,

Recognizing the existence of possible adverse effects, in the short and long term, of air pollution including transboundary air pollution,

Concerned that a rise in the level of emissions of air pollutants within the region as forecast may increase such adverse effects,

Recognizing the need to study the implications of the long-range transport of air pollutants and the need to seek solutions for the problems identified,

Affirming their willingness to reinforce active international co-operation to develop appropriate national policies and by means of exchange of information, consultation, research and monitoring, to co-ordinate national action for combating air pollution including long-range transboundary air pollution,

Have agreed as follows:

Article 1
Definitions

For the purposes of the present Convention:

(a) 'air pollution' means the introduction by man, directly or indirectly, of substances or energy into the air resulting in deleterious effects of such a nature as to endanger human health, harm living resources and ecosystems and material property and impair or interfere with amenities and other legitimate uses of the environment, and 'air pollutants' shall be construed accordingly;

(b) 'Long-range transboundary air pollution' means air pollution whose physical origin is situated wholly or in part within the area under the national jurisdiction of one State and which has adverse effects in the area under the jurisdiction of another State at such a distance that it is not generally possible to distinguish the contribution of individual emission sources or groups of sources.

Fundamental Principles
Article 2

The Contracting Parties, taking due account of the facts and problems involved, are determined to protect man and his environment against air pollution and shall endeavour to limit and, as far as possible, gradually reduce and prevent air pollution including long-range transboundary air pollution.

Article 3

The Contracting Parties, within the framework of the present Convention, shall by means of exchanges of information, consultation, research and monitoring, develop without undue delay policies and strategies which shall serve as a means of combating the discharge of air pollutants, taking into account efforts already made at national and international levels.

Article 4

The Contracting Parties shall exchange information on and review their policies, scientific activities and technical measures aimed at combating, as far as possible, the discharge of air pollutants which may have adverse effects, thereby contributing to the reduction of air pollution including long-range transboundary air pollution.

Article 5

Consultations shall be held, upon request, at an early stage between, on the one hand, Contracting parties which are actually affected by or exposed to a significant risk of long-range transboundary air pollution and, on the other hand, Contracting Parties within which and subject to whose jurisdiction a significant contribution to long-range transboundary air pollution originates, or could originate, in connexion with activities carried on or contemplated therein.

Article 6
Air Quality Management

Taking into account articles 2 to 5, the ongoing research, exchange of information and monitoring and the results thereof, the cost and effectiveness of local and other remedies and, in order to combat air pollution, in particular that originating from new or rebuilt installations, each Contracting Party undertakes to develop the best policies and strategies including air quality management systems and, as part of them, control measures compatible with balanced development, in particular by using the best available technology which is economically feasible and low- and non-waste technology.

Article 7
Research and Development

The Contracting Parties, as appropriate to their needs, shall initiate and co-operate in the conduct of research into and/or development of:

(a) existing and proposed technologies for reducing emissions of sulphur compounds and other major air pollutants, including technical and economic feasibility, and environmental consequences;

(b) instrumentation and other techniques for monitoring and measuring emission rates and ambient concentrations of air pollutants;

(c) improved models for a better understanding of the transmission of long-range transboundary air pollutants;

(d) the effects of sulphur compounds and other major air pollutants on human health and the environment, including agriculture, forestry, materials, aquatic and other natural ecosystems and visibility, with a view to establishing a scientific basis for dose/effect relationships designed to protect the environment;

(e) the economic, social and environmental assessment of alternative measures for attaining environmental objectives including the reduction of long-range transboundary air pollution;

(f) education and training programmes related to the environmental aspects of pollution by sulphur compounds and other major air pollutants.

Article 8
Exchange of Information

The Contracting Parties, within the framework of the Executive Body referred to in article 10 and bilaterally, shall, in their common interests, exchange available information on:

(a) data on emissions at periods of time to be agreed upon, of agreed air pollutants, starting with sulphur dioxide, coming from grid-units of agreed size; or on the fluxes of agreed air pollutants, starting with sulphur dioxide, across national borders, at distances and at periods of time to be agreed upon;

(b) major changes in national policies and in general industrial development, and their potential impact, which would be likely to cause significant changes in long-range transboundary air pollution;

(c) control techniques for reducing air pollution relevant to long-range transboundary air pollution;

(d) the projected cost of the emission control of sulphur compounds and other major air pollutants on a national scale;

(e) meteorological and physico-chemical data relating to the processes during transmission;

(f) physico-chemical and biological data relating to the effects of long-range transboundary air pollution and the extent of the damage[1] which these data indicate can be attributed to long-range transboundary air pollution;

(g) national, subregional and regional policies and strategies for the control of sulphur compounds and other major air pollutants.

Article 9
Implementation and Further Development of the Co-operative Programme for the Monitoring and Evaluation of the Long-range Transmission of Air Pollutants in Europe

The Contracting Parties stress the need for the implementation of the existing 'Co-operative programme for the monitoring and evaluation of the long-range transmission of air pollutants in Europe' (hereinafter referred to as EMEP) and, with regard to the further development of this programme, agree to emphasize:

(a) the desirability of Contracting Parties joining in and fully implementing EMEP which, as a first step, is based on the monitoring of sulphur dioxide and related substances;

(b) the need to use comparable or standardized procedures for monitoring whenever possible;

(c) the desirability of basing the monitoring programme on the framework of both national and international programmes. The establishment of monitoring stations and the collection of data shall be carried out under the national jurisdiction of the country in which the monitoring stations are located;

(d) the desirability of establishing a framework for a co-operative environmental monitoring programme, based on and taking into

---

[1] The present Convention does not contain a rule on State liability as to damage.

account present and future national, subregional, regional and other international programmes;

(e) the need to exchange data on emissions at periods of time to be agreed upon, of agreed air pollutants, starting with sulphur dioxide, coming from grid-units of agreed size; or on the fluxes of agreed air pollutants, starting with sulphur dioxide, across national borders, at distances and at periods of time to be agreed upon. The method, including the model, used to determine the fluxes, as well as the method, including the model, used to determine the transmission of air pollutants based on the emissions per grid-unit, shall be made available and periodically reviewed, in order to improve the methods and the models;

(f) their willingness to continue the exchange and periodic updating of national data on total emissions of agreed air pollutants, starting with sulphur dioxide;

(g) the need to provide meteorological and physico-chemical data relating to processes during transmission;

(h) the need to monitor chemical components in other media such as water, soil and vegetation, as well as a similar monitoring programme to record effects on health and environment;

(i) the desirability of extending the national EMEP networks to make them operational for control and surveillance purposes.

Article 10
Executive Body

1. The representatives of the Contracting Parties shall, within the framework of the Senior Advisers to ECE Governments on Environmental Problems, constitute the Executive Body of the present Convention, and shall meet at least annually in that capacity.

2. The Executive Body shall:

(a) review the implementation of the present Convention;

(b) establish, as appropriate, working groups to consider matters related to the implementation and development of the present Convention and to this end to prepare appropriate studies and other documentation and to submit recommendations to be considered by the Executive Body;

(c) fulfill such other functions as may be appropriate under the provisions of the present Convention.

3. The Executive Body shall utilize the Steering Body for the EMEP to play an integral part in the operation of the present Convention, in particular with regard to data collection and scientific co-operation.

4. The Executive Body, in discharging its functions, shall, when it deems appropriate, also make use of information from other relevant international organizations.

Article 11
Secretariat

The Executive Secretary of the Economic Commission for Europe shall carry out, for the Executive Body, the following secretariat functions:

(a) to convene and prepare the meetings of the Executive Body;
(b) to transmit to the Contracting Parties reports and other information received in accordance with the provisions of the present Convention;
(c) to discharge the functions assigned by the Executive Body.

Article 12
Amendments to the Convention

1. Any Contracting Party may propose amendments to the present Convention.

2. The text of proposed amendments shall be submitted in writing to the Executive Secretary of the Economic Commission for Europe, who shall communicate them to all Contracting Parties. The Executive Body shall discuss proposed amendments at its next annual meeting provided that such proposals have been circulated by the Executive Secretary of the Economic Commission for Europe to the Contracting Parties at least ninety days in advance.

3. An amendment to the present Convention shall be adopted by consensus of the representatives of the Contracting Parties, and shall enter into force for the Contracting Parties which have accepted it on the ninetieth day after the date on which two-thirds of the Contracting Parties have deposited their instruments of acceptance with the depositary. Thereafter, the amendment shall enter into force for any other Contracting Party on the ninetieth day after the date on which that Contracting Party deposits its instrument of acceptance of the amendment.

Article 13
Settlement of Disputes

If a dispute arises between two or more Contracting Parties to the present Convention as to the interpretation or application of the Convention, they shall seek a solution by negotiation or by any other method of dispute settlement acceptable to the parties to the dispute.

Article 14
Signature

1. The present Convention shall be open for signature at the United Nations Office at Geneva from 13 to 16 November 1979 on the occasion of the High-level Meeting within the framework of the Economic Commission for Europe on the Protection of the Environment, by the member States of the Economic Commission for Europe as well as States having consultative

status with the Economic Commission for Europe, pursuant to paragraph 8 of Economic and Social Council resolution 36 (IV) of 28 March 1947, and by regional economic integration organizations, constituted by sovereign States members of the Economic Commission for Europe, which have competence in respect of the negotiation, conclusion and application of international agreements in matters covered by the present Convention.

2. In matters within their competence, such regional economic integration organizations shall, on their own behalf, exercise the rights and fulfil the responsibilities which the present Convention attributes to their member States. In such cases, the member States of these organizations shall not be entitled to exercise such rights individually.

Article 15
Ratification, Acceptance, Approval and Accession

1. The present Convention shall be subject to ratification, acceptance or approval.

2. The present Convention shall be open for accession as from 17 November 1979 by the States and organizations referred to in article 14, paragraph 1.

3. The instruments of ratification, acceptance, approval or accession shall be deposited with the Secretary-General of the United Nations, who will perform the functions of the depositary.

Article 16
Entry into Force

1. The present Convention shall enter into force on the nineteenth day after the date of deposit of the twenty-fourth instrument of ratification, acceptance, approval or accession.

2. For each Contracting Party which ratifies, accepts or approves the present Convention or accedes thereto after the deposit of the twenty-fourth instrument of ratification, acceptance, approval or accession, the Convention shall enter into force on the nineteenth day after the date of deposit by such Contracting Party of its instrument of ratification, acceptance, approval or accession.

Article 17
Withdrawal

At any time after five years from the date on which the present Convention has come into force with respect to a Contracting Party, that Contracting Party may withdraw from the Convention by giving written notification to the depositary. Any such withdrawal shall take effect on the nineteenth day after the date of its receipt by the depositary.

Article 18
Authentic Texts

The original of the present Convention, of which the English, French and Russian texts are equally authentic, shall be deposited with the Secretary-General of the United Nations.

In witness whereof the undersigned, being duly authorized thereto, have signed the present Convention.

DONE at Geneva, this thirteenth day of November, one thousand nine hundred and seventy-nine.

TEXT OF 1994 PROTOCOL

The Parties,

Determined to implement the Convention on Long-range Transboundary Air Pollution,

Concerned that emissions of sulphur and other air pollutants continue to be transported across international boundaries and, in exposed parts of Europe and North America, are causing widespread damage to natural resources of vital environmental and economic importance, such as forests, soils and waters, and to materials, including historic monuments, and, under certain circumstances, have harmful effects on human health,

Resolved to take precautionary measures to anticipate, prevent or minimize emissions of air pollutants and mitigate their adverse effects,

Convinced that where there are threats of serious or irreversible damage, lack of full scientific certainty should not be used as a reason for postponing such measures, taking into account that such precautionary measures to deal with emissions of air pollutants should be cost-effective,

Mindful that measures to control emissions of sulphur and other air pollutants would also contribute to the protection of the sensitive Arctic environment,

Considering that the predominant sources of air pollution contributing to the acidification of the environment are the combustion of fossil fuels for energy production, and the main technological processes in various industrial sectors, as well as transport, which lead to emissions of sulphur, nitrogen oxides, and other pollutants,

Conscious of the need for a cost-effective regional approach to combating air pollution that takes account of the variations in effects and abatement costs between countries,

Desiring to take further and more effective action to control and reduce sulphur emissions,

Cognizant that any sulphur control policy, however cost-effective it may be at the regional level, will result in a relatively heavy economic burden on countries with economies that are in transition to a market economy,

Bearing in mind that measures taken to reduce sulphur emissions should not constitute a means of arbitrary or unjustifiable discrimination or a disguised restriction on international competition and trade,

Taking into consideration existing scientific and technical data on emissions, atmospheric processes and effects on the environment of sulphur oxides, as well as on abatement costs,

Aware that, in addition to emissions of sulphur, emissions of nitrogen oxides and of ammonia are also causing acidification of the environment,

Noting that under the United Nations Framework Convention on Climate Change, adopted in New York on 9 May 1992, there is agreement to establish national policies and take corresponding measures to combat climate change, which can be expected to lead to reductions of sulphur emissions,

Affirming the need to ensure environmentally sound and sustainable development,

Recognizing the need to continue scientific and technical cooperation to elaborate further the approach based on critical loads and critical levels, including efforts to assess several air pollutants and various effects on the environment, materials and human health,

Underlining that scientific and technical knowledge is developing and that it will be necessary to take such developments into account when reviewing the adequacy of the obligations entered into under the present Protocol and deciding on further action,

Acknowledging the protocol on the Reduction of Sulphur Emissions or Their Transboundary Fluxes by at least 30 per cent, adopted in Helsinki on 8 July 1985, and the measures already taken by many countries which have had the effect of reducing sulphur emissions,

Have agreed as follows:

Article 1
Definitions

For the purposes of the present Protocol,

1. 'Convention' means the Convention on Long-range Transboundary Air Pollution, adopted in Geneva on 13 November 1979;

2. 'EMEP' means the Cooperative Programme for Monitoring and Evaluation of the Long-range Transmission of Air Pollutants in Europe;

3. 'Executive Body' means the Executive Body for the Convention constituted under article 10, paragraph 1, of the Convention;

4. 'Commission' means the United Nations Economic Commission for Europe;

5. 'Parties' means, unless the context otherwise requires, the Parties to the present Protocol;

6. 'Geographical scope of EMEP' means the area defined in article 1, paragraph 4, of the Protocol to the 1979 Convention on Long-range Transboundary Air Pollution on Long-term Financing of the Cooperative Programme for Monitoring and Evaluation of the Long-range Transmission of Air Pollutants in Europe (EMEP), adopted in Geneva on 28 September 1984;

7. 'SOMA' means a sulphur oxides management area designated in annex III under the conditions laid down in article 2, paragraph 3;

8. 'Critical load' means a quantitative estimate of an exposure to one or more pollutants below which significant harmful effects on specified sensitive elements of the environment do not occur, according to present knowledge;

9. 'Critical levels' means the concentration of pollutants in the atmosphere above which direct adverse effects on receptors, such as human beings, plants, ecosystems or materials, may occur, according to present knowledge;

10. 'Critical sulphur deposition' means a quantitative estimate of the exposure to oxidized sulphur compounds, taking into account the effects of base cation uptake and base cation deposition, below which significant harmful effects on specified sensitive elements of the environment do not occur, according to present knowledge;

11. 'Emission' means the discharge of substances into the atmosphere;

12. 'Sulphur emissions' means all emissions of sulphur compounds expressed as kilotonnes of sulphur dioxide (kt SO_2) to the atmosphere originating from anthropogenic sources excluding from ships in international traffic outside territorial waters;

13. 'Fuel' means any solid, liquid or gaseous combustible material with the exception of domestic refuse and toxic or dangerous waste;

14. 'Stationary combustion source' means any technical apparatus or group of technical apparatus that is co-located on a common site and is or could be discharging waste gases through a common stack, in which fuels are oxidized in order to use the heat generated;

15. 'Major new stationary combustion source' means any stationary combustion source the construction or substantial modification of which is authorized after 31 December 1995 and the thermal input of which, when operating at rated capacity, is at least 50 MW_{th}. It is a matter for the competent national authorities to decide whether a modification is substantial or not, taking into account such factors as the environmental benefits of the modification;

16. 'Major existing stationary combustion source' means any existing stationary combustion source the thermal input of which, when operating at rated capacity, is at least 50 MW_{th};

17. 'Gas oil' means any petroleum product within HS 2710, or any petroleum product which, by reason of its distillation limits, falls within the category of middle distillates intended for use as fuel and of which at least 85% by volume, including distillation losses, distils at 350°C;

18. 'Emission limit value' means the permissible concentration of sulphur compounds expressed as sulphur dioxide in the waste gases from a stationary combustion source expressed in terms of mass per volume of the waste gases expressed in mg SO_2/Nm^3, assuming an oxygen content by volume in the waste gas of 3% in the case of liquid and gaseous fuels and 6% in the case of solid fuels;

19. 'Emission limitation' means the permissible total quantity of sulphur compounds expressed as sulphur dioxide discharged from a combustion source or group of combustion sources located either on a common site or within a defined geographical area, expressed in kilotonnes per year;

20. 'Desulphurization rate' means the ratio of the quantity of sulphur which is separated at the combustion source site over a given period to the quantity of sulphur contained in the fuel which is introduced into the combustion source facilities and which is used over the same period;

21. 'Sulphur budget' means a matrix of calculated contributions to the deposition of oxidized sulphur compounds in receiving areas, originating from the emissions from specified areas.

Article 2
Basic Obligations

1. The Parties shall control and reduce their sulphur emissions in order to protect human health and the environment from adverse effects, in particular acidifying effects, and to ensure, as far as possible, without entailing excessive costs, that depositions of oxidized sulphur compounds in the long term do not exceed critical loads for sulphur given, in annex I, as critical sulphur depositions, in accordance with present scientific knowledge.

2. As a first step, the Parties shall, as a minimum, reduce and maintain their annual sulphur emissions in accordance with the timing and levels specified in annex II.

3. In addition, any Party:

   (a) Whose total land area is greater than 2 million square kilometres,
   (b) Which has committed itself under paragraph 2 above to a national sulphur emission ceiling no greater than the lesser of its 1990 emissions or its obligation in the 1985 Helsinki Protocol on the Reduction of Sulphur Emissions or Their Transboundary Fluxes by at least 30 per cent, as indicated in annex II,
   (c) Whose annual sulphur emissions that contribute to acidification in areas under the jurisdiction of one or more other Parties originate

only from within areas under its jurisdiction that are listed as SOMAs in annex III, and has presented documentation to this effect, and

(d) Which has specified upon signature of, or accession to, the present Protocol its intention to act in accordance with this paragraph,

shall, as a minimum, reduce and maintain its annual sulphur emissions in the area so listed in accordance with the timing and levels specified in annex II.

4. Furthermore, the Parties shall make use of the most effective measures for the reduction of sulphur emissions, appropriate in their particular circumstances, for new and existing sources, which include, *inter alia*:

— Measures to increase energy efficiency,
— Measures to increase the use of renewable energy,
— Measures to reduce the sulphur content of particular fuels and to encourage the use of fuel with a low sulphur content, including the combined use of high-sulphur with low-sulphur or sulphur-free fuel,
— Measures to apply best available control technologies not entailing excessive cost,

using the guidance in annex IV.

5. Each Party, except those Parties subject to the United States/Canada Air Quality Agreement of 1991, shall as a minimum:

(a) Apply emission limit values at least as stringent as those specified in annex V to all major new stationary combustion sources,
(b) No later than 1 July 2004 apply, as far as possible without entailing excessive costs, emission limit values at least as stringent as those specified in annex V to those major existing stationary combustion sources the thermal input of which is above 500 MW_{th} taking into account the remaining lifetime of a plant, calculated from the date of entry into force of the present Protocol, or apply equivalent emission limitations or other appropriate provisions, provided that these achieve the sulphur emission ceilings specified in annex II and, subsequently, further approach the critical loads as given in annex I, and no later than 1 July 2004 apply emission limit values or emission limitations to those major existing stationary combustion sources the thermal input of which is between 50 and 500 MW_{th} using annex V as guidance,
(c) No later than two years after the date of entry into force of the present Protocol apply national standards for the sulphur content of gas oil at least as stringent as those specified in annex V. In cases where the supply of gas oil cannot otherwise be ensured, a State may extend the time period given in this subparagraph to a period of up to ten years. In this case it shall specify, in a declaration to be

deposited together with the instrument of ratification, acceptance, approval or accession, its intention to extend the time period.

6. The Parties may, in addition, apply economic instruments to encourage the adoption of cost-effective approaches to the reduction of sulphur emissions.

7. The Parties to this protocol may, at a session of the Executive Body, in accordance with rules and conditions which the Executive Body shall elaborate and adopt, decide whether two or more Parties may jointly implement the obligations set out in annex II. These rules and conditions shall ensure the fulfilment of the obligations set out in paragraph 2 above and also promote the achievement of the environmental objectives set out in paragraph 1 above.

8. The Parties shall, subject to the outcome of the first review provided for under article 8 and no later than one year after the completion of that review, commence negotiations on further obligations to reduce emissions.

Article 3
Exchange of Technology

1. The Parties shall, consistent with their national laws, regulations and practices, facilitate the exchange of technologies and techniques, including those that increase energy efficiency, the use of renewable energy and the processing of low-sulphur fuels, to reduce sulphur emissions, particularly through the promotion of:

(a) The commercial exchange of available technology,
(b) Direct industrial contacts and cooperation, including joint ventures,
(c) The exchange of information and experience,
(d) The provision of technical assistance.

2. In promoting the activities specified in paragraph 1 above, the Parties shall create favourable conditions by facilitating contacts and cooperation among appropriate organizations and individuals in the private and public sectors that are capable of providing technology, design and engineering services, equipment or finance.

3. The Parties shall, no later than six months after the date of entry into force of the present Protocol, commence consideration of procedures to create more favourable conditions for the exchange of technology to reduce sulphur emissions.

Article 4
National Strategies, Policies, Programmes, Measures and Information

1. Each Party shall, in order to implement its obligations under article 2:

(a) Adopt national strategies, policies and programmes, no later than six months after the present Protocol enters into force for it, and

(b) Take and apply national measures

to control and reduce its sulphur emissions.

2. Each Party shall collect and maintain information on:

(a) Actual levels of sulphur emissions, and of ambient concentrations and depositions of oxidized sulphur and other acidifying compounds, taking into account, for those Parties within the geographical scope of EMEP, the work plan of EMEP, and

(b) The effects of depositions of oxidized sulphur and other acidifying compounds.

Article 5
Reporting

1. Each Party shall report, through the Executive Secretary of the Commission, to the Executive Body, on a periodic basis as determined by the Executive Body, information on:

(a) The implementation of national strategies, policies, programmes and measures referred to in article 4, paragraph 1,

(b) The levels of national annual sulphur emissions, in accordance with guidelines adopted by the Executive Body, containing emission data for all relevant source categories, and

(c) The implementation of other obligations that it has entered into under the present Protocol,

in conformity with a decision regarding format and content to be adopted by the Parties at a session of the Executive Body. The terms of this decision shall be reviewed as necessary to identify any additional elements regarding the format and/or content of the information that are to be included in the reports.

2. Each Party within the geographical scope of EMEP shall report, through the Executive Secretary of the Commission, to EMEP, on a periodic basis to be determined by the Steering Body of EMEP and approved by the Parties at a session of the Executive Body, information on the levels of sulphur emissions with temporal and spatial resolution as specified by the Steering Body of EMEP.

3. In good time before each annual session of the Executive Body, EMEP shall provide information on:

(a) Ambient concentrations and deposition of oxidized sulphur compounds, and

(b) Calculations of sulphur budgets.

Parties in areas outside the geographical scope of EMEP shall make available similar information if requested to do so by the Executive Body.

4. The Executive Body shall, in accordance with article 10, paragraph 2(b), of the Convention, arrange for the preparation of information on the effects of depositions of oxidized sulphur and other acidifying compounds.

5. The Parties shall, at sessions of the Executive Body, arrange for the preparation, at regular intervals, of revised information on calculated and internationally optimized allocations of emission reductions for the States within the geographical scope of EMEP, with integrated assessment models, with a view to reducing further, for the purposes of article 2, paragraph 1, of the present Protocol, the difference between actual depositions of oxidized sulphur compounds and critical load values.

Article 6
Research, Development and Monitoring

The Parties shall encourage research, development, monitoring and cooperation related to:

(a) The international harmonization of methods for the establishment of critical loads and critical levels and the elaboration of procedures for such harmonization,

(b) The improvement of monitoring techniques and systems and of the modelling of transport, concentrations and deposition of sulphur compounds,

(c) Strategies for the further reduction of sulphur emissions based on critical loads and critical levels as well as on technical developments, and the improvement of integrated assessment modelling to calculate internationally optimized allocations of emission reductions taking into account an equitable distribution of abatement costs,

(d) The understanding of the wider effects of sulphur emissions on human health, the environment, in particular acidification, and materials, including historic and cultural monuments, taking into account the relationship between sulphur oxides, nitrogen oxides, ammonia, volatile organic compounds and tropospheric ozone,

(e) Emission abatement technologies, and technologies and techniques to enhance energy efficiency, energy conservation and the use of renewable energy,

(f) The economic evaluation of benefits for the environment and human health resulting from the reduction of sulphur emissions.

Article 7
Compliance

1. An Implementation Committee is hereby established to review the implementation of the present Protocol and compliance by the Parties with their obligations. It shall report to the Parties at sessions of the Executive

Body and may make such recommendations to them as it considers appropriate.

2. Upon consideration of a report, and any recommendations, of the Implementation Committee, the Parties, taking into account the circumstances of a matter and in accordance with Convention practice, may decide upon and call for action to bring about full compliance with the present Protocol, including measures to assist a Party's compliance with the Protocol, and to further the objectives of the Protocol.

3. The Parties shall, at the first session of the Executive Body after the entry into force of the present Protocol, adopt a decision that sets out the structure and functions of the Implementation Committee as well as procedures for its review of compliance.

4. The application of the compliance procedure shall be without prejudice to the provisions of article 9 of the present Protocol.

Article 8
Reviews by the Parties at Sessions of the Executive Body

1. The Parties shall, at sessions of the Executive Body, pursuant to article 10, paragraph 2(a), of the Convention, review the information supplied by the Parties and EMEP, the data on the effects of depositions of sulphur and other acidifying compounds and the reports of the Implementation Committee referred to in article 7, paragraph 1, of the present Protocol.

2. (a) The Parties shall, at sessions of the Executive Body, keep under review the obligations set out in the present Protocol, including:
   (i) Their obligations in relation to their calculated and internationally optimized allocations of emission reductions referred to in article 5, paragraph 5, and
   (ii) The adequacy of the obligations and the progress made towards the achievement of the objectives of the present Protocol,
   (b) Reviews shall take into account the best available scientific information on acidification, including assessments of critical loads, technological developments, changing economic conditions and the fulfilment of the obligations on emission levels,
   (c) In the context of such reviews, any Party whose obligations on sulphur emission ceilings under annex II hereto do not conform to the calculated and internationally optimized allocations of emission reductions for that Party, required to reduce the difference between depositions of sulphur in 1990 and critical sulphur depositions within the geographical scope of EMEP by at least 60%, shall make every effort to undertake revised obligations,
   (d) The procedures, methods and timing for such reviews shall be specified by the Parties at a session of the Executive Body. The first such review shall be completed in 1997.

Article 9
Settlement of Disputes

1. In the event of a dispute between any two or more Parties concerning the interpretation or application of the present Protocol, the Parties concerned shall seek a settlement of the dispute through negotiation or any other peaceful means of their own choice. The parties to the dispute shall inform the Executive Body of their dispute.

2. When ratifying, accepting, approving or acceding to the present Protocol, or at any time thereafter, a Party which is not a regional economic integration organization may declare in a written instrument submitted to the Depositary that, in respect of any dispute concerning the interpretation or application of the Protocol, it recognizes one or both of the following means of dispute settlement as compulsory *ipso facto* and without agreement, in relation to any Party accepting the same obligation:

    (a) Submission of the dispute to the International Court of Justice,
    (b) Arbitration in accordance with procedures to be adopted by the Parties at a session of the Executive Body as soon as practicable, in an annex on arbitration.

A Party which is a regional economic integration organization may make a declaration with like effect in relation to arbitration in accordance with the procedures referred to in subparagraph (b) above.

3. A declaration made under paragraph 2 above shall remain in force until it expires in accordance with its terms or until three months after written notice of its revocation has been deposited with the Depositary.

4. A new declaration, a notice of revocation or the expiry of a declaration shall not in any way affect proceedings pending before the International Court of Justice or the arbitral tribunal, unless the parties to the dispute agree otherwise.

5. Except in a case where the parties to a dispute have accepted the same means of dispute settlement under paragraph 2, if after twelve months following notification by one Party to another that a dispute exits between them, the Parties concerned have not been able to settle their dispute through the means mentioned in paragraph 1 above, the dispute shall be submitted, at the request of any of the parties to the dispute, to conciliation.

6. For the purpose of paragraph 5, a conciliation commission shall be created. The commission shall be composed of an equal number of members appointed by each party concerned or, where parties in conciliation share the same interest, by the group sharing that interest, and a chairman chosen jointly by the members so appointed. The commission shall render a recommendatory award, which the parties shall consider in good faith.

Article 10
Annexes

The annexes to the present Protocol shall form an integral part of the Protocol. Annexes I and IV are recommendatory in character.

Article 11
Amendments and Adjustments

1. Any Party may propose amendments to the present Protocol. Any Party to the Convention may propose an adjustment to annex II to the present Protocol to add to it its name, together with emission levels, sulphur emission ceilings and percentage emission reductions.

2. Such proposed amendments and adjustments shall be submitted in writing to the Executive Secretary of the Commission, who shall communicate them to all Parties. The Parties shall discuss the proposed amendments and adjustments at the next session of the Executive Body, provided that those proposals have been circulated by the Executive Secretary to the Parties at least ninety days in advance.

3. Amendments to the present Protocol and to its annexes II, III and V shall be adopted by consensus of the Parties present at a session of the Executive Body, and shall enter into force for the Parties which have accepted them on the ninetieth day after the date on which two-thirds of the Parties have deposited with the Depositary their instruments of acceptance thereof. Amendments shall enter into force for any other Party on the ninetieth day after the date on which that Party has deposited its instrument of acceptance thereof.

4. Amendments to the annexes to the present Protocol, other than to the annexes referred to in paragraph 3 above, shall be adopted by consensus of the Parties present at a session of the Executive Body. On the expiry of ninety days from the date of its communication by the Executive Secretary of the Commission, an amendment to any such annex shall become effective for those Parties which have not submitted to the Depositary a notification in accordance with the provisions of paragraph 5 below, provided that at least sixteen Parties have not submitted such a notification.

5. Any Party that is unable to approve an amendment to an annex, other than to an annex referred to in paragraph 3 above, shall so notify the Depositary in writing within ninety days from the date of the communication of its adoption. The Depositary shall without delay notify all Parties of any such notification received. A Party may at any time substitute an acceptance for its previous notification and, upon deposit of an instrument of acceptance with the Depositary, the amendment to such an annex shall become effective for that Party.

6. Adjustments to annex II shall be adopted by consensus of the Parties present at a session of the Executive Body and shall become effective for all

Parties to the present Protocol on the ninetieth day following the date on which the Executive Secretary of the Commission notifies those Parties in writing of the adoption of the adjustment.

Article 12
Signature

1. The present Protocol shall be open for signature at Oslo on 14 June 1994, then at United Nations Headquarters in New York until 12 December 1994 by States members of the Commission as well as States having consultative status with the Commission, pursuant to paragraph 8 of Economic and Social Council resolution 36 (IV) of 28 March 1947, and by regional economic integration organizations, constituted by sovereign States members of the Commission, which have competence in respect of the negotiation, conclusion and application of international agreements in matters covered by the Protocol, provided that the States and organizations concerned are Parties to the Convention and are listed in annex II.

2. In matters within their competence, such regional economic integration organizations shall, on their own behalf, exercise the rights and fulfil the responsibilities which the present Protocol attributes to their member States. In such cases, the member States of these organizations shall not be entitled to exercise such rights individually.

Article 13
Ratification, Acceptance, Approval and Accession

1. The present Protocol shall be subject to ratification, acceptance or approval by Signatories.

2. The present Protocol shall be open for accession as from 12 December 1994 by the States and organizations that meet the requirements of article 12, paragraph 1.

Article 14
Depositary

The instruments of ratification, acceptance, approval or accession shall be deposited with the Secretary-General of the United Nations, who will perform the functions of Depositary.

Article 15
Entry into Force

1. The present Protocol shall enter into force on the ninetieth day following the date on which the sixteenth instrument of ratification, acceptance, approval or accession has been deposited with the Depositary.

2. For each State and organization referred to in article 12, paragraph 1, which ratifies, accepts or approves the present Protocol or accedes thereto after the deposit of the sixteenth instrument of ratification, acceptance, approval or accession, the Protocol shall enter into force on the ninetieth

day following the date of deposit by such Party of its instrument of ratification, acceptance, approval or accession.

Article 16
Withdrawal

At any time after five years from the date on which the present Protocol has come into force with respect to a Party, that Party may withdraw from it by giving written notification to the Depositary. Any such withdrawal shall take effect on the ninetieth day following the date of its receipt by the Depositary, or on such later date as may be specified in the notification of the withdrawal.

Article 17
Authentic Texts

The original of the present Protocol, of which the English, French and Russian texts are equally authentic, shall be deposited with the Secretary-General of the United Nations.

In witness whereof the undersigned, being duly authorized thereto, have signed the present Protocol.

DONE at Oslo, this fourteenth day of June one thousand nine hundred and ninety-four.

[ANNEX I OMITTED]

Annex II

Sulphur Emission Ceilings and Percentage Emission Reductions

The sulphur emission ceilings listed in the table below give the obligations referred to in paragraphs 2 and 3 of article 2 of the present Protocol. The 1980 and 1990 emission levels and the percentage emission reductions listed are given for information purposes only.

	Emission levels kt SO_2 per year		Sulphur emission ceilings[1] kt SO_2 per year			Percentage emission reductions (base year 1980[2])		
	1980	1990	2000	2005	2010	2000	2005	2010
Austria	397	90	78			80		
Belarus	740		456	400	370	38	46	50
Belgium	828	443	248	232	215	70	72	74
Bulgaria	2,050	2,020	1,374	1,230	1,127	33	40	45

	Emission levels kt SO$_2$ per year		Sulphur emission ceilings[1] kt SO$_2$ per year			Percentage emission reductions[2] (base year 1980[2])		
	1980	1990	2000	2005	2010	2000	2005	2010
Canada—national	4,614	3,700	3,200			30		
—SOMA	3,245		1,750			46		
Croatia	150	160	133	125	117	11	17	22
Czech Republic	2,257	1,876	1,128	902	632	50	60	72
Denmark	451	180	90			80		
Finland	584	260	116			80		
France	3,348	1,202	868	770	737	74	77	78
Germany	7,494	5,803	1,300	990		83	87	
Greece	400	510	595	580	570	0	3	4
Hungary	1,632	1,010	898	816	653	45	50	60
Ireland	222	168	155			30		
Italy	3,800		1,330	1,042		65	73	
Liechtenstein	0.4	0.1	0.1			75		
Luxembourg	24		10			58		
Netherlands	466	207	106			77		
Norway	142	54	34			76		
Poland	4,100	3,210	2,583	2,173	1,397	37	47	66
Portugal	266	284	304	294		0	3	
Russian Federation[3]	7,161	4,460	4,440	4,297	4,297	38	40	40
Slovakia	843	539	337	295	240	60	65	72
Slovenia	235	195	130	94	71	45	60	70
Spain	3,319	2,316	2,143			35		
Sweden	507	130	100			80		
Switzerland	126	62	66			52		
Ukraine	3,850		2,310			40		
United Kingdom	4,898	3,780	2,449	1,470	980	50	70	80
European Community	25,513		9,598			62		

[1] If, in a given year before 2005, a Party finds that, due to a particularly cold winter, a particularly dry summer and an unforeseen short-term loss of capacity in the power supply system, domestically or in a neighbouring country, it cannot comply with its obligations under this annex, it may fulfil those obligations by averaging its national annual sulphur emissions for the year in question, the year preceding that year and the year following it, provided that the emission level in any single year is not more than 20% above the sulphur emission ceiling.

The reason for exceedance in any given year and the method by which the three-year average figure will be achieved, shall be reported to the Implementation Committee.

[2] For Greece and Portugal percentage emission reductions given are based on the sulphur emission ceilings indicated for the year 2000.

[3] European part within the EMEP area.

Annex III

Designation of Sulphur Oxides Management Areas (SOMAs)

The following SOMA is listed for the purposes of the present Protocol:
South-east Canada SOMA
This is an area of 1 million km² which includes all the territory of the provinces of Prince Edward Island, Nova Scotia and New Brunswick, all the territory of the province of Quebec south of a straight line between Havre-St. Pierre on the north coast of the Gulf of Saint Lawrence and the point where the Quebec-Ontario boundary intersects the James Bay coastline, and all the territory of the province of Ontario south of a straight line between the point where the Ontario-Quebec boundary intersects the James Bay coastline and Nipigon River near the north shore of Lake Superior.

[ANNEXES IV AND V OMITTED]

5. NUCLEAR RISKS

Convention on Early Notification of a Nuclear Accident, Vienna,
26 September 1986

This Convention, adopted shortly after the Chernobyl reactor accident, imposes on parties a duty to notify other states likely to be affected by transboundary releases of 'radiological safety significance' so as to enable them to take all possible precautionary measures. In addition to the practice of states supporting such an obligation, and reflected in a number of bilateral agreements, IAEA had developed guidelines on reporting of incidents and information exchange in 1985, but these were non-binding: IAEA/INFCIRC/321: Guidelines on Reportable Events, etc. A number of states, including the Soviet Union and the United Kingdom, applied the 1986 Convention provisionally pending ratification, and several agreements apply its provisions bilaterally. Despite the looseness of its terminology and the range of excluded occurrences, the Convention does seem to justify the conclusion that the principle of timely notification is a customary obligation. The same principle has also been applied in the case of accidents affecting nuclear powered merchant ships or spacecraft.

The Convention entered into force on 27 October 1986 and had sixty-eight parties on 1 January 1995. For text see 25 *ILM* (1986) 1377; Misc. 3 (1989), Cm. 566. Reservations are not prohibited. For reservations or declarations made on signature or ratification see UN, *Multilateral Treaties Deposited with the Secretary-General*, UN Doc. ST/LEG/SER. E/(Current year). See generally P. W. Birnie and A. E. Boyle, *International Law and the Environment* (Oxford, 1992), 364ff; P. Cameron, et al, *Nuclear Energy Law* (London, 1988), 19ff; A. Adede, The *IAEA Notification and Assistance Conventions* (Dordrecht, 1987); G. Handl, 'Transboundary Nuclear Accidents: the Post-Chernobyl Multilateral Legislative Agenda', 15 *Ecol. LQ* (1988) 203.

TEXT

The States Parties to This Convention,

Aware that nuclear activities are being carried out in a number of States,

Noting that comprehensive measures have been and are being taken to ensure a high revel of safety in nuclear activities, aimed at preventing nuclear accidents and minimizing the consequences of any such accident, should it occur,

Desiring to strengthen further international co-operation in the safe development and use of nuclear energy,

Convinced of the need for States to provide relevant information about nuclear accidents as early as possible in order that transboundary radiological consequences can be minimized,

Noting the usefulness of bilateral and multilateral arrangements on information exchange in this area,

Have Agreed as follows:

Article 1
Scope of application

1. This Convention shall apply in the event of any accident involving facilities or activities of a State Party or of persons or legal entities under its jurisdiction or control, referred to in paragraph 2 below, from which a release of radioactive material occurs or is likely to occur and has resulted or may result in an international transboundary release that could be of radiological safety significance for another State.

2. The facilities and activities referred to in paragraph 1 are the following:

(a) any nuclear reactor wherever located;
(b) any nuclear fuel cycle facility;
(c) any radioactive waste management facility;
(d) the transport and storage of nuclear fuels or radioactive wastes;
(e) the manufacture, use, storage, disposal and transport of radioisotopes for agricultural, industrial, medical and related scientific and research purposes; and
(f) the use of radioisotopes for power generation in space objects.

Article 2
Notification and information

In the event of an accident specified in article 1 (hereinafter referred to as a 'nuclear accident'), the State Party referred to in that article shall:

(a) forthwith notify, directly or through the International Atomic Energy Agency (hereinafter referred to as the 'Agency'), those States which are or may be physically affected as specified in article 1 and the Agency of the nuclear accident, its nature, the time of its occurrence and its exact location where appropriate; and
(b) promptly provide the States referred to in sub-paragraph (a), directly or through the Agency, and the Agency with such available information relevant to minimizing the radiological consequences in those States, as specified in article 5.

Article 3
Other nuclear accidents

With a view to minimizing the radiological consequences, States Parties may notify in the event of nuclear accidents other than those specified in article 1.

Article 4
Functions of the Agency

The Agency shall:

(a) forthwith inform States Parties, Member States, other States which are or may be physically affected as specified in article 1 and relevant international intergovernmental organizations (hereinafter referred to as 'international organizations') of a notification received pursuant to sub-paragraph (a) of article 2; and

(b) promptly provide any State Party, Member State or relevant international organization, upon request, with the information received pursuant to sub-paragraph (b) of article 2.

Article 5
Information to be provided

1. The information to be provided pursuant to sub-paragraph (b) of article 2 shall comprise the following data as then available to the notifying State Party:

(a) the time, exact location where appropriate, and the nature of the nuclear accident;

(b) the facility or activity involved;

(c) the assumed or established cause and the foreseeable development of the nuclear accident relevant to the transboundary release of the radioactive materials;

(d) the general characteristics of the radioactive release, including, as far as is practicable and appropriate, the nature, probable physical and chemical form and the quantity, composition and effective height of the radioactive release;

(e) information on current and forecast meteorological and hydrological conditions, necessary for forecasting the transboundary release of the radioactive materials;

(f) the results of environmental monitoring relevant to the transboundary release of the radioactive materials;

(g) the off-site protective measures taken or planned;

(h) the predicted behaviour over time of the radioactive release.

2. Such information shall be supplemented at appropriate intervals by further relevant information on the development of the emergency situation, including its foreseeable or actual termination.

3. Information received pursuant to sub-paragraph (b) of article 2 may be used without restriction, except when such information is provided in confidence by the notifying State Party.

Article 6
Consultations

A State Party providing information pursuant to sub-paragraph (b) of article 2 shall, as far as is reasonably practicable, respond promptly to a request for further information or consultations sought by an affected State Party with a view to minimizing the radiological consequences in that State.

Article 7
Competent authorities and points of contact

1. Each State Party shall make known to the Agency and to other States Parties, directly or through the Agency, its competent authorities and point of contact responsible for issuing and receiving the notification and information referred to in article 2. Such points of contact and a focal point within the Agency shall be available continuously.

2. Each State Party shall promptly inform the Agency of any changes that may occur in the information referred to in paragraph 1.

3. The Agency shall maintain an up-to-date list of such national authorities and points of contact as well as points of contact of relevant international organizations and shall provide it to States Parties and Member States and to relevant international organizations.

Article 8
Assistance to States Parties

The Agency shall, in accordance with its Statute and upon a request of a State Party which does not have nuclear activities itself and borders on a State having an active nuclear programme but not Party, conduct investigations into the feasibility and establishment of an appropriate radiation monitoring system in order to facilitate the achievement of the objectives of this Convention.

Article 9
Bilateral and multilateral arrangements

In furtherance of their mutual interests, States Parties may consider, where deemed appropriate, the conclusion of bilateral or multilateral arrangements relating to the subject matter of this Convention.

Article 10
Relationship to other international agreements

This Convention shall not affect the reciprocal rights and obligations of States Parties under existing international agreements which relate to the matters covered by this Convention, or under future international agreements concluded in accordance with the object and purpose of this Convention.

Article 11
Settlement of disputes

1. In the event of a dispute between States Parties, or between a State Party and the Agency, concerning the interpretation or application of this Convention, the parties to the dispute shall consult with a view to the settlement of the dispute by negotiation or by any other peaceful means of settling disputes acceptable to them.

2. If a dispute of this character between States Parties cannot be settled within one year from the request for consultation pursuant to paragraph 1, it shall, at the request of any party to such dispute, by submitted to arbitration or referred to the International Court of Justice for decision. Where a dispute is submitted to arbitration, if, within six months from the date of the request, the parties to the dispute are unable to agree on the organization of the arbitration, a party may request the President of the International Court of Justice or the Secretary-General of the United Nations to appoint one or more arbitrators. In cases of conflicting requests by the parties to the dispute, the request to the Secretary-General of the United Nations shall have priority.

3. When signing, ratifying, accepting, approving or acceding to this Convention, a State may declare that it does not consider itself bound by either or both of the dispute settlement procedures provided for in paragraph 2. The other States Parties shall not be bound by a dispute settlement procedure provided for in paragraph 2 with respect to a State Party for which such a declaration is in force.

4. A State Party which has made a declaration in accordance with paragraph 3 may at any time withdraw it by notification to the depositary.

Article 12
Entry into force

1. This Convention shall be open for signature by all States and Namibia, represented by the United Nations Council for Namibia, at the Headquarters of the International Atomic Energy Agency in Vienna and at the Headquarters of the United Nations in New York, from 26 September 1986 and 6 October 1986 respectively, until its entry into force or for twelve months, whichever period is longer.

2. A State and Namibia, represented by the United Nations Council for Namibia, may express its consent to be bound by this Convention either by signature, or by deposit of an instrument of ratification, acceptance or approval following signature made subject of ratification, acceptance or approval, or by deposit of an instrument of accession. The instruments of ratification, acceptance, approval or accession shall be deposited with the depositary.

3. This Convention shall enter into force thirty days after consent to be bound has been expressed by three States.

4. For each State expressing consent to be bound by this Convention after its entry into force, this Convention shall enter into force for that State thirty days after the date of expression of consent.

5. (a) This Convention shall be open for accession, as provided for in this article, by international organizations and regional integration organizations constituted by sovereign States, which have competence in respect of the negotiation, conclusion and application of

international agreements in matters covered by this Convention.

(b) In matters within their competence such organizations shall, on their own behalf, exercise the rights and fulfil the obligations which this Convention attributes to States Parties.

(c) When depositing its instrument of accession, such an organization shall communicate to the depositary a declaration indicating the extent of its competence in respect of matters covered by this Convention.

(d) Such an organization shall not hold any vote additional to those of its Member States.

Article 13
Provisional application

A State may, upon signature or at any later date before this Convention enters into force for it, declare that it will apply this Convention provisionally.

Article 14
Amendments

1. A State Party may propose amendments to this Convention. The proposed amendment shall be submitted to the depositary who shall circulate it immediately to all other States Parties.

2. If a majority of the States Parties request the depositary to convene a conference to consider the proposed amendments, the depositary shall invite all States Parties to attend such a conference to begin not sooner than thirty days after the invitations are issued. Any amendment adopted at the conference by a two-thirds majority of all States Parties shall be laid down in a protocol which is open to signature in Vienna and New York by all States Parties.

3. The protocol shall enter into force thirty days after consent to be bound has been expressed by three States. For each State expressing consent to be bound by the protocol after its entry into force, the protocol shall enter into force for that State thirty days after the date of expression of consent.

Article 15
Denunciation

1. A State Party may denounce this Convention by written notification to the depositary.

2. Denunciation shall take effect one year following the date on which the notification is received by the depositary.

Article 16
Depositary

1. The Director General of the Agency shall be the depositary of this Convention.

2. The Director General of the Agency shall promptly notify States Parties and all other States of:

(a) each signature of this Convention or any protocol of amendment;
(b) each deposit of an instrument of ratification, acceptance, approval or accession concerning this Convention or any protocol of amendment;
(c) any declaration or withdrawal thereof in accordance with article 11;
(d) any declaration of provisional application of this Convention in accordance with article 13;
(e) the entry into force of this Convention and of any amendment thereto; and
(f) any denunciation made under article 15.

Article 17
Authentic texts and certified copies

The original of this Convention, of which the Arabic, Chinese, English, French, Russian and Spanish texts are equally authentic, shall be deposited with the Director General of the International Atomic Energy Agency who shall send certified copies to States Parties and all other States.

IN WITNESS WHEREOF the undersigned, being duly authorized, have signed this Convention, open for signature as provided for in paragraph 1 of article 12.

ADOPTED by the General Conference of the International Atomic Energy Agency meeting in special session at Vienna on the twenty-sixth day of September one thousand nine hundred and eighty-six.

Convention on Nuclear Safety, Vienna, 17 June 1994

Negotiation of a Nuclear Safety Convention was authorized in 1991 by IAEA General Conference resolution GC (XXXV)/RES/553 and UNGA Resolution 46/16. Following the recommendations of an Expert Group convened by the IAEA Director General, the Convention does not require parties to adopt any of the relevant IAEA Safety Standards nor does it take the form of a framework convention with provision for further regulatory protocols. Instead it affirms that 'responsibility for nuclear safety rests with the State having jurisdiction over a nuclear installation' and requires each party to establish and maintain a national legislative and regulatory framework for the safety of nuclear installations, including a system of licensing and inspection. Parties are also required to take 'appropriate' steps with regard to human factors, quality assurance, assessment, radiation protection, emergency preparedness, siting, design, construction, and operation of installations. Reports on implementation measures are reviewed by meetings of the contracting parties. Reservations are not prohibited. The Convention requires twenty-two parties for entry into force, including seventeen with at least one nuclear installation. It does not affect the existing limited regulatory powers which IAEA possesses with respect to certain installations under its Statute.

The Convention is *repr.* 33 *ILM* (1994) 1518 and IAEA/INFCIRC 449 (1994). For background information see IAEA/GOV/2567 and IAEA/GOV/INF/723. An annex to the Final Act contains clarifications on various matters, *repr.* IAEA/INFCIRC/449/Add. 1, Attachment, Annex and 33 *ILM* (1994) 1525. Fifty-two states had signed by November 15 1994. See also 1980 Convention on Physical Protection of Nuclear Material, 18 *ILM* (1979) 1419; 1986 Convention on Assistance in the Case of a Nuclear Accident or Radiological Emergency, 25 *ILM* (1986) 1377. See generally P. W. Birnie and A. E. Boyle, *International Law and the Environment* (Oxford, 1992) Ch. 9; L. de la Fayette, 'International Environmental Law and the Problem of Nuclear Safety', 5 *JEL* (1993) 31; G. Handl, 'Transboundary Nuclear Accidents: the Post-Chernobyl Multilateral Legislative Agenda', 15 *Ecol. LQ* (1988) 203; M. T. Kamminga, The IAEA Convention on Nuclear Safety, 44 *ICLQ* (1995), pt. 4.

TEXT

Preamble

The Contracting Parties

(i) *Aware* of the importance to the international community of ensuring that the use of nuclear energy is safe, well regulated and environmentally sound;

(ii) *Reaffirming* the necessity of continuing to promote a high level of nuclear safety worldwide;

(iii) *Reaffirming* that responsibility for nuclear safety rests with the State having jurisdiction over a nuclear installation;

(iv) *Desiring* to promote an effective nuclear safety culture;

(v) *Aware* that accidents at nuclear installations have the potential for transboundary impacts;

(vi) *Keeping in mind* the Convention on the Physical Protection of Nuclear Material (1979), the Convention on Early Notification of a Nuclear Accident (1986), and the Convention on Assistance in the Case of a Nuclear Accident or Radiological Emergency (1986);

(vii) *Affirming* the importance of international co-operation for the enhancement of nuclear safety through existing bilateral and multilateral mechanisms and the establishment of this incentive Convention;

(viii) *Recognizing* that this Convention entails a commitment to the application of fundamental safety principles for nuclear installations rather than of detailed safety standards and that there are internationally formulated safety guidelines which are updated from time to time and so can provide guidance on contemporary means of achieving a high level of safety;

(ix) *Affirming* the need to begin promptly the development of an international convention on the safety of radioactive waste management as soon as the ongoing process to develop waste management safety fundamentals has resulted in broad international agreement;

(x) *Recognizing* the usefulness of further technical work in connection with the safety of other parts of the nuclear fuel cycle, and that this work may, in time, facilitate the development of current or future international instruments;

Have Agreed as follows:

Chapter 1. Objectives, Definitions and Scope of Application

Article 1
Objectives

The objectives of this Convention are:

(i) to achieve and maintain a high level of nuclear safety worldwide through the enhancement of national measures and international co-operation including, where appropriate, safety-related technical co-operation;

(ii) to establish and maintain effective defences in nuclear installations against potential radiological hazards in order to protect individuals, society and the environment from harmful effects of ionizing radiation from such installations;

(iii) to prevent accidents with radiological consequences and to mitigate such consequences should they occur.

Article 2
Definitions

For the purpose of this Convention:

(i) 'nuclear installation' means for each Contracting Party any land-based civil nuclear power plant under its jurisdiction including such storage, handling and treatment facilities for radioactive materials as are on the same site and are directly related to the operation of the nuclear power plant. Such a plant ceases to be a nuclear installation when all nuclear fuel elements have been removed permanently from the reactor core and have been stored safely in accordance with approved procedures, and a decommissioning programme has been agreed to by the regulatory body.

(ii) 'regulatory body' means for each Contracting Party any body or bodies given the legal authority by that Contracting Party to grant licences and to regulate the siting, design, design, construction, commissioning, operation or decommissioning of nuclear installations.

(iii) 'licence' means any authorization granted by the regulatory body to the applicant to have the responsibility for the siting, design, construction, commissioning, operation or decommissioning of a nuclear installation.

Article 3
Scope of Application

This Convention shall apply to the safety of nuclear installations.

Chapter 2. Obligations
(a) General Provisions

Article 4
Implementing Measures

Each Contracting Party shall take, within the framework of its national law, the legislative, regulatory and administrative measures and other steps necessary for implementing its obligations under this Convention.

Article 5
Reporting

Each Contracting Party shall submit for review, prior to each meeting referred to in Article 20, a report on the measures it has taken to implement each of the obligations of this Convention.

Article 6
Existing Nuclear Installations

Each Contracting Party shall take the appropriate steps to ensure that the safety of nuclear installations existing at the time the Convention enters into force for that Contracting Party is reviewed as soon as possible. When necessary in the context of this Convention, the Contracting Party shall ensure that all reasonably practicable improvements are made as a matter of urgency to upgrade the safety of the nuclear installation. If such upgrading cannot be achieved, plans should be implemented to shut down the nuclear installation as soon as practically possible. The timing of the shut-down may take into account the whole energy context and possible alternatives as well as the social, environmental and economic impact.

(b) Legislation and regulation

Article 7
Legislative and Regulatory Framework

1. Each Contracting Party shall establish and maintain a legislative and regulatory framework to govern the safety of nuclear installations.

2. The legislative and regulatory framework shall provide for:

   (i) the establishment of applicable national safety requirements and regulations;
   (ii) a system of licensing with regard to nuclear installations and the prohibition of the operation of a nuclear installation without a licence;
   (iii) a system of regulatory inspection and assessment of nuclear installations to ascertain compliance with applicable regulations and the terms of licences;
   (iv) the enforcement of applicable regulations and of the terms of licences, including suspension, modification or revocation.

Article 8
Regulatory Body

1. Each Contracting Party shall establish or designate a regulatory body entrusted with the implementation of the legislative and regulatory framework referred to in Article 7, and provided with adequate authority, competence and financial and human resources to fulfil its assigned responsibilities.

2. Each Contracting Party shall take the appropriate steps to ensure an effective separation between the functions of the regulatory body and those

of any other body or organization concerned with the promotion or utiliz-ation of nuclear energy.

Article 9
Responsibility of the Licence Holder

Each Contracting Party shall ensure that prime responsibility for the safety of a nuclear installation rests with the holder of the relevant licence and shall take the appropriate steps to ensure that each such licence holder meets its responsibility.

(c) General Safety Considerations

Article 10
Priority to Safety

Each Contracting Party shall take the appropriate steps to ensure that all organizations engaged in activities directly related to nuclear installations shall establish policies that give due priority to nuclear safety.

Article 11
Financial and Human Resources

1. Each Contracting Party shall take the appropriate steps to ensure that adequate financial resources are available to support the safety of each nuclear installation throughout its life.
2. Each Contracting Party shall take the appropriate steps to ensure that sufficient numbers of qualified staff with appropriate education, training and retraining are available for all safety-related activities in or for each nuclear installation, throughout its life.

Article 12
Human Factors

Each Contracting Party shall take the appropriate steps to ensure that the capabilities and limitations of human performance are taken into account throughout the life of a nuclear installation.

Article 13
Quality Assurance

Each Contracting Party shall take the appropriate steps to ensure that quality assurance programmes are established and implemented with a view to providing confidence that specified requirements for all activities important to nuclear safety are satisfied throughout the life of a nuclear installation.

Article 14
Assessment and Verification of Safety

Each Contracting Party shall take the appropriate steps to ensure that:

(i) comprehensive and systematic safety assessments are carried out before the construction and commissioning of a nuclear installation and throughout its life. Such assessments shall be well documented, subsequently updated in the light of operating experience and significant new safety information, and reviewed under the authority of the regulatory body;

(ii) verification by analysis, surveillance, testing and inspection is carried out to ensure that the physical state and the operation of a nuclear installation continue to be in accordance with its design, applicable national safety requirements, and operational limits and conditions.

Article 15
Radiation Protection

Each Contracting Party shall take the appropriate steps to ensure that in all operational states the radiation exposure to the workers and the public caused by a nuclear installation shall be kept as low as reasonably achievable and that no individual shall be exposed to radiation doses which exceed prescribed national dose limits.

Article 16
Emergency Preparedness

1. Each Contracting Party shall take the appropriate steps to ensure that there are on-site and off-site emergency plans that are routinely tested for nuclear installations and cover the activities to be carried out in the event of an emergency.
For any new nuclear installation, such plans shall be prepared and tested before it commences operation above a low power level agreed by the regulatory body.

2. Each Contracting Party shall take the appropriate steps to ensure that, insofar as they are likely to be affected by a radiological emergency, its own population and the competent authorities of the States in the vicinity of the nuclear installation are provided with appropriate information for emergency planning and response.

3. Contracting Parties which do not have a nuclear installation on their territory, insofar as they are likely to be affected in the event of a radiological emergency at a nuclear installation in the vicinity, shall take the appropriate steps for the preparation and testing of emergency plans for their territory that cover the activities to be carried out in the event of such an emergency.

(d) Safety of Installations

Article 17
Siting

Each Contracting Party shall take the appropriate steps to ensure that appropriate procedures are established and implemented:

  (i) for evaluating all relevant site-related factors likely to affect the safety of a nuclear installation for its projected lifetime;

  (ii) for evaluating the likely safety impact of a proposed nuclear installation on individuals, society and the environment;

  (iii) for re-evaluating as necessary all relevant factors referred to in subparagraphs (i) and (ii) so as to ensure the continued safety acceptability of the nuclear installation;

  (iv) for consulting Contracting Parties in the vicinity of a proposed nuclear installation, insofar as they are likely to be affected by that installation and, upon request providing the necessary information to such Contracting Parties, in order to enable them to evaluate and make their own assessment of the likely safety impact on their own territory of the nuclear installation.

Article 18
Design and Construction

Each Contracting Party shall take the appropriate steps to ensure that:

  (i) the design and construction of a nuclear installation provides for several reliable levels and methods of protection (defense in depth) against the release of radioactive materials, with a view to preventing the occurrence of accidents and to mitigating their radiological consequences should they occur;

  (ii) the technologies incorporated in the design and construction of a nuclear installation are proven by experience or qualified by testing or analysis;

  (iii) the design of a nuclear installation allows for reliable, stable and easily manageable operation, with specific consideration of human factors and the man-machine interface.

Article 19
Operation

Each Contracting Party shall take the appropriate steps to ensure that:

  (i) the initial authorization to operate a nuclear installation is based upon an appropriate safety analysis and a commissioning programme demonstrating that the installation, as constructed, is consistent with design and safety requirements;

(ii)   operational limits and conditions derived from the safety analysis, tests and operational experience are defined and revised as necessary for identifying safe boundaries for operation;

(iii)   operation, maintenance, inspection and testing of a nuclear installation are conducted in accordance with approved procedures;

(iv)   procedures are established for responding to anticipated operational occurrences and to accidents;

(v)   necessary engineering and technical support in all safety-related fields is available throughout the lifetime of a nuclear installation;

(vi)   incidents significant to safety are reported in a timely manner by the holder of the relevant licence to the regulatory body;

(vii)   programmes to collect and analyse operating experience are established, the results obtained and the conclusions drawn are acted upon and that existing mechanisms are used to share important experience with international bodies and with other operating organizations and regulatory bodies;

(viii) the generation of radioactive waste resulting from the operation of a nuclear installation is kept to the minimum practicable for the process concerned, both in activity and in volume, and any necessary treatment and storage of spent fuel and waste directly related to the operation and on the same site as that of the nuclear installation take into consideration conditioning and disposal.

Chapter 3. Meetings of the Contracting Parties

Article 20
Review Meetings

1. The Contracting Parties shall hold meetings (hereinafter referred to as 'review meetings') for the purpose of reviewing the reports submitted pursuant to Article 5 in accordance with the procedures adopted under Article 22.

2. Subject to the provisions of Article 24 sub-groups comprised of representatives of Contracting Parties may be established and may function during the review meetings as deemed necessary for the purpose of reviewing specific subjects contained in the reports.

3. Each Contracting Party shall have a reasonable opportunity to discuss the reports submitted by other Contracting Parties and to seek clarification of such reports.

Article 21
Timetable

1. A preparatory meeting of the Contracting Parties shall be held not later than six months after the date of entry into force of this Convention.

2. At this preparatory meeting, the Contracting Parties shall determine the date for the first review meeting. This review meeting shall be held as soon as possible, but not later than thirty months after the date of entry into force of this Convention.

3. At each review meeting, the Contracting Parties shall determine the date for the next such meeting. The interval between review meetings shall not exceed three years.

Article 22
Procedural Arrangements

1. At the preparatory meeting held pursuant to Article 21 the Contracting Parties shall prepare and adopt by consensus Rules of Procedure and Financial Rules. The Contracting Parties shall establish in particular and in accordance with the Rules of Procedure:

   (i) guidelines regarding the form and structure of the reports to be submitted pursuant to Article 5;

  (ii) a date for the submission of such reports;

 (iii) the process for reviewing such reports.

2. At review meetings the Contracting Parties may, if necessary, review the arrangements established pursuant to sub-paragraphs (i)–(iii) above, and adopt revisions by consensus unless otherwise provided for in the Rules of Procedure. They may also amend the Rules of Procedure and the Financial Rules, by consensus.

Article 23
Extraordinary Meetings

An extraordinary meeting of the Contracting Parties shall be held:

   (i) if so agreed by a majority of the Contracting Parties present and voting at a meeting, abstentions being considered as voting; or

  (ii) at the written request of a Contracting Party, within six months of this request having been communicated to the Contracting Parties and notification having been received by the secretariat referred to in Article 28, that the request has been supported by a majority of the Contracting Parties.

Article 24
Attendance

1. Each Contracting Party shall attend meetings of the Contracting Parties and be represented at such meetings by one delegate, and by such alternates, experts and advisers as it deems necessary.

2. The Contracting Parties may invite, by consensus, any intergovernmental organization which is competent in respect of matters governed by this Convention to attend, as an observer, any meeting, or specific sessions

thereof. Observers shall be required to accept in writing, and in advance, the provisions of Article 27.

Article 25
Summary Reports

The Contracting Parties shall adopt, by consensus, and make available to the public a document addressing issues discussed and conclusions reached during a meeting.

Article 26
Languages

1. The languages of meetings of the Contracting Parties shall be Arabic, Chinese, English, French, Russian and Spanish unless otherwise provided in the Rules of Procedure.

2. Reports submitted pursuant to Article 5 shall be prepared in the national language of the submitting Contracting Party or in a single designated language to be agreed in the Rules of Procedure. Should the report be submitted in a national language other than the designated language, a translation of the report into the designated language shall be provided by the Contracting Party.

3. Notwithstanding the provisions of paragraph 2, if compensated, the secretariat will assume the translation into the designated language of reports submitted in any other language of the meeting.

Article 27
Confidentiality

1. The provisions of this Convention shall not affect the rights and obligations of the Contracting Parties under their law to protect information from disclosure. For the purposes of this Article, 'information' includes, *inter alia,* (i) personal data; (ii) information protected by intellectual property rights or by industrial or commercial confidentiality; and (iii) information relating to national security or to the physical protection of nuclear materials or nuclear installations.

2. When, in the context of this Convention, a Contracting Party provides information identified by it as protected as described in paragraph 1, such information shall be used only for the purposes for which it has been provided and its confidentiality shall be respected.

3. The content of the debates during the reviewing of the reports by the Contracting Parties at each meeting shall be confidential.

Article 28
Secretariat

1. The International Atomic Energy Agency, (hereinafter referred to as the 'Agency') shall provide the secretariat for the meetings of the Contracting Parties.

2. The secretariat shall:

    (i) convene, prepare and service the meetings of the Contracting Parties;

    (ii) transmit to the Contracting Parties information received or prepared in accordance with the provisions of this Convention.

The costs incurred by the Agency in carrying out the functions referred to in sub-paragraphs (i) and (ii) above shall be borne by the Agency as part of its regular budget.

3. The Contracting Parties may, by consensus, request the Agency to provide other services in support of meetings of the Contracting Parties. The Agency may provide such services if they can be undertaken within its programme and regular budget. Should this not be possible, the Agency may provide such services if voluntary funding is provided from another source.

Chapter 4. Final Clauses and Other Provisions

Article 29
Resolution of Disagreements

In the event of a disagreement between two or more Contracting Parties concerning the interpretation or application of this Convention, the Contracting Parties shall consult within the framework of a meeting of the Contracting Parties with a view to resolving the disagreement.

Article 30
Signature, Ratification, Acceptance, Approval, Accession

1. This Convention shall be open for signature by all States at the Headquarters of the Agency in Vienna from 20 September 1994 until its entry into force.

2. This Convention is subject to ratification, acceptance or approval by the signatory States.

3. After its entry into force, this Convention shall be open for accession by all States.

4. (i) This Convention shall be open for signature or accession by regional organizations of an integration or other nature, provided that any such organization is constituted by sovereign States and has competence in respect of the negotiation, conclusion and application of international agreements in matters covered by this Convention.

    (ii) In matters within their competence, such organizations shall, on their own behalf, exercise the rights and fulfil the responsibilities which this Convention attributes to States Parties.

(iii) When becoming party to this Convention, such an organization shall communicate to the Depositary referred to in Article 34, a declaration indicating which States are members thereof, which articles of this Convention apply to it, and the extent of its competence in the field covered by those articles.

(iv) Such an organization shall not hold any vote additional to those of its Member States.

5. Instruments of ratification, acceptance, approval or accession shall be deposited with the Depositary.

Article 31
Entry into Force

1. This Convention shall enter into force on the ninetieth day after the date of deposit with the Depositary of the twenty-second instrument of ratification, acceptance or approval, including the instruments of seventeen States, each having at least one nuclear installation which has achieved criticality in a reactor core.

2. For each State or regional organization of an integration or other nature which ratifies, accepts, approves or accedes to this Convention after the date of deposit of the last instrument required to satisfy the conditions set forth in paragraph 1, this Convention shall enter into force on the ninetieth day after the date of deposit with the Depositary of the appropriate instrument by such a State or organization.

Article 32
Amendments to the Convention

1. Any Contracting Party may propose an amendment to this Convention. Proposed amendments shall be considered at a review meeting or an extraordinary meeting.

2. The text of any proposed amendment and the reasons for it shall be provided to the Depositary who shall communicate the proposal to the Contracting Parties promptly and at least ninety days before the meeting for which it is submitted for consideration. Any comments received on such a proposal shall be circulated by the Depositary to the Contracting Parties.

3. The Contracting Parties shall decide after consideration of the proposed amendment whether to adopt it by consensus, or, in the absence of consensus, to submit it to a Diplomatic Conference. A decision to submit a proposed amendment to a Diplomatic Conference shall require a two-thirds majority vote of the Contracting Parties present and voting at the meeting, provided that at least one half of the Contracting Parties are present at the time of voting. Abstentions shall be considered as voting.

4. The Diplomatic Conference to consider and adopt amendments to this

Convention shall be convened by the Depositary and held no later than one year after the appropriate decision taken in accordance with paragraph 3 of this Article. The Diplomatic Conference shall make every effort to ensure amendments are adopted by consensus. Should this not be possible, amendments shall be adopted with a two-thirds majority of all Contracting Parties.

5. Amendments to this Convention adopted pursuant to paragraphs 3 and 4 above shall be subject to ratification, acceptance, approval, or confirmation by the Contracting Parties and shall enter into force for those Contracting Parties which have ratified, accepted, approved or confirmed them on the ninetieth day after the receipt by the Depositary of the relevant instruments by at least three-fourths of the Contracting Parties. For a Contracting Party which subsequently ratifies, accepts, approves or confirms the said amendments, the amendments will enter into force on the ninetieth day after that Contracting Party has deposited its relevant instrument.

Article 33
Denunciation

1. Any Contracting Party may denounce this Convention by written notification to the Depositary.

2. Denunciation shall take effect one year following the date of the receipt of the notification by the Depositary, or on such later date as may be specified in the notification.

Article 34
Depositary

1. The Director General of the Agency shall be the Depositary of this Convention.

2. The Depositary shall inform the Contracting Parties of:

   (i) the signature of this Convention and of the deposit of instruments of ratification, acceptance, approval or accession, in accordance with Article 30;
   (ii) the date on which the Convention enters into force, in accordance with Article 31;
   (iii) the notifications of denunciation of the Convention and the date thereof, made in accordance with Article 33;
   (iv) the proposed amendments to this Convention submitted by Contracting Parties, the amendments adopted by the relevant Diplomatic Conference or by the meeting of the Contracting Parties, and the date of entry into force of the said amendments, in accordance with Article 32.

Article 35
Authentic Texts

The original of this Convention of which the Arabic, Chinese, English, French, Russian and Spanish texts are equally authentic, shall be deposited with the Depositary, who shall send certified copies thereof to the Contracting Parties.

Annex to the Final Act of the Diplomatic Conference
Some Clarification with Respect to Procedural and Financial
Arrangements, National Reports and the Conduct of Review Meetings,
Envisaged in the Convention on Nuclear Safety

1. Introduction

1.1 This document contains come clarification with respect to procedural and financial arrangements, national reports and the conduct of review meetings. It is understood that this document is not exhaustive and does not bind the Contracting Parties to the Convention on Nuclear Safety.

1.2 The basic principle underlying this clarification is that all provisions in the Rules of Procedure and the Financial Rules should be in strict conformity with the provisions of the Convention.

1.3 Nothing in the implementation of the Convention should dilute the national responsibility for nuclear safety.

2. National reports

In accordance with Article 5 of the Convention, national reports should, as applicable, address each obligation separately. The reports should demonstrate how each obligation has been met, with specific references to—*inter alia*—legislation, procedures and design criteria. When a report states that a particular obligation has not been met, that report should also state what measures are being taken or planned to meet that obligation.

3. Conduct of review meetings

The purpose of review meetings referred to in Article 20 of the Convention is the review by experts of national reports. The review process should:

• include in-depth study of all national reports, to be conducted by each party before the meeting, as it deems appropriate;
• be carried out through discussion among experts at the meeting;
• take into consideration the technical characteristics of different types of nuclear installation and the likely radiological impact of potential accidents;

- identify problems, concerns, uncertainties, or omissions in national reports, focusing on the most significant problems or concerns in order to ensure efficient and fruitful debate at the meetings; and
- identify technical information and opportunities for technical cooperation in the interest of resolving safety problems identified.

4. Rules of Procedure for the meeting of the Parties

4.1 Equitable representation: Paramount importance should be given to technical competence in the election of chairmen and officers. Consideration should also be given to the overall membership of the Convention, including the geographical distribution of the Contracting Parties.

4.2 Decision-making: Every effort should be made to take decisions by consensus.

4.3 Confidentiality: The Rules of Procedure should be formulated so as to ensure that the provisions of Article 27 are applied to all participants.

5. Financial rules

5.1 Costs to the secretariat: All costs to the secretariat, referred to in Article 28 of the Convention, should be kept to a minimum. The Agency should be requested to provide other services in support of the meeting of the Contracting Parties, only if such services are deemed essential.

5.2 Costs to the Contracting Parties: In order to encourage the widest possible adherence to the Convention, the costs of preparing for and participating in review meetings should, while maintaining the effectiveness of the review, be limited by—*inter alia*—the following means:

- limiting the frequency of review meetings; and
- limiting the duration of the preparatory meeting and of review meetings.

6. TRADE IN HAZARDOUS WASTES AND SUBSTANCES

Convention on the Control of Transboundary Movements of Hazardous
Wastes and their Disposal, Basel, 22 March 1989

This is a global convention developed by UNEP and intended to minimize and
control international trade in hazardous waste. It places on exporting and importing states a shared responsibility for environmentally sound management and
disposal of such wastes, while affirming the sovereign right of any state to prohibit
imports. It is published with annexes in 28 *ILM* (1989) 657; 19 *EPL* (1989) 68; UN
Doc. UNEP/WG.190/4. The annexes are not reproduced here. UNEP's Cairo
Guidelines and Principles of Environmentally Sound Management of Hazardous
Wastes, 1985, UNEP/WG.122/3, *repr.* 16 *EPL* (1986) 31, formed the basis for the
Convention and give some guidance on the meaning of 'environmentally sound
management.' For examples of regional conventions which provide a more restric-
tive regime for imports to developing countries, see Convention on the Ban of the
Import into Africa and Control of Transboundary Movement and Management of
Hazardous Wastes within Africa, Bamako, 29 January 1991, *repr.* 30 *ILM* (1991)
775; 4th Lomé Convention, 1989, Article 39 and Annexes VIII–X, *repr.* 29 *ILM*
(1990) 783. Trade in waste within or involving the European Union is regulated by
Council Regulation 259/93/EEC of 1 February 1993, *repr.* 4 *YIEL* (1993) 713; OJL
30/1–28 (6 February 1993).

The Basel Convention entered into force on 5 May 1992 and had 82 parties in
1993. For parties and declarations see UN, *Multilateral Treaties Deposited with the
Secretary-General*, UN Doc. ST/LEG/SER.E/(current year). For proceedings of
meetings of the parties see *Report of the First Meeting of the Conference of the Parties*,
UNEP/CHW.1.24 (1992). The Second Meeting of the Conference of the Parties,
held in 1994, decided to phase out trade in hazardous wastes between OECD and
non-OECD countries: *Report*, UNEP/CHW. 2/30.

On the Convention, see D. P. Hackett, 'An Assessment of the Basel Conven-
tion . . .' 5 *Am U JILP* (1990) 291; M. Bothe, 'International Regulation of
Transboundary Movement of Hazardous Waste', 33 *Germ. YIL* (1990) 422; K.
Kummer, 'The International Regulation of Transboundary Traffic in Hazardous
Waste: The 1989 Basel Convention', 41 *ICLQ* (1992) 530; *id., International Manage-
ment of Hazardous Wastes* (OUP, 1995); J. T. Smith, 'The Challenges of Environmen-
tally Sound and Efficient Regulation of Waste—The Need for Enhanced
International Understanding', 5 *JEL* (1993) 91; I. Rummel-Bulska, 'The Basel
Convention: A Global Approach for the Management of Hazardous Wastes', 24 *EPL*
(1994) 13; and generally, P. W. Birnie and A. E. Boyle, *International Law and the
Environment* (Oxford, 1992), 332ff; G. Handl and R. Lutz, 'An International Policy
Perspective on Trade of Hazardous Materials and Technologies', 30 *Harv. ILJ*
(1989) 359. See also UN, *Report of the Secretary-General on Illegal Traffic in Toxic and
Dangerous Products and Wastes*, UN Doc. A/44/362 (1989).

TEXT

Preamble

The Parties to this Convention,

Aware of the risk of damage to human health and the environment caused by hazardous wastes and other wastes and the transboundary movement thereof,

Mindful of the growing threat to human health and the environment posed by the increased generation and complexity, and transboundary movement of hazardous wastes and other wastes,

Mindful also that the most effective way of protecting human health and the environment from the dangers posed by such wastes is the reduction of their generation to a minimum in terms of quantity and/or hazard potential,

Convinced that States should take necessary measures to ensure that the management of hazardous wastes and other wastes including their transboundary movement and disposal is consistent with the protection of human health and the environment whatever the place of their disposal,

Noting that States should ensure that the generator should carry out duties with regard to the transport and disposal of hazardous wastes and other wastes in a manner that is consistent with the protection of the environment, whatever the place of disposal,

Fully recognizing that any State has the sovereign right to ban the entry or disposal of foreign hazardous wastes and other wastes in its territory,

Recognizing also the increasing desire for the prohibition of transboundary movements of hazardous wastes and their disposal in other States, especially developing countries,

Convinced that hazardous wastes and other wastes should, as far as is compatible with environmentally sound and efficient management, be disposed of in the State where they were generated,

Aware also that transboundary movements of such wastes from the State of their generation to any other State should be permitted only when conducted under conditions which do not endanger human health and the environment, and under conditions in conformity with the provisions of this Convention,

Considering that enhanced control of transboundary movement of hazardous wastes and other wastes will act as an incentive for their environmentally sound management and for the reduction of the volume of such transboundary movement,

Convinced that States should take measures for the proper exchange of information on and control of the transboundary movement of hazardous wastes and other wastes from and to those States,

Noting that a number of international and regional agreements have addressed the issue of protection and preservation of the environment with regard to the transit of dangerous goods,

Taking into account the Declaration of the United Nations Conference on the Human Environment (Stockholm, 1972), the Cairo Guidelines and Principles for the Environmentally Sound Management of Hazardous Wastes adopted by the Governing Council of the United Nations Environment Programme (UNEP) by decision 14/30 of 17 June 1987, the Recommendations of the United Nations Committee of Experts on the Transport of Dangerous Goods (formulated in 1957 and updated biennially), relevant recommendations, declarations, instruments and regulations adopted within the United Nations system and the work and studies done within other international and regional organizations,

Mindful of the spirit, principles, aims and functions of the World Charter for Nature adopted by the General Assembly of the United Nations at its thirty-seventh session (1982) as the rule of ethics in respect of the protection of the human environment and the conservation of natural resources,

Affirming that States are responsible for the fulfilment of their international obligations concerning the protection of human health and protection and preservation of the environment, and are liable in accordance with international law,

Recognizing that in the case of a material breach of the provisions of this Convention or any protocol thereto the relevant international law of treaties shall apply,

Aware of the need to continue the development and implementation of environmentally sound low-waste technologies, recycling options, good house-keeping and management systems with a view to reducing to a minimum the generation of hazardous wastes and other wastes,

Aware also of the growing international concern about the need for stringent control of transboundary movement of hazardous wastes and other wastes, and of the need as far as possible to reduce such movement to a minimum,

Concerned about the problem of illegal transboundary traffic in hazardous wastes and other wastes,

Taking into account also the limited capabilities of the developing countries to manage hazardous wastes and other wastes,

Recognizing the need to promote the transfer of technology for the sound management of hazardous wastes and other wastes produced locally, particularly to the developing countries in accordance with the spirit of the Cairo Guidelines and decision 14/16 of the Governing Council of UNEP on Promotion of the transfer of environmental protection technology,

Recognizing also that hazardous wastes and other wastes should be transported in accordance with relevant international conventions and recommendations,

Convinced also that the transboundary movement of hazardous wastes and other wastes should be permitted only when the transport and the ultimate disposal of such wastes is environmentally sound, and

Determined to protect, by strict control, human health and the environment against the adverse effects which may result from the generation and management of hazardous wastes and other wastes,

Have agreed as follows:

Article 1
Scope of the Convention

1. The following wastes that are subject to transboundary movement shall be 'hazardous wastes' for the purposes of this Convention:

    (a) Wastes that belong to any category contained in Annex I, unless they do not possess any of the characteristics contained in Annex III; and

    (b) Wastes that are not covered under paragraph (a) but are defined as, or are considered to be, hazardous wastes by the domestic legislation of the Party of export, import or transit.

2. Wastes that belong to any category contained in Annex II that are subject to transboundary movement shall be 'other wastes' for the purposes of this Convention.

3. Wastes which, as a result of being radioactive, are subject to other international control systems, including international instruments, applying specifically to radioactive materials, are excluded from the scope of this Convention.

4. Wastes which derive from the normal operations of a ship, the discharge of which is covered by another international instrument, are excluded from the scope of this Convention.

Article 2
Definitions

For the purposes of this Convention:

1. 'Wastes' are substances or objects which are disposed of or are intended to be disposed of or are required to be disposed of by the provisions of national law;

2. 'Management' means the collection, transport and disposal of hazardous wastes or other wastes, including after-care of disposal sites;

3. 'Transboundary movement' means any movement of hazardous wastes or other wastes from an area under the national jurisdiction of one State to or through an area under the national jurisdiction of another State or to or through an area not under the national jurisdiction of any State, provided at least two States are involved in the movement;

4. 'Disposal' means any operation specified in Annex IV to this Convention;

5. 'Approved site or facility' means a site or facility for the disposal of hazardous wastes or other wastes which is authorized or permitted to operate for this purpose by a relevant authority of the State where the site or facility is located;

6. 'Competent authority' means one governmental authority designated by a Party to be responsible, within such geographical areas as the Party may think fit, for receiving the notification of a transboundary movement of hazardous wastes or other wastes, and any information related to it, and for responding to such a notification, as provided in Article 6;

7. 'Focal point' means the entity of a Party referred to in Article 5 responsible for receiving and submitting information as provided for in Articles 13 and 16;

8. 'Environmentally sound management of hazardous wastes or other wastes' means taking all practicable steps to ensure that hazardous wastes or other wastes are managed in a manner which will protect human health and the environment against the adverse effects which may result from such wastes;

9. 'Area under the national jurisdiction of a State' means any land, marine area or airspace within which a State exercises administrative and regulatory responsibility in accordance with international law in regard to the protection of human health or the environment;

10. 'State of export' means a Party from which a transboundary movement of hazardous wastes or other wastes is planned to be initiated or is initiated;

11. 'State of import' means a Party to which a transboundary movement of hazardous wastes or other wastes is planned or takes place for the purpose of disposal therein or for the purpose of loading prior to disposal in an area not under the national jurisdiction of any State;

12. 'State of transit' means any State, other than the State of export or import, through which a movement of hazardous wastes or other wastes is planned or takes place;

13. 'States concerned' means Parties which are States of export or import, or transit States, whether or not Parties;

14. 'Person' means any natural or legal person;

15. 'Exporter' means any person under the jurisdiction of the State of export who arranges for hazardous wastes or other wastes to be exported;

16. 'Importer' means any person under the jurisdiction of the State of import who arranges for hazardous wastes or other wastes to be imported;

17. 'Carrier' means any person who carries out the transport of hazardous wastes or other wastes;

18. 'Generator' means any person whose activity produces hazardous wastes or other wastes or, if that person is not known, the person who is in possession and/or control of those wastes;

19. 'Disposer' means any person to whom hazardous wastes or other wastes are shipped and who carries out the disposal of such wastes;

20. 'Political and/or economic integration organization' means an organization constituted by sovereign States to which its member States have transferred competence in respect of matters governed by this Convention and which has been duly authorized, in accordance with its internal procedures, to sign, ratify, accept, approve, formally confirm or accede to it;

21. 'Illegal traffic' means any transboundary movement of hazardous wastes or other wastes as specified in Article 9.

Article 3
National Definitions of Hazardous Wastes

1. Each Party shall, within six months of becoming a Party to this Convention, inform the Secretariat of the Convention of the wastes, other than those listed in Annexes I and II, considered or defined as hazardous under its national legislation and of any requirements concerning transboundary movement procedures applicable to such wastes.

2. Each Party shall subsequently inform the Secretariat of any significant changes to the information it has provided pursuant to paragraph 1.

3. The Secretariat shall forthwith inform all Parties of the information it has received pursuant to paragraphs 1 and 2.

4. Parties shall be responsible for making the information transmitted to them by the Secretariat under paragraph 3 available to their exporters.

Article 4
General Obligations

1. (a) Parties exercising their right to prohibit the import of hazardous wastes or other wastes for disposal shall inform the other Parties of their decision pursuant to Article 13.

   (b) Parties shall prohibit or shall not permit the export of hazardous wastes and other wastes to the Parties which have prohibited the import of such wastes, when notified pursuant to subparagraph (a) above.

   (c) Parties shall prohibit or shall not permit the export of hazardous wastes and other wastes if the State of import does not consent in writing to the specific import, in the case where that State of import has not prohibited the import of such wastes.

2. Each Party shall take the appropriate measures to:

   (a) Ensure that the generation of hazardous wastes and other wastes within it is reduced to a minimum, taking into account social, technological and economic aspects;

   (b) Ensure the availability of adequate disposal facilities, for the environmentally sound management of hazardous wastes and other wastes, that shall be located, to the extent possible, within it, whatever the place of their disposal;

(c) Ensure that persons involved in the management of hazardous wastes or other wastes within it take such steps as are necessary to prevent pollution due to hazardous wastes and other wastes arising from such management and, if such pollution occurs, to minimize the consequences thereof for human health and the environment;

(d) Ensure that the transboundary movement of hazardous wastes and other wastes is reduced to the minimum consistent with the environmentally sound and efficient management of such wastes, and is conducted in a manner which will protect human health and the environment against the adverse effects which may result from such movement;

(e) Not allow the export of hazardous wastes or other wastes to a State or group of States belonging to an economic and/or political integration organization that are Parties, particularly developing countries, which have prohibited by their legislation all imports, or if it has reason to believe that the wastes in question will not be managed in an environmentally sound manner, according to criteria to be decided on by the Parties at their first meeting;

(f) Require that information about a proposed transboundary movement of hazardous wastes and other wastes be provided to the States concerned, according to Annex V A, to state clearly the effects of the proposed movement on human health and the environment;

(g) Prevent the import of hazardous wastes and other wastes if it has reason to believe that the wastes in question will not be managed in an environmentally sound manner;

(h) Co-operate in activities with other Parties and interested organizations, directly and through the Secretariat, including the dissemination of information on the transboundary movement of hazardous wastes and other wastes, in order to improve the environmentally sound management of such wastes and to achieve the prevention of illegal traffic.

3. The Parties consider that illegal traffic in hazardous wastes or other wastes is criminal.

4. Each Party shall take appropriate legal, administrative and other measures to implement and enforce the provisions of this Convention, including measures to prevent and punish conduct in contravention of the Convention.

5. A Party shall not permit hazardous wastes or other wastes to be exported to a non-Party or to be imported from a non-Party.

6. The Parties agree not to allow the export of hazardous wastes or other wastes for disposal within the area south of 60° South latitude, whether or not such wastes are subject to transboundary movement.

7. Furthermore, each Party shall:

(a) Prohibit all persons under its national jurisdiction from transporting or disposing of hazardous wastes or other wastes unless such persons are authorized or allowed to perform such types of operations;

(b) Require that hazardous wastes and other wastes that are to be the subject of a transboundary movement be packaged, labelled, and transported in conformity with generally accepted and recognized international rules and standards in the field of packaging, labelling, and transport, and that due account is taken of relevant internationally recognized practices;

(c) Require that hazardous wastes and other wastes be accompanied by a movement document from the point at which a transboundary movement commences to the point of disposal.

8. Each Party shall require that hazardous wastes or other wastes, to be exported, are managed in an environmentally sound manner in the State of import or elsewhere. Technical guidelines for the environmentally sound management of wastes subject to this Convention shall be decided by the Parties at their first meeting.

9. Parties shall take the appropriate measures to ensure that the transboundary movement of hazardous wastes and other wastes only be allowed if:

(a) The State of export does not have the technical capacity and the necessary facilities, capacity or suitable disposal sites in order to dispose of the wastes in question in an environmentally sound and efficient manner; or

(b) The wastes in question are required as a raw material for recycling or recovery industries in the State of import; or

(c) The transboundary movement in question is in accordance with other criteria to be decided by the Parties, provided those criteria do not differ from the objectives of this Convention.

10. The obligation under this Convention of States in which hazardous wastes and other wastes are generated to require that those wastes are managed in an environmentally sound manner may not under any circumstances be transferred to the States of import or transit.

11. Nothing in this Convention shall prevent a Party from imposing additional requirements that are consistent with the provisions of this Convention, and are in accordance with the rules of international law, in order better to protect human health and the environment.

12. Nothing in this Convention shall affect in any way the sovereignty of States over their territorial sea established in accordance with international law, and the sovereign rights and the jurisdiction which States have in their exclusive economic zones and their continental shelves in accordance with international law, and the exercise by ships and aircraft of all States of navigational rights and freedoms as provided for in international law and as reflected in relevant international instruments.

13. Parties shall undertake to review periodically the possibilities for the reduction of the amount and/or the pollution potential of hazardous wastes and other wastes which are exported to other States, in particular to developing countries.

Article 5
Designation of Competent Authorities and Focal Point

To facilitate the implementation of this Convention, the Parties shall:

1. Designate or establish one or more competent authorities and one focal point. One competent authority shall be designated to receive the notification in case of a State of transit.

2. Inform the Secretariat, within three months of the date of the entry into force of this Convention for them, which agencies they have designated as their focal point and their competent authorities.

3. Inform the Secretariat, within one month of the date of decision, of any changes regarding the designation made by them under paragraph 2 above.

Article 6
Transboundary Movement between Parties

1. The State of export shall notify, or shall require the generator or exporter to notify, in writing, through the channel of the competent authority of the State of export, the competent authority of the States concerned of any proposed transboundary movement of hazardous wastes or other wastes. Such notification shall contain the declarations and information specified in Annex V A, written in a language acceptable to the State of import. Only one notification needs to be sent to each State concerned.

2. The State of import shall respond to the notifier in writing, consenting to the movement with or without conditions, denying permission for the movement, or requesting additional information. A copy of the final response of the State of import shall be sent to the competent authorities of the States concerned which are Parties.

3. The State of export shall not allow the generator or exporter to commence the transboundary movement until it has received written confirmation that:

(a) The notifier has received the written consent of the State of import; and

   (b) The notifier has received from the State of import confirmation of the existence of a contract between the exporter and the disposer specifying environmentally sound management of the wastes in question.

4. Each state of transit which is a Party shall promptly acknowledge to the notifier receipt of the notification. It may subsequently respond to the notifier in writing, within 60 days, consenting to the movement with or without conditions, denying permission for the movement, or requesting additional information. The State of export shall not allow the transboundary movement to commence until it has received the written consent of the State of transit. However, if at any time a Party decides not to require prior written consent, either generally or under specific conditions, for transit transboundary movements of hazardous wastes or other wastes, or modifies its requirements in this respect, it shall forthwith inform the other Parties of its decision pursuant to Article 13. In this latter case, if no response is received by the State of export within 60 days of the receipt of a given notification by the State of transit, the State of export may allow the export to proceed through the State of transit.

5. In the case of a transboundary movement of wastes where the wastes are legally defined as or considered to be hazardous wastes only:

   (a) By the State of export, the requirements of paragraph 9 of this Article that apply to the importer or disposer and the State of import shall apply *mutatis mutandis* to the exporter and State of export respectively;

   (b) By the State of import, or by the States of import and transit which are Parties, the requirements of paragraphs 1, 3, 4 and 6 of this Article that apply to the exporter and State of export shall apply *mutatis mutandis* to the importer or disposer and State of import, respectively; or

   (c) By any State of transit which is a Party, the provisions of paragraph 4 shall apply to such State.

6. The State of export may, subject to the written consent of the States concerned, allow the generator or the exporter to use a general notification where hazardous wastes or other wastes having the same physical and chemical characteristics are shipped regularly to the same disposer via the same customs office of exit of the State of export via the same customs office of entry of the State of import, and, in the case of transit, via the same customs office of entry and exit of the State or States of transit.

7. The States concerned may make their written consent to the use of the general notification referred to in paragraph 6 subject to the supply of certain information, such as the exact quantities or periodical lists of hazardous wastes or other wastes to be shipped.

8. The general notification and written consent referred to in paragraphs 6 and 7 may cover multiple shipments of hazardous wastes or other wastes during a maximum period of 12 months.

9. The Parties shall require that each person who takes charge of a transboundary movement of hazardous wastes or other wastes sign the movement document either upon delivery or receipt of the wastes in question. They shall also require that the disposer inform both the exporter and the competent authority of the State of export of receipt by the disposer of the wastes in question and, in due course, of the completion of disposal as specified in the notification. If no such information is received within the State of export, the competent authority of the State of export or the exporter shall so notify the State of import.

10. The notification and response required by this Article shall be transmitted to the competent authority of the Parties concerned or to such governmental authority as may be appropriate in the case of non-Parties.

11. Any transboundary movement of hazardous wastes or other wastes shall be covered by insurance, bond or other guarantee as may be required by the State of import or any State of transit which is a Party.

Article 7
Transboundary Movement from a Party through States Which Are not Parties

Paragraph 2 of Article 6 of the Convention shall apply *mutatis mutandis* to transboundary movement of hazardous wastes or other wastes from a Party through a State or States which are not Parties.

Article 8
Duty to Re-import

When a transboundary movement of hazardous wastes or other wastes to which the consent of the States concerned has been given, subject to the provisions of this Convention, cannot be completed in accordance with the terms of the contract, the State of export shall ensure that the wastes in question are taken back into the State of export, by the exporter, if alternative arrangements cannot be made for their disposal in an environmentally sound manner, within 90 days from the time that the importing State informed the State of export and the Secretariat, or such other period of time as the States concerned agree. To this end, the State of export and any Party of transit shall not oppose, hinder or prevent the return of those wastes to the State of export.

Article 9
Illegal Traffic

1. For the purpose of this Convention, any transboundary movement of hazardous wastes or other wastes:

   (a) without notification pursuant to the provisions of this Convention to all States concerned; or

   (b) without the consent pursuant to the provisions of this Convention of a State concerned; or

(c) with consent obtained from States concerned through falsification, misrepresentation or fraud; or

(d) that does not conform in a material way with the documents; or

(e) that results in deliberate disposal (e.g. dumping) of hazardous wastes or other wastes in contravention of this Convention and of general principles of international law,

shall be deemed to be illegal traffic.

2. In case of a transboundary movement of hazardous wastes or other wastes deemed to be illegal traffic as the result of conduct on the part of the exporter or generator, the State of export shall ensure that the wastes in question are:

(a) taken back by the exporter or the generator or, if necessary, by itself into the State of export, or, if impracticable,

(b) are otherwise disposed of in accordance with the provisions of this Convention, within 30 days from the time the State of export has been informed about the illegal traffic or such other period of time as States concerned may agree. To this end the Parties concerned shall not oppose, hinder or prevent the return of those wastes to the State of export.

3. In the case of a transboundary movement of hazardous wastes or other wastes deemed to be illegal traffic as the result of conduct on the part of the importer or disposer, the State of import shall ensure that the wastes in question are disposed of in an environmentally sound manner by the importer or disposer or, if necessary, by itself within 30 days from the time the illegal traffic has come to the attention of the State of import or such other period of time as the States concerned may agree. To this end, the Parties concerned shall co-operate, as necessary in the disposal of the wastes in an environmentally sound manner.

4. In cases where the responsibility for the illegal traffic cannot be assigned either to the exporter or generator or to the importer or disposer, the Parties concerned or other Parties, as appropriate, shall ensure, through co-operation, that the wastes in question are disposed of as soon as possible in an environmentally sound manner either in the State of export or the State of import or elsewhere as appropriate.

5. Each Party shall introduce appropriate national/domestic legislation to prevent and punish illegal traffic. The Parties shall co-operate with a view to achieving the objects of this Article.

Article 10
International Co-operation

1. The Parties shall co-operate with each other in order to improve and achieve environmentally sound management of hazardous wastes and other wastes.

2. To this end, the Parties shall:

(a) Upon request, make available information, whether on a bilateral or multilateral basis, with a view to promoting the environmentally sound management of hazardous wastes and other wastes, including harmonization of technical standards and practices for the adequate management of hazardous wastes and other wastes;

(b) Co-operate in monitoring the effects of the management of hazardous wastes on human health and the environment;

(c) Co-operate, subject to their national laws, regulations and policies, in the development and implementation of new environmentally sound low-waste technologies and the improvement of existing technologies with a view to eliminating, as far as practicable, the generation of hazardous wastes and other wastes and achieving more effective and efficient methods of ensuring their management in an environmentally sound manner, including the study of the economic, social and environmental effects of the adoption of such new or improved technologies;

(d) Co-operate actively, subject to their national laws, regulations and policies, in the transfer of technology and management systems related to the environmentally sound management of hazardous wastes and other wastes. They shall also co-operate in developing the technical capacity among Parties, especially those which may need and request technical assistance in this field;

(e) Co-operate in developing appropriate technical guidelines and/or codes of practice.

3. The Parties shall employ appropriate means to co-operate in order to assist developing countries in the implementation of subparagraphs a, b, c and d of paragraph 2 of Article 4.

4. Taking into account the needs of developing countries, co-operation between Parties and the competent international organizations is encouraged to promote, *inter alia*, public awareness, the development of sound management of hazardous wastes and other wastes and the adoption of new low-waste technologies.

Article 11
Bilateral, Multilateral and Regional Agreements

1. Notwithstanding, the provisions of Article 4, paragraph 5, Parties may enter into bilateral, multilateral, or regional agreements or arrangements regarding transboundary movement of hazardous wastes or other wastes with Parties or non-Parties provided that such agreements or arrangements do not derogate from the environmentally sound management of hazardous wastes and other wastes as required by this Convention. These agreements or arrangements shall stipulate provisions which are not less environmentally sound than those provided for by

this Convention in particular taking into account the interests of developing countries.

2. Parties shall notify the Secretariat of any bilateral, multilateral or regional agreements or arrangements referred to in paragraph 1 and those which they have entered into prior to the entry into force of this Convention for them, for the purpose of controlling transboundary movements of hazardous wastes and other wastes which take place entirely among the Parties to such agreements. The provisions of this Convention shall not affect transboundary movements which take place pursuant to such agreements provided that such agreements are compatible with the environmentally sound management of hazardous wastes and other wastes as required by this Convention.

Article 12
Consultations on Liability

The Parties shall co-operate with a view to adopting, as soon as practicable, a protocol setting out appropriate rules and procedures in the field of liability and compensation for damage resulting from the transboundary movement and disposal of hazardous wastes and other wastes.

Article 13
Transmission of Information

1. The Parties shall, whenever it comes to their knowledge, ensure that, in the case of an accident occurring during the transboundary movement of hazardous wastes or other wastes or their disposal, which are likely to present risks to human health and the environment in other States, those States are immediately informed.

2. The Parties shall inform each other, through the Secretariat, of:

(a) Changes regarding the designation of competent authorities and/or focal points, pursuant to Article 5;

(b) Changes in their national definition of hazardous wastes, pursuant to Article 3;

and, as soon as possible,

(c) Decisions made by them not to consent totally or partially to the import of hazardous wastes or other wastes for disposal within the area under their national jurisdiction;

(d) Decisions taken by them to limit or ban the export of hazardous wastes or other wastes;

(e) Any other information required pursuant to paragraph 4 of this Article.

3. The Parties, consistent with national laws and regulations, shall transmit, through the Secretariat, to the Conference of the Parties established under

Article 15, before the end of each calendar year, a report on the previous calendar year, containing the following information:

(a) Competent authorities and focal points that have been designated by them pursuant to Article 5;

(b) Information regarding transboundary movements of hazardous wastes or other wastes in which they have been involved, including:

    (i) The amount of hazardous wastes and other wastes exported, their category, characteristics, destination, any transit country and disposal method as stated on the response to notification;

    (ii) The amount of hazardous wastes and other wastes imported, their category, characteristics, origin, and disposal methods;

    (iii) Disposals which did not proceed as intended;

    (iv) Efforts to achieve a reduction of the amount of hazardous wastes or other wastes subject to transboundary movement;

(c) Information on the measures adopted by them in implementation of this Convention;

(d) Information on available qualified statistics which have been compiled by them on the effects on human health and the environment of the generation, transportation and disposal of hazardous wastes or other wastes;

(e) Information concerning bilateral, multilateral and regional agreements and arrangements entered into pursuant to Article 11 of this Convention;

(f) Information on accidents occurring during the transboundary movement and disposal of hazardous wastes and other wastes and on the measures undertaken to deal with them;

(g) Information on disposal options operated within the area of their national jurisdiction;

(h) Information on measures undertaken for development of technologies for the reduction and/or elimination of production of hazardous wastes and other wastes: and

(i) Such other matters as the Conference of the Parties shall deem relevant.

4. The Parties, consistent with national laws and regulations, shall ensure that copies of each notification concerning any given transboundary movement of hazardous wastes or other wastes, and the response to it, are sent to the Secretariat when a Party that considers that its environment may be affected by that transboundary movement has requested that this should be done.

Article 14
Financial Aspects

1. The Parties agree that, according to the specific needs of different

regions and subregions, regional or sub-regional centres for training and technology transfers regarding the management of hazardous wastes and other wastes and the minimization of their generation should be established. The Parties shall decide on the establishment of appropriate funding mechanisms of a voluntary nature.

2. The Parties shall consider the establishment of a revolving fund to assist on an interim basis in case of emergency situations to minimize damage from accidents arising from transboundary movements of hazardous wastes and other wastes or during the disposal of those wastes.

Article 15
Conference of the Parties

1. A Conference of the Parties is hereby established. The first meeting of the Conference of the Parties shall be convened by the Executive Director of UNEP not later than one year after the entry into force of this Convention. Thereafter, ordinary meetings of the Conference of the Parties shall be held at regular intervals to be determined by the Conference at its first meeting.

2. Extraordinary meetings of the Conference of the Parties shall be held at such other times as may be deemed necessary by the Conference or at the written request of any Party, provided that, within six months of the request being communicated to them by the Secretariat, it is supported by at least one-third of the Parties.

3. The Conference of the Parties shall by consensus agree upon and adopt rules of procedure for itself and for any subsidiary body it may establish, as well as financial rules to determine in particular the financial participation of the Parties under this Convention.

4. The Parties at their first meeting shall consider any additional measures needed to assist them in fulfilling their responsibilities with respect to the protection and the preservation of the marine environment in the context of this Convention.

5. The Conference of the Parties shall keep under continuous review and evaluation the effective implementation of this Convention, and, in addition, shall:

(a) Promote the harmonization of appropriate policies, strategies and measures for minimizing harm to human health and the environment by hazardous wastes and other wastes;

(b) Consider and adopt, as required, amendments to this Convention and its annexes, taking into consideration, *inter alia*, available scientific, technical, economic and environmental information;

(c) Consider and undertake any additional action that may be required for the achievement of the purposes of this Convention in the light of experience gained in its operation and in the operation of the agreements and arrangements envisaged in Article 11;

(d) Consider and adopt protocols as required; and

(e) Establish such subsidiary bodies as are deemed necessary for the implementation of this Convention.

6. The United Nations, its specialized agencies, as well as any State not party to this Convention, may be represented as observers at meetings of the Conference of the Parties. Any other body or agency, whether national or international, governmental or non-governmental, qualified in fields relating to hazardous wastes or other wastes which has informed the Secretariat of its wish to be represented as an observer at a meeting of the Conference of the Parties, may be admitted unless at least one-third of the Parties present object. The admission and participation of observers shall be subject to the rules of procedure adopted by the Conference of the Parties.

7. The Conference of the Parties shall undertake three years after the entry into force of this Convention, and at least every six years thereafter, an evaluation of its effectiveness and, if deemed necessary, to consider the adoption of a complete or partial ban of transboundary movements of hazardous wastes and other wastes in light of the latest scientific, environmental, technical and economic information.

Article 16
Secretariat

1. The functions of the Secretariat shall be:

(a) To arrange for and service meetings provided for in Articles 15 and 17;

(b) To prepare and transmit reports based upon information received in accordance with Articles 3, 4, 6, 11 and 13 as well as upon information derived from meetings of subsidiary bodies established under Article 15 as well as upon, as appropriate, information provided by relevant intergovernmental and non-governmental entities;

(c) To prepare reports on its activities carried out in implementation of its functions under this Convention and present them to the Conference of the Parties;

(d) To ensure the necessary coordination with relevant international bodies, and in particular to enter into such administrative and contractual arrangements as may be required for the effective discharge of its functions;

(e) To communicate with focal points and competent authorities established by the Parties in accordance with Article 5 of this Convention;

(f) To compile information concerning authorized national sites and facilities of Parties available for the disposal of their hazardous wastes

and other wastes and to circulate this information among Parties;
(g) To receive and convey information from and to Parties on:
— sources of technical assistance and training;
— available technical and scientific know-how;
— sources of advice and expertise; and
— availability of resources with a view to assisting them, upon request, in such areas as:
  — the handling of the notification system of this Convention;
  — the management of hazardous wastes and other wastes;
  — environmentally sound technologies relating to hazardous wastes and other wastes, such as low- and non-waste technology;
  — the assessment of disposal capabilities and sites;
  — the monitoring of hazardous wastes and other wastes; and
  — emergency responses;
(h) To provide Parties, upon request, with information on consultants or consulting firms having the necessary technical competence in the field, which can assist them to examine a notification for a transboundary movement, the concurrence of a shipment of hazardous wastes or other wastes with the relevant notification, and/or the fact that the proposed disposal facilities for hazardous wastes or other wastes are environmentally sound, when they have reason to believe that the wastes in question will not be managed in an environmentally sound manner. Any such examination would not be at the expense of the Secretariat;
(i) To assist Parties upon request in their identification of cases of illegal traffic and to circulate immediately to the Parties concerned any information it has received regarding illegal traffic;
(j) To co-operate with Parties and with relevant and competent international organizations and agencies in the provision of experts and equipment for the purpose of rapid assistance to States in the event of an emergency situation; and
(k) To perform such other functions relevant to the purposes of this Convention as may be determined by the Conference of the Parties.

2. The secretariat functions will be carried out on an interim basis by UNEP until the completion of the first meeting of the Conference of the Parties held pursuant to Article 15.

3. At its first meeting, the Conference of the Parties shall designate the Secretariat from among those existing competent intergovernmental organizations which have signified their willingness to carry out the secretariat functions under this Convention. At this meeting, the Conference of the Parties shall also evaluate the implementation by the interim Secretariat of the functions assigned to it, in particular under paragraph 1 above, and decide upon the structures appropriate for those functions.

Article 17
Amendment of the Convention

1. Any Party may propose amendments to this Convention and any Party to a protocol may propose amendments to that protocol. Such amendments shall take due account, *inter alia*, of relevant scientific and technical considerations.

2. Amendments to this Convention shall be adopted at a meeting of the Conference of the Parties. Amendments to any protocol shall be adopted at a meeting of the Parties to the protocol in question. The text of any proposed amendment to this Convention or to any protocol, except as may otherwise be provided in such protocol, shall be communicated to the Parties by the Secretariat at least six months before the meeting at which it is proposed for adoption. The Secretariat shall also communicate proposed amendments to the Signatories to this Convention for information.

3. The Parties shall make every effort to reach agreement on any proposed amendment to this Convention by consensus. If all efforts at consensus have been exhausted, and no agreement reached, the amendment shall as a last resort be adopted by a three-fourths majority vote of the Parties present and voting at the meeting, and shall be submitted by the Depositary to all Parties for ratification, approval, formal confirmation or acceptance.

4. The procedure mentioned in paragraph 3 above shall apply to amendments to any protocol, except that a two-thirds majority of the Parties to that protocol present and voting at the meeting shall suffice for their adoption.

5. Instruments of ratification, approval, formal confirmation or acceptance of amendments shall be deposited with the Depositary. Amendments adopted in accordance with paragraphs 3 or 4 above shall enter into force between Parties having accepted them on the ninetieth day after the receipt by the Depositary of their instrument of ratification, approval, formal confirmation or acceptance by at least three-fourths of the Parties who accepted the amendments to the protocol concerned, except as may otherwise be provided in such protocol. The amendments shall enter into force for any other Party on the ninetieth day after that Party deposits its instrument of ratification, approval, formal confirmation or acceptance of the amendments.

6. For the purpose of this Article, 'Parties present and voting' means Parties present and casting an affirmative or negative vote.

Article 18
Adoption and Amendment of Annexes

1. The annexes to this Convention or to any protocol shall form an integral part of this Convention or of such protocol, as the case may be and, unless

expressly provided otherwise, a reference to this Convention or its protocols constitutes at the same time a reference to any annexes thereto. Such annexes shall be restricted to scientific, technical and administrative matters.

2. Except as may be otherwise provided in any protocol with respect to its annexes, the following procedure shall apply to the proposal, adoption and entry into force of additional annexes to this Convention or of annexes to a protocol:

(a) Annexes to this Convention and its protocols shall be proposed and adopted according to the procedure laid down in Article 17, paragraphs 2, 3 and 4;

(b) Any Party that is unable to accept an additional annex to this Convention or an annex to any protocol to which it is Party shall so notify the Depositary, in writing, within six months from the date of the communication of the adoption by the Depositary. The Depositary shall without delay notify all Parties of any such notification received. A Party may at any time substitute an acceptance for a previous declaration of objection and the annexes shall thereupon enter into force for that Party;

(c) On the expiry of six months from the date of the circulation of the communication by the Depositary, the annex shall become effective for all Parties to this Convention or to any protocol concerned, which have not submitted a notification in accordance with the provision of subparagraph (b) above.

3. The proposal, adoption and entry into force of amendments to annexes to this Convention or to any protocol shall be subject to the same procedure as for the proposal, adoption and entry into force of annexes to the Convention or annexes to a protocol. Annexes and amendments thereto shall take due account, *inter alia*, of relevant scientific and technical considerations.

4. If an additional annex or an amendment to an annex involves an amendment to this Convention or to any protocol, the additional annex or amended annex shall not enter into force until such time as the amendment to this Convention or to the protocol enters into force.

Article 19
Verification

Any Party which has reason to believe that another Party is acting or has acted in breach of its obligations under this Convention may inform the Secretariat thereof, and in such an event, shall simultaneously and immediately inform, directly or through the Secretariat, the Party against whom the allegations are made. All relevant information should be submitted by the Secretariat to the Parties.

Article 20
Settlement of Disputes

1. In case of a dispute between Parties as to the interpretation or application of, or compliance with, this Convention or any protocol thereto, they shall seek a settlement of the dispute through negotiation or any other peaceful means of their own choice.

2. If the Parties concerned cannot settle their dispute through the means mentioned in the preceding paragraph, the dispute, if the parties to the dispute agree, shall be submitted to the International Court of Justice or to the arbitration under the conditions set out in Annex VI on Arbitration. However, failure to reach common agreement on submission of the dispute to the International Court of Justice or to arbitration shall not absolve the Parties from the responsibility of continuing to seek to resolve it by the means referred to in paragraph 1.

3. When ratifying, accepting, approving, formally confirming or acceding to this Convention, or at any time thereafter, a State or political and/or economic integration organization may declare that it recognizes as compulsory *ipso facto* and without special agreement, in relation to any Party accepting the same obligation:

   (a) submission of the dispute to the International Court of Justice; and/or
   (b) arbitration in accordance with the procedures set out in Annex VI. Such declaration shall be notified in writing to the Secretariat which shall communicate it to the Parties.

Article 21
Signature

This Convention shall be open for signature by States, by Namibia, represented by the United Nations Council for Namibia, and by political and/or economic integration organizations, in Basel on 22 March 1989, at the Federal Department of Foreign Affairs of Switzerland in Berne from 23 March 1989 to 30 June 1989 and at United Nations Headquarters in New York from 1 July 1989 to 22 March 1990.

Article 22
Ratification, Acceptance, Formal Confirmation or Approval

1. This Convention shall be subject to ratification, acceptance or approval by States and by Namibia, represented by the United Nations Council for Namibia, and to formal confirmation or approval by political and/or economic integration organizations. Instruments of ratification, acceptance, formal confirmation, or approval shall be deposited with the Depositary.

2. Any organization referred to in paragraph 1 above which becomes a Party to this Convention without any of its member States being a Party shall be bound by all the obligations under the Convention. In the case of

such organizations, one or more of whose member States is a Party to the Convention, the organization and its member States shall decide on their respective responsibilities for the performance of their obligations under the Convention. In such cases, the organization and the member States shall not be entitled to exercise rights under the Convention concurrently.

3. In their instruments of formal confirmation or approval, the organizations referred to in paragraph 1 above shall declare the extent of their competence with respect to the matters governed by the Convention. These organizations shall also inform the Depositary, who will inform the Parties of any substantial modification in the extent of their competence.

Article 23
Accession

1. This Convention shall be open for accession by States, by Namibia, represented by the United Nations Council for Namibia, and by political and/or economic integration organizations from the day after the date on which the Convention is closed for signature. The instruments of accession shall be deposited with the Depositary.

2. In their instruments of accession, the organizations referred to in paragraph 1 above shall declare the extent of their competence with respect to the matters governed by the Convention. These organizations shall also inform the Depositary of any substantial modification in the extent of their competence.

3. The provisions of Article 22 paragraph 2, shall apply to political and/or economic integration organizations which accede to this Convention.

Article 24
Right to vote

1. Except as provided for in paragraph 2 below, each Contracting Party to this Convention shall have one vote.

2. Political and/or economic integration organizations, in matters within their competence, in accordance with Article 22, paragraph 3, and Article 23, paragraph 2, shall exercise their right to vote with a number of votes equal to the number of their member States which are Parties to the Convention or the relevant protocol. Such organizations shall not exercise their right to vote if their member States exercise theirs, and vice versa.

Article 25
Entry into Force

1. This Convention shall enter into force on the ninetieth day after the date of deposit of the twentieth instrument of ratification, acceptance, formal confirmation, approval or accession.

2. For each State or political and/or economic integration organization which ratifies, accepts, approves or formally confirms this Convention or

accedes thereto after the date of the deposit of the twentieth instrument of ratification, acceptance, approval, formal confirmation or accession, it shall enter into force on the ninetieth day after the date of deposit by such State or political and/or economic integration organization of its instrument of ratification, acceptance, approval, formal confirmation or accession.

3. For the purposes of paragraphs 1 and 2 above, any instrument deposited by a political and/or economic integration organization shall not be counted as additional to those deposited by member States of such organization.

Article 26
Reservations and Declarations

1. No reservation or exception may be made to this Convention.

2. Paragraph 1 of this Article does not preclude a State or political and/or economic integration organization, when signing, ratifying, accepting, approving, formally confirming or acceding to this Convention, from making declarations or statements, however phrased or named, with a view, *inter alia*, to the harmonization of its laws and regulations with the provisions of this Convention, provided that such declarations or statements do not purport to exclude or to modify the legal effects of the provisions of the Convention in their application to that State.

Article 27
Withdrawal

1. At any time after three years from the date on which this Convention has entered into force for a Party, that Party may withdraw from the Convention by giving written notification to the Depositary.

2. Withdrawal shall be effective one year from receipt of notification by the Depositary, or on such later date as may be specified in the notification.

Article 28
Depository

The Secretary-General of the United Nations shall be the Depository of this Convention and of any protocol thereto.

Article 29
Authentic texts

The original Arabic, Chinese, English, French, Russian and Spanish texts of this Convention are equally authentic.

In Witness whereof the undersigned, being duly authorized to that effect, have signed this Convention.

[ANNEXES I–VI OMITTED]

7. INTERNATIONAL WATERCOURSES

Convention on the Protection and Use of Transboundary Watercourses and Lakes, Helsinki, 17 March 1992

Negotiated under the auspices of the UN Economic Commission for Europe, this treaty is important because it is the first to codify on a regional basis rules governing the protection and use of international watercourses. In certain respects it draws on existing international law, and on some of the work of the International Law Commission (q.v.). This is most evident in its provisions on the control of pollution, on equitable and reasonable utilization, and on co-operation. The Convention is progressive, however, in requiring ecologically sound and rational water management, conservation and restoration of ecosystems, application of the precautionary principle and the polluter pays principle, and in defining 'best available technology' for the purpose of pollution control. The Convention has been signed by twenty-six states; 9 parties 30 January 1995, not in force. Reservations are not prohibited. For parties, reservations, and declarations see UN, *Multilateral Treaties Deposited with the Secretary-General* UN Doc/ST/LEG/SER.E.

The text is *repr.* 31 *ILM* (1992) 1312. For background material see ECE, *Report of the Working Party on Water Problems*, 5th Special Session, ENVWA/WP.3/CRP.9 (1991) and Draft Convention ENVWA/WP.3/R.19/Rev. 1(1991). See generally A. Nollkaemper, *The Legal Regime for Transboundary Water Pollution: Between Discretion and Constraint* (Dordrecht, 1993).

TEXT

Preamble

The Parties to this Convention,

Mindful that the protection and use of transboundary watercourses and international lakes are important and urgent tasks, the effective accomplishment of which can only be ensured by enhanced cooperation,

Concerned over the existence and threats of adverse effects, in the short or long term, of changes in the conditions of transboundary watercourses and international lakes on the environment, economies and well-being of the member countries of the Economic Commission for Europe (ECE),

Emphasizing the need for strengthened national and international measures to prevent, control and reduce the release of hazardous substances into the aquatic environment and to abate eutrophication and acidification, as well as pollution of the marine environment, in particular coastal areas, from land-based sources,

Commending the efforts already undertaken by the ECE Governments to strengthen cooperation, on bilateral and multilateral levels, for the prevention, control and reduction of transboundary pollution, sustainable water management, conservation of water resources and environmental protection,

Recalling the pertinent provisions and principles of the Declaration of the Stockholm Conference on the Human Environment, the Final Act of the Conference on Security and Cooperation in Europe (CSCE), the Concluding Documents of the Madrid and Vienna Meetings of Representatives of the Participating States of the CSCE, and the Regional Strategy for Environmental Protection and Rational Use of Natural Resources in ECE Member Countries covering the Period up to the Year 2000 and Beyond,

Conscious of the role of the United Nations Economic Commission for Europe in promoting international cooperation for the prevention, control and reduction of transboundary water pollution and sustainable use of transboundary waters, and in this regard recalling the ECE Declaration of Policy on Prevention and Control of Water Pollution, including Transboundary Pollution; the ECE Declaration of Policy on the Rational Use of Water; the ECE Principles Regarding Cooperation in the Field of Transboundary Waters; the ECE Charter on Groundwater Management; and the Code of Conduct on Accidental Pollution of Transboundary Inland Waters,

Referring to decisions I(42) and I(44) adopted by the Economic Commission for Europe at its forty-second and forty-fourth sessions, respectively, and the outcome of the CSCE Meeting on the Protection of the Environment (Sofia, Bulgaria, 16 October–3 November 1989),

Emphasizing that cooperation between member countries in regard to the protection and use of transboundary waters shall be implemented primarily through the elaboration of agreements between countries bordering the same waters, especially where no such agreements have yet been reached,

Have agreed as follows:

Article 1
Definitions

For the purposes of this Convention,

1. 'Transboundary waters' means any surface or ground waters which mark, cross or are located on boundaries between two or more States; wherever transboundary waters flow directly into the sea, these transboundary waters end at a straight line across their respective mouths between points on the low-water line of their banks;

2. 'Transboundary impact' means any significant adverse effect on the environment resulting from a change in the conditions of transboundary waters caused by a human activity, the physical origin of which is situated wholly or in part within an area under the jurisdiction of a Party, within an area under the jurisdiction of another Party. Such effects on the environ-

ment include effects on human health and safety, flora, fauna, soil, air, water, climate, landscape and historical monuments or other physical structures or the interaction among these factors; they also include effects on the cultural heritage or socio-economic conditions resulting from alterations to those factors;

3. 'Party' means, unless the text otherwise indicates, a Contracting Party to this Convention;

4. 'Riparian Parties' means the Parties bordering the same transboundary waters;

5. 'Joint body' means any bilateral or multilateral commission or other appropriate institutional arrangements for cooperation between the Riparian Parties;

6. 'Hazardous substances' means substances which are toxic, carcinogenic, mutagenic, teratogenic or bio-accumulative, especially when they are persistent;

7. 'Best available technology' (the definition is contained in annex I to this Convention).

Part I
Provisions Relating to All Parties

Article 2
General Provisions

1. The Parties shall take all appropriate measures to prevent, control and reduce any transboundary impact.

2. The Parties shall, in particular, take all appropriate measures:

   (a) To prevent, control and reduce pollution of waters causing or likely to cause transboundary impact;

   (b) To ensure that transboundary waters are used with the aim of ecologically sound and rational water management, conservation of water resources and environmental protection;

   (c) To ensure that transboundary waters are used in a reasonable and equitable way, taking into particular account their transboundary character, in the case of activities which cause or are likely to cause transboundary impact;

   (d) To ensure conservation and, where necessary, restoration of ecosystems.

3. Measures for the prevention, control and reduction of water pollution shall be taken, where possible, at source.

4. These measures shall not directly or indirectly result in a transfer of pollution to other parts of the environment.

5. In taking the measures referred to in paragraphs 1 and 2 of this article, the Parties shall be guided by the following principles:

(a) The precautionary principle, by virtue of which action to avoid the potential transboundary impact of the release of hazardous substances shall not be postponed on the ground that scientific research has not fully proved a causal link between those substances, on the one hand, and the potential transboundary impact, on the other hand;

(b) The polluter-pays principle, by virtue of which costs of pollution prevention, control and reduction measures shall be borne by the polluter;

(c) Water resources shall be managed so that the needs of the present generation are met without compromising the ability of future generations to meet their own needs.

6. The Riparian Parties shall cooperate on the basis of equality and reciprocity, in particular through bilateral and multilateral agreements, in order to develop harmonized policies, programmes and strategies covering the relevant catchment areas, or parts thereof, aimed at the prevention, control and reduction of transboundary impact and aimed at the protection of the environment of transboundary waters or the environment influenced by such waters, including the marine environment.

7. The application of this Convention shall not lead to the deterioration of environmental conditions nor lead to increased transboundary impact.

8. The provisions of this Convention shall not affect the right of Parties individually or jointly to adopt and implement more stringent measures than those set down in this Convention.

Article 3
Prevention, Control and Reduction

1. To prevent, control and reduce transboundary impact, the Parties shall develop, adopt, implement and, as far as possible, render compatible relevant legal, administrative, economic, financial and technical measures, in order to ensure, *inter alia*, that:

(a) The emission of pollutants is prevented, controlled and reduced at source through the application of, *inter alia*, low- and non-waste technology;

(b) Transboundary waters are protected against pollution from point sources through the prior licensing of waste-water discharges by the competent national authorities, and that the authorized discharges are monitored and controlled;

(c) Limits for waste-water discharges stated in permits are based on the best available technology for discharges of hazardous substances;

(d) Stricter requirements, even leading to prohibition in individual cases, are imposed when the quality of the receiving water or the ecosystem so requires;

(e) At least biological treatment or equivalent processes are applied to municipal waste water, where necessary in a step-by-step approach;

(f) Appropriate measures are taken, such as the application of the best available technology, in order to reduce nutrient inputs from industrial and municipal sources;

(g) Appropriate measures and best environmental practices are developed and implemented for the reduction of inputs of nutrients and hazardous substances from diffuse sources, especially where the main sources are from agriculture (guidelines for developing best environmental practices are given in annex II to this Convention);

(h) Environmental impact assessment and other means of assessment are applied;

(i) Sustainable water-resources management, including the application of the ecosystems approach, is promoted;

(j) Contingency planning is developed;

(k) Additional specific measures are taken to prevent the pollution of groundwaters;

(l) The risk of accidental pollution is minimized.

2. To this end, each Party shall set emission limits for discharges from point sources into surface waters based on the best available technology, which are specifically applicable to individual industrial sectors or industries from which hazardous substances derive. The appropriate measures mentioned in paragraph 1 of this article to prevent, control and reduce the input of hazardous substances from point and diffuse sources into waters, may, *inter alia*, include total or partial prohibition of the production or use of such substances. Existing lists of such industrial sectors or industries and of such hazardous substances in international conventions or regulations, which are applicable in the area covered by this Convention, shall be taken into account.

3. In addition, each Party shall define, where appropriate, water-quality objectives and adopt water-quality criteria for the purpose of preventing, controlling and reducing transboundary impact. General guidance for developing such objectives and criteria is given in annex III to this Convention. When necessary, the Parties shall endeavour to update this annex.

Article 4
Monitoring

The Parties shall establish programmes for monitoring the conditions of transboundary waters.

Article 5
Research and Development

The Parties shall cooperate in the conduct of research into and development of effective techniques for the prevention, control and reduction of transboundary impact. To this effect, the Parties shall, on a bilateral and/or multilateral basis, taking into account research activities pursued in relevant international forums, endeavour to initiate or intensify specific research programmes, where necessary, aimed, *inter alia*, at:

(a) Methods for the assessment of the toxicity of hazardous substances and the noxiousness of pollutants;
(b) Improved knowledge on the occurrence, distribution and environmental effects of pollutants and the processes involved;
(c) The development and application of environmentally sound technologies, production and consumption patterns;
(d) The phasing out and/or substitution of substances likely to have transboundary impact;
(e) Environmentally sound methods of disposal of hazardous substances;
(f) Special methods for improving the conditions of transboundary waters;
(g) The development of environmentally sound water-construction works and water-regulation techniques;
(h) The physical and financial assessment of damage resulting from transboundary impact.

The results of these research programmes shall be exchanged among the Parties in accordance with article 6 of this Convention.

Article 6
Exchange of Information

The Parties shall provide for the widest exchange of information, as early as possible, on issues covered by the provisions of this Convention.

Article 7
Responsibility and Liability

The Parties shall support appropriate international efforts to elaborate rules, criteria and procedures in the field of responsibility and liability.

Article 8
Protection of Information

The provisions of this Convention shall not affect the rights or the obligations of Parties in accordance with their national legal systems and applicable supranational regulations to protect information related to industrial and commercial secrecy, including intellectual property, or national security.

Part II
Provisions Relating to Riparian Parties

Article 9
Bilateral and Multilateral Cooperation

1. The Riparian Parties shall on the basis of equality and reciprocity enter into bilateral or multilateral agreements or other arrangements, where these do not yet exist, or adapt existing ones, where necessary to eliminate the contradictions with the basic principles of this Convention, in order to define their mutual relations and conduct regarding the prevention, control and reduction of transboundary impact. The Riparian Parties shall specify the catchment area, or part(s) thereof, subject to cooperation. These agreements or arrangements shall embrace relevant issues covered by this Convention, as well as any other issues on which the Riparian Parties may deem it necessary to cooperate.

2. The agreements or arrangements mentioned in paragraph 1 of this article shall provide for the establishment of joint bodies. The tasks of these joint bodies shall be, *inter alia*, and without prejudice to relevant existing agreements or arrangements, the following:

(a) To collect, compile and evaluate data in order to identify pollution sources likely to cause transboundary impact;

(b) To elaborate joint monitoring programmes concerning water quality and quantity;

(c) To draw up inventories and exchange information on the pollution sources mentioned in paragraph 2(a) of this article;

(d) To elaborate emission limits for waste water and evaluate the effectiveness of control programmes;

(e) To elaborate joint water-quality objectives and criteria having regard to the provisions of article 3, paragraph 3 of this Convention, and to propose relevant measures for maintaining and, where necessary, improving the existing water quality;

(f) To develop concerted action programmes for the reduction of pollution loads from both point sources (e.g. municipal and industrial sources) and diffuse sources (particularly from agriculture);

(g) To establish warning and alarm procedures;

(h) To serve as a forum for the exchange of information on existing and planned uses of water and related installations that are likely to cause transboundary impact;

(i) To promote cooperation and exchange of information on the best available technology in accordance with the provisions of article 13 of this Convention, as well as to encourage cooperation in scientific research programmes;

(j) To participate in the implementation of environmental impact assessments relating to transboundary waters, in accordance with appropriate international regulations.

3. In cases where a coastal State, being Party to this Convention, is directly and significantly affected by transboundary impact, the Riparian Parties can, if they all so agree, invite that coastal State to be involved in an appropriate manner in the activities of multilateral joint bodies established by Parties riparian to such transboundary waters.

4. Joint bodies according to this Convention shall invite joint bodies, established by coastal States for the protection of the marine environment directly affected by transboundary impact, to cooperate in order to harmonize their work and to prevent, control and reduce the transboundary impact.

5. Where two or more joint bodies exist in the same catchment area, they shall endeavour to coordinate their activities in order to strengthen the prevention, control and reduction of transboundary impact within that catchment area.

Article 10
Consultations

Consultations shall be held between the Riparian Parties on the basis of reciprocity, good faith and good-neighbourliness, at the request of any such Party. Such consultations shall aim at cooperation regarding the issues covered by the provisions of this Convention. Any such consultations shall be conducted through a joint body established under article 9 of this Convention, where one exists.

Article 11
Joint Monitoring and Assessment

1. In the framework of general cooperation mentioned in article 9 of this Convention, or specific arrangements, the Riparian Parties shall establish and implement joint programmes for monitoring the conditions of transboundary waters, including floods and ice drifts, as well as transboundary impact.

2. The Riparian Parties shall agree upon pollution parameters and pollutants whose discharges and concentration in transboundary waters shall be regularly monitored.

3. The Riparian Parties shall, at regular intervals, carry out joint or coordinated assessments of the conditions of transboundary waters and the effectiveness of measures taken for the prevention, control and reduction of transboundary impact. The results of these assessments shall be made available to the public in accordance with the provisions set out in article 16 of this Convention.

4. For these purposes, the Riparian Parties shall harmonize rules for the setting up and operation of monitoring programmes, measurement systems, devices, analytical techniques, data processing and evaluation procedures, and methods for the registration of pollutants discharged.

Article 12
Common Research and Development

In the framework of general cooperation mentioned in article 9 of this Convention, or specific arrangements, the Riparian Parties shall undertake specific research and development activities in support of achieving and maintaining the water-quality objectives and criteria which they have agreed to set and adopt.

Article 13
Exchange of Information between Riparian Parties

1. The Riparian Parties shall, within the framework of relevant agreements or other arrangements according to article 9 of this Convention, exchange reasonably available data, *inter alia*, on:

    (a) Environmental conditions of transboundary waters;
    (b) Experience gained in the application and operation of best available technology and results of research and development;
    (c) Emission and monitoring data;
    (d) Measures taken and planned to be taken to prevent, control and reduce transboundary impact;
    (e) Permits or regulations for waste-water discharges issued by the competent authority or appropriate body.

2. In order to harmonize emission limits, the Riparian Parties shall undertake the exchange of information on their national regulations.

3. If a Riparian Party is requested by another Riparian Party to provide data or information that is not available, the former shall endeavour to comply with the request but may condition its compliance upon the payment, by the requesting Party, of reasonable charges for collecting and, where appropriate, processing such data or information.

4. For the purposes of the implementation of this Convention, the Riparian Parties shall facilitate the exchange of best available technology, particularly through the promotion of: the commercial exchange of available technology; direct industrial contacts and cooperation, including joint ventures; the exchange of information and experience; and the provision of technical assistance. The Riparian Parties shall also undertake joint training programmes and the organization of relevant seminars and meetings.

Article 14
Warning and Alarm Systems

The Riparian Parties shall without delay inform each other about any critical situation that may have transboundary impact. The Riparian Parties shall set up, where appropriate, and operate coordinated or joint communication, warning and alarm systems with the aim of obtaining and transmitting information. These systems shall operate on the basis of compatible data transmission and treatment procedures and facilities to be agreed upon by the Riparian Parties. The Riparian Parties shall inform each other about competent authorities or points of contact designated for this purpose.

Article 15
Mutual Assistance

1. If a critical situation should arise, the Riparian Parties shall provide mutual assistance upon request, following procedures to be established in accordance with paragraph 2 of this article.

2. The Riparian Parties shall elaborate and agree upon procedures for mutual assistance addressing, *inter alia*, the following issues:

   (a) The direction, control, coordination and supervision of assistance;
   (b) Local facilities and services to be rendered by the Party requesting assistance, including, where necessary, the facilitation of border-crossing formalities;
   (c) Arrangements for holding harmless, indemnifying and/or compensating the assisting Party and/or its personnel, as well as for transit through territories of third Parties, where necessary;
   (d) Methods of reimbursing assistance services.

Article 16
Public Information

1. The Riparian Parties shall ensure that information on the conditions of transboundary waters, measures taken or planned to be taken to prevent, control and reduce transboundary impact, and the effectiveness of those measures, is made available to the public. For this purpose, the Riparian Parties shall ensure that the following information is made available to the public:

   (a) Water-quality objectives;
   (b) Permits issued and the conditions required to be met;
   (c) Results of water and effluent sampling carried out for the purposes of monitoring and assessment, as well as results of checking compliance with the water-quality objectives or the permit conditions.

2. The Riparian Parties shall ensure that this information shall be available

to the public at all reasonable times for inspection free of charge, and shall provide members of the public with reasonable facilities for obtaining from the Riparian Parties, on payment of reasonable charges, copies of such information.

Part III
Institutional and Final Provisions

Article 17
Meeting of Parties

1. The first meeting of the Parties shall be convened no later than one year after the date of the entry into force of this Convention. Thereafter, ordinary meetings shall be held every three years, or at shorter intervals as laid down in the rules of procedure. The Parties shall hold an extraordinary meeting if they so decide in the course of an ordinary meeting or at the written request of any Party, provided that, within six months of it being communicated to all Parties, the said request is supported by at least one-third of the Parties.

2. At their meetings, the Parties shall keep under continuous review the implementation of this Convention, and, with this purpose in mind, shall:

(a) Review the policies for and methodological approaches to the protection and use of transboundary waters of the Parties with a view to further improving the protection and use of transboundary waters;

(b) Exchange information regarding experience gained in concluding and implementing bilateral and multilateral agreements or other arrangements regarding the protection and use of transboundary waters to which one or more of the Parties are party;

(c) Seek, where appropriate, the services of relevant ECE bodies as well as other competent international bodies and specific committees in all aspects pertinent to the achievement of the purposes of this Convention;

(d) At their first meeting, consider and by consensus adopt rules of procedure for their meetings;

(e) Consider and adopt proposals for amendments to this Convention;

(f) Consider and undertake any additional action that may be required for the achievement of the purposes of this Convention.

Article 18
Right to Vote

1. Except as provided for in paragraph 2 of this article, each Party to this Convention shall have one vote.

2. Regional economic integration organizations, in matters within their

competence, shall exercise their right to vote with a number of votes equal to the number of their member States which are Parties to this Convention. Such organizations shall not exercise their right to vote if their member States exercise theirs, and vice versa.

Article 19
Secretariat

The Executive Secretary of the Economic Commission for Europe shall carry out the following secretariat functions:

    (a) The convening and preparing of meetings of the Parties;
    (b) The transmission to the Parties of reports and other information received in accordance with the provisions of this Convention;
    (c) The performance of such other functions as may be determined by the Parties.

Article 20
Annexes

Annexes to this Convention shall constitute an integral part thereof.

Article 21
Amendments to the Convention

1. Any Party may propose amendments to this Convention.

2. Proposals for amendments to this Convention shall be considered at a meeting of the Parties.

3. The text of any proposed amendment to this Convention shall be submitted in writing to the Executive Secretary of the Economic Commission for Europe, who shall communicate it to all Parties at least ninety days before the meeting at which it is proposed for adoption.

4. An amendment to the present Convention shall be adopted by consensus of the representatives of the Parties to this Convention present at a meeting of the Parties, and shall enter into force for the Parties to the Convention which have accepted it on the ninetieth day after the date on which two-thirds of those Parties have deposited with the Depositary their instruments of acceptance of the amendment. The amendment shall enter into force for any other Party on the ninetieth day after the date on which that Party deposits its instrument of acceptance of the amendment.

Article 22
Settlement of Disputes

1. If a dispute arises between two or more Parties about the interpretation or application of this Convention, they shall seek a solution by negotiation or by any other means of dispute settlement acceptable to the parties to the dispute.

2. When signing, ratifying, accepting, approving or acceding to this Convention, or at any time thereafter, a Party may declare in writing to the Depositary that, for a dispute not resolved in accordance with paragraph 1 of this article, it accepts one or both of the following means of dispute settlement as compulsory in relation to any Party accepting the same obligation:

(a) Submission of the dispute to the International Court of Justice;

(b) Arbitration in accordance with the procedure set out in annex IV.

3. If the parties to the dispute have accepted both means of dispute settlement referred to in paragraph 2 of this article, the dispute may be submitted only to the International Court of Justice, unless the parties agree otherwise.

Article 23
Signature

This Convention shall be open for signature at Helsinki from 17 to 18 March 1992 inclusive, and thereafter at United Nations Headquarters in New York until 18 September 1992, by States members of the Economic Commission for Europe as well as States having consultative status with the Economic Commission for Europe pursuant to paragraph 8 of Economic and Social Council resolution 36 (IV) of 28 March 1947, and by regional economic integration organizations constituted by sovereign States members of the Economic Commission for Europe to which their member States have transferred competence over matters governed by this Convention, including the competence to enter into treaties in respect of these matters.

Article 24
Depositary

The Secretary-General of the United Nations shall act as the Depositary of this Convention.

Article 25
Ratification, Acceptance, Approval and Accession

1. This Convention shall be subject to ratification, acceptance or approval by signatory States and regional economic integration organizations.

2. This Convention shall be open for accession by the States and organizations referred to in article 23.

3. Any organization referred to in article 23 which becomes a Party to this Convention without any of its member States being a Party shall be bound by all the obligations under this Convention. In the case of such organizations, one or more of whose member States is a Party to this Convention, the organization and its member States shall decide on

their respective responsibilities for the performance of their obligations under this Convention. In such cases, the organization and the member States shall not be entitled to exercise rights under this Convention concurrently.

4. In their instruments of ratification, acceptance, approval or accession, the regional economic integration organizations referred to in article 23 shall declare the extent of their competence with respect to the matters governed by this Convention. These organizations shall also inform the Depositary of any substantial modification to the extent of their competence.

Article 26
Entry into Force

1. This Convention shall enter into force on the ninetieth day after the date of deposit of the sixteenth instrument of ratification, acceptance, approval or accession.

2. For the purposes of paragraph 1 of this article, any instrument deposited by a regional economic integration organization shall not be counted as additional to those deposited by States members of such an organization.

3. For each State or organization referred to in article 23 which ratifies, accepts or approves this Convention or accedes thereto after the deposit of the sixteenth instrument of ratification, acceptance, approval or accession, the Convention shall enter into force on the ninetieth day after the date of deposit by such State or organization of its instrument of ratification, acceptance, approval or accession.

Article 27
Withdrawal

At any time after three years from the date on which this Convention has come into force with respect to a Party, that Party may withdraw from the Convention by giving written notification to the Depositary. Any such withdrawal shall take effect on the ninetieth day after the date of its receipt by the Depositary.

Article 28
Authentic Texts

The original of this Convention, of which the English, French and Russian texts are equally authentic, shall be deposited with the Secretary-General of the United Nations.

IN WITNESS WHEREOF the undersigned, being duly authorized thereto, have signed this Convention.

DONE at Helsinki, this seventeenth day of March one thousand nine hundred and ninety-two.

Annex I
Definition of the Term 'Best Available Technology'

1. The term 'best available technology' is taken to mean the latest stage of development of processes, facilities or methods of operation which indicate the practical suitability of a particular measure for limiting discharges, emissions and waste. In determining whether a set of processes, facilities and methods of operation constitute the best available technology in general or individual cases, special consideration is given to:

(a) Comparable processes, facilities or methods of operation which have recently been successfully tried out;
(b) Technological advances and changes in scientific knowledge and understanding;
(c) The economic feasibility of such technology;
(d) Time limits for installation in both new and existing plants;
(e) The nature and volume of the discharges and effluents concerned;
(f) Low- and non-waste technology.

2. It therefore follows that what is 'best available technology' for a particular process will change with time in the light of technological advances, economic and social factors, as well as in the light of changes in scientific knowledge and understanding.

Annex II
Guidelines for Developing Best Environmental Practices

1. In selecting for individual cases the most appropriate combination of measures which may constitute the best environmental practice, the following graduated range of measures should be considered:

(a) Provision of information and education to the public and to users about the environmental consequences of the choice of particular activities and products, their use and ultimate disposal;
(b) The development and application of codes of good environmental practice which cover all aspects of the product's life;
(c) Labels informing users of environmental risks related to a product, its use and ultimate disposal;
(d) Collection and disposal systems available to the public;
(e) Recycling, recovery and reuse;
(f) Application of economic instruments to activities, products or groups of products;
(g) A system of licensing, which involves a range of restrictions or a ban.

2. In determining what combination of measures constitute best environmental practices, in general or in individual cases, particular consideration should be given to:

    (a) The environmental hazard of:
        (i) The product;
        (ii) The product's production;
        (iii) The product's use;
        (iv) The product's ultimate disposal;
    (b) Substitution by less polluting processes or substances;
    (c) Scale of use;
    (d) Potential environmental benefit or penalty of substitute materials or activities;
    (e) Advances and changes in scientific knowledge and understanding;
    (f) Time limits for implementation;
    (g) Social and economic implications.

3. It therefore follows that best environmental practices for a particular source will change with time in the light of technological advances, economic and social factors, as well as in the light of changes in scientific knowledge and understanding.

Annex III
Guidelines for Developing Water-quality Objectives and Criteria

Water-quality objectives and criteria shall:

    (a) Take into account the aim of maintaining and, where necessary, improving the existing water quality;
    (b) Aim at the reduction of average pollution loads (in particular hazardous substances) to a certain degree within a certain period of time;
    (c) Take into account specific water-quality requirements (raw water for drinking-water purposes, irrigation, etc.);
    (d) Take into account specific requirements regarding sensitive and specially protected waters and their environment, e.g. lakes and groundwater resources;
    (e) Be based on the application of ecological classification methods and chemical indices for the medium- and long-term review of water-quality maintenance and improvement;
    (f) Take into account the degree to which objectives are reached and the additional protective measures, based on emission limits, which may be required in individual cases.

Annex IV
Arbitration

1. In the event of a dispute being submitted for arbitration pursuant to article 22, paragraph 2 of this Convention, a party or parties shall notify the secretariat of the subject-matter of arbritration and indicate, in particular, the articles of this Convention whose interpretation or application is at issue. The secretariat shall forward the information received to all Parties to this Convention.

2. The arbitral tribunal shall consist of three members. Both the claimant party or parties and the other party or parties to the dispute shall appoint an arbitrator, and the two arbitrators so appointed shall designate by common agreement the third arbitrator, who shall be the president of the arbitral tribunal. The latter shall not be a national of one of the parties to the dispute, nor have his or her usual place of residence in the territory of one of these parties, nor be employed by any of them, nor have dealt with the case in any other capacity.

3. If the president of the arbitral tribunal has not been designated within two months of the appointment of the second arbitrator, the Executive Secretary of the Economic Commission for Europe shall, at the request of either party to the dispute, designate the president within a further two-month period.

4. If one of the parties to the dispute does not appoint an arbitrator within two months of the receipt of the request, the other party may so inform the Executive Secretary of the Economic Commission for Europe, who shall designate the president of the arbitral tribunal within a further two-month period. Upon designation, the president of the arbitral tribunal shall request the party which has not appointed an arbitrator to do so within two months. If it fails to do so within that period, the president shall so inform the Executive Secretary of the Economic Commission for Europe, who shall make this appointment within a further two-month period.

5. The arbitral tribunal shall render its decision in accordance with international law and the provisions of this Convention.

6. Any arbitral tribunal constituted under the provisions set out in this annex shall draw up its own rules of procedure.

7. The decisions of the arbitral tribunal, both on procedure and on substance, shall be taken by majority vote of its members.

8. The tribunal may take all appropriate measures to establish the facts.

9. The parties to the dispute shall facilitate the work of the arbitral tribunal and, in particular, using all means at their disposal, shall:

(a) Provide it with all relevant documents, facilities and information;

(b) Enable it, where necessary, to call witnesses or experts and receive their evidence.

10. The parties and the arbitrators shall protect the confidentiality of any information they receive in confidence during the proceedings of the arbitral tribunal.

11. The arbitral tribunal may, at the request of one of the parties, recommend interim measures of protection.

12. If one of the parties to the dispute does not appear before the arbitral tribunal or fails to defend its case, the other party may request the tribunal to continue the proceedings and to render its final decision. Absence of a party or failure of a party to defend its case shall not constitute a bar to the proceedings.

13. The arbitral tribunal may hear and determine counter-claims arising directly out of the subject-matter of the dispute.

14. Unless the arbitral tribunal determines otherwise because of the particular circumstances of the case, the expenses of the tribunal, including the remuneration of its members, shall be borne by the parties to the dispute in equal shares. The tribunal shall keep a record of all its expenses, and shall furnish a final statement thereof to the parties.

15. Any Party to this Convention which has an interest of a legal nature in the subject-matter of the dispute, and which may be affected by a decision in the case, may intervene in the proceedings with the consent of the tribunal.

16. The arbitral tribunal shall render its award within five months of the date on which it is established, unless it finds it necessary to extend the time limit for a period which should not exceed five months.

17. The award of the arbitral tribunal shall be accompanied by a statement of reasons. It shall be final and binding upon all parties to the dispute. The award will be transmitted by the arbitral tribunal to the parties to the dispute and to the secretariat. The secretariat will forward the information received to all Parties to this Convention.

18. Any dispute which may arise between the parties concerning the interpretation or execution of the award may be submitted by either party to the arbitral tribunal which made the award or, if the latter cannot be seized thereof, to another tribunal constituted for this purpose in the same manner as the first.

ILC Draft Articles on the Non-navigational Uses of International Watercourses, 1994

The draft articles reproduced here were adopted by the International Law Commission at its 46th Session in 1994. In resolution 49/52 the UN General Assembly at its 49th Session decided to convene an international conference in 1996 to elaborate a framework convention on the law of the non-navigational uses of international watercourses based on the Commission's draft, following an opportunity for written comments and observations by states. The Commission's draft represents the first attempt since the ILA's Helsinki Rules, *repr.* ILA, *Fifty Second Report* (1966) 485, to codify and develop the law of international watercourses. The present articles are significant with regard to environmental issues in several ways. Part III establishes a system of notification and consultation on the possible effects of planned measures on the condition of a watercourse. These articles differ only in detail from existing customary law and are supported by significant state practice. Part IV includes obligations of ecosystem protection, pollution prevention, and protection of the marine environment which are now more widely reflected in regional treaties, in the 1982 UNCLOS, and in the contemporary development of international environmental law, including the law on land-based sources of marine pollution. In Part II general principles of equitable utilization and an obligation not to cause significant harm are formulated in terms which draw heavily on a study of existing treaties and state practice. The Commission has endorsed these general principles as representing established international law. Not surprisingly the standard of care which the Commission derives from these sources is not one of strict liability for damage but does require diligent conduct to prevent adverse effects. The permissibility of harm which results despite meeting this standard of conduct must then be judged on equitable criteria, and must be consistent with 'adequate protection' of the watercourse.

The Commission's work is based solidly on precedent, and, as far as possible, on the material evidence of state practice. It is both exhaustive and authoritative, and represents an important guide to the contemporary law. For background material and consideration of the work of earlier ILC rapporteurs, see UN, *Yearbook of the ILC* from 1974 to 1991. The 1994 draft articles are reproduced from UN Doc. A/CN.4/L492 and Add. 1 (1994). For commentary see 1st and 2nd Reports of the Special Rapporteur, UN Docs. A/CN.4/451 (1993) and A/CN.4/462 (1994) and Reports of the Commission in II *Yearbook of the ILC* (1993), (1994). The 1991 text of the draft articles is discussed in 3 *Col. JIELP* (1992), 1–334. See generally P. W. Birnie and A. E. Boyle, *International Law and the Environment* (Oxford, 1992) 215ff; J. Lammers, *Pollution of International Watercourses* (The Hague, 1984).

TEXT

Part I
Introduction

Article 1
Scope of the present articles

1. The present articles apply to uses of international watercourses and of

their waters for purposes other than navigation and to measures of conservation and management related to the uses of those watercourses and their waters.

2. The use of international watercourses for navigation is not within the scope of the present articles except in so far as other uses affect navigation or are affected by navigation.

Article 2
Use of terms

For the purposes of the present articles:

(a) 'international watercourse' means a watercourse, parts of which are situated in different States;
(b) 'watercourse' means a system of surface waters and groundwaters constituting by virtue of their physical relationship a unitary whole and normally flowing into a common terminus;
(c) 'watercourse State' means a State in whose territory part of an international watercourse is situated.

Article 3
Watercourse agreements

1. Watercourse States may enter into one or more agreements, hereinafter referred to as 'watercourse agreements', which apply and adjust the provisions of the present articles to the characteristics and uses of a particular international watercourse or part thereof.

2. Where a watercourse agreement is concluded between two or more watercourse States, it shall define the waters to which it applies. Such an agreement may be entered into with respect to an entire international watercourse or with respect to any part thereof or a particular project, programme or use, provided that the agreement does not adversely affect, to a significant extent, the use by one or more other watercourse States of the waters of the watercourse.

3. Where a watercourse State considers that adjustment or application of the provisions of the present articles is required because of the characteristics and uses of a particular international watercourse, watercourse States shall consult with a view to negotiating in good faith for the purpose of concluding a watercourse agreement or agreements.

Article 4
Parties to watercourse agreements

1. Every watercourse State is entitled to participate in the negotiation of and to become a party to any watercourse agreement that applies to the entire international watercourse, as well as to participate in any relevant consultations.

2. A watercourse State whose use of an international watercourse may be affected to a significant extent by the implementation of a proposed watercourse agreement that applies only to a part of the watercourse or to a particular project, programme or use is entitled to participate in consultations on, and in the negotiation of, such an agreement, to the extent that its use is thereby affected, and to become a party thereto.

Part II
General Principles

Article 5
Equitable and reasonable utilization and participation

1. Watercourse States shall in their respective territories utilize an international watercourse in an equitable and reasonable manner. In particular, an international watercourse shall be used and developed by watercourse States with a view to attaining optimal utilization thereof and benefits therefrom consistent with adequate protection of the watercourse.

2. Watercourse States shall participate in the use, development and protection of an international watercourse in an equitable and reasonable manner. Such participation includes both the right to utilize the watercourse and the duty to cooperate in the protection and development thereof, as provided in the present articles.

Article 6
Factors relevant to equitable and reasonable utilization

1. Utilization of an international watercourse in an equitable and reasonable manner within the meaning of article 5 requires taking into account all relevant factors and circumstances, including:

(a) geographic, hydrographic, hydrological, climatic, ecological and other factors of a natural character;
(b) the social and economic needs of the watercourse States concerned;
(c) the population dependent on the watercourse in each watercourse State;
(d) the effects of the use or uses of the watercourse in one watercourse State on other watercourse States;
(e) existing and potential uses of the watercourse;
(f) conservation, protection, development and economy of use of the water resources of the watercourse and the costs of measures taken to that effect;
(g) the availability of alternatives, of corresponding value, to a particular planned or existing use.

2. In the application of article 5 or paragraph 1 of this article, watercourse States concerned shall, when the need arises, enter into consultations in a spirit of cooperation.

Article 7
Obligation not to cause significant harm

1. Watercourse States shall exercise due diligence to utilize an international watercourse in such a way as not to cause significant harm to other watercourse States.

2. Where, despite the exercise of due diligence, significant harm is caused to another watercourse State, the State whose use causes the harm shall, in the absence of agreement to such use, consult with the State suffering such harm over:

    (a) the extent to which such use has proved equitable and reasonable taking into account the factors listed in article 6;

    (b) the question of ad hoc adjustments to its utilization, designed to eliminate or mitigate any such harm caused and, where appropriate, the question of compensation.

Article 8
General obligation to cooperate

Watercourse States shall cooperate on the basis of sovereign equality, territorial integrity and mutual benefit in order to attain optimal utilization and adequate protection of an international watercourse.

Article 9
Regular exchange of data and information

1. Pursuant to article 8, watercourse States shall on a regular basis exchange readily available data and information on the condition of the watercourse, in particular that of a hydrological, meteorological, hydrogeological and ecological nature, as well as related forecasts.

2. If a watercourse State is requested by another watercourse State to provide data or information that is not readily available, it shall employ its best efforts to comply with the request but may condition its compliance upon payment by the requesting State of the reasonable costs of collecting and, where appropriate, processing such data or information.

3. Watercourse States shall employ their best efforts to collect and, where appropriate, to process data and information in a manner which facilitates its utilization by the other watercourse States to which it is communicated.

Article 10
Relationship between different kinds of uses

1. In the absence of agreement or custom to the contrary, no use of an

international watercourse enjoys inherent priority over other uses.

2. In the event of a conflict between uses of an international watercourse, it shall be resolved with reference to the principles and factors set out in articles 5 to 7, with special regard being given to the requirements of vital human needs.

Part III
Planned Measures

Article 11
Information concerning planned measures

Watercourse States shall exchange information and consult each other on the possible effects of planned measures on the condition of an international watercourse.

Article 12
Notification concerning planned measures with possible adverse effects

Before a watercourse State implements or permits the implementation of planned measures which may have a significant adverse effect upon other watercourse States, it shall provide those States with timely notification thereof. Such notification shall be accompanied by available technical data and information in order to enable the notified States to evaluate the possible effects of the planned measures.

Article 13
Period for reply to notification
Unless otherwise agreed:

(a) a watercourse State providing a notification under article 12 shall allow the notified States a period of six months within which to study and evaluate the possible effects of the planned measures and to communicate the findings to it;

(b) this period shall, at the request of a notified State for which the evaluation of the planned measure poses special difficulty, be extended for a period not exceeding six months.

Article 14
Obligations of the notifying State during the period for reply

During the period referred to in article 13, the notifying State shall cooperate with the notified States by providing them, on request, with any additional data and information that is available and necessary for an accurate evaluation, and shall not implement or permit the implementation of the planned measures without the consent of the notified States.

Article 15
Reply to notification

1. The notified States shall communicate their findings to the notifying State as early as possible.

2. If a notified State finds that implementation of the planned measures would be inconsistent with the provisions of articles 5 or 7, it shall communicate this finding to the notifying State within the period applicable pursuant to article 13, together with a documented explanation setting forth the reasons for the finding.

Article 16
Absence of reply to notification

1. If, within the period applicable pursuant to article 13, the notifying State receives no communication under paragraph 2 of article 15, it may, subject to its obligations under articles 5 and 7, proceed with the implementation of the planned measures, in accordance with the notification and any other data and information provided to the notified States.

2. Any claim to compensation by a notified State which has failed to reply may be offset by the costs incurred by the notifying State for action undertaken after the expiration of the time for a reply which would not have been undertaken if the notified State had objected within the period applicable pursuant to article 13.

Article 17
Consultations and negotiations concerning planned measures

1. If a communication is made under paragraph 2 of article 15, the notifying State and the State making the communication shall enter into consultations and, if necessary, negotiations with a view to arriving at an equitable resolution of the situation.

2. The consultations and negotiations shall be conducted on the basis that each State must in good faith pay reasonable regard to the rights and legitimate interests of the other State.

3. During the course of the consultations and negotiations, the notifying State shall, if so requested by the notified State at the time it makes the communication, refrain from implementing or permitting the implementation of the planned measures for a period not exceeding six months.

Article 18
Procedures in the absence of notification

1. If a watercourse State has serious reason to believe that another watercourse State is planning measures that may have a significant adverse effect upon it, the former State may request the latter to apply the provisions of

article 12. The request shall be accompanied by a documented explanation setting forth its reasons.

2. In the event that the State planning the measures nevertheless finds that it is not under an obligation to provide a notification under article 12, it shall so inform the other State, providing a documented explanation setting forth the reasons for such finding. If this finding does not satisfy the other State, the two States shall, at the request of that other State, promptly enter into consultations and negotiations in the manner indicated in paragraphs 1 and 2 of article 17.

3. During the course of the consultations and negotiations, the State planning the measures shall, if so requested by the other State at the time it requests the initiation of consultations and negotiations, refrain from implementing or permitting the implementation of those measures for a period not exceeding six months.

Article 19
Urgent implementation of planned measures

1. In the event that the implementation of planned measures is of the utmost urgency in order to protect public health, public safety or other equally important interests, the State planning the measures may, subject to articles 5 and 7, immediately proceed to implementation, notwithstanding the provisions of article 14 and paragraph 3 of article 17.

2. In such cases, a formal declaration of the urgency of the measures shall be communicated to the other watercourse States referred to in article 12 together with the relevant data and information.

3. The State planning the measures shall, at the request of any of the States referred to in paragraph 2, promptly enter into consultations and negotiations with it in the manner indicated in paragraphs 1 and 2 of article 17.

Part IV
Protection, Preservation and Management

Article 20
Protection and preservation of ecosystems

Watercourse States shall, individually or jointly, protect and preserve the ecosystems of international watercourses.

Article 21
Prevention, reduction and control of pollution

1. For the purposes of this article, 'pollution of an international watercourse' means any detrimental alteration in the composition or quality of

the waters of an international watercourse which results directly or indirectly from human conduct.

2. Watercourse States shall, individually or jointly, prevent, reduce and control pollution of an international watercourse that may cause significant harm to other watercourse States or to their environment, including harm to human health or safety, to the use of the waters for any beneficial purpose or to the living resources of the watercourse. Watercourse States shall take steps to harmonize their policies in this connection.

3. Watercourse States shall, at the request of any of them, consult with a view to establishing lists of substances, the introduction of which into the waters of an international watercourse is to be prohibited, limited, investigated or monitored.

Article 22
Introduction of alien or new species

Watercourse States shall take all measures necessary to prevent the introduction of species, alien or new, into an international watercourse which may have effects detrimental to the ecosystem of the watercourse resulting in significant harm to other watercourse States.

Article 23
Protection and preservation of the marine environment

Watercourse States shall, individually or jointly, take all measures with respect to an international watercourse that are necessary to protect and preserve the marine environment, including estuaries, taking into account generally accepted international rules and standards.

Article 24
Management

1. Watercourse States shall, at the request of any of them, enter into consultations concerning the management of an international watercourse, which may include the establishment of a joint management mechanism.

2. For the purposes of this article, 'management' refers, in particular, to:

   (a) planning the sustainable development of an international watercourse and providing for the implementation of any plans adopted; and
   (b) otherwise promoting rational and optimal utilization, protection and control of the watercourse.

Article 25
Regulation

1. Watercourse States shall cooperate, where appropriate, to respond to

needs or opportunities for regulation of the flow of the waters of an international watercourse.

2. Unless otherwise agreed, watercourse States shall participate on an equitable basis in the construction and maintenance or defrayal of the costs of such regulation works as they may have agreed to undertake.

3. For the purpose of this article, 'regulation' means the use of hydraulic works or any other continuing measure to alter, vary or otherwise control the flow of the waters of an international watercourse.

Article 26
Installations

1. Watercourse States shall, within their respective territories, employ their best efforts to maintain and protect installations, facilities and other works related to an international watercourse.

2. Watercourse States shall, at the request of any of them which has serious reason to believe that it may suffer significant adverse effects, enter into consultations with regard to:

(a) the safe operation or maintenance of installations, facilities or other works related to an international watercourse; or

(b) the protection of installations, facilities or other works from wilful or negligent acts or the forces of nature.

Part V
Harmful Conditions and Emergency Situations

Article 27
Prevention and mitigation of harmful conditions

Watercourse States shall, individually or jointly, take all appropriate measures to prevent or mitigate conditions that may be harmful to other watercourse States, whether resulting from natural causes or human conduct, such as flood or ice conditions, water-borne diseases, siltation, erosion, salt-water intrusion, drought or desertification.

Article 28
Emergency situations

1. For the purposes of this article, 'emergency' means a situation that causes, or poses an imminent threat of causing, serious harm to watercourse States or other States and that results suddenly from natural causes, such as floods, the breaking up of ice, landslides or earthquakes, or from human conduct, such as industrial accidents.

2. A watercourse State shall, without delay and by the most expeditious means available, notify other potentially affected States and competent

international organizations of any emergency originating within its territory.

3. A watercourse State within whose territory an emergency originates shall, in cooperation with potentially affected States and, where appropriate, competent international organizations, immediately take all practicable measures necessitated by the circumstances to prevent, mitigate and eliminate harmful effects of the emergency.

4. When necessary, watercourse States shall jointly develop contingency plans for responding to emergencies, in cooperation, where appropriate, with other potentially affected States and competent international organizations.

Part VI
Miscellaneous Provisions

Article 29
International watercourses and installations in time of armed conflict

International watercourses and related installations, facilities and other works shall enjoy the protection accorded by the principles and rules of international law applicable in international and internal armed conflict and shall not be used in violation of those principles and rules.

Article 30
Indirect procedures

In cases where there are serious obstacles to direct contacts between watercourse States, the States concerned shall fulfil their obligations of cooperation provided for in the present articles, including exchange of data and information, notification, communication, consultations and negotiations, through any direct procedure accepted by them.

Article 31
Data and information vital to national defence or security

Nothing in the present articles obliges a watercourse State to provide data or information vital to its national defence or security. Nevertheless, that State shall cooperate in good faith with the other watercourse States with a view to providing as much information as possible under the circumstances.

Article 32
Non-discrimination

Unless the watercourse States concerned have agreed otherwise for the protection of the interests of persons, natural or juridical, who have suffered or are under a serious threat of suffering significant transboundary harm as a result of activities related to an international watercourse, a watercourse State shall not discriminate on the basis of nationality or residence or place where the injury occurred, in granting to such persons, in accordance with its legal system, access to judicial or other procedures, or a right to claim compensation or other relief in respect of significant harm caused by such activities carried on under its jurisdiction.

Article 33
Settlement of disputes

In the absence of an applicable agreement between the watercourse States concerned, any watercourse dispute concerning a question of fact or the interpretation or application of the present articles shall be settled in accordance with the following provisions:

(a) If such a dispute arises, the States concerned shall expeditiously enter into consultations and negotiations with a view to arriving at equitable solutions of the dispute, making use, as appropriate, of any joint watercourse institutions that may have been established by them.

(b) If the States concerned have not arrived at a settlement of the disputes through consultations and negotiations, at any time after six months from the date of the request for consultations and negotiations, they shall at the request of any of them have recourse to impartial fact-finding or, if agreed upon by the States concerned, mediation or conciliation.

   (i) Unless otherwise agreed, a Fact-Finding Commission shall be established, composed of one member nominated by each State concerned and in addition a member not having the nationality of any of the States concerned chosen by the nominated members who shall serve as Chairman.

  (ii) If the members nominated by States are unable to agree on a Chairman within four months of the request for the establishment of the Commission, any State concerned may request the Secretary-General of the United Nations to appoint the Chairman. If one of the States fails to nominate a member within four months of the initial request pursuant to paragraph (b), any other State concerned may request the Secretary-General of the United Nations to appoint a person who shall not have the nationality of any of the States concerned, who shall constitute a single member Commission.

 (iii) The Commission shall determine its own procedure.

 (iv) The States concerned have the obligation to provide the Commission with such information as it may require and, on request, to permit the Commission to have access to their respective territory and to inspect any facilities, plant, equipment, construction or natural feature relevant for the purpose of its inquiry.

(v) The Commission shall adopt its report by a majority vote, unless it is a single member Commission, and shall submit that report to the States concerned setting forth its findings and the reasons therefor and such recommendations as it deems appropriate.

(vi) The expenses of the Commission shall be borne equally by the States concerned.

(c) If, after 12 months from the initial request for fact-finding, mediation or conciliation or, if a fact-finding, mediation or conciliation commission has been established, six months after receipt of a report from the Commission, whichever is the later, the States concerned have been unable to settle the dispute, they may by agreement submit the dispute to arbitration or judicial settlement.

8. CONSERVATION OF NATURE AND LIVING RESOURCES

Convention for the Protection of the World Cultural and Natural Heritage, Paris, 16 November 1972

The Convention was negotiated under the auspices of the United Nations Educational, Scientific and Cultural Organization (UNESCO) and was adopted on 16 November 1972 by the General Conference of UNESCO at its seventeenth session held in Paris. It entered into force on 17 December 1975. The text is *repr.* in 27 *UST* 37 *TIAS* 8226; 11 *ILM* (1972) 1358; *UKTS* 2 (1985) Cmnd. 9424. The Convention had 132 parties in 1993; reservations have been entered by thirteen states. For the background to the Convention see *Protection of Mankind's Cultural Heritage, Sites and Monuments* (UNESCO, Paris, 1970); R. L. Meyer, 'Travaux Préparatoires for the UNESCO World Heritage Convention', 2 *Earth Law Journal* (1976) 45; Operational Guidelines for the Implementation of the World Heritage Convention, UNESCO Doc. WH C/2; Report of the Rapporteur, *World Heritage Committee*, UNESCO Doc. CC81/ Conf. 003/6; 008/2; UNESCO Doc. SC/83/Conf. 009/8; Doc. CLT 82/ Conf. U15/7.

The Convention requires states to conserve elements of world heritage, which can include natural areas of outstanding environmental interest situated in their territory. It establishes a World Heritage Committee and provides procedures for listing such sites on a World Heritage List as well as establishing a World Heritage Fund for assisting the conservation of listed sites. It recognises that the international community has a duty to conserve heritage of universal value. UNESCO has also adopted various relevant recommendations which define the principles and standards governing national action and list the measures required: see *Conventions and Recommendations of UNESCO concerning the Protection of the Cultural Heritage* (UNESCO, Paris, 1983), 75–94. For analysis of the World Heritage Convention's usefulness in protecting the environment, see S. Lyster, *International Wildlife Law,* (Cambridge, 1985), 208–38; P. W. Birnie and A. E. Boyle, *International Law and the Environment,* (Oxford, 1992), 59–60, 458, 468–70; L. Caldwell, *International Environmental Policy* (2nd edn., Durham, 1990), 90–3.

TEXT

The General Conference of the United Nations Educational, Scientific and Cultural Organization meeting in Paris from 17 October to 21 November 1972, at its seventeenth session,

Noting that the cultural heritage and the natural heritage are increasingly threatened with destruction not only by the traditional causes of decay, but also by changing social and economic conditions which aggravate the situation with even more formidable phenomena of damage or destruction,

Considering that deterioration or disappearance of any item of the cultural or natural heritage constitutes a harmful impoverishment of the heritage of all the nations of the world,

Considering that protection of this heritage at the national level often remains incomplete because of the scale of the resources which it requires and of the insufficient economic, scientific and technical resources of the country where the property to be protected is situated,

Recalling that the Constitution of the Organization provides that it will maintain, increase and diffuse knowledge, by assuring the conservation and protection of the world's heritage, and recommending to the nations concerned the necessary international conventions,

Considering that the existing international conventions, recommendations and resolutions concerning cultural and natural property demonstrate the importance, for all the peoples of the world, of safeguarding this unique and irreplaceable property, to whatever people it may belong,

Considering that parts of the cultural or natural heritage are of outstanding interest and therefore need to be preserved as part of the world heritage of mankind as a whole,

Considering that, in view of the magnitude and gravity of the new dangers threatening them, it is incumbent on the international community as a whole to participate in the protection of the cultural and natural heritage of outstanding universal value, by the granting of collective assistance which, although not taking the place of action by the State concerned, will serve as an effective complement thereto,

Considering that it is essential for this purpose to adopt new provisions in the form of a convention establishing an effective system of collective protection of the cultural and natural heritage of outstanding universal value, organized on a permanent basis and in accordance with modern scientific methods,

Having decided, at its sixteenth session, that this question should be made the subject of an international convention,

Adopts this sixteenth day of November 1972 this Convention.

I. Definitions of the Cultural and the Natural Heritage

Article 1

For the purposes of this Convention, the following shall be considered as 'cultural heritage':

monuments: architectural works, works of monumental sculpture and painting, elements or structures of an archaeological nature, inscriptions, cave dwellings and combinations of features, which are of outstanding universal value from the point of view of history, art or science;

groups of buildings: groups of separate or connected buildings which, because of their architecture, their homogeneity or their place in the landscape, are of outstanding universal value from the point of view of history, art or science;

sites: works of man or the combined works of nature and of man, and areas including archeological sites which are of outstanding universal value from the historical, aesthetic, ethnological or anthropological points of view.

Article 2

For the purposes of this Convention, the following shall be considered as 'natural heritage':

natural features consisting of physical and biological formations or groups of such formations, which are of outstanding universal value from the aesthetic or scientific point of view;

geological and physiographical formations and precisely delineated areas which constitute the habitat of threatened species of animals and plants of outstanding universal value from the point of view of science or conservation;

natural sites or precisely delineated areas of outstanding universal value from the point of view of science, conservation or natural beauty.

Article 3

It is for each State Party to this Convention to identify and delineate the different properties situated on its territory mentioned in Articles 1 and 2 above.

II. National Protection and International Protection of the Cultural and Natural Heritage

Article 4

Each State Party to this Convention recognizes that the duty of ensuring the identification, protection, conservation, presentation and transmission to future generations of the cultural and natural heritage referred to in Articles 1 and 2 and situated on its territory, belongs primarily to that State. It will do all it can to this end, to the utmost of its own resources and, where appropriate, with any international assistance and co-operation, in particular, financial, artistic, scientific and technical, which it may be able to obtain.

Article 5

To ensure that effective and active measures are taken for the protection, conservation and presentation of the cultural and natural heritage situated on its territory, each State Party to this Convention shall endeavour, in so far as possible, and as appropriate for each country:

(a) to adopt a general policy which aims to give the cultural and natural

heritage a function in the life of the community and to integrate the
protection of that heritage into comprehensive planning
programmes;

(b) to set up within its territories, where such services do not exist, one
or more services for the protection, conservation and presentation
of the cultural and natural heritage with an appropriate staff and
possessing the means to discharge their functions;

(c) to develop scientific and technical studies and research and to
work out such operating methods as will make the State capable of
counteracting the dangers that threaten its cultural or natural
heritage;

(d) to take the appropriate legal, scientific, technical, administrative
and financial measures necessary for the identification, protection, conservation, presentation and rehabilitation of this heritage; and

(e) to foster the establishment or development of national or regional
centres for training in the protection, conservation and presentation
of the cultural and natural heritage and to encourage scientific
research in this field.

Article 6

1. Whilst fully respecting the sovereignty of the States on whose territory
the cultural and natural heritage mentioned in Articles 1 and 2 is situated,
and without prejudice to property rights provided by national legislation,
the States Parties to this Convention recognize that such heritage constitutes a world heritage for whose protection it is the duty of the international
community as a whole to co-operate.

2. The States Parties undertake, in accordance with the provisions of this
Convention, to give their help in the identification, protection, conservation and preservation of the cultural and natural heritage referred to in
paragraphs 2 and 4 of Article 11 if the States on whose territory it is situated
so request.

3. Each State Party to this Convention undertakes not to take any deliberate measures which might damage directly or indirectly the cultural and
natural heritage referred to in Articles 1 and 2 situated on the territory of
other States Parties to this Convention.

Article 7

For the purpose of this Convention, international protection of the world
cultural and natural heritage shall be understood to mean the establishment of a system of international co-operation and assistance designed to
support States Parties to the Convention in their efforts to conserve and
identify that heritage.

III. Intergovernmental Committee for the Protection of the World Cultural and Natural Heritage

Article 8

1. An Intergovernmental Committee for the Protection of the Cultural and Natural Heritage of Outstanding Universal Value, called 'the World Heritage Committee', is hereby established within the United Nations Educational, Scientific and Cultural Organization. It shall be composed of 15 States Parties to the Convention, elected by States Parties to the Convention meeting in general assembly during the ordinary session of the General Conference of the United Nations Educational, Scientific and Cultural Organization. The number of States members of the Committee shall be increased to 21 as from the date of the ordinary session of the General Conference following the entry into force of this Convention for at least 40 States.

2. Election of members of the Committee shall ensure an equitable representation of the different regions and cultures of the world.

3. A representative of the International Centre for the Study of the Preservation and Restoration of Cultural Property (Rome Centre), a representative of the International Council of Monuments and Sites (ICOMOS) and a representative of the International Union for Conservation of Nature and Natural Resources (IUCN), to whom may be added, at the request of States Parties to the Convention meeting in general assembly during the ordinary sessions of the General Conference of the United Nations Educational, Scientific and Cultural Organization, representatives of other intergovernmental or non-governmental organizations, with similar objectives, may attend the meetings of the Committee in an advisory capacity.

Article 9

1. The term of office of States members of the World Heritage Committee shall extend from the end of the ordinary session of the General Conference during which they are elected until the end of its third subsequent ordinary session.

2. The term of office of one-third of the members designated at the time of the first election shall, however, cease at the end of the first ordinary session of the General Conference following that at which they were elected; and the term of office of a further third of the members designated at the same time shall cease at the end of the second ordinary session of the General Conference following that at which they were elected. The names of these members shall be chosen by lot by the President of the General Conference of the United Nations Educational, Scientific and Cultural Organization after the first election.

3. States members of the Committee shall choose as their representatives persons qualified in the field of the cultural or natural heritage.

Article 10

1. The World Heritage Committee shall adopt its Rules of Procedure.

2. The Committee may at any time invite public or private organizations or individuals to participate in its meetings for consultation on particular problems.

3. The Committee may create such consultative bodies as it deems necessary for the performance of its functions.

Article 11

1. Every State Party to this Convention shall, in so far as possible, submit to the World Heritage Committee an inventory of property forming part of the cultural and natural heritage, situated in its territory and suitable for inclusion in the list provided for in paragraph 2 of this Article. This inventory, which shall not be considered exhaustive, shall include documentation about the location of the property in question and its significance.

2. On the basis of the inventories submitted by States in accordance with paragraph 1, the Committee shall establish, keep up to date and publish, under the title of 'World Heritage List', a list of properties forming part of the cultural heritage and natural heritage, as defined in Articles 1 and 2 of this Convention, which it considers as having outstanding universal value in terms of such criteria as it shall have established. An updated list shall be distributed at least every two years.

3. The inclusion of a property in the World Heritage List requires the consent of the State concerned. The inclusion of a property situated in a territory, sovereignty or jurisdiction over which is claimed by more than one State shall in no way prejudice the rights of the parties to the dispute.

4. The Committee shall establish, keep up to date and publish, whenever circumstances shall so require, under the title of 'List of World Heritage in Danger', a list of the property appearing in the World Heritage List for the conservation of which major operations are necessary and for which assistance has been requested under this Convention. This list shall contain an estimate of the cost of such operations. The list may include only such property forming part of the cultural and natural heritage as is threatened by serious and specific dangers, such as the threat of disappearance caused by accelerated deterioration, large-scale public or private projects or rapid urban or tourist development projects; destruction caused by changes in the use or ownership of the land; major alterations due to unknown causes; abandonment for any reason whatsoever; the outbreak or the threat of an armed conflict; calamities and cataclysms; serious fires, earthquakes, land-

slides; volcanic eruptions; changes in water level, floods, and tidal waves. The Committee may at any time, in case of urgent need, make a new entry in the List of World Heritage in Danger and publicize such entry immediately.

5. The Committee shall define the criteria on the basis of which a property belonging to the cultural or natural heritage may be included in either of the lists mentioned in paragraphs 2 and 4 of this Article.

6. Before refusing a request for inclusion in one of the two lists mentioned in paragraphs 2 and 4 of this Article, the Committee shall consult the State Party in whose territory the cultural or natural property in question is situated.

7. The Committee shall, with the agreement of the States concerned, co-ordinate and encourage the studies and research needed for the drawing up of the lists referred to in paragraphs 2 and 4 of this Article.

Article 12

The fact that a property belonging to the cultural or natural heritage has not been included in either of the two lists mentioned in paragraphs 2 and 4 of Article 11 shall in no way be construed to mean that it does not have an outstanding universal value for purposes other than those resulting from inclusion in these lists.

Article 13

1. The World Heritage Committee shall receive and study requests for international assistance formulated by States Parties to this Convention with respect to property forming part of the cultural or natural heritage, situated in their territories, and included or potentially suitable for inclusion in the lists referred to in paragraphs 2 and 4 of Article 11. The purpose of such requests may be to secure the protection, conservation, presentation or rehabilitation of such property.

2. Requests for international assistance under paragraph 1 of this Article may also be concerned with identification of cultural or natural property defined in Articles 1 and 2, when preliminary investigations have shown that further inquiries would be justified.

3. The Committee shall decide on the action to be taken with regard to these requests, determine where appropriate, the nature and extent of its assistance, and authorize the conclusion, on its behalf, of the necessary arrangements with the government concerned.

4. The Committee shall determine an order of priorities for its operations. It shall in so doing bear in mind the respective importance for the world cultural and natural heritage of the property requiring protection, the need to give international assistance to the property most representative of a natural environment or of the genius and the history of the peoples of the

world, the urgency of the work to be done, the resources available to the States on whose territory the threatened property is situated and in particular the extent to which they are able to safeguard such property by their own means.

5. The Committee shall draw up, keep up to date and publicize a list of property for which international assistance has been granted.

6. The Committee shall decide on the use of the resources of the Fund established under Article 15 of this Convention. It shall seek ways of increasing these resources and shall take all useful steps to this end.

7. The Committee shall co-operate with international and national governmental and non-governmental organizations having objectives similar to those of this Convention. For the implementation of its programmes and projects, the Committee may call on such organizations, particularly the International Centre for the Study of the Preservation and Restoration of Cultural Property (the Rome Centre), the International Council of Monuments and Sites (ICOMOS) and the International Union for Conservation of Nature and Natural Resources (IUCN), as well as on public and private bodies and individuals.

8. Decisions of the Committee shall be taken by a majority of two-thirds of its members present and voting. A majority of the members of the Committee shall constitute a quorum.

Article 14

1. The World Heritage Committee shall be assisted by a Secretariat appointed by the Director-General of the United Nations Educational, Scientific and Cultural Organization.

2. The Director-General of the United Nations Educational, Scientific and Cultural Organization, utilizing to the fullest extent possible the services of the International Centre for the Study of the Preservation and the Restoration of Cultural Property (the Rome Centre), the International Council of Monuments and Sites (ICOMOS) and the International Union for Conservation of Nature and Natural Resources (IUCN) in their respective areas of competence and capability, shall prepare the Committee's documentation and the agenda of its meetings and shall have the responsibility for the implementation of its decisions.

IV. Fund for the Protection of the World Cultural and Natural Heritage

Article 15

1. A Fund for the Protection of the World Cultural and Natural Heritage of Outstanding Universal Value, called 'the World Heritage Fund', is hereby established.

2. The Fund shall constitute a trust fund, in conformity with the provisions of the Financial Regulations of the United Nations Educational, Scientific and Cultural Organization.

3. The resources of the Fund shall consist of:

(a) compulsory and voluntary contributions made by the States Parties to this Convention,

(b) contributions, gifts or bequests which may be made by:
  (i) other States;
  (ii) the United Nations Educational, Scientific and Cultural Organization, other organizations of the United Nations system, particularly the United Nations Development Programme or other intergovernmental organizations;
  (iii) public or private bodies or individuals;

(c) any interest due on the resources of the Fund;

(d) funds raised by collections and receipts from events organized for the benefit of the Fund; and

(e) all other resources authorized by the Fund's regulations, as drawn up by the World Heritage Committee.

4. Contributions to the Fund and other forms of assistance made available to the Committee may be used only for such purposes as the Committee shall define. The Committee may accept contributions to be used only for a certain programme or project, provided that the Committee shall have decided on the implementation of such programme or project. No political conditions may be attached to contributions made to the Fund.

Article 16

1. Without prejudice to any supplementary voluntary contribution, the States Parties to this Convention undertake to pay regularly, every two years, to the World Heritage Fund, contributions, the amount of which, in the form of a uniform percentage applicable to all States, shall be determined by the General Assembly of States Parties to the Convention, meeting during the sessions of the General Conference of the United Nations Educational, Scientific and Cultural Organization. This decision of the General Assembly requires the majority of the States Parties present and voting, which have not made the declaration referred to in paragraph 2 of this Article. In no case shall the compulsory contribution of States Parties to the Convention exceed 1% of the contribution to the Regular Budget of the United Nations Educational, Scientific and Cultural Organization.

2. However, each State referred to in Article 31 or in Article 32 of this Convention may declare, at the time of the deposit of its instrument of ratification, acceptance or accession, that it shall not be bound by the provisions of paragraph 1 of this Article.

3. A State Party to the Convention which has made the declaration referred to in paragraph 2 of this Article may at any time withdraw the said declaration by notifying the Director-General of the United Nations Educational, Scientific and Cultural Organization. However, the withdrawal of the declaration shall not take effect in regard to the compulsory contribution due by the State until the date of the subsequent General Assembly of States Parties to the Convention.

4. In order that the Committee may be able to plan its operations effectively, the contributions of States Parties to this Convention which have made the declaration referred to in paragraph 2 of this Article, shall be paid on a regular basis, at least every two years, and should not be less than the contributions which they should have paid if they had been bound by the provisions of paragraph 1 of this Article.

5. Any State Party to the Convention which is in arrears with the payment of its compulsory or voluntary contribution for the current year and the calendar year immediately preceding it shall not be eligible as a Member of the World Heritage Committee, although this provision shall not apply to the first election. The terms of office of any such State which is already a member of the Committee shall terminate at the time of the elections provided for in Article 8, paragraph 1 of this Convention.

Article 17

The States Parties to this Convention shall consider or encourage the establishment of national, public and private foundations or associations whose purpose is to invite donations for the protection of the cultural and natural heritage as defined in Articles 1 and 2 of this Convention.

Article 18

The States Parties to this Convention shall give their assistance to international fund-raising campaigns organized for the World Heritage Fund under the auspices of the United Nations Educational, Scientific and Cultural Organization. They shall facilitate collections made by the bodies mentioned in paragraph 3 of Article 15 for this purpose.

V. Conditions and Arrangements for International Assistance

Article 19

Any State Party to this Convention may request international assistance for property forming part of the cultural or natural heritage of outstanding universal value situated within its territory. It shall submit with its request such information and documentation provided for in Article 21 as it has in its possession and as will enable the Committee to come to a decision.

Article 20

Subject to the provisions of paragraph 2 of Article 13, subparagraph (c) of Article 22 and Article 23, international assistance provided for by this Convention may be granted only to property forming part of the cultural and natural heritage which the World Heritage Committee has decided, or may decide, to enter in one of the lists mentioned in paragraphs 2 and 4 of Article 11.

Article 21

1. The World Heritage Committee shall define the procedure by which requests to it for international assistance shall be considered and shall specify the content of the request, which should define the operation contemplated, the work that is necessary, the expected cost thereof, the degree of urgency and the reasons why the resources of the State requesting assistance do not allow it to meet all the expenses. Such requests must be supported by experts' reports whenever possible.

2. Requests based upon disasters or natural calamities should, by reason of the urgent work which they may involve, be given immediate priority consideration by the Committee, which should have a reserve fund at its disposal against such contingencies.

3. Before coming to a decision, the Committee shall carry out such studies and consultations as it deems necessary.

Article 22

Assistance granted by the World Heritage Committee may take the following forms:

    (a) studies concerning the artistic, scientific and technical problems raised by the protection, conservation, presentation and rehabilitation of the cultural and natural heritage, as defined in paragraph 2 and 4 of Article 11 of this Convention;

    (b) provision of experts, technicians and skilled labour to ensure that the approved work is correctly carried out;

    (c) training of staff and specialists at all levels in the field of identification, protection, conservation, presentation and rehabilitation of the cultural and natural heritage;

    (d) supply of equipment which the State concerned does not possess or is not in a position to acquire;

    (e) low-interest or interest-free loans which might be repayable on a longer-term basis;

    (f) the granting, in exceptional cases and for special reasons, of non-repayable subsidies.

Article 23

The World Heritage Committee may also provide international assistance to national or regional centres for the training of staff and specialists at all levels in the field of identification, protection, conservation, presentation and rehabilitation of the cultural and natural heritage.

Article 24

International assistance on a large scale shall be preceded by detailed scientific, economic and technical studies. These studies shall draw upon the most advanced techniques for the protection, conservation, presentation and rehabilitation of the natural and cultural heritage and shall be consistent with the objectives of this Convention. The studies shall also seek means of making rational use of the resources available in the State concerned.

Article 25

As a general rule, only part of the cost of work necessary shall be borne by the international community. The contribution of the State benefiting from international assistance shall constitute a substantial share of the resources devoted to each programme or project, unless its resources do not permit this.

Article 26

The World Heritage Committee and the recipient State shall define in the agreement they conclude the conditions in which a programme or project for which international assistance under the terms of this Convention is provided, shall be carried out. It shall be the responsibility of the State receiving such international assistance to continue to protect conserve and present the property so safeguarded, in observance of the conditions laid down by the agreement.

VI. Educational Programmes

Article 27

1. The States Parties to this Convention shall endeavour by all appropriate means, and in particular by educational and information programmes, to strengthen appreciation and respect by their peoples of the cultural and natural heritage defined in Articles 1 and 2 of the Convention.

2. They shall undertake to keep the public broadly informed of the dangers threatening this heritage and of activities carried on in pursuance of this Convention.

Article 28

States Parties to this Convention which receive international assistance under the Convention shall take appropriate measures to make known the importance of the property for which assistance has been received and the role played by such assistance.

VII. Reports

Article 29

1. The States Parties to this Convention shall, in the reports which they submit to the General Conference of the United Nations Educational, Scientific and Cultural Organization on dates and in a manner to be determined by it, give information on the legislative and administrative provisions which they have adopted and other action which they have taken for the application of this Convention, together with details of the experience acquired in this field.

2. These reports shall be brought to the attention of the World Heritage Committee.

3. The Committee shall submit a report on its activities at each of the ordinary sessions of the General Conference of the United Nations Educational, Scientific and Cultural Organization.

VIII. Final Clauses

Article 30

This Convention is drawn up in Arabic, English, French, Russian and Spanish, the five texts being equally authoritative.

Article 31

1. This Convention shall be subject to ratification or acceptance by States members of the United Nations Educational, Scientific and Cultural Organization in accordance with their respective constitutional procedures.

2. The instruments of ratification or acceptance shall be deposited with the Director-General of the United Nations Educational, Scientific and Cultural Organization.

Article 32

1. This Convention shall be open to accession by all States not members of the United Nations Educational, Scientific and Cultural Organization

which are invited by the General Conference of the Organization to accede to it.

2. Accession shall be effected by the deposit of an instrument of accession with the Director-General of the United Nations Educational, Scientific and Cultural Organization.

Article 33

This Convention shall enter into force three months after the date of the deposit of the twentieth instrument of ratification, acceptance or accession, but only with respect to those States which have deposited their respective instruments of ratification, acceptance or accession on or before that date. It shall enter into force with respect to any other State three months after the deposit of its instrument of ratification, acceptance or accession.

Article 34

The following provisions shall apply to those States Parties to this Convention which have a federal or non-unitary constitutional system:

    (a) with regard to the provisions of this Convention, the implementation of which comes under the legal jurisdiction of the federal or central legislative power, the obligations of the federal or central government shall be the same as for those States Parties which are not federal States;

    (b) with regard to the provisions of this Convention, the implementation of which comes under the legal jurisdiction of individual constituent States, countries, provinces or cantons that are not obliged by the constitutional system of the federation to take legislative measures, the federal government shall inform the competent authorities of such States, countries, provinces or cantons of the said provisions, with its recommendation for their adoption.

Article 35

1. Each State Party to this Convention may denounce the Convention.

2. The denunciation shall be notified by an instrument in writing, deposited with the Director-General of the United Nations Educational, Scientific and Cultural Organization.

3. The denunciation shall take effect twelve months after the receipt of the instrument of denunciation. It shall not affect the financial obligations of the denouncing State until the date on which the withdrawal takes effect.

Article 36

The Director-General of the United Nations Educational, Scientific and Cultural Organization shall inform the States members of the Organization, the States not members of the Organization which are referred to in

Article 32, as well as the United Nations, of the deposit of all the instruments of ratification, acceptance, or accession provided for in Articles 31 and 32, and of the denunciations provided for in Article 35.

Article 37

1. This Convention may be revised by the General Conference of the United Nations Educational, Scientific and Cultural Organization. Any such revision shall, however, bind only the States which shall become Parties to the revising convention.

2. If the General Conference should adopt a new convention revising this Convention in whole or in part, then, unless the new convention otherwise provides, this Convention shall cease to be open to ratification, acceptance or accession, as from the date on which the new revising convention enters into force.

Article 38

In conformity with Article 102 of the Charter of the United Nations, this Convention shall be registered with the Secretariat of the United Nations at the request of the Director-General of the United Nations Educational, Scientific and Cultural Organization.

DONE at Paris, this twenty-third day of November 1972, in two authentic copies bearing the signature of the President of the seventeenth session of the General Conference and of the Director-General of the United Nations Educational, Scientific and Cultural Organization, which shall be deposited in the archives of the United Nations Educational, Scientific and Cultural Organization, and certified true copies of which shall be delivered to all the States referred to in Articles 31 and 32 as well as to the United Nations.

United Nations Convention on Biological Diversity, Nairobi, 22 June 1992

The Convention was negotiated between 1987 and 1992 under the auspices of UNEP following preparatory work by IUCN and FAO. An Intergovernmental Negotiating Committee (INC) for a Convention on Biological Diversity was established in 1991. The Convention was adopted on 22 May 1992 in Nairobi, and was opened for signature at the UN Conference on Environment and Development (UNCED) held in Rio de Janeiro from June 3–14 1992. It was signed at UNCED by 157 states and the European Community and subsequently by a further nine states. Thirty ratifications were required for entry into force, which took place on 29 December 1993. As of 31 January 1995, 179 states had signed the Convention, and 102 states and the European Union have ratified, acceded to or approved it. The text is *repr.* in 31 ILM (1992) 818; *Misc.* 3(1993), C. 2127; S. Johnson (ed.), *The Earth Summit: The United Nations Conference on Environment and Development* (Dordrecht, 1993).

The Convention's aim is to provide a broad global framework for development of measures to conserve the Earth's biodiversity, within which states parties will themselves develop the measures necessary to achieve the objectives which it sets out. It does not list species or habitats to be protected. States are required to develop a national strategy and plan a programme for conservation of biodiversity and suitable use of biological resources. The possibility of further negotiation of annexes and protocols is emphasised.

No reservations are permitted but some developed states (France, Italy, UK) made Declarations on signing the Convention indicating their understanding of the meaning of provisions relating to funding viz. that neither paragraph 1 of Article 21 nor Article 20 authorises the Conferences of the Parties to take decisions concerning the amount, nature, frequency or size of the contributions of the Parties under the Convention. The EU also made a declaration on approving the Convention on 21 December 1993 stressing the importance of transfer of technology and biotechnology to ensure conservation and sustainable use of biological diversity and the need for compliance with intellectual property rights. The EU stated that it and its Member States would encourage use of the financial mechanisms established by the Convention to promote voluntary transfer of intellectual property rights by European operators. Chile, Cuba, Switzerland, and Papua New Guinea made declarations on other aspects on ratification.

The Intergovernmental Committee for the Convention on Biological Diversity met for the first time from 11–15 October 1993 in Geneva and again in Nairobi from 9–20 May 1994 to consider various issues preparatory to the entry into force of the Convention and the convening of the first meeting of the Conference of the Parties, held in Nassau from 28 November–1 December 1994. For detailed explanation of the Convention's negotiating history and provisions, including a bibliography, see L. Glowka, F. Burhenne-Guilmin, H. Synge, *A Guide to The Convention on Biological Diversity*, Envir. Policy and Law Paper No. 30 (IUCN Environmental Law Centre, Gland, 1994). For a commentary on the Convention, see A. Boyle, 'The Convention on Biological Diversity', in L. Campiglio, L. Pineschi, D. Siniscalco, and T. Treves (eds.), *The Environment After Rio: International Law and Economics* (London, 1994) 114ff; F. Burhenne and S. Casey-Lefkowitz, 'The Convention on Biological Diversity: A Hard won Global Achievement', 3 YBIEL (1992) 42–59; S. Bilderbeck, (ed.) *Biodiversity and International Law* (Amsterdam, 1992); M. Bowman and C. Redgwell (eds.), *International Law and the Protection of Biological*

Diversity (London, 1995). For UNEP follow-up see *Report of Panel I: Priorities for Action for Conservation and Sustainable Use of Bio-Diversity and Agenda for Scientific and Technological Research*, UNEP/Bio.Div./Panels./Def. 1 (28 April 1993); *Reports of Panel II, Evaluation of Potential Economic Implications of Conservation of Biological Diversity and its Sustainable Use and Evaluation of Biological and Genetic Resources*, UNEP/Bio.Div./ Panels/Inf.2 (28 April 1993); *Report of Panel IV, Consideration of Need for and Modalities of a Protocol Setting Out Appropriate Procedures Including, in particular, Advance Informed Agreement in the Field of Safe Transfer, Handling and Use of Any Living Modified Organism Resulting from Bio-technology that may have Adverse Effect on the Conservation and Use of Biological Diversity*, UNEP/Bio.Div./ Panels/ Inf.4 (28 April 1993).

For First Meeting of the Conference of the Parties, see I Environmental Law, February 1995, p. 23 (UNEP): see also *Report of Intergovernmental Committee on the Convention on Biological Diversity on the Work of its First Session*, UNEP/CBD/COP/1/3, 21 September 1994; and *Second Session*, UNEP/CBD/COP/1/4, 21 September 1994.

TEXT

Preamble

The Contracting Parties,

Conscious of the intrinsic value of biological diversity and of the ecological, genetic, social, economic, scientific, educational, cultural, recreational and aesthetic values of biological diversity and its components,

Conscious also of the importance of biological diversity for evolution and for maintaining life sustaining systems of the biosphere,

Affirming that the conservation of biological diversity is a common concern of humankind,

Reaffirming that States have sovereign rights over their own biological resources,

Reaffirming also that States are responsible for conserving their biological diversity and for using their biological resources in a sustainable manner,

Concerned that biological diversity is being significantly reduced by certain human activities,

Aware of the general lack of information and knowledge regarding biological diversity and of the urgent need to develop scientific, technical and institutional capacities to provide the basic understanding upon which to plan and implement appropriate measures,

Noting that it is vital to anticipate, prevent and attack the causes of significant reduction or loss of biological diversity at source,

Noting also that where there is a threat of significant reduction or loss of biological diversity, lack of full scientific certainty should not be used as a reason for postponing measures to avoid or minimize such a threat,

Noting further that the fundamental requirement for the conservation of biological diversity is the *in-situ* conservation of ecosystems and natural habitats and the maintenance and recovery of viable populations of species in their natural surroundings,

Noting further that *ex-situ* measures, preferably in the country of origin, also have an important role to play,

Recognizing the close and traditional dependence of many indigenous and local communities embodying traditional lifestyles on biological resources, and the desirability of sharing equitably benefits arising from the use of traditional knowledge, innovations and practices relevant to the conservation of biological diversity and the sustainable use of its components,

Recognizing also the vital role that women play in the conservation and sustainable use of biological diversity and affirming the need for the full participation of women at all levels of policy-making and implementation for biological diversity conservation,

Stressing the importance of, and the need to promote, international, regional and global cooperation among States and intergovernmental organizations and the non-governmental sector for the conservation of biological diversity and the sustainable use of its components,

Acknowledging that the provision of new and additional financial resources and appropriate access to relevant technologies can be expected to make a substantial difference in the world's ability to address the loss of biological diversity,

Acknowledging further that special provision is required to meet the needs of developing countries, including the provision of new and additional financial resources and appropriate access to relevant technologies,

Noting in this regard the special conditions of the least developed countries and small island States,

Acknowledging that substantial investments are required to conserve biological diversity and that there is the expectation of a broad range of environmental, economic and social benefits from those investments,

Recognizing that economic and social development and poverty eradication are the first and overriding priorities of developing countries,

Aware that conservation and sustainable use of biological diversity is of critical importance for meeting the food, health and other needs of the growing world population, for which purpose access to and sharing of both genetic resources and technologies are essential,

Noting that, ultimately, the conservation and sustainable use of biological diversity will strengthen friendly relations among States and contribute to peace for humankind,

Desiring to enhance and complement existing international arrangements for the conservation of biological diversity and sustainable use of its components, and

Determined to conserve and sustainably use biological diversity for the benefit of present and future generations,

Have agreed as follows:

Article 1
Objectives

The objectives of this Convention, to be pursued in accordance with its relevant provisions, are the conservation of biological diversity, the sustainable use of its components and the fair and equitable sharing of the benefits arising out of the utilization of genetic resources, including by appropriate access to genetic resources and by appropriate transfer of relevant technologies, taking into account all rights over those resources and to technologies, and by appropriate funding.

Article 2
Use of Terms

For the purposes of this Convention:

'*Biological diversity*' means the variability among living organisms from all sources including, *inter alia*, terrestrial, marine and other aquatic ecosystems and the ecological complexes of which they are part; this includes diversity within species, between species and of ecosystems.

'*Biological resources*' includes genetic resources, organisms or parts thereof, populations, or any other biotic component of ecosystems with actual or potential use or value for humanity.

'*Biotechnology*' means any technological application that uses biological systems, living organisms, or derivatives thereof, to make or modify products or processes for specific use.

'*Country of origin of genetic resources*' means the country which possesses those genetic resources in *in-situ* conditions.

'*Country providing genetic resources*' means the country supplying genetic resources collected from *in-situ* sources, including populations of both wild and domesticated species, or taken from *ex-situ* sources, which may or may not have originated in that country.

'*Domesticated or cultivated species*' means species in which the evolutionary process has been influenced by humans to meet their needs.

'*Ecosystem*' means a dynamic complex of plant, animal and micro-organism communities and their non-living environment interacting as a functional unit.

'*Ex-situ conservation*' means the conservation of components of biological diversity outside their natural habitats.

'*Genetic material*' means any material of plant, animal, microbial or other origin containing functional units of heredity.

'*Genetic resources*' means genetic material of actual or potential value.

'*Habitat*' means the place or type of site where an organism or population naturally occurs.

'*In-situ conditions*' means conditions where genetic resources exist within ecosystems and natural habitats, and, in the case of domesticated or cultivated species, in the surroundings where they have developed their distinctive properties.

'*In-situ conservation*' means the conservation of ecosystems and natural habitats and the maintenance and recovery of viable populations of species in their natural surroundings and, in the case of domesticated or cultivated species, in the surroundings where they have developed their distinctive properties.

'*Protected area*' means a geographically defined area which is designated or regulated and managed to achieve specific conservation objectives.

'*Regional economic integration organization*' means an organization constituted by sovereign States of a given region, to which its member States have transferred competence in respect of matters governed by this Convention and which has been duly authorized, in accordance with its internal procedures, to sign, ratify, accept, approve or accede to it.

'*Sustainable use*' means the use of components of biological diversity in a way and at a rate that does not lead to the long-term decline of biological diversity, thereby maintaining its potential to meet the needs and aspirations of present and future generations.

'*Technology*' includes biotechnology.

Article 3
Principle

States have, in accordance with the Charter of the United Nations and the principles of international law, the sovereign right to exploit their own resources pursuant to their own environmental policies, and the responsibility to ensure that activities within their jurisdiction or control do not cause damage to the environment of other States or of areas beyond the limits of national jurisdiction.

Article 4
Jurisdictional Scope

Subject to the rights of other States, and except as otherwise expressly provided in this Convention, the provisions of this Convention apply, in relation to each Contracting Party:

    (a) In the case of components of biological diversity, in areas within the limits of its national jurisdiction; and

    (b) In the case of processes and activities, regardless of where their effects occur, carried out under its jurisdiction or control, within the area of its national jurisdiction or beyond the limits of national jurisdiction.

Article 5
Cooperation

Each Contracting Party shall, as far as possible and as appropriate, cooperate with other Contracting Parties, directly or, where appropriate, through competent international organizations, in respect of areas beyond national jurisdiction and on other matters of mutual interest, for the conservation and sustainable use of biological diversity.

Article 6
General Measures for Conservation and Sustainable Use

Each Contracting Party shall, in accordance with its particular conditions and capabilities:

(a) Develop national strategies, plans or programmes for the conservation and sustainable use of biological diversity or adapt for this purpose existing strategies, plans or programmes which shall reflect, *inter alia*, the measures set out in this Convention relevant to the Contracting Party concerned; and

(b) Integrate, as far as possible and as appropriate, the conservation and sustainable use of biological diversity into relevant sectoral or cross-sectoral plans, programmes and policies.

Article 7
Identification and Monitoring

Each Contracting Party shall, as far as possible and as appropriate, in particular for the purposes of Articles 8 to 10:

(a) Identify components of biological diversity important for its conservation and sustainable use having regard to the indicative list of categories set down in Annex I;

(b) Monitor, through sampling and other techniques, the components of biological diversity identified pursuant to subparagraph (a) above, paying particular attention to those requiring urgent conservation measures and those which offer the greatest potential for sustainable use;

(c) Identify processes and categories of activities which have or are likely to have significant adverse impacts on the conservation and sustainable use of biological diversity, and monitor their effects through sampling and other techniques; and

(d) Maintain and organize, by any mechanism, data derived from identification and monitoring activities pursuant to subparagraphs (a), (b) and (c) above.

Article 8
In-situ *Conservation*

Each Contracting Party shall, as far as possible and as appropriate:

(a) Establish a system of protected areas or areas where special measures need to be taken to conserve biological diversity;

(b) Develop, where necessary, guidelines for the selection, establishment and management of protected areas or areas where special measures need to be taken to conserve biological diversity;

(c) Regulate or manage biological resources important for the conservation of biological diversity whether within or outside protected areas, with a view to ensuring their conservation and sustainable use;

(d) Promote the protection of ecosystems, natural habitats and the maintenance of viable populations of species in natural surroundings;

(e) Promote environmentally sound and sustainable development in areas adjacent to protected areas with a view to furthering protection of these areas;

(f) Rehabilitate and restore degraded ecosystems and promote the recovery of threatened species, *inter alia*, through the development and implementation of plans or other management strategies;

(g) Establish or maintain means to regulate, manage or control the risks associated with the use and release of living modified organisms resulting from biotechnology which are likely to have adverse environmental impacts that could affect the conservation and sustainable use of biological diversity, taking also into account the risks to human health;

(h) Prevent the introduction of, control or eradicate those alien species which threaten ecosystems, habitats or species;

(i) Endeavour to provide the conditions needed for compatibility between present uses and the conservation of biological diversity and the sustainable use of its components;

(j) Subject to its national legislation, respect, preserve and maintain knowledge, innovations and practices of indigenous and local communities embodying traditional lifestyles relevant for the conservation and sustainable use of biological diversity and promote their wider application with the approval and involvement of the holders of such knowledge, innovations and practices and encourage the equitable sharing of the benefits arising from the utilization of such knowledge, innovations and practices;

(k) Develop or maintain necessary legislation and/or other regulatory provisions for the protection of threatened species and populations;

(l) Where a significant adverse effect on biological diversity has been determined pursuant to Article 7, regulate or manage the relevant processes and categories of activities; and

(m) Cooperate in providing financial and other support for *in-situ* conservation outlined in subparagraphs (a) to (l) above, particularly to developing countries.

Article 9
Ex-situ *Conservation*

Each Contracting Party shall, as far as possible and as appropriate, and predominantly for the purpose of complementing *in-situ* measures:

(a) Adopt measures for the *ex-situ* conservation of components of biological diversity, preferably in the country of origin of such components;

(b) Establish and maintain facilities for *ex-situ* conservation of and research on plants, animals and micro-organisms, preferably in the country of origin of genetic resources;

(c) Adopt measures for the recovery and rehabilitation of threatened species and for their reintroduction into their natural habitats under appropriate conditions;

(d) Regulate and manage collection of biological resources from natural habitats for *ex-situ* conservation purposes so as not to threaten ecosystems and *in-situ* populations of species, except where special temporary *ex-situ* measures are required under subparagraph (c) above; and

(e) Cooperate in providing financial and other support for *ex-situ* conservation outlined in subparagraphs (a) to (d) above and in the establishment and maintenance of *ex-situ* conservation facilities in developing countries.

Article 10
Sustainable Use of Components of Biological Diversity

Each Contracting Party shall, as far as possible and as appropriate:

(a) Integrate consideration of the conservation and sustainable use of biological resources into national decision-making;

(b) Adopt measures relating to the use of biological resources to avoid or minimize adverse impacts on biological diversity;

(c) Protect and encourage customary use of biological resources in accordance with traditional cultural practices that are compatible with conservation or sustainable use requirements;

(d) Support local populations to develop and implement remedial action in degraded areas where biological diversity has been reduced; and

(e) Encourage cooperation between its governmental authorities and its private sector in developing methods for sustainable use of biological resources.

Article 11
Incentive Measures

Each Contracting Party shall, as far as possible and as appropriate, adopt economically and socially sound measures that act as incentives for the conservation and sustainable use of components of biological diversity.

Article 12
Research and Training

The Contracting Parties, taking into account the special needs of developing countries, shall:

(a) Establish and maintain programmes for scientific and technical education and training in measures for the identification, conservation and sustainable use of biological diversity and its components and provide support for such education and training for the specific needs of developing countries;

(b) Promote and encourage research which contributes to the conservation and sustainable use of biological diversity, particularly in developing countries, *inter alia*, in accordance with decisions of the Conference of the Parties taken in consequence of recommendations of the Subsidiary Body on Scientific, Technical and Technological Advice; and

(c) In keeping with the provisions of Articles 16, 18 and 20, promote and cooperate in the use of scientific advances in biological diversity research in developing methods for conservation and sustainable use of biological resources.

Article 13
Public Education and Awareness

The Contracting Parties shall:

(a) Promote and encourage understanding of the importance of, and the measures required for, the conservation of biological diversity, as well as its propagation through media, and the inclusion of these topics in educational programmes; and

(b) Cooperate, as appropriate, with other States and international organizations in developing educational and public awareness programmes, with respect to conservation and sustainable use of biological diversity.

Article 14
Impact Assessment and Minimizing Adverse Impacts

1. Each Contracting Party, as far as possible and as appropriate, shall:

   (a) Introduce appropriate procedures requiring environmental impact assessment of its proposed projects that are likely to have significant adverse effects on biological diversity with a view to avoiding or minimizing such effects and, where appropriate, allow for public participation in such procedures;

   (b) Introduce appropriate arrangements to ensure that the environmental consequences of its programmes and policies that are likely to have significant adverse impacts on biological diversity are duly taken into account;

   (c) Promote, on the basis of reciprocity, notification, exchange of information and consultation on activities under their jurisdiction or control which are likely to significantly affect adversely the biological diversity of other States or areas beyond the limits of national jurisdiction, by encouraging the conclusion of bilateral, regional or multilateral arrangements, as appropriate;

   (d) In the case of imminent or grave danger or damage, originating under its jurisdiction or control, to biological diversity within the area under jurisdiction of other States or in areas beyond the limits of national jurisdiction, notify immediately the potentially affected States of such danger or damage, as well as initiate action to prevent or minimize such danger or damage; and

   (e) Promote national arrangements for emergency responses to activities or events, whether caused naturally or otherwise, which present a grave and imminent danger to biological diversity and encourage international cooperation to supplement such national efforts and, where appropriate and agreed by the States or regional economic integration organizations concerned, to establish joint contingency plans.

2. The Conference of the Parties shall examine, on the basis of studies to be carried out, the issue of liability and redress, including restoration and compensation, for damage to biological diversity, except where such liability is a purely internal matter.

Article 15
Access to Genetic Resources

1. Recognizing the sovereign rights of States over their natural resources, the authority to determine access to genetic resources rests with the national governments and is subject to national legislation.

2. Each Contracting Party shall endeavour to create conditions to facilitate access to genetic resources for environmentally sound uses by other Con-

tracting Parties and not to impose restrictions that run counter to the objectives of this Convention.

3. For the purpose of this Convention, the genetic resources being provided by a Contracting Party, as referred to in this Article and Articles 16 and 19, are only those that are provided by Contracting Parties that are countries of origin of such resources or by the Parties that have acquired the genetic resources in accordance with this Convention.

4. Access, where granted, shall be on mutually agreed terms and subject to the provisions of this Article.

5. Access to genetic resources shall be subject to prior informed consent of the Contracting Party providing such resources, unless otherwise determined by that Party.

6. Each Contracting Party shall endeavour to develop and carry out scientific research based on genetic resources provided by other Contracting Parties with the full participation of, and where possible in, such Contracting Parties.

7. Each Contracting Party shall take legislative, administrative or policy measures, as appropriate, and in accordance with Articles 16 and 19 and, where necessary, through the financial mechanism established by Articles 20 and 21 with the aim of sharing in a fair and equitable way the results of research and development and the benefits arising from the commercial and other utilization of genetic resources with the Contracting Party providing such resources. Such sharing shall be upon mutually agreed terms.

Article 16
Access to and Transfer of Technology

1. Each Contracting Party, recognizing that technology includes biotechnology, and that both access to and transfer of technology among Contracting Parties are essential elements for the attainment of the objectives of this Convention, undertakes subject to the provisions of this Article to provide and/or facilitate access for and transfer to other Contracting Parties of technologies that are relevant to the conservation and sustainable use of biological diversity or make use of genetic resources and do not cause significant damage to the environment.

2. Access to and transfer of technology referred to in paragraph 1 above to developing countries shall be provided and/or facilitated under fair and most favourable terms, including on concessional and preferential terms where mutually agreed, and, where necessary, in accordance with the financial mechanism established by Articles 20 and 21. In the case of technology subject to patents and other intellectual property rights, such access and transfer shall be provided on terms which recognize and are

consistent with the adequate and effective protection of intellectual property rights. The application of this paragraph shall be consistent with paragraphs 3, 4 and 5 below.

3. Each Contracting Party shall take legislative, administrative or policy measures, as appropriate, with the aim that Contracting Parties, in particular those that are developing countries, which provide genetic resources are provided access to and transfer of technology which makes use of those resources, on mutually agreed terms, including technology protected by patents and other intellectual property rights, where necessary, through the provisions of Articles 20 and 21 and in accordance with international law and consistent with paragraphs 4 and 5 below.

4. Each Contracting Party shall take legislative, administrative or policy measures, as appropriate, with the aim that the private sector facilitates access to, joint development and transfer of technology referred to in paragraph 1 above for the benefit of both governmental institutions and the private sector of developing countries and in this regard shall abide by the obligations included in paragraphs 1, 2 and 3 above.

5. The Contracting Parties, recognizing that patents and other intellectual property rights may have an influence on the implementation of this Convention, shall cooperate in this regard subject to national legislation and international law in order to ensure that such rights are supportive of and do not run counter to its objectives.

Article 17
Exchange of Information

1. The Contracting Parties shall facilitate the exchange of information, from all publicly available sources, relevant to the conservation and sustainable use of biological diversity, taking into account the special needs of developing countries.

2. Such exchange of information shall include exchange of results of technical, scientific and socio-economic research, as well as information on training and surveying programmes, specialized knowledge, indigenous and traditional knowledge as such and in combination with the technologies referred to in Article 16, paragraph 1. It shall also, where feasible, include repatriation of information.

Article 18
Technical and Scientific Cooperation

1. The Contracting Parties shall promote international technical and scientific cooperation in the field of conservation and sustainable use of biological diversity, where necessary, through the appropriate international and national institutions.

2. Each Contracting Party shall promote technical and scientific cooper-

ation with other Contracting Parties, in particular developing countries, in implementing this Convention, *inter alia*, through the development and implementation of national policies. In promoting such cooperation, special attention should be given to the development and strengthening of national capabilities, by means of human resources development and institution building.

3. The Conference of the Parties, at its first meeting, shall determine how to establish a clearing-house mechanism to promote and facilitate technical and scientific cooperation.

4. The Contracting Parties shall, in accordance with national legislation and policies, encourage and develop methods of cooperation for the development and use of technologies, including indigenous and traditional technologies, in pursuance of the objectives of this Convention. For this purpose, the Contracting Parties shall also promote cooperation in the training of personnel and exchange of experts.

5. The Contracting Parties shall, subject to mutual agreement, promote the establishment of joint research programmes and joint ventures for the development of technologies relevant to the objectives of this Convention.

Article 19
Handling of Biotechnology and Distribution of its Benefits

1. Each Contracting Party shall take legislative, administrative or policy measures, as appropriate, to provide for the effective participation in biotechnological research activities by those Contracting Parties, especially developing countries, which provide the genetic resources for such research, and where feasible in such Contracting Parties.

2. Each Contracting Party shall take all practicable measures to promote and advance priority access on a fair and equitable basis by Contracting Parties, especially developing countries, to the results and benefits arising from biotechnologies based upon genetic resources provided by those Contracting Parties. Such access shall be on mutually agreed terms.

3. The Parties shall consider the need for and modalities of a protocol setting out appropriate procedures, including, in particular, advance informed agreement, in the field of the safe transfer, handling and use of any living modified organism resulting from biotechnology that may have adverse effect on the conservation and sustainable use of biological diversity.

4. Each Contracting Party shall, directly or by requiring any natural or legal person under its jurisdiction providing the organisms referred to in paragraph 3 above, provide any available information about the use and safety regulations required by that Contracting Party in handling such organisms,

as well as any available information on the potential adverse impact of the specific organisms concerned to the Contracting Party into which those organisms are to be introduced.

Article 20
Financial Resources

1. Each Contracting Party undertakes to provide, in accordance with its capabilities, financial support and incentives in respect of those national activities which are intended to achieve the objectives of this Convention, in accordance with its national plans, priorities and programmes.

2. The developed country Parties shall provide new and additional financial resources to enable developing country Parties to meet the agreed full incremental costs to them of implementing measures which fulfil the obligations of this Convention and to benefit from its provisions and which costs are agreed between a developing country Party and the institutional structure referred to in Article 21, in accordance with policy, strategy, programme priorities and eligibility criteria and an indicative list of incremental costs established by the Conference of the Parties. Other Parties, including countries undergoing the process of transition to a market economy, may voluntarily assume the obligations of the developed country Parties. For the purpose of this Article, the conference of the Parties, shall at its first meeting establish a list of developed country Parties and other Parties which voluntarily assume the obligations of the developed country Parties. The Conference of the Parties shall periodically review and if necessary amend the list. Contributions from other countries and sources on a voluntary basis would also be encouraged. The implementation of these commitments shall take into account the need for adequacy, predictability and timely flow of funds and the importance of burden-sharing among the contributing Parties included in the list.

3. The developed country Parties may also provide, and developing country Parties avail themselves of, financial resources related to the implementation of this Convention through bilateral, regional and other multilateral channels.

4. The extent to which developing country Parties will effectively implement their commitments under this Convention will depend on the effective implementation by developed country Parties of their commitments under this Convention related to financial resources and transfer of technology and will take fully into account the fact that economic and social development and eradication of poverty are the first and overriding priorities of the developing country Parties.

5. The Parties shall take full account of the specific needs and special situation of least developed countries in their actions with regard to funding and transfer of technology.

6. The Contracting Parties shall also take into consideration the special conditions resulting from the dependence on, distribution and location of, biological diversity within developing country Parties, in particular small island States.

7. Consideration shall also be given to the special situation of developing countries, including those that are most environmentally vulnerable, such as those with arid and semi-arid zones, coastal and mountainous areas.

Article 21
Financial Mechanism

1. There shall be a mechanism for the provision of financial resources to developing country Parties for purposes of this Convention on a grant or concessional basis the essential elements of which are described in this Article. The mechanism shall function under the authority and guidance of, and be accountable to, the Conference of the Parties for purposes of this Convention. The operations of the mechanism shall be carried out by such institutional structure as may be decided upon by the Conference of the Parties at its first meeting. For purposes of this Convention, the Conference of the Parties shall determine the policy, strategy, programme priorities and eligibility criteria relating to the access to and utilization of such resources. The contributions shall be such as to take into account the need for predictability, adequacy and timely flow of funds referred to in Article 20 in accordance with the amount of resources needed to be decided periodically by the Conference of the Parties and the importance of burden-sharing among the contributing Parties included in the list referred to in Article 20, paragraph 2. Voluntary contributions may also be made by the developed country Parties and by other countries and sources. The mechanism shall operate within a democratic and transparent system of governance.

2. Pursuant to the objectives of this Convention, the Conference of the Parties shall at its first meeting determine the policy, strategy and programme priorities, as well as detailed criteria and guidelines for eligibility for access to and utilization of the financial resources including monitoring and evaluation on a regular basis of such utilization. The Conference of the Parties shall decide on the arrangements to give effect to paragraph 1 above after consultation with the institutional structure entrusted with the operation of the financial mechanism.

3. The Conference of the Parties shall review the effectiveness of the mechanism established under this Article, including the criteria and guidelines referred to in paragraph 2 above, not less than two years after the entry into force of this Convention and thereafter on a regular basis. Based on such review, it shall take appropriate action to improve the effectiveness of the mechanism if necessary.

4. The Contracting Parties shall consider strengthening existing financial

institutions to provide financial resources for the conservation and sustainable use of biological diversity.

Article 22
Relationship with Other International Conventions

1. The provisions of this Convention shall not affect the rights and obligations of any Contracting Party deriving from any existing international agreement, except where the exercise of those rights and obligations would cause a serious damage or threat to biological diversity.

2. Contracting Parties shall implement this Convention with respect to the marine environment consistently with the rights and obligations of States under the law of the sea.

Article 23
Conference of the Parties

1. A Conference of the Parties is hereby established. The first meeting of the Conference of the Parties shall be convened by the Executive Director of the United Nations Environment Programme not later than one year after the entry into force of this Convention. Thereafter, ordinary meetings of the Conference of the Parties shall be held at regular intervals to be determined by the Conference at its first meeting.

2. Extraordinary meetings of the Conference of the Parties shall be held at such other times as may be deemed necessary by the Conference, or at the written request of any Party, provided that, within six months of the request being communicated to them by the Secretariat, it is supported by at least one-third of the Parties.

3. The Conference of the Parties shall by consensus agree upon and adopt rules of procedure for itself and for any subsidiary body it may establish, as well as financial rules governing the funding of the Secretariat. At each ordinary meeting, it shall adopt a budget for the financial period until the next ordinary meeting.

4. The Conference of the Parties shall keep under review the implementation of this Convention, and, for this purpose, shall:

(a) Establish the form and the intervals for transmitting the information to be submitted in accordance with Article 26 and consider such information as well as reports submitted by any subsidiary body;

(b) Review scientific, technical and technological advice on biological diversity provided in accordance with Article 25;

(c) Consider and adopt, as required, protocols in accordance with Article 28;

(d) Consider and adopt, as required, in accordance with Articles 29 and 30, amendments to this Convention and its annexes;

(e) Consider amendments to any protocol, as well as to any annexes thereto, and, if so decided, recommend their adoption to the parties to the protocol concerned;

(f) Consider and adopt, as required, in accordance with Article 30, additional annexes to this Convention;

(g) Establish such subsidiary bodies, particularly to provide scientific and technical advice, as are deemed necessary for the implementation of this Convention;

(h) Contact, through the Secretariat, the executive bodies of conventions dealing with matters covered by this Convention with a view to establishing appropriate forms of cooperation with them; and

(i) Consider and undertake any additional action that may be required for the achievement of the purposes of this Convention in the light of experience gained in its operation.

5. The United Nations, its specialized agencies and the International Atomic Energy Agency, as well as any State not Party to this Convention, may be represented as observers at meetings of the Conference of the Parties. Any other body or agency, whether governmental or non-governmental, qualified in fields relating to conservation and sustainable use of biological diversity, which has informed the Secretariat of its wish to be represented as an observer at a meeting of the Conference of the Parties, may be admitted unless at least one-third of the Parties present object. The admission and participation of observers shall be subject to the rules of procedure adopted by the Conference of the Parties.

Article 24
Secretariat

1. A secretariat is hereby established. Its functions shall be:

(a) To arrange for and service meetings of the Conference of the Parties provided for in Article 23;

(b) To perform the functions assigned to it by any protocol;

(c) To prepare reports on the execution of its functions under this Convention and present them to the Conference of the Parties;

(d) To coordinate with other relevant international bodies and, in particular to enter into such administrative and contractual arrangements as may be required for the effective discharge of its functions; and

(e) To perform such other functions as may be determined by the Conference of the Parties.

2. At its first ordinary meeting, the Conference of the Parties shall designate the secretariat from amongst those existing competent international organizations which have signified their willingness to carry out the secretariat functions under this Convention.

Article 25
Subsidiary Body on Scientific, Technical and Technological Advice

1. A subsidiary body for the provision of scientific, technical and technological advice is hereby established to provide the Conference of the Parties and, as appropriate, its other subsidiary bodies with timely advice relating to the implementation of this Convention. This body shall be open to participation by all Parties and shall be multidisciplinary. It shall comprise government representatives competent in the relevant field of expertise. It shall report regularly to the Conference of the Parties on all aspects of its work.

2. Under the authority of and in accordance with guidelines laid down by the Conference of the Parties, and upon its request, this body shall:

    (a) Provide scientific and technical assessments of the status of biological diversity;

    (b) Prepare scientific and technical assessments of the effects of types of measures taken in accordance with the provisions of this Convention;

    (c) Identify innovative, efficient and state-of-the-art technologies and know-how relating to the conservation and sustainable use of biological diversity and advise on the ways and means of promoting development and/or transferring such technologies;

    (d) Provide advice on scientific programmes and international cooperation in research and development related to conservation and sustainable use of biological diversity; and

    (e) Respond to scientific, technical, technological and methodological questions that the Conference of the Parties and its subsidiary bodies may put to the body.

3. The functions, terms of reference, organization and operation of this body may be further elaborated by the Conference of the Parties.

Article 26
Reports

1. Each Contracting Party shall, at intervals to be determined by the Conference of the Parties, present to the Conference of the Parties, reports on measures which it has taken for the implementation of the provisions of this Convention and their effectiveness in meeting the objectives of this Convention.

Article 27
Settlement of Disputes

1. In the event of a dispute between Contracting Parties concerning the interpretation or application of this Convention, the parties concerned shall seek solution by negotiation.

2. If the parties concerned cannot reach agreement by negotiation, they may jointly seek the good offices of , or request mediation by, a third party.

3. When ratifying, accepting, approving or acceding to this Convention, or at any time thereafter, a State or regional economic integration organization may declare in writing to the Depositary that for a dispute not resolved in accordance with paragraph 1 or paragraph 2 above, it accepts one or both of the following means of dispute settlement as compulsory:

    (a) Arbitration in accordance with the procedure laid down in Part 1 of Annex II;

    (b) Submission of the dispute to the International Court of Justice.

4. If the parties to the dispute have not, in accordance with paragraph 3 above, accepted the same or any procedure, the dispute shall be submitted to conciliation in accordance with Part 2 of Annex II unless the parties otherwise agree.

5. The provisions of this Article shall apply with respect to any protocol except as otherwise provided in the protocol concerned.

Article 28
Adoption of Protocols

1. The Contracting Parties shall cooperate in the formulation and adoption of protocols to this Convention.

2. Protocols shall be adopted at a meeting of the Conference of the Parties.

3. The text of any proposed protocol shall be communicated to the Contracting Parties by the Secretariat at least six months before such a meeting.

Article 29
Amendment of the Convention or Protocols

1. Amendments to this Convention may be proposed by any Contracting Party. Amendments to any protocol may be proposed by any Party to that protocol.

2. Amendments to this Convention shall be adopted at a meeting of the Conference of the Parties. Amendments to any protocol shall be adopted at a meeting of the Parties to the Protocol in question. The text of any proposed amendment to this Convention or to any protocol, except as may otherwise be provided in such protocol, shall be communicated to the Parties to the instrument in question by the secretariat at least six months before the meeting at which it is proposed for adoption. The secretariat shall also communicate proposed amendments to the signatories to this Convention for information.

3. The Parties shall make every effort to reach agreement on any proposed amendment to this Convention or to any protocol by consensus. If all efforts at consensus have been exhausted, and no agreement reached, the amendment shall as a last resort be adopted by a two-thirds majority vote of the Parties to the instrument in question present and voting at the meeting, and shall be submitted by the Depositary to all Parties for ratification, acceptance or approval.

4. Ratification, acceptance or approval of amendments shall be notified to the Depositary in writing. Amendments adopted in accordance with paragraph 3 above shall enter into force among Parties having accepted them on the ninetieth day after the deposit of instruments of ratification, acceptance or approval by at least two-thirds of the Contracting Parties to this Convention or of the Parties to the protocol concerned, except as may otherwise be provided in such protocol. Thereafter the amendments shall enter into force for any other Party on the ninetieth day after that Party deposits its instrument of ratification, acceptance or approval of the amendments.

5. For the purposes of this Article, 'Parties present and voting' means Parties present and casting an affirmative or negative vote.

Article 30
Adoption and Amendment of Annexes

1. The annexes to this Convention or to any protocol shall form an integral part of the Convention or of such protocol, as the case may be, and, unless expressly provided otherwise, a reference to this Convention or its protocols constitutes at the same time a reference to any annexes thereto. Such annexes shall be restricted to procedural, scientific, technical and administrative matters.

2. Except as may be otherwise provided in any protocol with respect to its annexes, the following procedure shall apply to the proposal, adoption and entry into force of additional annexes to this Convention or of annexes to any protocol:

   (a) Annexes to this Convention or to any protocol shall be proposed and adopted according to the procedure laid down in Article 29;
   (b) Any Party that is unable to approve an additional annex to this Convention or an annex to any protocol to which it is Party shall so notify the Depositary, in writing, within one year from the date of the communication of the adoption by the Depositary. The Depositary shall without delay notify all Parties of any such notification received. A Party may at any time withdraw a previous declaration of objection and the annexes shall thereupon enter into force for that Party subject to subparagraph (c) below;

(c) On the expiry of one year from the date of the communication of the adoption by the Depositary, the annex shall enter into force for all Parties to this Convention or to any protocol concerned which have not submitted a notification in accordance with the provisions of subparagraph (b) above.

3. The proposal, adoption and entry into force of amendments to annexes to this Convention or to any protocol shall be subject to the same procedure as for the proposal, adoption and entry into force of annexes to the Convention or annexes to any protocol.

4. If an additional annex or an amendment to an annex is related to an amendment to this Convention or to any protocol, the additional annex or amendment shall not enter into force until such time as the amendment to the Convention or to the protocol concerned enters into force.

Article 31
Right to Vote

1. Except as provided for in paragraph 2 below, each Contracting Party to this Convention or to any protocol shall have one vote.

2. Regional economic integration organizations, in matters within their competence, shall exercise their right to vote with a number of votes equal to the number of their member States which are Contracting Parties to this Convention or the relevant protocol. Such organizations shall not exercise their right to vote if their member States exercise theirs, and vice versa.

Article 32
Relationship between this Convention and Its Protocols

1. A State or a regional economic integration organization may not become a party to a protocol unless it is, or becomes at the same time, a Contracting Party to this Convention.

2. Decisions under any protocol shall be taken only by the Parties to the protocol concerned. Any Contracting Party that has not ratified, accepted or approved a protocol may participate as an observer in any meeting of the parties to that protocol.

Article 33
Signature

This Convention shall be open for signature at Rio de Janeiro by all States and any regional economic integration organization from 5 June 1992 until 14 June 1992, and at the United Nations Headquarters in New York from 15 June 1992 to 4 June 1993.

Article 34
Ratification, Acceptance or Approval

1. This Convention and any protocol shall be subject to ratification, acceptance or approval by States and by regional economic integration organizations. Instruments of ratification, acceptance or approval shall be deposited with the Depositary.

2. Any organization referred to in paragraph 1 above which becomes a Contracting Party to this Convention or any protocol without any of its member States being a Contracting Party shall be bound by all the obligations under the Convention or the protocol, as the case may be. In the case of such organizations, one or more of whose member States is a Contracting Party to this Convention or relevant protocol, the organization and its member States shall decide on their respective responsibilities for the performance of their obligations under the Convention or protocol, as the case may be. In such cases, the organization and the member States shall not be entitled to exercise rights under the Convention or relevant protocol concurrently.

3. In their instruments of ratification, acceptance or approval, the organizations referred to in paragraph 1 above shall declare the extent of their competence with respect to the matters governed by the Convention or the relevant protocol. These organizations shall also inform the Depositary of any relevant modification in the extent of their competence.

Article 35
Accession

1. This Convention and any protocol shall be open for accession by States and by regional economic integration organizations from the date on which the Convention or the protocol concerned is closed for signature. The instruments of accession shall be deposited with the Depositary.

2. In their instruments of accession, the organizations referred to in paragraph 1 above shall declare the extent of their competence with respect to the matters governed by the Convention or the relevant protocol. These organizations shall also inform the Depositary of any relevant modification in the extent of their competence.

3. The provisions of Article 34, paragraph 2, shall apply to regional economic integration organizations which accede to this Convention or any protocol.

Article 36
Entry Into Force

1. This Convention shall enter into force on the ninetieth day after the

date of deposit of the thirtieth instrument of ratification, acceptance, approval or accession.

2. Any protocol shall enter into force on the ninetieth day after the date of deposit of the number of instruments of ratification, acceptance, approval or accession, specified in that protocol, has been deposited.

3. For each Contracting Party which ratifies, accepts or approves this Convention or accedes thereto after the deposit of the thirtieth instrument of ratification, acceptance, approval or accession, it shall enter into force on the ninetieth day after the date of deposit by such Contracting Party of its instrument of ratification, acceptance, approval or accession.

4. Any protocol, except as otherwise provided in such protocol, shall enter into force for a Contracting Party that ratifies, accepts or approves that protocol or accedes thereto after its entry into force pursuant to paragraph 2 above, on the ninetieth day after the date on which that Contracting Party deposits its instrument of ratification, acceptance, approval or accession, or on the date on which this Convention enters into force for that Contracting Party, whichever shall be the later.

5. For the purposes of paragraphs 1 and 2 above, any instrument deposited by a regional economic integration organization shall not be counted as additional to those deposited by member States of such organization.

Article 37
Reservations

No reservations may be made to this Convention.

Article 38
Withdrawals

1. At any time after two years from the date on which this Convention has entered into force for a Contracting Party, that Contracting Party may withdraw from the Convention by giving written notification to the Depositary.

2. Any such withdrawal shall take place upon expiry of one year after the date of its receipt by the Depositary, or on such later date as may be specified in the notification of the withdrawal.

3. Any Contracting Party which withdraws from this Convention shall be considered as also having withdrawn from any protocol to which it is party.

Article 39
Financial Interim Arrangements

Provided that it has been fully restructured in accordance with the requirements of Article 21, the Global Environment Facility of the United Nations

Development Programme, the United Nations Environment Programme and the International Bank for Reconstruction and Development shall be the institutional structure referred to in Article 21 on an interim basis, for the period between the entry into force of this Convention and the first meeting of the Conference of the Parties or until the Conference of the Parties decides which institutional structure will be designated in accordance with Article 21.

Article 40
Secretariat Interim Arrangements

The secretariat to be provided by the Executive Director of the United Nations Environment Programme shall be the secretariat referred to in Article 24, paragraph 2, on an interim basis for the period between the entry into force of this Convention and the first meeting of the Conference of the Parties.

Article 41
Depositary

The Secretary-General of the United Nations shall assume the functions of Depositary of this Convention and any protocols.

Article 42
Authentic Texts

The original of this Convention, of which the Arabic, Chinese, English, French, Russian and Spanish texts are equally authentic, shall be deposited with the Secretary-General of the United Nations.

IN WITNESS WHEREOF the undersigned, being duly authorized to that effect, have signed this Convention.

DONE at Rio de Janeiro on this fifth day of June, one thousand nine hundred and ninety-two.

Annex I

Identification and Monitoring

1. Ecosystems and habitats: containing high diversity, large numbers of endemic or threatened species, or wilderness; required by migratory species; of social, economic, cultural or scientific importance; or, which are representative, unique or associated with key evolutionary or other biological processes;

2. Species and communities which are: threatened; wild relatives of domesticated or cultivated species; of medicinal, agricultural or other economic

value; or social, scientific or cultural importance; or importance for research into the conservation and sustainable use of biological diversity, such as indicator species; and

3. Described genomes and genes of social, scientific or economic importance.

[ANNEX II: OMITTED]

Convention on International Trade in Endangered Species of Wild Flora and Fauna, Washington, 3 March 1973

This Convention (known as CITES) prohibits or regulates among its parties trade in endangered species listed in three Appendices (not reproduced), and to a more limited extent, trade with non-parties. It institutes a system of permits for import and export of such species and products derived therefrom. States are permitted to enter reservations concerning particular listings. The Convention requires parties to establish national Management and Scientific Committees to administer this system. The Convention entered into force on 1 July 1975 and had 130 parties by 31 January 1995, thirty of which had entered reservations. The text reproduced here includes amendments made in 1979. For the unamended text of the Convention see 12 *ILM* (1973) 1055; *UKTS* 101 (1976) Cmnd. 6647; 27 *UST* 1087 *TIAS* 8249; 993 *UNTS* 243. The Convention followed the enactment of the United States Endangered Species Conservation Act 1969. The proposal for conclusion of a treaty was endorsed by the United Nations Conference on the Human Environment in 1972, which recommended that on its entry into force the secretariat functions should be undertaken by UNEP. These functions are now carried out on behalf of UNEP by the IUCN. The Secretariat can be contacted at 6 Rue de Marpas, P.O. Box 78, 1000 Lausanne 9, Switzerland.

Meetings of the Conference of the Parties are generally held biennially. Nine meetings have been held to date, viz.: the First, in Berne (1976), the Second, in San Jose (1978), the Third, in New Delhi (1981), the Fourth, in Gaborone (1983), the Fifth, in Buenos Aires (1985), the Sixth, in Ottawa (1986), the Seventh, in Lausanne (1989), the Eighth, in Kyoto (1992), the Ninth, in Fort Lauderdale (1994). The last developed new biological criteria for amendment of Appendices I and II and repealed various earlier resolutions. It also considered a Secretariat *Report on Review of Alleged Infractions and other Problems of Interpretation of the Convention*, CITES Doc. 9. 22, 1994. Reports of the proceedings of these meetings, incorporating details of the amendments made to the Appendices, which are reconsidered and amended at each meeting, recommendations and other resolutions adopted, are obtainable from the CITES Secretariat. The Appendices are not reproduced here.

The Convention has been amended twice: first by amendment of Article XI, para. 3(a) done at Bonn, 22 June 1979 (text in *The Marine Mammal Commission Compendium of Selected Treaties*, Vol. 2. (Washington D.C., 1994) 655); secondly by amendment done at Gaborone, 30 April 1983, to Article XXI (MMC Compendium 656–7). The 1979 amendments to Article XI(3)(a) came into force for all parties which had indicated their acceptance of them on 13 April 1987. States which have accepted the Convention after that date accept it as amended. The 1983 amendments to Article XXI have not yet come into force, and are not reproduced here.

For discussion of CITES see D. Favre, *Convention on Trade in Endangered Species* (Dordrecht, 1980), *passim*; S. Lyster, *International Wildlife Law* (Cambridge, 1985), 239ff; *id.* 29 *Nat Res J.* (1989) 979ff; C. de Klemm, 29 *Nat Res J.* (1989) 953ff; P. W. Birnie and A. E. Boyle, *International Law and the Environment* (Oxford, 1992), Ch. 12, esp. 475–80; D. Harland, *Killing Game: International Law and the African Elephant* (Westport, 1994).

TEXT

The Contracting States,

Recognizing that wild fauna and flora in their many beautiful and varied forms are an irreplaceable part of the natural systems of the earth which must be protected for this and the generations to come;

Conscious of the ever-growing value of wild fauna and flora from aesthetic, scientific, cultural, recreational and economic points of view;

Recognizing that peoples and States are and should be the best protectors of their own wild fauna and flora;

Recognizing, in addition, that international cooperation is essential for the protection of certain species of wild fauna and flora against overexploitation through international trade;

Convinced of the urgency of taking appropriate measures to this end;

Have agreed as follows:

Article I
Definitions

For the purpose of the present Convention, unless the context otherwise requires:

(a) 'Species' means any species, sub-species, or geographically separate population thereof;

(b) 'Specimen' means;
   (i) an animal or plant, whether alive or dead;
   (ii) in the case of an animal: for species included in Appendices I and II, any readily recognizable part or derivative thereof; and for species included in Appendix III, any readily recognizable part or derivative thereof specified in Appendix III in relation to the species; and
   (iii) in the case of a plant: for species included in Appendix I, any readily recognizable part or derivative thereof; and for species included in Appendices II and III, any readily recognizable part or derivative thereof specified in Appendices II and III in relation to the species;

(c) 'Trade' means export, re-export, import and introduction from the sea;

(d) 'Re-export' means export of any specimen that has previously been imported;

(e) 'Introduction from the sea' means transportation into a State of specimens of any species which were taken in the marine environment not under the jurisdiction of any State;

(f) 'Scientific Authority' means a national scientific authority designated in accordance with Article IX;

(g) 'Management Authority' means a national management authority designated in accordance with Article IX;

(h) 'Party' means a State for which the present Convention has entered into force.

Article II
Fundamental Principles

1. Appendix I shall include all species threatened with extinction which are or may be affected by trade. Trade in specimens of these species must be subject to particularly strict regulation in order not to endanger further their survival and must only be authorized in exceptional circumstances.

2. Appendix II shall include:

(a) all species which although not necessarily now threatened with extinction may become so unless trade in specimens of such species is subject to strict regulation in order to avoid utilization incompatible with their survival; and

(b) other species which must be subject to regulation in order that trade in specimens of certain species referred to in subparagraph (a) of this paragraph may be brought under effective control.

3. Appendix III shall include all species which any Party identifies as being subject to regulation within its jurisdiction for the purposes of preventing or restricting exploitation, and as needing the co-operation of other Parties in the control of trade.

4. The Parties shall not allow trade in specimens of species included in Appendices I, II and III except in accordance with the provisions of the present Convention.

Article III
Regulation of Trade in Specimens of Species Included in Appendix I

1. All trade in speciments of species included in Appendix I shall be in accordance with the provisions of this Article.

2. The export of any specimen of a species included in Appendix I shall require the prior grant and presentation of an export permit. An export permit shall only be granted when the following conditions have been met:

(a) a Scientific Authority of the State of export has advised that such export will not be detrimental to the survival of that species;

(b) a Management Authority of the State of export is satisfied that the specimen was not obtained in contravention of the laws of that State for the protection of fauna and flora;

(c) a Management Authority of the State of export is satisfied that any living specimen will be so prepared and shipped as to minimize the risk of injury, damage to health or cruel treatment; and

(d) a Management Authority of the State of export is satisfied that an import permit has been granted for the specimen.

3. The import of any specimen of a species included in Appendix I shall require the prior grant and presentation of an import permit and either an export permit or a re-export certificate. An import permit shall only be granted when the following conditions have been met:

(a) a Scientific Authority of the State of import has advised that the import will be for purposes which are not detrimental to the survival of the species involved;

(b) a Scientific Authority of the State of import is satisfied that the proposed recipient of a living specimen is suitably equipped to house and care for it; and

(c) a Management Authority of the State of import is satisfied that the specimen is not to be used for primarily commercial purposes.

4. The re-export of any specimen of a species included in Appendix I shall require the prior grant and presentation of a re-export certificate. A re-export certificate shall only be granted when the following conditions have been met:

(a) a Management Authority of the State of re-export is satisfied that the specimen was imported into that State in accordance with the provisions of the present Convention;

(b) a Management Authority of the State of re-export is satisfied that any living specimen will be so prepared and shipped as to minimize the risk of injury, damage to health or cruel treatment; and

(c) a Management Authority of the State of re-export is satisfied that an import permit has been granted for any living specimen.

5. The introduction from the sea of any specimen of a species included in Appendix I shall require the prior grant of a certificate from a Management Authority of the State of introduction. A certificate shall only be granted when the following conditions have been met:

(a) a Scientific Authority of the State of introduction advises that the introduction will not be detrimental to the survival of the species involved;

(b) a Management Authority of the State of introduction is satisfied that the proposed recipient of a living specimen is suitably equipped to house and care for it; and

(c) a Management Authority of the State of introduction is satisfied that the specimen is not to be used for primarily commercial purposes.

Article IV
Regulation of Trade in Specimens of Species Included in Appendix II

1. All trade in specimens of species included in Appendix II shall be in accordance with the provisions of this Article.

2. The export of any specimen of a species included in Appendix II shall require the prior grant and presentation of an export permit. An export permit shall only be granted when the following conditions have been met:

   (a) a Scientific Authority of the State of export has advised that such export will not be detrimental to the survival of that species;

   (b) a Management Authority of the State of export is satisfied that the specimen was not obtained in contravention of the laws of that State for the protection of fauna and flora; and

   (c) a Management Authority of the State of export is satisfied that any living specimen will be so prepared and shipped as to minimize the risk of injury, damage to health or cruel treatment.

3. A Scientific Authority in each Party shall monitor both the export permits granted by that State for specimens of species included in Appendix II and the actual exports of such specimens. Whenever a Scientific Authority determines that the export of specimens of any such species should be limited in order to maintain that species throughout its range at a level consistent with its role in the ecosystems in which it occurs and well above the level at which that species might become eligible for inclusion in Appendix I, the Scientific Authority shall advise the appropriate Management Authority of suitable measures to be taken to limit the grant of export permits for specimens of that species.

4. The import of any specimen of a species included in Appendix II shall require the prior presentation of either an export permit or a re-export certificate.

5. The re-export of any specimen of a species included in Appendix II shall require the prior grant and presentation of a re-export certificate. A re-export certificate shall only be granted when the following conditions have been met:

   (a) a Management Authority of the State of re-export is satisfied that the specimen was imported into that State in accordance with the provisions of the present Convention; and

   (b) a Management Authority of the State of re-export is satisfied that any living specimen will be so prepared and shipped as to minimize the risk of injury, damage to health or cruel treatment.

6. The introduction from the sea of any specimen of a species included in Appendix II shall require the prior grant of a certificate from a Management Authority of the State of introduction. A certificate shall only be granted when the following conditions have been met:

   (a) a Scientific Authority of the State of introduction advises that the introduction will not be detrimental to the survival of the species involved; and

(b) a Management Authority of the State of introduction is satisfied that any living specimen will be so handled as to minimize the risk of injury, damage to health or cruel treatment.

7. Certificates referred to in paragraph 6 of this Article may be granted on the advice of a Scientific Authority, in consultation with other national scientific authorities or, when appropriate, international scientific authorities, in respect of periods not exceeding one year for total numbers of specimens to be introduced in such periods.

Article V
Regulation of Trade in Specimens of Species Included in Appendix III

1. All trade in specimens of species included in Appendix III shall be in accordance with the provisions of this Article.

2. The export of any specimen of a species included in Appendix III from any State which has included that species in Appendix III shall require the prior grant and presentation of an export permit. An export permit shall only be granted when the following conditions have been met:

(a) a Management Authority of the State of export is satisfied that the specimen was not obtained in contravention of the laws of that State for the protection of fauna and flora; and

(b) a Management Authority of the State of export is satisfied that any living specimen will be so prepared and shipped as to minimize the risk of injury, damage to health or cruel treatment.

3. The import of any specimen of a species included in Appendix III shall require, except in circumstances to which paragraph 4 of this Article applies, the prior presentation of a certificate of origin and, where the import is from a State which has included that species in Appendix III, an export permit.

4. In the case of re-export, a certificate granted by the Management Authority of the State of re-export that the specimen was processed in that State or is being re-exported shall be accepted by the State of import as evidence that the provisions of the present Convention have been complied with in respect of the specimen concerned.

Article VI
Permits and Certificates

1. Permits and certificates granted under the provisions of Articles III, IV and V shall be in accordance with the provisions of this Article.

2. An export permit shall contain the information specified in the model set forth in Appendix IV, and may only be used for export within a period of six months from the date on which it was granted.

3. Each permit or certificate shall contain the title of the present Convention, the name and any identifying stamp of the Management Authority granting it and a control number assigned by the Management Authority.

4. Any copies of a permit or certificate issued by a Management Authority shall be clearly marked as copies only and no such copy may be used in place of the original, except to the extent endorsed thereon.

5. A separate permit or certificate shall be required for each consignment of specimens.

6. A Management Authority of the State of import of any specimen shall cancel and retain the export permit or re-export certificate and any corresponding import permit presented in respect of the import of that specimen.

7. Where appropriate and feasible a Management Authority may affix a mark upon any specimen to assist in identifying the specimen. For these purposes 'mark' means any indelible imprint, lead seal or other suitable means of identifying a specimen, designed in such a way as to render its imitation by unauthorized persons as difficult as possible.

Article VII
Exemptions and Other Special Provisions Relating to Trade

1. The provisions of Articles III, IV and V shall not apply to the transit or trans-shipment of specimens through or in the territory of a Party while the specimens remain in Customs control.

2. Where a Management Authority of the State of export or re-export is satisfied that a specimen was acquired before the provisions of the present Convention applied to that specimen, the provisions of Articles III, IV and V shall not apply to that specimen where the Management Authority issues a certificate to that effect.

3. The provisions of Articles III, IV and V shall not apply to specimens that are personal or household effects. This exemption shall not apply where:

    (a) in the case of specimens of a species included in Appendix I, they were acquired by the owner outside his State of usual residence, and are being imported into that State; or

    (b) in the case of specimens of species included in Appendix II:
        (i) they were acquired by the owner outside his State of usual residence and in a State where removal from the wild occurred;
        (ii) they are being imported into the owner's State of usual residence; and
        (iii) the State where removal from the wild occurred requires the

prior grant of export permits before any export of such specimens; unless a Management Authority is satisfied that the specimens were acquired before the provisions of the present Convention applied to such specimens.

4. Specimens of an animal species included in Appendix I bred in captivity for commercial purposes, or of a plant species included in Appendix I artificially propagated for commerical purposes, shall be deemed to be specimens of species included in Appendix II.

5. Where a Management Authority of the State of export is satisfied that any specimen of an animal species was bred in captivity or any specimen of a plant species was artificially propagated, or is a part of such an animal or plant or was derived therefrom, a certificate by that Management Authority to that effect shall be accepted in lieu of any of the permits or certificates required under the provisions of Articles III, IV or V.

6. The provisions of Articles III, IV and V shall not apply to the non-commercial loan, donation or exchange between scientists or scientific institutions registered by a Management Authority of their State, of herbarium specimens, other preserved, dried or embedded museum specimens, and live plant material which carry a label issued or approved by a Management Authority.

7. A Management Authority of any State may waive the requirements of Articles III, IV and V and allow the movement without permits or certificates of specimens which form part of a travelling zoo, circus, menagerie, plant exhibition or other travelling exhibition provided that:

(a) the exporter or importer registers full details of such specimens with that Management Authority;
(b) the specimens are in either of the categories specified in paragraphs 2 and 5 of this Article; and
(c) the Management Authority is satisfied that any living specimen will be so transported and cared for as to minimize the risk of injury, damage to health or cruel treatment.

Article VIII
Measures to be Taken by the Parties

1. The Parties shall take appropriate measures to enforce the provisions of the present Convention and to prohibit trade in specimens in violation thereof. These shall include measures:

(a) to penalize trade in, or possession of, such specimens, or both; and
(b) to provide for the confiscation or return to the State of export of such specimens.

2. In addition to the measures taken under paragraph 1 of this Article a Party may, when it deems it necessary, provide for any method of internal

reimbursement for expenses incurred as a result of the confiscation of a specimen traded in violation of the measures taken in the application of the provisions of the present Convention.

3. As far as possible, the Parties shall ensure that specimens shall pass through any formalities required for trade with a minimum of delay. To facilitate such passage, a Party may designate ports of exit and ports of entry at which specimens must be presented for clearance. The Parties shall ensure further that all living specimens, during any period of transit, holding or shipment, are properly cared for so as to minimize the risk of injury, damage to health or cruel treatment.

4. Where a living specimen is confiscated as a result of measures referred to in paragraph 1 of this Article:

  (a) the specimen shall be entrusted to a Management Authority of the State of confiscation;
  (b) the Management Authority shall, after consultation with the State of export, return the specimen to that State at the expense of that State, or to a rescue centre or such other place as the Management Authority deems appropriate and consistent with the purposes of the present Convention; and
  (c) the Management Authority may obtain the advice of a Scientific Authority, or may, wherever it considers it desirable, consult the Secretariat in order to facilitate the decision under sub-paragraph (b) of this paragraph, including the choice of a rescue centre or other place.

5. A rescue centre as referred to in paragraph 4 of this Article means an institution designated by a Management Authority to look after the welfare of living specimens, particularly those that have been confiscated.

6. Each Party shall maintain records of trade in specimens of species included in Appendices I, II and III which shall cover:

  (a) the names and addresses of exporters and importers; and
  (b) the number and type of permits and certificates granted; the States with which such trade occurred; the numbers or quantities and types of specimens, names of species as included in Appendices I, II and III and, where applicable, the size and sex of the specimens in question.

7. Each Party shall prepare periodic reports on its implementation of the present Convention and shall transmit to the Secretariat:

  (a) an annual report containing a summary of the information specified in sub-paragraph (b) of paragraph 6 of this Article; and
  (b) a biennial report on legislative, regulatory and administrative measures taken to enforce the provisions of the present Convention.

8. The information referred to in paragraph 7 of this Article shall be available to the public where this is not inconsistent with the law of the Party concerned.

Article IX
Management and Scientific Authorities

1. Each Party shall designate for the purposes of the present Convention:

   (a) one or more Management Authorities competent to grant permits or certificates on behalf of that Party; and
   (b) one or more Scientific Authorities.

2. A State depositing an instrument of ratification, acceptance, approval or accession shall at that time inform the Depositary Government of the name and address of the Management Authority authorized to communicate with other Parties and with the Secretariat.

3. Any changes in the designations or authorizations under the provisions of this Article shall be communicated by the Party concerned to the Secretariat for transmission to all other Parties.

4. Any Management Authority referred to in paragraph 2 of this Article shall if so requested by the Secretariat or the Management Authority of another Party, communicate to it impression of stamps, seals or other devices used to authenticate permits or certificates.

Article X
Trade With States Not Party to the Convention

Where export or re-export is to, or import is from, a State not a Party to the present Convention, comparable documentation issued by the competent authorities in that State which substantially conforms with the requirements of the present Convention for permits and certificates may be accepted in lieu thereof by any Party.

Article XI
Conference of the Parties

1. The Secretariat shall call a meeting of the Conference of the Parties not later than two years after the entry into force of the present Convention.

2. Thereafter the Secretariat shall convene regular meetings at least once every two years, unless the Conference decides otherwise, and extraordinary meetings at any time on the written request of a least one-third of the Parties.

3. At meetings, whether regular or extraordinary, the Parties shall review the implementation of the present Convention and may:

   (a) make such provision as may be necessary to enable the Secretariat to carry out its duties, and adopt financial provisions;

(b) consider and adopt amendments to Appendices I and II in accordance with Article XV;

(c) review the progress made towards the restoration and conservation of the species included in Appendices I, II and III;

(d) receive and consider any reports presented by the Secretariat or by any Party; and

(e) where appropriate, make recommendations for improving the effectiveness of the present Convention.

4. At each regular meeting, the Parties may determine the time and venue of the next regular meeting to be held in accordance with the provisions of paragraph 2 of this Article.

5. At any meeting, the Parties may determine and adopt rules of procedure for the meeting.

6. The United Nations, its Specialized Agencies and the International Atomic Energy Agency, as well as any State not a Party to the present Convention, may be represented at meetings of the Conference by observers, who shall have the right to participate but not to vote.

7. Any body or agency technically qualified in protection, conservation or management of wild fauna and flora, in the following categories, which has informed the Secretariat of its desire to be represented at meetings of the Conference by observers, shall be admitted unless at least one-third of the Parties present object:

(a) international agencies or bodies, either governmental or non-governmental, and national governmental agencies and bodies; and

(b) national non-governmental agencies or bodies which have been approved for this purpose by the State in which they are located.

Once admitted, these observers shall have the right to participate but not to vote.

Article XII
The Secretariat

1. Upon entry into force of the present Convention, a Secretariat shall be provided by the Executive Director of the United Nations Environment Programme. To the extent and in the manner he considers appropriate, he may be assisted by suitable intergovernmental or non-governmental international or national agencies and bodies technically qualified in protection, conservation and management of wild fauna and flora.

2. The functions of the Secretariat shall be:

(a) to arrange for and service meetings of the Parties;

(b) to perform the functions entrusted to it under the provisions of Articles XV and XVI of the present Convention;

(c) to undertake scientific and technical studies in accordance with programmes authorized by the Conference of the Parties as will contribute to the implementation of the present Convention, including studies concerning standards for appropriate preparation and shipment of living specimens and the means of identifying specimens;

(d) to study the reports of Parties and to request from Parties such further information with respect thereto as it deems necessary to ensure implementation of the present Convention;

(e) to invite the attention of the Parties to any matter pertaining to the aims of the present Convention;

(f) to publish periodically and distribute to the Parties current editions of Appendices I, II and III together with any information which will facilitate identification of specimens of species included in those Appendices;

(g) to prepare annual reports to the Parties on its work and on the implementation of the present Convention and such other reports as meetings of the Parties may request;

(h) to make recommendations for the implementation of the aims and provisions of the present Convention, including the exchange of information of a scientific or technical nature;

(i) to perform any other function as may be entrusted to it by the Parties.

Article XIII
International Measures

1. When the Secretariat in the light of information received is satisfied that any species included in Appendices I or II is being affected adversely by trade in specimens of that species or that the provisions of the present Convention are not being effectively implemented, it shall communicate such information to the authorized Management Authority of the Party or Parties concerned.

2. When any Party receives a communication as indicated in paragraph 1 of this Article, it shall, as soon as possible, inform the Secretariat of any relevant facts insofar as its laws permit and, where appropriate, propose remedial action. Where the Party considers that an inquiry is desirable, such inquiry may be carried out by one or more persons expressly authorized by the Party.

3. The information provided by the Party or resulting from any inquiry as specified in paragraph 2 of this Article shall be reviewed by the next Conference of the Parties which may make whatever recommendations it deems appropriate.

Article XIV
Effect on Domestic Legislation and International Conventions

1. The provisions of the present Convention shall in no way affect the right of Parties to adopt:

   (a) stricter domestic measures regarding the conditions for trade, taking, possession or transport of specimens of species included in Appendices I, II and III, or the complete prohibition thereof; or

   (b) domestic measures restricting or prohibiting trade, taking possession, or transport of species not included in Appendices I, II or III.

2. The provisions of the present Convention shall in no way affect the provisions of any domestic measures or the obligations of Parties deriving from any treaty, convention, or international agreement relating to other aspects of trade, taking, possession, or transport of specimens which is in force or subsequently may enter into force for any Party including any measure pertaining to the Customs, public health, veterinary or plant quarantine fields.

3. The provisions of the present Convention shall in no way affect the provisions of, or the obligations deriving from, any treaty, convention or international agreement concluded or which may be concluded between States creating a union or regional trade agreement establishing or maintaining a common external customs control and removing customs controls between the parties thereto insofar as they relate to trade among the States members of that union or agreement.

4. A State Party to the present Convention, which is also a Party to any other treaty, convention or international agreement which is in force at the time of the coming into force of the present Convention and under the provisions of which protection is afforded to marine species included in Appendix II, shall be relieved of the obligations imposed on it under the provisions of the present Convention with respect to trade in specimens of species included in Appendix II that are taken by ships registered in that State and in accordance with the provisions of such other treaty, convention or international agreement.

5. Notwithstanding the provisions of Articles III, IV and V, any export of a specimen taken in accordance with paragraph 4 of this Article shall only require a certificate from a Management Authority of the State of introduction to the effect that the specimen was taken in accordance with the provisions of the other treaty, convention or international agreement in question.

6. Nothing in the present Convention shall prejudice the codification and development of the law of the sea by the United Nations Conference on the Law of the Sea convened pursuant to Resolution 2750 C (XXV) of the

General Assembly of the United Nations nor the present or future claims and legal views of any State concerning the law of the sea and the nature and extent of coastal and flag State jurisdiction.

Article XV
Amendments to Appendices I and II

1. The following provisions shall apply in relation to amendments to Appendices I and II at meetings of the Conference of the Parties:

  (a) Any Party may propose an amendment to Appendix I or II for consideration at the next meeting. The text of the proposed amendment shall be communicated to the Secretariat at least 150 days before the meeting. The Secretariat shall consult the other Parties and interested bodies on the amendment in accordance with the provisions of sub-paragraphs (b) and (c) of paragraph 2 of this Article and shall communicate the response to all Parties not later than 30 days before the meeting.
  (b) Amendments shall be adopted by a two-thirds majority of Parties present and voting. For these purposes 'Parties present and voting' means Parties present and casting an affirmative or negative vote. Parties abstaining from voting shall not be counted among the two-thirds required for adopting an amendment.
  (c) Amendments adopted at a meeting shall enter into force 90 days after that meeting for all Parties except those which make a reservation in accordance with paragraph 3 of this Article.

2. The following provisions shall apply in relation to amendments to Appendices I and II between meetings of the Conference of the Parties:

  (a) Any Party may propose an amendment to Appendix I and II for consideration between meetings by the postal procedures set forth in this paragraph.
  (b) For marine species, the Secretariat shall, upon receiving the text of the proposed amendment, immediately communicate it to the Parties. It shall also consult intergovernmental bodies having a function in relation to those species especially with a view to obtaining scientific data these bodies may be able to provide and to ensuring co-ordination with any conservation measures enforced by such bodies. The Secretariat shall communicate the views expressed and data provided by these bodies and its own findings and recommendations to the Parties as soon as possible.
  (c) For species other than marine species, the Secretariat shall, upon receiving the text of the proposed amendments, immediately communicate it to the Parties, and, as soon as possible thereafter, its own recommendations.

(d) Any Party may, within 60 days of the date on which the Secretariat communicated its recommendations to the Parties under sub-paragraphs (b) or (c) of this paragraph, transmit to the Secretariat any comments on the proposed amendment together with any relevant scientific data and information.

(e) The Secretariat shall communicate the replies received together with its own recommendations to the Parties as soon as possible.

(f) If no objection to the proposed amendment is received by the Secretariat within 30 days of the date the replies and recommendations were communicated under the provisions of sub-paragraph (e) of this paragraph, the amendment shall enter into force 90 days later for all Parties except those which make a reservation in accordance with paragraph 3 of this Article.

(g) If an objection by any Party is received by the Secretariat the proposed amendment shall be submitted to a postal vote in accordance with the provisions of sub-paragraphs (h), (i) and (j) of this paragraph.

(h) The Secretariat shall notify the Parties that notification of objection has been received.

(i) Unless the Secretariat receives the votes for, against or in abstention from at least one-half of the Parties within 60 days of the date of notification under sub-paragraph (h) of this paragraph, the proposed amendment shall be referred to the next meeting of the Conference for further consideration.

(j) Provided that votes are received from one-half of the Parties, the amendment shall be adopted by a two-thirds majority of Parties casting an affirmative or negative vote.

(k) The Secretariat shall notify all Parties of the result of the vote.

(l) If the proposed amendment is adopted it shall enter into force 90 days after the date of the notification by the Secretariat of its acceptance for all Parties except those which make a reservation in accordance with paragraph 3 of this Article.

3. During the period of 90 days provided for by sub-paragraph (c) of paragraph 1 or sub-paragraph (l) of paragraph 2 of this Article any Party may by notification in writing to the Depositary Government make a reservation with respect to the amendment. Until such reservation is withdrawn the Party shall be treated as a State not a Party to the present Convention with respect to trade in the species concerned.

Article XVI
Appendix III and Amendments Thereto

1. Any Party may at any time submit to the Secretariat a list of species which it identifies as being subject to regulation within its jurisdiction for the

purpose mentioned in paragraph 3 of Article II. Appendix III shall include the names of the Parties submitting the species for inclusion therein, the scientific names of the species so submitted, and any parts or derivatives of the animals or plants concerned that are specified in relation to the species for the purposes of sub-paragraph (b) of Article I.

2. Each list submitted under the provisions of paragraph 1 of this Article shall be communicated to the Parties by the Secretariat as soon as possible after receiving it. The list shall take effect as part of Appendix III 90 days after the date of such communication. At any time after the communication of such list, any Party may by notification in writing to the Depositary Government enter a reservation with respect to any species or any parts or derivatives, and until such reservation is withdrawn, the State shall be treated as a State not a Party to the present Convention with respect to trade in the species or part or derivative concerned.

3. A Party which has submitted a species for inclusion in Appendix III may withdraw it at any time by notification to the Secretariat which shall communicate the withdrawal to all Parties. The withdrawal shall take effect 30 days after the date of such communication.

4. Any Party submitting a list under the provisions of paragraph 1 of this Article shall submit to the Secretariat a copy of all domestic laws and regulations applicable to the protection of such species, together with any interpretations which the Party may deem appropriate or the Secretariat may request. The Party shall, for as long as the species in question is included in Appendix III, submit any amendments of such laws and regulations or any new interpretations as they are adopted.

Article XVII
Amendment of the Convention

1. An extraordinary meeting of the Conference of the Parties shall be convened by the Secretariat on the written request of at least one-third of the Parties to consider and adopt amendments to the present Convention. Such amendments shall be adopted by a two-thirds majority of Parties present and voting. For these purposes 'Parties present and voting' means Parties present and casting an affirmative or negative vote. Parties abstaining from voting shall not be counted among the two-thirds required for adopting an amendment.

2. The text of any proposed amendment shall be communicated by the Secretariat to all Parties at least 90 days before the meeting.

3. An amendment shall enter into force for the Parties which have accepted it 60 days after two-thirds of the Parties have deposited an instrument of acceptance of the amendment with the Depositary Government. Thereafter, the amendment shall enter into force for any other Party

60 days after that Party deposits its instrument of acceptance of the amendment.

Article XVIII
Resolution of Disputes

1. Any dispute which may arise between two or more Parties with respect to the interpretation or application of the provisions of the present Convention shall be subject to negotiation between the Parties involved in the dispute.

2. If the dispute cannot be resolved in accordance with paragraph 1 of this Article, the Parties may, by mutual consent, submit the dispute to arbitration, in particular that of the Permanent Court of Arbitration at The Hague, and the Parties submitting the dispute shall be bound by the arbitral decision.

Article XIX
Signature

The present Convention shall be open for signature at Washington until 30 April 1973 and thereafter at Berne until 31 December 1974.

Article XX
Ratification, Acceptance, Approval

The present Convention shall be subject to ratification, acceptance or approval. Instruments of ratification, acceptance or approval shall be deposited with the Government of the Swiss Confederation which shall be the Depositary Government.

Article XXI
Accession

The present Convention shall be open indefinitely for accession. Instruments of accession shall be deposited with the Depositary Government.

Article XXII
Entry into Force

1. The present Convention shall enter into force 90 days after the date of deposit of the tenth instrument of ratification, acceptance, approval or accession, with the Depositary Government.

2. For each State which ratifies, accepts or approves the present Convention or accedes thereto after the deposit of the tenth instrument of ratification, acceptance, approval or accession, the present Convention shall enter into force 90 days after the deposit by such State of its instrument of ratification, acceptance, approval or accession.

Article XXIII
Reservations

1. The provisions of the present Convention shall not be subject to general reservations. Specific reservations may be entered in accordance with the provisions of this Article and Articles XV and XVI.

2. Any State may, on depositing its instrument of ratification, acceptance, approval or accession, enter a specific reservation with regard to:

    (a) any species included in Appendix I, II, III; or

    (b) any parts or derivatives specified in relation to a species included in Appendix III.

3. Until a Party withdraws its reservation entered under the provisions of this Article, it shall be treated as a State not a Party to the present Convention with respect to trade in the particular species or parts or derivatives specified in such reservation.

Article XXIV
Denunciation

Any Party may denounce the present Convention by written notification to the Depositary Government at any time. The denunciation shall take effect twelve months after the Depositary Government has received the notification.

Article XXV
Depositary

1. The original of the present Convention, in the Chinese, English, French, Russian and Spanish languages, each version being equally authentic, shall be deposited with the Depositary Government, which shall transmit certified copies thereof to all States that have signed it or deposited instruments of accession to it.

2. The Depositary Government shall inform all signatory and acceding States and the Secretariat of signatures, deposit of instruments of ratification, acceptance, approval or accession, entry into force of the present Convention, amendments thereto, entry and withdrawal of reservations and notifications of denunciation.

3. As soon as the present Convention enters into force, a certified copy thereof shall be transmitted by the Depositary Government to the Secretariat of the United Nations for registration and publication in accordance with Article 102 of the Charter of the United Nations.

    IN WITNESS WHEREOF the undersigned Plenipotentiaries, being duly authorized to that effect, have signed the present Convention.

    DONE at Washington this third day of March, one thousand nine hundred and seventy-three.

Convention on the Conservation of Migratory Species of Wild Animals, Bonn, 23 June 1979

This Convention, which provides a framework for further actions by its parties, both aims to protect migratory species as such during their transboundary migrations and to conserve their habitats. Species are listed on its two Appendices according to their level of endangerment or other threats to survival. It defines such species in terms of entire populations of wild animals or any geographically separate parts thereof that cyclically and predictably cross national boundaries. It also introduces the concepts of 'conservation status', which it defines as the sum of the influences acting on such species that may affect their long term distribution and abundance, and of 'Range States'. It requires conclusion of further formal 'AGREEMENTS' (sic) by the Range States of species which, *inter alia*, have 'unfavourable conservation status'. The Convention was drafted under the auspices of the IUCN. For the full text of the Convention see 19 *ILM* (1980) 15; *Misc.* 11 (1980), Cmnd. 7888; S. Lyster, *International Wildlife Law* (Cambridge, 1985), 411–27. The Convention requires widespread ratification and implementation by Range States to make it effective. As at 31 January 1995 it had only forty-four parties; two AGREEMENTS had been concluded, viz. Agreement on the Conservation of Seals in the Wadden Sea, done at Bonn, 16 October 1990, in force 1 October 1991; and Agreement on the Conservation of Small Cetaceans of the Baltic and North Seas (ASCOBANS), done at New York, 17 March 1992 (texts in MMC *Compendium* Vol. II, 1607–11 and 1612–17 respectively).

The negotiation of the Convention is described in 'Explanatory Notes on Revised Draft Convention on the Conservation of Migratory Species of Wild Animals', *Convention on the Conservation of Migratory Species of Wild Animals* (Federal Ministry of Food, Agriculture, and Forestry of the Federal Republic of Germany, 1979) and in the *Report of the US Delegation to the Conference to Conclude a Convention on the Conservation of Migratory Species of Wild Animals* (Washington D.C., 1979).

Amendments to the Appendices were made at the Conferences of the Parties held in: 1985 (in force 24 January 1980); 1988 (in force 12 January 1989); and 1991 (in force 18 July 1992). The text of the Appendices as amended at 31 December 1988 is found in UKTS 87 (1990), Cmnd. 1332 (not reproduced). Details of these and the agreements concluded under the Convention are given in the proceedings of the Conference of the Parties published by the Secretariat, which is located in Bonn.

For discussion of the operation of the Convention see R. Osterwoldt, 'Implementation and Enforcement Issues in the Protection of Migratory Species', 29 *Nat Res J.* (1989) 1028ff; S. Lyster, *International Wildlife Law* (Cambridge, 1985), 278ff; J. Johnson, 'The Bonn Convention and The Law of the Sea Convention: Conservation of Marine Mammals', in A. Soons (ed.) *Implementation of the Law of the Sea Convention through International Institutions* (Honolulu, 1990), 363ff; P.W. Birnie and A. E. Boyle, *International Law and the Environment* (Oxford, 1992), Ch. 12, esp. 470–80.

TEXT

The Contracting Parties,

Recognizing that wild animals in their innumerable forms are an irreplaceable part of the earth's natural system which must be conserved for the good of mankind;

Aware that each generation of man holds the resources of the earth for future generations and has an obligation to ensure that this legacy is conserved and, where utilized, is used wisely;

Conscious of the ever-growing value of wild animals from environmental, ecological, genetic, scientific, aesthetic, recreational, cultural, educational, social and economic points of view;

Concerned particularly with those species of wild animals that migrate across or outside national jurisdictional boundaries;

Recognizing that the States are and must be the protectors of the migratory species of wild animals that live within or pass through their national jurisdictional boundaries;

Convinced that conservation and effective management of migratory species of wild animals require the concerted action of all States within the national jurisdictional boundaries of which such species spend any part of their life cycles;

Recalling Recommendation 32 of the Action Plan adopted by the United Nations Conference on the Human Environment (Stockholm, 1972) and noted with satisfaction at the Twenty-seventh Session of the General Assembly of the United Nations;

Have Agreed as follows:

Article I
Interpretation

1. For the purpose of this Convention:
   (a) 'Migratory species' means the entire population or any geographically separate part of the population of any species or lower taxon of wild animals, a significant proportion of whose members cyclically and predictably cross one or more national jurisdictional boundaries;
   (b) 'Conservation status of a migratory species' means the sum of the influences acting on the migratory species that may affect its long-term distribution and abundance;
   (c) 'Conservation status' will be taken as 'favourable' when:
      (1) population dynamics data indicate that the migratory species is maintaining itself on a long-term basis as a viable component of its ecosystems;
      (2) the range of the migratory species is neither currently being reduced, nor is likely to be reduced, on a long-term basis;
      (3) there is, and will be in the foreseeable future, sufficient habitat to maintain the population of the migratory species on a long-term basis; and
      (4) the distribution and abundance of the migratory species approach historic coverage and levels to the extent that potentially

suitable ecosystems exist and to the extent consistent with wise wildlife management;

(d) 'Conservation status' will be taken as 'unfavourable' if any of the conditions set out in sub-paragraph (c) of this paragraph is not met;

(e) 'Endangered' in relation to a particular migratory species means that the migratory species is in danger of extinction throughout all or a significant portion of its range;

(f) 'Range' means all the areas of land or water that a migratory species inhabits, stays in temporarily, crosses or overflies at any time on its normal migration route;

(g) 'Habitat' means any area in the range of a migratory species which contains suitable living conditions for that species;

(h) 'Range State' in relation to a particular migratory species means any State (and where appropriate any other Party referred to under sub-paragraph (k) of this paragraph) that exercises jurisdiction over any part of the range of that migratory species, or a State, flag vessels of which are engaged outside national jurisdictional limits in taking that migratory species;

(i) 'Taking' means taking, hunting, fishing, capturing, harassing, deliberate killing, or attempting to engage in any such conduct;

(j) 'AGREEMENT' means an international agreement relating to the conservation of one or more migratory species as provided for in Articles IV and V of this Convention; and

(k) 'Party' means a State or any regional economic integration organization constituted by sovereign States which has competence in respect of the negotiation, conclusion and application of international agreements in matters covered by this Convention for which this Convention is in force.

2. In matters within their competence, the regional economic integration organizations which are Parties to this Convention shall in their own name exercise the rights and fulfil the responsibilities which this Convention attributes to their member States. In such cases the member States of these organizations shall not be entitled to exercise such rights individually.

3. Where this Convention provides for a decision to be taken by either a two-thirds majority or a unanimous decision of 'the Parties present and voting' this shall mean 'the Parties present and casting an affirmative or negative vote'. Those abstaining from voting shall not be counted amongst 'the Parties present and voting' in determining the majority.

Article II
Fundamental Principles

1. The Parties acknowledge the importance of migratory species being conserved and of Range States agreeing to take action to this end whenever

possible and appropriate, paying special attention to migratory species the conservation status of which is unfavourable, and taking individually or in co-operation appropriate and necessary steps to conserve such species and their habitat.

2. The Parties acknowledge the need to take action to avoid any migratory species becoming endangered.

3. In particular, the Parties:

   (a) should promote, co-operate in and support research relating to migratory species;
   (b) shall endeavour to provide immediate protection for migratory species included in Appendix I; and
   (c) shall endeavour to conclude AGREEMENTS covering the conservation and management of migratory species included in Appendix II.

Article III
Endangered Migratory Species: Appendix I

1. Appendix I shall list migratory species which are endangered.

2. A migratory species may be listed in Appendix I provided that reliable evidence, including the best scientific evidence available, indicates that the species is endangered.

3. A migratory species may be removed from Appendix I when the Conference of the Parties determines that:

   (a) reliable evidence, including the best scientific evidence available, indicates that the species is no longer endangered, and
   (b) the species is not likely to become endangered again because of loss of protection due to its removal from Appendix I.

4. Parties that are Range States of a migratory species listed in Appendix I shall endeavour:

   (a) to conserve and, where feasible and appropriate, restore those habitats of the species which are of importance in removing the species from danger of extinction;
   (b) to prevent, remove, compensate for or minimize, as appropriate, the adverse effects of activities or obstacles that seriously impede or prevent the migration of the species; and
   (c) to the extent feasible and appropriate, to prevent, reduce or control factors that are endangering or are likely to further endanger the species, including strictly controlling the introduction of, or controlling or eliminating, already introduced exotic species.

5. Parties that are Range States of a migratory species listed in Appendix I shall prohibit the taking of animals belonging to such species. Exceptions may be made to this prohibition only if:

(a) the taking is for scientific purposes;

(b) the taking is for the purpose of enhancing the propagation or survival of the affected species;

(c) the taking is to accommodate the needs of traditional subsistence users of such species; or

(d) extraordinary circumstances so require;

provided that such exceptions are precise as to content and limited in space and time. Such taking should not operate to the disadvantage of the species.

6. The Conferences of the Parties may recommend to the Parties that are Range States of a migratory species listed in Appendix I that they take further measures considered appropriate to benefit the species.

7. The Parties shall as soon as possible inform the Secretariat of any exceptions made pursuant to paragraph 5 of this Article.

Article IV
Migratory Species to be the Subject to Agreements: Appendix II

1. Appendix II shall list migratory species which have an unfavourable conservation status and which require international agreements for their conservation and management, as well as those which have a conservation status which would significantly benefit from the international co-operation that could be achieved by an international agreement.

2. If the circumstances so warrant, a migratory species may be listed both in Appendix I and Appendix II.

3. Parties that are Range States of migratory species listed in Appendix II shall endeavour to conclude AGREEMENTS where these would benefit the species and should give priority to those species in an unfavourable conservation status.

4. Parties are encouraged to take action with a view to concluding AGREEMENTS for any population or any geographically separate part of the population of any species or lower taxon of wild animals, members of which periodically cross one or more national jurisdictional boundaries.

5. The Secretariat shall be provided with a copy of each AGREEMENT concluded pursuant to the provisions of this Article.

Article V
Guidelines for AGREEMENTS

1. The object of each AGREEMENT shall be to restore the migratory species concerned to a favourable conservation status or to maintain it in such a status. Each AGREEMENT should deal with those aspects of the conservation and management of the migratory species concerned which serve to achieve that object.

2. Each AGREEMENT should cover the whole of the range of the migratory species concerned and should be open to accession by all Range States of that species, whether or not they are Parties to this Convention.

3. An AGREEMENT should, wherever possible, deal with more than one migratory species.

4. Each AGREEMENT should:

(a) identify the migratory species covered;

(b) describe the range and migration route of the migratory species;

(c) provide for each Party to designate its national authority concerned with the implementation of the AGREEMENT;

(d) establish, if necessary, appropriate machinery to assist in carrying out the aims of the AGREEMENT, to monitor its effectiveness, and to prepare reports for the Conference of the Parties;

(e) provide for procedures for the settlement of disputes between Parties to the AGREEMENT; and

(f) at a minimum, prohibit, in relation to a migratory species of the Order Cetacea, any taking that is not permitted for that migratory species under any other multilateral agreement and provide for accession to the AGREEMENT by States that are not Range States of that migratory species.

5. Where appropriate and feasible, each AGREEMENT should provide for but not be limited to:

(a) periodic review of the conservation status of the migratory species concerned and the identification of the factors which may be harmful to that status;

(b) co-ordinated conservation and management plans;

(c) research into the ecology and population dynamics of the migratory species concerned, with special regard to migration;

(d) the exchange of information on the migratory species concerned, special regard being paid to the exchange of the results of research and of relevant statistics;

(e) conservation and, where required and feasible, restoration of the habitats of importance in maintaining a favourable conservation status, and protection of such habitats from disturbances, including strict control of the introduction of, or control of already introduced, exotic species detrimental to the migratory species;

(f) maintenance of a network of suitable habitats appropriately disposed in relation to the migration routes;

(g) where it appears desirable, the provision of new habitats favourable to the migratory species or reintroduction of the migratory species into favourable habitats;

(h) elimination of, to the maximum extent possible, or compensation for activities and obstacles which hinder or impede migration;

(i) prevention, reduction or control of the release into the habitat of the migratory species of substances harmful to that migratory species;

(j) measures based on sound ecological principles to control and manage the taking of the migratory species;

(k) procedures for co-ordinating action to suppress illegal taking;

(l) exchange of information on substantial threats to the migratory species;

(m) emergency procedures whereby conservation action would be considerably and rapidly strengthened when the conservation status of the migratory species is seriously affected; and

(n) making the general public aware of the contents and aims of the AGREEMENT.

Article VI
Range States

1. A list of the Range States of migratory species listed in Appendices I and II shall be kept up to date by the Secretariat using information it has received from the Parties.

2. The Parties shall keep the Secretariat informed as to which of the migratory species listed in Appendices I and II they consider they are Range States, including provision of information on their flag vessels engaged outside national jurisdictional limits in taking the migratory species concerned and, where possible, future plans in respect of such taking.

3. The Parties which are Range States for migratory species listed in Appendix I or Appendix II should inform the Conference of the Parties through the Secretariat, at least six months prior to each ordinary meeting of the Conference, on measures that they are taking to implement the provisions of this Convention for these species.

Article VII
The Conference of the Parties

1. The Conference of the Parties shall be the decision-making organ of this Convention.

2. The Secretariat shall call a meeting of the Conference of the Parties not later than two years after the entry into force of this Convention.

3. Thereafter the Secretariat shall convene ordinary meetings of the Conference of the Parties at intervals of not more than three years, unless the Conference decides otherwise, and extraordinary meetings at any time on the written request of at least one-third of the Parties.

4. The Conference of the Parties shall establish and keep under review the financial regulations of this Convention. The Conference of the Parties shall, at each of its ordinary meetings, adopt the budget for the next

financial period. Each Party shall contribute to this budget according to a scale to be agreed upon by the Conference. Financial regulations, including the provisions on the budget and the scale of contributions as well as their modifications, shall be adopted by unanimous vote of the Parties present and voting.

5. At each of its meetings the Conference of the Parties shall review the implementation of this Convention and may in particular:

(a) review and assess the conservation status of migratory species;

(b) review the progress made towards the conservation of migratory species, especially those listed in Appendices I and II;

(c) make such provision and provide such guidance as may be necessary to enable the Scientific Council and the Secretariat to carry out their duties;

(d) receive and consider any reports presented by the Scientific Council, the Secretariat, any Party or any standing body established pursuant to an AGREEMENT;

(e) make recommendations to the Parties for improving the conservation status of migratory species and review the progress being made under AGREEMENTS;

(f) in those cases where an AGREEMENT has not been concluded, make recommendations for the convening of meetings of the Parties that are Range States of a migratory species or group of migratory species to discuss measures to improve the conservation status of the species;

(g) make recommendations to the Parties for improving the effectiveness of this Convention; and

(h) decide on any additional measure that should be taken to implement the objectives of this Convention.

6. Each meeting of the Conference of the Parties should determine the time and venue of the next meeting.

7. Any meeting of the Conference of the Parties shall determine and adopt rules of procedure for that meeting. Decisions at a meeting of the Conference of the Parties shall require a two-thirds majority of the Parties present and voting, except where otherwise provided for by this Convention.

8. The United Nations, its Specialized Agencies, the International Atomic Energy Agency, as well as any State not a party to this Convention and, for each AGREEMENT, the body designated by the parties to that AGREE-MENT, may be represented by observers at meetings of the Conference of the Parties.

9. Any agency or body technically qualified in protection, conservation and management of migratory species, in the following categories, which has informed the Secretariat of its desire to be represented at meetings of the Conference of the Parties by observers, shall be admitted unless at least

one-third of the Parties present object:

(a) international agencies or bodies, either governmental or non-governmental, and national governmental agencies and bodies; and

(b) national non-governmental agencies or bodies which have been approved for this purpose by the State in which they are located.

Once admitted, these observers shall have the right to participate but not to vote.

Article VIII
The Scientific Council

1. At its first meeting, the Conference of the Parties shall establish a Scientific Council to provide advice on scientific matters.

2. Any Party may appoint a qualified expert as a member of the Scientific Council. In addition, the Scientific Council shall include as members qualified experts selected and appointed by the Conference of the Parties; the number of these experts, the criteria for their selection and the terms of their appointments shall be as determined by the Conference of the Parties.

3. The Scientific Council shall meet at the request of the Secretariat as required by the Conference of the Parties.

4. Subject to the approval of the Conference of the Parties, the Scientific Council shall establish its own rules of procedure.

5. The Conference of the Parties shall determine the functions of the Scientific Council, which may include:

(a) providing scientific advice to the Conference of the Parties, to the Secretariat, and, if approved by the Conference of the Parties, to any body set up under this Convention or an AGREEMENT or to any Party;

(b) recommending research and the co-ordination of research on migratory species, evaluating the results of such research in order to ascertain the conservation status of migratory species and reporting to the Conference of the Parties on such status and measures for its improvement;

(c) making recommendations to the Conference of the Parties as to the migratory species to be included in Appendices I or II, together with an indication of the range of such migratory species;

(d) making recommendations to the Conference of the Parties as to specific conservation and management measures to be included in AGREEMENTS on migratory species; and

(e) recommending to the Conference of the Parties solutions to problems relating to the scientific aspects of the implementation of this Convention, in particular with regard to the habitats of migratory species.

Article IX
The Secretariat

1. For the purposes of this Convention a Secretariat shall be established.

2. Upon entry into force of this Convention, the Secretariat is provided by the Executive Director of the United Nations Environment Programme. To the extent and in the manner he considers appropriate, he may be assisted by suitable intergovernmental and non-governmental, international or national agencies and bodies technically qualified in protection, conservation and management of wild animals.

3. If the United Nations Environment Programme is no longer able to provide the Secretariat, the Conference of the Parties shall make alternative arrangements for the Secretariat.

4. The functions of the Secretariat shall be:

(a) to arrange for and service meetings:
   (i) of the Conference of the Parties, and
   (ii) of the Scientific Council;
(b) to maintain liaison with and promote liaison between the Parties, the standing bodies set up under AGREEMENTS and other international organizations concerned with migratory species;
(c) to obtain from any appropriate source reports and other information which will further the objectives and implementation of this Convention and to arrange for the appropriate dissemination of such information;
(d) to invite the attention of the Conference of the Parties to any matter pertaining to the objectives of this Convention;
(e) to prepare for the Conference of the Parties reports on the work of the Secretariat and on the implementation of this Convention;
(f) to maintain and publish a list of Range States of all migratory species included in Appendices I and II;
(g) to promote, under the direction of the Conference of the Parties, the conclusion of AGREEMENTS,
(h) to maintain and make available to the Parties a list of AGREEMENTS and, if so required by the Conference of the Parties, to provide any information on such AGREEMENTS;
(i) to maintain and publish a list of the recommendations made by the Conference of the Parties pursuant to subparagraphs (e), (f) and (g) of paragraph 5 of Article VII or of decisions made pursuant to sub-paragraph (h) of that paragraph;
(j) to provide for the general public information concerning this Convention and its objectives; and
(k) to perform any other function entrusted to it under this Convention or by the Conference of the Parties.

Article X
Amendment of the Convention

1. This Convention may be amended at any ordinary or extraordinary meeting of the Conference of the Parties.

2. Proposals for amendment may be made by any Party.

3. The text of any proposed amendment and the reasons for it shall be communicated to the Secretary at least one hundred and fifty days before the meeting at which it is to be considered and shall promptly be communicated by the Secretary to all Parties. Any comments on the text by the Parties shall be communicated to the Secretariat not less than sixty days before the meeting begins. The Secretariat shall, immediately after the last day for submission of comments, communicate to the Parties all comments submitted by that day.

4. Amendments shall be adopted by a two-thirds majority of Parties present and voting.

5. An amendment adopted shall enter into force for all Parties which have accepted it on the first day of the third month following the date on which two-thirds of the Parties have deposited an instrument of acceptance with the Depositary. For each Party which deposits an instrument of acceptance after the date on which two-thirds of the Parties have deposited an instrument of acceptance, the amendment shall enter into force for that Party on the first day of the third month following the deposit of its instrument of acceptance.

Article XI
Amendment of the Appendices

1. Appendices I and II may be amended at any ordinary or extraordinary meeting of the Conference of the Parties.

2. Proposals for amendment may be made by any Party.

3. The text of any proposed amendment and the reasons for it, based on the best scientific evidence available, shall be communicated to the Secretariat at least 150 days before the meeting and shall promptly be communicated by the Secretariat to all Parties. Any comments on the text by the Parties shall be communicated to the Secretariat not less than 60 days before the meeting begins. The Secretariat shall, immediately after the last day for submission of comments, communicate to the Parties all comments submitted by that day.

4. Amendments shall be adopted by a two-thirds majority of Parties present and voting.

5. An amendment to the Appendices shall enter into force for all Parties 90 days after the meeting of the Conference of the Parties at which it was

adopted, except for those Parties which make a reservation in accordance with paragraph 6 of this Article.

6. During the period of 90 days provided for in paragraph 5 of this Article, any Party may by notification in writing to the Depositary make a reservation with respect to the amendment. A reservation to an amendment may be withdrawn by written notification to the Depositary and thereupon the amendment shall enter into force for that Party 90 days after the reservation is withdrawn.

Article XII
Effect on International Conventions and Other Legislation

1. Nothing in this Convention shall prejudice the codification and development of the law of the sea by the United Nations Conference on the Law of the Sea convened pursuant to Resolution 2750 C (XXV) of the General Assembly of the United Nations nor the present or future claims and legal views of any State concerning the law of the sea and the nature and extent of coastal and flag State jurisdiction.

2. The provisions of this Convention shall in no way affect the rights or obligations of any Party deriving from any existing treaty convention or agreement.

3. The provisions of this Convention shall in no way affect the right of Parties to adopt stricter domestic measures concerning the conservation of migratory species listed in Appendices I and II or to adopt domestic measures concerning the conservation of species not listed in Appendices I and II.

Article XIII
Settlement of Disputes

1. Any dispute which may arise between two or more Parties with respect to the interpretation or application of the provisions of this Convention shall be subject to negotiation between the Parties involved in the dispute.

2. If the dispute cannot be resolved in accordance with paragraph 1 of this Article, the Parties may, by mutual consent, submit the dispute to arbitration, in particular that of the Permanent Court of Arbitration at The Hague, and the Parties submitting the dispute shall be bound by the arbitral decision.

Article XIV
Reservations

1. The provisions of this Convention shall not be subject to general reservations. Specific reservations may be entered in accordance with the provisions of this Article and Article XI.

2. Any State or any regional economic integration organization may, on depositing its instrument of ratification, acceptance, approval or accession, enter a specific reservation with regard to the presence on either Appendix I or Appendix II or both, of any migratory species and shall then not be regarded as a Party in regard to the subject of that reservation until ninety days after the Depositary has transmitted to the Parties notification that such reservation has been withdrawn.

Article XV
Signature

This Convention shall be open for signature at Bonn for all States and any regional economic integration organization until the twenty-second day of June 1980.

Article XVI
Ratification, Acceptance, Approval

This Convention shall be subject to ratification, acceptance or approval. Instruments of ratification, acceptance or approval shall be deposited with the Government of the Federal Republic of Germany, which shall be the Depositary.

Article XVII
Accession

After the twenty-second day of June 1980 this Convention shall be open for accession by all non-signatory States and any regional economic integration organization. Instruments of accession shall be deposited with the Depositary.

Article XVIII
Entry into Force

1. This Convention shall enter into force on the first day of the third month following the date of deposit of the fifteenth instrument of ratification, acceptance, approval or accession with the Depositary.

2. For each State or each regional economic integration organization which ratifies, accepts or approves this Convention or accedes thereto after the deposit of the fifteenth instrument of ratification, acceptance, approval or accession, this Convention shall enter into force on the first day of the third month following the deposit by such State or such organization of its instrument of ratification, acceptance, approval or accession.

Article XIX
Denunciation

Any Party may denounce this Convention by written notification to the Depositary at any time. The denunciation shall take effect twelve months after the Depositary has received the notification.

Article XX
Depositary

1. The original of this Convention, in the English, French, German, Russian and Spanish languages, each version being equally authentic, shall be deposited with the Depositary. The Depositary shall transmit certified copies of each of these versions to all States and all regional economic integration organizations that have signed the Convention or deposited instruments of accession to it.

2. The Depositary shall, after consultation with the Governments concerned, prepare official versions of the text of this Convention in the Arabic and Chinese languages.

3. The Depositary shall inform all signatory and acceding States and all signatory and acceding regional economic integration organizations and the Secretariat of signatures, deposit of instruments of ratification, acceptance, approval or accession, entry into force of this Convention, amendments thereto, specific reservations and notifications of denunciation.

4. As soon as this Convention enters into force, a certified copy thereof shall be transmitted by the Depositary to the Secretariat of the United Nations for registration and publication in accordance with Article 102 of the Charter of the United Nations.

IN WITNESS WHEREOF the undersigned, being duly authorized to the effect, have signed the present Convention.

DONE at Bonn, this 23rd day of June 1979.

Convention on Wetlands of International Importance, Ramsar, 2 February 1971

The need for an international convention to protect wetlands was recognised by an International Conference on Wetlands convened at Les-Saintes-Maries-de-la-Mer, France, jointly by the IUCN, the International Council for Bird Protection (ICBP), and the International Wild Fowl Research Bureau (IWRB), in 1962. Work began on compiling a list of European and North African wetlands of international import-ance to form the basis of a convention. The proposal was further developed at European meetings on water fowl conservation held in Scotland in 1963 and in the Netherlands in 1966, and a preliminary draft of a convention was produced prior to an International Regional Meeting on Conservation of Wild Fowl Resources held in Leningrad in 1968, which decided to accelerate adoption of a convention. The final text was adopted by an international conference held in Ramsar, Iran, on 2 February 1971, with the support of UNESCO's Man in the Biosphere Programme; see *Proceedings of the International Conference on Conservation of Wetlands of International Importance* (IWRB, 1972). The Convention entered into force on 21 December 1975 and had eighty-eight parties at 31 January 1995. The unamended text is found in 996 *UNTS* 245; *UKTS* 34 (1976), Cmnd. 6465; 11 *ILM* (1972) 963; *TIAS* 11084; T. Davies (ed.) *Key Texts* (Ramsar Bureau, Gland, 1994). The amended text is reproduced here.

The Convention requires parties to conserve wetlands, *inter alia*, as habitats of distinctive ecosystems and to designate Wetlands of International Importance for inclusion in a list thereof to be maintained by the IUCN. As of December 31 1994, 718 Wetlands have been so designated totalling 43,798,762 hectares. The number of ratifications by developing states has increased following a recommendation adopted in 1987 to make it more attractive for them to do by stressing the value of wetlands and the need for wise use rather than emphasising the need for protection measures as such, and the institution in 1990 of a Small Wetlands Conservation Fund to assist conservation of listed wetlands.

At a meeting of the parties in Heilenhaten, Germany, 1974, convened by the IWRB, criteria for designation of wetlands were agreed. Since then five Conferences on the Conservation of Wetlands and Water Fowl have been held as at 31 December 1994: the First in Cagliari, Italy, 24–29 November 1980; the Second in Groningen, The Netherlands, 7–12 May 1984; the Third in Regina, Canada, 27 May–5 June 1987; simultaneously an Extraordinary Conference was held there to adopt the funding and secretariat amendments referred to below. A Fourth Conference was held in Montreal, France, 27 June–4 July 1990 at which further amendments to the criteria for designating sites were approved. The Fifth Conference was held at Kushiro, Japan, 9–16 June 1993 and a Sixth is planned in Brisbane, Australia, in 1996. The Reports of the proceedings of the conferences are published by the Ramsar Bureau. The Conferences of the Parties have addressed various problems created by the ambiguities of the Convention's provisions and gaps therein. The 1971 Convention provided neither for a permanent secretariat nor procedures for amending the Convention. The Convention has been amended twice: first, by a Protocol to provide for amendment and approve equally authentic, different language versions of the Convention, done at Paris, 3 December 1982, *repr. Misc.* 1 (1984), Cmnd. 9113; 22 *ILM* (1983) 698. It entered into force on 1 October 1986 and is binding on all parties except Algeria, Belgium, Suriname, Uruguay, and Yugoslavia. Secondly, by amendments to the Convention done at Regina, 3 June 1987 by an Extraordinary Conference, to enable the Bureau to convene a regular

Conference of the Parties to review and promote the Convention. These amendments entered into force on 1 May 1994; text in Marine Mammal Commission, *Compendium of Selected Treaties*, vol. 1 (Washington D.C., 1994), 585–6. The Independent Bureau established by the 1987 amendments maintains offices at IUCN, Rue Mauverney 28, CH–1196 Gland, Switzerland. Its small office at the International Water Fowl Research Bureau, The New Grounds, Slimbridge, Gloucs., GL2 7BT, UK, collects information on listed sites.

For further discussion, see S. Lyster, *International Wildlife Law* (Cambridge, 1985) 183–207; D. Navid, 'The International Law of Migratory Species: The Ramsar Convention', 29 *Nat Res J.* (1989) 1001–6; 20 *IUCN Bull.* 4–6 (1989), 'Special Report on Wetlands'; Ramsar Bureau, quarterly *Newsletter of the Convention on Wetlands of International Importance*; P. W. Birnie and A. E. Boyle, *International Law and the Environment* (Oxford University Press, Oxford, 1992), 465–8.

TEXT

The Contracting Parites,

Recognizing the interdependence of man and his environment;

Considering the fundamental ecological functions of wetlands as regulators of water regimes and as habitats supporting a characteristic flora and fauna, especially waterfowl;

Being convinced that wetlands constitute a resource of great economic, cultural, scientific and recreational value, the loss of which would be irreparable;

Desiring to stem the progressive encroachment on and loss of wetlands now and in the future;

Recognizing that waterfowl in their seasonal migrations may transcend frontiers and so should be regarded as an international resource;

Being confident that the conservation of wetlands and their flora and fauna can be ensured by combining far-sighted national policies with coordinated international action;

Have Agreed as follows:

Article 1

1. For the purpose of this Convention wetlands are areas of marsh, fen, peatland or water, whether natural or artificial, permanent or temporary, with water that is static or flowing, fresh, brackish or salt, including areas of marine water the depth of which at low tide does not exceed six metres.

2. For the purpose of this Convention waterfowl are birds ecologically dependent on wetlands.

Article 2

1. Each Contracting Party shall designate suitable wetlands within its territory for inclusion in a List of Wetlands of International Importance, hereinafter referred to as 'the List' which is maintained by the bureau established under Article 8. The boundaries of each wetland shall be

precisely described and also delimited on a map and they may incorporate riparian and coastal zones adjacent to the wetlands, and islands or bodies of marine water deeper than six metres at low tide lying within the wetlands, especially where these have importance as waterfowl habital.

2. Wetlands should be selected for the List on account of their international significance in terms of ecology, botany, zoology, limnology or hydrology. In the first instance wetlands of international importance to waterfowl at any season should be included.

3. The inclusion of a wetland in the List does not prejudice the exclusive sovereign rights of the Contracting Party in whose territory the wetland is situated.

4. Each Contracting Party shall designate at least one wetland to be included in the List when signing this Convention or when depositing its instrument of ratification or accession, as provided in Article 9.

5. Any Contracting Party shall have the right to add to the List further wetlands situated within its territory, to extend the boundaries of those wetlands already included by it in the List, or, because of its urgent national interests, to delete or restrict the boundaries of wetlands already included by it in the List and shall, at the earliest possible time, inform the organization or government responsible for the continuing bureau duties specified in Article 8 of any such changes.

6. Each Contracting Party shall consider its international responsibilities for the conservation, management and wise use of migratory stocks of waterfowl, both when designating entries for the List and when exercising its right to change entries in the List relating to wetlands within its territory.

Article 3

1. The Contracting Parties shall formulate and implement their planning so as to promote the conservation of the wetlands included in the List, and as far as possible the wise use of wetlands in their territory.

2. Each Contracting Party shall arrange to be informed at the earliest possible time if the ecological character of any wetland in its territory and included in the List has changed, is changing or is likely to change as the result of technological developments, pollution or other human interference. Information on such changes shall be passed without delay to the organization or government responsible for the continuing bureau duties specified in Article 8.

Article 4

1. Each Contracting Party shall promote the conservation of wetlands and waterfowl by establishing nature reserves on wetlands, whether they are included in the List or not, and provide adequately for their wardening.

2. Where a Contracting Party in its urgent national interest, deletes or restricts the boundaries of a wetland included in the List, it should as far as possible compensate for any loss of wetland resources, and in particular it should create additional nature reserves for waterfowl and for the protection, either in the same area or elsewhere, of an adequate portion of the original habitat.

3. The Contracting Parties shall encourage research and the exchange of data and publications regarding wetlands and their flora and fauna.

4. The Contracting Parties shall endeavour through management to increase waterfowl populations on appropriate wetlands.

5. The Contracting Parties shall promote the training of personnel competent in the fields of wetland research, management and wardening.

Article 5

The Contracting Parties shall consult with each other about implementing obligations arising from the Convention especially in the case of a wetland extending over the territories of more than one Contracting Party or where a water system is shared by Contracting Parties.

They shall at the same time endeavour to coordinate and support present and future policies and regulations concerning the conservation of wetlands and their flora and fauna.

Article 6

1. There shall be established a Conference of the Contracting Parties to review and promote the implementation of this Convention. The bureau referred to in Article 8, paragraph 1, shall convene ordinary meetings of the Conference of the Contracting Parties at intervals of not more than three years, unless the Conference decides otherwise, and extraordinary meetings at the written request of at least one third of the Contracting Parties. Each ordinary meeting of the Conference of the Contracting Parties shall determine the time and venue of the next ordinary meeting.

2. These Conferences of the Contracting Parties shall be competent:

   (a) to discuss the implementation of this Convention;
   (b) to discuss additions to and changes in the List;
   (c) to consider information regarding changes in the ecological character of wetlands included in the List provided in accordance with paragraph 2 of Article 3;
   (d) to make general or specific recommendations to the Contracting Parties regarding the conservation, management and wise use of wetlands and their flora and fauna;
   (e) to request relevant international bodies to prepare reports and statistics on matters which are essentially international in character affecting wetlands.

(f) to adopt other recommendations, or resolutions, to promote the functioning of this Convention.

3. The Contracting Parties shall ensure that those responsible at all levels for wetlands management shall be informed of, and take into consideration, recommendations of such Conferences concerning the conservation, management and wise use of wetlands and their flora and fauna.

4. The Conference of the Contracting Parties shall adopt rules of procedure for each of its meetings.

5. The Conference of the Contracting Parties shall establish and keep under review the financial regulations of this Convention. At each of its ordinary meetings, it shall adopt the budget for the next financial period by a two-thirds majority of Contracting Parties present and voting.

6. Each Contracting Party shall contribute to the budget according to a scale of contributions adopted by unanimity of the Contracting Parties present and voting at a meeting of the ordinary Conference of the Contracting Parties.

Article 7

1. The representatives of the Contracting Parties at such Conferences should include persons who are experts on wetlands or waterfowl by reason of knowledge and experience gained in scientific, administrative or other appropriate capacities.

2. Each of the Contracting Parties represented at a Conference shall have one vote, recommendations, resolutions and decisions being adopted by a simple majority of the Contracting Parties present and voting, unless otherwise provided for in this Convention.

Article 8

1. The International Union for the Conservation of Nature and Natural Resources shall perform the continuing bureau duties under this Convention until such time as another organization or government is appointed by a majority of two-thirds of all Contracting Parties.

2. The continuing bureau duties shall be, *inter alia*:

   (a) to assist in the convening and organizing of Conferences specified in Article 6;

   (b) to maintain the List of Wetlands of International Importance and to be informed by the Contracting Parties of any additions, extensions, deletions or restrictions concerning wetlands included in the List provided in accordance with paragraph 5 of Article 2;

   (c) to be informed by the Contracting Parties of any changes in the ecological character of wetlands included in the List provided in accordance with paragraph 2 of Article 3;

(d) to forward notification of any alterations to the List, or changes in character of wetlands included therein, to all Contracting Parties and to arrange for these matters to be discussed at the next Conference;

(e) to make known to the Contracting Party concerned, the recommendations of the Conferences in respect of such alterations to the List or of changes in the character of wetlands included therein.

Article 9

1. This Convention shall remain open for signature indefinitely.

2. Any member of the United Nations or of one of the Specialized Agencies or of the International Atomic Energy Agency or Party to the Statute of the International Court of Justice may become a Party to this Convention by:

(a) signature without reservation as to ratification;

(b) signature subject to ratification followed by ratification;

(c) accession.

3. Ratification or accession shall be effected by the deposit of an instrument of ratification or accession with the Director-General of the United Nations Educational, Scientific and Cultural Organization (hereinafter referred to as 'the Depository').

Article 10

1. This Convention shall enter into force four months after seven States have become Parties to this Convention in accordance with paragraph 2 of Article 9.

2. Thereafter this Convention shall enter into force for each Contracting Party four months after the day of its signature without reservation as to ratification, or its deposit of an instrument of ratification or accession.

Article 10 Bis

1. This Convention may be amended at a meeting of the Contracting Parites convened for that purpose in accordance with this Article.

2. Proposals for amendment may be made by any Contracting Party.

3. The text of any proposed amendment and the reasons for it shall be communicated to the organization or government performing the continuing bureau duties under the Convention (hereinafter referred to as 'the Bureau') and shall promptly be communicated by the Bureau to all Contracting Parties. Any comments on the text by the Contracting Parties shall be communicated to the Bureau within three months of the date on which amendments were communicated to the Contracting Parties by the Bureau.

The Bureau shall, immediately after the last day for submission of comments, communicate to the Contracting Parties all comments submitted by that day.

4. A meeting of Contracting Parties to consider an amendment communicated in accordance with paragraph 3 shall be convened by the Bureau upon the written request of one-third of the Contracting Parties. The Bureau shall consult the Parties concerning the time and venue of the meeting.

5. Amendments shall be adopted by a two-thirds majority of the Contracting Parties present and voting.

6. An amendment adopted shall enter into force for the Contracting Parties which have accepted it on the first day of the fourth month following the date on which two-thirds of the Contracting Parties have deposited an instrument of acceptance with the Depository. For each Contracting Party which deposits an instrument of acceptance after the date on which two-thirds of the Contracting Parties have deposited an instrument of acceptance, the amendment shall enter into force on the first day of the fourth month following the date of the deposit of its instrument of acceptance.

Article 11

1. This Convention shall continue in force for an indefinite period.

2. Any Contracting Party may denounce this Convention after a period of five years from the date on which it entered into force for that Party by giving written notice thereof to the Depository. Denunciation shall take effect four months after the day on which notice thereof is received by the Depository.

Article 12

1. The Depository shall inform all States that have signed and acceded to this Convention as soon as possible of:

    (a) signatures to the Convention;
    (b) deposits of instruments of ratification of this Convention;
    (c) deposits of instruments of accession to this Convention;
    (d) the date of entry into force of this Convention;
    (e) notifications of denunciation of this Convention.

2. When this Convention has entered into force, the Depository shall have it registered with the Secretariat of the United Nations in accordance with Article 102 of the Charter.

IN WITNESS WHEREOF, the undersigned, being duly authorized to that effect, have signed this Convention.

DONE at Ramsar this 2nd day of February 1971, in a single original in the English, French, German and Russian languages, all texts being equally authentic, which shall be deposited with the Depository which shall send true copies thereof to all Contracting Parties.

Convention on the Conservation of European Wildlife and Natural Habitats, Berne, 19 September 1979

The Convention was negotiated under the auspices of the Council of Europe to overcome the inadequacies of the piecemeal and outdated existing European Conventions, which focused mainly on birds and hunting controls, and to provide for co-operation among States. The recognition in its preamble of a valuable natural heritage 'that needs to be preserved and handed on to future generations' reflects a then new approach to nature conservation, as does its awareness that conservation of natural habitats is a vital component of conservation of wild flora and fauna. The Convention was concluded in Berne, Switzerland on 19 September 1979, and entered into force on 1 June 1982. As at 31 January 1995 it had thirty-one parties including the European Community, eight of which had entered reservations. The text can be found in *ETS* 104; *UKTS* 56 (1982), Cmnd. 8738; 28 Rüster 40; Kiss 509. For background to the negotiation of the treaty, see: *Explanatory Report Concerning the Convention* (Council of Europe, Strasbourg 1979); *Report of the Meetings of the Interim Committee of the Convention on the Conservation of European Wildlife and Natural Habitats*, CE Doc. T–US (1981); L. K. Caldwell, *International Environmental Policy* (2nd edn. Durham, N. C., 1990). Parties are required to take measures to maintain populations of wild flora and fauna, especially endangered and vulnerable species listed on the Appendices of the Convention, though exceptions are permitted and states can on ratification make reservations regarding species listed in the Appendices, or in relation to any of their dependent territories to which they have specifically extended the Convention's application. They are also required to ensure the conservation of habitats of species listed and endangered natural habitats. The Convention is administered by the Council of Europe.

A Standing Committee of Contracting States oversees and reviews its application. It approved amendments to Appendices I and II on 11 December 1987, which entered into force on 12 March 1988, subject to objections to particular species by Finland, Norway, Turkey, and the UK. Norway subsequently withdrew its objections in respect to some species. Amendments to Appendix I were adopted on 11 January 1991 and entered into force on 12 April 1991, subject to objections in respect of particular species by Denmark and Norway. Further amendments were adopted on 6 December 1991 and entered into force on 7 May 1992, subject to objections in respect of particular species by France and Greece. Reports of the Meetings of the Standing Committee are obtainable from the Council of Europe. The Appendices are not reproduced here.

The Convention has been implemented by the European Community through the EC Directives on the Conservation of Natural Habitats of Wild Fauna and Flora, 92/43 EEC, O J L206, 22 July 1992, 116 and on Conservation of Wild Birds, 79/419/EEC, O J L103, 27 August 1979, 50. For discussion see S. Lyster, *International Wildlife Law* (Cambridge, 1983), 112–29; P. W. Birnie and A. E. Boyle, *International Law and the Enviroment* (Oxford, 1992), 443–89, esp. 446–7, 481.

TEXT

Preamble

The Member States of the Council of Europe and the other signatories hereto,

Considering that the aim of the Council of Europe is to achieve a greater unity between its members;

Considering the wish of the Council of Europe to co-operate with other States in the field of nature conservation;

Recognizing that wild flora and fauna constitute a natural heritage of aesthetic, scientific, cultural, recreational, economic and intrinsic value that needs to be preserved and handed on to future generations;

Recognizing the essential role played by wild flora and fauna in maintaining biological balances;

Noting that numerous species of wild flora and fauna are being seriously depleted and that some of them are threatened with extinction;

Aware that the conservation of natural habitats is a vital component of the protection and conservation of wild flora and fauna;

Recognizing that the conservation of wild flora and fauna should be taken into consideration by the governments in their national goals and programmes, and that international co-operation should be established to protect migratory species in particular;

Bearing in mind the widespread requests for common action made by governments or by international bodies, in particular the requests expressed by the United Nations Conference on the Human Environment 1972 and the Consultative Assembly of the Council of Europe;

Desiring particularly to follow, in the field of wildlife conservation, the recommendations of Resolution No. 2 of the Second European Ministerial Conference on the Environment;

Have Agreed as follows:

Chapter I

General Provisions

Article 1

1. The aims of this Convention are to conserve wild flora and fauna and their natural habitats, especially those species and habitats whose conservation requires the co-operation of several States, and to promote such co-operation.

2. Particular emphasis is given to endangered and vulnerable species, including endangered and vulnerable migratory species.

Article 2

The Contracting Parties shall take requisite measures to maintain the population of wild flora and fauna at, or adapt it to, a level which corresponds in particular to ecological, scientific and cultural requirements, while taking account of economic and recreational requirements and the needs of sub-species, varieties or forms at risk locally.

Article 3

1. Each Contracting Party shall take steps to promote national policies for the conservation of wild flora, wild fauna and natural habitats, with particular attention to endangered and vulnerable species, especially endemic ones, and endangered habitats, in accordance with the provisions of this Convention.

2. Each Contracting Party undertakes, in its planning and development policies and in its measures against pollution, to have regard to the conservation of wild flora and fauna.

3. Each Contracting Party shall promote education and disseminate general information on the need to conserve species of wild flora and fauna and their habitats.

Chapter II

Protection of Habitats

Article 4

1. Each Contracting Party shall take appropriate and necessary legislative and administrative measures to ensure the conservation of the habitats of the wild flora and fauna species, especially those specified in Appendices I and II, and the conservation of endangered natural habitats.

2. The Contracting Parties in their planning and development policies shall have regard to the conservation requirements of the areas protected under the preceding paragraph, so as to avoid or minimise as far as possible any deterioration of such areas.

3. The Contracting Parties undertake to give special attention to the protection of areas that are of importance for the migratory species specified in Appendices II and III and which are appropriately situated in relation to migration routes, as wintering, staging, feeding, breeding or moulting areas.

4. The Contracting Parties undertake to co-ordinate as appropriate their efforts for the protection of the natural habitats referred to in this Article when these are situated in frontier areas.

Chapter III

Protection of Species

Article 5

Each Contracting Party shall take appropriate and necessary legislative and administrative measures to ensure the special protection of the wild flora species specified in Appendix I. Deliberate picking, collecting, cutting or uprooting of such plants shall be prohibited. Each Contracting Party shall, as appropriate, prohibit the possession or sale of these species.

Article 6

Each Contracting Party shall take appropriate and necessary legislative and administrative measures to ensure the special protection of the wild fauna species specified in Appendix II. The following will in particular be prohibited for these species:

    (a) all forms of deliberate capture and keeping and deliberate killing;
    (b) the deliberate damage to or destruction of breeding or resting sites;
    (c) the deliberate disturbance of wild fauna, particularly during the period of breeding, rearing and hibernation, insofar as disturbance would be significant in relation to the objectives of this Convention;
    (d) the deliberate destruction or taking of eggs from the wild or keeping these eggs even if empty;
    (e) the possession of and internal trade in these animals, alive or dead, including stuffed animals and any readily recognizable part or derivative thereof, where this would contribute to the effectiveness of the provisions of this Article.

Article 7

1. Each Contracting Party shall take appropriate and necessary legislative and administrative measures to ensure the protection of the wild fauna species specified in Appendix III.

2. Any exploitation of wild fauna specified in Appendix III shall be regulated in order to keep the populations out of danger, taking into account the requirements of Article 2.

3. Measures to be taken shall include:

    (a) closed seasons and/or other procedures regulating the exploitation;
    (b) the temporary or local prohibition of exploitation, as appropriate, in order to restore satisfactory population levels;

(c) the regulation as appropriate of sale, keeping for sale, transport for sale or offering for sale of live and dead wild animals.

Article 8

In respect of the capture or killing of wild fauna species specified in Appendix III and in cases where, in accordance with Article 9, exceptions are applied to species specified in Appendix II, Contracting Parties shall prohibit the use of all indiscriminate means of capture and killing and the use of all means capable of causing local disappearance of, or serious disturbance to, populations of a species, and in particular, the means specified in Appendix IV.

Article 9

1. Each Contracting Party may make exceptions from the provisions of Articles 4, 5, 6, 7 and from the prohibition of the use of the means mentioned in Article 8 provided that there is no other satisfactory solution and that the exception will not be detrimental to the survival of the population concerned:

— for the protection of flora and fauna;
— to prevent serious damage to crops, livestock, forests, fisheries, water and other forms of property;
— in the interests of public health and safety, air safety or other overriding public interests;
— for the purposes of research and education, of repopulation, of reintroduction and for the necessary breeding;
— to permit, under strictly supervised conditions, on a selective basis and to a limited extent, the taking, keeping or other judicious exploitation of certain wild animals and plants in small numbers.

2. The Contracting Parties shall report every two years to the Standing Committee on the exceptions made under the preceding paragraph. These reports must specify:

— the populations which are or have been subject to the exceptions and, when practical, the number of specimens involved;
— the means authorised for the killing or capture;
— the conditions of risk and the circumstances of time and place under which such exceptions were granted;
— the authority empowered to declare that these conditions have been fulfilled, and to take decisions in respect of the means that may be used, their limits and the persons instructed to carry them out;
— the controls involved.

Chapter IV

Special Provisions for Migratory Species

Article 10

1. The Contracting Parties undertake, in addition to the measures specified in Articles 4, 6, 7 and 8, to co-ordinate their efforts for the protection of the migratory species specified in Appendices II and III whose range extends into their territories.

2. The Contracting Parties shall take measures to seek to ensure that the closed seasons and/or other procedures regulating the exploitation established under paragraph 3.*a* of Article 7 are adequate and approximately disposed to meet the requirements of the migratory species specified in Appendix III.

Chapter V

Supplementary Provisions

Article 11

1. In carrying out the provisions of the Convention, the Contracting Parties undertake:

    (a) to co-operate whenever appropriate and in particular where this would enhance the effectiveness of measures taken under other articles of this Convention;

    (b) to encourage and co-ordinate research related to the purposes of this Convention.

2. Each Contracting Party undertakes:

    (a) to encourage the reintroduction of native species of wild flora and fauna when this would contribute to the conservation of an endangered species, provided that a study is first made in the light of the experiences of other Contracting Parties to establish that such reintroduction would be effective and acceptable;

    (b) to strictly control the introduction of non-native species.

3. Each Contracting Party shall inform the Standing Committee of the species receiving complete protection on its territory and not included in Appendices I and II.

Article 12

The Contracting Parties may adopt stricter measures for the conservation of wild flora and fauna and their natural habitats than those provided under this Convention.

Chapter VI

Standing Committee

Article 13

1. For the purposes of this Convention, a Standing Committee shall be set up.

2. Any Contracting Party may be represented on the Standing Committee by one or more delegates. Each delegation shall have one vote. Within the areas of its competence, the European Economic Community shall exercise its right to vote with a number of votes equal to the number of its member States which are Contracting Parties to this Convention; the European Economic Community shall not exercise its right to vote in cases where the member States concerned exercise theirs, and conversely.

3. Any member State of the Council of Europe which is not a Contracting Party to the Convention may be represented on the Committee as an observer.

The Standing Committee may, by unanimous decision, invite any non-member State of the Council of Europe which is not a Contracting Party to the Convention to be represented by an observer at one of its meetings.

Any body or agency technically qualified in the protection, conservation or management of wild fauna and flora and their habitats, and belonging to one of the following categories:

(a) international agencies or bodies, either governmental or non-governmental, and national governmental agencies or bodies;

(b) national non-governmental agencies or bodies which have been approved for this purpose by the State in which they are located, may inform the Secretary-General of the Council of Europe, at least three months before the meeting of the Committee, of its wish to be represented at that meeting by observers. They shall be admitted unless, at least one month before the meeting, one-third of the Contracting Parties have informed the Secretary General of their objection.

4. The Standing Committee shall be convened by the Secretary General of the Council of Europe. Its first meeting shall be held within one year of the date of the entry into force of the Convention. It shall subsequently meet at least every two years and whenever a majority of the Contracting Parties so request.

5. A majority of the Contracting Parties shall constitute a quorum for holding a meeting of the Standing Committee.

6. Subject to the provisions of the Convention, the Standing Committee shall draw up its own Rules of Procedure.

Article 14

1. The Standing Committee shall be responsible for following the application of this Convention. It may in particular:

— keep under review the provisions of this Convention, including its Appendices, and examine any modifications necessary;
— make recommendations to the Contracting Parties concerning measures to be taken for the purposes of this Convention;
— recommend the appropriate measures to keep the public informed about the activities undertaken within the framework of this Convention;
— make recommendations to the Committee of Ministers concerning non-member States of the Council of Europe to be invited to accede to this Convention;
— make any proposal for improving the effectiveness of this Convention, including proposals for the conclusion, with the States which are not Contracting Parties to the Convention, of agreements that would enhance the effective conservation of species or groups of species.

2. In order to discharge its functions, the Standing Committee may, on its own initiative, arrange for meetings of groups of experts.

Article 15

After each meeting, the Standing Committee shall forward to the Committee of Ministers of the Council of Europe a report on its work and on the functioning of the Convention.

Chapter VII

Amendments

Article 16

1. Any amendment to the articles of this Convention proposed by a Contracting Party or the Committee of Ministers shall be communicated to the Secretary General of the Council of Europe and forwarded by him at least two months before the meeting of the Standing Committee to the member States of the Council of Europe, to any signatory, to any Contracting Party, to any State invited to sign this Convention in accordance with the provisions of Article 19 and to any State invited to accede to it in accordance with the provisions of Article 20.

2. Any amendment proposed in accordance with the provisions of the preceding paragraph shall be examined by the Standing Committee which:

(a) for amendments to Articles 1 to 12, shall submit the text adopted by a three-quarters majority of the votes cast of the Contracting Parties for acceptance;

(b) for amendments to Articles 13 to 24, shall submit the text adopted by a three-quarters majority of the votes cast to the Committee of Ministers for approval. After its approval, this text shall be forwarded to the Contracting Parties for acceptance.

3. Any amendment shall enter into force on the thirtieth day after all the Contracting Parties have informed the Secretary General that they have accepted it.

4. The provisions of paragraphs 1, 2.a and 3 of this Article shall apply to the adoption of new Appendices to this Convention.

Article 17

1. Any amendment to the Appendices of this Convention proposed by a Contracting Party or the Committee of Ministers shall be communicated to the Secretary General of the Council of Europe and forwarded by him at least two months before the meeting of the Standing Committee to the member States of the Council of Europe, to any signatory, to any Contracting Party, to any State invited to sign this Convention in accordance with the provisions of Article 19 and to any State invited to accede to it in accordance with the provisions of Article 20.

2. Any amendment proposed in accordance with the provisions of the preceding paragraph shall be examined by the Standing Committee, which may adopt it by a two-thirds majority of the Contracting Parties. The text adopted shall be forwarded to the Contracting Parties.

3. Three months after its adoption by the Standing Committee and unless one-third of the Contracting Parties have notified objections, any amendment shall enter into force for those Contracting Parties which have not notified objections.

Chapter VIII

Settlement of Disputes

Article 18

1. The Standing Committee shall use its best endeavours to facilitate a friendly settlement of any difficulty to which the execution of this Convention may give rise.

2. Any dispute between Contracting Parties concerning the interpretation

or application of this Convention which has not been settled on the basis of the provisions of the preceding paragraph or by negotiation between the parties concerned shall, unless the said parties agree otherwise, be submitted, at the request of one of them, to arbitration. Each party shall designate an arbitrator and the two arbitrators shall designate a third arbitrator. Subject to the provisions of paragraph 3 of this Article, if one of the parties has not designated its arbitrator within the three months following the request for arbitration, he shall be designated at the request of the other party by the President of the European Court of Human Rights within a further three months period. The same procedure shall be observed if the arbitrators cannot agree on the choice of the third arbitrator within the three months following the designation of the two first arbitrators.

3. In the event of a dispute between two Contracting Parties one of which is a member State of the European Economic Community, the latter itself being a Contracting Party, the other Contracting Party shall address the request for arbitration both to the member State and to the Community, which jointly, shall notify it, within two months of receipt of the request, whether the member State or the Community, or the member and the Community jointly, shall be party to the dispute. In the absence of such notification within the said time limit, the member State and the Community shall be considered as being one and the same party to the dispute for the purposes of the application of the provisions governing the constitution and procedure of the arbitration tribunal. The same shall apply when the member State and the Community jointly present themselves as party to the dispute.

4. The arbitration tribunal shall draw up its own Rules of Procedure. Its decisions shall be taken by majority vote. Its award shall be final and binding.

5. Each party to the dispute shall bear the expenses of the arbitrator designated by it and the parties shall share equally the expenses of the third arbitrator, as well as other costs entailed by the arbitration.

Chapter IX

Final Provisions

Article 19

1. This Convention shall be open for signature by the member States of the Council of Europe and non-member States which have participated in its elaboration and by the European Economic Community.

Up until the date when the Convention enters into force, it shall also be open for signature by any other State so invited by the Committee of Ministers.

The Convention is subject to ratification, acceptance or approval. Instruments of ratification, acceptance or approval shall be deposited with the Secretary General of the Council of Europe.

2. The Convention shall enter into force on the first day of the month following the expiry of a period of three months after the date on which five States, including at least four member States of the Council of Europe, have expressed their consent to be bound by the Convention in accordance with the provisions of the preceding paragraph.

3. In respect of any signatory State or the European Economic Community which subsequently express their consent to be bound by it, the Convention shall enter into force on the first day of the month following the expiry of a period of three months after the date of the deposit of the instrument of ratification, acceptance or approval.

Article 20

1. After the entry into force of this Convention, the Committee of Ministers of the Council of Europe, after consulting the Contracting Parties, may invite to accede to the Convention any non-member State of the Council which, invited to sign in accordance with the provisions of Article 19, has not yet done so, and any other non-member State.

2. In respect of any acceding State, the Convention shall enter into force on the first day of the month following the expiry of a period of three months after the date of the deposit of the instrument of accession with the Secretary General of the Council of Europe.

Article 21

1. Any State may, at the time of signature or when depositing its instrument of ratification, acceptance, approval or accession, specify the territory or territories to which this Convention shall apply.

2. Any Contracting Party may, when depositing its instrument of ratification, acceptance, approval or accession or at any later date, by declaration addressed to the Secretary General of the Council of Europe, extend the application of this Convention to any other territory specified in the declaration and for whose international relations it is responsible or on whose behalf it is authorized to give undertakings.

3. Any declaration made under the preceding paragraph may, in respect of any territory mentioned in such declaration, be withdrawn by notification addressed to the Secretary General. Such withdrawal shall become effective

on the first day of the month following the expiry of a period of six months after the date of receipt of the notification by the Secretary General.

Article 22

1. Any State may, at the time of signature or when depositing its instrument of ratification, acceptance, approval or accession, make one or more reservations regarding certain species specified in Appendices I to III and/or, for certain species mentioned in the reservation or reservations, regarding certain means or methods of killing, capture and other exploitation listed in Appendix IV. No reservations of a general nature may be made.

2. Any Contracting Party which extends the application of this Convention to a territory mentioned in the declaration referred to in paragraph 2 of Article 21 may, in respect of the territory concerned, make one or more reservations in accordance with the provisions of the preceding paragraph.

3. No other reservation may be made.

4. Any Contracting Party which has made a reservation under paragraph 1 and 2 of this Article may wholly or partly withdraw it by means of a notification addressed to the Secretary General of the Council of Europe. Such withdrawal shall take effect as from the date of receipt of the notification by the Secretary General.

Article 23

1. Any Contracting Party may, at any time, denounce this Convention by means of a notification addressed to the Secretary General of the Council of Europe.

2. Such denunciation shall become effective on the first day of the month following the expiry of a period of six months after the date of receipt of the notification by the Secretary General.

Article 24

The Secretary General of the Council of Europe shall notify the member States of the Council of Europe, any signatory State, the European Economic Community if a signatory of this Convention and any Contracting Party of:

  (a) any signature;
  (b) the deposit of any instrument of ratification, acceptance, approval or accession;
  (c) any date of entry into force of this Convention in accordance with Articles 19 and 20;
  (d) any information forwarded under the provisions of paragraph 3 of Article 13;
  (e) any report established in pursuance of the provisions of Article 15;

(f) any amendment or any new Appendix adopted in accordance with Articles 16 and 17 and the date on which the amendment or new Appendix comes into force;

(g) any declaration made under the provisions of paragraphs 2 and 3 of Article 21;

(h) any reservation made under the provisions of paragraphs 1 and 2 of Article 22;

(i) the withdrawal of any reservation carried out under the provisions of paragaph 4 of Article 22;

(j) any notification made under the provisions of Article 23 and the date on which the denunciation takes effect.

IN WITNESS WHEREOF the undersigned, being duly authorised thereto, have signed this Convention.

DONE at Bern, this 19th day of September 1979, in English and French, both texts being equally authentic, in a single copy which shall be deposited in the archives of the Council of Europe. The Secretary General of the Council of Europe shall transmit certified copies to each member State of the Council of Europe, to any signatory State, to the European Economic Community if a signatory and to any State invited to sign this Convention or to accede thereto.

Protocol to the Antarctic Treaty on Environmental Protection, Madrid, 4 October 1991

The Antarctic Treaty was concluded in Washington, D. C., December 1959; in force 23 June 1961; text in 402 *UNTS* 71; *UKTS* 97 (1961), Cmnd. 1535; 12 *UST* 794 *TIAS* 4780. It did not specifically provide for environmental protection as such, though some provisions do protect Antarctica from certain threats.

However, its Consultative Parties subsequently adopted various Recommendations directed to protection of specific areas, sources of environmental damage or potentially damaging activities. These included Agreed Measures for the Conservation of Antarctic Fauna and Flora (Rec. III/8, Third Consultative Meeting 1964); Recommendations on 'Sites of Special Scientific Interest' 1975 (Recs. VIII–3 and VIII–7, adopted at the Eighth Consultative Meeting 1975); Recommendations on tourism (from 1966 onwards) and a ban on nuclear waste disposal in 1975. During this period two conservatory treaties were also adopted. The Convention for Conservation of Antarctic Seals was concluded in London in 1973 and entered into force 11 March 1978 (1080 *UNTS* 175; *UKTS* 45 (1978), Cmnd. 7209; 29 *UST* 441 *TIAS* 8826; 11 *ILM* (1972) 251). The Convention on the Conservation of Antarctic Marine Living Resources (q.v.) was concluded in Canberra, 20 May 1980 (*UKTS* 48 (1982), Cmnd. 8714; *TIAS* 10240; 19 *ILM* (1980) 837; in force 7 April 1981). For discussion of these conventions see S. Lyster, *International Wildlife Law*, (Cambridge, 1985), 48–61 and 156–82 respectively. For an unofficial collection of Antarctic measures see *Handbook of the Antarctic Treaty System*, (6th edn., Cambridge, 1989).

A Convention on the Regulation of Antarctic Mineral Resource Activities (CRAMRA), was concluded at Wellington, 2 June 1988; *Misc.* (1989), Cmnd. 885; 27 *ILM* (1988) 368. CRAMRA provided a legal framework for such activities, though subject to stringent environmental conditions and procedures. (For details, see E. Sciso, 'Are Mineral Resource Activities Still Compatible with the Protection of the Antarctic Environment?' in F. Francioni (ed.) *International Environmental Law for Antarctica* (Milan, 1992), 259–82; J. Verhoeven, P. Sands and M. Bruce (eds.), *The Antarctic Environment and International Law* (London, 1992), 21–6. CRAMRA required ratification by all states claiming sovereignty in Antarctica for entry into force, but environmental pressure led two of these, France and Australia, to announce in 1989 that they were postponing signature. As a result it has not entered into force and is now unlikely to do so.

Following negotiation of more protective environmental measures during 1987–1991, including Rec. XIV–2 (1987) on environmental impact assessment and Rec. XV–1 (1989) on environmental monitoring, it was decided in response to growing environmental concern to adopt a comprehensive environmental Protocol to the 1959 Convention, rather than the other alternatives put forward, viz. adoption of further Recommendations or adoption of a separate convention (Rec. XVI–10, Final Report, Sixteenth Antarctic Treaty Consultative Meeting, Bonn, October 7–18, 1991, pp. 117ff). For details of the Madrid Protocol negotiation, principles and system, see F. Francioni, 'The Madrid Protocol on the Protection of the Antarctica Environment', in Francioni (ed.). op. cit. supra., 1–30, and other contributions therein; and Verhoeven, Sands, and Bruce, op. cit., *passim.*

The Protocol designates Antarctica as 'a natural reserve, devoted to peace and science' (Article 2) and goes beyond the scope of the 1959 Treaty and CRAMRA in requiring 'comprehensive protection of the Antarctic environment and dependent and associated ecosystems'. As a compromise between proposals for a permanent ban and those for a short term prohibition only, the Protocol bans mineral activities for fifty years, following which modification of the ban will require the support of a majority of the Parties, including three-quarters of the States which were Antarctic Treaty Consultative Parties (ATCPs) at the time of adoption of the Protocol. Entry into force of the Protocol also requires ratification by all states which were ATCPs at that date (Article 23). The Protocol is not yet in force; as at 31 January 1995 it had been ratified by fourteen States. It requires ratification by all of the twenty-six ATCPs for entry into force.

TEXT

Preamble

The States Parties to this Protocol to the Antarctic Treaty, hereinafter referred to as the Parties,

Convinced of the need to enhance the protection of the Antarctic environment and dependent and associated ecosystems;

Convinced of the need to strengthen the Antarctic Treaty system so as to ensure that Antarctica shall continue forever to be used exclusively for peaceful purposes and shall not become the scene or object of international discord;

Bearing in mind the special legal and political status of Antarctica and the special responsibility of the Antarctic Treaty Consultative Parties to ensure that all activities in Antarctica are consistent with the purposes and principles of the Antarctic Treaty;

Recalling the designation of Antarctica as a Special Conservation Area and other measures adopted under the Antarctic Treaty system to protect the Antarctic environment and dependent and associated ecosystems;

Acknowledging further the unique opportunities Antarctica offers for scientific monitoring of and research on processes of global as well as regional importance;

Reaffirming the conservation principles of the Convention on the Conservation of Antarctic Marine Living Resources;

Convinced that the development of a comprehensive regime for the protection of the Antarctic environment and dependent and associated ecosystems is in the interest of mankind as a whole;

Desiring to supplement the Antarctic Treaty to this end;

Have agreed as follows:

Article 1
Definitions

For the purposes of this Protocol:

(a) 'The Antarctic Treaty' means the Antarctic Treaty done at Washington on 1 December 1959;

(b) 'Antarctic Treaty area' means the area to which the provisions of the Antarctic Treaty apply in accordance with Article VI of that Treaty;

(c) 'Antarctic Treaty Consultative Meetings' means the meetings referred to in Article IX of the Antarctic Treaty;

(d) 'Antarctic Treaty Consultative Parties' means the Contracting Parties to the Antarctic Treaty entitled to appoint representatives to participate in the meetings referred to in Article IX of that Treaty;

(e) 'Antarctic Treaty system' means the Antarctic Treaty, the measures in effect under that Treaty, its associated separate international instruments in force and the measures in effect under those instruments;

(f) 'Arbitral Tribunal' means the Arbitral Tribunal established in accordance with the Schedule to this Protocol, which forms an integral part thereof;

(g) 'Committee' means the Committee for Environmental Protection established in accordance with Article 11.

Article 2
Objective and Designation

The Parties commit themselves to the comprehensive protection of the Antarctic environment and dependent and associated ecosystems and hereby designate Antarctica as a natural reserve, devoted to peace and science.

Article 3
Environmental Principles

1. The protection of the Antarctic environment and dependent and associated ecosystems and the intrinsic value of Antarctica, including its wilderness and aesthetic values and its value as an area for the conduct of scientific research, in particular research essential to understanding the global environment, shall be fundamental considerations in the planning and conduct of all activities in this Antarctic Treaty area.

2. To this end:

(a) activities in the Antarctic Treaty area shall be planned and conducted so as to limit adverse impacts on the Antarctic environment and dependent and associated ecosystems;

(b) activities in the Antarctic Treaty area shall be planned and conducted so as to avoid:
   (i) adverse effects on climate or weather patterns;
   (ii) significant adverse effects on air or water quality;
   (iii) significant changes in the atmospheric, terrestrial (including aquatic), glacial or marine environments;
   (iv) detrimental changes in the distribution, abundance or productivity of species or populations of species of fauna and flora;

(v) further jeopardy to endangered or threatened species or populations of such species; or

(vi) degradation of, or substantial risk to, areas of biological, scientific, historic, aesthetic or wilderness significance;

(c) activities in the Antarctic Treaty area shall be planned and conducted on the basis of information sufficient to allow prior assessments of, and informed judgments about, their possible impacts on the Antarctic environment and dependent and associated ecosystems and on the value of Antarctica for the conduct of scientific research; such judgments shall take full account of:

(i) the scope of the activity, including its area, duration and intensity;

(ii) the cumulative impacts of the activity, both by itself and in combination with other activities in the Antarctic Treaty area;

(iii) whether the activity will detrimentally affect any other activity in the Antarctic Treaty area;

(iv) whether technology and procedures are available to provide for environmentally safe operations;

(v) whether there exists the capacity to monitor key environmental parameters and ecosystem components so as to identify and provide early warning of any adverse effects of the activity and to provide for such modification of operating procedures as may be necessary in the light of the results of monitoring or increased knowledge of the Antarctic environment and dependent and associated ecosystems; and

(vi) whether there exists the capacity to respond promptly and effectively to accidents, particularly those with potential environmental effects;

(d) regular and effective monitoring shall take place to allow assessment of the impacts of ongoing activities, including the verification of predicted impacts;

(e) regular and effective monitoring shall take place to facilitate early detection of the possible unforeseen effects of activities carried on both within and outside the Antarctic Treaty area on the Antarctic environment and dependent and associated ecosystems.

3. Activities shall be planned and conducted in the Antarctic Treaty area so as to accord priority to scientific research and to preserve the value of Antarctica as an area for the conduct of such research, including research essential to understanding the global environment.

4. Activities undertaken in the Antarctic Treaty area pursuant to scientific research programmes, tourism and all other governmental and non-governmental activities in the Antarctic Treaty area for which advance notice is required in accordance with Article VII (5)

of the Antarctic Treaty, including associated logistic support activities, shall:

(a) take place in a manner consistent with the principles in this Article; and

(b) be modified, suspended or cancelled if they result in or threaten to result in impacts upon the Antarctic environment or dependent or associated ecosystems inconsistent with those principles.

Article 4
Relationship with the Other Components of the Antarctic Treaty System

1. This Protocol shall supplement the Antarctic Treaty and shall neither modify nor amend that Treaty.

2. Nothing in this Protocol shall derogate from the rights and obligations of the Parties to this Protocol under the other international instruments in force within the Antarctic Treaty system.

Article 5
Consistency with the Other Components of the Antarctic Treaty System

The Parties shall consult and co-operate with the Contracting Parties to the other international instruments in force within the Antarctic Treaty system and their respective institutions with a view to ensuring the achievement of the objectives and principles of this Protocol and avoiding any interference with the achievement of the objectives and principles of those instruments or any inconsistency between the implementation of those instruments and of this Protocol.

Article 6
Co-operation

1. The Parties shall co-operate in the planning and conduct of activities in the Antarctic Treaty area. To this end, each Party shall endeavour to:

(a) promote co-operative programmes of scientific, technical and educational value, concerning the protection of the Antarctic environment and dependent and associated ecosystems;

(b) provide appropriate assistance to other Parties in the preparation of environmental impact assessments;

(c) provide to other Parties upon request information relevant to any potential environmental risk and assistance to minimize the effects of accidents which may damage the Antarctic environment or dependent and associated ecosystems;

(d) consult with other Parties with regard to the choice of sites for prospective stations and other facilities so as to avoid the cumulative impacts caused by their excessive concentration in any location;

(e) where appropriate, undertake joint expeditions and share the use of stations and other facilities; and

(f) carry out such steps as may be agreed upon at Antarctic Treaty Consultative Meetings.

2. Each Party undertakes, to the extent possible, to share information that may be helpful to other Parties in planning and conducting their activities in the Antarctic Treaty area, with a view to the protection of the Antarctic environment and dependent and associated ecosystems.

3. The Parties shall co-operate with those Parties which may exercise jurisdiction in areas adjacent to the Antarctic Treaty area with a view to ensuring that activities in the Antarctic Treaty area do not have adverse environmental impacts on those areas.

Article 7
Prohibition of Mineral Resource Activities

Any activity relating to mineral resources, other than scientific research, shall be prohibited.

Article 8
Environmental Impact Assessment

1. Proposed activities referred to in paragraph 2 below shall be subject to the procedures set out in Annex I for prior assessment of the impacts of those activities on the Antarctic environment or on dependent or associated ecosystems according to whether those activities are identified as having:

(a) less than a minor or transitory impact;

(b) a minor or transitory impact; or

(c) more than a minor or transitory impact.

2. Each Party shall ensure that the assessment procedures set out in Annex I are applied in the planning processes leading to decisions about any activities undertaken in the Antarctic Treaty area pursuant to scientific research programmes, tourism and all other governmental and non-governmental activities in the Antarctic Treaty area for which advance notice is required under Article VII(5) of the Antarctic Treaty, including associated logistic support activities.

3. The assessment procedures set out in Annex I shall apply to any change in an activity whether the change arises from an increase or decrease in the intensity of an existing activity, from the addition of an activity, the decommissioning of a facility, or otherwise.

4. Where activities are planned jointly by more than one Party, the Parties involved shall nominate one of their number to coordinate the implementation of the environmental impact assessment procedures set out in Annex I.

Article 9
Annexes

1. The Annexes to this Protocol shall form an integral part thereof.

2. Annexes, additional to Annexes I–IV, may be adopted and become effective in accordance with Article IX of the Antarctic Treaty.

3. Amendments and modifications to Annexes may be adopted and become effective in accordance with Article IX of the Antarctic Treaty, provided that any Annex may itself make provision for amendments and modifications to become effective on an accelerated basis.

4. Annexes and any amendments and modifications thereto which have become effective in accordance with paragraphs 2 and 3 above shall, unless an Annex itself provides otherwise in respect of the entry into effect of any amendment or modification thereto, become effective for a Contracting Party to the Antarctic Treaty which is not an Antarctic Treaty Consultative Party, or which was not an Antarctic Treaty Consultative Party at the time of the adoption, when notice of approval of that Contracting Party has been received by the Depositary.

5. Annexes shall, except to the extent that an Annex provides otherwise, be subject to the procedures for dispute settlement set out in Articles 18 to 20.

Article 10
Antarctic Treaty Consultative Meetings

1. Antarctic Treaty Consultative Meetings shall, drawing upon the best scientific and technical advice available:

 (a) define, in accordance with the provisions of this Protocol, the general policy for the comprehensive protection of the Antarctic environment and dependent and associated ecosystems; and
 (b) adopt measures under Article IX of the Antarctic Treaty for the implementation of this Protocol.

2. Antarctic Treaty Consultative Meetings shall review the work of the Committee and shall draw fully upon its advice and recommendations in carrying out the tasks referred to in paragraph 1 above, as well as upon the advice of the Scientific Committee on Antarctic Research.

Article 11
Committee for Environmental Protection

1. There is hereby established the Committee for Environmental Protection.

2. Each Party shall be entitled to be a member of the Committee and to appoint a representative who may be accompanied by experts and advisers.

3. Observer status in the Committee shall be open to any Contracting Party to the Antarctic Treaty which is not a Party to this Protocol.

4. The Committee shall invite the President of the Scientific Committee on Antarctic Research and the Chairman of the Scientific Committee for the Conservation of Antarctic Marine Living Resources to participate as observers at its sessions. The Committee may also, with the approval of the Antarctic Treaty Consultative Meeting, invite such other relevant scientific, environmental and technical organisations which can contribute to its work to participate as observers at its sessions.

5. The Committee shall present a report on each of its sessions to the Antarctic Treaty Consultative Meeting. The report shall cover all matters considered at the session and shall reflect the views expressed. The report shall be circulated to the Parties and to observers attending the session, and shall thereupon be made publicly available.

6. The Committee shall adopt its rules of procedure which shall be subject to approval by the Antarctic Treaty Consultative Meeting.

Article 12
Functions of the Committee

1. The functions of the Committee shall be to provide advice and formulate recommendations to the Parties in connection with the implementation of this Protocol including the operation of its Annexes, for consideration at Antarctic Treaty Consultative Meetings, and to perform such other functions as may be referred to it by the Antarctic Treaty Consultative Meetings. In particular, it shall provide advice on:

    (a) the effectiveness of measures taken pursuant to this Protocol;

    (b) the need to update, strengthen or otherwise improve such measures;

    (c) the need for additional measures, including the need for additional Annexes, where appropriate;

    (d) the application and implementation of the environmental impact assessment procedures set out in Article 8 and Annex I;

    (e) means of minimising or mitigating environmental impacts of activities in the Antarctic Treaty area;

    (f) procedures for situations requiring urgent action, including response action in environmental emergencies;

    (g) the operation and further elaboration of the Antarctic Protected Area system;

    (h) inspection procedures, including formats for inspection reports and checklists for the conduct of inspections;

    (i) the collection, archiving, exchange and evaluation of information related to environmental protection;

    (j) the state of the Antarctic environment; and

(k) the need for scientific research, including environmental monitoring, related to the implementation of this Protocol.

2. In carrying out its functions, the Committee shall, as appropriate, consult with the Scientific Committee on Antarctic Research, the Scientific Committee for the Conservation of Antarctic Marine Living Resources and other relevant scientific, environmental and technical organizations.

Article 13
Compliance with this Protocol

1. Each Party shall take appropriate measures within its competence, including the adoption of laws and regulations, administrative actions and enforcement measures, to ensure compliance with this Protocol.

2. Each Party shall exert appropriate efforts, consistent with the Charter of the United Nations, to the end that no one engages in any activity contrary to this Protocol.

3. Each Party shall notify all other Parties of the measures it takes pursuant to paragraphs 1 and 2 above.

4. Each Party shall draw the attention of all other Parties to any activity which in its opinion affects the implementation of the objectives and principles of this Protocol.

5. The Antarctic Treaty Consultative Meetings shall draw the attention of any State which is not a Party to this Protocol to any activity undertaken by that State, its agencies, instrumentalities, natural or juridical persons, ships, aircraft or other means of transport which affects the implementation of the objectives and principles of this Protocol.

Article 14
Inspection

1. In order to promote the protection of the Antarctic environment and dependent and associated ecosystems, and to ensure compliance with this Protocol, the Antarctic Treaty Consultative Parties shall arrange, individually or collectively, for inspections by observers to be made in accordance with Article VII of the Antarctic Treaty.

2. Observers are:

(a) observers designated by any Antarctic Treaty Consultative Party who shall be nationals of that Party; and
(b) any observers designated at Antarctic Treaty Consultative Meetings to carry out inspections under procedures to be established by an Antarctic Treaty Consultative Meeting.

3. Parties shall co-operate fully with observers undertaking inspections, and shall ensure that during inspections, observers are given access to all

parts of stations, installations, equipment, ships and aircraft open to inspection under Article VII(3) of the Antarctic Treay, as well as to all records maintained thereon which are called for pursuant to this Protocol.

4. Reports of inspections shall be sent to the Parties whose stations, installations, equipment, ships or aircraft are covered by the reports. After those Parties have been given the opportunity to comment, the reports and any comments thereon shall be circulated to all the Parties and to the Committee, considered at the next Antarctic Treaty Consultative Meeting, and thereafter made publicly available.

Article 15
Emergency Response Action

1. In order to respond to environmental emergencies in the Antarctic Treaty area, each Party agrees to:

(a) provide for prompt and effective response action to such emergencies which might arise in the performance of scientific research programmes, tourism and all other governmental and non-governmental activities in the Antarctic Treaty area for which advance notice is required under Article VII(5) of the Antarctic Treaty, including associated logistic support activities; and

(b) establish contingency plans for response to incidents with potential adverse effects on the Antarctic environment or dependent and associated ecosystems.

2. To this end, the Parties shall:

(a) co-operate in the formulation and implementation of such contingency plans; and

(b) establish procedures for immediate notification of, and co-operative response to, environmental emergencies.

3. In the implementation of this Article, the Parties shall draw upon the advice of the appropriate international organisations.

Article 16
Liability

Consistent with the objectives of this Protocol for the comprehensive protection of the Antarctic environment and dependent and associated ecosystems, the Parties undertake to elaborate rules and procedures relating to liability for damage arising from activities taking place in the Antarctic Treaty area and covered by this Protocol. Those rules and procedures shall be included in one or more Annexes to be adopted in accordance with Article 9(2).

Article 17
Annual Report by Parties

1. Each Party shall report annually on the steps taken to implement this Protocol. Such reports shall include notifications made in accordance with Article 13(3), contingency plans established in accordance with Article 15 and any other notifications and information called for pursuant to this Protocol for which there is no other provision concerning the circulation and exchange of information.

2. Reports made in accordance with paragraph 1 above shall be circulated to all Parties and to the Committee, considered at the next Antarctic Treaty Consultative Meeting, and made publicly available.

Article 18
Dispute Settlement

If a dispute arises concerning the interpretation or application of this Protocol, the parties to the dispute shall, at the request of any one of them, consult among themselves as soon as possible with a view to having the dispute resolved by negotiation, inquiry, mediation, conciliation, arbitration, judicial settlement or other peaceful means to which the parties to the dispute agree.

Article 19
Choice of Dispute Settlement Procedure

1. Each Party, when signing, ratifying, accepting, approving or acceding to this Protocol, or at any time thereafter, may choose, by written declaration, one or both of the following means for the settlement of disputes concerning the interpretation or application of Articles 7, 8 and 15 and, except to the extent that an Annex provides otherwise, the provisions of any Annex and, insofar as it relates to these Articles and provisions, Article 13:

   (a) the International Court of Justice;
   (b) the Arbitral Tribunal.

2. A declaration made under paragraph 1 above shall not affect the operation of Article 18 and Article 20(2).

3. A Party which has not made a declaration under paragraph 1 above or in respect of which a declaration is no longer in force shall be deemed to have accepted the competence of the Arbitral Tribunal.

4. If the parties to a dispute have accepted the same means for the settlement of a dispute, the dispute may be submitted only to that procedure, unless the parties otherwise agree.

5. If the parties to a dispute have not accepted the same means for the settlement of a dispute, or if they have both accepted both means, the dispute may be submitted only to the Arbitral Tribunal, unless the parties otherwise agree.

6. A declaration made under paragraph 1 above shall remain in force until it expires in accordance with its terms or until three months after written notice of revocation has been deposited with the Depositary.

7. A new declaration, a notice of revocation or the expiry of a declaration shall not in any way affect proceedings pending before the International Court of Justice or the Arbitral Tribunal, unless the parties to the dispute otherwise agree.

8. Declarations and notices referred to in this article shall be deposited with the Depositary who shall transmit copies thereof to all Parties.

Article 20
Dispute Settlement Procedure

1. If the parties to a dispute concerning the interpretation or application of Articles 7, 8 or 15, or except to the extent that an Annex provides otherwise, the provisions of any Annex or, insofar as it relates to these Articles and provisions, Article 13, have not agreed on a means for resolving it within 12 months of the request for consultation pursuant to Article 18, the dispute shall be referred, at the request of any party to the dispute, for settlement in accordance with the procedure determined by Article 19(4) and (5).

2. The Arbitral Tribunal shall not be competent to decide or rule upon any matter within the scope of Article IV of the Antarctic Treaty. In addition, nothing in this Protocol shall be interpreted as conferring competence or jurisdiction on the International Court of Justice or any other tribunal established for the purpose of settling disputes between Parties to decide or otherwise rule upon any matters within the scope of Article IV of the Antarctic Treaty.

Article 21
Signature

This Protocol shall be open for signature at Madrid on the 4th October 1991 and thereafter at Washington until the 3rd of October 1992 by any State which is a Contracting Party to the Antarctic Treaty.

Article 22
Ratification, Acceptance, Approval or Accession

1. This Protocol is subject to ratification, acceptance or approval by signatory States.

2. After the 3rd of October 1992 this Protocol shall be open for accession by any State which is a Contracting Party to the Antarctic Treaty.

3. Instruments of ratification, acceptance, approval or accession shall be deposited with the Government of the United States of America, hereby designated as the Depositary.

4. After the date on which this Protocol has entered into force, the Antarctic Treaty Consultative Parties shall not act upon a notification re-

garding the entitlement of a Contracting Party to the Antarctic Treaty to appoint representatives to participate in Antarctic Treaty Consultative Meetings in accordance with Article IX(2) of the Antarctic Treaty unless that Contracting Party has first ratified, accepted, approved or acceded to this Protocol.

Article 23
Entry into Force

1. This Protocol shall enter into force on the thirtieth day following the date of deposit of instruments of ratification, acceptance, approval or accession by all States which are Antarctic Treaty Consultative Parties at the date on which this Protocol is adopted.

2. For each Contracting Party to the Antarctic Treaty which, subsequent to the data of entry into force of this Protocol, deposits an instrument of ratification, acceptance, approval or accession, this Protocol shall enter into force on the thirtieth day following such deposit.

Article 24
Reservations

Reservations to this Protocol shall not be permitted.

Article 25
Modification or Amendment

1. Without prejudice to the provisions of Article 9, this Protocol may be modified or amended at any time in accordance with the procedures set forth in Article XII(1)(a) and (b) of the Antarctic Treaty.

2. If, after expiration of 50 years from the date of entry into force of this Protocol, any of the Antarctic Treaty Consultative Parties so requests by a communication addressed to the Depositary, a conference shall be held as soon as practicable to review the operation of this Protocol.

3. A modification or amendment proposed at any Review Conference called pursuant to paragraph 2 above shall be adopted by a majority of the Parties, including three-fourths of the States which are Antarctic Treaty Consultative Parties at the time of adoption of this Protocol.

4. A modification or amendment adopted pursuant to paragraph 3 above shall enter into force upon ratification, acceptance, approval or accession by three-fourths of the Antarctic Treaty Consultative Parties, including ratification, acceptance, approval or accession by all States which are Antarctic Treaty Consultative Parties at the time of adoption of this Protocol.

5. (a) With respect to Article 7, the prohibition on Antarctic mineral resource activities contained therein shall continue unless there is in force a binding legal regime on Antarctic mineral resource activities that includes an agreed means for determining whether, and, if so,

under which conditions, any such activities would be acceptable. This regime shall fully safeguard the interests of all States referred to in Article IV of the Antarctic Treaty and apply the principles thereof. Therefore, if a modification or amendment to Article 7 is proposed at a Review Conference referred to in paragraph 2 above, it shall include such a binding legal regime.

(b) If any such modification or amendment has not entered into force within 3 years of the date of its adoption, any Party may at any time thereafter notify to the Depositary of its withdrawal from this Protocol, and such withdrawal shall take effect 2 years after receipt of the notification by the Depositary.

Article 26
Notifications by the Depositary

The Depositary shall notify all Contracting Parties to the Antarctic Treaty of the following:

(a) signatures of this Protocol and the deposit of instruments of ratification, acceptance, approval or accession;

(b) the date of entry into force of this Protocol and any additional Annex thereto;

(c) the date of entry into force of any amendment or modification to this Protocol;

(d) the deposit of declarations and notices pursuant to Article 19; and

(e) any notification received pursuant to Article 25(5)(b).

Article 27
Authentic Texts and Registration with the United Nations

1. This Protocol, done in the English, French, Russian and Spanish languages, each version being equally authentic, shall be deposited in the archives of the Government of the United States of America, which shall transmit duly certified copies thereof to all Contracting Parties to the Antarctic Treaty.

2. This Protocol shall be registered by the Depositary pursuant to Article 102 of the Charter of the United Nations.

DONE at Madrid on 4 October 1991.

Schedule to the Protocol
Arbitration

Article 1

1. The Arbitral Tribunal shall be constituted and shall function in accordance with the Protocol, including this Schedule.

2. The Secretary referred to in this Schedule is the Secretary General of the Permanent Court of Arbitration.

Article 2

1. Each Party shall be entitled to designate up to three Arbitrators, at least one of whom shall be designated within three months of the entry into force of the Protocol for that Party. Each Arbitrator shall be experienced in Antarctic affairs, have thorough knowledge of international law and enjoy the highest reputation for fairness, competence and integrity. The names of the persons so designated shall constitute the list of Arbitrators. Each Party shall at all times maintain the name of at least one Arbitrator on the list.

2. Subject to paragraph 3 below, an Arbitrator designated by a Party shall remain on the list for a period of five years and shall be eligible for redesignation by that Party for additional five year periods.

3. A Party which designated an Arbitrator may withdraw the name of that Arbitrator from the list. If an Arbitrator dies or if a Party for any reason withdraws from the list the name of an Arbitrator designated by it, the Party which designated the Arbitrator in question shall notify the Secretary promptly. An Arbitrator whose name is withdrawn from the list shall continue to serve on any Arbitral Tribunal to which that Arbitrator has been appointed until the completion of proceedings before the Arbitral Tribunal.

4. The Secretary shall ensure that an up-to-date list is maintained of the Arbitrators designated pursuant to this Article.

Article 3

1. The Arbitral Tribunal shall be composed of three Arbitrators who shall be appointed as follows:

    (a) The party to the dispute commencing the proceedings shall appoint one Arbitrator, who may be its national, from the list referred to in Article 2. This appointment shall be included in the notification referred to in Article 4.

    (b) Within 40 days of the receipt of that notification, the other party to the dispute shall appoint the second Arbitrator, who may be its national, from the list referred to in Article 2.

    (c) Within 60 days of the appointment of the second Arbitrator, the parties to the dispute shall appoint by agreement the third Arbitrator from the list referred to in Article 2. The third Arbitrator shall not be either a national of a party to the dispute, or a person designated for the list referred to in Article 2 by a party to the dispute, or of the same nationality as either of the first two Arbitrators. The third Arbitrator shall be the Chairperson of the Arbitral Tribunal.

(d) If the second Arbitrator has not been appoined within the pre-scribed period, or if the parties to the dispute have not reached agreement within the prescribed period on the appointment of the third Arbitrator, the Arbitrator or Arbitrators shall be appointed, at the request of any party to the dispute and within 30 days of the receipt of such request, by the President of the International Court of Justice from the list referred to in Article 2 and subject to the conditions prescribed in subparagraphs (b) and (c) above. In per-forming the functions accorded him or her in this subparagraph, the President of the Court shall consult the parties to the dispute.

(e) If the President of the International Court of Justice is unable to perform the functions accorded him or her in subparagraph (d) above or is a national of a party to the dispute, the functions shall be performed by the Vice-President of the Court, except that if the Vice-President is unable to perform the functions or is a national of a party to the dispute the functions shall be performed by the next most senior member of the Court who is available and is not a national of a party to the dispute.

2. Any vacancy shall be filled in the manner prescribed for the initial appointment.

3. In any dispute involving more than two Parties, those Parties having the same interest shall appoint one Arbitrator by agreement within the period specified in paragraph 1(b) above.

Article 4

The party to the dispute commencing proceedings shall so notify the other party or parties to the dispute and the Secretary in writing. Such notification shall include a statement of the claim and the grounds on which it is based. The notification shall be transmitted by the Secretary to all Parties.

Article 5

1. Unless the parties to the dispute agree otherwise, arbitration shall take place at The Hague, where the records of the Arbitral Tribunal shall be kept. The Arbitral Tribunal shall adopt its own rules of procedure. Such rules shall ensure that each party to the dispute has a full opportunity to be heard and to present its case and shall also ensure that the proceedings are conducted expeditiously.

2. The Arbitral Tribunal may hear and decide counterclaims arising out of the dispute.

Article 6

1. The Arbitral Tribunal, where it considers that *prima facie* it has jurisdiction under the Protocol, may:

    (a) at the request of any party to a dispute, indicate such provisional measures as it considers necessary to preserve the respective rights of the parties to the dispute;

    (b) prescribe any provisional measures which it considers appropriate under the circumstances to prevent serious harm to the Antarctic environment or dependent or associated ecosystems.

2. The parties to the dispute shall comply promptly with any provisional measures prescribed under paragraph 1(b) above pending an award under Article 10.

3. Notwithstanding the time period in Article 20 of the Protocol, a party to a dispute may at any time, by notification to the other party or parties to the dispute and to the Secretary in accordance with Article 4, request that the Arbitral Tribunal be constituted as a matter of exceptional urgency to indicate or prescribe emergency provisional measures in accordance with this Article. In such case, the Arbitral Tribunal shall be constituted as soon as possible in accordance with Article 3, except that the time periods in Article 3(1)(b), (c) and (d) shall be reduced to 14 days in each case. The Arbitral Tribunal shall decide upon the request for emergency provisional measures within two months of the appointment of its Chairperson.

4. Following a decision by the Arbitral Tribunal upon a request for emergency provisional measures in accordance with paragraph 3 above, settlement of the dispute shall proceed in accordance with Articles 12, 19 and 20 of the Protocol.

Article 7

Any Party which believes it has a legal interest, whether general or individual, which may be substantially affected by the award of an Arbitral Tribunal, may, unless the Arbitral Tribunal decides otherwise, intervene in the proceedings.

Article 8

The parties to the dispute shall facilitate the work of the Arbitral Tribunal and, in particular, in accordance with their law and using all means at their disposal, shall provide it with all relevant documents and information, and enable it, when necessary, to call witnesses or experts and receive their evidence.

Article 9

If one of the parties to the dispute does not appear before the Arbitral Tribunal or fails to defend its case, any other party to the dispute may request the Arbitral Tribunal to continue the proceedings and make its award.

Article 10

1. The Arbitral Tribunal shall, on the basis of the provisions of the Protocol and other applicable rules and principles of international law that are not incompatible with such provisions, decide such disputes as are submitted to it.

2. The Arbitral Tribunal may decide, *ex aequo et bono*, a dispute submitted to it, if the parties to the dispute so agree.

Article 11

1. Before making its award, the Arbitral Tribunal shall satisfy itself that it has competence in respect of the dispute and that the claim or counter-claim is well founded in fact and law.

2. The award shall be accompanied by a statement of reasons for the decision and shall be communicated to the Secretary who shall transmit it to all Parties.

3. The award shall be final and binding on the parties to the dispute and on any Party which intervened in the proceedings and shall be complied with without delay. The Arbitral Tribunal shall interpret the award at the request of a party to the dispute or of any intervening Party.

4. The award shall have no binding force except in respect of that particular case.

5. Unless the Arbitral Tribunal decides otherwise, the expenses of the Arbitral Tribunal, including the remuneration of the Arbitrators, shall be borne by the parties to the dispute in equal shares.

Article 12

All decisions of the Arbitral Tribunal, including those referred to in Articles 5, 6 and 11, shall be made by a majority of the Arbitrators who may not abstain from voting.

Article 13

This Schedule may be amended or modified by a measure adopted in accordance with Article IX(1) of the Antarctic Treaty. Unless the measure specifies otherwise, the amendment or modification shall be deemed to have been approved. and shall become effective, one year after the close of the Antarctic Treaty Consultative Meeting at which it was adopted, unless one or more of the Antarctic Treaty Consultative Parties notifies the Depositary, within that time period, that it wishes an extension of that period or that it is unable to approve the measure.

2. Any amendment or modification of this Schedule which becomes effective in accordance with paragraph 1 above shall thereafter become effective

as to any other Party when notice of approval by it has been received by the Depositary.

Annex I

Environmental Impact Assessment

Article 1
Preliminary Stage

1. The environmental impacts of proposed activities referred to in Article 8 of the Protocol shall, before their commencement, be considered in accordance with appropriate national procedures.
2. If an activity is determined as having less than a minor or transitory impact, the activity may proceed forthwith.

Article 2
Initial Environmental Evaluation

1. Unless it has been determined that an activity will have less than a minor or transitory impact, or unless a Comprehensive Environmental Evaluation is being prepared in accordance with Article 3, an Initial Environmental Evaluation shall be prepared. It shall contain sufficient detail to assess whether a proposed activity may have more than a minor or transitory impact and shall include:

    (a) a description of the proposed activity, including its purpose, location, duration, and intensity; and

    (b) consideration of alternatives to the proposed activity and any impacts that the activity may have, including consideration of cumulative impacts in the light of existing and known planned activities.

2. If an Initial Environmental Evaluation indicates that a proposed activity is likely to have no more than a minor or transitory impact, the activity may proceed, provided that appropriate procedures, which may include monitoring, are put in place to assess and verify the impact of the activity.

Article 3
Comprehensive Environmental Evaluation

1. If an Initial Environmental Evaluation indicates or if it is otherwise determined that a proposed activity is likely to have more than a minor or transitory impact, a Comprehensive Environmental Evaluation shall be prepared.
2. A Comprehensive Environmenal Evaluation shall include:

(a) a description of the proposed activity including its purpose, location, duration and intensity, and possible alternatives to the activity, including the alternative of not proceeding, and the consequences of those alternatives;

(b) a description of the initial environmental reference state with which predicted changes are to be compared and a prediction of the future environmental reference state in the absence of the proposed activity;

(c) a description of the methods and data used to forecast the impacts of the proposed activity;

(d) estimation of the nature, extent, duration, and intensity of the likely direct impacts of the proposed activity;

(e) consideration of possible indirect or second order impacts of the proposed activity;

(f) consideration of cumulative impacts of the proposed activity in the light of existing activities and other known planned activities;

(g) identification of measures, including monitoring programmes, that could be taken to minimise or mitigate impacts of the proposed activity and to detect unforeseen impacts and that could provide early warning of any adverse effects of the activity as well as to deal promptly and effectively with accidents;

(h) identification of unavoidable impacts of the proposed activity;

(i) consideration of the effects of the proposed activity on the conduct of scientific research and on other existing uses and values;

(j) an identification of gaps in knowledge and uncertainties encountered in compiling the information required under this paragraph;

(k) a non-technical summary of the information provided under this paragraph; and

(l) the name and address of the person or organization which prepared the Comprehensive Environmental Evaluation and the address to which comments thereon should be directed.

3. The draft Comprehensive Enviromental Evaluation shall be made publicly available and shall be circulated to all Parties, which shall also make it publicly available, for comment. A period of 90 days shall be allowed for the receipt of comments.

4. The draft Comprehensive Environmental Evaluation shall be forwarded to the Committee at the same time as it is circulated to the Parties, and at least 120 days before the next Antarctic Treaty Consultative Meeting, for consideration as appropriate.

5. No final decision shall be taken to proceed with the proposed activity in the Antarctic Treaty area unless there has been an opportunity for consideration of the draft Comprehensive Environmental Evaluation by the Antarctic Treaty Consultative Meeting on the advice of the Committee,

provided that no decision to proceed with a proposed activity shall be delayed through the operation of this paragraph for longer than 15 months from the date of circulation of the draft Comprehensive Environmental Evaluation.

6. A final Comprehensive Environmental Evaluation shall address and shall include or summarise comments received on the draft Comprehensive Environmental Evaluation. The final Comprehensive Environmental Evaluation, notice of any decisions relating thereto, and any evaluation of the significance of the predicted impacts in relation to the advantages of the proposed activity, shall be circulated to all Parties, which shall also make them publicly available, at least 60 days before the commencement of the proposed activity in the Antarctic Treaty area.

Article 4
Decisions to be Based on Comprehensive Environmental Evaluations

Any decision on whether a proposed activity, to which Article 3 applies, should proceed, and, if so, whether in its original or in a modified form, shall be based on the Comprehensive Environmental Evaluation as well as other relevant considerations.

Article 5
Monitoring

1. Procedures shall be put in place, including appropriate monitoring of key environmental indicators, to assess and verify the impact of any activity that proceeds following the completion of a Comprehensive Environmental Evaluation.

2. The procedures referred to in paragraph 1 above and in Article 2(2) shall be designed to provide a regular and verifiable record of the impacts of the activity in order, *inter alia*, to:

(a) enable assessments to be made of the extent to which such impacts are consistent with the Protocol; and
(b) provide information useful for minimising or mitigating impacts, and, where appropriate, information on the need for suspension, cancellation or modification of the activity.

Article 6
Circulation of Information

1. The following information shall be circulated to the Parties, forwarded to the Committee and made publicly available:

(a) a description of the procedures referred to in Article 1;
(b) an annual list of any Initial Environmental Evaluations prepared in accordance with Article 2 and any decisions taken in consequence thereof;

(c) significant information obtained, and any action taken in consequence thereof, from procedures put in place in accordance with Articles 2(2) and 5; and

(d) information referred to in Article 3(6).

2. Any Initial Environmental Evaluation prepared in accordance with Article 2 shall be made available on request.

Article 7
Cases of Emergency

1. This Annex shall not apply in cases of emergency relating to the safety of human life or of ships, aircraft or equipment and facilities of high value, or the protection of the environment, which require an activity to be undertaken without completion of the procedures set out in this Annex.

2. Notice of activities undertaken in cases of emergency, which would otherwise have required preparation of a Comprehensive Environmental Evaluation, shall be circulated immediately to all Parties and to the Committee and a full explanation of the activities carried out shall be provided within 90 days of those activities.

Article 8
Amendment or Modification

1. This Annex may be amended or modified by a measure adopted in accordance with Article IX(1) of the Antarctic Treaty. Unless the measure specifics otherwise, the amendment or modification shall be deemed to have been approved, and shall become effective, one year after the close of the Antarctic Treaty Consultative Meeting at which it was adopted, unless one or more of the Antarctic Treaty Consultative Parties notifies the Depositary, within that period, that it wishes an extension of that period or that it is unable to approve the measure.

2. Any amendment or modification of this Annex which becomes effective in accordance with paragraph 1 above shall thereafter become effective as to any other Party when notice of approval by it has been received by the Depositary.

Annex II

Conservation of Antarctic Fauna and Flora

Article 1
Definitions

For the purposes of this Annex:

(a) 'native mammal' means any member of any species belonging to the Class Mammalia, indigenous to the Antarctic Treaty area or occurring there seasonally through natural migrations:

(b) 'native bird' means any member, at any stage of its life cycle (including eggs), of any species of the Class Aves indigenous to the Antarctic Treaty area or occurring there seasonally through natural migrations;

(c) 'native plant' means any terrestrial or freshwater vegetation, including bryophytes, lichens, fungi and algae, at any stage of its life cycle (including seeds, and other propagules), indigenous to the Antarctic Treaty area;

(d) 'native invertebrate' means any terrestrial or freshwater invertebrate, at any stage of its life cycle, indigenous to the Antarctic Treaty area;

(e) 'appropriate authority' means any person or agency authorized by a Party to issue permits under this Annex;

(f) 'permit' means a formal permission in writing issued by an appropriate authority;

(g) 'take' or 'taking' means to kill, injure, capture, handle or molest, a native mammal or bird, or to remove or damage such quantities of native plants that their local distribution or abundance would be significantly affected;

(h) 'harmful interference' means:
   (i) flying or landing helicopters or other aircraft in a manner that disturbs concentrations of birds and seals;
   (ii) using vehicles or vessels, including hovercraft and small boats, in a manner that disturbs concentrations of birds and seals;
   (iii) using explosives or firearms in a manner that disturbs concentrations of birds and seals;
   (iv) wilfully disturbing breeding or moulting birds or concentrations of birds and seals by persons on foot;
   (v) significantly damaging concentrations of native terrestrial plants by landing aircraft, driving vehicles, or walking on them, or by other means; and
   (vi) any activity that results in the significant adverse modification of habitats of any species or population of native mammal, bird, plant or invertebrate.

(i) 'International Convention for the Regulation of Whaling' means the Convention done at Washington on 2 December 1946.

Article 2
Cases of Emergency

1. This Annex shall not apply in cases of emergency relating to the safety of human life or of ships, aircraft, or equipment and facilities of high value, or the protection of the environment.

2. Notice of activities undertaken in cases of emergency shall be circulated immediately to all Parties and to the Committee.

Article 3
Protection of Native Fauna and Flora

1. Taking or harmful interference shall be prohibited, except in accordance with a permit.

2. Such permits shall specify the authorized activity, including when, where and by whom it is to be conducted and shall be issued only in the following circumstances:

   (a) to provide specimens for scientific study or scientific information;
   (b) to provide specimens for museums, herbaria, zoological and botanical gardens, or other educational or cultural institutions or uses; and
   (c) to provide for unavoidable consequences of scientific activities not otherwise authorized under sub-paragraphs (a) or (b) above, or of the construction and operation of scientific support facilities.

3. The issue of such permits shall be limited so as to ensure that:

   (a) no more native mammals, birds, or plants are taken than are strictly necessary to meet the purposes set forth in paragraph 2 above;
   (b) only small numbers of native mammals or birds are killed and in no case more native mammals or birds are killed from local populations than can, in combination with other permitted takings, normally be replaced by natural reproduction in the following season; and
   (c) the diversity of species, as well as the habitats essential to their existence, and the balance of the ecological systems existing within the Antarctic Treaty area are maintained.

4. Any species of native mammals, birds and plants listed in Appendix A to this Annex shall be designated 'Specially Protected Species', and shall be accorded special protection by the Parties.

5. A permit shall not be issued to take a Specially Protected Species unless the taking:

   (a) is for a compelling scientific purpose;
   (b) will not jeopardize the survival or recovery of that species or local population; and
   (c) uses non-lethal techniques where appropriate.

6. All taking of native mammals and birds shall be done in the manner that involves the least degree of pain and suffering practicable.

Article 4
Introduction of Non-native Species, Parasites and Disease

1. No species of animal or plant not native to the Antarctic Treaty area shall be introduced onto land or ice shelves, or into water in the Antarctic Treaty area except in accordance with a permit.

2. Dogs shall not be introduced onto land or ice shelves and dogs currently in those areas shall be removed by 1 April 1994.

3. Permits under paragraph 1 above shall be issued to allow the importation only of the animals and plants listed in Appendix B to this Annex and shall specify the species, numbers and, if appropriate, age and sex and precautions to be taken to prevent escape or contact with native fauna and flora.

4. Any plant or animal for which a permit has been issued in accordance with paragraphs 1 and 3 above, shall, prior to expiration of the permit, be removed from the Antarctic Treaty area or be disposed of by incineration or equally effective means that eliminates risk to native fauna or flora. The permit shall specify this obligation. Any other plant or animal introduced into the Antarctic Treaty area not native to that area, including any progeny, shall be removed or disposed of, by incineration or by equally effective means, so as to be rendered sterile, unless it is determined that they pose no risk to native flora or fauna.

5. Nothing in this Article shall apply to the importation of food into the Antarctic Treaty area provided that no live animals are imported for this purpose and all plants and animal parts and products are kept under carefully controlled conditions and disposed of in accordance with Annex III to the Protocol and Appendix C to this Annex.

6. Each Party shall require that precautions, including those listed in Appendix C to this Annex, be taken to prevent the introduction of micro-organisms (e.g., viruses, bacteria, parasites, yeasts, fungi) not present in the native fauna and flora.

Article 5
Information

Each Party shall prepare and make available information setting forth, in particular, prohibited activities and providing lists of Specially Protected Species and relevant Protected Areas to all those persons present in or intendng to enter the Antarctic Treaty area with a view to ensuring that such persons understand and observe the provisions of this Annex.

Article 6
Exchange of Information

1. The Parties shall make arrangements for:

(a) collecting and exchanging records (including records of permits) and statistics concerning the numbers of quantities of each species of native mammal, bird or plant taken annually in the Antarctic Treaty area;

(b) obtaining and exchanging information as to the status of native mammals, birds, plants, and invertebrates in the Antarctic Treaty area, and the extent to which any species or population needs protection;

(c) establishing a common form in which this information shall be submitted by Parties in accordance with paragraph 2 below.

2. Each Party shall inform the other Parties as well as the Committee before the end of November of each year of any step taken pursuant to paragraph 1 above and of the number and nature of permits issued under this Annex in the preceding period of 1 July to 30 June.

Article 7
Relationship with Other Agreements Outside the Antarctic Treaty System

Nothing in this Annex shall derogate from the rights and obligations of Parties under the International Convention for the Regulation of Whaling.

Article 8
Review

The Parties shall keep under continuing review measures for the conservation of Antarctic fauna and flora, taking into account any recommendations from the Committee.

Article 9
Amendment or Modification

1. This Annex may be amended or modified by a measure adopted in accordance with Article IX(1) of the Antarctic Treaty. Unless the measure specifies otherwise, the amendment or modification shall be deemed to have been approved, and shall become effective, one year after the close of the Antarctic Treaty Consultative Meeting at which it was adopted, unless one or more of the Antarctic Treaty Consultative Parties notifies the Depositary, within that time period, that it wishes an extension of that period or that it is unable to approve the measure.

2. Any amendment or modification of this Annex which becomes effective in accordance with paragraph 1 above shall thereafter become effective as to any other Party when notice of approval by it has been received by the Depositary.

Appendices to the Annex

Appendix A:
Specially Protected Species

All species of the genus *Arctocephalus*, Fur Seals, *Ommatophoca rossii*, Ross Seal.

Appendix B:
Importation of Animals and Plants

The following animals and plants may be imported into the Antarctic Treaty area in accordance with permits issued under Article 4 of this Annex:
  (a) domestic plants; and
  (b) laboratory animals and plants including viruses, bacteria, yeasts and fungi.

Appendix C:
Precautions to Prevent Introduction of Micro-organisms

1. Poultry. No live poultry or other living birds shall be brought into the Antarctic Treaty area. Before dressed poultry is packaged for shipment to the Antarctic Treaty area, it shall be inspected for evidence of disease, such as Newcastle's Disease, tuberculosis, and yeast infection. Any poultry or parts not consumed shall be removed from the Antarctic Treaty area or disposed of by incineration or equivalent means that eliminates risks to native flora and fauna.

2. The importation of non-sterile soil shall be avoided to the maximum extent practicable.

Annex III

Waste Disposal and Waste Management

Article 1
General Obligations

1. This Annex shall apply to activities undertaken in the Antarctic Treaty area pursuant to scientific research programmes, tourism and all other governmental and non-governmental activities in the Antarctic Treaty area for which advance notice is required under Article VII(5) of the Antarctic Treaty, including associated logistic support activities.

2. The amount of wastes produced or disposed of in the Antarctic Treaty area shall be reduced as far as practicable so as to minimise impact on the

Antarctic environment and to minimise interference with the natural values of Antarctica, with scientific research and with other uses of Antarctica which are consistent with the Antarctic Treaty.

3. Waste storage, disposal and removal from the Antarctic Treaty area, as well as recycling and source reduction, shall be essential considerations in the planning and conduct of activities in the Antarctic Treaty area.

4. Wastes removed from the Antarctic Treaty area shall, to the maximum extent practicable, be returned to the country from which the activities generating the waste were organized or to any other country in which arrangements have been made for the disposal of such wastes in accordance with relevant international agreements.

5. Past and present waste disposal sites on land and abandoned work sites of Antarctic activities shall be cleaned up by the generator of such wastes and the user of such sites. This obligation shall not be interpreted as requiring:

(a) the removal of any structure designated as a historic site or monument; or

(b) the removal of any structure or waste material in circumstances where the removal by any practical option would result in greater adverse environmental impact than leaving the structure or waste material in its existing location.

Article 2
Waste Disposal by Removal from the Antarctic Treaty Area

1. The following wastes, if generated after entry into force of this Annex, shall be removed from the Antarctic Treaty area by the generator of such wastes:

(a) radio-active materials;

(b) electrical batteries;

(c) fuel, both liquid and solid;

(d) wastes containing harmful levels of heavy metals or acutely toxic or harmful persistent compounds;

(e) poly-vinyl chloride (PVC), polyurethane foam, polystyrene foam, rubber and lubricating oils, treated timbers and other products which contain additives that could produce harmful emissions if incinerated;

(f) all other plastic wastes, except low density polyethylene containers (such as bags for storing wastes), provided that such containers shall be incinerated in accordance with Article 3(1);

(g) fuel drums; and

(h) other solid, non-combustible wastes;

provided that the obligation to remove drums and solid non-combustible wastes contained in subparagraphs (g) and (h) above shall not apply in circumstances where the removal of such wastes by any practical option would result in greater adverse environmental impact than leaving them in their existing locations.

2. Liquid wastes which are not covered by paragraph 1 above and sewage and domestic liquid wastes, shall, to the maximum extent practicable, be removed from the Antarctic Treaty area by the generator of such wastes.

3. The following wastes shall be removed from the Antarctic Treaty area by the generator of such wastes, unless incinerated, autoclaved or otherwise treated to be made sterile:

  (a) residues of carcasses of imported animals;
  (b) laboratory culture of micro-organisms and plant pathogens; and
  (c) introduced avian products.

Article 3
Waste Disposal by Incineration

1. Subject to paragraph 2 below, combustible wastes, other than those referred to in Article 2(1), which are not removed from the Antarctic Treaty area shall be burnt in incinerators which to the maximum extent practicable reduce harmful emissions. Any emission standards and equipment guidelines which may be recommended by, *inter alia*, the Committee and the Scientific Committee on Antarctic Research shall be taken into account. The solid residue of such incineration shall be removed from the Antarctic Treaty area.

2. All open burning of wastes shall be phased out as soon as practicable, but not later than the end of the 1998/1999 season. Pending the completion of such phase-out, when it is necessary to dispose of wastes by open burning, allowance shall be made for the wind direction and speed and the type of wastes to be burnt to limit particulate deposition and to avoid such deposition over areas of special biological, scientific, historic, aesthetic or wilderness significance including, in particular, areas accorded protection under the Antarctic Treaty.

Article 4
Other Waste Disposal on Land

1. Wastes not removed or disposed of in accordance with Articles 2 and 3 shall not be disposed of onto ice-free areas or into fresh water systems.

2. Sewage, domestic liquid wastes and other liquid wastes not removed from the Antarctic Treaty area in accordance with Article 2, shall, to the maximum extent practicable, not be disposed of onto sea ice, ice shelves or the grounded ice-sheet, provided that such wastes which are generated by stations located inland on ice shelves or on the grounded ice-sheet may be

disposed of in deep ice pits where such disposal is the only practicable option. Such pits shall not be located on known ice-flow lines which terminate at ice-free areas or in areas of high ablation.

3. Wastes generated at field camps shall, to the maximum extent practicable, be removed by the generator of such wastes to supporting stations or ships for disposal in accordance with this Annex.

Article 5
Disposal of Waste in the Sea

1. Sewage and domestic liquid wastes may be discharged directly into the sea, taking into account the assimilative capacity of the receiving marine environment and provided that:

   (a) such discharge is located, wherever practicable, where conditions exist for initial dilution and rapid dispersal; and
   (b) large quantities of such wastes (generated in a station where the average weekly occupancy over the austral summer is approximately 30 individuals or more) shall be treated at least by maceration.

2. The by-product of sewage treatment by the Rotary Biological Contacter process or similar processes may be disposed of into the sea provided that such disposal does not adversely affect the local environment, and provided also that any such disposal at sea shall be in accordance with Annex IV to the Protocol.

Article 6
Storage of Waste

All wastes to be removed from the Antarctic Treaty area, or otherwise disposed of, shall be stored in such a way as to prevent their dispersal into the environment.

Article 7
Prohibited Products

No polychlorinated biphenyls (PCBs), non-sterile soil, polystyrene beads, chips or similar forms of packaging, or pesticides (other than those required for scientific, medical or hygiene purposes) shall be introduced onto land or ice shelves or into water in the Antarctic Treaty area.

Article 8
Waste Management Planning

1. Each Party which itself conducts activities in the Antarctic Treaty area shall, in respect of those activities, establish a waste disposal classification system as a basis for recording wastes and to facilitate studies aimed at evaluating the environmental impacts of scientific activity and associated logistic support. To that end, wastes produced shall be classified as:

(a) sewage and domestic liquid wastes (Group 1);
(b) other liquid wastes and chemicals, including fuels and lubricants (Group 2);
(c) solids to be combusted (Group 3);
(d) other solid wastes (Group 4); and
(e) radioactive material (Group 5).

2. In order to reduce further the impact of waste on the Antarctic environment, each such Party shall prepare and annually review and update its waste management plans (including waste reduction, storage and disposal), specifying for each fixed site, for field camps generally, and for each ship (other than small boats that are part of the operations of fixed sites or of ships and taking into account existing management plans for ships):

(a) programmes for cleaning up existing waste disposal sites and abandoned work sites;
(b) current and planned waste management arrangements, including final disposal;
(c) current and planned arrangements for analysing the environmental effects of waste and waste management; and
(d) other efforts to minimise any environmental effects of wastes and waste management.

3. Each such Party shall, as far as is practicable, also prepare an inventory of locations of past activities (such as traverses, fuel depots, field bases, crashed aircraft) before the information is lost, so that such locations can be taken into account in planning future scientific programmes (such as snow chemistry, pollutants in lichens or ice core drilling).

Article 9
Circulation and Review of Waste Management Plans

1. The waste management plans prepared in accordance with Article 8, reports on their implementation, and the inventories referred to in Article 8(3), shall be included in the annual exchanges of information in accordance with Articles III and VII of the Antarctic Treaty and related Recommendations under Article IX of the Antarctic Treaty.

2. Each Party shall send copies of its waste management plans, and reports on their implementation and review, to the Committee.

3. The Committee may review waste management plans and reports thereon and may offer comments, including suggestions for minimising impacts and modifications and improvement to the plans, for the consideration of the Parties.

4. The Parties may exchange information and provide advice on, *inter alia*, available low waste technologies, reconversion of existing installations, spe-

cial requirements for effluents, and appropriate disposal and discharge methods.

Article 10
Management Practices

Each Party shall:

    (a) designate a waste management official to develop and monitor waste management plans; in the field, this responsibility shall be delegated to an appropriate person at each site;

    (b) ensure that members of its expeditions receive training designed to limit the impact of its operations on the Antarctic environment and to inform them of requirements of this Annex; and

    (c) discourage the use of poly-vinyl chloride (PVC) products and ensure that its expeditions to the Antarctic Treaty area are advised of any PVC products they may introduce in the Antarctic Treaty area in order that they may be removed subsequently in accordance with this Annex.

Article 11
Review

This Annex shall be subject to regular review in order to ensure that it is updated to reflect improvement in waste disposal technology and procedures and to ensure thereby maximum protection of the Antarctic environment.

Article 12
Cases of Emergency

1. This Annex shall not apply in cases of emergency relating to the safety of human life or of ships, aircraft or the protection of the environment.

2. Notice of activities undertaken in cases of emergency shall be circulated immediately to all Parties and to the Committee.

Article 13
Amendment or Modification

1. This Annex may be amended or modified by a measure adopted in accordance with Article IX(1) of the Antarctic Treaty. Unless the measure specifies otherwise, the amendment or modification shall be deemed to have been approved, and shall become effective, one year after the close of the Antarctic Treaty Consultative Meeting at which it was adopted, unless one or more of the Antarctic Treaty Consultative Parties notifies the Depositary, within that time period, that it wishes an extension of that period or that it is unable to approve the amendment.

2. Any amendment or modification of this Annex which becomes effective in accordance with paragraph 1 above shall thereafter become effective as to any other Party when notice of approval by it has been received by the Depositary.

Annex IV

Prevention of Marine Pollution

Article 1
Definitions

For the purpose of this Annex:

    (a) 'discharge' means any release howsoever caused from a ship and includes any escape, disposal, spilling, leaking, pumping, emitting or emptying;

    (b) 'garbage' means all kinds of victual, domestic and operational waste excluding fresh fish and parts thereof, generated during the normal operation of the ship, except those substances which are covered by Articles 3 and 4;

    (c) 'MARPOL 73/78' means the International Convention for the Prevention of Pollution from Ships, 1973, as amended by the Protocol of 1978 relating thereto and by any other amendment in force thereafter;

    (d) 'noxious liquid substance' means any noxious liquid substance as defined in Annex II of MARPOL 73/78;

    (e) 'oil' means petroleum in any form including crude oil, fuel oil, sludge, oil refuse and refined oil products (other than petrochemicals which are subject to the provisions of Article 4);

    (f) 'oily mixture' means a mixture with any oil content; and

    (g) 'ship' means a vessel of any type whatsoever operating in the marine environment and includes hydrofoil boats, air-cushion vehicles, submersibles, floating craft and fixed or floating platforms.

Article 2
Application

This Annex applies, with respect to each Party, to ships entitled to fly its flag and to any other ship engaged in or supporting its Antarctic operations, while operating in the Antarctic Treaty area.

Article 3
Discharge of Oil

1. Any discharge into the sea of oil or oily mixture shall be prohibited, except in cases permitted under Annex I of MARPOL 73/78. While oper-

ating in the Antarctic Treaty area, ships shall retain on board all sludge, dirty ballast, tank washing waters and other oily residues and mixtures which may not be discharged into the sea. Ships shall discharge these residues only outside the Antarctic Treaty area, at reception facilities or as otherwise permitted under Annex I of MARPOL 73/78.

2. This Article shall not apply to:

    (a) the discharge into the sea of oil or oily mixture resulting from damage to a ship or its equipment:

        (i) provided that all reasonable precautions have been taken after the occurrence of the damage or discovery of the discharge for the purpose of preventing or minimising the discharge; and

        (ii) except if the owner or the Master acted either with intent to cause damage, or recklessly and with the knowledge that damage would probably result; or

    (b) the discharge into the sea of substances containing oil which are being used for the purpose of combating specific pollution incidents in order to minimise the damage from pollution.

Article 4
Discharge of Noxious Liquid Substances

The discharge into the sea of any noxious liquid substance, and any other chemical or other substances, in quantities or concentrations that are harmful to the marine environment, shall be prohibited.

Article 5
Disposal of Garbage

1. The disposal into the sea of all plastics, including but not limited to synthetic ropes, synthetic fishing nets, and plastic garbage bags, shall be prohibited.

2. The disposal into the sea of all other garbage, including paper products, rags, glass, metal, bottles, crockery, incineration ash, dunnage, lining and packing materials, shall be prohibited.

3. The disposal into the sea of food wastes may be permitted when they have been passed through a comminuter or grinder, provided that such disposal shall, except in cases permitted under Annex V of MARPOL 73/78, be made as far as practicable from land and ice shelves but in any case not less than 12 nautical miles from the nearest land or ice shelf. Such comminuted or ground food wastes shall be capable of passing through a screen with openings no greater than 25 millimeters.

4. When a substance or material covered by this article is mixed with other such substance or material for discharge or disposal, having different disposal or discharge requirements, the most stringent disposal or discharge requirements shall apply.

5. The provisions of paragraphs 1 and 2 above shall not apply to:

   (a) the escape of garbage resulting from damage to a ship or its equipment provided all reasonable precautions have been taken, before and after the occurrence of the damage, for the purpose of preventing or minimising the escape; or

   (b) the accidental loss of synthetic fishing nets, provided all reasonable precautions have been taken to prevent such loss.

6. The Parties shall, where appropriate, require the use of garbage record books.

Article 6
Discharge of Sewage

1. Except where it would unduly impair Antarctic operations:

   (a) each Party shall eliminate all discharge into the sea of untreated sewage ('sewage' being defined in Annex IV of MARPOL 73/78) within 12 nautical miles of land or ice shelves;

   (b) beyond such distance, sewage stored in a holding tank shall not be discharged instantaneously but at a moderate rate and, where practicable, while the ship is en route at a speed of no less than 4 knots.

This paragraph does not apply to ships certified to carry not more than 10 persons.

2. The Parties shall, where appropriate, require the use of sewage record books.

Article 7
Cases of Emergency

1. Articles 3, 4, 5 and 6 of this Annex shall not apply in cases of emergency relating to the safety of a ship and those on board or saving life at sea.

2. Notice of activities undertaken in cases of emergency shall be circulated immediately to all Parties and to the Committee.

Article 8
Effect on Dependent and Associated Ecosystems

In implementing the provisions of this Annex, due consideration shall be given to the need to avoid detrimental effects on dependent and associated ecosystems, outside the Antarctic Treaty area.

Article 9
Ship Retention Capacity and Reception Facilities

1. Each Party shall undertake to ensure that all ships entitled to fly its flag and any other ship engaged in or supporting its Antarctic operations,

before entering the Antarctic Treaty area, are fitted with a tank or tanks of sufficient capacity on board for the retention of all sludge, dirty ballast, tank washing water and other oily residues and mixtures, and have sufficient capacity on board for the retention of garbage, while operating in the Antarctic Treaty area and have concluded arrangements to discharge such oily residues and garbage at reception facility after leaving that area. Ships shall also have sufficient capacity on board for the retention of noxious liquid substances.

2. Each Party at whose ports ships depart en route to or arrive from the Antarctic Treaty area undertakes to ensure that as soon as practicable adequate facilities are provided for the reception of all sludge, dirty ballast, tank washing water, other oily residues and mixtures, and garbage from ships, without causing undue delay, and according to the needs of the ships using them.

3. Parties operating ships which depart to or arrive from the Antarctic Treaty area at ports of other Parties shall consult with those Parties with a view to ensuring that the establishment of port reception facilities does not place an inequitable burden on Parties adjacent to the Antarctic Treaty area.

Article 10
Design, Construction, Manning and Equipment of Ships

In the design, construction, manning and equipment of ships engaged in or supporting Antarctic operations, each Party shall take into account the objectives of this Annex.

Article 11
Sovereign Immunity

1. This Annex shall not apply to any warship, naval auxiliary or other ship owned or operated by a State and used, for the time being, only on government non-commercial service. However, each Party shall ensure by the adoption of appropriate measures not impairing the operations or operational capabilities of such ships owned or operated by it, that such ships act in a manner consistent, so far as is reasonable and practicable, with this Annex.

2. In applying paragraph 1 above, each Party shall take into account the importance of protecting the Antarctic environment.

3. Each Party shall inform the other Parties of how it implements this provision.

4. The dispute settlement procedure set out in Articles 18 to 20 of the Protocol shall not apply to this Article.

Article 12
Preventive Measures and Emergency Preparedness and Response

1. In order to respond more effectively to marine pollution emergencies or the threat thereof in the Antarctic Treaty area, the Parties, in accordance with Article 15 of the Protocol, shall develop contingency plans for marine pollution response in the Antarctic Treaty area, including contingency plans for ships (other than small boats that are part of the operations of fixed sites or of ships) operating in the Antarctic Treaty area, paticularly ships carrying oil as cargo, and for oil spills, originating from coastal installations, which enter into the marine environment. To this end they shall:

   (a) co-operate in the formulation and implementation of such plans; and
   (b) draw on the advice of the Committee, the International Maritime Organization and other international organizations.

2. The Parties shall also establish procedures for co-operative response to pollution emergencies and shall take appropriate response actions in accordance with such procedures.

Article 13
Review

The Parties shall keep under continuous review the provisions of this Annex and other measures to prevent, reduce and respond to pollution of the Antarctic marine environment, including any amendments and new regulations adopted under MARPOL 73/78, with a view to achieving the objectives of this Annex.

Article 14
Relationship with MARPOL 73/78

With respect to those Parties which are also Parties to MARPOL 73/78, nothing in this Annex shall derogate from the specific rights and obligations thereunder.

Article 15
Amendment or Modification

1. This Annex may be amended or modified by a measure adopted in accordance with Article IX(1) of the Antarctic Treaty. Unless the measure specifies otherwise, the amendment or modification shall be deemed to have been approved, and shall become effective, one year after the close of the Antarctic Treaty Consultative Meeting at which it was adopted, unless one or more of the Antarctic Treaty Consultative Parties notifies the De-

positary, within that time period, that it wishes an extension of that period or that it is unable to approve the measure.

2. Any amendment or modification of this Annex which becomes effective in accordance with paragraph 1 above shall thereafter become effective as to any other Party when notice of approval by it has been received by the Depositary.

Annex V

Area Protection and Management

Article 1
Definitions

For the purposes of this Annex:

(a) 'appropriate authority' means any person or agency authorised by a Party to issue permits under this Annex;

(b) 'permit' means a formal permission in writing issued by an appropriate authority;

(c) 'Management Plan' means a plan to manage the activities and protect the special value or values in an Antarctic Specially Protected Area or an Antarctic Specially Managed Area.

Articles 2
Objectives

For the purposes set out in this Annex, any area, including any marine area, may be designated as an Antarctic Specially Protected Area or an Antarctic Specially Managed Area. Activities in those Areas shall be prohibited, restricted or managed in accordance with Management Plans adopted under the provisions of this Annex.

Article 3
Antarctic Specially Protected Areas

1. Any area, including any marine area, may be designated as an Antarctic Specially Protected Area to protect outstanding environmental, scientific, historic, aesthetic or wilderness values, any combination of those values, or ongoing or planned scientific research.

2. Parties shall seek to identify, within a systematic environmental-geographical framework, and to include in the series of Antarctic Specially Protected Areas:

(a) areas kept inviolate from human interference so that future comparisons may be possible with localities that have been affected by human activities;

(b) representative examples of major terrestrial, including glacial and aquatic, ecosystems and marine ecosystems;

(c) areas with important or unusual assemblages of species, including major colonies of breeding native birds or mammals;

(d) the type locality or only known habitat of any species;

(e) areas of particular interest to ongoing or planned scientific research;

(f) examples of outstanding geological, glaciological or geomorphological features;

(g) areas of outstanding aesthetic and wilderness value;

(h) sites or monuments of recognised historic value; and

(i) such other areas as may be appropriate to protect the values set out in paragraph 1 above.

3. Specially Protected Areas and Sites of Special Scientific Interest designated as such by past Antarctic Treaty Consultative Meetings are hereby designated as Antarctic Specially Protected Areas and shall be renamed and renumbered accordingly.

4. Entry into an Antarctic Specially Protected Area shall be prohibited except in accordance with a permit issued under Article 7.

Article 4
Antarctic Specially Managed Areas

1. Any area, including any marine area, where activities are being conducted or may in the future be conducted, may be designated as an Antarctic Specially Managed Area to assist in the planning and co-ordination of activities, avoid possible conflicts, improve co-operation between Parties or minimise environmental impacts.

2. Antarctic Specially Managed Areas may include:

(a) areas where activities pose risks of mutual interference or cumulative environmental impacts; and

(b) sites or monuments of recognised historic value.

3. Entry into an Antarctic Specially Managed Area shall not require a permit.

4. Notwithstanding paragraph 3 above, an Antarctic Specially Managed Area may contain one or more Antarctic Specially Protected Areas, entry into which shall be prohibited except in accordance with a permit issued under Article 7.

Article 5
Management Plans

1. Any Party, the Committee, the Scientific Committee for Antarctic Research or the Commission for the Conservation of Antarctic Marine Living Resources may propose an area for designation as an Antarctic Specially

Protected Area or an Antarctic Specially Managed Area by submitting a proposed Management Plan to the Antarctic Treaty Consultative Meeting.

2. The area proposed for designation shall be of sufficient size to protect the values for which the special protection or management is required.

3. Proposed Management Plans shall include, as appropriate:

   (a) a description of the value or values for which special protection or management is required;

   (b) a statement of the aims and objectives of the Management Plan for the protection or management of those values;

   (c) management activities which are to be undertaken to protect the values for which special protection or management is required;

   (d) a period of designation, if any;

   (e) a description of the area, including:

      (i) the geographical co-ordinates, boundary markers and natural features that delineate the area;

     (ii) access to the area by land, sea or air including marine approaches and anchorages, pedestrian and vehicular routes within the area, and aircraft routes and landing areas;

    (iii) the location of structures, including scientific stations, research or refuge facilities, both within the area and near to it; and

    (iv) the location in or near the area of other Antarctic Specially Protected Areas or Antarctic Specially Managed Areas designated under this Annex, or other protected areas designated in accordance with measures adopted under other components of the Antarctic Treaty System;

   (f) the identification of zones within the area, in which activities are to be prohibited, restricted or managed for the purpose of achieving the aims and objectives referred to in subparagraph (b) above;

   (g) maps and photographs that show clearly the boundary of the area in relation to surrounding features and key features within the area;

   (h) supporting documentation;

   (i) in respect of an area proposed for designation as an Antarctic Specially Protected Area, a clear description of the conditions under which permits may be granted by the appropriate authority regarding:

      (i) access to a movement within or over the area;

     (ii) activities which are or may be conducted within the area, including restrictions on time and place;

    (iii) the installation, modification, or removal of structures;

    (iv) the location of field camps;

    (v) restrictions on materials and organisms which may be brought into the area;

    (vi) the taking of or harmful interference with native flora and fauna;

   (vii) the collection or removal of anything not brought into the area by the permit-holder;

  (viii) the disposal of waste;

   (ix) measures that may be necessary to ensure that the aims and objectives of the Management Plan can continue to be met; and

    (x) requirements for reports to be made to the appropriate authority regarding visits to the area;

(j) in respect of an area proposed for designation as an Antarctic Specially Managed Area. a code of conduct regarding;

    (i) access to and movement within or over the area;

   (ii) activities which are or may be conducted within the area, including restrictions on time and place;

  (iii) the installation, modification, or removal of structures;

  (iv) the location of field camps;

   (v) the taking of or harmful interference with native flora and fauna;

  (vi) the collection or removal of anything not brought into the area by the visitor;

  (vii) the disposal of waste; and

  (viii) any requirements for reports to be made to the appropriate authority regarding visits to the area; and

(k) provisions relating to the circumstances in which Parties should seek to exchange information in advance of activities which they propose to conduct.

Article 6
Designation Procedures

1. Proposed Management Plans shall be forwarded to the Committee, the Scientific Committee on Antarctic Research and, as appropriate, to the Commission for the Conservation of Antarctic Marine Living Resources. In formulating its advice to the Antarctic Treaty Consultative Meeting, the Committee shall take into account any comments provided by the Scientific Committee on Antarctic Research and, as appropriate, by the Commission for the Conservation of Antarctic Marine Living Resources. Thereafter Management Plans may be approved by the Antarctic Treaty Consultative Parties by a measure adopted at an Antarctic Treaty Consultative Meeting in accordance with Article IX(1) of the Antarctic Treaty. Unless the measure specifies otherwise, the Plan shall be deemed to have been approved 90 days after the close of the Antarctic Treaty Consultative Meeting at which it was adopted, unless one or more of the Consultative Parties notifies the Depositary, within that time period,

that it wishes an extension of that period or is unable to approve the measure.

2. Having regard to the provisions of Articles 4 and 5 of the Protocol, no marine area shall be designated as an Antarctic Specially Protected Area or an Antarctic Specially Managed Area without the prior approval of the Commission for the Conservation of Antarctic Marine Living Resources.

3. Designation of an Antarctic Specially Protected Area or an Antarctic Specially Managed Area shall be for an indefinite period unless the Management Plan provides otherwise. A review of a Management Plan shall be initiated at least every five years. The Plan shall be updated as necessary.

4. Management Plans may be amended or revoked in accordance with paragraph 1 above.

5. Upon approval Management Plans shall be circulated promptly by the Depositary to all Parties. The Depositary shall maintain a record of all currently approved Management Plans.

Article 7
Permits

1. Each Party shall appoint an appropriate authority to issue permits to enter and engage in activities within an Antarctic Specially Protected Area in accordance with the requirements of the Management Plan relating to that Area. The permit shall be accompanied by the relevant sections of the Management Plan and shall specify the extent and location of the Area, the authorised activities and when, where and by whom the activities are authorised and any other conditions imposed by the Management Plan.

2. In the case of a Specially Protected Area designated as such by past Antarctic Treaty Consultative Meetings which does not have a Management Plan, the appropriate authority may issue a permit for a compelling scientific purpose which cannot be served elsewhere and which will not jeopardise the natural ecological system in that Area.

3. Each Party shall require a permit-holder to carry a copy of the permit while in the Antarctic Specially Protected Area concerned.

Article 8
Historic Sites and Monuments

1. Sites or monuments of recognised historic value which have been designated as Antarctic Specially Protected Areas or Antarctic Specially Managed Areas, or which are located within such Areas, shall be listed as Historic Sites and Monuments.

2. Any Party may propose a site or monument of recognised historic value which has not been designated as an Antarctic Specially Protected Area or

an Antarctic Specially Managed Area, or which is not located within such an Area, for listing as a Historic Site or Monument. The proposal for listing may be approved by the Antarctic Treaty Consultative Parties by a measure adopted at an Antarctic Treaty Consultative Meeting in accordance with Article IX(1) of the Antarctic Treaty. Unless the measure specifies otherwise, the proposal shall be deemed to have been approved 90 days after the close of the Antarctic Treaty Consultative Meeting at which it was adopted, unless one or more of the Consultative Parties notifies the Depositary, within that time period, that it wishes an extension of that period or is unable to approve the measure.

3. Existing Historic Sites and Monuments which have been listed as such by previous Antarctic Treaty Consultative Meetings shall be included in the list of Historic Sites and Monuments under this Article.

4. Listed Historic Sites and Monuments shall not be damaged, removed or destroyed.

5. The list of Historic Sites and Monuments may be amended in accordance with paragraph 2 above. The Depositary shall maintain a list of current Historic Sites and Monuments.

Article 9
Information and Publicity

1. With a view to ensuring that all persons visiting or proposing to visit Antarctica understand and observe the provisions of this Annex, each Party shall make available information setting forth, in particular:

   (a) the location of Antarctic Specially Protected Areas and Antarctic Specially Managed Areas;
   (b) listing and maps of those Areas;
   (c) the Management Plans, including listings of prohibitions relevant to each Area;
   (d) the location of Historic Sites and Monuments and any relevant prohibition or restriction.

2. Each Party shall ensure that the location and, if possible, the limits, of Antarctic Specially Protected Areas, Antarctic Specially Managed Areas and Historic Sites and Monuments are shown on its topographic maps, hydrographic charts and in other relevant publications.

3. Parties shall co-operate to ensure that, where appropriate, the boundaries of Antarctic Specially Protected Areas, Antarctic Specially Managed Areas and Historic Sites and Monuments are suitably marked on the site.

Article 10
Exchange of Information

1. The Parties shall make arrangements for:

(a) collecting and exchanging records, including records of permits and reports of visits, including inspection visits, to Antarctic Specially Protected Areas and reports of inspection visits, to Antarctic Specially Managed Areas;

(b) obtaining and exchanging information on any significant change or damage to any Antarctic Specially Managed Area, Antarctic Specially Protected Area or Historic Site or Monument; and

(c) establishing common forms in which records and information shall be submitted by Parties in accordance with paragraph 2 below.

2. Each Party shall inform the other Parties and the Committee before the end of November of each year of the number and nature of permits issued under this Annex in the preceding period of 1 July to 30 June.

3. Each Party conducting, funding, or authorising research or other activities in Antarctic Specially Protected Areas or Antarctic Specially Managed Areas shall maintain a record of such activities and in the annual exchange of information in accordance with the Treaty shall provide summary descriptions of the activities conducted by persons subject to its jurisdiction in such areas in the preceding year.

4. Each Party shall inform the other Parties and the Committee before the end of November each year of measures it has taken to implement this Annex, including any site inspections and any steps it has taken to address instances of activities in contravention of the provisions of the approved Management Plan for an Antarctic Specially Protected Area or Antarctic Specially Managed Area.

Article 11
Cases of Emergency

1. The restrictions laid down and authorised by this Annex shall not apply in cases of emergency involving safety of human life or of ships, aircraft, or equipment and facilities of high value or the protection of the environment.

2. Notice of activities undertaken in cases of emergency shall be circulated immediately to all Parties and to the Committee.

Article 12
Amendment or Modification

1. This Annex may be amended or modified by a measure adopted in accordance with Article IX(1) of the Antarctic Treaty. Unless the measure specifies otherwise, the amendment or modification shall be deemed to have been approved, and shall become effective, one year after the close of the Antarctic Treaty Consultative Meeting at which it was adopted, unless one or more of the Antarctic Treaty Consultative Parties notifies the De-

positary, within that time period, that it wishes an extension of that period or that it is unable to approve the measure.

2. Any amendment or modification of this Annex which becomes effective in accordance with paragraph 1 above shall thereafter become effective as to any other Party when notice of approval by it has been received by the Depositary.

Convention to Combat Desertification in Those Countries Experiencing Drought and/or Desertification, Particularly in Africa, Paris, 17 June 1994

Desertification has been defined by UNCED as 'land degradation in arid, semi-arid and dry sub-humid areas resulting from various factors, including climate variations and human activities' (Agenda 21, para 12.2). UNEP and other concerned bodies and conferences at the regional and international level had drawn attention to the increasingly serious socio-economic consequences for many years. At its Third Session in 1975 the UNEP General Council proposed the convening of an international conference on desertification. The UN General Assembly instructed UNEP and UNDP to convene a UN Conference on Desertification (UNGA Resolution 3511 (XXX), 15 December 1975) which took place in Nairobi, from 29 August – 9 September 1977 and was co-ordinated informally with the United Nations Water Conference, held in Mar del Plata, Argentina, 14–25 March 1977. The Conference made various recommendations calling for more ecologically sound land-use priorities which took realistic account of climatic conditions and adopted a Plan of Action (see *Report of the United Nations Conference on Desertification*, UN Doc. A/CONF. 74/36 (1977); M. K. Tolba, 'The United Nations Conference on Desertification: A Review', 6 *Mazingara* (1982) 14–23; M.R. Biswas, 'UN Conference on Desertification in Retrospect', 5 *Envtl Consvn* (1978) 69–70, 247–62; 6 *Envtl Consvn* (1979) 160–1). These recommendations were subsequently promoted by various agencies, including UNESCO, FAO, the Permanent Inter-State Committee on Drought Control in the Sahel, and the UN Sudano-Sahelian Office. UNEP also established a Consultation Group for Desertification Control (DESCON) to assist its existing Desertification Unit. The Action Plan, however, was not effectively implemented, the spread of desertification continued, and the adverse transfrontier consequences of certain activities became more apparent. The demands by some states for further action at the international level grew; many states, however, resisted proposals that an international convention should be concluded, regarding this as an invasion of sovereignty. It was not possible, therefore, at UNCED to adopt a convention, but agreement was reached on an international definition of desertification and a programme to address the complex underlying problems. Agenda 21's provisions on Combating Desertification and Drought recommended that further effort should be made to negotiate an international convention, and this led the UN General Assembly at its 47th Session in 1992 to establish an Intergovernmental Negotiating Committee (INC) for the Elaboration of an International Convention to Combat Desertification in Those Countries Experiencing Serious Drought and/or Desertification, Particularly in Africa (UNGA Res 47/188 of 22 December 1992, text in 23 *EPL* (1993) 43–4). Its first (organisational) session took place in New York from 26–29 January 1993, at which socio-economic and funding issues were discussed (for details, see 23 *EPL* (1993), 202), and a target date of June 1994 for conclusion of the convention was set.

The first substantive session of the INC was held in Nairobi from 24 May–3 June 1993. Its progress was reported to the First Substantive Session of the Commission on Sustainable Development (q.v.). Elements of a convention based on a background paper prepared by the INC Secretariat were discussed. Delegates were anxious to avoid conflict and overlap with other environmental conventions, especially those on Climate Change (q.v.) and Biodiversity (q.v.). Disagreement remained on the timing of negotiations on specific regional instruments which it was agreed should form an integral part of the convention. It was agreed that one on Africa should be concluded as soon as the convention structure was established and should be an integral part thereof, and that others would follow (23 *EPL* (1993) 202–3).

A Second Session of the INC was held in Geneva from 13–24 September 1993. The framework and most of the elements of the proposed convention were discussed (24 *EPL* (1994) 8–12). For the outcome of this session see Draft Decision submitted by the Chairman on the Basis of Informal Consultations held on draft decisions, UN Doc. A/AC. 241/L. 12, in 24 *EPL* (1994) 36–7. The INC emphasised that in view of the global dimension, the complexities of the problems of desertification and drought, and the particular conditions of each region, an effective convention should deal with the specific needs of the regions, particularly in Africa. It annexed a draft resolution for adoption by the UN General Assembly which included, *inter alia*, a request for the INC to complete negotiation of such a convention by June 1994 (text in 24 *EPL* (1994) 36–7). Though considerable progress in resolving differences was made at the Third and Fourth Sessions (for details, see 24 *EPL* (1994) 60 and 145–6 respectively), some problems remained, including provision of financial resources and mechanisms. These were resolved at the INC's Fifth Session held in Paris from 6–17 June 1994, and the Convention was adopted on 17 June 1994, with four regional annexes (for Africa; Latin America and the Caribbean; Asia; and the Northern Mediterranean). Only Annex 1 is reproduced.

Two Resolutions recommending urgent action for Africa and interim arrangements to apply in the period between adoption and entry into force were also adopted. The 49th Session of the UN General Assembly is to review the implementation of the resolutions and the Convention and to provide for the continued functioning of the Secretariat in the interim period and of the INC until the first meeting of the Conference of the Parties. The INC held its Sixth Session in New York from 9–10 January 1995.

The text of the Convention and its four Annexes is found in 33 *ILM* (1994) 1332–82 and, without the annexes, in 24 *EPL* (1994) 283–4. As of 31 January 1995, thirty-seven States have signed the Convention; seven have ratified (Argentina, Australia, Ecuador, France, Peru, Spain, Sweden). For the background to the 1974 UN Conference on Desertification see L. Caldwell, *International Environmental Policy*, 1st edn., (Durham N. C., 1984), 216–18; for the background to the 1994 Convention and remaining problems, see 6 *Our Planet* (1994) 1–31, esp. A. Henrati, 'Taking Effective Action', 5–7; B. Kjellen, 'A New Departure?', 8–9.

TEXT

   The Parties to this Convention,

Affirming that human beings in affected or threatened areas are at the centre of concerns to combat desertification and mitigate the effects of drought,

Reflecting the urgent concern of the international community, including States and international organizations, about the adverse impacts of desertification and drought,

Aware that arid, semi-arid and dry sub-humid areas together account for a significant proportion of the Earth's land area and are the habitat and source of livelihood for a large segment of its population,

Acknowledging that desertification and drought are problems of global dimension in that they affect all regions of the world and that joint action of the international community is needed to combat desertification and/or mitigate the effects of drought,

Noting the high concentration of developing countries, notably the least developed countries, among those experiencing serious drought and/or desertification, and the particularly tragic consequences of these phenomena in Africa,

Noting also that desertification is caused by complex interactions among physical, biological, political, social, cultural and economic factors,

Considering the impact of trade and relevant aspects of international economic relations on the ability of affected countries to combat desertification adequately,

Conscious that sustainable economic growth, social development and poverty eradication are priorities of affected developing countries, particularly in Africa, and are essential to meeting sustainability objectives,

Mindful that desertification and drought affect sustainable development through their interrelationships with important social problems such as poverty, poor health and nutrition, lack of food security, and those arising from migration, displacement of persons and demographic dynamics,

Appreciating the significance of the past efforts and experience of States and international organizations in combating desertification and mitigating the effects of drought, particularly in implementing the Plan of Action to Combat Desertification which was adopted at the United Nations Conference on Desertification in 1977,

Realizing that, despite efforts in the past, progress in combating desertification and mitigating the effects of drought has not met expectations and that a new and more effective approach is needed at all levels within the framework of sustainable development,

Recognizing the validity and relevance of decisions adopted at the United Nations Conference on Environment and Development, particularly of Agenda 21 and its chapter 12, which provide a basis for combating desertification,

Reaffirming in this light the commitments of developed countries as contained in paragraph 13 of chapter 33 of Agenda 21,

Recalling General Assembly resolution 47/188, particularly the priority in it prescribed for Africa, and all other relevant United Nations resolutions, decisions and programmes on desertification and drought, as well as relevant declarations by African countries and those from other regions,

Reaffirming the Rio Declaration on Environment and Development which states, in its Principle 2, that States have, in accordance with the Charter of the United Nations and the principles of international law, the sovereign right to exploit their own resources pursuant to their own environmental and developmental policies, and the responsibility to ensure that activities within their jurisdiction or control do not cause damage to the environment of other States or of areas beyond the limits of national jurisdiction,

Recognizing that national Governments play a critical role in combating desertification and mitigating the effects of drought and that progress in that respect depends on local implementation of action programmes in affected areas,

Recognizing also the importance and necessity of international cooperation and partnership in combating desertification and mitigating the effects of drought,

Recognizing the importance of the provision to affected developing countries, particularly in Africa, of effective means, *inter alia* substantial financial resources, including new and additional funding, and access to technology, without which it will be difficult for them to implement fully their commitments under this Convention,

Expressing concern over the impact of desertification and drought on affected countries in Central Asia and the Transcaucasus,

Stressing the important role played by women in regions affected by desertification and/or drought, particularly in rural areas of developing countries, and the importance of ensuring the full participation of both men and women at all levels in programmes to combat desertification and mitigate the effects of drought,

Emphasizing the special role of non-governmental organizations and other major groups in programmes to combat desertification and mitigate the effects of drought,

Bearing in mind the relationship between desertification and other environmental problems of global dimension facing the international and national communities,

Bearing also in mind the contribution that combating desertification can make to achieving the objectives of the United Nations Framework Convention on Climate Change, the Convention on Biological Diversity and other related environmental conventions,

Believing that strategies to combat desertification and mitigate the effects of drought will be most effective if they are based on sound systematic observation and rigorous scientific knowledge and if they are continuously re-evaluated,

Recognizing the urgent need to improve the effectiveness and coordination of international cooperation to facilitate the implementation of national plans and priorities,

Determined to take appropriate action in combating desertification and mitigating the effects of drought for the benefit of present and future generations,

Have agreed as follows:

Part I
Introduction

Article 1
Use of terms

For the purposes of this Convention:

(a) 'desertification' means land degradation in arid, semi-arid and dry sub-humid areas resulting from various factors, including climatic variations and human activities;

(b) 'combating desertification' includes activities which are part of the integrated development of land in arid, semi-arid and dry sub-humid areas for sustainable development which are aimed at:
  (i) prevention and/or reduction of land degradation;
  (ii) rehabilitation of partly degraded land; and
  (iii) reclamation of desertified land;

(c) 'drought' means the naturally occurring phenomenon that exists when precipitation has been significantly below normal recorded levels, causing serious hydrological imbalances that adversely affect land resource production systems;

(d) 'mitigating the effects of drought' means activities related to the prediction of drought and intended to reduce the vulnerability of society and natural systems to drought as it relates to combating desertification;

(e) 'land' means the terrestrial bio-productive system that comprises soil, vegetation, other biota, and the ecological and hydrological processes that operate within the system;

(f) 'land degradation' means reduction or loss, in arid, semi-arid and dry sub-humid areas, of the biological or economic productivity and complexity of rainfed cropland, irrigated cropland, or range, pasture, forest and woodlands resulting from land uses or from a process or combination of processes, including processes arising from human activities and habitation patterns, such as:
  (i) soil erosion caused by wind and/or water;
  (ii) deterioration of the physical, chemical and biological or economic properties of soil; and
  (iii) long-term loss of natural vegetation;

(g) 'arid, semi-arid and dry sub-humid areas' means areas, other than polar and sub-polar regions, in which the ratio of annual precipitation to potential evapotranspiration falls within the range from 0.05 to 0.65;

(h) 'affected areas' means arid, semi-arid and/or dry sub-humid areas affected or threatened by desertification;

(i) 'affected countries' means countries whose lands include, in whole or in part, affected areas;

(j) 'regional economic integration organization' means an organization constituted by sovereign States of a given region which has competence in respect of matters governed by this Convention and has been duly authorized, in accordance with its internal procedures, to sign, ratify, accept, approve or accede to this Convention;

(k) 'developed country Parties' means developed country Parties and regional economic integration organizations constituted by developed countries.

Article 2
Objective

1. The objective of this Convention is to combat desertification and mitigate the effects of drought in countries experiencing serious drought and/or desertification, particularly in Africa, through effective action at all levels, supported by international cooperation and partnership arrangements, in the framework of an integrated approach which is consistent with Agenda 21, with a view to contributing to the achievement of sustainable development in affected areas.

2. Achieving this objective will involve long-term integrated strategies that focus simultaneously, in affected areas, on improved productivity of land, and the rehabilitation, conservation and sustainable management of land and water resources, leading to improved living conditions, in particular at the community level.

Article 3
Principles

In order to achieve the objective of this Convention and to implement its provisions, the Parties shall be guided, *inter alia*, by the following:

(a) the Parties should ensure that decisions on the design and implementation of programmes to combat desertification and/or mitigate the effects of drought are taken with the participation of populations and local communities and that an enabling environment is created at higher levels to facilitate action at national and local levels;

(b) the Parties should, in a spirit of international solidarity and partnership, improve cooperation and coordination at subregional, regional and international levels, and better focus financial, human, organizational and technical resources where they are needed;

(c) the Parties should develop, in a spirit of partnership, cooperation among all levels of government, communities, non-governmental organizations and landholders to establish a better understanding of the nature and value of land and scarce water resources in affected areas and to work towards their sustainable use; and

(d) the Parties should take into full consideration the special needs and circumstances of affected developing country Parties, particularly the least developed among them.

Part II
General Provisions

Article 4
General obligations

1. The Parties shall implement their obligations under this Convention, individually or jointly, either through existing or prospective bilateral and multilateral arrangements or a combination thereof, as appropriate, emphasizing the need to coordinate efforts and develop a coherent long-term strategy at all levels.

2. In pursuing the objective of this Convention, the Parties shall:

(a) adopt an integrated approach addressing the physical, biological and socio-economic aspects of the processes of desertification and drought;

(b) give due attention, within the relevant international and regional bodies, to the situation of affected developing country Parties with regard to international trade, marketing arrangements and debt with a view to establishing an enabling international economic environment conducive to the promotion of sustainable development;

(c) integrate strategies for poverty eradication into efforts to combat desertification and mitigate the effects of drought;

(d) promote cooperation among affected country Parties in the fields of environmental protection and the conservation of land and water resources, as they relate to desertification and drought;

(e) strengthen subregional, regional and international cooperation;

(f) cooperate within relevant intergovernmental organizations;

(g) determine institutional mechanisms, if appropriate, keeping in mind the need to avoid duplication; and

(h) promote the use of existing bilateral and multilateral financial mechanisms and arrangements that mobilize and channel substantial financial resources to affected developing country Parties in combating desertification and mitigating the effects of drought.

3. Affected developing country Parties are eligible for assistance in the implementation of the Convention.

Article 5
Obligations of affected country Parties

In addition to their obligations pursuant to Article 4, affected country Parties undertake to:

(a) give due priority to combating desertification and mitigating the effects of drought, and allocate adequate resources in accordance with their circumstances and capabilities;
(b) establish strategies and priorities, within the framework of sustainable development plans and/or policies, to combat desertification and mitigate the effects of drought;
(c) address the underlying causes of desertification and pay special attention to the socio-economic factors contributing to desertification processes;
(d) promote awareness and facilitate the participation of local populations, particularly women and youth, with the support of non-governmental organizations, in efforts to combat desertification and mitigate the effects of drought; and
(e) provide an enabling environment by strengthening, as appropriate, relevant existing legislation and, where they do not exist, enacting new laws and establishing long-term policies and action programmes.

Article 6
Obligations of developed country Parties

In addition to their general obligations pursuant to Article 4, developed country Parties undertake to:

(a) actively support, as agreed, individually or jointly, the efforts of affected developing country Parties, particularly those in Africa, and the least developed countries, to combat desertification and mitigate the effects of drought;
(b) provide substantial financial resources and other forms of support to assist affected developing country Parties, particularly those in Africa, effectively to develop and implement their own long-term plans and strategies to combat desertification and mitigate the effects of drought;
(c) promote the mobilization of new and additional funding pursuant to Article 20, paragraph 2(b);
(d) encourage the mobilization of funding from the private sector and other non-governmental sources; and
(e) promote and facilitate access by affected country Parties, particularly affected developing country Parties, to appropriate technology, knowledge and know-how.

Article 7
Priority for Africa

In implementing this Convention, the Parties shall give priority to affected African country Parties, in the light of the particular situation prevailing in that region, while not neglecting affected developing country Parties in other regions.

Article 8
Relationship with other conventions

1. The Parties shall encourage the coordination of activities carried out under this Convention and, if they are Parties to them, under other relevant international agreements, particularly the United Nations Framework Convention on Climate Change and the Convention on Biological Diversity, in order to derive maximum benefit from activities under each agreement while avoiding duplication of effort. The Parties shall encourage the conduct of joint programmes, particularly in the fields of research, training, systematic observation and information collection and exchange, to the extent that such activities may contribute to achieving the objectives of the agreements concerned.

2. The provisions of this Convention shall not affect the rights and obligations of any Party deriving from a bilateral, regional or international agreement into which it has entered prior to the entry into force of this Convention for it.

Part III
Action Programmes, Scientific and Technical Cooperation and
Supporting Measures

SECTION 1: ACTION PROGRAMMES

Article 9
Basic approach

1. In carrying out their obligations pursuant to Article 5, affected developing country Parties and any other affected country Party in the framework of its regional implementation annex or, otherwise, that has notified the Permanent Secretariat in writing of its intention to prepare a national action programme, shall, as appropriate, prepare, make public and implement national action programmes, utilizing and building, to the extent possible, on existing relevant successful plans and programmes, and subregional and regional action programmes, as the central element of the strategy to combat desertification and mitigate the effects of drought. Such programmes shall be updated through a continuing participatory process on the basis of lessons from field action, as well as the results of research. The preparation of national action programmes shall be closely interlinked with other efforts to formulate national policies for sustainable development.

2. In the provision by developed country Parties of different forms of assistance under the terms of Article 6, priority shall be given to supporting,

as agreed, national, sub-regional and regional action programmes of affected developing country Parties, particularly those in Africa, either directly or through relevant multilateral organizations or both.

3. The Parties shall encourage organs, funds and programmes of the United Nations system and other relevant intergovernmental organizations, academic institutions, the scientific community and non-governmental organizations in a position to cooperate, in accordance with their mandates and capabilities, to support the elaboration, implementation and follow-up of action programmes.

Article 10
National action programmes

1. The purpose of national action programmes is to identify the factors contributing to desertification and practical measures necessary to combat desertification and mitigate the effects of drought.

2. National action programmes shall specify the respective roles of government, local communities and land users and the resources available and needed. They shall, *inter alia*:

(a) incorporate long-term strategies to combat desertification and mitigate the effects of drought, emphasize implementation and be integrated with national policies for sustainable development;

(b) allow for modifications to be made in response to changing circumstances and be sufficiently flexible at the local level to cope with different socio-economic, biological and geo-physical conditions;

(c) give particular attention to the implementation of preventive measures for lands that are not yet degraded or which are only slightly degraded;

(d) enhance national climatological, meteorological and hydrological capabilities and the means to provide for drought early warning;

(e) promote policies and strengthen institutional frameworks which develop cooperation and coordination, in a spirit of partnership, between the donor community, governments at all levels, local populations and community groups, and facilitate access by local populations to appropriate information and technology;

(f) provide for effective participation at the local, national and regional levels of non-governmental organizations and local populations; both women and men, particularly resource users, including farmers and pastoralists and their representative organizations, in policy planning, decision-making, and implementation and review of national action programmes; and

(g) require regular review of, and progress reports on, their implementation.

3. National action programmes may include, *inter alia*, some or all of the following measures to prepare for and mitigate the effects of drought:

  (a) establishment and/or strengthening, as appropriate, of early warning systems, including local and national facilities and joint systems at the subregional and regional levels, and mechanisms for assisting environmentally displaced persons;

  (b) strengthening of drought preparedness and management, including drought contingency plans at the local, national, subregional and regional levels, which take into consideration seasonal to interannual climate predictions;

  (c) establishment and/or strengthening, as appropriate, of food security systems, including storage and marketing facilities, particularly in rural areas;

  (d) establishment of alternative livelihood projects that could provide incomes in drought prone areas; and

  (e) development of sustainable irrigation programmes for both crops and livestock.

4. Taking into account the circumstances and requirements specific to each affected country Party, national action programmes include, as appropriate, *inter alia*, measures in some or all of the following priority fields as they relate to combating desertification and mitigating the effects of drought in affected areas and to their populations: promotion of alternative livelihoods and improvement of national economic environments with a view to strengthening programmes aimed at the eradication of poverty and at ensuring food security, demographic dynamics, sustainable management of natural resources, sustainable agricultural practices, development and efficient use of various energy sources, institutional and legal frameworks, strengthening of capabilities for assessment and systematic observation, including hydrological and meteorological services, and capacity building, education and public awareness.

Article 11
Subregional and regional action programmes

Affected country parties shall consult and cooperate to prepare, as appropriate, in accordance with relevant regional implementation annexes, subregional and/or regional action programmes to harmonize, complement and increase the efficiency of national programmes. The provisions of Article 10 shall apply *mutatis mutandis* to subregional and regional programmes. Such cooperation may include agreed joint programmes for the sustainable management of transboundary natural resources, scientific and technical cooperation, and strengthening of relevant institutions.

Article 12
International cooperation

Affected country Parties, in collaboration with other Parties and the international community, should cooperate to ensure the promotion of an enabling international environment in the implementation of the Convention. Such cooperation should also cover fields of techology transfer as well as scientific research and development, information collection and dissemination and financial resources.

Article 13
Support for the elaboration and implementation of action programmes

1. Measures to support action programmes pursuant to Article 9 include, *inter alia*:

   (a) financial cooperation to provide predictability for action programmes, allowing for necessary long-term planning;
   (b) elaboration and use of cooperation mechanisms which better enable support at the local level, including action through non-governmental organizations, in order to promote the replicability of successful pilot programme activities where relevant;
   (c) increased flexibility in project design, funding and implementation in keeping with the experimental, iterative approach indicated for participatory action at the local community level; and
   (d) as appropriate, administrative and budgetary procedures that increase the efficiency of cooperation and of support programmes.

2. In providing such support to affected developing country Parties, priority shall be given to African country Parties and to least developed country Parties.

Article 14
Coordination in the elaboration and implementation of action programmes

1. The Parties shall work closely together, directly and through relevant intergovernmental organizations, in the elaboration and implementation of action programmes.

2. The Parties shall develop operational mechanisms, particularly at the national and field levels, to ensure the fullest possible coordination among developed country Parties, developing country Parties and relevant intergovernmental and non-governmental organizations, in order to avoid duplication, harmonize interventions and approaches, and maximize the impact of assistance. In affected developing country Parties, priority will be given to coordinating activities related to international cooperation in order to maximize the efficient use of resources, to ensure responsive

assistance, and to facilitate the implementation of national action programmes and priorities under this Convention.

Article 15
Regional implementation annexes

Elements for incorporation in action programmes shall be selected and
adapted to the socio-economic, geographical and climatic factors applicable to affected country Parties or regions, as well as to their level of
development. Guidelines for the preparation of action programmes and
their exact focus and content for particular subregions and regions are set
out in the regional implementation annexes.

SECTION 2: SCIENTIFIC AND TECHNICAL COOPERATION

Article 16
Information collection, analysis and exchange

The Parties agree, according to their respective capabilities, to integrate
and coordinate the collection, analysis and exchange of relevant short term
and long term data and information to ensure systematic observation of
land degradation in affected areas and to understand better and assess the
processes and effects of drought and desertification. This would help ac-
complish, *inter alia*, early warning and advance planning for periods of
adverse climatic variation in a form suited for practical application by users
at all levels, including especially local populations. To this end, they shall,
as appropriate:

(a) facilitate and strengthen the functioning of the global network of
institutions and facilities for the collection, analysis and exchange of
information, as well as for systematic observation at all levels, which
shall, *inter alia*:
  (i) aim to use compatible standards and systems;
  (ii) encompass relevant data and stations, including in remote
areas;
  (iii) use and disseminate modern technology for data collection,
transmission and assessment on land degradation; and
  (iv) link national, subregional and regional data and information
centres more closely with global information sources;
(b) ensure that the collection, analysis and exchange of information
address the needs of local communities and those of decision makers, with a view to resolving specific problems, and that local
communities are involved in these activities;
(c) support and further develop bilateral and multilateral programmes
and projects aimed at defining, conducting, assessing and financing

the collection, analysis and exchange of data and information, including, *inter alia*, integrated sets of physical, biological, social and
economic indicators;

(d) make full use of the expertise of competent intergovernmental and
non-governmental organizations, particularly to disseminate relevant information and experiences among target groups in different
regions;

(e) give full weight to the collection, analysis and exchange of socio-
economic data, and their integration with physical and biological
data;

(f) exchange and make fully, openly and promptly available information from all publicly available sources relevant to combating
desertification and mitigating the effects of drought; and

(g) subject to their respective national legislation and/or policies, exchange information on local and traditional knowledge, ensuring
adequate protection for it and providing appropriate return from
the benefits derived from it, on an equitable basis and on mutually
agreed terms, to the local populations concerned.

Article 17
Research and development

1. The Parties undertake, according to their respective capabilities, to
promote technical and scientific cooperation in the fields of combating
desertification and mitigating the effects of drought through appropriate
national, subregional, regional and international institutions. To this end,
they shall support research activities that:

(a) contribute to increased knowledge of the processes leading to
desertification and drought and the impact of, and distinction between, causal factors, both natural and human, with a view to combating desertification and mitigating the effects of drought, and
achieving improved productivity as well as sustainable use and management of resources;

(b) respond to well defined objectives, address the specific needs of local
populations and lead to the identification and implementation of
solutions that improve the living standards of people in affected
areas;

(c) protect, integrate, enhance and validate traditional and local
knowledge, know-how and practices, ensuring, subject to their
respective national legislation and/or policies, that the owners of
that knowledge will directly benefit on an equitable basis and
on mutually agreed terms from any commercial utilization of
it or from any technological development derived from that
knowledge;

(d) develop and strengthen national, subregional and regional research capabilities in affected developing country Parties, particularly in Africa, including the development of local skills and the strengthening of appropriate capacities, especially in countries with a weak research base, giving particular attention to multidisciplinary and participative socio-economic research;

(e) take into account, where relevant, the relationship between poverty, migration caused by environmental factors, and desertification;

(f) promote the conduct of joint research programmes between national, subregional, regional and international research organizations, in both the public and private sectors, for the development of improved, affordable and accessible technologies for sustainable development through effective participation of local populations and communities; and

(g) enhance the availability of water resources in affected areas, by means of, *inter alia*, cloud-seeding.

2. Research priorities for particular regions and subregions, reflecting different local conditions, should be included in action programmes. The Conference of the Parties shall review research priorities periodically on the advice of the Committee on Science and Technology.

Article 18
Transfer, acquisition, adaptation and development of technology

1. The Parties undertake, as mutually agreed and in accordance with their respective national legislation and/or policies, to promote, finance and/or facilitate the financing of the transfer, acquisition, adaptation and development of environmentally sound, economically viable and socially acceptable technologies relevant to combating desertification and/or mitigating the effects of drought, with a view to contributing to the achievement of sustainable development in affected areas. Such cooperation shall be conducted bilaterally or multilaterally, as appropriate, making full use of the expertise of intergovernmental and non-governmental organizations. The Parties shall, in particular:

(a) fully utilize relevant existing national, subregional, regional and international information systems and clearing-houses for the dissemination of information on available technologies, their sources, their environmental risks and the broad terms under which they may be acquired;

(b) facilitate access, in particular by affected developing country Parties, on favourable terms, including on concessional and preferential terms, as mutually agreed, taking into account the need to protect intellectual property rights, to technologies most suitable to practical application for specific needs of local populations, paying special attention to the social, cultural, economic and environmental impact of such technology;

(c) facilitate technology cooperation among affected country Parties through financial assistance or other appropriate means;

(d) extend technology cooperation with affected developing country Parties, including, where relevant, joint ventures, especially to sectors which foster alternative livelihoods; and

(e) take appropriate measures to create domestic market conditions and incentives, fiscal or otherwise, conducive to the development, transfer, acquisition and adaptation of suitable technology, knowledge, know-how and practices, including measures to ensure adequate and effective protection of intellectual property rights.

2. The Parties shall, according to their respective capabilities, and subject to their respective national legislation and/or policies, protect, promote and use in particular relevant traditional and local technology, knowledge, know-how and practices and, to that end, they undertake to:

(a) make inventories of such technology, knowledge, know-how and practices and their potential uses with the participation of local populations, and disseminate such information, where appropriate, in cooperation with relevant intergovernmental and non-governmental organizations;

(b) ensure that such technology, knowledge, know-how and practices are adequately protected and that local populations benefit directly, on an equitable basis and as mutually agreed, from any commercial utilization of them or from any technological development derived therefrom;

(c) encourage and actively support the improvement and dissemination of such technology, knowledge, know-how and practices or of the development of new technology based on them; and

(d) facilitate, as appropriate, the adaptation of such technology, knowledge, know-how and practices to wide use and integrate them with modern technology, as appropriate.

SECTION 3: SUPPORTING MEASURES

Article 19
Capacity building, education and public awareness

1. The Parties recognize the significance of capacity building — that is to say, institution building, training and development of relevant local and national capacities — in efforts to combat desertification and mitigate the effects of drought. They shall promote, as appropriate, capacity-building:

(a) through the full participation at all levels of local people, particularly at the local level, especially women and youth, with the cooperation of non-governmental and local organizations;

(b) by strengthening training and research capacity at the national level in the field of desertification and drought;

(c) by establishing and/or strengthening support and extension services to disseminate relevant technology methods and techniques more effectively, and by training field agents and members of rural organizations in participatory approaches for the conservation and sustainable use of natural resources;

(d) by fostering the use and dissemination of the knowledge, know-how and practices of local people in technical cooperation programmes, wherever possible;

(e) by adapting, where necessary, relevant environmentally sound technology and traditional methods of agriculture and pastoralism to modern socio-economic conditions;

(f) by providing appropriate training and technology in the use of alternative energy sources, particularly renewable energy resources, aimed particularly at reducing dependence on wood for fuel;

(g) through cooperation, as mutually agreed, to strengthen the capacity of affected developing country Parties to develop and implement programmes in the field of collection, analysis and exchange of information pursuant to Article 16;

(h) through innovative ways of promoting alternative livelihoods, including training in new skills;

(i) by training of decision makers, managers, and personnel who are responsible for the collection and analysis of data for the dissemination and use of early warning information on drought conditions and for food production;

(j) through more effective operation of existing national institutions and legal frameworks and, where necessary, creation of new ones, along with strengthening of strategic planning and management; and

(k) by means of exchange visitor programmes to enhance capacity building in affected country Parties through a long-term, interactive process of learning and study.

2. Affected developing country Parties shall conduct, in cooperation with other Parties and competent intergovernmental and non-governmental organizations, as appropriate, an interdisciplinary review of available capacity and facilities at the local and national levels, and the potential for strengthening them.

3. The Parties shall cooperate with each other and through competent intergovernmental organizations, as well as with non-governmental organizations, in undertaking and supporting public awareness and educa-

tional programmes in both affected and, where relevant, unaffected country Parties to promote understanding of the causes and effects of
desertification and drought and of the importance of meeting the objective
of this Convention. To that end, they shall:

(a) organize awareness campaigns for the general public;

(b) promote, on a permanent basis, access by the public to relevant
information, and wide public participation in education and awareness activities;

(c) encourage the establishment of associations that contribute to public awareness;

(d) develop and exchange educational and public awareness material,
where possible in local languages, exchange and second experts to
train personnel of affected developing country Parties in carrying
out relevant education and awareness programmes, and fully utilize
relevant educational material available in competent international
bodies;

(e) assess educational needs in affected areas, elaborate appropriate
school curricula and expand, as needed, educational and adult lit-
eracy programmes and opportunities for all, in particular for girls
and women, on the identification, conservation and sustainable use
and management of the natural resources of affected areas; and

(f) develop interdisciplinary participatory programmes integrating
desertification and drought awareness into educational systems and
in non-formal, adult, distance and practical educational programmes.

4. The Conference of the Parties shall establish and/or strengthen networks of regional education and training centres to combat desertification
and mitigate the effects of drought. These networks shall be coordinated by
an institution created or designated for that purpose, in order to train
scientific, technical and management personnel and to strengthen existing
institutions responsible for education and training in affected country
Parties, where appropriate, with a view to harmonizing programmes and to
organizing exchanges of experience among them. These networks shall
cooperate closely with relevant intergovernmental and non-governmental
organizations to avoid duplication of effort.

Article 20
Financial resources

1. Given the central importance of financing to the achievement of the
objective of the Convention, the Parties, taking into account their capabilities, shall make every effort to ensure that adequate financial resources are
available for programmes to combat desertification and mitigate the effects
of drought.

2. In this connection, developed country Parties, while giving priority to affected African country Parties without neglecting affected developing country Parties in other regions, in accordance with Article 7, undertake to:

(a) mobilize substantial financial resources, including grants and concessional loans, in order to support the implementation of programmes to combat desertification and mitigate the effects of drought;

(b) promote the mobilization of adequate, timely and predictable financial resources, including new and additional funding from the Global Environment Facility of the agreed incremental costs of those activities concerning desertification that relate to its four focal areas, in conformity with the relevant provisions of the Instrument establishing the Global Environment Facility;

(c) facilitate through international cooperation the transfer of technology, knowledge and know-how; and

(d) explore, in cooperation with affected developing country Parties, innovative methods and incentives for mobilizing and channelling resources, including those of foundations, non-governmental organizations and other private sector entities, particularly debt swaps and other innovative means which increase financing by reducing the external debt burden of affected developing country Parties, particularly those in Africa.

3. Affected developing country Parties, taking into account their capabilities, undertake to mobilize adequate financial resources for the implementation of their national action programmes.

4. In mobilizing financial resources, the Parties shall seek full use and continued qualitative improvement of all national, bilateral and multilateral funding sources and mechanisms, using consortia, joint programmes and parallel financing, and shall seek to involve private sector funding sources and mechanisms, including those of non-governmental organizations. To this end, the Parties shall fully utilize the operational mechanisms developed pursuant to Article 14.

5. In order to mobilize the financial resources necessary for affected developing country Parties to combat desertification and mitigate the effects of drought, the Parties shall:

(a) rationalize and strengthen the management of resources already allocated for combating desertification and mitigating the effects of drought by using them more effectively and efficiently, assessing their successes and shortcomings, removing hindrances to their effective use and, where necessary, re-orienting programmes in light of the integrated long-term approach adopted pursuant to this Convention;

(b) give due priority and attention within the governing bodies of multi-lateral financial institutions, facilities and funds, including regional development banks and funds, to supporting affected developing country Parties, particularly those in Africa, in activities which advance implementation of the Convention, notably action pro-grammes they undertake in the framework of regional implemen-tation annexes; and

(c) examine ways in which regional and sub-regional cooperation can be strengthened to support efforts undertaken at the national level.

6. Other country Parties are encouraged to provide, on a voluntary basis, knowledge, know-how and techniques related to desertification and/or financial resources to affected developing country Parties.

7. The full implementation by affected developing country Parties, particu-larly those in Africa, of their obligations under the Convention will be greatly assisted by the fulfilment by developed country Parties of their obligations under the Convention, including in particular those regarding financial resources and transfer of technology. In fulfilling their obli-gations, developed country Parties should take fully into account that economic and social development and poverty eradication are the first priorities of affected developing country Parties, particularly those in Africa.

Article 21
Financial mechanisms

1. The Conference of the Parties shall promote the availability of financial mechanisms and shall encourage such mechanisms to seek to maximize the availability of funding for affected developing country Parties, particularly those in Africa, to implement the Convention. To this end, the Conference of the Parties shall consider for adoption *inter alia* approaches and policies that:

(a) facilitate the provision of necessary funding at the national, subregional, regional and global levels for activities pursuant to relevant provisions of the Convention;

(b) promote multiple-source funding approaches, mechanisms and ar-rangements and their assessment, consistent with Article 20;

(c) provide on a regular basis, to interested Parties and relevant inter-governmental and non-governmental organizations, information on available sources of funds and on funding patterns in order to facilitate coordination among them;

(d) facilitate the establishment, as appropriate, of mechanisms, such as national desertification funds, including those involving the partici-pation of non-governmental organizations, to channel financial resources rapidly and efficiently to the local level in affected developing country Parties; and

(e) strengthen existing funds and financial mechanisms at the sub-regional and regional levels, particularly in Africa, to support more effectively the implementation of the Convention.

2. The Conference of the Parties shall also encourage the provision, through various mechanisms within the United Nations system and through multilateral financial institutions, of support at the national, sub-regional and regional levels to activities that enable developing country Parties to meet their obligations under the Convention.

3. Affected developing country Parties shall utilize, and where necessary, establish and/or strengthen, national coordinating mechanisms, integrated in national development programmes, that would ensure the efficient use of all available financial resources. They shall also utilize participatory processes involving non-governmental organizations, local groups and the private sector, in raising funds, in elaborating as well as implementing programmes and in assuring access to funding by groups at the local level. These actions can be enhanced by improved coordination and flexible programming on the part of those providing assistance.

4. In order to increase the effectiveness and efficiency of existing financial mechanisms, a Global Mechanism to promote actions leading to the mobilization and channelling of substantial financial resources, including for the transfer of technology, on a grant basis, and/or on concessional or other terms, to affected developing country Parties, is hereby established. This Global Mechanism shall function under the authority and guidance of the Conference of the Parties and be accountable to it.

5. The Conference of the Parties shall identify, at its first ordinary session, an organization to house the Global Mechanism. The Conference of the Parties and the organization it has identified shall agree upon modalities for this Global Mechanism to ensure *inter alia* that such Mechanism:

(a) identifies and draws up an inventory of relevant bilateral and multilateral cooperation programmes that are available to implement the Convention;

(b) provides advice, on request, to Parties on innovative methods of financing and sources of financial assistance and on improving the coordination of cooperation activities at the national level;

(c) provides interested Parties and relevant intergovernmental and non-governmental organizations with information on available sources of funds and on funding patterns in order to facilitate coordination among them; and

(d) reports to the Conference of the Parties, beginning at its second ordinary session, on its activities.

6. The Conference of the Parties shall, at its first session, make appropriate arrangements with the organization it has identified to house the Global Mechanism for the administrative operations of such Mechanism, drawing to the extent possible on existing budgetary and human resources.

7. The Conference of the Parties shall, at its third ordinary session, review the policies, operational modalities and activities of the Global Mechanism accountable to it pursuant to paragraph 4, taking into account the provisions of Article 7. On the basis of this review, it shall consider and take appropriate action.

Part IV

Institutions

Article 22
Conference of the Parties

1. A Conference of the Parties is hereby established.

2. The Conference of the Parties is the supreme body of the Convention. It shall make, within its mandate, the decisions necessary to promote its effective implementation. In particular, it shall:

(a) regularly review the implementation of the Convention and the functioning of its institutional arrangements in the light of the experience gained at the national, subregional, regional and international levels and on the basis of the evolution of scientific and technological knowledge;

(b) promote and facilitate the exchange of information on measures adopted by the Parties, and determine the form and timetable for transmitting the information to be submitted pursuant to Article 26, review the reports and make recommendations on them;

(c) establish such subsidiary bodies as are deemed necessary for the implementation of the Convention;

(d) review reports submitted by its subsidiary bodies and provide guidance to them;

(e) agree upon and adopt, by consensus, rules of procedure and financial rules for itself and any subsidiary bodies;

(f) adopt amendments to the Convention pursuant to Articles 30 and 31;

(g) approve a programme and budget for its activities, including those of its subsidiary bodies, and undertake necessary arrangements for their financing;

(h) as appropriate, seek the cooperation of, and utilize the services of and information provided by, competent bodies or agencies, whether national or international, intergovernmental or non-governmental;

(i) promote and strengthen the relationship with other relevant conventions while avoiding duplication of effort; and

(j) exercise such other functions as may be necessary for the achievement of the objective of the Convention.

3. The Conference of the Parties shall, at its first session, adopt its own rules of procedure, by consensus, which shall include decision-making procedures for matters not already covered by decision-making procedures stipulated in the Convention. Such procedures may include specified majorities required for the adoption of particular decisions.

4. The first session of the Conference of the Parties shall be convened by the interim secretariat referred to in Article 35 and shall take place not later than one year after the date of entry into force of the Convention. Unless otherwise decided by the Conference of the Parties, the second, third and fourth ordinary sessions shall be held yearly, and thereafter, ordinary sessions shall be held every two years.

5. Extraordinary sessions of the Conference of the Parties shall be held at such other times as may be decided either by the Conference of the Parties in ordinary session or at the written request of any Party, provided that, within three months of the request being communicated to the Parties by the Permanent Secretariat, it is supported by at least one-third of the Parties.

6. At each ordinary session, the Conference of the Parties shall elect a Bureau. The structure and functions of the Bureau shall be determined in the rules of procedure. In appointing the Bureau, due regard shall be paid to the need to ensure equitable geographical distribution and adequate representation of affected country Parties, particularly those in Africa.

7. The United Nations, its specialized agencies and any State member thereof or observers thereto not Party to the Convention, may be represented at sessions of the Conference of the Parties as observers. Any body or agency, whether national or international, governmental or non-governmental, which is qualified in matters covered by the Convention, and which has informed the Permanent Secretariat of its wish to be represented at a session of the Conference of the Parties as an observer, may be so admitted unless at least one-third of the Parties present object. The admission and participation of observers shall be subject to the rules of procedure adopted by the Conference of the Parties.

8. The Conference of the Parties may request competent national and international organizations which have relevant expertise to provide it with information relevant to Article 16, paragraph (g), Article 17, paragraph 1 (c) and Article 18, paragraph 2(b).

Article 23
Permanent Secretariat

1. A permanent Secretariat is hereby established.

2. The functions of the Permanent Secretariat shall be:

   (a) to make arrangements for sessions of the Conference of the Parties and its subsidiary bodies established under the Convention and to provide them with services as required;

   (b) to compile and transmit reports submitted to it;

   (c) to facilitate assistance to affected developing country Parties, on request, particularly those in Africa, in the compilation and communication of information required under the Convention;

   (d) to coordinate its activities with the secretariats of other relevant international bodies and conventions;

   (e) to enter, under the guidance of the Conference of the Parties, into such administrative and contractual arrangements as may be required for the effective discharge of its functions;

   (f) to prepare reports on the execution of its functions under this Convention and present them to the Conference of the Parties; and

   (g) to perform such other secretariat functions as may be determined by the Conference of the Parties.

3. The Conference of the Parties, at its first session, shall designate a Permanent Secretariat and make arrangements for its functioning.

Article 24
Committee on Science and Technology

1. A Committee on Science and Technology is hereby established as a subsidiary body of the Conference of the Parties to provide it with information and advice on scientific and technological matters relating to combating desertification and mitigating the effects of drought. The Committee shall meet in conjunction with the ordinary sessions of the Conference of the Parties and shall be multidisciplinary and open to the participation of all Parties. It shall be composed of government representatives competent in the relevant fields of expertise. The Conference of the Parties shall decide, at its first session, on the terms of reference of the Committee.

2. The Conference of the Parties shall establish and maintain a roster of independent experts with expertise and experience in the relevant fields. The roster shall be based on nominations received in writing from the Parties, taking into account the need for a multidisciplinary approach and broad geographical representation.

3. The Conference of the Parties may, as necessary, appoint *ad hoc* panels to provide it, through the Committee, with information and advice on

specific issues regarding the state of the art in fields of science and technology relevant to combating desertification and mitigating the effects of drought. These panels shall be composed of experts whose names are taken from the roster, taking into account the need for a multidisciplinary approach and broad geographical representation. These experts shall have scientific backgrounds and field experience and shall be appointed by the Conference of the Parties on the recommendation of the Committee. The Conference of the Parties shall decide on the terms of reference and the modalities of work of these panels.

Article 25
Networking of institutions, agencies and bodies

1. The Committee on Science and Technology shall, under the supervision of the Conference of the Parties, make provision for the undertaking of a survey and evaluation of the relevant existing networks, institutions, agencies and bodies willing to become units of a network. Such a network shall support the implementation of the Convention.

2. On the basis of the results of the survey and evaluation referred to in paragraph 1, the Committee on Science and Technology shall make recommendations to the Conference of the Parties on ways and means to facilitate and strengthen networking of the units at the local, national and other levels, with a view to ensuring that the thematic needs set out in Articles 16 to 19 are addressed.

3. Taking into account these recommendations, the Conference of the Parties shall:

   (a) identify those national, subregional, regional and international units that are most appropriate for networking, and recommend operational procedures, and a time frame, for them; and

   (b) identify the units best suited to facilitating and strengthening such networking at all levels.

Part V
Procedures

Article 26
Communication of information

1. Each Party shall communicate to the Conference of the Parties for consideration at its ordinary sessions, through the Permanent Secretariat, reports on the measures which it has taken for the implementation of the Convention. The Conference of the Parties shall determine the timetable for submission and the format of such reports.

2. Affected country Parties shall provide a description of the strategies

established pursuant to Article 5 and of any relevant information on their implementation.

3. Affected country Parties which implement action programmes pursuant to Articles 9 to 15 shall provide a detailed description of the programmes and of their implementation.

4. Any group of affected country Parties may make a joint communication on measures taken at the subregional and/or regional levels in the framework of action programmes.

5. Developed country Parties shall report on measures taken to assist in the preparation and implementation of action programmes, including information on the financial resources they have provided, or are providing, under the Convention.

6. Information communicated pursuant to paragraphs 1 to 4 shall be transmitted by the Permanent Secretariat as soon as possible to the Conference of the Parties and to any relevant subsidiary body.

7. The Conference of the Parties shall facilitate the provision to affected developing countries, particularly those in Africa, on request, of technical and financial support in compiling and communicating information in accordance with this Article, as well as identifying the technical and financial needs associated with action programmes.

Article 27
Measures to resolve questions on implementation

The Conference of the Parties shall consider and adopt procedures and institutional mechanisms for the resolution of questions that may arise with regard to the implementation of the Convention.

Article 28
Settlement of disputes

1. Parties shall settle any dispute between them concerning the interpretation or application of the Convention through negotiation or other peaceful means of their own choice.

2. When ratifying, accepting, approving, or acceding to the Convention, or at any time thereafter, a Party which is not a regional economic integration organization may declare in a written instrument submitted to the Depositary that, in respect of any dispute concerning the interpretation or application of the Convention, it recognizes one or both of the following means of dispute settlement as compulsory in relation to any Party accepting the same obligation:

  (a) arbitration in accordance with a procedure adopted by the Conference of the Parties in an annex as soon as practicable;
  (b) submission of the dispute to the International Court of Justice.

3. A Party which is a regional economic integration organization may make a declaration with like effect in relation to arbitration in accordance with the procedure referred to in paragraph 2(a).

4. A declaration made pursuant to paragraph 2 shall remain in force until it expires in accordance with its terms or until three months after written notice of its revocation has been deposited with the Depositary.

5. The expiry of a declaration, a notice of revocation or a new declaration shall not in any way affect proceedings pending before an arbitral tribunal or the International Court of Justice unless the Parties to the dispute otherwise agree.

6. If the Parties to a dispute have not accepted the same or any procedure pursuant to paragraph 2 and if they have not been able to settle their dispute within twelve months following notification by one Party to another that a dispute exists between them, the dispute shall be submitted to conciliation at the request of any Party to the dispute, in accordance with procedure adopted by the Conference of the Parties in an annex as soon as practicable.

Article 29
Status of annexes

1. Annexes form an integral part of the Convention and, unless expressly provided otherwise, a reference to the Convention also constitutes a reference to its annexes.

2. The Parties shall interpret the provisions of the annexes in a manner that is in conformity with their rights and obligations under the Articles of this Convention.

Article 30
Amendments to the Convention

1. Any Party may propose amendments to the Convention.

2. Amendments to the Convention shall be adopted at an ordinary session of the Conference of the Parties. The text of any proposed amendment shall be communicated to the Parties by the Permanent Secretariat at least six months before the meeting at which it is proposed for adoption. The Permanent Secretariat shall also communicate proposed amendments to the signatories to the Convention.

3. The Parties shall make every effort to reach agreement on any proposed amendment to the Convention by consensus. If all efforts at consensus have been exhausted and no agreement reached, the amendment shall, as a last resort, be adopted by a two-thirds majority vote of the Parties present and voting at the meeting. The adopted amendment shall be communicated by the Permanent Secretariat to the Depositary, who shall circulate it to all Parties for their ratification, acceptance, approval or accession.

4. Instruments of ratification, acceptance, approval or accession in respect

of an amendment shall be deposited with the Depositary. An amendment adopted pursuant to paragraph 3 shall enter into force for those Parties having accepted it on the ninetieth day after the date of receipt by the Depositary of an instrument of ratification, acceptance, approval or accession by at least two-thirds of the Parties to the Convention which were Parties at the time of the adoption of the amendment.

5. The amendment shall enter into force for any other Party on the ninetieth day after the date on which that Party deposits with the Depositary its instrument of ratification, acceptance or approval of, or accession to the said amendment.

6. For the purposes of this Article and Article 31, 'Parties present and voting' means Parties present and casting an affirmative or negative vote.

Article 31
Adoption and amendment of annexes

1. Any additional annex to the Convention and any amendment to an annex shall be proposed and adopted in accordance with the procedure for amendment of the Convention set forth in Article 30, provided that, in adopting an additional regional implementation annex or amendment to any regional implementation annex, the majority provided for in that Article shall include a two-thirds majority vote of the Parties of the region concerned present and voting. The adoption or amendment of an annex shall be communicated by the Depositary to all Parties.

2. An annex, other than an additional regional implementation annex, or an amendment to an annex, other than an amendment to any regional implementation annex, that has been adopted in accordance with paragraph 1, shall enter into force for all Parties to the Convention six months after the date of communication by the Depositary to such Parties of the adoption of such annex or amendment, except for those Parties that have notified the Depositary in writing within that period of their non-acceptance of such annex or amendment. Such annex or amendment shall enter into force for Parties which withdraw their notification of non-acceptance on the ninetieth day after the date on which withdrawal of such notification has been received by the Depositary.

3. An additional regional implementation annex or amendment to any regional implementation annex that has been adopted in accordance with paragraph 1, shall enter into force for all Parties to the Convention six months after the date of the communication by the Depositary to such Parties of the adoption of such annex or amendment, except with respect to:

    (a) any Party that has notified the Depositary in writing, within such six month period, of its non-acceptance of that additional regional implementation annex or of the amendment to the regional implementation annex, in which case such annex or amendment shall enter into force for Parties which withdraw their notification of non-acceptance on the ninetieth day after the date on which withdrawal of such notification has been received by the Depositary; and

(b) any Party that has made a declaration with respect to additional regional implementation annexes or amendments to regional implementation annexes in accordance with Article 34, paragraph 4, in which case any such annex or amendment shall enter into force for such a Party on the ninetieth day after the date of deposit with the Depositary of its instrument of ratification, acceptance, approval or accession with respect to such annex or amendment.

4. If the adoption of an annex or an amendment to an annex involves an amendment to the Convention, that annex or amendment to an annex shall not enter into force until such time as the amendment to the Convention enters into force.

Article 32
Right to vote

1. Except as provided for in paragraph 2, each Party to the Convention shall have one vote.

2. Regional economic integration organizations, in matters within their competence, shall exercise their right to vote with a number of votes equal to the number of their member States that are Parties to the Convention. Such an organization shall not exercise its right to vote if any of its member States exercises its right, and vice versa.

Part VI
Final Provisions

Article 33
Signature

This Convention shall be opened for signature at Paris, on 14–15 October 1994, by States Members of the United Nations or any of its specialized agencies or that are Parties to the Statute of the International Court of Justice and by regional economic integration organizations. It shall remain open for signature, thereafter, at the United Nations Headquarters in New York until 13 October 1995.

Article 34
Ratification, acceptance, approval and accession

1. The Convention shall be subject to ratification, acceptance, approval or accession by States and by regional economic integration organizations. It

shall be open for accession from the day after the date on which the Convention is closed for signature. Instruments of ratification, acceptance, approval or accession shall be deposited with the Depositary.

2. Any regional economic integration organization which becomes a Party to the Convention without any of its member States being a Party to the Convention shall be bound by all the obligations under the Convention. Where one or more member States of such an organization are also Party to the Convention, the organization and its member States shall decide on their respective responsibilities for the performance of their obligations under the Convention. In such cases, the organization and the member States shall not be entitled to exercise rights under the Convention concurrently.

3. In their instruments of ratification, acceptance, approval or accession, regional economic integration organizations shall declare the extent of their competence with respect to the matters governed by the Convention. They shall also promptly inform the Depositary, who shall in turn inform the Parties, of any substantial modification in the extent of their competence.

4. In its instrument of ratification, acceptance, approval or accession, any Party may declare that, with respect to it, any additional regional implementation annex or any amendment to any regional implementation annex shall enter into force only upon the deposit of its instrument of ratification, acceptance, approval or accession with respect thereto.

Article 35
Interim arrangements

The secretariat functions referred to in Article 23 will be carried out on an interim basis by the secretariat established by the General Assembly of the United Nations in its resolution 47/188 of 22 December 1992, until the completion of the first session of the Conference of the Parties.

Article 36
Entry into force

1. The Convention shall enter into force on the ninetieth day after the date of deposit of the fiftieth instrument of ratification, acceptance, approval or accession.

2. For each State or regional economic integration organization ratifying, accepting, approving or acceding to the Convention after the deposit of the fiftieth instrument of ratification, acceptance, approval or accession, the Convention shall enter into force on the ninetieth day after the date of deposit by such State or regional economic integration organization of its instrument of ratification, acceptance, approval or accession.

3. For the purposes of paragraphs 1 and 2, any instrument deposited by a regional economic integration organization shall not be counted as additional to those deposited by States members of the organization.

Article 37
Reservations

No reservations may be made to this Convention.

Article 38
Withdrawal

1. At any time after three years from the date on which the Convention has entered into force for a Party, that Party may withdraw from the Convention by giving written notification to the Depositary.

2. Any such withdrawal shall take effect upon expiry of one year from the date of receipt by the Depositary of the notification of withdrawal, or on such later date as may be specified in the notification of withdrawal.

Article 39
Depositary

The Secretary-General of the United Nations shall be the Depositary of the Convention.

Article 40
Authentic texts

The original of the present Convention, of which the Arabic, Chinese, English, French, Russian and Spanish texts are equally authentic, shall be deposited with the Secretary-General of the United Nations.

IN WITNESS WHEREOF the undersigned, being duly authorized to that effect, have signed the present Convention.

DONE AT Paris, this 17th day of June one thousand nine hundred and ninety-four.

Annex I
Regional Implementation Annex for Africa

Article 1
Scope

This Annex applies to Africa, in relation to each Party and in conformity with the Convention, in particular its Article 7, for the purpose of combating desertification and/or mitigating the effects of drought in its arid, semi-arid and dry sub-humid areas.

Article 2
Purpose

The purpose of this Annex, at the national, subregional and regional levels in Africa and in the light of its particular conditions, is to:

(a) identify measures and arrangements, including the nature and processes of assistance provided by developed country Parties, in accordance with the relevant provisions of the Convention;

(b) provide for the efficient and practical implementation of the Convention to address conditions specific to Africa; and

(c) promote processes and activities relating to combating desertification and/or mitigating the effects of drought within the arid, semi-arid and dry sub-humid areas of Africa.

Article 3
Particular conditions of the African region

In carrying out their obligations under the Convention, the Parties shall, in the implementation of this Annex, adopt a basic approach that takes into consideration the following particular conditions of Africa:

(a) the high proportion of arid, semi-arid and dry sub-humid areas;

(b) the substantial number of countries and populations adversely affected by desertification and by the frequent recurrence of severe drought;

(c) the large number of affected countries that are landlocked;

(d) the widespread poverty prevalent in most affected countries, the large number of least developed countries among them, and their need for significant amounts of external assistance, in the form of grants and loans on concessional terms, to pursue their development objectives;

(e) the difficult socio-economic conditions, exacerbated by deteriorating and fluctuating terms of trade, external indebtedness and political instability, which induce internal, regional and international migrations;

(f) the heavy reliance of populations on natural resources for subsistence which, compounded by the effects of demographic trends and factors, a weak technological base and unsustainable production practices, contributes to serious resource degradation;

(g) the insufficient institutional and legal frameworks, the weak infrastructural base and the insufficient scientific, technical and educational capacity, leading to substantial capacity building requirements; and

(h) the central role of actions to combat desertification and/or mitigate the effects of drought in the national development priorities of affected African countries.

Article 4
Commitments and obligations of African country Parties

1. In accordance with their respective capabilities, African country Parties undertake to:

(a) adopt the combating of desertification and/or the mitigation of the effects of drought as a central strategy in their efforts to eradicate poverty;

(b) promote regional cooperation and integration, in a spirit of solidarity and partnership based on mutual interest, in programmes and activities to combat desertification and/or mitigate the effects of drought;

(c) rationalize and strengthen existing institutions concerned with desertification and drought and involve other existing institutions, as appropriate, in order to make them more effective and to ensure more efficient use of resources;

(d) promote the exchange of information on appropriate technology, knowledge, know-how and practices between and among them; and

(e) develop contingency plans for mitigating the effects of drought in areas degraded by desertification and/or drought.

2. Pursuant to the general and specific obligations set out in Articles 4 and 5 of the Convention, affected African country Parties shall aim to:

(a) make appropriate financial allocations from their national budgets consistent with national conditions and capabilities and reflecting the new priority Africa has accorded to the phenomenon of desertification and/or drought;

(b) sustain and strengthen reforms currently in progress toward greater decentralization and resource tenure as well as reinforce participation of local populations and communities; and

(c) identify and mobilize new and additional national financial resources, and expand, as a matter of priority, existing national capabilities and facilities to mobilize domestic financial resources.

Article 5
Commitments and obligations of developed country Parties

1. In fulfilling their obligations pursuant to Articles 4, 6 and 7 of the Convention, developed country Parties shall give priority to affected African country Parties and, in this context, shall:

(a) assist them to combat desertification and/or mitigate the effects of drought by, *inter alia*, providing and/or facilitating access to financial and/or other resources, and promoting, financing and/or facilitating the financing of the transfer, adaptation and access to appropriate environmental technologies and know-how, as mutually agreed and in accordance with national policies, taking into account their adoption of poverty eradication as a central strategy;

(b) continue to allocate significant resources and/or increase resources to combat desertification and/or mitigate the effects of drought; and

(c) assist them in strengthening capacities to enable them to improve their institutional frameworks, as well as their scientific and technical capabilities, information collection and analysis, and research and development for the purpose of combating desertification and/or mitigating the effects of drought.

2. Other country Parties may provide, on a voluntary basis, technology, knowledge and know-how relating to desertification and/or financial resources, to affected African country Parties. The transfer of such knowledge, know-how and techniques is facilitated by international cooperation.

Article 6
Strategic planning framework for sustainable development

1. National action programmes shall be a central and integral part of a broader process of formulating national policies for the sustainable development of affected African country Parties.

2. A consultative and participatory process involving appropriate levels of government, local populations, communities and non-governmental organizations shall be undertaken to provide guidance on a strategy with flexible planning to allow maximum participation from local populations and communities. As appropriate, bilateral and multilateral assistance agencies may be involved in this process at the request of an affected African country Party.

Article 7
Timetable for preparation of action programmes

Pending entry into force of this Convention, the African country Parties, in cooperation with other members of the international community, as appropriate, shall, to the extent possible, provisionally apply those provisions of the Convention relating to the preparation of national, subregional and regional action programmes.

Article 8
Content of national action programmes

1. Consistent with Article 10 of the Convention, the overall strategy of national action programme shall emphasize integrated local development programmes for affected areas, based on participatory mechanisms and on

integration of strategies for poverty eradication into efforts to combat desertification and mitigate the effects of drought. The programmes shall aim at strengthening the capacity of local authorities and ensuring the active involvement of local populations, communities and groups, with emphasis on education and training, mobilization of non-governmental organizations with proven expertise and strengthening of decentralized governmental structures.

2. National action programmes shall, as appropriate, include the following general features:

(a) the use, in developing and implementing national action programmes, of past experiences in combating desertification and/or mitigating the effects of drought, taking into account social, economic and ecological conditions;

(b) the identification of factors contributing to desertification and/or drought and the resources and capacities available and required, and the setting up of appropriate policies and institutional and other responses and measures necessary to combat those phenomena and/or mitigate their effects; and

(c) the increase in participation of local populations and communities, including women, farmers and pastoralists, and delegation to them of more responsibility for management.

3. National action programmes shall also, as appropriate, include the following:

(a) measures to improve the economic environment with a view to eradicating poverty:
   (i) increasing incomes and employment opportunities, especially for the poorest members of the community, by:
      — developing markets for farm and livestock products;
      — creating financial instruments suited to local needs;
      — encouraging diversification in agriculture and the setting-up of agricultural enterprises; and
      — developing economic activities of a para-agricultural or non-agricultural type;
   (ii) improving the long-term prospects of rural economies by the creation of:
      — incentives for productive investment and access to the means of production; and
      — price and tax policies and commercial practices that promote growth;
   (iii) defining and applying population and migration policies to reduce population pressure on land; and

       (iv) promoting the use of drought resistant crops and the appli-
cation of integrated dry-land farming systems for food security
purposes;

(b) measures to conserve natural resources:

       (i) ensuring integrated and sustainable management of natural
resources, including:

— agricultural land and pastoral land;

— vegetation cover and wildlife;

— forests;

— water resources; and

— biological diversity;

      (ii) training with regard to, and strengthening, public awareness
and environmental education campaigns and disseminating
knowledge of techniques relating to the sustainable management of natural resources; and

     (iii) ensuring the development and efficient use of diverse energy
sources, the promotion of alternative sources of energy, particularly solar energy, wind energy and bio-gas, and specific
arrangements for the transfer, acquisition and adaptation of
relevant technology to alleviate the pressure on fragile natural
resources;

(c) measures to improve institutional organization:

       (i) defining the roles and responsibilities of central government
and local authorities within the framework of a land use planning policy;

      (ii) encouraging a policy of active decentralization, devolving re-
sponsibility for management and decision-making to local
authorities, and encouraging initiatives and the assumption of
responsibility by local communities and the establishment of
local structures; and

     (iii) adjusting, as appropriate, the institutional and regulatory
framework of natural resource management to provide security
of land tenure for local populations;

(d) measures to improve knowledge of desertification:

       (i) promoting research and the collection, processing and ex-
change of information on the scientific, technical and socio-
economic aspects of desertification;

      (ii) improving national capabilities in research and in the collec-
tion, processing, exchange and analysis of information so as to
increase understanding and to translate the results of the analysis into operational terms; and

     (iii) encouraging the medium and long-term study of:

— socio-economic and cultural trends in affected areas;

— qualitative and quantitative trends in natural resources; and

— the interaction between climate and desertification; and
(e) measures to monitor and assess the effects of drought:
  (i) developing strategies to evaluate the impacts of natural climate variability on regional drought and desertification and/or to utilize predictions of climate variability on seasonal to interannual time scales in efforts to mitigate the effects of drought;
  (ii) improving early warning and response capacity, efficiently managing emergency relief and food aid, and improving food stocking and distribution systems, cattle protection schemes and public works and alternative livelihoods for drought prone areas; and
  (iii) monitoring and assessing ecological degradation to provide reliable and timely information on the process and dynamics of resource degradation in order to facilitate better policy formulations and responses.

Article 9
Preparation of national action programmes and implementation and evaluation indicators

Each affected African country Party shall designate an appropriate national coordinating body to function as a catalyst in the preparation, implementation and evaluation of its national action programme. This coordinating body shall, in the light of Article 3 and as appropriate:

(a) undertake an identification and review of actions, beginning with a locally driven consultation process, involving local populations and communities and with the cooperation of local administrative authorities, developed country Parties and intergovernmental and non-governmental organizations, on the basis of initial consultations of those concerned at the national level;
(b) identify and analyze the constraints, needs and gaps affecting development and sustainable land use and recommend practical measures to avoid duplication by making full use of relevant ongoing efforts and promote implementation of results;
(c) facilitate, design and formulate project activities based on interactive, flexible approaches in order to ensure active participation of the population in affected areas, to minimize the negative impact of such activities, and to identify and prioritize requirements for financial assistance and technical cooperation;
(d) establish pertinent, quantifiable and readily verifiable indicators to ensure the assessment and evaluation of national action programmes, which encompass actions in the short, medium and long terms, and of the implementation of such programmes; and

(e) prepare progress reports on the implementation of the national action programmes.

Article 10
Organizational framework of subregional action programmes

1. Pursuant to Article 4 of the Convention, African country Parties shall cooperate in the preparation and implementation of subregional action programmes for central, eastern, northern, southern and western Africa and, in that regard, may delegate the following responsibilities to relevant subregional intergovernmental organizations:

(a) acting as focal points for preparatory activities and coordinating the implementation of the subregional action programmes;

(b) assisting in the preparation and implementation of national action programmes;

(c) facilitating the exchange of information, experience and know-how as well as providing advice on the review of national legislation; and

(d) any other responsibilities relating to the implementation of subregional action programmes.

2. Specialized subregional institutions may provide support, upon request, and/or be entrusted with the responsibility to coordinate activities in their respective fields of competence.

Article 11
Content and preparation of subregional action programmes

Subregional action programmes shall focus on issues that are better addressed at the subregional level. They shall establish, where necessary, mechanisms for the management of shared natural resources. Such mechanisms shall effectively handle transboundary problems associated with desertification and/or drought and shall provide support for the harmonious implementation of national action programmes. Priority areas for subregional action programmes shall, as appropriate, focus on:

(a) joint programmes for the sustainable management of transboundary natural resources through bilateral and multilateral mechanisms, as appropriate;

(b) coordination of programmes to develop alternative energy sources;

(c) cooperation in the management and control of pests as well as of plant and animal diseases;

(d) capacity building, education and public awareness activities that are better carried out or supported at the subregional level;

(e) scientific and technical cooperation, particularly in the climatological, meteorological and hydrological fields, including networking for data collection and assessment, information sharing and project monitoring, and coordination and prioritization of research and development activities;

(f) early warning systems and joint planning for mitigating the effects of drought, including measures to address the problems resulting from environmentally induced migrations;

(g) exploration of ways of sharing experiences, particularly regarding participation of local populations and communities, and creation of an enabling environment for improved land use management and for use of appropriate technologies;

(h) strengthening of the capacity of subregional organizations to coordinate and provide technical services, as well as establishment, reorientation and strengthening of subregional centres and institutions; and

(i) development of policies in fields, such as trade, which have impact upon affected areas and populations, including policies for the coordination of regional marketing regimes and for common infrastructure.

Article 12
Organizational framework of the regional action programme

1. Pursuant to Article 11 of the Convention, African country Parties shall jointly determine the procedures for preparing and implementing the regional action programme.

2. The Parties may provide appropriate support to relevant African regional institutions and organizations to enable them to assist African country Parties to fulfil their responsibilities under the Convention.

Article 13
Content of the regional action programme

The regional action programme includes measures relating to combating desertification and/or mitigating the effects of drought in the following priority areas, as appropriate:

(a) development of regional cooperation and coordination of subregional action programmes for building regional consensus on key policy areas, including through regular consultations of subregional organizations;

(b) promotion of capacity building in activities which are better implemented at the regional level;

(c) the seeking of solutions with the international community to global economic and social issues that have an impact on affected areas taking into account Article 4, paragraph 2(b) of the Convention;

(d) promotion among the affected country Parties of Africa and its subregions, as well as with other affected regions, of exchange of

information and appropriate techniques, technical know-how and
relevant experience;

(e) promotion of scientific and technological cooperation particularly
in the fields of climatology, meteorology, hydrology, water resource
development and alternative energy sources;

(f) coordination of sub-regional and regional research activities and
identification of regional priorities for research and development;

(g) coordination of networks for systematic observation and assessment
and information exchange, as well as their integration into world
wide networks; and

(h) coordination of and reinforcement of sub-regional and regional
early warning systems and drought contingency plans.

Article 14
Financial resources

1. Pursuant to Article 20 of the Convention and Article 4, paragraph 2,
affected African country Parties shall endeavour to provide a
macroeconomic framework conducive to the mobilization of financial resources and shall develop policies and establish procedures to channel
resources more effectively to local development programmes, including
through non-governmental organizations, as appropriate.

2. Pursuant to Article 21, paragraphs 4 and 5 of the Convention, the
Parties agree to establish an inventory of sources of funding at the
national, subregional, regional and international levels to ensure the rational use of existing resources and to identify gaps in resource allocation,
to facilitate implementation of the action programmes. The inventory shall
be regularly reviewed and up-dated.

3. Consistent with Article 7 of the Convention, the developed country
Parties shall continue to allocate significant resources and/or increased
resources and other forms of assistance to affected African country Parties
on the basis of partnership agreements and arrangements referred to in
Article 18, giving, *inter alia*, due attention to matters related to debt, international trade and marketing arrangements in accordance with Article 4,
paragraph 2(b) of the Convention.

Article 15
Financial Mechanisms

1. Consistent with Article 7 of the Convention and considering the particular situation prevailing in this region, the Parties shall pay special attention
to the implementation in Africa of the provisions of Article 21, paragraph
1(d) and (e) of the Convention, notably by:

(a) facilitating the establishment of mechanisms, such as national
desertification funds, to channel financial resources to the local
level; and

(b) strengthening existing funds and financial mechanisms at the subregional and regional levels.

2. Consistent with Articles 20 and 21 of the Convention, the Parties which are also members of the governing bodies of relevant regional and subregional financial institutions, including the African Development Bank and the African Development Fund, shall promote efforts to give due priority and attention to the activities of those institutions that advance the implementation of this Annex.

3. The Parties shall streamline, to the extent possible, procedures for channelling funds to affected African country Parties.

Article 16
Technical assistance and cooperation

The Parties undertake, in accordance with their respective capabilities, to rationalize technical assistance to, and cooperation with, African country Parties with a view to increasing project and programme effectiveness by, *inter alia*:

(a) limiting the costs of support measures and backstopping, especially overhead costs, so that, in any case, such costs shall only represent an appropriately low percentage of the total cost of the project so as to maximize project efficiency;

(b) giving preference to the utilization of competent national experts or, where necessary, competent experts from within the subregion and/or region, in project design, preparation and implementation, and to the building of local expertise where it does not exist; and

(c) effectively managing and coordinating, as well as efficiently utilizing, technical assistance to be provided.

Article 17
Transfer, acquisition, adaptation and access to environmentally sound technology

In implementing Article 18 of the Convention relating to transfer, acquisition, adaptation and development of technology, the Parties undertake to give priority to African country Parties and, as necessary, to develop with them new models of partnership and cooperation with a view to strengthening capacity building in the fields of scientific research and development and information collection and dissemination to enable them to implement their strategies to combat desertification and mitigate the effects of drought.

Article 18
Coordination and partnership agreements

1. African country Parties shall coordinate the preparation, negotiation and implementation of national, subregional and regional action pro-

grammes. They may involve, as appropriate, other Parties and relevant intergovernmental and non-governmental organizations in this process.

2. The objectives of such coordination shall be to ensure that financial and technical cooperation is consistent with the Convention and to provide the necessary continuity in the use and administration of resources.

3. African country Parties shall organize consultative processes at the national, subregional and regional levels. These consultative processes may:

  (a) serve as a forum to negotiate and conclude partnership agreements based on national, subregional and regional action programmes; and

  (b) specify the contribution of African country Parties and other members of the consultative groups to the programmes and identify priorities and agreements on implementation and evaluation indicators, as well as funding arrangements for implementation.

4. The Permanent Secretariat may, at the request of African country Parties, pursuant to Article 23 of the Convention, facilitate the convocation of such consultative processes by:

  (a) providing advice on the organization of effective consultative arrangements, drawing on experiences from other such arrangements;

  (b) providing information to relevant bilateral and multilateral agencies concerning consultative meetings or processes, and encouraging their active involvement; and

  (c) providing other information that may be relevant in establishing or improving consultative arrangements.

5. The subregional and regional coordinating bodies shall, *inter alia*:

  (a) recommend appropriate adjustments to partnership agreements;

  (b) monitor, assess and report on the implementation of the agreed subregional and regional programmes; and

  (c) aim to ensure efficient communication and cooperation among African country Parties.

6. Participation in the consultative groups shall, as appropriate, be open to Governments, interested groups and donors, relevant organs, funds and programmes of the United Nations system, relevant subregional and regional organizations, and representatives of relevant non-governmental organizations. Participants of each consultative group shall determine the modalities of its management and operation.

7. Pursuant to Article 14 of the Convention, developed country Parties are encouraged to develop, on their own initiative, an informal process of consultation and coordination among themselves, at the country,

subregional and regional levels, and, at the request of an affected African country Party or of an appropriate subregional or regional organization, to participate in a national, subregional or regional consultative process that would evaluate and respond to assistance needs in order to facilitate implementation.

Article 19
Follow-up arrangements

Follow-up of this annex shall be carried out by African country Parties in accordance with the Convention as follow:

(a) at the national level, by a mechanism the composition of which should be determined by each affected African country Party and which shall include representatives of local communities and shall function under the supervision of the national coordinating body referred to in Article 9;

(b) at the subregional level, by a multidisciplinary scientific and technical consultative committee, the composition and modalities of operation of which shall be determined by the African country Parties of the subregion concerned; and

(c) at the regional level, by mechanisms defined in accordance with the relevant provisions of the Treaty establishing the African Economic Community, and by an African Scientific and Technical Advisory Committee.

[ANNEXES II–IV OMITTED]

International Tropical Timber Agreement, Geneva, 26 January 1994

World Forestry Congresses from the 1960s onwards repeatedly warned of the ecological consequences of excessive destruction of tropical forests. Such global concerns led to calls from developed states for international regulation. Developing states, however, stressed their right to exploit the natural resources within territory over which they had sovereignty, on which see Treaty of the Amazonian Co-operation of 1978 (text in 17 *ILM* (1978) 1045) re-iterating that this right to develop forest resources was subject only to restrictions arising from international agreement.

The impact of the UNCHE Declaration of Principles governing the Human Environment, especially Principle 21, and Recommendations 24–32 concerning forests in the UNCHE Action Plan led from 1972 onwards to the development of various strategies to limit destruction and preserve biological diversity. Following proposals emerging through FAO's consultation group on international agricultural research and its International Board for Plant Genetic Resources, and UNEP's Ecosystem Task Force acting in co-operation with the International Council for Agro-Forestry, and studies under the auspices of IUCN, UNEP sponsored a global meeting on deforestation in Libreville, Gabon, in 1980. Nine African States also held a meeting at Yaoundé, Cameroon, in 1980 and agreed on articles of a treaty designed to improve forest management. Following UNESCO initiatives, with UNEP backing, a regional centre for Scientific Information and Documentation in Tropical Ecology was established in Yaoundé. After six years of negotiation under the auspices of UNCTAD and an FAO/UNEP Tropical Forest Assessment in 1982, an International Tropical Timber Agreement was concluded at Geneva in 1983, in the form of a commodity agreement establishing the International Tropical Timber Organisation (ITTO) (text in UN Doc TD–Timber–11, 25 November 1983). The forty-three parties to this comprised twenty-five timber producers and eighteen timber consumers. It aimed to limit the export of timber and encourage sustainable use, but was subsequently regarded as inadequate in many respects. Moreover although tropical forest states in Latin America and the Caribbean recognised the need to protect and preserve the cultural, economic, and ecological heritage of the Amazonian regions and to co-operate with other countries, they called also for developed states to co-operate by providing finance and technology, and reserved the right to set their own priorities, consistent with sovereignty over their resources. (See the Amazon Declaration, 6 May 1989, Manaus, Brazil; Declaration of Brasilia on the Environment, 31 March 1989; *repr.* in R. Churchill and D. Freestone (eds), *International Law and Global Climate Change*, (London, 1991), 324–5 and 320–22 respectively).

As concern grew, especially in relation to the role of tropical forest in the climate change process, the World Bank, UNEP, FAO, and the World Resources Institute in 1985 established a Tropical Forest Action Plan (FAO, Rome, 1989) to provide a broad framework for action backed by financial support. In response to the 1987 report of the World Commission on Environment and Development (*Our Common Future*, Oxford, 1987), a proposal for the conclusion of an international convention to put the conservation and management of forests on a more sustainable basis was put forward in 1989 by an FAO working party. During negotiations leading to adoption by ITTO of 'Criteria for and Measurements of Sustainable Forest Management' (Decision 3(XII) of the ITTO Council, Doc. ITTC (XII) 14, 14 May 1992), the addition to the forthcoming UNCED Climate Change Convention of a protocol on forests was proposed. During the UNCED preparatory processes various proposals and drafts were introduced (see in particular FAO Committee on Forestry, Proposal for an International Convention on Conservation and Development of Forests, Tenth Session, Rome, 24–28 September 1990, Doc. COFO–96/3(a), September 1990). The contentious nature of the issues involved and the divergent North/South positions thereon prevented progress and G. A. Resolution 44/22 convening UNCED merely referred to deforestation problems without calling for conclusion of any international agreement (paras 12(d) and 15(f)). During the UNCED Preparatory Commissions and at UNCED itself a group of developing states from South East Asia, Latin America, and Africa, led by Malaysia, strongly resisted the Northern States pressure for a convention. The 'Non-Legally Binding Authoritative Statement of Principles for a Global Consensus on the Management, Conservation and Sustainable Development of all Types of Forests' finally adopted by UNCED represented the resultant compromise (see UN Doc. A/CONF. 151/PC/ WG 1/L.18/ Rev. 1 Decision 2/13, reproduced in 31 *ILM* (1992) 881; 4 *EPL* (1992) 269–291); see also relevant provisions of UNCED Agenda 21 (UN Doc A/ CONF. 151/26, vol. II, 13 August 1992, paras. 24–41; UN Doc. A/CONF. 151/26, Vol. III, 14 August 1992, paras. 111–117). The preamble to the Forest Principles stresses that they are to be applied to all types of forest in all regions and climatic zones. Principle 1 repeats Stockhom Declaration, Principle 21, and stresses the need for increased international co-operation and equitable sharing of the additional costs of conservation policies. Principle 2 recognises that states have the sovereign right to 'utilize, manage and develop their forests in accordance with their development needs' but in a manner consistent with sustainable development. Principle 4 recognizes the role of forests in maintaining ecological balance and processes at local, national, regional, and global levels. Principle 10 notes that new and additional financial resources should be provided to developing countries, though without reference to any specific mechanism for achieving this aim. Environmentalists criticized the Principles as over-emphasising development of forests but developing countries welcomed the recognition of their national interests. See F. Yamin and P. Flint, 3 *YBIEL* (1992) 327–8.

The issues continued to be discussed at regional meetings post-UNCED, such as the Ministerial Conference for the Protection of Forests in Europe, Helsinki 16–17 June 1993, 5 *EPL* (1993) 231–5, and a 1993 Montreal workshop held under the auspices of the Conference on Security and Co-operation. A regional Convention for Management and Conservation of Natural Forest Ecosystems was also concluded at Guatemala City, 29 October 1993 (4 *YBIEL* (1993) Doc. 13). Following adoption of the 'Cartagena Commitment' ('A New Partnership for Development: The Cartagena Commitment', Final Document of the Eighth Session of UNCTAD, Cartagena de Indias, 8–25 February 1992), negotiations at the international level to conclude a successor agreement to the ITTA, which was due to expire in March 1994, continued under UNCTAD auspices at the United Nations Conference for the Renegotiation of the International Tropical Timber Agreement. (See also Background, Status, and Operation of the International Tropical Timber Agreement, 1983, and Recent Developments of Relevance to the Negotiation of a Successor Agreement, Doc. TD/Timber, 2/3, 26 February 1993.) The Conference participants were again divided on North/South lines similar to those prevailing in previous negotiations except that the tropical timber producing States now relied on the UNCED declarations and resolutions and the Forest Principles. The Conference was, however, able to agree on adoption of a new ITTA on 26 January 1994. It was opened for signature at the United Nations, New York, on 1 April 1994. (Text *repr.* in 33 *ILM* (1994) 1016–1042.)

As of 12 July 1994, seven States had become signatories (Congo, Ecuador, Gabon, Indonesia, Panama, Togo, United States of America). The new ITTA continues the ITTO (Article 3). It covers some aspects of trade in timber in general, as well as tropical timber (Article 1). Trade in timber and its import and use are not restricted or banned (Article 36); and the commitment made in Bali, Indonesia, by ITTO members in May 1990 that 'by the year 2000, the total exports of tropical timber products should come from sustainably managed resources' was reaffirmed (Preamble). The Preamble notes that timber-consuming States entered into a separate commitment to this outside the new ITTA ('Formal Statement by Consumer Members', Doc. TD/Timber 2/1 6, 21 January 1994 circulated and published with the Final Act). It also establishes 'The Bali Partnership Fund' to assist sustainable management (Article 21), based on Principle 10 of the Forest Principles. For further discussion see H. M. Schally, 'Forests: Towards an International Legal Regime?' 4 *YBIEL* (1993) 30–50; B. Johnson, *Responding to Tropical Deforestation*, An Osborn Center Research Paper (World Wildlife Fund UK/US, Baltimore, 1991); J. Woodliffe, 'Tropical Forests', in R. Churchill and D. Freestone (eds.) *International Law and Global Climate Change* (London, 1991) 57–74.

TEXT

Preamble

The Parties to this Agreement,

Recalling the Declaration and the Programme of Action on the Establishment of A New International Economic Order; the Integrated Programme for Commodities; A New Partnership for Development: the Cartagena Commitment and the relevant objectives contained in the Spirit of Cartagena,

Recalling the International Tropical Timber Agreement, 1983, and *recognizing* the work of the International Tropical Timber Organization and its achievements since its inception, including a strategy for achieving international trade in tropical timber from sustainably managed sources,

Recalling further the Rio Declaration on Environment and Development, the Non-Legally Binding Authoritative Statement of Principles for a Global Consensus on the Management, Conservation and Sustainable Development of all Types of Forests, and the relevant Chapters of Agenda 21 as adopted by the United Nations Conference on Environment and Development in June 1992, in Rio de Janeiro; the United Nations Framework Convention on Climate Change; and the Convention on Biological Diversity,

Recognizing the importance of timber to the economies of countries with timber-producing forests,

Further recognizing the need to promote and apply comparable and appropriate guidelines and criteria for the management, conservation and sustainable development of all types of timber-producing forests,

Taking into account the linkages of tropical timber trade and the international timber market and the need for taking a global perspective in order to improve transparency in the international timber market,

Noting the commitment of all members, made in Bali, Indonesia, in May 1990, to achieve exports of tropical timber products from sustainably managed sources by the year 2000 and *recognizing* Principle 10 of the Non-Legally Binding Authoritative Statement of Principles for a Global Consensus on the Management, Conservation and Sustainable Development of all Types of Forests which states that new and additional financial resources should be provided to developing countries to enable them to sustainably manage, conserve and develop their forests, including through afforestation, reforestation and combating deforestation and forest and land degradation,

Noting also the statement of commitment to maintain, or achieve by the year 2000, the sustainable management of their respective forests made by consuming members who are parties to the International Tropical Timber Agreement, 1983 at the fourth session of the United Nations Conference for the Negotiation of a Successor Agreement to the International Tropical Timber Agreement, 1983 in Geneva on 21 January 1994,

Desiring to strengthen the framework of international cooperation and policy development between members in finding solutions to the problems facing the tropical timber economy,

Have agreed as follows:

Chapter I. Objectives

Article 1
Objectives

Recognizing the sovereignty of members over their natural resources, as defined in Principle 1(a) of the Non-Legally Binding Authoritative Statement of Principles for a Global Consensus on the Management, Conservation and Sustainable Development of all Types of Forests, the objectives of the International Tropical Timber Agreement, 1994 (hereinafter referred to as 'this Agreement') are:

(a) To provide an effective framework for consultation, international cooperation and policy development among all members with regard to all relevant aspects of the world timber economy;

(b) To provide a forum for consultation to promote non-discriminatory timber trade practices;

(c) To contribute to the process of sustainable development;

(d) To enhance the capacity of members to implement a strategy for achieving exports of tropical timber and timber products from sustainably managed sources by the year 2000;

(e) To promote the expansion and diversification of international trade in tropical timber from sustainable sources by improving the structural conditions in international markets, by taking into account, on the one hand, a long-term increase in consumption and continuity of supplies, and, on the other, prices which reflect the costs of sustainable forest management and which are remunerative and equitable for members, and the improvement of market access;

(f) To promote and support research and development with a view to improving forest management and efficiency of wood utilization as well as increasing the capacity to conserve and enhance other forest values in timber-producing tropical forests;

(g) To develop and contribute towards mechanisms for the provision of new and additional financial resources and expertise needed to enhance the capacity of producing members to attain the objectives of this Agreement;

(h) To improve market intelligence with a view to ensuring greater transparency in the international timber market, including the gathering, compilation, and dissemination of trade-related data, including data related to species being traded;

(i) To promote increased and further processing of tropical timber from sustainable sources in producing member countries with a view to promoting their industrialization and thereby increasing their employment opportunities and export earnings;

(j) To encourage members to support and develop industrial tropical timber reforestation and forest management activities as well as rehabilitation of degraded forest land, with due regard for the interests of local communities dependent on forest resources;

(k) To improve marketing and distribution of tropical timber exports from sustainably managed sources;

(l) To encourage members to develop national policies aimed at sustainable utilization and conservation of timber-producing forests and their genetic resources and at maintaining the ecological balance in the regions concerned, in the context of tropical timber trade;

(m) To promote the access to, and transfer of, technologies and technical cooperation to implement the objectives of this Agreement, including on concessional and preferential terms and conditions, as mutually agreed; and

(n) To encourage information-sharing on the international timber market.

Chapter II. Definitions

Article 2
Definitions

For the purposes of this Agreement:

1. 'Tropical timber' means non-coniferous tropical wood for industrial uses, which grows or is produced in the countries situated between the Tropic of Cancer and the Tropic of Capricorn. The term covers logs, sawnwood, veneer sheets and plywood. Plywood which includes in some measure conifers of tropical origin shall also be covered by this definition;

2. 'Further processing' means the transformation of logs into primary wood products, semi-finished and finished products made wholly or almost wholly of tropical timber;

3. 'Member' means a Government or an intergovernmental organization referred to in article 5 which has consented to be bound by this Agreement whether it is in force provisionally or definitively;

4. 'Producing member' means any country with tropical forest resources and/or a net exporter of tropical timber in volume terms which is listed in annex A and which becomes a party to this Agreement, or any country with tropical forest resources and/or a net exporter of tropical timber in volume terms which is not so listed and which becomes a party to this Agreement and which the Council, with the consent of that country, declares to be a producing member;

5. 'Consuming member' means any country listed in annex B which becomes a party to this Agreement, or any country not so listed which becomes a party to this Agreement and which the Council, with the consent of that country, declares to be a consuming member;

6. 'Organization' means the International Tropical Timber Organization established in accordance with article 3;

7. 'Council' means the International Tropical Timber Council established in accordance with article 6;

8. 'Special vote' means a vote requiring at least two-thirds of the votes cast by producing members present and voting and at least 60 per cent of the votes cast by consuming members present and voting, counted separately, on condition that these votes are cast by at least half of the producing members present and voting and at least half of the consuming members present and voting;

9. 'Simple distributed majority vote' means a vote requiring more than half of the votes cast by producing members present and voting and more than half of the votes cast by consuming members present and voting, counted separately;

10. 'Financial year' means the period from 1 January to 31 December inclusive;

11. 'Freely usable currencies' means the deutsche mark, the French franc, the Japanese yen, the pound sterling, the United States dollar and any other currency which has been designated from time to time by a competent international monetary organization as being in fact widely used to

make payments for international transactions and widely traded in the principal exchange markets.

Chapter III. Organization and Administration

Article 3
Headquarters and structure of the International Tropical Timber Organization

1. The International Tropical Timber Organization established by the International Tropical Timber Agreement, 1983 shall continue in being for the purposes of administering the provisions and supervising the operation of this Agreement.

2. The Organization shall function through the Council established under article 6, the committees and other subsidiary bodies referred to in article 26 and the Executive Director and staff.

3. The headquarters of the Organization shall be in Yokohama, unless the Council, by special vote, decides otherwise.

4. The headquarters of the Organization shall at all times be located in the territory of a member.

Article 4
Membership in the Organization

There shall be two categories of membership in the Organization, namely:

(a) Producing; and
(b) Consuming.

Article 5
Membership by intergovernmental organizations

1. Any reference in this Agreement to 'Governments' shall be construed as including the European Community and any other intergovernmental organization having responsibilities in respect of the negotiation, conclusion and application of international agreements, in particular commodity agreements. Accordingly, any reference in this Agreement to signature, ratification, acceptance or approval, or to notification of provisional application, or to accession shall, in the case of such intergovernmental organizations, be construed as including a reference to signature, ratification, acceptance or approval, or to notification of provisional application, or to accession, by such intergovernmental organizations.

2. In the case of voting on matters within their competence, such intergovernmental organizations shall vote with a number of votes equal to the total number of votes attributable to their member States in accordance with article 10. In such cases, the member States of such inter-

governmental organizations shall not be entitled to exercise their individual voting rights.

Chapter IV. International Tropical Timber Council

Article 6
Composition of the International Tropical Timber Council

1. The highest authority of the Organization shall be the International Tropical Timber Council, which shall consist of all the members of the Organization.

2. Each member shall be represented in the Council by one representative and may designate alternates and advisers to attend sessions of the Council.

3. An alternate representative shall be empowered to act and vote on behalf of the representative during the latter's absence or in special circumstances.

Article 7
Powers and functions of the Council

1. The Council shall exercise all such powers and perform or arrange for the performance of all such functions as are necessary to carry out the provisions of this Agreement.

2. The Council shall, by special vote, adopt such rules and regulations as are necessary to carry out the provisions of this Agreement and as are consistent therewith, including its own rules of procedure and the financial rules and staff regulations of the Organization. Such financial rules shall, *inter alia*, govern the receipt and expenditure of funds under the Administrative Account, the Special Account and the Bali Partnership Fund. The Council may, in its rules of procedure, provide for a procedure whereby it may, without meeting, decide specific questions.

3. The Council shall keep such records as are required for the performance of its functions under this Agreement.

Article 8
Chairman and Vice-Chairman of the Council

1. The Council shall elect for each calendar year a Chairman and a Vice-Chairman, whose salaries shall not be paid by the Organization.

2. The Chairman and the Vice-Chairman shall be elected, one from among the representatives of producing members and the other from among the representatives of consuming members. These offices shall alternate each year between the two categories of members, provided, however, that this shall not prohibit the re-election of either or both, under exceptional circumstances, by special vote of the Council.

3. In the temporary absence of the Chairman, the Vice-Chairman shall act in his place. In the temporary absence of both the Chairman and the Vice-Chairman, or in the absence of one or both of them for the rest of the term for which they were elected, the Council may elect new officers from among the representatives of the producing members and/or from among the representatives of the consuming members, as the case may be, on a temporary basis or for the rest of the term for which the predecessor or predecessors were elected.

Article 9
Sessions of the Council

1. As a general rule, the Council shall hold at least one regular session a year.

2. The Council shall meet in special session whenever it so decides or at the request of:

(a) The Executive Director, in agreement with the Chairman of the Council; or
(b) A majority of producing members or a majority of consuming members; or
(c) Members holding at least 500 votes.

3. Sessions of the Council shall be held at the headquarters of the Organization unless the Council, by special vote, decides otherwise. If on the invitation of any member the Council meets elsewhere than at the headquarters of the Organization, that member shall pay the additional cost of holding the meeting away from headquarters.

4. Notice of any sessions and the agenda for such sessions shall be communicated to members by the Executive Director at least six weeks in advance, except in cases of emergency, when notice shall be communicated at least seven days in advance.

Article 10
Distribution of votes

1. The producing members shall together hold 1,000 votes and the consuming members shall together hold 1,000 votes.

2. The votes of the producing members shall be distributed as follows:

(a) Four hundred votes shall be distributed equally among the three producing regions of Africa, Asia-Pacific and Latin America. The votes thus allocated to each of these regions shall then be distributed equally among the producing members of that region;
(b) Three hundred votes shall be distributed among the producing members in accordance with their respective shares of the total tropical forest resources of all producing members; and

(c) Three hundred votes shall be distributed among the producing members in proportion to the average of the values of their respective net exports of tropical timber during the most recent three-year period for which definitive figures are available.

3. Notwithstanding the provisions of paragraph 2 of this article, the total votes allocated to the producing members from the African region, calculated in accordance with paragraph 2 of this article, shall be distributed equally among all producing members from the African region. If there are any remaining votes, each of these votes shall be allocated to a producing member from the African region: the first to the producing member which is allocated the highest number of votes calculated in accordance with paragraph 2 of this article, the second to the producing member which is allocated the second highest number of votes, and so on until all the remaining votes have been distributed.

4. For purposes of the calculation of the distribution of votes under paragraph 2(b) of this article, 'tropical forest resources' means productive closed broad-leaved forests as defined by the Food and Agriculture Organization (FAO).

5. The votes of the consuming members shall be distributed as follows: each consuming member shall have 10 initial votes: the remaining votes shall be distributed among the consuming members in proportion to the average volume of their respective net imports of tropical timber during the three-year period commencing four calendar years prior to the distribution of votes.

6. The Council shall distribute the votes for each financial year at the beginning of its first session of that year in accordance with the provisions of this article. Such distribution shall remain in effect for the rest of that year, except as provided for in paragraph 7 of this article.

7. Whenever the membership of the Organization changes or when any member has its voting rights suspended or restored under any provision of this Agreement, the Council shall redistribute the votes within the affected category or categories of members in accordance with the provisions of this article. The Council shall, in that event, decide when such redistribution shall become effective.

8. There shall be no fractional votes.

Article 11
Voting procedure of the Council

1. Each member shall be entitled to cast the number of votes it holds and no member shall be entitled to divide its votes. A member may, however, cast differently from such votes any votes which it is authorized to cast under paragraph 2 of this article.

2. By written notification to the Chairman of the Council, any producing member may authorize, under its own responsibility, any other producing member, and any consuming member may authorize, under its own responsibility, any other consuming member, to represent its interests and to cast its votes at any meeting of the Council.

3. When abstaining, a member shall be deemed not to have cast its votes.

Article 12
Decisions and recommendations of the Council

1. The Council shall endeavour to take all decisions and to make all recommendations by consensus. If consensus cannot be reached, the Council shall take all decisions and make all recommendations by a simple distributed majority vote, unless this Agreement provides for a special vote.

2. Where a member avails itself of the provisions of article 11, paragraph 2, and its votes are cast at a meeting of the Council, such member shall, for the purposes of paragraph 1 of this article, be considered as present and voting.

Article 13
Quorum for the Council

1. The quorum for any meeting of the Council shall be the presence of a majority of members of each category referred to in article 4, provided that such members hold at least two-thirds of the total votes in their respective categories.

2. If there is no quorum in accordance with paragraph 1 of this article on the day fixed for the meeting and on the following day, the quorum on the subsequent days of the session shall be the presence of a majority of members of each category referred to in article 4, provided that such members hold a majority of the total votes in their respective categories.

3. Representation in accordance with article 11, paragraph 2, shall be considered as presence.

Article 14
Cooperation and coordination with other organizations

1. The Council shall make arrangements as appropriate for consultations and cooperation with the United Nations and its organs, including the United Nations Conference on Trade and Development (UNCTAD) and the Commission on Sustainable Development (CSD), intergovernmental organizations, including the General Agreement on Tariffs and Trade (GATT) and the Convention on International Trade in Endangered Species of Wild Fauna and Flora (CITES), and non-governmental organizations.

2. The Organization shall, to the maximum extent possible, utilize the facilities, services and expertise of existing intergovernmental, govern-

mental or non-governmental organizations, in order to avoid duplication of efforts in achieving the objectives of this Agreement and to enhance the complementarity and the efficiency of their activities.

Article 15
Admission of observers

The Council may invite any non-member Government or any of the organizations referred to in article 14, article 20 and article 29, interested in the activities of the Organization to attend as observers any of the meetings of the Council.

Article 16
Executive Director and staff

1. The Council shall, by special vote, appoint the Executive Director.

2. The terms and conditions of appointment of the Executive Director shall be determined by the Council.

3. The Executive Director shall be the chief administrative officer of the Organization and shall be responsible to the Council for the administration and operation of this Agreement in accordance with decisions of the Council.

4. The Executive Director shall appoint the staff in accordance with regulations to be established by the Council. The Council shall, by special vote, decide the number of executive and professional staff the Executive Director may appoint. Any changes in the number of executive and professional staff shall be decided by the Council by special vote. The staff shall be responsible to the Executive Director.

5. Neither the Executive Director nor any member of the staff shall have any financial interest in the timber industry or trade, or associated commercial activities.

6. In the performance of their duties, the Executive Director and staff shall not seek or receive instructions from any member or from any authority external to the Organization. They shall refrain from any action which might reflect adversely on their positions as international officials ultimately responsible to the Council. Each member shall respect the exclusively international character of the responsibilities of the Executive Director and staff and shall not seek to influence them in the discharge of their responsibilities.

Chapter V. Privileges and Immunities

Article 17
Privileges and immunities

1. The Organization shall have legal personality. It shall in particular have

the capacity to contract, to acquire and dispose of movable and immovable property, and to institute legal proceedings.

2. The status, privileges and immunities of the Organization, of its Executive Director, its staff and experts, and of representatives of members while in the territory of Japan shall continue to be governed by the Headquarters Agreement between the Government of Japan and the International Tropical Timber Organization signed at Tokyo on 27 February 1988, with such amendments as may be necessary for the proper functioning of this Agreement.

3. The Organization may conclude, with one or more countries, agreements to be approved by the Council relating to such capacity, privileges and immunities as may be necessary for the proper functioning of this Agreement.

4. If the headquarters of the Organization is moved to another country, the member in question shall, as soon as possible, conclude with the Organization a headquarters agreement to be approved by the Council. Pending the conclusion of such an Agreement, the Organization shall request the new host Government to grant, within the limits of its national legislation, exemption from taxation on remuneration paid by the Organization to its employees, and on the assets, income and other property of the Organization.

5. The headquarters agreement shall be independent of this Agreement. It shall, however, terminate:

(a) By agreement between the host Government and the Organization;
(b) In the event of the headquarters of the Organization being moved from the country of the host Government; or
(c) In the event of the Organization ceasing to exist.

Chapter VI. Finance

Article 18
Financial accounts

1. There shall be established:

(a) The Administrative Account;
(b) The Special Account;
(c) The Bali Partnership Fund; and
(d) Such other accounts as the Council shall deem appropriate and necessary.

2. The Executive Director shall be responsible for the administration of these accounts and the Council shall make provision therefore in the financial rules of the Organization.

Article 19
Administrative Account

1. The expenses necessary for the administration of this Agreement shall be brought into the Administrative Account and shall be met by annual contributions paid by members in accordance with their respective constitutional or institutional procedures and assessed in accordance with paragraphs 3, 4 and 5 this article.

2. The expenses of delegations to the Council, the committees and any other subsidiary bodies of the Council referred to in article 26 shall be met by the members concerned. In cases where a member requests special services from the Organization, the Council shall require that member to pay the costs of such services.

3. Before the end of each financial year, the Council shall approve the administrative budget of the Organization for the following financial year and shall assess the contribution of each member to that budget.

4. The contribution of each member to the administrative budget for each financial year shall be in the proportion which the number of its votes at the time the administrative budget for that financial year is approved bears to the total votes of all the members. In assessing contributions, the votes of each member shall be calculated without regard to the suspension of any member's voting rights or any redistribution of votes resulting therefrom.

5. The initial contribution of any member joining the Organization after the entry into force of this Agreement shall be assessed by the Council on the basis of the number of votes to be held by that member and the period remaining in the current financial year, but the assessment made upon other members from the current financial year shall not thereby be altered.

6. Contributions to administrative budgets shall become due on the first day of each financial year. Contributions of members in respect of the financial year in which they join the Organization shall be due on the date on which they become members.

7. If a member has not paid its full contribution to the administrative budget within four months after such contribution becomes due in accordance with paragraph 6 of this article, the Executive Director shall request that member to make payment as quickly as possible. If that member has still not paid its contribution within two months after such request, that member shall be requested to state the reasons for its inability to make payment. If at the expiry of seven months from the due date of contribution, that member has still not paid its contribution, its voting rights shall be suspended until such time as it has paid in full its contribution, unless the Council, by special vote, decides otherwise. If, on the contrary, a member has paid its full contribution to the administrative budget within four months after such contribution becomes due in accordance with paragraph

6 of this article, the member's contribution shall receive a discount as may be established by the Council in the financial rules of the Organization.

8. A member whose rights have been suspended under paragraph 7 of this article shall remain liable to pay its contribution.

Article 20
Special Account

1. There shall be established two sub-accounts under the Special Account:

    (a) The Pre-Project Sub-Account; and
    (b) The Project Sub-Account.

2. The possible sources of finance for the Special Account may be:

    (a) The Common Fund for Commodities;
    (b) Regional and international financial institutions; and
    (c) Voluntary contributions.

3. The resources of the Special Account shall be used only for approved pre-projects or projects.

4. All expenditures under the Pre-Project Sub-Account shall be reimbursed from the Project Sub-Account if projects are subsequently approved and funded. If within six months of the entry into force of this Agreement the Council does not receive any funds for the Pre-Project Sub-Account, it shall review the situation and take appropriate action.

5. All receipts pertaining to specific identifiable pre-projects or projects under the Special Account shall be brought into that Account. All expenditures incurred on such pre-projects or projects, including remuneration and travel expenses of consultants and experts, shall be charged to the same Account.

6. The Council shall, by special vote, establish terms and conditions on which it would, when and where appropriate, sponsor projects for loan financing, where a member or members have voluntarily assumed full obligations and responsibilities for such loans. The Organization shall have no obligations for such loans.

7. The Council may nominate and sponsor any entity with the consent of that entity, including a member or members, to receive loans for the financing of approved projects and to undertake all the obligations involved, except that the Organization shall reserve to itself the right to monitor the use of resources and to follow up on the implementation of projects so financed. However, the Organization shall not be responsible for guarantees voluntarily provided by individual members or other entities.

8. No member shall be responsible by reason of its membership in the

Organization for any liability arising from borrowing or lending by any other member or entity in connection with projects.

9. In the event that voluntary unearmarked funds are offered to the Organization, the Council may accept such funds. Such funds may be utilized for approved pre-projects and projects.

10. The Executive Director shall endeavour to seek, on such terms and conditions as the Council may decide, adequate and assured finance for pre-projects and projects approved by the Council.

11. Contributions for specified approved projects shall be used only for the projects for which they were originally intended, unless otherwise decided by the Council in agreement with the contributor. After the completion of a project, the Organization shall return to each contributor for specific projects the balance of any funds remaining pro rata to each contributor's share in the total of the contributions originally made available for financing that project, unless otherwise agreed to by the contributor.

Article 21
The Bali Partnership Fund

1. A Fund for sustainable management of tropical timber-producing forests is hereby established to assist producing members to make the investments necessary to achieve the objective of article 1(d) of this Agreement.

2. The Fund shall be constituted by:

(a) Contributions from donor members;
(b) Fifty per cent of income earned as a result of activities related to the Special Account;
(c) Resources from other private and public sources which the Organization may accept consistent with its financial rules.

3. Resources of the Fund shall be allocated by the Council only for pre-projects and projects for the purpose set out in paragraph 1 of this article and approved in accordance with article 25.

4. In allocating resources of the Fund, the Council shall take into account:

(a) The special needs of members whose forestry sectors' contribution to their economies is adversely affected by the implementation of the strategy for achieving the exports of tropical timber and timber products from sustainably managed sources by the year 2000;
(b) The needs of members with significant forest areas who establish conservation programmes in timber-producing forests.

5. The Council shall examine annually the adequacy of the resources available to the Fund and endeavour to obtain additional resources needed by producing members to achieve the purpose of the Fund. The ability of

members to implement the strategy referred to in paragraphy 4(a) of this article will be influenced by the availability of resources.

6. The Council shall establish policies and financial rules for the operation of the Fund, including rules covering the settlement of accounts on termination or expiry of this Agreement.

Article 22
Forms of payment

1. Contributions to the Administrative Account shall be payable in freely usable currencies and shall be exempt from foreign-exchange restrictions.

2. Financial contributions to the Special Account and the Bali Partnership Fund shall be payable in freely usable currencies and shall be exempt from foreign-exchange restrictions.

3. The Council may also decide to accept other forms of contributions to the Special Account or the Bali Partnership Fund, including scientific and technical equipment or personnel, to meet the requirements of approved projects.

Article 23
Audit and publication of accounts

1. The Council shall appoint independent auditors for the purpose of auditing the accounts of the Organization.

2. Independently audited statements of the Administrative Account, of the Special Account and of the Bali Partnership Fund shall be made available to members as soon as possible after the close of each financial year, but not later than six months after that date, and be considered for approval by the Council at its next session, as appropriate. A summary of the audited accounts and balance sheet shall thereafter be published.

Chpater VII. Operational Activities

Article 24
Policy work of the Organization

In order to achieve the objectives set out in article 1, the Organization shall undertake policy work and project activities in the areas of Economic Information and Market Intelligence, Reforestation and Forest Management and Forest Industry, in a balanced manner, to the extent possible integrating policy work and project activities.

Article 25
Project activities of the Organization

1. Bearing in mind the needs of developing countries, members may submit pre-project and project proposals to the Council in the fields of re-

search and development, market intelligence, further and increased wood processing in producing member countries, and reforestation and forest management. Pre-projects and projects should contribute to the achievement of one or more of the objectives of this Agreement.

2. The Council, in approving pre-projects and projects, shall take into account:

(a) Their relevance to the objectives of this Agreement;
(b) Their environmental and social effects;
(c) The desirability of maintaining an appropriate geographical balance;
(d) The interests and characteristics of each of the developing producing regions;
(e) The desirability of equitable distribution of resources among the fields referred to in paragraph 1 of this article;
(f) Their cost-effectiveness; and
(g) The need to avoid duplication of efforts.

3. The Council shall establish a schedule and procedure for submitting, appraising, and prioritizing pre-projects and projects seeking funding from the Organization, as well as for their implementation, monitoring and evaluation. The Council shall decide on the approval of pre-projects and projects for financing or sponsorship in accordance with article 20 or article 21.

4. The Executive Director may suspend disbursement of the Organization's funds to a pre-project or project if they are being used contrary to the project document or in cases of fraud, waste, neglect or mismanagement. The Executive Director will provide to the Council at its next session a report for its consideration. The Council shall take appropriate action.

5. The Council may, by special vote, terminate its sponsorship of any pre-project or project.

Article 26
Establishment of Committees

1. The following are hereby established as Committees of the Organization:

(a) Committee on Economic Information and Market Intelligence;
(b) Committee on Reforestation and Forest Management;
(c) Committee on Forest Industry; and
(d) Committee on Finance and Administration.

2. The Council may, by special vote, establish such other committees and subsidiary bodies as it deems appropriate and necessary.

3. Participation in each of the committees shall be open to all members. The rules of procedure of the committees shall be decided by the Council.

4. The committees and subsidiary bodies referred to in paragraphs 1 and 2 of this article shall be responsible to, and work under the general direction of, the Council. Meetings of the committees and subsidiary bodies shall be convened by the Council.

Article 27
Functions of the Committees

1. The Committee on Economic Information and Market Intelligence shall:

   (a) Keep under review the availability and quality of statistics and other information required by the Organization;
   (b) Analyse the statistical data and specific indicators as decided by the Council for the monitoring of international timber trade;
   (c) Keep under continuous review the international timber market, its current situation and short-term prospects on the basis of the data mentioned in subparagraph (b) above and other relevant information, including information related to undocumented trade;
   (d) Make recommendations to the Council on the need for, and nature of, appropriate studies on tropical timber, including prices, market elasticity, market substitutability, marketing of new products, and long-term prospects of the international tropical timber market, and monitor and review any studies commissioned by the Council;
   (e) Carry out any other tasks related to the economic, technical and statistical aspects of timber assigned to it by the Council;
   (f) Assist in provision of technical cooperation to developing member countries to improve their relevant statistical services.

2. The Committee on Reforestation and Forest Management shall:

   (a) Promote cooperation between members as partners in development of forest activities in member countries, *inter alia*, in the following areas:
       (i) Reforestation;
       (ii) Rehabilitation;
       (iii) Forest management;
   (b) Encourage the increase of technical assistance and transfer of technology in the fields of reforestation and forest management to developing countries;
   (c) Follow up ongoing activities in this field, and identify and consider problems and possible solutions to them in cooperation with the competent organizations;
   (d) Review regularly the future needs of international trade in industrial tropical timber and, on this basis, identify and consider appropriate possible schemes and measures in the field of reforestation, rehabilitation and forest management;

(e) Facilitate the transfer of knowledge in the field of reforestation and forest management with the assistance of competent organizations;

(f) Coordinate and harmonize these activities for cooperation in the field of reforestation and forest management with relevant activities pursued elsewhere, such as those under the auspices of the Food and Agriculture Organization of the United Nations (FAO), the United Nations Environment Programme (UNEP), the World Bank, the United Nations Development Programme (UNDP), regional development banks and other competent organizations.

3. The Committee on Forest Industry shall:

(a) Promote cooperation between member countries as partners in the development of processing activities in producing member countries, *inter alia*, in the following areas:
   (i) Product development through transfer of technology;
   (ii) Human resources development and training;
   (iii) Standardization of nomenclature of tropical timber;
   (iv) Harmonization of specifications of processed products;
   (v) Encouragement of investment and joint ventures; and
   (vi) Marketing, including the promotion of lesser known and lesser used species;

(b) Promote the exchange of information in order to facilitate structural changes involved in increased and further processing in the interests of all member countries, in particular developing member countries;

(c) Follow up ongoing activities in this field, and identify and consider problems and possible solutions to them in cooperation with the competent organizations;

(d) Encourage the increase of technical cooperation for the processing of tropical timber for the benefit of producing member countries.

4. In order to promote the policy and project work of the Organization in a balanced manner, the Committee on Economic Information and Market Intelligence, the Committee on Reforestation and Forest Management and the Committee on Forest Industry shall each:

(a) Be responsible for ensuring the effective appraisal, monitoring and evaluation of pre-projects and projects;

(b) Make recommendations to the Council relating to pre-projects and projects;

(c) Follow up the implementation of pre-projects and projects and provide for the collection and dissemination of their results as widely as possible for the benefit all members;

(d) Develop and advance policy ideas to the Council;

(e) Review regularly the results of project and policy work and make

recommendations to the Council on the future of the Organization's programme;

(f) Review regularly the strategies, criteria and priority areas for programme development and project work contained in the Organization's Action Plan and recommend revisions to the Council;

(g) Take account of the need to strengthen capacity building and human resource development in member countries;

(h) Carry out any other task related to the objectives of this Agreement
assigned to them by the Council.

5. Research and development shall be a common function of the Committees referred to in paragraphs 1, 2, and 3 of this article.

6. The Committee on Finance and Administration shall:

(a) Examine and make recommendations to the Council regarding the
approval of the Organization's administrative budget proposals and
the management operations of the Organization;

(b) Review the assets of the Organization to ensure prudent asset management and that the Organization has sufficient reserves to carry
out its work;

(c) Examine and make recommendations to the Council on the budgetary implications of the Organization's annual work programme, and
the actions that might be taken to secure the resources needed to
implement it;

(d) Recommend to the Council the choice of independent auditors and
review the independent audited statements;

(e) Recommend to the Council any modifications it may judge necessary to the Rules of Procedure or the Financial Rules;

(f) Review the Organization's revenues and the extent to which they
constrain the work of the Secretariat.

Chapter VIII. Relationship with the Common Fund for Commodities

Article 28
Relationship with the Common Fund for Commodities

The Organization shall take full advantage of the facilities of the Common
Fund for Commodities.

Chapter IX. Statistics, Studies and Information

Article 29
Statistics, studies and information

1. The Council shall establish close relationships with relevant intergovernmental, governmental and non-governmental organizations, in order to

help ensure the availability of recent reliable data and information on the trade in tropical timber, as well as relevant information on non-tropical timber and on the management of timber-producing forests. As deemed necessary for the operation of this Agreement, the Organization, in cooperation with such organizations, shall compile, collate and, where relevant, publish statistical information on production, supply, trade, stocks, consumption and market prices of timber, the extent of timber resources and the management of timber-producing forests.

2. Members shall, to the fullest extent possible not inconsistent with their national legislation, furnish, within a reasonable time, statistics and information on timber, its trade and the activities aimed at achieving sustainable management of timber-producing forests as well as other relevant information as requested by the Council. The Council shall decide on the type of information to be provided under this paragraph and on the format in which it is to be presented.

3. The Council shall arrange to have any relevant studies undertaken of the trends and of short- and long-term problems of the international timber markets and of the progress towards the achievement of sustainable management of timber-producing forests.

Article 30
Annual report and review

1. The Council shall, within six months after the close of each calendar year, publish an annual report on its activities and such other information as it considers appropriate.

2. The Council shall annually review and assess:

   (a) The international timber situation;
   (b) Other factors, issues and developments considered relevant to achieve the objectives of this Agreement.

3. The review shall be carried out in the light of:

   (a) Information supplied by members in relation to national production, trade, supply, stocks, consumption and prices of timber;
   (b) Other statistical data and specific indicators provided by members as requested by the Council;
   (c) Information supplied by members on their progress towards the sustainable management of their timber-producing forests;
   (d) Such other relevant information as may be available to the Council either directly or through the organizations in the United Nations system and intergovernmental, governmental or non-governmental organizations.

4. The Council shall promote the exchange of views among member countries regarding:

(a) The status of sustainable management of timber-producing forests and related matters in member countries;

(b) Resource flows and requirements in relation to objectives, criteria and guidelines set by the Organization.

5. Upon request, the Council shall endeavour to enhance the technical capacity of member countries, in particular developing member countries, to obtain the data necessary for adequate information-sharing, including the provision of resources for training and facilities to members.

6. The results of the review shall be included in the reports of the Council's deliberations.

Chapter X. Miscellaneous

Article 31
Complaints and disputes

Any complaint that a member has failed to fulfil its obligations under this Agreement and any dispute concerning the interpretation or applicaton of this Agreement shall be referred to the Council for decision. Decisions of the Council on these matters shall be final and binding.

Article 32
General obligations of members

1. Members shall, for the duration of this Agreement, use their best endeavours and cooperate to promote the attainment of its objectives and to avoid any action contrary thereto.

2. Members undertake to accept and carry out the decisions of the Council under the provisions of this Agreement and shall refrain from implementing measures which would have the effect of limiting or running counter to them.

Article 33
Relief from obligations

1. Where it is necessary on account of exceptional circumstances or emergency or *force majeure* not expressly provided for in this Agreement, the Council may, by special vote, relieve a member of an obligation under this Agreement if it is satisfied by an explanation from that member regarding the reasons why the obligation cannot be met.

2. The Council, in granting relief to a member under paragraph 1 of this article, shall state explicitly the terms and conditions on which, and the period for which, the member is relieved of such obligation, and the reasons for which the relief is granted.

Article 34
Differential and remedial measures and special measures

1. Developing importing members whose interests are adversely affected by measures taken under this Agreement may apply to the Council for appropriate differential and remedial measures. The Council shall consider taking appropriate measures in accordance with section III, paragraphs 3 and 4, of resolution 93 (IV) of the United Nations Conference on Trade and Development.

2. Members in the category of least developed countries as defined by the United Nations may apply to the Council for special measures in accordance with section III, paragraph 4, of resolution 93 (IV) and with paragraphs 56 and 57 of the Paris Declaration and Programme of Action for the Least Developed Countries for the 1990s.

Article 35
Review

The Council shall review the scope of this Agreement four years after its entry into force.

Article 36
Non-discrimination

Nothing in this Agreement authorizes the use of measures to restrict or ban international trade in, and in particular as they concern imports of and utilization of, timber and timber products.

Chapter XI. Final Provisions

Article 37
Depositary

The Secretary-General of the United Nations is hereby designated as the depositary of this Agreement.

Article 38
Signature, ratification, acceptance and approval

1. This Agreement shall be open for signature, at United Nations Headquarters from 1 April 1994 until one month after the date of its entry into force, by Governments invited to the United Nations Conference for the Negotiation of a Successor Agreement to the International Tropical Timber Agreement, 1983.

2. Any Government referred to in paragraph 1 of this article may:

(a) At the time of signing this Agreement, declare that by such signature it expresses its consent to be bound by this Agreement (definitive signature); or

(b) After signing this Agreement, ratify, accept or approve it by the deposit of an instrument to that effect with the depositary.

Article 39
Accession

1. This Agreement shall be open for accession by the Governments of all States upon conditions established by the Council, which shall include a time-limit for the deposit of instruments of accession. The Council may, however, grant extensions of time to Governments which are unable to accede by the time-limit set in the conditions of accession.

2. Accession shall be effected by the deposit of an instrument of accession with the depositary.

Article 40
Notification of provisional application

A signatory Government which intends to ratify, accept or approve this Agreement, or a Government for which the Council has established conditions for accession but which has not yet been able to deposit its instrument, may, at any time, notify the depositary that it will apply this Agreement provisionally either when it enters into force in accordance with article 41, or, if it is already in force, at a specified date.

Article 41
Entry into force

1. This Agreement shall enter into force definitively on 1 February 1995 or on any date thereafter, if 12 Governments of producing countries holding at least 55 per cent of the total votes as set out in annex A to this Agreement, and 16 Governments of consuming countries holding at least 70 per cent of the total votes as set out in annex B to this Agreement have signed this Agreement definitively or have ratified, accepted or approved it or acceded thereto pursuant to article 38, paragraph 2, or article 39.

2. If this Agreement has not entered into force definitively on 1 February 1995, it shall enter into force provisionally on that date or on any date within seven months thereafter, if 10 Governments of producing countries holding at least 50 per cent of the total votes as set out in annex A to this Agreement, and 14 Governments of consuming countries holding at least 65 per cent of the total votes as set out in annex B to this Agreement have signed this Agreement definitively or have ratified, accepted or approved it pursuant to article 38, paragraph 2, or have notified the depositary under article 40 that they will apply this Agreement provisionally.

3. If the requirements for entry into force under paragraph 1 or paragraph 2 of this article have not been met on 1 September 1995, the Secretary-General of the United Nations shall invite those Governments which have signed this Agreement definitively or have ratified, accepted or approved it pursuant to article 38, paragraph 2, or have notified the depositary that they will apply this Agreement provisionally, to meet at the earliest time practicable to decide whether to put this Agreement into force provisionally or definitively among themselves in whole or in part. Governments which decide to put this Agreement into force provisionally among themselves may meet from time to time to review the situation and decide whether this Agreement shall enter into force definitively among themselves.

4. For any Government which has not notified the depositary under article 40 that it will apply this Agreement provisionally and which deposits its instrument of ratification, acceptance, approval or accession after the entry into force of this Agreement, this Agreement shall enter into force on the date of such deposit.

5. The Executive Director of the Organization shall convene the Council as soon as possible after the entry into force of this Agreement.

Article 42
Amendments

1. The Council may, by special vote, recommend an amendment of this Agreement to members.

2. The Council shall fix a date by which members shall notify the depositary of their acceptance of the amendment.

3. An amendment shall enter into force 90 days after the depositary has received notifications of acceptance from members constituting at least two-thirds of the producing members and accounting for at least 75 per cent of the votes of the producing members, and from members constituting at least two-thirds of the consuming members and accounting for at least 75 per cent of the votes of the consuming members.

4. After the depositary informs the Council that the requirements for entry into force of the amendment have been met, and notwithstanding the provisions of paragraph 2 of this article relating to the date fixed by the Council, a member may still notify the depositary of its acceptance of the amendment, provided that such notification is made before the entry into force of the amendment.

5. Any member which has not notified its acceptance of an amendment by the date on which such amendment enters into force shall cease to be a party to this Agreement as from that date, unless such member has satisfied the Council that its acceptance could not be obtained in time owing to difficulties in completing its constitutional or institutional procedures, and

the Council decides to extend for that member the period for acceptance of the amendment. Such member shall not be bound by the amendment before it has notified its acceptance thereof.

6. If the requirments for the entry into force of the amendment have not been met by the date fixed by the Council in accordance with paragraph 2 of this article, the amendment shall be considered withdrawn.

Article 43
Withdrawal

1. A member may withdraw from this Agreement at any time after the entry into force of this Agreement by giving written notice of withdrawal to the depositary. That member shall simultaneously inform the Council of the action it has taken.

2. Withdrawal shall become effective 90 days after the notice is received by the depositary.

3. Financial obligations to the Organization incurred by a member under this Agreement shall not be terminated by its withdrawal.

Article 14
Exclusion

If the Council decides that any member is in breach of its obligations under this Agreement and decides further that such breach significantly impairs the operation of this Agreement, it may, by special vote, exclude that member from this Agreement. The Council shall immediately so notify the depositary. Six months after the date of the Council's decision, that member shall cease to be a party to this Agreement.

Article 45
Settlement of accounts with withdrawing or excluded members or members unable to accept an amendment

1. The Council shall determine any settlement of accounts with a member which ceases to be a party to this Agreement owing to:

  (a) Non-acceptance of an amendment to this Agreement under article 42;
  (b) Withdrawal from this Agreement under article 43; or
  (c) Exclusion from this Agreement under article 44.

2. The Council shall retain any contribution paid to the Administrative Account, to the Special Account or to the Bali Partnership Fund by a member which ceases to be a party to this Agreement.

3. A member which has ceased to be a party to this Agreement shall not be entitled to any share of the proceeds of liquidation or the other assets of the Organization. Nor shall such member be liable for payment of any

part of the deficit, if any, of the Organization upon termination of this Agreement.

Article 46
Duration, extension and termination

1. This Agreement shall remain in force for a period of four years after its entry into force unless the Council, by special vote, decides to extend, renegotiate or terminate it in accordance with the provisions of this article.

2. The Council may, by special vote, decide to extend this Agreement for two periods of three years each.

3. If, before the expiry of the four-year period referred to in paragraph 1 of this article, or before the expiry of an extension period referred to in paragraph 2 of this article, as the case may be, a new agreement to replace this Agreement has been negotiated but has not yet entered into force either definitively or provisionally, the Council may, by special vote, extend this Agreement until the provisional or definitive entry into force of the new agreement.

4. If a new agreement is negotiated and enters into force during any period of extension of this Agreement under paragraph 2 or paragraph 3 of this article, this Agreement, as extended, shall terminate upon the entry into force of the new agreement.

5. The Council may at any time, by special vote, decide to terminate this Agreement with effect from such date as it may determine.

6. Notwithstanding the termination of this Agreement, the Council shall continue in being for a period not exceeding 18 months to carry out the liquidation of the Organization, including the settlement of accounts, and, subject to relevant decisions to be taken by special vote, shall have during that period such powers and functions as may be necessary for these purposes.

7. The Council shall notify the depositary of any decision taken under this article.

Article 47
Reservations

Reservations may not be made with respect to any of the provisions of this Agreement.

Article 48
Supplementary and transitional provisions

1. This Agreement shall be the successor to the International Tropical Timber Agreement, 1983.

2. All acts by or on behalf of the Organization or any of its organs under the International Tropical Timber Agreement, 1983, which are in effect on

the date of entry into force of this Agreement and the terms of which do not provide for expiry on that date shall remain in effect unless changed under the provisions of this Agreement.

IN WITNESS WHEREOF the undersigned, being duly authorized thereto, have affixed their signatures under this Agreement on the dates indicated.

DONE at Geneva, on twenty-six January, one thousand nine hundred and ninety-four, the text of this Agreement in the Arabic, Chinese, English, French, Russian and Spanish languages being equally authentic.

Annex A

List of producing countries with tropical forest resources and/or net exporters of tropical timber in volume terms, and allocation of votes for the purposes of article 41

Bolivia	21
Brazil	133
Cameroon	23
Colombia	24
Congo	23
Costa Rica	9
Côte d'Ivoire	23
Dominican Republic	9
Ecuador	14
El Salvador	9
Equatorial Guinea	23
Gabon	23
Ghana	23
Guyana	14
Honduras	9
India	34
Indonesia	170
Liberia	23
Malaysia	139
Mexico	14
Myanmar	33
Panama	10
Papua New Guinea	28
Paraguay	11
Peru	25
Philippines	25
Tanzania, United Republic of	23
Thailand	20
Togo	23
Trinidad and Tobago	9
Venezuela	10
Zaire	23
Total	1,000

Annex B

List of consuming countries and allocation of votes for the purposes of article 41

Afghanistan	10
Algeria	13
Australia	18
Austria	11
Bahrain	11
Bulgaria	10
Canada	12
Chile	10
China	36
Egypt	14
European Community	(302)
Belgium/Luxembourg	26
Denmark	11
France	44
Germany	35
Greece	13
Ireland	13
Italy	35
Netherlands	40
Portugal	18
Spain	25
United Kingdom	42
Finland	10
Japan	320
Nepal	10
New Zealand	10
Norway	10
Republic of Korea	97
Russian Federation	13
Slovakia	11
Sweden	10
Switzerland	11
United States of America	51
Total	1,000

9. CONSERVATION OF MARINE LIVING RESOURCES

International Convention for the Regulation of Whaling, Washington,
2 December 1946, with Schedule

The need to regulate internationally commercial whaling activities was appreciated
from 1927 onwards when declines in several of the stocks of the major species of
whales that were the target of the whaling industry gave rise to fears that the great
expansion in the industry, especially in Antarctica, was leading to commercial
extinction. The first proposals for a convention originated during the preparations
for the League of Nations Conference on the Law of the Sea, held in The Hague in
1930. Following consultations between the League's committees and the International Council for the Exploration of the Sea (ICES), a draft Convention for the
Regulation of Whaling, prepared by a League committee of experts, was adopted,
following amendment, in 1931 and came into force on 16 January 1935. It was
signed by twenty-six States and ratified by eighteen; text in 155 *LNTS* 349; for details
see W. R. Vallance, 'International Convention for the Regulation of Whaling', 31
AJIL (1937) 112–19; P. Birnie, *International Regulation of Whaling*, (2 vols.), (Dobbs
Ferry, 1985), 109–18; J. E. Scarff, 'The International Management of Whales,
Dolphins and Porpoises: An Interdisciplinary Assessment', 6 *ELQ* (1977) 323–427,
571–638; L. Leonard, 'Recent Negotiations toward the International Regulation of
Whaling', 35 *AJIL* (1941) 90ff. Though it was innovatory in applying to all waters of
the world (Article 9) and involving various conservatory measures, it had many
defects, e.g. it specifically protected only right whales, made no provision for
enforcement, and neither set quotas nor established any institutions to oversee
regulation. Inter-company agreements concluded between 1932–36 to limit oil
production by fixing an overall quota related to the oil obtained from each whale
species did not prove effective. A new International Convention for the Regulation
of Whaling was therefore adopted on 7 June 1937 (190 *LNTS* 79; 34 *AJIL* (1940),
supp., 106). It introduced further measures but failed to stop over-exploitation; a
Protocol amending the International Whaling Agreement was therefore adopted
on 24 June 1938 (196 *LNTS* 131) involving some minor improvements. Whaling
greatly decreased during World War II but as the industry gradually resumed
further Protocols were adopted on 7 February 1944 (UK Misc. No 1 (1944), Cmnd.
6510); 5 October 1945 (148 *UNTS* 1143); 15 March 1946[UKTS 44 (1946) Cmnd.
6941]. They had little impact, *inter alia* because the conferences were *ad hoc* and the
Protocols neither attracted ratification by all whaling states, or even by the same
states on each occasion (for details of this period see J. N. Tønnessen and A. O.
Johnson, *The History of Modern Whaling*, (London, 1982), 472–98; Birnie, op.cit,
130–41).

Following World War II, previously rejected proposals for establishment of a
permanent international body with powers to regulate whaling were revived. The
issue was discussed at the 1945 London Conference, and at a further International
Whaling Conference held in Washington in November 1946, at which a new draft
Convention submitted by the United States of America, drawing on fisheries conventions concluded by that date, was adopted, with some amendments (see Birnie,
op.cit., 165–264 for analysis of provisions). The International Whaling Convention
1946 was, at that time, more innovatory than most of the models on which it was
based. Its Preamble recognised 'The interests of the nations of the world in safe-

guarding for future generations the great natural resources represented by whale stocks'; it regarded achievement of an 'optimum level' of stocks as an objective in the 'common interest'; it required catching to be limited to those species best able to sustain exploitation, and stated the Convention's objective as 'proper and effective conservation and development of whale stocks' to enable orderly development of the industry on the basis of the principles of the earlier agreements. Its substantive articles established a Commission of representatives of each contracting Government with power to amend, on the basis of scientific findings (Article V), a Schedule of Regulations that forms an integral part of the Convention. The ICRW applies in all waters world-wide (Article I). The text of the Convention is found at 161 *UNTS* 143; 1 *UST* 281 *TIAS* 18409 and 2052; *UKTS* 5(1949), Cmnd. 7604; *UKTS* 36 (1950), Cmnd. 7989; *UKTS* 68(1959), Cmnd. 849. It was amended by Protocol concluded in Washington on 2 December 1956 (338 *UNTS* 366; *UKTS* 22 (1957), Cmnd. 49; 10 *UST* 952 *TIAS* 4228), in force 4 May 1959.

For the subsequent practice of the Whaling Commission see the *Reports of Meetings of the International Whaling Commission,* IWC, The Red House, Station Road, Histon, Cambridge, CB4 7NP; for discussion of progress from the First to Thirty Fifth (1983) Meetings see Birnie, op.cit., *passim.* Major changes were introduced in 1974 following the adoption by the UN Conference on the Human Environment of a Resolution calling for a ten year moratorium on whaling. Since 1982 the IWC has set quotas for all commercially exploited stocks of whales at zero, but subject to the possibility of future review. Norway and the Russian Federation have maintained objections to this. The Convention had 40 parties at 31 January, 1995.

At the Forty Sixth Meeting, held in Mexico City, 23–27 May 1994, a new Revised Management Procedure was accepted, completing the main scientific component in the development of a Revised Management Scheme for commercial baleen whaling, which will, when it is finalised, address *inter alia* the problems of providing more effective supervision and control, cessation of illegal trade in whale products, under reporting of catch data, and effects of environmental degradation and humane killing. The revised text of the Convention and the 1994 Schedule are reproduced.

TEXT

The Governments whose duly authorized representatives have subscribed hereto,

Recognizing the interest of the nations of the world in safeguarding for future generations the great natural resources represented by the whale stocks;

Considering that the history of whaling has seen over-fishing of one area after another and of one species of whale after another to such a degree that it is essential to protect all species of whales from further over-fishing;

Recognizing that the whale stocks are susceptible of natural increases if whaling is properly regulated, and that increases in the size of whale stocks will permit increases in the numbers of whales which may be captured without endangering these natural resources;

Recognizing that it is in the common interest to achieve the optimum level of whale stocks as rapidly as possible without causing widespread economic and nutritional distress;

Recognizing that in the course of achieving these objectives, whaling operations should be confined to those species best able to sustain exploitation in order to give an interval for recovery to certain species of whales now depleted in numbers;

Desiring to establish a system of international regulation for the whale fisheries to ensure proper and effective conservation and development of whale stocks on the basis of the principles embodied in the provisions of the International Agreement for the Regulation of Whaling signed in London on 8 June 1937, and the protocols to that Agreement signed in London on 24 June 1938, and 26 November 1945; and

Having decided to conclude a convention to provide for the proper conservation of whale stocks and thus make possible the orderly development of the whaling industry;

Have Agreed as follows:

Article I

1. This Convention includes the Schedule attached thereto which forms an integral part thereof. All references to 'Convention' shall be understood as including the said Schedule either in its present terms or as amended in accordance with the provisions of Article V.

2. This Convention applies to factory ships, land stations, and whale catchers under the jurisdiction of the Contracting Governments, and to all waters in which whaling is prosecuted by such factory ships, land stations, and whale catchers.

Article II

As used in this Convention:

1. 'factory ship' means a ship in which or on which whales are treated whether wholly or in part;

2. 'land station' means a factory on the land at which whales are treated whether wholly or in part;

3. 'whale catcher' means a helicopter, or other aircraft, or a ship used for the purpose of hunting, taking, killing, towing, holding on to, or scouting for whales;

4. 'Contracting Government' means any Government which has deposited an instrument of ratification or has given notice of adherence to this Convention.

Article III

1. The Contracting Governments agree to establish an International Whaling Commission, hereinafter referred to as the Commission, to be composed of one member from each Contracting Government. Each member

shall have one vote and may be accompanied by one or more experts and advisers.

2. The Commission shall elect from its own members a Chairman and Vice-Chairman and shall determine its own Rules of Procedure. Decisions of the Commission shall be taken by a simple majority of those members voting except that a three-fourths majority of those members voting shall be required for action in pursuance of Article V. The Rules of Procedure may provide for decisions otherwise than at meetings of the Commission.

3. The Commission may appoint its own Secretary and staff.

4. The Commission may set up, from among its own members and experts or advisers, such committees as it considers desirable to perform such functions as it may authorize.

5. The expenses of each member of the Commission and of his experts and advisers shall be determined and paid by his own Government.

6. Recognizing that specialized agencies related to the United Nations will be concerned with the conservation and development of whale fisheries and the products arising therefrom and desiring to avoid duplication of functions, the Contracting Governments will consult among themselves within two years after the coming into force of this Convention to decide whether the Commission shall be brought within the framework of a specialized agency related to the United Nations.

7. In the meantime the Government of the United Kingdom of Great Britain and Northern Ireland shall arrange, in consultation with the other Contracting Governments, to convene the first meeting of the Commission, and shall initiate the consultation referred to in paragraph 6 above.

8. Subsequent meetings of the Commission shall be convened as the Commission may determine.

Article IV

1. The Commission may either in collaboration with or through independent agencies of the Contracting Governments or other public or private agencies, establishments, or organizations, or independently

   (a) encourage, recommend, or if necessary, organize studies and investigations relating to whales and whaling;
   (b) collect and analyze statistical information concerning the current condition and trend of the whale stocks and the effects of whaling activities thereon;
   (c) study, appraise, and disseminate information concerning methods of maintaining and increasing the populations of whale stocks.

2. The Commission shall arrange for the publication of reports of its activities, and it may publish independently or in collaboration with the International Bureau for Whaling Statistics at Sandefjord in Norway and

other organizations and agencies such reports as it deems appropriate, as well as statistical, scientific, and other pertinent information relating to whales and whaling.

Article V

1. The Commission may amend from time to time the provisions of the Schedule by adopting regulations with respect to the conservation and utilization of whale resources, fixing (a) protected and unprotected species; (b) open and closed seasons; (c) open and closed waters, including the designation of sanctuary areas; (d) size limits for each species; (e) time, methods, and intensity of whaling (including the maximum catch of whales to be taken in any one season); (f) types and specifications of gear and apparatus and appliances which may be used; (g) methods of measurement; (h) catch returns and other statistical and biological records; and (i) methods of inspection.

2. These amendments of the Schedule (a) shall be such as are necessary to carry out the objectives and purposes of this Convention and to provide for the conservation, development, and optimum utilization of the whale resources; (b) shall be based on scientific findings; (c) shall not involve restrictions on the number or nationality of factory ships or land stations, nor allocate specific quotas to any factory ship or land station or to any group of factory ships or land stations; and (d) shall take into consideration the interests of the consumers of whale products and the whaling industry.

3. Each of such amendments shall become effective with respect to the Contracting Governments ninety days following notification of the amendment by the Commission to each of the Contracting Governments, except that (a) if any Government presents to the Commission objection to any amendment prior to the expiration of this ninety-day period, the amendment shall not become effective with respect to any of the Governments for an additional ninety days; (b) thereupon, any other Contracting Government may present objection to the amendment at any time prior to the expiration of the additional ninety-day period, or before the expiration of thirty days from the date of receipt of the last objection received during such additional ninety-day period, whichever date shall be the later; and (c) thereafter, the amendment shall become effective with respect to all Contracting Governments which have not presented objection but shall not become effective with respect to any Government which has so objected until such date as the objection is withdrawn. The Commission shall notify each Contracting Government immediately upon receipt of each objection and withdrawal and each Contracting Government shall acknowledge receipt of all notifications of amendments, objections, and withdrawals.

4. No amendments shall become effective before 1 July 1949.

Article VI

The Commission may from time to time make recommendations to any or all Contracting Governments on any matters which relate to whales or whaling and to the objectives and purposes of this Convention.

Article VII

The Contracting Governments shall ensure prompt transmission to the International Bureau of Whaling Statistics at Sandefjord in Norway, or to such other body as the Commission may designate, of notifications and statistical and other information required by this Convention in such form and manner as may be prescribed by the Commission.

Article VIII

1. Notwithstanding anything contained in this Convention, any Contracting Government may grant to any of its nationals a special permit authorizing that national to kill, take, and treat whales for purposes of scientific research subject to such restrictions as to number and subject to such other conditions as the Contracting Government thinks fit, and the killing, taking, and treating of whales in accordance with the provisions of this Article shall be exempt from the operation of this Convention. Each Contracting Government shall report at once to the Commission all such authorizations which it has granted. Each Contracting Government may at any time revoke any such special permit which it has granted.

2. Any whales taken under these special permits shall so far as practicable be processed and the proceeds shall be dealt with in accordance with directions issued by the Government by which the permit was granted.

3. Each Contracting Government shall transmit to such body as may be designated by the Commission, in so far as practicable, and at intervals of not more than one year, scientific information available to that Government with respect to whales and whaling, including the results of research conducted pursuant to paragraph 1 of this Article and to Article IV.

4. Recognizing that continuous collection and analysis of biological data in connection with the operations of factory ships and land stations are indispensable to sound and constructive management of the whale fisheries, the Contracting Governments will take all practicable measures to obtain such data.

Article IX

1. Each Contracting Government shall take appropriate measures to ensure the application of the provisions of this Convention and the punishment of infractions against the said provisions in operations carried out by persons or by vessels under its jurisdiction.

2. No bonus or other remuneration calculated with relation to the results of their work shall be paid to the gunners and crews of whale catchers in respect of any whales the taking of which is forbidden by this Convention.

3. Prosecution for infractions against or contraventions of this Convention shall be instituted by the Government having jurisdiction over the offence.

4. Each Contracting Government shall transmit to the Commission full details of each infraction of the provisions of this Convention by persons or vessels under the jurisdiction of that Government as reported by its inspectors. This information shall include a statement of measures taken for dealing with the infraction and of penalties imposed.

Article X

1. This Convention shall be ratified and the instruments of ratification shall be deposited with the Government of the United States of America.

2. Any Government which has not signed this Convention may adhere thereto after it enters into force by a notification in writing to the Government of the United States of America.

3. The Government of the United States of America shall inform all other signatory Governments and all adhering Governments of all ratifications deposited and adherences received.

4. This Convention shall, when instruments of ratification have been deposited by at least six signatory Governments, which shall include the Governments of the Netherlands, Norway, the Union of Soviet Socialist Republics, the United Kingdom of Great Britain and Northern Ireland, and the United States of America, enter into force with respect to those Governments and shall enter into force with respect to each Government which subsequently ratifies or adheres on the date of the deposit of its instrument of ratification or the receipt of its notification of adherence.

5. The provisions of the Schedule shall not apply prior to 1 July 1948. Amendments to the Schedule adopted pursuant to Article V shall not apply prior to 1 July 1949.

Article XI

Any Contracting Government may withdraw from this Convention on June thirtieth of any year by giving notice on or before January first of the same year to the depositary Government, which upon receipt of such a notice shall at once communicate it to the other Contracting Governments. Any other Contracting Government may, in like manner, within one month of the receipt of a copy of such a notice from the depositary Government, give notice of withdrawal, so that the Convention shall cease to be in force on June thirtieth of the same year with respect to the Government giving such notice of withdrawal.

This Convention shall bear the date on which it is opened for signature and shall remain open for signature for a period of fourteen days thereafter.

IN WITNESS WHEREOF the undersigned, being duly authorized, have signed this Convention.

DONE in Washington this second day of December 1946, in the English language, the original of which shall be deposited in the archives of the Government of the United States of America. The Government of the United States of America shall transmit certified copies thereof to all the other signatory and adhering Governments.

TEXT OF SCHEDULE (AS AMENDED BY THE COMMISSION AT THE 46TH ANNUAL MEETING, MAY 1994, AND REPLACING THAT DATED OCTOBER 1993)

I. Interpretation

1. The following expressions have the meanings respectively assigned to them, that is to say:

A. *Baleen whales*
'baleen whale' means any whale which has baleen or whale bone in the mouth, i.e. any whale other than a toothed whale.

'blue whale' (*Balaenoptera musculus*) means any whale known as blue whale, Sibbald's rorqual, or sulphur bottom, and including pygmy blue whale.

'bowhead whale' (*Balaena mysticetus*) means any whale known as bowhead, Arctic right whale, great polar whale, Greenland right whale, Greenland whale.

'Bryde's whale' (*Balaenoptera edeni, B. brydei*) means any whale known as Bryde's whale.

'fin whale' (*Balaenoptera physalus*) means any whale known as common finback, common rorqual, fin whale, herring whale, or true fin whale.

'gray whale' (*Eschrichtius robustus*) means any whale known as gray whale, California gray, devil fish, hard head, mussel digger, gray back, or rip sack.

'humpback whale' (*Megaptera novaeangliae*) means any whale known as bunch, humpback, humpback whale, humpbacked whale, hump whale or hunchbacked whale.

'minke whale' (*Balaenoptera acutorostrata, B. bonaerensis*) means any whale known as lesser rorqual, little piked whale, minke whale, pike-headed whale or sharp headed finner.

'pygmy right whale' (*Caperea marginata*) means any whale known as southern pygmy right whale or pygmy right whale.

'right whale' (*Eubalaena glacialis. E. australis*) means any whale known as Atlantic right whale, Arctic right whale, Biscayan right whale, Nordkaper, North Atlantic right whale, North Cape whale, Pacific right whale, or southern right whale.

'sei whale' (*Balaenoptera borealis*) means any whale known as sei whale, Rudolphi's rorqual, pollack whale, or coalfish whale.

B. Toothed whales

'toothed whale' means any whale which has teeth in the jaws.

'beaked whale' means any whale belonging to the genus *Mesoplodon*, or any whale known as Cuvier's beaked whale (*Ziphius cavirostris*), or Shepherd's beaked whale (*Tasmacetus shepherdi*).

'bottlenose whale' means any whale known as Baird's beaked whale (*Berardius bairdii*), Arnoux's whale (*Berardius arnuxii*), southern bottlenose whale (*Hyperoodon planifrons*), or northern bottlenose whale (*Hyperoodon ampullatus*).

'killer whale' (*Orcinus orca*) means any whale known as killer whale or orca.

'pilot whale' means any whale known as long-finned pilot whale (*Globicephala melaena*) or short-finned pilot whale (*G. macrorhynchus*).

'sperm whale' (*Physeter macrocephalus*) means any whale known as sperm whale, spermacet whale, cachalot or pot whale.

C. General

'strike' means to penetrate with a weapon used for whaling.

'land' means to retrieve to a factory ship, land station, or other place where a whale can be treated.

'take' means to flag, buoy or make fast to a whale catcher.

'lose' means to either strike or take but not to land.

'dauhval' means any unclaimed dead whale found floating.

'lactating whale' means (a) with respect to baleen whales—a female which has any milk present in a mammary gland, (b) with respect to sperm whales—a female which has milk present in a mammary gland the maximum thickness (depth) of which is 10 cm or more. This measurement shall be at the mid ventral point of the mammary gland perpendicular to the body axis, and shall be logged to the nearest centimetre; that is to say, any gland between 9.5 cm and 10.5 cm shall be logged as 10 cm. The measurement of any gland which falls on an exact 0.5 centimetre shall be logged at the next 0.5 centimetre, e.g. 10.5 cm shall be logged as 11.0 cm. However, notwithstanding these criteria, a whale shall not be considered a lactating whale if scientific (histological or other biological) evidence is presented to the appropriate national authority establishing that the whale could not at that point in its physical cycle have had a calf dependent on it for milk.

'small-type whaling' means catching operations using powered vessels with mounted harpoon guns hunting exclusively for minke, bottlenose, beaked, pilot or killer whales.

II. Seasons

Factory Ship Operations

2. (a) It is forbidden to use a factory ship or whale catcher attached thereto for the purpose of taking or treating baleen whales except minke whales, in any waters south of 40° South Latitude except during the period from 12th December to 7th April following, both days inclusive.

   (b) It is forbidden to use a factory ship or whale catcher attached thereto for the purpose of taking or treating sperm or minke whales, except as permitted by the Contracting Governments in accordance with sub-paragraphs (c) and (d) of this paragraph, and paragraph 5.

   (c) Each Contracting Government shall declare for all factory ships and whale catchers attached thereto under its jurisdiction, an open season or seasons not to exceed eight months out of any period of twelve months during which the taking or killing of sperm whales by whale catchers may be permitted; provided that a separate open season may be declared for each factory ship and the whale catchers attached thereto.

   (d) Each Contracting Government shall declare for all factory ships and whale catchers attached thereto under its jurisdiction one continuous open season not to exceed six months out of any period of twelve months during which the taking or killing of minke whales by the whale catchers may be permitted provided that:
      (1) a separate open season may be declared for each factory ship and the whale catchers attached thereto;
      (2) the open season need not necessarily include the whole or any part of the period declared for other baleen whales pursuant to sub-paragraph (a) of this paragraph.

3. It is forbidden to use a factory ship which has been used during a season in any waters south of 40° South Latitude for the purpose of treating baleen whales, except minke whales, in any other area except the North Pacific Ocean and its dependent waters north of the Equator for the same purpose within a period of one year from the termination of that season: provided that catch limits in the North Pacific Ocean and dependent waters are established as provided in paragraphs 12 and 16 of this Schedule and provided that this paragraph shall not apply to a ship which has been used

during the season solely for freezing or salting the meat and entrails of whales intended for human food or feeding animals.

Land Station Operations

4. (a) It is forbidden to use a whale catcher attached to a land station for the purpose of killing or attempting to kill baleen and sperm whales except as permitted by the Contracting Government in accordance with sub-paragraphs (b), (c) and (d) of this paragraph.

   (b) Each Contracting Government shall declare for all land stations under its jurisdiction, and whale catchers attached to such land stations, one open season during which the taking or killing of baleen whales, except minke whales, by the whale catchers shall be permitted. Such open season shall be for a period of not more than six consecutive months in any period of twelve months and shall apply to all land stations under the jurisdiction of the Contracting Government: provided that a separate open season may be declared for any land station used for the taking or treating of baleen whales, except minke whales, which is more than 1,000 miles from the nearest land station used for the taking or treating of baleen whales, except minke whales, under the jurisdiction of the same Contracting Government.

   (c) Each Contracting Government shall declare for all land stations under its jurisdiction and for whale catchers attached to such land stations, one open season not to exceed eight continuous months in any one period of twelve months, during which the taking or killing of sperm whales by the whale catchers shall be permitted, provided that a separate open season may be declared for any land station used for the taking or treating of sperm whales which is more than 1,000 miles from the nearest land station used for the taking or treating of sperm whales under the jurisdiction of the same Contracting Government.

   (d) Each Contracting Government shall declare for all land stations under its jurisdiction and for whale catchers attached to such land stations one open season not to exceed six continuous months in any period of twelve months during which the taking or killing of minke whales by the whale catchers shall be permitted (such period not being necessarily concurrent with the period declared for other baleen whales, as provided for in sub-paragraph (b) of this paragraph); provided that a separate open season may be declared for any land station used for the taking or treating of minke whales which is more than 1,000 miles from the nearest land station used for the taking or treating of minke whales under the jurisdiction of the same Contracting Government.

Except that a separate open season may be declared for any land station used for the taking or treating of minke whales which is located in an area having oceanographic conditions clearly distinguishable from those of the area in which are located the other land stations used for the taking or treating of minke whales under the jurisdiction of the same Contracting Government; but the declaration of a separate open season by virtue of the provisions of this sub-paragraph shall not cause thereby the period of time covering the open seasons declared by the same Contracting Government to exceed nine continuous months of any twelve months.

(e) The prohibitions contained in this paragraph shall apply to all land stations as defined in Article II of the Whaling Convention of 1946.

Other Operations

5. Each Contracting Government shall declare for all whale catchers under its jurisdiction not operating in conjunction with a factory ship or land station one continuous open season not to exceed six months out of any period of twelve months during which the taking or killing of minke whales by such whale catchers may be permitted. Notwithstanding this paragraph one continuous open season not to exceed nine months may be implemented so far as Greenland is concerned.

III. Capture

6. The killing for commercial purposes of whales, except minke whales, using the cold grenade harpoon shall be forbidden from the beginning of the 1980/81 pelagic and 1981 coastal seasons. The killing for commercial purposes of minke whales using the cold grenade harpoon shall be forbidden from the beginning of the 1982/83 pelagic and the 1983 coastal seasons.[1]

7. (a) In accordance with Article V(I)(c) of the Convention, commercial whaling, whether by pelagic operations or from land stations, is prohibited in a region designated as the Indian Ocean Sanctuary. This comprises the waters of the Northern Hemisphere from the coast of Africa to 100°E, including the Red and Arabian Seas and the Gulf of Oman; and the waters of the Southern Hemisphere in the sector from 20°E to 130°E, with the Southern boundary set at 55°S.

---

[1] The Governments of Brazil, Iceland, Japan, Norway and the Union of Soviet Socialist Republics lodged objections to the second sentence of paragraph 6 within the prescribed period. For all other Contracting Governments this sentence came into force on 8 March 1982.

Norway withdrew its objection on 9 July 1985 and Brazil on 8 January 1992.

Iceland withdrew from the Convention with effect from 30 June 1992.

The objections of Japan and the Russian Federation not having been withdrawn, this sentence is not binding upon these governments.

This prohibition applies irrespective of such catch limits for baleen or toothed whales as may from time to time be determined by the Commission. This prohibition shall be reviewed by the Commission at its Annual Meeting in 2002.

(b) In accordance with Article V(I)(c) of the Convention, commercial whaling, whether by pelagic operations or from land stations, is prohibited in a region designated as the Southern Ocean Sanctuary. This Sanctuary comprises the waters of the Southern Hemisphere southwards of the following line: starting from 40°S, 50°W; thence due east to 20°E; thence due south to 55°S; thence due east to 130°E; thence due north to 40°S; thence due east to 130°W; thence due south to 60°S; thence due east to 50°W; thence due north to the point of beginning. This prohibition applies irrespective of the conservation status of baleen and toothed whale stocks in this Sanctuary, as may from time to time be determined by the Commission. However, this prohibition shall be reviewed ten years after its initial adoption and at succeeding ten year intervals, and could be revised at such times by the Commission. Nothing in this sub-paragraph is intended to prejudice the special legal and political status of Antarctica.[2,3]

Area Limits for Factory Ships

8. It is forbidden to use a factory ship or whale catcher attached thereto, for the purpose of taking or treating baleen whales, except minke whales, in any of the following areas:

(a) in the waters north of 66°N, except that from 150°E eastwards as far as 140°W, the taking or killing of baleen whales by a factory ship or whale catcher shall be permitted between 66°N and 72°N;

(b) in the Atlantic Ocean and its dependent waters north of 40°S;

(c) in the Pacific Ocean and its dependent waters east of 150°W between 40°S and 35°N;

(d) in the Pacific Ocean and its dependent waters west of 150°W between 40°S and 20°N;

(e) in the Indian Ocean and its dependent waters north of 40°S.

---

[2] The Government of Japan lodged an objection within the prescribed period to paragraph 7(b) to the extent that it applies to the Antarctic minke whale stocks.

The Government of the Russian Federation also lodged an objection to paragraph 7(b) within the prescribed period but withdrew it on 26 October 1994.

For all Contracting Governments except Japan paragraph 7(b) came into force on 6 December 1994.

[3] Paragraph 7(b) contains a provision for review of the Southern Ocean Sanctuary 'ten years after its initial adoption'. Paragraph 7(b) was adopted at the 46th (1994) Annual Meeting. Therefore, the first review is due in 2004.

Classification of Areas and Divisions
9. (a) Classification of Areas
    Areas relating to Southern Hemisphere baleen whales except
    Bryde's whales are those waters between the ice-edge and the Equa-
    tor and between the meridians of longitude listed in Table 1.
  (b) Classification of Divisions
    Divisions relating to Southern Hemisphere sperm whales are those
    waters between the ice-edge and the Equator and between the mer-
    idians of longitude listed in Table 3.
  (c) Geographical boundaries in the North Atlantic
    The geographical boundaries for the fin, minke and sei whale stocks
    in the North Atlantic are:

Fin whale stocks

Nova Scotia
South and West of a line through:
47°N 54°W, 46°N 54°30'W,
46°N 42°W, 20°N 42°W.

North Norway
North and East of a line through:
74°N 22°W, 74°N 3°E, 68°N 3°E,
67°N 0°, 67°N 14°E.

Newfoundland–Labrador
West of a line through:
75°N 73°30'W, 69°N 59°W,
61°N 59°W, 52°20'N 42°W,
46°N 42°W and
North of a line through:
46°N 42°W, 46°N 54°30'W,
47°N 54°W.

West Norway–Faroe Islands
South of a line through:
67°N 14°E, 67°N 0°, 60°N 18°W, and
North of a line through:
61°N 16°W, 61°N 0°, Thyborøn
(western entrance to Limfjorden,
Denmark).

West Greenland
East of a line through:
75°N 73°30'W, 69°N 59°W,
61°N 59°W, 52°20'N 42°W,
and West of a line through:
52°20'N 42°W, 59°N 42°W,
59°N 44°W, Kap Farvel.

Spain–Portugal–British Isles
South of a line through:
Thyborøn (Denmark). 61°N 0°,
61°N 16°W, and East of a line
through: 63°N 11°W, 60°N 18°W,
22°N 18°W.

East Greenland–Iceland
East of a line through:
Kap Farvel (South Greenland).
59°N 44°W, 59°N 42°W, 20°N 42°W,
and West of a line through:
20°N 18°W, 60°N 18°W, 68°N 3°E,
74°N 3°E, and South of 74°N.

Minke whale stocks

Canadian East Coast
West of a line through:
75°N 73°30′W, 69°N 59°W,
61°N 59°W, 52°20′N 42°W,
20°N, 42°W,

Central
East of a line through:
Kap Farvel (South Greenland),
59°N 44°W, 59°N 42°W, 20°N 42°W
and West of a line through:
20°N 18°W, 60°N 18°W, 68°N 3°E,
74°N 3°E, and South of 74°N.

West Greenland
East of a line through:
75°N 73°30′W, 69°N 59°W,
61°N 59°W, 52°20′N 42°W, and
West of a line through:
52°20′N 42°W, 59°N 42°W,
59°N 44°W, Kap Farvel.

Northeastern
East of a line through:
20°N 18°W, 60°N 18°W, 68°N 3°E,
74°N 3°E, and North of a line
through: 74°N 3°E, 74°N 22°W.

Sei whale stocks

Nova Scotia
South and West of a line through:
47°N 54°W, 46°N 54°30′W,
46°N 42°W, 20°N 42°W.

Eastern
East of a line through:
20°N 18°W, 60°N 18°W, 68°N 3°E,
74°N 3°E,
and North of a line through:
74°N 3°E, 74°N 22°W.

Iceland–Denmark Strait
East of a line through:
Kap Farvel (South Greenland),
59°N 44°W, 59°N 42°W, 20°N 42°W,
and West of a line through:
20°N 18°W, 60°N 18°W, 68°N 3°E,
74°N 3°E, and South of 74°N.

   (d) Geographical boundaries in the North Pacific
      The geographical boundaries for the sperm, Bryde's and minke
      whale stocks in the North Pacific are:

Sperm whale stocks
  Western Division
    West of a line from the ice-edge south along the 180° meridian of
longitude to 180°, 50°N, then east along the 50°N parallel of latitude to
160°W, 50°N, then south along the 160°W meridian of longitude to 160°W,
40°N, then east along the 40°N parallel of latitude to 150°W, 40°N, then
south along the 150°W meridian of longitude to the Equator.

Eastern Division
East of the line described above.

Bryde's whale stocks

East China Sea
West of the Ryukyu Island chain

Eastern
East of 160°W
(excluding the Peruvian stock area)

Western
West of 160°W
(excluding the East China Sea
stock area)

Minke whale stocks

Sea of Japan–Yellow Sea–
East China Sea
West of a line through
the Philippine Islands, Taiwan,
Ryukyu Islands, Kyushu, Honshu,
Hokkaido and Sakhalin Island,
north of the Equator

Okhotsk Sea–West Pacific
East of the Sea of Japan–Yellow Sea–
East China Sea stock and west of
180° north of the Equator

Remainder
East of the Okhotsk Sea–West
Pacific stock. north of the Equator

(e) Geographical boundaries for Bryde's whale stocks in the Southern
Hemisphere

Southern Indian Ocean
20°E to 130°E
South of the Equator

Solomon Islands
150°E to 170°E
20°S to the Equator

Peruvian
110°W to the South American
coast 10°S to 10°N

Eastern South Pacific
150°W to 70°W
South of the Equator
(excluding the Peruvian stock area)

Western South Pacific
130°E to 150°W
South of the Equator
(excluding the Solomon Islands
stock area)

South Atlantic
70°W to 20°E
South of the Equator (excluding the
South African inshore stock area)

South African Inshore
South African coast west of 27°E
and out to the 200 metre isobath

Classification of Stocks

10. All stocks of whales shall be classified in one of three categories according to the advice of the Scientific Committee as follows:

(a) A Sustained Management Stock (SMS) is a stock which is not more than 10 per cent of Maximum Sustainable Yield (hereinafter referred to as MSY) stock level below MSY stock level, and not more than 20 per cent above that level; MSY being determined on the basis of the number of whales.

When a stock has remained at a stable level for a considerable period under a regime of approximately constant catches, it shall be classified as a Sustained Management Stock in the absence of any positive evidence that it should be otherwise classified.

Commercial whaling shall be permitted on Sustained Management Stocks according to the advice of the Scientific Committee. These stocks are listed in Tables 1, 2 and 3 of this Schedule.

For stocks at or above the MSY stock level, the permitted catch shall not exceed 90 per cent of the MSY. For stocks between the MSY stock level and 10 per cent below that level, the permitted catch shall not exceed the number of whales obtained by taking 90 per cent of the MSY and reducing that number by 10 per cent for every 1 per cent by which the stock falls short of the MSY stock level.

(b) An Initial Management Stock (IMS) is a stock more than 20 per cent of MSY stock level above MSY stock level. Commercial whaling shall be permitted on Initial Management Stocks according to the advice of the Scientific Committee as to measures necessary to bring the stocks to the MSY stock level and then optimum level in an efficient manner and without risk of reducing them below this level. The permitted catch for such stocks will not be more than 90 per cent of MSY as far as this is known, or, where it will be more appropriate, catching effort shall be limited to that which will take 90 per cent of MSY in a stock at MSY stock level.

In the absence of any positive evidence that a continuing higher percentage will not reduce the stock below the MSY stock level no more than 5 per cent of the estimated initial exploitable stock shall be taken in any one year. Exploitation should not commence until an estimate of stock size has been obtained which is satisfactory in the view of the Scientific Committee. Stocks classified as Initial Management Stock are listed in Tables 1, 2 and 3 of this Schedule. [OMITTED—Ed.]

(c) A Protection Stock (PS) is a stock which is below 10 per cent of MSY stock level below MSY stock level.

There shall be no commercial whaling on Protection Stocks. Stocks so classified are listed in Tables 1, 2 and 3 of this Schedule. [OMITTED—Ed.]

(d) Notwithstanding the other provisions of paragraph 10 there shall be a moratorium on the taking, killing or treating of whales, except minke whales, by factory ships or whale catchers attached to factory ships. This moratorium applies to sperm whales, killer whales and baleen whales, except minke whales.

(e) Notwithstanding the other provisions of paragraph 10, catch limits for the killing for commercial purposes of whales from all stocks for the 1986 coastal and the 1985/86 pelagic seasons and thereafter shall be zero. This provision will be kept under review, based upon the best scientific advice, and by 1990 at the latest the Commission will undertake a comprehensive assessment of the effects of this decision on whale stocks and consider modification of this provision and the establishment of other catch limits.[1]

Baleen Whale Catch Limits

11. The number of baleen whales taken in the Southern Hemisphere in the 1994/95 pelagic season and the 1995 coastal season shall not exceed the limits shown in Tables 1 and 2. [OMITTED—Ed.]

12. The number of baleen whales taken in the North Pacific Ocean and dependent waters in 1995 and in the North Atlantic Ocean in 1995 shall not exceed the limits shown in Tables 1 and 2. [OMITTED—Ed.]

13. (a) Notwithstanding the provisions of paragraph 10, catch limits for aboriginal subsistence whaling to satisfy aboriginal subsistence need for the 1984 whaling season and each whaling season thereafter shall be established in accordance with the following principles:

(1) For stocks at or above MSY level, aboriginal subsistence catches shall be permitted so long as total removals do not exceed 90 per cent of MSY.

(2) For stocks below the MSY level but above a certain minimum level, aboriginal subsistence catches shall be permitted so long as they are set at levels which will allow whale stocks to move to the MSY level.[2]

---

[1] The Governments of Japan, Norway, Peru and the Union of Soviet Socialist Republics lodged objection to paragraph 10(e) within the prescribed period. For all other Contracting Governments this paragraph came into force on 3 February 1983. Peru withdrew its objection on 22 July 1983.

The Government of Japan withdrew its objections with effect from 1 May 1987 with respect to commercial pelagic whaling: from 1 October 1987 with respect to commercial coastal whaling for minke and Bryde's whales: and from 1 April 1988 with respect to commercial coastal sperm whaling.

The objections of Norway and the Russian Federation not having been withdrawn, the paragraph is not binding upon these Governments.

[2] The Commission, on advice of the Scientific Committee, shall establish as far as possible (a) a minimum stock level for each stock below which whales shall not be taken, and (b) a rate of increase towards the MSY level for each stock. The Scientific Committee shall advise on a minimum stock level and on a range of rates of increase towards the MSY level under different catch regimes.

(3) The above provisions will be kept under review, based upon the best scientific advice, and by 1990 at the latest the Commission will undertake a comprehensive assessment of the effects of these provisions on whale stocks and consider modification.

(b) Catch limits for aboriginal subsistence whaling are as follows:

(1) The taking of bowhead whales from the Bering–Chukchi–Beaufort Seas stock by aborigines is permitted, but only when the meat and products of such whales are to be used exclusively for local consumption by the aborigines and further provided that:

  (i) For the years 1995, 1996, 1997 and 1998, the number of bowhead whales landed shall not exceed 204, and the number of bowheads struck shall not exceed 68 in 1995, 67 in 1996, 66 in 1997, and 65 in 1998, except that any unused portion of the strike quota for each year shall be carried forward from that year and added to the strike quota of any subsequent years, provided that no more than 10 strikes shall be added to the strike quota for any one year.

  (ii) It is forbidden to strike, take or kill calves or any bowhead whale accompanied by a calf.

  (iii) This provision shall be reviewed annually by the Commission in light of the advice of the Scientific Committee.

(2) The taking of gray whales from the Eastern stock in the North Pacific is permitted, but only by aborigines or a Contracting Government on behalf of aborigines, and then only when the meat and products of such whales are to be used exclusively for local consumption by the aborigines.

  (i) The number of gray whales taken in accordance with this sub-paragraph in each of the years 1995, 1996 and 1997 shall not exceed the limit shown in Table 1. [OMITTED—Ed.]

  (ii) This provision shall be reviewed annually by the Commission in light of the advice of the Scientific Committee.

(3) The taking by aborigines of minke whales from the West Greenland and Central stocks and fin whales from the West Greenland stock is permitted and then only when the meat and products are to be used exclusively for local consumption.

  (i) The number of fin whales from the West Greenland stock and minke whales from the Central stock taken in accordance with this sub-paragraph shall not exceed the limits shown in Table 1. [OMITTED—Ed.]

  (ii) For each of the years 1995, 1996 and 1997, the number of minke whales struck from the West Greenland stock shall not exceed 165, and the total number of whales struck shall not exceed 465 in these three years.

(4) For the seasons 1993/94 to 1995/96 the taking of 2[1] humpback whales each season is permitted by Bequians of St Vincent and The Grenadines, but only when the meat and products of such whales are to be used exclusively for local consumption in St Vincent and The Grenadines.

14. It is forbidden to take or kill suckling calves or female whales accompanied by calves.

Baleen Whale Size Limits

15. (a) It is forbidden to take or kill any sei or Bryde's whales below 40 feet (12.2 metres) in length except that sei and Bryde's whales of not less than 35 feet (10.7 metres) may be taken for delivery to land stations, provided that the meat of such whales is to be used for local consumption as human or animal food.

   (b) It is forbidden to take or kill any fin whales below 57 feet (17.4 metres) in length in the Southern Hemisphere, and it is forbidden to take or kill fin whales below 55 feet (16.8 metres) in the Northern Hemisphere; except that fin whales of not less than 55 feet (16.8 metres) may be taken in the Southern Hemisphere for delivery to land stations and fin whales of not less than 50 feet (15.2 metres) may be taken in the Northern Hemisphere for delivery to land stations, provided that, in each case the meat of such whales is to be used for local consumption as human or animal food.

Sperm Whale Catch Limits

16. Catch limits for sperm whales of both sexes shall be set at zero in the Southern Hemisphere for the 1981/82 pelagic season and 1982 coastal seasons and following seasons, and at zero in the Northern Hemisphere for the 1982 and following coastal seasons; except that the catch limits for the 1982 coastal season and following seasons in the Western Division of the North Pacific shall remain undetermined and subject to decision by the Commission following special or annual meetings of the Scientific Committee. These limits shall remain in force until such time as the Commission, on the basis of the scientific information which will be reviewed annually, decides otherwise in accordance with the procedures followed at that time by the Commission.

17. It is forbidden to take or kill suckling calves or female whales accompanied by calves.

---

[1] Each year this figure will be reviewed and if necessary amended on the basis of the advice of the Scientific Committee.

Sperm Whale Size Limits

18. (a) It is forbidden to take or kill any sperm whales below 30 feet (9.2 metres) in length except in the North Atlantic Ocean where it is forbidden to take or kill any sperm whales below 35 feet (10.7 metres).

    (b) It is forbidden to take or kill any sperm whale over 45 feet (13.7 metres) in length in the Southern Hemisphere north of 40° South Latitude during the months of October to January inclusive.

    (c) It is forbidden to take or kill any sperm whale over 45 feet (13.7 metres) in length in the North Pacific Ocean and dependent water south of 40° North Latitude during the months of March to June inclusive.

IV. Treatment

19. (a) It is forbidden to use a factory ship or a land station for the purpose of treating any whales which are classified as Protection Stocks in paragraph 10 or are taken in contravention of paragraphs 2, 3, 4, 5, 6, 7, 8, 11, 12, 14, 16 and 17 of this Schedule, whether or not taken by whale catchers under the jurisdiction of a Contracting Government.

    (b) All other whales taken, except minke whales, shall be delivered to the factory ship or land station and all parts of such whales shall be processed by boiling or otherwise, except the internal organs, whale bone and flippers of all whales, the meat of sperm whales and parts of whales intended for human food or feeding animals. A Contracting Government may in less developed regions exceptionally permit treating of whales without use of land stations, provided that such whales are fully utilised in accordance with this paragraph.

    (c) Complete treatment of the carcases of 'dauhval' and of whales used as fenders will not be required in cases where the meat or bone of such whales is in bad condition.

20. (a) The taking of whales for treatment by a factory ship shall be so regulated or restricted by the master or person in charge of the factory ship that no whale carcase (except of a whale used as a fender, which shall be processed as soon as is reasonably practicable) shall remain in the sea for a longer period than thirty-three hours from the time of killing to the time when it is hauled up for treatment.

    (b) Whales taken by all whale catchers, whether for factory ships or land stations, shall be clearly marked so as to identify the catcher and to indicate the order of catching.

V. Supervision and Control

21. (a) There shall be maintained on each factory ship at least two inspectors of whaling for the purpose of maintaining twenty-four hour inspection provided that at least one such inspector shall be maintained on each catcher functioning as a factory ship. These inspectors shall be appointed and paid by the Government having jurisdiction over the factory ship; provided that inspectors need not be appointed to ships which, apart from the storage of products, are used during the season solely for freezing or salting the meat and entrails of whales intended for human food or feeding animals.

   (b) Adequate inspection shall be maintained at each land station. The inspectors serving at each land station shall be appointed and paid by the Government having jurisdiction over the land station.

   (c) There shall be received such observers as the member countries may arrange to place on factory ships and land stations or groups of land stations of other member countries. The observers shall be appointed by the Commission acting through its Secretary and paid by the Government nominating them.

22. Gunners and crews of factory ships, land stations, and whale catchers, shall be engaged on such terms that their remuneration shall depend to a considerable extent upon such factors as the species, size and yield of whales and not merely upon the number of the whales taken. No bonus or other remuneration shall be paid to the gunners or crews of whale catchers in respect of the taking of lactating whales.

23. Whales must be measured when at rest on deck or platform after the hauling out wire and grasping device have been released, by means of a tape-measure made of a non-stretching material. The zero end of the tape-measure shall be attached to a spike or stable device to be positioned on the deck or platform abreast of one end of the whale. Alternatively the spike may be stuck into the tail fluke abreast of the apex of the notch. The tape-measure shall be held taut in a straight line parallel to the deck and the whale's body, and other than in exceptional circumstances along the whale's back, and read abreast of the other end of the whale. The ends of the whale for measurement purposes shall be the tip of the upper jaw, or in sperm whales the most forward part of the head, and the apex of the notch between the tail flukes.

Measurements shall be logged to the nearest foot or 0.1 metre. That is to say, any whale between 75 feet 6 inches and 76 feet 6 inches shall be logged as 76 feet, and any whale between 76 feet 6 inches and 77 feet 6 inches shall be logged as 77 feet. Similarly, any whale between 10.15 metres and 10.25 metres shall be logged as 10.2 metres, and any whale between 10.25 metres and 10.35 metres shall be logged as 10.3 metres. The measurement of any whale which falls on an exact half foot or 0.05 metre shall be logged at the next half foot or 0.05 metre, e.g. 76 feet 6 inches precisely shall be logged as 77 feet and 10.25 metres precisely shall be logged as 10.3 metres.

VI. Information Required

24. (a) All whale catchers operating in conjunction with a factory ship shall report by radio to the factory ship:
    (1) the time when each whale is taken
    (2) its species, and
    (3) its marking effected pursuant to paragraph 20(b).
    (b) The information specified in sub-paragraph (a) of this paragraph shall be entered immediately by a factory ship in a permanent record which shall be available at all times for examination by the whaling inspectors; and in addition there shall be entered in such permanent record the following information as soon as it becomes available:
    (1) time of hauling up for treatment
    (2) length, measured pursuant to paragraph 23
    (3) sex
    (4) if female, whether lactating
    (5) length and sex of foetus, if present, and
    (6) a full explanation of each infraction.
    (c) A record similar to that described in sub-paragraph (b) of this paragraph shall be maintained by land stations, and all of the information mentioned in the said sub-paragraph shall be entered therein as soon as available.
    (d) A record similar to that described in sub-paragraph (b) of this paragraph shall be maintained by 'small-type whaling' operations conducted from shore or by pelagic fleets, and all of this information mentioned in the said sub-paragraph shall be entered therein as soon as available.

25. (a) All Contracting Governments shall report to the Commission for all whale catchers operating in conjunction with factory ships and land stations the following information:
    (1) methods used to kill each whale, other than a harpoon, and in particular compressed air
    (2) number of whales struck but lost.
    (b) A record similar to that described in sub-paragraph (a) of this paragraph shall be maintained by vessels engaged in 'small-type whaling' operations and by native peoples taking species listed in paragraph 1, and all the information mentioned in the said sub-paragraph shall be entered therein as soon as available,

and forwarded by Contracting Governments to the Commission.

26. (a) Notification shall be given in accordance with the provisions of Article VII of the Convention, within two days after the end of each calendar week, of data on the number of baleen whales by species taken in any waters south of 40° South Latitude by all factory ships or whale catchers attached thereto under the jurisdiction of each Contracting Government, provided that when the number of each of these species taken is deemed by the Secretary to the International Whaling Commission to have reached 85 per cent of whatever total catch limit is imposed by the Commission notification shall be given as aforesaid at the end of each day of data on the number of each of these species taken.

(b) If it appears that the maximum catches of whales permitted by paragraph 11 may be reached before 7 April of any year, the Secretary to the International Whaling Commission shall determine, on the basis of the data provided, the date on which the maximum catch of each of these species shall be deemed to have been reached and shall notify the master of each factory ship and each Contracting Government of that date not less than four days in advance thereof. The taking or attempting to take baleen whales, so notified, by factory ships or whale catchers attached thereto shall be illegal in any waters south of 40° South Latitude after midnight of the date so determined.

(c) Notification shall be given in accordance with the provisions of Article VII of the Convention of each factory ship intending to engage in whaling operations in any waters south of 40° South Latitude.

27. Notification shall be given in accordance with the provisions of Article VII of the Convention with regard to all factory ships and catcher ships of the following statistical information:

(a) concerning the number of whales of each species taken, the number thereof lost, and the number treated at each factory ship or land station, and

(b) as to the aggregate amounts of oil of each grade and quantities of meal, fertiliser (guano), and other products derived from them, together with

(c) particulars with respect to each whale treated in the factory ship, land station or 'small-type whaling' operations as to the date and approximate latitude and longitude of taking, the species and sex of the whale, its length and, if it contains a foetus, the length and sex, if ascertainable, of the foetus.

The data referred to in (a) and (c) above shall be verified at the time of the tally and there shall also be notification to the Commission of any information which may be collected or obtained concerning the calving grounds and migration of whales.

28. (a) Notification shall be given in accordance with the provisions of Article VII of the Convention with regard to all factory ships and catcher ships of the following statistical information:

    (1) The name and gross tonnage of each factory ship.
    (2) For each catcher ship attached to a factory ship or land station:
        (i) the dates on which each is commissioned and ceases whaling for the season
        (ii) the number of days on which each is at sea on the whaling grounds each season
        (iii) the gross tonnage, horsepower, length and other characteristics of each; vessels used only as low boats should be specified.
    (3) A list of the land stations which were in operation during the period concerned, and the number of miles searched per day by aircraft, if any.

    (b) The information required under paragraph (a)(2)(iii) should also be recorded together with the following information, in the log book format shown in Appendix A, and forwarded to the Commission:

    (1) where possible the time spent each day on different components of the catching operation
    (2) any modifications of the measures in paragraphs (a)(2)(i)–(iii) or (b)(1) or data from other suitable indicators of fishing effort for 'small-type whaling' operations.

29. (a) Where possible all factory ships and land stations shall collect from each whale taken and report on:

    (1) both ovaries or the combined weight of both testes
    (2) at least one ear plug, or one tooth (preferably first mandibular).

    (b) Where possible similar collections to those described in sub-paragraph (a) of this paragraph shall be undertaken and reported by 'small-type whaling' operations conducted from shore or by pelagic fleets.

    (c) All specimens collected under sub-paragraphs (a) and (b) shall be properly labelled with platform or other identification number of the whale and be appropriately preserved.

    (d) Contracting Governments shall arrange for the analysis as soon as possible of the tissue samples and specimens collected under sub-paragraphs (a) and (b) and report to the Commission on the results of such analyses.

30. A Contracting Government shall provide the Secretary to the International Whaling Commission with proposed scientific permits before they are issued and in sufficient time to allow the Scientific Committee to review and comment on them. The proposed permits should specify:

(a) objectives of the research;
(b) number, sex, size and stock of the animals to be taken;
(c) opportunities for participation in the research by scientists of other nations; and
(d) possible effect on conservation of stock.

Proposed permits shall be reviewed and commented on by the Scientific Committee at Annual Meetings when possible. When permits would be granted prior to the next Annual Meeting, the Secretary shall send the proposed permits to members of the Scientific Committee by mail for their comment and review. Preliminary results of any research resulting from the permits should be made available at the next Annual Meeting of the Scientific Committee.

31. A Contracting Government shall transmit to the Commission copies of all its official laws and regulations relating to whales and whaling and changes in such laws and regulations.

United Nations Convention on the Law of the Sea 1982,
Parts V and VII (excerpts)

For background to this Convention see supra, Chapter 3. Articles 55–75, 86–9 and 116–120 of the United Nations Law of the Sea Convention deal specifically with living resources found within the Exclusive Economic Zone (EEZ) and in the High Seas. They lay down, *inter alia*, the conditions on which fishing activities take place in these areas. In the EEZ fishing is subject to the exclusive jurisdiction of the Coastal State which has sovereign rights over the exploration and exploitation of the living resources therein. This is, however, subject to the duties, *inter alia*, set out in Articles 61 and 62, which include the taking of measures to ensure their conservation and management and to promote optimum utilization.

On the high seas (Article 86 (1)(e)) the doctrine of freedom of fishing prevails but subject to the requirement that *all* States observe the duties set out in Articles 116–120, including that they 'co-operate with each other in conservation and management' and 'enter into negotiations with a view to' achieving these ends.

Both sets of articles represent compromises achieved during the UNCLOS negotiations. For the drafting history of Articles 61–73 see M. Nordquist, S. N. Nandan, and S. Rosenne (eds.) *United Nations Convention on the Law of the Sea 1982: A Commentary*, vol. II (Dordrecht/Boston/London, 1993), and for Articles 116–120, ibid, vol. III. For preparatory material, see Third United Nations Conference on the Law of the Sea: Official Records, 17 vols. (1975–84). There is considerable evidence in state practice both from the conclusion of multi-lateral and bi-lateral agreements and enactment of national legislation, that Articles 61–73 are widely accepted; for details see *The Marine Mammal Commission Compendium of Treaties, International Agreements, and Other Relevant Documents on Marine Resources Wildlife and the Environment* (3 vols.) (Washington D.C., 1994); *Coastal State Requirements for Foreign Fishing*, FAO Legislative Study 21, Rev. 4 (FAO, Rome, 1993); *Law of the Sea Bulletin* (1–26 *et seq*), UN Division for Ocean Affairs and the Law of the Sea, Office of Legal Affairs. State practice in relation to Articles 116–120 is less clear; some conventions regulating conservation of specific species or fisheries in specific areas of the high seas have been concluded (see op. cit. supra.), but not all States engaged in high seas are party to these and disputes concerning their interpretation are increasing; for examples, see W. T. Burke, *The New International Law of Fisheries: UNCLOS 1982 and Beyond* (Oxford, 1994), *passim*.

Stocks that straddle EEZs, the high seas, or both, have given rise to problems. Conflicts arose between distant water fishing states and coastal states, especially in relation to stocks straddling Canada's EEZ, when vessels fishing on the high seas did not observe international conservation measures in force under international agreements. These disputes derive from ambiguities inherent in the provisions of Article 63 relating to straddling stocks and Articles 116–119 concerning conservation of high seas fisheries. Following recommendations made in UNCED, *Agenda 21*, Chapter 17, a Code of Conduct for Responsible Fishing was being negotiated under the auspices of FAO in 1995, to include the 1993 FAO Agreement to Promote Compliance with International Conservation and Management Measures by Fishing Vessels on the High Seas (q.v.). Negotiations were also still in progress in 1995 within the United Nations Conference on Straddling Fish Stocks aimed at adopting a Code or Agreement on this issue (for progress see C. Higginson, 'The UN Conference on High Seas Fishing', 2 *RECIEL* (1993) 237–44; 'First Steps to a Convention on Fish Stocks', 23 *EPL* (1993) 238–40; 'Fish Stocks: Revised Negotiating Text', 24 *EPL* (1994) 142–44.)

Increasing use of large drift nets on the high seas led the UN General Assembly to adopt Resolutions expressing concern (UNGA Resolution 44/225 (1989); UNGA Resolution 46/215 (1991), 31 *ILM* (1992) 241). For a comprehensive UN Secretariat study of the high seas regime see Report of the Secretary-General, UN Doc. A/48/451 (1993). A regional convention for the Prohibition of Fishing with Long Drift Nets in the South Pacific, was concluded at Wellington, 23 November 1989 (text in 29 *ILM* (1990) 1449; Marine Mammal Commission, *Compendium* (Washington D.C., 1994) 1350–1359). For driftnetting, see D. Johnston, 'The Driftnetting Problem in the Pacific Ocean: Legal Considerations and Diplomatic Options', 21 *ODIL* (1990) 5ff.; for a different view see W. Burke, op. cit; 86–7; 102–7; 109; 117–18; 180–1.

It is notable that the UNCLOS does not define the term 'conservation'. This was defined in the Convention and Fishing and Conservation of the Living Resources of the High Seas, done at Geneva, 29 April 1958; 559 *UNTS* 285; *UKTS* 39 (1966), Cmnd. 3028; 17 *UST* 138 *TIAS* 5969; text and notes on travaux préparatoires in I. Brownlie (ed.) *Basic Documents in International Law* (Oxford, 1983), 85–6; for background see D. Johnson, *International Law of Fisheries* (New Haven, 1965), 108–16. This Convention is still in effect for thirty-six parties, but for those party to the UNCLOS the latter will prevail (UNCLOS Article 311). The definition of 'conservation of the living resources of the high seas' in the 1958 Convention (Article 2) in terms of 'the aggregate of measures rendering possible the optimum sustainable yield from those resources so as to secure a maximum supply of food and other marine products' has been largely superseded in the light of the State practice referred to above based on the UNCLOS text, which takes more account of environmental factors: see especially the Revised Management Procedures adopted by the International Whaling Commission at its 46th Meeting (q.v.). There is an exceptionally large bibliography on fisheries, including marine mammals, anadromous and catadromous species, and migratory species in general; for details see UN, *The Law of the Sea: A Select Bibliography*, 1966–88, and annual UN bibliographies from 1985 onwards, UN Division for Ocean Affairs and the Law of the Sea, Office of Legal Affairs; see also its publications on *Law of the Sea: national legislation on the exclusive economic zone, the economic zone and the exclusive fisheries zone*, (1986); *Law of the Sea: current developments in State Practice* (No. II), (1989); *The law of the sea: the regime of high seas fisheries—status and prospects*, (1992); *The law of the sea: national legislation on the exclusive economic zone*, (1993). For a succinct account of the development of fisheries law up to 1988, see R. R. Churchill and V. Lowe, *The Law of the Sea*, 2nd edn. (Manchester, 1988), 223–40; for environmental aspects see P. W. Birnie and A. E. Boyle, *International Law and the Environment* (Oxford, 1992), 417–42 and 490–542. For extension of Canadian legislation to straddling stocks see Canadian Coastal Fisheries Protection Act (as amended in 1994), 33 *ILM* (1994) 1383–88; see also J. Gilliland Dalton, 'The Chilean Mar Presencial: A Harmless Concept or a Dangerous Precedent' 8 *Marine and Coastal Law* (1993) 399–403.

TEXT OF PART V ON EXCLUSIVE ECONOMIC ZONE

Article 55
Specific legal régime of the exclusive economic zone

The exclusive economic zone is an area beyond and adjacent to the territorial sea, subject to the specific legal régime established in this Part, under which the rights and jurisdiction of the coastal State and the rights and freedoms of other States are governed by the relevant provisions of this Convention.

Article 56
Rights, jurisdiction and duties of the coastal State in the exclusive economic zone

1. In the exclusive economic zone, the coastal State has:

   (a) sovereign rights for the purpose of exploring and exploiting, conserving and managing the natural resources, whether living or non-living, of the waters superjacent to the sea-bed and of the sea-bed and its subsoil, and with regard to other activities for the economic exploitation and exploration of the zone, such as the production of energy from the water, currents and winds;
   (b) jurisdiction as provided for in the relevant provisions of this Convention with regard to:
      (i) the establishment and use of artificial islands, installations and structures;
      (ii) marine scientific research;
      (iii) the protection and preservation of the marine environment;
   (c) other rights and duties provided for in this Convention.

2. In exercising its rights and performing its duties under this Convention in the exclusive economic zone, the coastal State shall have due regard to the rights and duties of other States and shall act in a manner compatible with the provisions of this Convention.

3. The rights set out in this article with respect to the sea-bed and subsoil shall be exercised in accordance with Part VI.

Article 57
Breadth of the exclusive economic zone

The exclusive economic zone shall not extend beyond 200 nautical miles from the baselines from which the breadth of the territorial sea is measured.

Article 58
Rights and duties of other States in the exclusive economic zone

1. In the exclusive economic zone, all States, whether coastal or land-locked, enjoy, subject to the relevant provisions of this Convention, the freedoms referred to in article 87 of navigation and overflight and of the laying of submarine cables and pipelines, and other internationally lawful uses of the sea related to these freedoms, such as those associated with the operation of ships, aircraft and submarine cables and pipelines, and compatible with the other provisions of this Convention.

2. Articles 88 to 115 and other pertinent rules of international law apply to

the exclusive economic zone in so far as they are not incompatible with this Part.

3. In exercising their rights and performing their duties under this Convention in the exclusive economic zone, States shall have due regard to the rights and duties of the coastal State and shall comply with the laws and regulations adopted by the coastal State in accordance with the provisions of this Convention and other rules of international law in so far as they are not incompatible with this Part.

Article 59
Basis for the resolution of conflicts regarding the attribution of rights and jurisdiction in the exclusive economic zone

In cases where this Convention does not attribute rights or jurisdiction to the coastal State or to other States within the exclusive economic zone, and a conflict arises between the interests of the coastal State and any other State or States, the conflict should be resolved on the basis of equity and in the light of all the relevant circumstances, taking into account the respective importance of the interests involved to the parties as well as to the international community as a whole.

Article 60
Artificial islands, installations and structures in the exclusive economic zone

1. In the exclusive economic zone, the coastal State shall have the exclusive right to construct and to authorize and regulate the construction, operation and use of:

(a) artificial islands;
(b) installations and structures for the purposes provided for in article 56 and other economic purposes;
(c) installations and structures which may interfere with the exercise of the rights of the coastal State in the zone.

2. The coastal State shall have exclusive jurisdiction over such artificial islands, installations and structures, including jurisdiction with regard to customs, fiscal, health, safety and immigration laws and regulations.

3. Due notice must be given of the construction of such artificial islands, installations or structures, and permanent means for giving warning of their presence must be maintained. Any installations or structures which are abandoned or disused shall be removed to ensure safety of navigation, taking into account any generally accepted international standards established in this regard by the competent international organization. Such removal shall also have due regard to fishing, the protection of the marine environment and the rights and duties of other States. Appropriate publicity shall be given to the depth, position and dimensions of any installations or structures not entirely removed.

4. The coastal State may, where necessary, establish reasonable safety zones around such artificial islands, installations and structures in which it may take appropriate measures to ensure the safety both of navigation and of the artificial islands, installations and structures.

5. The breadth of the safety zones shall be determined by the coastal State, taking into account applicable international standards. Such zones shall be designed to ensure that they are reasonably related to the nature and function of the artificial islands, installations or structures, and shall not exceed a distance of 500 metres around them, measured from each point of their outer edge, except as authorized by generally accepted international standards or as recommended by the competent international organization. Due notice shall be given of the extent of safety zones.

6. All ships must respect these safety zones and shall comply with generally accepted international standards regarding navigation in the vicinity of artificial islands, installations, structures and safety zones.

7. Artificial islands, installations and structures and the safety zones around them may not be established where interference may be caused to the use of recognized sea lanes essential to international navigation.

8. Artificial islands, installations and structures do not possess the status of islands. They have no territorial sea of their own, and their presence does not affect the delimitation of the territorial sea, the exclusive economic zone or the continental shelf.

Article 61
Conservation of the living resources

1. The coastal State shall determine the allowable catch of the living resources in its exclusive economic zone.

2. The coastal State, taking into account the best scientific evidence available to it, shall ensure through proper conservation and management measures that the maintenance of the living resources in the exclusive economic zone is not endangered by over-exploitation. As appropriate, the coastal State and competent international organizations, whether subregional, regional or global, shall co-operate to this end.

3. Such measures shall also be designed to maintain or restore populations of harvested species at levels which can produce the maximum sustainable yield, as qualified by relevant environmental and economic factors, including the economic needs of coastal fishing communities and the special requirements of developing States, and taking into account fishing patterns, the interdependence of stocks and any generally recommended international minimum standards, whether subregional, regional or global.

4. In taking such measures the coastal State shall take into consideration the effects on species associated with or dependent upon harvested species

with a view to maintaining or restoring populations of such associated or dependent species above levels at which their reproduction may become seriously threatened.

5. Available scientific information, catch and fishing effort statistics, and other data relevant to the conservation of fish stocks shall be contributed and exchanged on a regular basis through competent international organizations, whether subregional, regional or global, where appropriate and with participation by all States concerned, including States whose nationals are allowed to fish in the exclusive economic zone.

Article 62
Utilization of the living resources

1. The coastal State shall promote the objective of optimum utilization of the living resources in the exclusive economic zone without prejudice to article 61.

2. The coastal State shall determine its capacity to harvest the living resources of the exclusive economic zone. Where the coastal State does not have the capacity to harvest the entire allowable catch, it shall, through agreements or other arrangements and pursuant to the terms, conditions, laws and regulations referred to in paragraph 4, give other States access to the surplus of the allowable catch, having particular regard to the provisions of articles 69 and 70, especially in relation to the developing States mentioned therein.

3. In giving access to other States to its exclusive economic zone under this article, the coastal State shall take into account all relevant factors, including, *inter alia*, the significance of the living resources of the area to the economy of the coastal State concerned and its other national interests, the provisions of articles 69 and 70, the requirements of developing States in the subregion or region in harvesting part of the surplus and the need to minimize economic dislocation in States whose nationals have habitually fished in the zone or which have made substantial efforts in research and identification of stocks.

4. Nationals of other States fishing in the exclusive economic zone shall comply with the conservation measures and with the other terms and conditions established in the laws and regulations of the coastal State. These laws and regulations shall be consistent with this Convention and may relate, *inter alia*, to the following:

(a) licensing of fishermen, fishing vessels and equipment, including payment of fees and other forms of remuneration, which, in the case of developing coastal States, may consist of adequate compensation in the field of financing, equipment and technology relating to the fishing industry;

   (b) determining the species which may be caught, and fixing quotas of catch, whether in relation to particular stocks or groups of stocks or catch per vessel over a period of time or to the catch by nationals of any State during a specified period;

   (c) regulating seasons and areas of fishing, the types, sizes and amount of gear, and the types, sizes and number of fishing vessels that may be used;

   (d) fixing the age and size of fish and other species that may be caught;

   (e) specifying information required of fishing vessels, including catch and effort statistics and vessel position reports;

   (f) requiring, under the authorization and control of the coastal State, the conduct of specified fisheries research programmes and regulating the conduct of such research, including the sampling of catches, disposition of samples and reporting of associated scientific data;

   (g) the placing of observers or trainees on board such vessels by the coastal State;

   (h) the landing of all or any part of the catch by such vessels in the ports of the coastal State;

   (i) terms and conditions relating to joint ventures or other co-operative arrangements;

   (j) requirements for the training of personnel and the transfer of fisheries technology, including enhancement of the coastal State's capability of undertaking fisheries research;

   (k) enforcement procedures.

5. Coastal States shall give due notice of conservation and management laws and regulations.

Article 63
Stocks occurring within the exclusive economic zones of two or more coastal States or both within the exclusive economic zone and in an area beyond and adjacent to it

1. Where the same stock or stocks of associated species occur within the exclusive economic zones of two or more coastal States, these States shall seek, either directly or through appropriate subregional or regional organizations, to agree upon the measures necessary to co-ordinate and ensure the conservation and development of such stocks without prejudice to the other provisions of this Part.

2. Where the same stock or stocks of associated species occur both within the exclusive economic zone and in an area beyond and adjacent to the zone, the coastal State and the States fishing for such stocks in the adjacent area shall seek, either directly or through appropriate subregional or regional organizations, to agree upon the measures necessary for the conservation of these stocks in the adjacent area.

Article 64
Highly migratory species

1. The coastal State and other States whose nationals fish in the region for the highly migratory species listed in Annex I shall co-operate directly or through appropriate international organizations with a view to ensuring conservation and promoting the objective of optimum utilization of such species throughout the region, both within and beyond the exclusive economic zone. In regions for which no appropriate international organization exists, the coastal State and other States whose nationals harvest these species in the region shall co-operate to establish such an organization and participate in its work.

2. The provisions of paragraph 1 apply in addition to the other provisions of this Part.

Article 65
Marine mammals

Nothing in this Part restricts the right of a coastal State or the competence of an international organization, as appropriate, to prohibit, limit or regulate the exploitation of marine mammals more strictly than provided for in this Part. States shall co-operate with a view to the conservation of marine mammals and in the case of cetaceans shall in particular work through the appropriate international organizations for their conservation, management and study.

Article 66
Anadromous stocks

1. States in whose rivers anadromous stocks originate shall have the primary interest in and responsibility for such stocks.

2. The State of origin of anadromous stocks shall ensure their conservation by the establishment of appropriate regulatory measures for fishing in all waters landward of the outer limits of its exclusive economic zone and for fishing provided for in paragraph 3(b). The State of origin may, after consultations with the other States referred to in paragraphs 3 and 4 fishing these stocks, establish total allowable catches for stocks originating in its rivers.

3. (a) Fisheries for anadromous stocks shall be conducted only in waters landward of the outer limits of exclusive economic zones, except in cases where this provision would result in economic dislocation for a State other than the State of origin. With respect to such fishing beyond the outer limits of the exclusive economic zone, States concerned shall maintain consultations with a view to achieving agreement on terms and conditions of such fishing giving due regard to

the conservation requirements and the needs of the State of origin in respect of these stocks.

(b) The State of origin shall co-operate in minimizing economic dislocation in such other States fishing these stocks, taking into account the normal catch and the mode of operations of such States, and all the areas in which such fishing has occurred.

(c) States referred to in subparagraph (b), participating by agreement with the State of origin in measures to renew anadromous stocks, particularly by expenditures for that purpose, shall be given special consideration by the State of origin in the harvesting of stocks originating in its rivers.

(d) Enforcement of regulations regarding anadromous stocks beyond the exclusive economic zone shall be by agreement between the State of origin and the other States concerned.

4. In cases where anadromous stocks migrate into or through the waters landward of the outer limits of the exclusive economic zone of a State other than the State of origin, such State shall co-operate with the State of origin with regard to the conservation and management of such stocks.

5. The State of origin of anadromous stocks and other States fishing these stocks shall make arrangements for the implementation of the provisions of this article, where appropriate, through regional organizations.

Article 67
Catadromous species

1. A coastal State in whose waters catadromous species spend the greater part of their life cycle shall have responsibility for the management of these species and shall ensure the ingress and egress of migrating fish.

2. Harvesting of catadromous species shall be conducted only in waters landward of the outer limits of exclusive economic zones. When conducted in exclusive economic zones, harvesting shall be subject to this article and the other provisions of this Convention concerning fishing in these zones.

3. In cases where catadromous fish migrate through the exclusive economic zone of another State, whether as juvenile or maturing fish, the management, including harvesting, of such fish shall be regulated by agreement between the State mentioned in paragraph 1 and the other State concerned. Such agreement shall ensure the rational management of the species and take into account the responsibilities of the State mentioned in paragraph 1 for the maintenance of these species.

Article 68
Sedentary species

This Part does not apply to sedentary species as defined in article 77, paragraph 4.

Article 69
Right of land-locked States

1. Land-locked States shall have the right to participate, on an equitable basis, in the exploitation of an appropriate part of the surplus of the living resources of the exclusive economic zones of coastal States of the same subregion or region, taking into account the relevant economic and geographical circumstances of all the States concerned and in conformity with the provisions of this article and of articles 61 and 62.

2. The terms and modalities of such participation shall be established by the States concerned through bilateral, subregional or regional agreements taking into account, *inter alia*:

   (a) the need to avoid effects detrimental to fishing communities or fishing industries of the coastal State;
   (b) the extent to which the land-locked State, in accordance with the provisions of this article, is participating or is entitled to participate under existing bilateral, subregional or regional agreements in the exploitation of living resources of the exclusive economic zones of other coastal States;
   (c) the extent to which other land-locked States and geographically disadvantaged States are participating in the exploitation of the living resources of the exclusive economic zone of the coastal State and the consequent need to avoid a particular burden for any single coastal State or a part of it;
   (d) the nutritional needs of the populations of the respective States.

3. When the harvesting capacity of a coastal State approaches a point which would enable it to harvest the entire allowable catch of the living resources in its exclusive economic zone, the coastal State and other States concerned shall co-operate in the establishment of equitable arrangements on a bilateral, subregional or regional basis to allow for participation of developing land-locked States of the same subregion or region in the exploitation of the living resources of the exclusive economic zones of coastal States of the subregion or region, as may be appropriate in the circumstances and on terms satisfactory to all parties. In the implementation of this provision the factors mentioned in paragraph 2 shall also be taken into account.

4. Developed land-locked States shall, under the provisions of this article, be entitled to participate in the exploitation of living resources only in the exclusive economic zones of developed coastal States of the same subregion or region having regard to the extent to which the coastal State, in giving access to other States to the living resources of its exclusive economic zone, has taken into account the need to minimize detrimental effects on fishing

communities and economic dislocation in States whose nationals have habitually fished in the zone.

5. The above provisions are without prejudice to arrangements agreed upon in subregions or regions where the coastal States may grant to land-locked States of the same subregion or region equal or preferential rights for the exploitation of the living resources in the exclusive economic zones.

Article 70
Right of geographically disadvantaged States

1. Geographically disadvantaged States shall have the right to participate, on an equitable basis, in the exploitation of an appropriate part of the surplus of the living resources of the exclusive economic zones of coastal States of the same subregion or region, taking into account the relevant economic and geographical circumstances of all the States concerned and in conformity with the provisions of this article and of articles 61 and 62.

2. For the purposes of this Part, 'geographically disadvantaged States' means coastal States, including States bordering enclosed or semi-enclosed seas, whose geographical situation makes them dependent upon the exploi-tation of the living resources of the exclusive economic zones of other States in the subregion or region for adequate supplies of fish for the nutritional purposes of their populations or parts thereof, and coastal States which can claim no exclusive economic zones of their own.

3. The terms and modalities of such participation shall be established by the States concerned through bilateral, subregional or regional agreements taking into account, *inter alia*:

(a) the need to avoid effects detrimental to fishing communities or fishing industries of the coastal State;
(b) the extent to which the geographically disadvantaged State, in ac-cordance with the provisions of this article, is participating or is entitled to participate under existing bilateral, subregional or re-gional agreements in the exploitation of living resources of the exclusive economic zones of other coastal States;
(c) the extent to which other geographically disadvantaged States and landlocked States are participating in the exploitation of the living resources of the exclusive economic zone of the coastal State and the consequent need to avoid a particular burden for any single coastal State or a part of it;
(d) the nutritional needs of the populations of the respective States.

4. When the harvesting capacity of a coastal State approaches a point which would enable it to harvest the entire allowable catch of the living resources in its exclusive economic zone, the coastal State and other States concerned shall co-operate in the establishment of equitable arrangements on a bilateral, subregional or regional basis to allow for participation of

developing geographically disadvantaged States of the same subregion or region in the exploitation of the living resources of the exclusive economic zones of coastal States of the subregion or region, as may be appropriate in the circumstances and on terms satisfactory to all parties. In the implementation of this provision the factors mentioned in paragraph 3 shall also be taken into account.

5. Developed geographically disadvantaged States shall, under the provisions of this article, be entitled to participate in the exploitation of living resources only in the exclusive economic zones of developed coastal States of the same subregion or region having regard to the extent to which the coastal State, in giving access to other States to the living resources of its exclusive economic zone, has taken into account the need to minimize detrimental effects on fishing communities and economic dislocation in States whose nationals have habitually fished in the zone.

6. The above provisions are without prejudice to arrangements agreed upon in subregions or regions where the coastal States may grant to geographically disadvantaged States of the same subregion or region equal or preferential rights for the exploitation of the living resources in the exclusive economic zones.

Article 71
Non-applicability of articles 69 and 70

The provisions of articles 69 and 70 do not apply in the case of a coastal State whose economy is overwhelmingly dependent on the exploitation of the living resources of its exclusive economic zone.

Article 72
Restrictions on transfer of rights

1. Rights provided under articles 69 and 70 to exploit living resources shall not be directly or indirectly transferred to third States or their nationals by lease or licence, by establishing joint ventures or in any other manner which has the effect of such transfer unless otherwise agreed by the States concerned.

2. The foregoing provision does not preclude the States concerned from obtaining technical or financial assistance from third States or international organizations in order to facilitate the exercise of the rights pursuant to articles 69 and 70, provided that it does not have the effect referred to in paragraph 1.

Article 73
Enforcement of laws and regulations of the coastal State

1. The coastal State may, in the exercise of its sovereign rights to explore, exploit, conserve and manage the living resources in the exclusive econ-

omic zone, take such measures, including boarding, inspection, arrest and judicial proceedings, as may be necessary to ensure compliance with the laws and regulations adopted by it in conformity with this Convention.

2. Arrested vessels and their crews shall be promptly released upon the posting of reasonable bond or other security.

3. Coastal State penalties for violations of fisheries laws and regulations in the exclusive economic zone may not include imprisonment, in the absence of agreements to the contrary by the States concerned, or any other form of corporal punishment.

4. In cases of arrest or detention of foreign vessels the coastal State shall promptly notify the flag State, through appropriate channels, of the action taken and of any penalties subsequently imposed.

Article 74
Delimitation of the exclusive economic zone between States with opposite or adjacent coasts

1. The delimitation of the exclusive economic zone between States with opposite or adjacent coasts shall be effected by agreement on the basis of international law, as referred to in Article 38 of the Statute of the International Court of Justice, in order to achieve an equitable solution.

2. If no agreement can be reached within a reasonable period of time, the States concerned shall resort to the procedures provided for in Part XV.

3. Pending agreement as provided for in paragraph 1, the States concerned, in a spirit of understanding and co-operation, shall make every effort to enter into provisional arrangements of a practical nature and, during this transitional period, not to jeopardize or hamper the reaching of the final agreement. Such arrangements shall be without prejudice to the final delimitation.

4. Where there is an agreement in force between the States concerned, questions relating to the delimitation of the exclusive economic zone shall be determined in accordance with the provisions of that agreement.

Article 75
Charts and lists of geographical co-ordinates

1. Subject to this Part, the outer limit lines of the exclusive economic zone and the lines of delimitation drawn in accordance with article 74 shall be shown on charts of a scale or scales adequate for ascertaining their position. Where appropriate, lists of geographical co-ordinates of points, specifying the geodetic datum, may be substituted for such outer limit lines or lines of delimitation.

2. The coastal State shall give due publicity to such charts or lists of geographical co-ordinates and shall deposit a copy of each such chart or list with the Secretary-General of the United Nations.

TEXT OF PART VII HIGH SEAS

Section 1. General Provisions

Article 86
Application of the provisions of this Part

The provisions of this Part apply to all parts of the sea that are not included in the exclusive economic zone, in the territorial sea or in the internal waters of a State, or in the archipelagic waters of an archipelagic State. This article does not entail any abridgement of the freedoms enjoyed by all States in the exclusive economic zone in accordance with article 58.

Article 87
Freedom of the high seas

1. The high seas are open to all States, whether coastal or land-locked. Freedom of the high seas is exercised under the conditions laid down by this Convention and by other rules of international law. It comprises, *inter alia*, both for coastal and land-locked States:

  (a) freedom of navigation;
  (b) freedom of overflight;
  (c) freedom to lay submarine cables and pipelines, subject to Part VI;
  (d) freedom to construct artificial islands and other installations permitted under international law, subject to Part VI;
  (e) freedom of fishing, subject to the conditions laid down in section 2;
  (f) freedom of scientific research, subject to Parts VI and XIII.

2. These freedoms shall be exercised by all States with due regard for the interests of other States in their exercise of the freedom of the high seas, and also with due regard for the rights under this Convention with respect to activities in the Area.

Article 88
Reservation of the high seas for peaceful purposes

The high seas shall be reserved for peaceful purposes.

Article 89
Invalidity of claims of sovereignty over the high seas

No State may validly purport to subject any part of the high seas to its sovereignty.

[ARTICLES 90–115 OMITTED]

Section 2. Conservation and Management of the Living Resources of the High Seas

Article 116
Right to fish on the high seas

All States have the right for their nationals to engage in fishing on the high seas subject to:

    (a) their treaty obligations;
    (b) the rights and duties as well as the interests of coastal States provided for, *inter alia*, in article 63, paragraph 2, and articles 64 to 67; and
    (c) the provisions of this section.

Article 117
Duty of States to adopt with respect to their nationals measures for the conservation of the living resources of the high seas

All States have the duty to take, or to co-operate with other States in taking, such measures for their respective nationals as may be necessary for the conservation of the living resources of the high seas.

Article 118
Co-operation of States in the conservation and management of living resources

States shall co-operate with each other in the conservation and management of living resources in the areas of the high seas. States whose nationals exploit indentical living resources, or different living resources in the same area, shall enter into negotiations with a view to taking the measures necessary for the conservation of the living resources concerned. They shall, as appropriate, cooperate to establish subregional or regional fisheries organizations to this end.

Article 119
Conservation of the living resources of the high seas

1. In determining the allowable catch and establishing other conservation measures for the living resources in the high seas, States shall:

    (a) take measures which are designed, on the best scientific evidence available to the States concerned, to maintain or restore populations of harvested species at levels which can produce the maximum sustainable yield, as qualified by relevant environmental and economic factors, including the special requirements of developing States, and taking into account fishing patterns, the interdependence of stocks and any generally recommended international minimum standards, whether subregional, regional or global;

(b) take into consideration the effects on species associated with or dependent upon harvested species with a view to maintaining or restoring populations of such associated or dependent species above levels at which their reproduction may become seriously threatened.

2. Available scientific information, catch and fishing effort statistics, and other data relevant to the conservation of fish stocks shall be contributed and exchanged on a regular basis through competent international organizations, whether subregional, regional or global, where appropriate and with participation by all States concerned.

3. States concerned shall ensure that conservation measures and their implementation do not discriminate in form or in fact against the fishermen of any State.

Article 120
Marine mammals

Article 65 also applies to the conservation and management of marine mammals in the high seas.

Convention on the Conservation of Antarctic Marine Living Resources, Canberra, 20 May 1980

The Antarctic Treaty, concluded in Washington D.C., 1 December 1959 (402 *UNTS* 71; *UKTS* 97 (1961), Cmnd. 1535; 12 *UST* 794 *TIAS* 4780) applies to the area south of 60° south latitude (Article VI) but does not directly address the exploration, exploitation, conservation or management of the living resources in this area. The Consultative Parties, exercising their power to recommend measures for the preservation and conservation of living resources in Antarctica (Article IX(1)(f)), adopted at their Consultative Meetings various measures, including a set of Agreed Measures for the Conservation of Antarctic Flora and Fauna adopted at the third Meeting of Consultative Parties in Brussels in 1964. These and other measures, including those on sealing, are found in the Marine Mammal Commission, *Compendium of Treaties* (Washington D.C., 1994), 8–371. Following exploration of commercial sealing possibilities by Norway in 1964, a Convention for the Conservation of Antarctic Seals was negotiated and adopted in London, 1 June 1972; in force 11 March 1978, 29 *UST* 441 *TIAS* 8826; 11 *ILM* (1972) 251; *UKTS* 45 (1978), Cmnd. 7209. It was the first international treaty to be concluded before exploitation of the resource concerned began; no sealing has taken place under it.

Fishing for krill (*Euphaisuea Superba*) in Antarctica by Japan and the USSR in the late 1960s and early 1970s led to negotiations on a regime to control fisheries before establishment of any major industry, and resulted in the conclusion of CCAMLR. The text is found in *UKTS* 48 (1982), Cmnd. 8714; 33 *UST* 3476 *TIAS* 10240; 19 *ILM* (1980) 841. The Convention had twenty-nine parties at 1 January 1994. It entered into force on 7 April 1982. It aims to conserve Antarctic marine living resources and includes within the term 'conservation' the 'rational use' thereof. It was especially notable in 1980 for introducing, unlike the UNCLOS fisheries articles (q.v.), an ecosystem approach. Its area of application is not limited to waters below 60° south, or to a 200 mile zone, but includes the fluctuating area within the Antarctic Convergence (Article I(2)). An ecological approach is also adopted for conservation and management within that area (Article II(3)). The Commission established by the Convention (Article VII) has adopted various conservatory measures. At its Seventh Meeting it adopted the System of Inspection (CCAMLR—VII para 124) required in the Convention (Article XXI). At the Eleventh Meeting it adopted a CCAMLR Scheme of International Scientific Observation (CCAMLR—XI (para 6.11). The Commission's Reports are obtainable from the Commission Headquarters at 25, Old Wharf, Hobart, Tasmania, Australia 7000. For discussion see J. Barnes, 'The Emerging Convention on the Conservation of Antarctic Marine Living Resources: An attempt to Meet the New Realities of Resources Exploitation in the Southern Ocean', in J. Charney (ed.), *The New Nationalism and the Use of Common Spaces: Issues in Marine Pollution and the Exploitation of Antarctica* (1982), 284; S. Lyster, *International Wildlife Law* (Cambridge, 1985), 156–82; D. Edwards and J. Heap, 'Convention on Conservation of Antarctic Marine Living Resources: A Commentary', 20 *Polar Record* No. 27 (1980) 354; M. Howard, 'The Convention on the Conservation of Antarctic Marine Living Resources: A Five Year Review', 38 *ICLQ* (1989) 104.

TEXT

The Contracting Parties,

Recognising the importance of safeguarding the environment and protecting the integrity of the ecosystem of the seas surrounding Antarctica;

Noting the concentration of marine living resources found in Antarctic waters and the increased interest in the possibilities offered by the utilization of these resources as a source of protein;

Conscious of the urgency of ensuring the conservation of Antarctic marine living resources;

Considering that it is essential to increase knowledge of the Antarctic marine ecosystem and its components so as to be able to base decisions on harvesting on sound scientific information;

Believing that the conservation of Antarctic marine living resources calls for international co-operation with due regard for the provisions of the Antarctic Treaty and with the active involvement of all States engaged in research or harvesting activities in Antarctic waters;

Recognising the prime responsibilities of the Antarctic Treaty Consultative Parties for the protection and preservation of the Antarctic environment and, in particular, their responsibilities under Article IX, paragraph 1 (f) of the Antarctic Treaty in respect of the preservation and conservation of living resources in Antarctica;

Recalling the action already taken by the Antarctic Treaty Consultative Parties including in particular the Agreed Measures for the Conservation of Antarctic Fauna and Flora, as well as the provisions of the Convention for the Conservation of Antarctic Seals;

Bearing in mind the concern regarding the conservation of Antarctic marine living resources expressed by the Consultative Parties at the Ninth Consultative Meeting of the Antarctic Treaty and the importance of the provisions of Recommendation IX-2 which led to the establishment of the present Convention;

Believing that it is in the interest of all mankind to preserve the waters surrounding the Antarctic continent for peaceful purposes only and to prevent their becoming the scene or object of international discord;

Recognising, in the light of the foregoing, that it is desirable to establish suitable machinery for recommending, promoting, deciding upon and coordinating the measures and scientific studies needed to ensure the conservation of Antarctic marine living organisms;

Have Agreed as follows:

Article I

1. This Convention applies to the Antarctic marine living resources of the area south of 60° South latitude and to the Antarctic marine living resources of the area between that latitude and the Antarctic Convergence which form part of the Antarctic marine ecosystem.

2. Antarctic marine living resources means the populations of fin fish,

molluscs, crustaceans and all other species of living organisms, including birds, found south of the Antarctic Convergence.

3. The Antarctic marine ecosystem means the complex of relationships of Antarctic marine living resources with each other and with their physical environment.

4. The Antarctic Convergence shall be deemed to be a line joining the following points along parallels of latitude and meridians of longitude: 50°S, 0°; 50°S, 30°E; 45°S, 30°E; 45°S, 80°E; 55°S, 80°E; 55°S, 150°E; 60°S, 150°E; 60°S, 50°W; 50°S, 50°W; 50°S, 0°.

Article II

1. The objective of this Convention is the conservation of Antarctic marine living resources.

2. For the purposes of this Convention, the term 'conservation' includes rational use.

3. Any harvesting and associated activities in the area to which this Convention applies shall be conducted in accordance with the provisions of this Convention and with the following principles of conservation:

   (a) prevention of decrease in the size of any harvested population to levels below those which ensure its stable recruitment. For this purpose its size should not be allowed to fall below a level close to that which ensures the greatest net annual increment;
   (b) maintenance of the ecological relationships between harvested, dependent and related populations of Antarctic marine living resources and the restoration of depleted populations to the levels defined in sub-paragraph (a) above; and
   (c) prevention of changes or minimization of the risk of changes in the marine ecosystem which are not potentially reversible over two or three decades, taking into account the state of available knowledge of the direct and indirect impact of harvesting, the effect of the introduction of alien species, the effects of associated activities on the marine ecosystem and of the effects of environmental changes, with the aim of making possible the sustained conservation of Antarctic marine living resources.

Article III

The Contracting Parties, whether or not they are Parties to the Antarctic Treaty, agree that they will not engage in any activities in the Antarctic Treaty area contrary to the principles and purposes of that Treaty and that, in their relations with each other, they are bound by the obligations contained in Articles I and V of the Antarctic Treaty.

Article IV

1. With respect to the Antarctic Treaty area, all Contracting Parties, whether or not they are Parties to the Antarctic Treaty, are bound by Articles IV and VI of the Antarctic Treaty in their relations with each other.

2. Nothing in this Convention and no acts or activities taking place while the present Convention is in force shall:

   (a) constitute a basis for asserting, supporting or denying a claim to territorial sovereignty in the Antarctic Treaty area or create any rights of sovereignty in the Antarctic Treaty area;

   (b) be interpreted as a renunciation or diminution by any Contracting Party of, or as prejudicing, any right or claim or basis of claim to exercise coastal state jurisdiction under international law within the area to which this Convention applies;

   (c) be interpreted as prejudicing the position of any Contracting Party as regards its recognition or non-recognition of any such right, claim or basis of claim;

   (d) affect the provision of Article IV, paragraph 2, of the Antarctic Treaty that no new claim, or enlargement of an existing claim, to territorial sovereignty in Antarctica shall be asserted while the Antarctic Treaty is in force.

Article V

1. The Contracting Parties which are not Parties to the Antarctic Treaty acknowledge the special obligations and responsibilities of the Antarctic Treaty Consultative Parties for the protection and preservation of the environment of the Antarctic Treaty area.

2. The Contracting Parties which are not Parties to the Antarctic Treaty agree that, in their activities in the Antarctic Treaty area, they will observe as and when appropriate the Agreed Measures for the Conservation of Antarctic Fauna and Flora and such other measures as have been recommended by the Antarctic Treaty Consultative Parties in fulfilment of their responsibility for the protection of the Antarctic environment from all forms of harmful human interference.

3. For the purposes of this Convention, 'Antarctic Treaty Consultative Parties' means the Contracting Parties to the Antarctic Treaty whose Representatives participate in meetings under Article IX of the Antarctic Treaty.

Article VI

Nothing in this Convention shall derogate from the rights and obligations of Contracting Parties under the International Convention for the Regulation of Whaling and the Convention for the Conservation of Antarctic Seals.

Article VII

1. The Contracting Parties hereby establish and agree to maintain the Commission for the Conservation of Antarctic Marine Living Resources (hereinafter referred to as 'the Commission').

2. Membership in the Commission shall be as follows:

   (a) each Contracting Party which participated in the meeting at which this Convention was adopted shall be a Member of the Commission;

   (b) each State Party which has acceded to this Convention pursuant to Article XXIX shall be entitled to be a Member of the Commission during such time as that acceding party is engaged in research or harvesting activities in relation to the marine living resources to which this Convention applies;

   (c) each regional economic integration organization which has acceded to this Convention pursuant to Article XXIX shall be entitled to be a Member of the Commission during such time as its States members are so entitled;

   (d) a Contracting Party seeking to participate in the work of the Commission pursuant to sub-paragraphs (b) and (c) above shall notify the Depositary of the basis upon which it seeks to become a Member of the Commission and of its willingness to accept conservation measures in force. The Depositary shall communicate to each Member of the Commission such notification and accompanying information. Within two months of receipt of such communication from the Depositary, any Member of the Commission may request that a special meeting of the Commission be held to consider the matter. Upon receipt of such request, the Depositary shall call such a meeting. If there is no request for a meeting, the Contracting Party submitting the notification shall be deemed to have satisfied the requirements for Commission Membership.

3. Each Member of the Commission shall be represented by one representative who may be accompanied by alternate representatives and advisers.

Article VIII

The Commission shall have legal personality and shall enjoy in the territory of each of the States Parties such legal capacity as may be necessary to perform its function and achieve the purposes of this Convention. The privileges and immunities to be enjoyed by the Commission and its staff in the territory of a State Party shall be determined by agreement between the Commission and the State Party concerned.

Article IX

1. The function of the Commission shall be to give effect to the objective and principles set out in Article II of this Convention. To this end, it shall:

    (a) facilitate research into and comprehensive studies of Antarctic marine living resources and of the Antarctic marine ecosystem;

    (b) compile data on the status of and changes in population of Antarctic marine living resources and on factors affecting the distribution, abundance and productivity of harvested species and dependent or related species or populations;

    (c) ensure the acquisition of catch and effort statistics on harvested populations;

    (d) analyse, disseminate and publish the information referred to in sub-paragraphs (b) and (c) above and the reports of the Scientific Committee;

    (e) identify conservation needs and analyse the effectiveness of conservation measures;

    (f) formulate, adopt and revise conservation measures on the basis of the best scientific evidence available, subject to the provisions of paragraph 5 of this Article;

    (g) implement the system of observation and inspection established under Article XXIV of this Convention;

    (h) carry out such other activities as are necessary to fulfil the objective of this Convention.

2. The conservation measures referred to in paragraph (f) above include the following:

    (a) the designation of the quantity of any species which may be harvested in the area to which this Convention applies;

    (b) the designation of regions and sub-regions based on the distribution of populations of Antarctic marine living resources;

    (c) the designation of the quantity which may be harvested from the populations of regions and sub-regions;

    (d) the designation of protected species;

    (e) the designation of the size, age and, as appropriate, sex of species which may be harvested;

    (f) the designation of open and closed seasons for harvesting;

    (g) the designation of the opening and closing of areas, regions or sub-regions for purposes of scientific study or conservation, including special areas for protection and scientific study;

    (h) regulation of the effort employed and methods of harvesting, including fishing gear, with a view, *inter alia*, to avoiding undue concentration of harvesting in any region or sub-region;

    (i) the taking of such other conservation measures as the Commission considers necessary for the fulfilment of the objective of this Convention, including measures concerning the effects of harvesting and associated activities on components of the marine ecosystem other than the harvested populations.

3. The Commission shall publish and maintain a record of all conservation measures in force.

4. In exercising its functions under paragraph 1 above, the Commission shall take full account of the recommendations and advice of the Scientific Committee.

5. The Commission shall take full account of any relevant measures or regulations established or recommended by the Consultative Meetings pursuant to Article IX of the Antarctic Treaty or by existing fisheries commissions responsible for species which may enter the area to which this Convention applies, in order that there shall be no inconsistency between the rights and obligations of a Contracting Party under such regulations or measures and conservation measures which may be adopted by the Commission.

6. Conservation measures adopted by the Commission in accordance with this Convention shall be implemented by Members of the Commission in the following manner:

  (a) the Commission shall notify conservation measures to all Members of the Commission;
  (b) conservation measures shall become binding upon all Members of the Commission 180 days after such notification, except as provided in sub-paragraphs (c) and (d) below;
  (c) if a Member of the Commission, within ninety days following the notification specified in sub-paragraph (a), notifies the Commission that it is unable to accept the conservation measure, in whole or in part, the measure shall not, to the extent stated, be binding upon that Member of the Commission;
  (d) in the event that any Member of the Commission invokes the procedure set forth in sub-paragraph (c) above, the Commission shall meet at the request of any Member of the Commission to review the conservation measure. At the time of such meeting and within thirty days following the meeting, any Member of the Commission shall have the right to declare that it is no longer able to accept the conservation measure, in which case the Member shall no longer be bound by such measure.

Article X

1. The Commission shall draw the attention of any State which is not a Party to this Convention to any activity undertaken by its nationals or vessels

which, in the opinion of the Commission, affects the implementation of the objective of this Convention.

2. The Commission shall draw the attention of all Contracting Parties to any activity which, in the opinion of the Commission, affects the implementation by a Contracting Party of the objective of this Convention or the compliance by that Contracting Party with its obligations under this Convention.

Article XI

The Commission shall seek to cooperate with Contracting Parties which may exercise jurisdiction in marine areas adjacent to the area to which this Convention applies in respect of the conservation of any stock or stocks of associated species which occur both within those areas and the area to which this Convention applies, with a view to harmonizing the conservation measures adopted in respect of such stocks.

Article XII

1. Decisions of the Commission on matters of substance shall be taken by consensus. The question of whether a matter is one of substance shall be treated as a matter of substance.

2. Decisions on matters other than those referred to in paragraph 1 above shall be taken by a simple majority of the Members of the Commission present and voting.

3. In Commission consideration of any item requiring a decision, it shall be made clear whether a regional economic integration organization will participate in the taking of the decision and, if so, whether any of its member States will also participate. The number of Contracting Parties so participating shall not exceed the number of member States of the regional economic integration organization which are members of the Commission.

4. In the taking of decisions pursuant to this Article, a regional economic integration organization shall have only one vote.

Article XIII

1. The headquarters of the Commission shall be established at Hobart, Tasmania, Australia.

2. The Commission shall hold a regular annual meeting. Other meetings shall also be held at the request of one-third of its members and as otherwise provided in this Convention. The first meeting of the Commission shall be held within three months of the entry into force of this Convention, provided that among the Contracting Parties there are at least two States conducting harvesting activities within the area to which this Convention applies. The first meeting shall, in any event, be held within one year of the entry into force of this Convention. The Depositary shall consult with

the signatory States regarding the first Commission meeting, taking into account that a broad representation of such States is necessary for the effective operation of the Commission.

3. The Depositary shall convene the first meeting of the Commission at the headquarters of the Commission. Thereafter, meetings of the Commission shall be held at its headquarters, unless it decides otherwise.

4. The Commission shall elect from among its members a Chairman and Vice-Chairman, each of whom shall serve for a term of two years and shall be eligible for re-election for one additional term. The first Chairman shall, however, be elected for an initial term of three years. The Chairman and Vice-Chairman shall not be representatives of the same Contracting Party.

5. The Commission shall adopt and amend as necessary the rules of procedure for the conduct of its meetings, except with respect to the matters dealt with in Article XII of this Convention.

6. The Commission may establish such subsidiary bodies as are necessary for the performance of its functions.

Article XIV

1. The Contracting Parties hereby establish the Scientific Committee for the Conservation of Antarctic Marine Living Resources (hereinafter referred to as 'the Scientific Committee') which shall be a consultative body to the Commission. The Scientific Committee shall normally meet at the headquarters of the Commission unless the Scientific Committee decides otherwise.

2. Each Member of the Commission shall be a member of the Scientific Committee and shall appoint a representative with suitable scientific qualifications who may be accompanied by other experts and advisers.

3. The Scientific Committee may seek the advice of other scientists and experts as may be required on an *ad hoc* basis.

Article XV

1. The Scientific Committee shall provide a forum for consultation and cooperation concerning the collection, study and exchange of information with respect to the marine living resources to which this Convention applies. It shall encourage and promote cooperation in the field of scientific research in order to extend knowledge of the marine living resources of the Antarctic marine ecosystem.

2. The Scientific Committee shall conduct such activities as the Commission may direct in pursuance of the objective of this Convention and shall:

    (a) establish criteria and methods to be used for determinations concerning the conservation measures referred to in Article IX of this Convention;

(b) regularly assess the status and trends of the populations of Antarctic marine living resources;

(c) analyse data concerning the direct and indirect effects of harvesting on the populations of Antarctic marine living resources;

(d) assess the effects of proposed changes in the methods or levels of harvesting and proposed conservation measures;

(e) transmit assessments, analyses, reports and recommendations to the Commission as requested or on its own initiative regarding measures and research to implement the objective of this Convention;

(f) formulate proposals for the conduct of international and national programmes of research into Antarctic marine living resources.

3. In carrying out its functions, the Scientific Committee shall have regard to the work of other relevant technical and scientific organizations and to the scientific activities conducted within the framework of the Antarctic Treaty.

Article XVI

1. The first meeting of the Scientific Committee shall be held within three months of the first meeting of the Commission. The Scientific Committee shall meet thereafter as often as may be necessary to fulfil its functions.

2. The Scientific Committee shall adopt and amend as necessary its rules of procedure. The rules and any amendments thereto shall be approved by the Commission. The rules shall include procedures for the presentation of minority reports.

3. The Scientific Committee may establish, with the approval of the Commission, such subsidiary bodies as are necessary for the performance of its functions.

Article XVII

1. The Commission shall appoint an Executive Secretary to serve the Commission and Scientific Committee according to such procedures and on such terms and conditions as the Commission may determine. His term of office shall be for four years and he shall be eligible for re-appointment.

2. The Commission shall authorize such staff establishment for the Secretariat as may be necessary and the Executive Secretary shall appoint, direct and supervise such staff according to such rules and procedures and on such terms and conditions as the Commission may determine.

3. The Executive Secretary and Secretariat shall perform the functions entrusted to them by the Commission.

Article XVIII

The official languages of the Commission and of the Scientific Committee shall be English, French, Russian and Spanish.

Article XIX

1. At each annual meeting, the Commission shall adopt by consensus its budget and the budget of the Scientific Committee.

2. A draft budget for the Commission and the Scientific Committee and any subsidiary bodies shall be prepared by the Executive Secretary and submitted to the Members of the Commission at least sixty days before the annual meeting of the Commission.

3. Each Member of the Commission shall contribute to the budget. Until the expiration of five years after the entry into force of this Convention, the contribution of each Member of the Commission shall be equal. Thereafter the contribution shall be determined in accordance with two criteria: the amount harvested and an equal sharing among all Members of the Commission. The Commission shall determine by consensus the proportion in which these two criteria shall apply.

4. The financial activities of the Commission and Scientific Committee shall be conducted in accordance with financial regulations adopted by the Commission and shall be subject to an annual audit by external auditors selected by the Commission.

5. Each Member of the Commission shall meet its own expenses arising from attendance at meetings of the Commission and of the Scientific Committee.

6. A Member of the Commission that fails to pay its contributions for two consecutive years shall not, during the period of its default, have the right to participate in the taking of decisions in the Commission.

Article XX

1. The Members of the Commission shall, to the greatest extent possible, provide annually to the Commission and to the Scientific Committee such statistical, biological and other data and information as the Commission and Scientific Committee may require in the exercise of their functions.

2. The Members of the Commission shall provide, in the manner and at such intervals as may be prescribed, information about their harvesting activities, including fishing areas and vessels, so as to enable reliable catch and effort statistics to be compiled.

3. The Members of the Commission shall provide to the Commission at such intervals as may be prescribed information on steps taken to implement the conservation measures adopted by the Commission.

4. The Members of the Commission agree that in any of their harvesting activities, advantage shall be taken of opportunities to collect data needed to assess the impact of harvesting.

Article XXI

1. Each Contracting Party shall take appropriate measures within its competence to ensure compliance with the provisions of this Convention and with conservation measures adopted by the Commission to which the Party is bound in accordance with Article IX of this Convention.

2. Each Contracting Party shall transmit to the Commission information on measures taken pursuant to paragraph 1 above, including the imposition of sanctions for any violation.

Article XXII

1. Each Contracting Party undertakes to exert appropriate efforts, consistent with the Charter of the United Nations, to the end that no one engages in any activity contrary to the objective of this Convention.

2. Each Contracting Party shall notify the Commission of any such activity which comes to its attention.

Article XXIII

1. The Commission and the Scientific Committee shall co-operate with the Antarctic Treaty Consultative Parties on matters falling within the competence of the latter.

2. The Commission and the Scientific Committee shall co-operate, as appropriate, with the Food and Agriculture Organisation of the United Nations and with other Specialised Agencies.

3. The Commission and the Scientific Committee shall seek to develop cooperative working relationships, as appropriate, with inter-governmental and non-governmental organizations which could contribute to their work, including the Scientific Committee on Antarctic Research, the Scientific Committee on Oceanic Research and the International Whaling Commission.

4. The Commission may enter into agreements with the organizations referred to in this Article and with other organizations as may be appropriate. The Commission and the Scientific Committee may invite such organizations to send observers to their meetings and to meetings of their subsidiary bodies.

Article XXIV

1. In order to promote the objective and ensure observance of the provisions of this Convention, the Contracting Parties agree that a system of observation and inspection shall be established.

2. The system of observation and inspection shall be elaborated by the Commission on the basis of the following principles:

(a) Contracting Parties shall co-operate with each other to ensure the effective implementation of the system of observation and inspection, taking account of the existing international practice. This system shall include, *inter alia*, procedures for boarding and inspection by observers and inspectors designated by the Members of the Commission and procedures for flag state prosecution and sanctions on the basis of evidence resulting from such boarding and inspections. A report of such prosecutions and sanctions imposed shall be included in the information referred to in Article XXI of this Convention;

(b) in order to verify compliance with measures adopted under this Convention, observation and inspection shall be carried out on board vessels engaged in scientific research or harvesting of marine living resources in the area to which this Convention applies, through observers and inspectors designated by the Members of the Commission and operating under terms and conditions to be established by the Commission;

(c) designated observers and inspectors shall remain subject to the jurisdiction of the Contracting Party of which they are nationals. They shall report to the Member of the Commission by which they have been designated which in turn shall report to the Commission.

3. Pending the establishment of the system of observation and inspection, the Members of the Commission shall seek to establish interim arrangements to designate observers and inspectors and such designated observers and inspectors shall be entitled to carry out inspections in accordance with the principles set out in paragraph 2 above.

Article XXV

1. If any dispute arises between two or more of the Contracting Parties concerning the interpretation or application of this Convention, those Contracting Parties shall consult among themselves with a view to having the dispute resolved by negotiation, inquiry, mediation, conciliation, arbitration, judicial settlement or other peaceful means of their own choice.

2. Any dispute of this character not so resolved shall, with the consent in each case of all Parties to the dispute, be referred for settlement to the International Court of Justice or to arbitration; but failure to reach agreement on reference to the International Court or to arbitration shall not absolve Parties to the dispute from the responsibility of continuing to seek to resolve it by any of the various peaceful means referred to in paragraph 1 above.

3. In cases where the dispute is referred to arbitration, the arbitral tribunal shall be constituted as provided in the Annex to this Convention.

Article XXVI

1. This Convention shall be open for signature at Canberra from 1 August to 31 December 1980 by the States participating in the Conference on the Conservation of Antarctic Marine Living Resources held at Canberra from 7 to 20 May 1980.

2. The States which so sign will be the original signatory States of the Convention.

Article XXVII

1. This Convention is subject to ratification, acceptance or approval by signatory States.

2. Instruments of ratification, acceptance or approval shall be deposited with the Government of Australia, hereby designated as the Depositary.

Article XXVIII

1. This Convention shall enter into force on the thirtieth day following the date of deposit of the eighth instrument of ratification, acceptance or approval by States referred to in paragraph 1 of Article XXVI of this Convention.

2. With respect to each State or regional economic integration organization which subsequent to the date of entry into force of this Convention deposits an instrument of ratification, acceptance, approval or accession, the Convention shall enter into force on the thirtieth day following such deposit.

Article XXIX

1. This Convention shall be open for accession by any State interested in research or harvesting activities in relation to the marine living resources to which this Convention applies.

2. This Convention shall be open for accession by regional economic integration organizations constituted by sovereign States which include among their members one or more States Members of the Commission and to which the States members of the organization have transferred, in whole or in part, competences with regard to the matters covered by this Convention. The accession of such regional economic integration organizations shall be the subject of consultations among Members of the Commission.

Article XXX

1. This Convention may be amended at any time.

2. If one-third of the Members of the Commission request a meeting to discuss a proposed amendment the Depositary shall call such a meeting.

3. An amendment shall enter into force when the Depositary has received instruments of ratification, acceptance or approval thereof from all the Members of the Commission.

4. Such amendment shall thereafter enter into force as to any other Contracting Party when notice of ratification, acceptance or approval by it has been received by the Depositary. Any such Contracting Party from which no such notice has been received within a period of one year from the date of entry into force of the amendment in accordance with paragraph 3 above shall be deemed to have withdrawn from this Convention.

Article XXXI

1. Any Contracting Party may withdraw from this Convention on 30 June of any year, by giving written notice not later than 1 January of the same year to the Depositary, which, upon receipt of such a notice, shall communicate it forthwith to the other Contracting Parties.

2. Any other Contracting Party may, within sixty days of the receipt of a copy of such a notice from the Depositary, give written notice of withdrawal to the Depositary in which case the Convention shall cease to be in force on 30 June of the same year with respect to the Contracting Party giving such notice.

3. Withdrawal from this Convention by any Member of the Commission shall not affect its financial obligations under this Convention.

Article XXXII

The Depositary shall notify all Contracting Parties of the following:

(a) signatures of this Convention and the deposit of instruments of ratification, acceptance, approval or accession;
(b) the date of entry into force of this Convention and of any amendment thereto.

Article XXXIII

1. This Convention, of which the English, French, Russian and Spanish texts are equally authentic, shall be deposited with the Government of Australia which shall transmit duly certified copies thereof to all signatory and acceding Parties.

2. This Convention shall be registered by the Depositary pursuant to Article 102 of the Charter of the United Nations.

Drawn up at Canberra this twentieth day of May 1980.

IN WITNESS WHEREOF the undersigned, being duly authorized, have signed this Convention.

Annex for an Arbitral Tribunal

The arbitral tribunal referred to in paragraph 3 of Article XXV shall be composed of three arbitrators who shall be appointed as follows: The Party commencing proceedings shall communicate the name of an arbitrator to the other Party which, in turn, within a period of forty days following such notification, shall communicate the name of the second arbitrator. The Parties shall, within a period of sixty days following the appointment of the second arbitrator, appoint the third arbitrator, who shall not be a national of either Party and shall not be of the same nationality as either of the first two arbitrators. The third arbitrator shall preside over the tribunal.

If the second arbitrator has not been appointed within the prescribed period, or if the Parties have not reached agreement within the prescribed period on the appointment of the third arbitrator, that arbitrator shall be appointed, at the request of either Party, by the Secretary-General of the Permanent Court of Arbitration, from among persons of international standing not having the nationality of a State which is a Party to this Convention. The arbitral tribunal shall decide where its headquarters will be located and shall adopt its own rules of procedure. The award of the arbitral tribunal shall be made by a majority of its members, who may not abstain from voting. Any Contracting Party which is not a Party to the dispute may intervene in the proceedings with the consent of the arbitral tribunal. The award of the arbitral tribunal shall be final and binding on all Parties to the dispute and on any Party which intervenes in the proceedings and shall be complied with without delay. The arbitral tribunal shall interpret the award at the request of one of the Parties to the dispute or of any intervening Party. Unless the arbitral tribunal determines otherwise because of the particular circumstances of the case, the expenses of the tribunal, including the remuneration of its members, shall be borne by the Parties to the dispute in equal shares.

TEXT OF DECLARATION INCLUDED IN THE FINAL ACT

The Conference at which the Convention on the Conservation of Antarctic Marine Living Resources was adopted decided to include in the Final Act the following declaration by France concerning the application of the Convention to waters adjacent to Kerguelen and Crozet over which France exercises jurisdiction and to waters adjacent to other islands situated within the field of application of the Convention over which the exercise of State sovereignty is recognised by all of the Parties:

'1. Measures for the conservation of Antarctic marine living resources of the waters adjacent to Kerguelen and Crozet, over which France has jurisdiction, adopted by France prior to the entry into force of the Convention, would remain in force after the entry into force of the Convention until modified by France acting within the framework of the Commission or otherwise.

2. After the Convention has come into force, each time the Commission should undertake examination of the conservation needs of the marine living resources of the general area in which the waters adjacent to Kerguelen and Crozet are to be found, it would be open to France either to agree that the waters in question should be included in the area of application of any specific conservation measure under consideration or to indicate that they should be excluded. In the latter event, the Commission would not proceed to the adoption of the specific conservation measure in a form applicable to the waters in question unless France removed its objection to it. France could also adopt such national measures as it might deem appropriate for the waters in question.

3. Accordingly, when specific conservation measures are considered within the framework of the Commission and with the participation of France, then:

    (a) France would be bound by any conservation measures adopted by consensus with its participation for the duration of those measures. This would not prevent France from promulgating national measures that were more strict than the Commission's measures or which dealt with other matters;

    (b) In the absence of consensus, France could promulgate any national measures which it might deem appropriate.

4. Conservation measures, whether national measures or measures adopted by the Commission, in respect of the waters adjacent to Kerguelen and Crozet, would be enforced by France. The system of observation and inspection foreseen by the Convention would not be implemented in the waters adjacent to Kerguelen and Crozet except as agreed by France and in the manner so agreed.

5. The understandings, set forth in paragraphs 1–4 above, regarding the application of the Convention to waters adjacent to the Islands of Kerguelen and Crozet, also apply to waters adjacent to the islands within the area to which this Convention applies over which the existence of State sovereignty is recognized by all Contracting Parties.'

No objection to the statement was made.

Agreement to Promote Compliance with International Conservation and Management Measures by Fishing Vessels on the High Seas, Rome, 24 November 1993

For the context and background to this agreement, which was not yet in force as at 31 January 1995, see commentary on 1982 UNCLOS Parts V and VII (supra). The text is found in 33 *ILM* (1994) 969–80; the agreement was opened for signature in October 1994. It arose from the ambiguities generated by the UNCLOS Articles 61–73 and 116–120. The need for an agreement to deter reflagging of fishing vessels to avoid internationally established controls on fishing on the high seas was noted at the Cancun Conference on Responsible Fishing held in April 1992. UNCED repeated this demand in the recommendations made in UNCED Agenda 21, Ch. 17, para. 17.50. The proposal was further supported by the FAO Technical Consultation on High Seas Fishing, held in Rome in September 1992, pursuant to the UNCED Recommendation. The 1993 agreement addresses the concerns of states that fishing on the high seas by states which do not participate in global or regional fisheries organizations or agreements of a conservatory nature, or whose vessels do not strictly observe agreements to which their flag states are party, or which allow reflagging of vessels to avoid conservation regimes, endangers the effectiveness of international fisheries agreements.

At its 102nd Session in November 1992, the FAO Council agreed that the issue of fishing vessels reflagging into flags of convenience to avoid compliance with internationally agreed conservation measures, while forming part of the issues that would be covered by the proposed Code of Conduct on Responsible Fishing, should be addressed immediately by FAO, that there was a need for an international agreement, and that if possible a draft text should be presented to the FAO Committee on Fisheries (COFI). At its 20th Session held in March 1993, COFI established an open-ended Working Group (WG) to review a draft agreement prepared by the Secretariat, aided by an informal group of invited experts. As the WG was unable to finalize a text, since the issues raised proved controversial, it suggested further review of the draft before submission to the Conference. At its 103rd Session in June 1993 the FAO Council established a Technical Committee to review the draft; FAO members who were not members of Council and observers from non-member States and interested fisheries management organizations were also invited to participate in the discussions. A revised text with various options was put to the Council which took note thereof. The draft agreement was brought before the 27th Session of Conference in November 1993 for its consideration and approval. Further consultations with governments of potential parties continued in the interim to try to resolve difficulties and the draft was also referred to the Sixty-first Session of the Committee on Constitutional and Legal Matters (CCLM) in October 1993. The draft was approved, subject to certain revisions, at the Council's 104th Session in November 1993 (see FAO Doc. C 93/26, August 1993) and submitted to the 27th Session of FAO Conference, Rome, 6–25 November 1993 as a Draft Agreement on the Flagging of Vessels Fishing on the High Seas to Promote Compliance with Internationally Agreed Conservation and Management Measures. The final Agreement is innovatory in many respects, calling on parties to maintain a record of fishing vessels authorized to fly their flag and to fish on the high seas (Article IV) and requiring them to take measures to ensure that their vessels do not engage in activities that undermine the effectiveness of international conservation and management measures (Article III); and to co-operate in its implementation, including exchanging information and evidence. It also requires a port State, into whose ports vessels flying the flag of another party enter, to notify the flag State if it has 'reasonable grounds' for believing that the vessels have committed a violation of the Agreement (Article V). Parties are also to make available to FAO specified information about vessels entered on their record (Article VI). Parties are also required to co-operate with FAO and other organizations to provide technical assistance to developing country parties to help them fulfil their obligations under the Agreement.

The Agreement requires twenty-five ratifications for entry into force; as of 31 January 1995 it had seven ratifications. For further background see P. Birnie, 'Reflagging of Fishing Vessels on the High Seas' and N. Bonucci, 'Towards an International Code of Conduct for Responsible Fishing', in 2 *RECIEL* (1993) 245–51 and 270–76 respectively.

TEXT

Preamble

The Parties to this Agreement,

Recognizing that all States have the right for their nationals to engage in fishing on the high seas, subject to the relevant rules of international law, as reflected in the United Nations Convention on the Law of the Sea,

Further recognizing that, under international law as reflected in the United Nations Convention on the Law of the Sea, all States have the duty to take, or to cooperate with other States in taking, such measures for their respective nationals as may be necessary for the conservation of the living resources of the high seas,

Acknowledging the right and interest of all States to develop their fishing sectors in accordance with their national policies, and the need to promote cooperation with developing countries to enhance their capabilities to fulfil their obligations under this Agreement,

Recalling that Agenda 21, adopted by the United Nations Conference on Environment and Development, calls upon States to take effective action, consistent with international law, to deter reflagging of vessels by their nationals as a means of avoiding compliance with applicable conservation and management rules for fishing activities on the high seas,

Further recalling that the Declaration of Cancun, adopted by the International Conference on Responsible Fishing, also calls on States to take action in this respect,

Bearing in mind that under Agenda 21, States commit themselves to the conservation and sustainable use of marine living resources on the high seas,

Calling upon States which do not participate in global, regional or subregional fisheries organizations or arrangements to join or, as appropriate, to enter into understandings with such organizations or with parties to such organizations or arrangements with a view to achieving compliance with international conservation and management measures,

Conscious of the duties of every State to exercise effectively its jurisdiction and control over vessels flying its flag, including fishing vessels and vessels engaged in the transhipment of fish,

Mindful that the practice of flagging or reflagging fishing vessels as a means of avoiding compliance with international conservation and management measures for living marine resources, and the failure of flag States to fulfil their responsibilities with respect to fishing vessels entitled to fly their flag, are among the factors that seriously undermine the effectiveness of such measures,

Realizing that the objective of this Agreement can be achieved through specifying flag States' responsibility in respect of fishing vessels entitled to fly their flags and operating on the high seas, including the authorization by the flag State of such operations, as well as through strengthened international cooperation and increased transparency through the exchange of information on high seas fishing,

Noting that this Agreement will form an integral part of the International Code of Conduct for Responsible Fishing called for in the Declaration of Cancun,

Desiring to conclude an international agreement within the framework of the Food and Agriculture Organization of the United Nations, hereinafter referred to as FAO, under Article XIV of the FAO Constitution,

Have agreed as follows:

Article I
Definitions

For the purposes of this Agreement:

(a) 'fishing vessel' means any vessel used or intended for use for the purposes of the commercial exploitation of living marine resources, including mother ships and any other vessels directly engaged in such fishing operations;

(b) 'international conservation and management measures' means measures to conserve or manage one or more species of living marine resources that are adopted and applied in accordance with the relevant rules of international law as reflected in the 1982 United Nations Convention on the Law of the Sea. Such measures may be adopted either by global, regional or subregional fisheries organizations, subject to the rights and obligations of their members, or by treaties or other international agreements;

(c) 'length' means
  (i) for any fishing vessel built after 18 July 1982, 96 per cent of the total length on a waterline at 85 per cent of the least moulded

depth measured from the top of the keel, or the length from the foreside of the stem to the axis of the rudder stock on that waterline, if that be greater. In ships designed with a rake of keel the waterline on which this length is measured shall be parallel to the designed waterline;

    (ii) for any fishing vessel built before 18 July 1982, registered length as entered on the national register or other record of vessels;

  (d) 'record of fishing vessels' means a record of fishing vessels in which are recorded pertinent details of the fishing vessel. It may constitute a separate record for fishing vessels or form part of a general record of vessels;

  (e) 'regional economic integration organization' means a regional economic integration organization to which its member States have transferred competence over matters covered by this Agreement, including the authority to make decisions binding on its member States in respect of those matters;

  (f) 'vessels entitled to fly its flag' and 'vessels entitled to fly the flag of a State', includes vessels entitled to fly the flag of a member State of a regional economic integration organization.

Article II
Application

1. Subject to the following paragraphs of this Article, this Agreement shall apply to all fishing vessels that are used or intended for fishing on the high seas.

2. A Party may exempt fishing vessels of less than 24 metres in length entitled to fly its flag from the application of this Agreement unless the Party determines that such an exemption would undermine the object and purpose of this Agreement, provided that such exemptions:

  (a) shall not be granted in respect of fishing vessels operating in fishing regions referred to in paragraph 3 below, other than fishing vessels that are entitled to fly the flag of a coastal State of that fishing region; and

  (b) shall not apply to the obligations undertaken by a Party under paragraph 1 of Article III, or paragraph 7 of Article VI of this Agreement.

3. Without prejudice to the provisions of paragraph 2 above, in any fishing region where bordering coastal States have not yet declared exclusive economic zones, or equivalent zones of national jurisdiction over fisheries, such coastal States as are Parties to this Agreement may agree, either directly or through appropriate regional fisheries organizations, to establish a minimum length of fishing vessels below which this Agreement shall

not apply in respect of fishing vessels flying the flag of any such coastal State and operating exclusively in such fishing region.

Article III
Flag State Responsibility

1. (a) Each Party shall take such measures as may be necessary to ensure that fishing vessels entitled to fly its flag do not engage in any activity that undermines the effectiveness of international conservation and management measures.

   (b) In the event that a Party has, pursuant to paragraph 2 of Article II, granted an exemption for fishing vessels of less than 24 metres in length entitled to fly its flag from the application of other provisions of this Agreement, such Party shall nevertheless take effective measures in respect of any such fishing vessel that undermines the effectiveness of international conservation and management measures. These measures shall be such as to ensure that the fishing vessel ceases to engage in activities that undermine the effectiveness of the international conservation and management measures.

2. In particular, no Party shall allow any fishing vessel entitled to fly its flag to be used for fishing on the high seas unless it has been authorized to be so used by the appropriate authority or authorities of that Party. A fishing vessel so authorized shall fish in accordance with the conditions of the authorization.

3. No Party shall authorize any fishing vessel entitled to fly its flag to be used for fishing on the high seas unless the Party is satisfied that it is able, taking into account the links that exist between it and the fishing vessel concerned, to exercise effectively its responsibilities under this Agreement in respect of that fishing vessel.

4. Where a fishing vessel that has been authorized to be used for fishing on the high seas by a Party ceases to be entitled to fly the flag of that Party, the authorization to fish on the high seas shall be deemed to have been cancelled.

5. (a) No Party shall authorize any fishing vessel previously registered in the territory of another Party that has undermined the effectiveness of international conservation and management measures to be used for fishing on the high seas, unless it is satisfied that

   (i) any period of suspension by another Party of an authorization for such fishing vessel to be used for fishing on the high seas has expired; and

   (ii) no authorization for such fishing vessel to be used for fishing on the high seas has been withdrawn by another Party within the last three years.

   (b) The provisions of subparagraph (a) above shall also apply in respect of fishing vessels previously registered in the territory of a State which is not a Party to this Agreement, provided that sufficient information is available to the Party concerned on the circumstances in which the authorization to fish was suspended or withdrawn.

(c) The provisions of subparagraph (a) and (b) shall not apply where the ownership of the fishing vessel has subsequently changed, and the new owner has provided sufficient evidence demonstrating that the previous owner or operator has no further legal, beneficial or financial interest in, or control of, the fishing vessel.

(d) Notwithstanding the provisions of subparagraphs (a) and (b) above, a Party may authorize a fishing vessel, to which those subparagraphs would otherwise apply, to be used for fishing on the high seas, where the Party concerned, after having taken into account all relevant facts, including the circumstances in which the fishing authorization has been withdrawn by the other Party or State, has determined that to grant an authorization to use the vessel for fishing on the high seas would not undermine the object and purpose of this Agreement.

6. Each Party shall ensure that all fishing vessels entitled to fly its flag that it has entered in the record maintained under Article IV are marked in such a way that they can be readily identified in accordance with generally accepted standards, such as the FAO Standard Specifications for the Marking and Identification of Fishing Vessels.

7. Each Party shall ensure that each fishing vessel entitled to fly its flag shall provide it with such information on its operations as may be necessary to enable the Party to fulfil its obligations under this Agreement, including in particular information pertaining to the area of its fishing operations and to its catches and landings.

8. Each Party shall take enforcement measures in respect of fishing vessels entitled to fly its flag which act in contravention of the provisions of this Agreement, including, where appropriate, making the contravention of such provisions an offence under national legislation. Sanctions applicable in respect of such contraventions shall be of sufficient gravity as to be effective in securing compliance with the requirements of this Agreement and to deprive offenders of the benefits accruing from their illegal activities. Such sanctions shall, for serious offences, include refusal, suspension or withdrawal of the authorization to fish on the high seas.

Article IV
Records of Fishing Vessels

Each Party shall, for the purposes of this Agreement, maintain a record of fishing vessels entitled to fly its flag and authorized to be used for fishing on the high seas, and shall take such measures as may be necessary to ensure that all such fishing vessels are entered in that record.

Article V
International Cooperation

1. The Parties shall cooperate as appropriate in the implementation of this Agreement, and shall, in particular, exchange information, including evidentiary material, relating to activities of fishing vessels in order to assist the flag State in identifying those fishing vessels flying its flag reported to have engaged in activities undermining international conservation and management measures, so as to fulfil its obligations under Article III.

2. When a fishing vessel is voluntarily in the port of a Party other than its flag State, that Party, where it has reasonable grounds for believing that the fishing vessel has been used for an activity that undermines the effectiveness of international conservation and management measures, shall promptly notify the flag State accordingly. Parties may make arrangements regarding the undertaking by port States of such investigatory measures as may be considered necessary to establish whether the fishing vessel has indeed been used contrary to the provisions of this Agreement.

3. The Parties shall, when and as appropriate, enter into cooperative agreements or arrangements of mutual assistance on a global, regional, subregional or bilateral basis so as to promote the achievement of the objectives of this Agreement.

Article VI
Exchange of Information

1. Each Party shall make readily available to FAO the following information with respect to each fishing vessel entered in the record required to be maintained under Article IV:

   (a) name of fishing vessel, registration number, previous names (if known), and port of registry;
   (b) previous flag (if any);
   (c) International Radio Call Sign (if any);
   (d) name and address of owner or owners;
   (e) where and when built;
   (f) type of vessel;
   (g) length.

2. Each Party shall, to the extent practicable, make available to FAO the following additional information with respect to each fishing vessel entered in the record required to be maintained under Article IV:

   (a) name and address of operator (manager) or operators (managers) (if any);

(b) type of fishing method or methods;
(c) moulded depth;
(d) beam;
(e) gross register tonnage;
(f) power of main engine or engines.

3. Each Party shall promptly notify to FAO any modifications to the information listed in paragraphs 1 and 2 of this Article.

4. FAO shall circulate periodically the information provided under paragraphs 1, 2, and 3 of this Article to all Parties, and, on request, individually to any Party. FAO shall also, subject to any restrictions imposed by the Party concerned regarding the distribution of information, provide such information on request individually to any global, regional or subregional fisheries organization.

5. Each Party shall also promptly inform FAO of—

(a) any additions to the record;
(b) any deletions from the record by reason of—
   (i) the voluntary relinquishment or non-renewal of the fishing authorization by the fishing vessel owner or operator;
   (ii) the withdrawal of the fishing authorization issued in respect of the fishing vessel under paragraph 8 of Article III;
   (iii) the fact that the fishing vessel concerned is no longer entitled to fly its flag;
   (iv) the scrapping, decommissioning or loss of the fishing vessel concerned; or
   (v) any other reason.

6. Where information is given to FAO under paragraph 5(b) above, the Party concerned shall specify which of the reasons listed in that paragraph is applicable.

7. Each Party shall inform FAO of:

(a) any exemption it has granted under paragraph 2 of Article II, the number and type of fishing vessel involved and the geographical areas in which such fishing vessels operate; and
(b) any agreement reached under paragraph 3 of Article II.

8. (a) Each Party shall report promptly to FAO all relevant information regarding any activities of fishing vessels flying its flag that undermine the effectiveness of international conservation and management measures, including the identity of the fishing vessel or vessels involved and measures imposed by the Party in respect of such activities. Reports on measures imposed by a Party may be subject to such limitations as may be required by national legislation with

respect to confidentiality, including, in particular, confidentiality regarding measures that are not yet final.

(b) Each Party, where it has reasonable grounds to believe that a fishing vessel not entitled to fly its flag has engaged in any activity that undermines the effectiveness of international conservation and management measures, shall draw this to the attention of the flag State concerned and may, as appropriate, draw it to the attention of FAO. It shall provide the flag State with full supporting evidence and may provide FAO with a summary of such evidence. FAO shall not circulate such information until such time as the flag State has had an opportunity to comment on the allegation and evidence submitted, or to object as the case may be.

9. Each Party shall inform FAO of any cases where the Party, pursuant to paragraph 5(d) of Article III, has granted an authorization notwithstanding the provisions of paragraph 5(a) or 5(b) of Article III. The information shall include pertinent data permitting the identification of the fishing vessel and the owner or operator and, as appropriate, any other information relevant to the Party's decision.

10. FAO shall circulate promptly the information provided under paragraphs 5, 6, 7, 8 and 9 of this Article to all Parties, and, on request, individually to any Party. FAO shall also, subject to any restrictions imposed by the Party concerned regarding the distribution of information, provide such information promptly on request individually to any global, regional or subregional fisheries organization.

11. The Parties shall exchange information relating to the implementation of this Agreement, including through FAO and other appropriate global, regional and subregional fisheries organizations.

Article VII
Cooperation with Developing Countries

The Parties shall cooperate, at a global, regional, subregional or bilateral level, and, as appropriate, with the support of FAO and other international or regional organizations, to provide assistance, including technical assistance, to Parties that are developing countries in order to assist them in fulfilling their obligations under this Agreement.

Article VIII
Non-parties

1. The Parties shall encourage any State not party to this Agreement to accept this Agreement and shall encourage any non-Party to adopt laws and regulations consistent with the provisions of this Agreement.

2. The Parties shall cooperate in a manner consistent with this Agreement and with international law to the end that fishing vessels entitled to fly the

flags of non-Parties do not engage in activities that undermine the effectiveness of international conservation and management measures.

3. The Parties shall exchange information amongst themselves, either directly or through FAO, with respect to activities of fishing vessels flying the flags of non-Parties that undermine the effectiveness of international conservation and management measures.

Article IX
Settlement of Disputes

1. Any Party may seek consultations with any other Party or Parties on any dispute with regard to the interpretation or application of the provisions of this Agreement with a view to reaching a mutually satisfactory solution as soon as possible.

2. In the event that the dispute is not resolved through these consultations within a reasonable period of time, the Parties in question shall consult among themselves as soon as possible with a view to having the dispute settled by negotiation, inquiry, mediation, conciliation, arbitration, judicial settlement or other peaceful means of their own choice.

3. Any dispute of this character not so resolved shall, with the consent of all Parties to the dispute, be referred for settlement to the International Court of Justice, to the International Tribunal for the Law of the Sea upon entry into force of the 1982 United Nations Convention on the Law of the Sea or to arbitration. In the case of failure to reach agreement on referral to the International Court of Justice, to the International Tribunal for the Law of the Sea or to arbitration, the Parties shall continue to consult and cooperate with a view to reaching settlement of the dispute in accordance with the rules of international law relating to the conservation of living marine resources.

Article X
Acceptance

1. This Agreement shall be open to acceptance by any Member or Associate Member of FAO, and to any non-member State that is a member of the United Nations, or of any of the specialized agencies of the United Nations or of the International Atomic Energy Agency.

2. Acceptance of this Agreement shall be effected by the deposit of an instrument of acceptance with the Director-General of FAO, hereinafter referred to as the Director-General.

3. The Director-General shall inform all Parties, all Members and Associate Members of FAO and the Secretary-General of the United Nations of all instruments of acceptance received.

4. When a regional economic integration organization becomes a Party to this Agreement, such regional economic integration organization shall, in

accordance with the provisions of Article II.7 of the FAO Constitution, as appropriate, notify such modifications or clarifications to its declaration of competence submitted under Article II.5 of the FAO Constitution as may be necessary in light of its acceptance of this Agreement. Any Party to this Agreement may, at any time, request a regional economic integration organization that is a Party to this Agreement to provide information as to which, as between the regional economic integration organization and its Member States, is responsible for the implementation of any particular matter covered by this Agreement. The regional economic integration organization shall provide this information within a reasonable time.

Article XI
Entry into Force

1. This Agreement shall enter into force as from the date of receipt by the Director-General of the twenty-fifth instrument of acceptance.

2. For the purpose of this Article, an instrument deposited by a regional economic integration organization shall not be counted as additional to those deposited by member States of such an organization.

Article XII
Reservations

Acceptance of this Agreement may be made subject to reservations which shall become effective only upon unanimous acceptance by all Parties to this Agreement. The Director-General shall notify forthwith all Parties of any reservation. Parties not having replied within three months from the date of the notification shall be deemed to have accepted the reservation. Failing such acceptance, the State or regional economic integration organization making the reservation shall not become a Party to this Agreement.

Article XIII
Amendments

1. Any proposal by a Party for the amendment of this Agreement shall be communicated to the Director-General.

2. Any proposed amendment of this Agreement received by the Director-General from a Party shall be presented to a regular or special session of the Conference for approval and, if the amendment involves important technical changes or imposes additional obligations on the Parties, it shall be considered by an advisory committee of specialists convened by FAO prior to the Conference.

3. Notice of any proposed amendment of this Agreement shall be transmitted to the Parties by the Director-General not later than the time when the agenda of the session of the Conference at which the matter is to be considered is dispatched.

4. Any such proposed amendment of this Agreement shall require the approval of the Conference and shall come into force as from the thirtieth day after acceptance by two-thirds of the Parties. Amendments involving new obligations for Parties, however, shall come into force in respect of each Party only on acceptance by it and as from the thirtieth day after such acceptance. Any amendment shall be deemed to involve new obligations for Parties unless the Conference, in approving the amendment, decides otherwise by consensus.

5. The instruments of acceptance of amendments involving new obligations shall be deposited with the Director-General, who shall inform all Parties of the receipt of acceptance and the entry into force of amendments.

6. For the purpose of this Article, an instrument deposited by a regional economic integration organization shall not be counted as additional to those deposited by member States of such an organization.

Article XIV
Withdrawal

Any Party may withdraw from this Agreement at any time after the expiry of two years from the date upon which the Agreement entered into force with respect to that Party, by giving written notice of such withdrawal to the Director-General who shall immediately inform all the Parties and the Members and Associate Members of FAO of such withdrawal. Withdrawal shall become effective at the end of the calendar year following that in which the notice of withdrawal has been received by the Director-General.

Article XV
Duties of the Depositary

The Director-General shall be the Depositary of this Agreement. The Depositary shall:

(a) send certified copies of this Agreement to each Member and Associate Member of FAO and to such non-member States as may become party to this Agreement;

(b) arrange for the registration of this Agreement, upon its entry into force, with the Secretariat of the United Nations in accordance with Article 102 of the Charter of the United Nations;

(c) inform each Member and Associate Member of FAO and any non-member States as may become Party to this Agreement of:

   (i) instruments of acceptance deposited in accordance with Article X;

   (ii) the date of entry into force of this Agreement in accordance with Article XI;

(iii) proposals for and the entry into force of amendments to this Agreement in accordance with Article XIII;

(iv) withdrawals from this Agreement pursuant to Article XIV.

Article XVI
Authentic Texts

The Arabic, Chinese, English, French, and Spanish texts of this Agreement are equally authentic.

10. INSTITUTIONS

UN General Assembly Resolution 47/191 (1992): Commission on Sustainable Development

The Commission on Sustainable Development (CSD) was established by the UN in 1992, following the Rio Conference on Environment and Development, as a functional Commission of ECOSOC. Elections to fill fifty-three seats on the Commission were first held in 1993. General Assembly Resolution 47/191 defines its mandate. Its primary role is to monitor, review and consider progress in the *implementation* of international environmental policy and law, as set out in Agenda 21 of the Report of UNCED, and in international conventions. It is also required to promote incorporation of the Rio Declaration on Environment and Development (q.v.) and of the non-legally binding Statement of Principles on Forests in implementing Agenda 21. These perhaps over-ambitious functions differentiate the CSD from UNEP (established by UNGA Resolution 2997 (XXVII) after the 1972 Stockholm Conference on the Human Environment) whose role it is to act as a 'catalytic' and advisory agent in the *development* of international environmental policy and law.

The resolution was adopted without a vote on 22 December 1992. For background material see UN, *Report of the UN Conference on Environment and Development* (1992), UN Doc. A/CONF. 151/26. vols. I–III, especially Ch. 38; *Report of the UN Secretary-General on Institutional Arrangements* (1992), UN Doc. A/47/598 and Add. 1. Reports of the annual proceedings of the Commission on Sustainable Development are published by ECOSOC. The Commission held its first substantive session in New York in June 1993. Its report is published as UN Doc. E/1993/25/Add. 1. Two intersessional *ad hoc* working groups were established, on financial flows and mechanisms, and on technology transfer and co-operation. Its second session was held in May 1994.

TEXT

Institutional arrangements to follow up the United Nations Conference on Environment and Development

The General Assembly,

Welcoming the adoption by the United Nations Conference on Environment and Development of Agenda 21,[1] in particular chapter 38, entitled 'International institutional arrangements', which contains a set of important recommendations on institutional arrangements to follow up the Conference,

Stressing the overall objective of the integration of environment and development issues at the national, subregional, regional and international

---

[1] See *Report of the United Nations Conference on Environment and Development, Rio de Janeiro, 3–14 June 1992* (A/CONF.151/26), vols. I, II and Corr. 1, and III.

levels, including the United Nations system institutional arrangements, and the specific objectives recommended by the Conference in paragraph 38.8 of Agenda 21,

Taking note of the report of the Secretary-General,[1] prepared with the assistance of the Secretary-General of the United Nations Conference on Environment and Development, on institutional arrangements to follow up the Conference, as well as the recommendations and proposals contained therein,

1. *Endorses* the recommendation on international institutional arrangements to follow up the United Nations Conference on Environment and Development as contained in chapter 38 of Agenda 21, particularly those on the establishment of a high-level Commission on Sustainable Development;

Commission on Sustainable Development

2. *Requests* the Economic and Social Council, at its organizational session for 1993, to set up a high-level Commission on Sustainable Development as a functional commission of the Council in accordance with Article 68 of the Charter of the United Nations in order to ensure the effective follow-up of the Conference, as well as to enhance international cooperation and rationalize the intergovernmental decision-making capacity for the integration of environment and development issues and to examine the progress of the implementation of Agenda 21 at the national, regional and international levels, fully guided by the principles of the Rio Declaration on Environment and Development[2] and all other aspects of the Conference, in order to achieve sustainable development in all countries;

3. *Recommends* that the Commission shall have the following functions, as agreed in paragraphs 38.13, 33.13 and 33.21 of Agenda 21:

   (a) To monitor progress in the implementation of Agenda 21 and activities related to the integration of environmental and developmental goals throughout the United Nations system through analysis and evaluation of reports from all relevant organs, organizations, programmes and institutions of the United Nations system dealing with various issues of environment and development, including those related to finance;

   (b) To consider information provided by Governments, including, for example, in the form of periodic communications or national re-

[1] A/47/598 and Add. 1.
[2] See *Report of the United Nations Conference on Environment and Development, Rio de Janeiro, 3–14 June 1992* (A/CONF.151/26), vol. I, chap. I.

ports regarding the activities they undertake to implement Agenda 21, the problems they face, such as problems related to financial resources and technology transfer, and other environment and development issues they find relevant;

(c) To review the progress in the implementation of the commitments contained in Agenda 21, including those related to the provision of financial resources and transfer of technology;

(d) To review and monitor regularly progress towards the United Nations target of 0.7 per cent of the gross national product of developed countries for official development assistance. This review process should systematically combine the monitoring of the implementation of Agenda 21 with the review of financial resources available;

(e) To review on a regular basis the adequacy of funding and mechanisms, including efforts to reach agreed objectives of chapter 33 of Agenda 21, including targets where applicable;

(f) To receive and analyse relevant input from competent non-governmental organizations, including the scientific and the private sector, in the context of the overall implementation of Agenda 21;

(g) To enhance the dialogue, within the framework of the United Nations, with non-governmental organizations and the independent sector, as well as other entities outside the United Nations system;

(h) To consider, where appropriate, information regarding the progress made in the implementation of environmental conventions, which could be made available by the relevant Conferences of Parties;

(i) To provide appropriate recommendations to the General Assembly, through the Economic and Social Council, on the basis of an integrated consideration of the reports and issues related to the implementation of Agenda 21;

(j) To consider, at an appropriate time, the results of the review to be conducted expeditiously by the Secretary-General of all recommendations of the Conference for capacity-building programmes, information networks, task forces and other mechanisms to support the integration of environment and development at regional and subregional levels;

4. *Also recommends* that the Commission shall:

(a) Promote the incorporation of the principles of the Rio Declaration on Environment and Development in the implementation of Agenda 21;

(b) Promote the incorporation of the Non-legally Binding Authoritative Statement of Principles for a Global Consensus on the Management, Conservation and Sustainable Development of All Types of Forests[1] in the implementation of Agenda 21, in particular in the context of the review of the implementation of chapter 11 thereof;

(c) Keep under review the implementation of Agenda 21, recognizing that it is a dynamic programme that could evolve over time, taking into account the agreement to review Agenda 21 in 1997, and make recommendations, as appropriate, on the need for new cooperative arrangements related to sustainable development to the Economic and Social Council and, through it, to the General Assembly;

5. *Decides* that the Commission, in the fulfilment of its functions, will also:

(a) Monitor progress in promoting, facilitating and financing, as appropriate, the access to and the transfer of environmentally sound technologies and corresponding know-how, in particular to developing countries, on favourable terms, including on concessional and preferential terms, as mutually agreed, taking into account the need to protect intellectual property rights as well as the special needs of developing countries for the implementation of Agenda 21;

(b) Consider issues related to the provision of financial resources from all available funding sources and mechanisms, as contained in paragraphs 33.13 to 33.16 of Agenda 21;

6. *Recommends* that the Commission consist of representatives of 53 States elected by the Economic and Social Council from among the Member States of the United Nations and its specialized agencies for three-year terms, with due regard to equitable geographical distribution. The regional allocation of seats could be the same as in the Commission on Science and Technology for Development, as decided in Economic and Social Council decision 1992/222 of 29 May 1992. Representation should be at a high level, including ministerial participation. Other Member States of the United Nations and its specialized agencies, as well as other observers of the United Nations, may participate in the Commission in the capacity of observer, in accordance with established practice;

7. *Also recommends* that the Commission should:

(a) Provide for representatives of various parts of the United Nations system and other intergovernmental organizations, including international financial institutions, the General Agreement on Tariffs and Trade, regional development banks, subregional financial institutions, relevant regional and subregional economic and technical cooperation organizations and regional economic integration organizations, to assist and advise the Commission in the performance of its functions within their respective areas of expertise and mandates, and participate actively in its deliberations; and provide for the European Economic Community, within its areas of competence, to participate—as will be appropriately defined in the rules

---

[1] See *Report of the United Nations Conference on Environment and Development, Rio de Janeiro, 3–14 June 1992* (A/CONF.151/26), vol. III.

of procedure of the Commission on Sustainable Development— fully, without the right to vote;

(b) Provide for non-governmental organizations, including those related to major groups as well as industry and the scientific and business communities, to participate effectively in its work and contribute within their areas of competence to its deliberations;

8. *Requests* the Secretary-General, in the light of paragraph 7 above, to submit, for the consideration of the Economic and Social Council at its organizational session for 1993, his proposals on the rules of procedure of the Commission, including those related to participation of relevant intergovernmental and non-governmental organizations, as recommended by the United Nations Conference on Environment and Development, taking into account the following:

(a) The procedures, while ensuring the intergovernmental nature of the Commission, should allow its members to benefit from the expertise and competence of relevant intergovernmental and nongovernmental organizations;

(b) The procedures should permit relevant intergovernmental organizations inside and outside the United Nations system, including multilateral financial institutions, to appoint special representatives to the Commission;

(c) The rules of procedure of the Economic and Social Council and the rules of procedure of its functional commissions;

(d) The rules of procedure of the United Nations Conference on Environment and Development;

(e) Decisions 1/1[1] and 2/1[2] of the Preparatory Committee for the United Nations Conference on Environment and Development;

(f) Paragraphs 38.11 and 38.44 of Agenda 21;

9. *Recommends* that the Commission on Sustainable Development shall meet once a year for a period of two to three weeks. The first substantive session of the Commission will be held in New York in 1993, without prejudice to the venue of its future sessions;

10. *Requests* the Committee on Conferences to consider the need for readjusting the calendar of meetings in order to take account of the interrelationship between the work of the Commission and the work of other relevant United Nations intergovernmental subsidiary organs, in order to ensure timely reporting to the Economic and Social Council;

11. *Recommends* that in 1993, as a transitional measure, the Commission hold a short organizational session in New York. At that session, the Com-

---

[1] *Official Records of the General Assembly, Forty-fifth Session, Supplement No. 46* (A/45/46), annex I.

[2] Ibid., *Forty-sixth Session, Supplement No. 48* (A/46/48), vol. I, annex I.

mission will elect the Bureau of the Commission, consisting of a chairperson, three vice-chairpersons and a rapporteur, coming from each of the regional groups, decide on the agenda of its first substantive session and consider all other organizational issues as may be necessary. The agenda of the organizational session of the Commission shall be decided on by the Economic and Social Council at its organizational session of 1993;

12. *Also recommends* that the Commission, at its first substantive session, adopt a multi-year thematic programme of its work that will provide a framework to assess progress achieved in the implementation of Agenda 21 and ensure an integrated approach to all of its environment and development components as well as linkages between sectoral and cross-sectoral issues. This programme could be of clusters that would integrate in an effective manner related sectoral and cross-sectoral components of Agenda 21 in such a way as to allow the Commission to review the progress of the implementation of the entire Agenda 21 by 1997. This programme of work could be adjusted, as the need may arise, at the future sessions of the Commission;

13. *Requests* the Secretary-General to submit his proposals for such a programme of work during the organizational session of the Commission;

14. *Recommends* that in order to carry out its functions and implement its work programme effectively the Commission consider organizing its work on the following lines:

(a) Financial resources, mechanisms, transfer of technology, capacity-building and other cross-sectoral issues;

(b) Review of implementation of Agenda 21 at the international level, as well as at the regional and national levels, including the means of implementation, in accordance with paragraph 12 above and the functions of the Commission, taking into account, where appropriate, information regarding the progress in the implementation of relevant environmental conventions;

(c) A high-level meeting, with ministerial participation, to have an integrated overview of the implementation of Agenda 21, to consider emerging policy issues and to provide necessary political impetus to the implementation of decisions of the United Nations Conference on Environment and Development and commitments contained therein.
    Review and consideration of implementation of Agenda 21 should be in an integrated manner;

15. *Requests* the Secretary-General to provide for each session of the Commission, in accordance with the programme of work mentioned in paragraph 12 above and in accordance with its organizational modalities, analytical reports containing information on relevant activities to implement Agenda 21, progress achieved and emerging issues to be addressed;

16. *Also requests* the Secretary-General to prepare, for the first substantive session of the Commission, reports containing information and proposals, as appropriate, on the following issues:

  (a) Initial financial commitments, financial flows and arrangements to give effect to the decisions of the Conference from all available funding sources and mechanisms;

  (b) Progress achieved in facilitating and promoting transfer of environmentally sound technologies, cooperation and capacity-building;

  (c) Progress in the incorporation of recommendations of the United Nations Conference on Environment and Development in the activities of international organizations and measures undertaken by the Administrative Committee on Coordination to ensure that sustainable development principles are incorporated into programmes and processes within the United Nations system;

  (d) Ways in which, upon request, the United Nations system and bilateral donors are assisting countries, particularly developing countries, in the preparation of national reports and national Agenda 21 action plans;

  (e) Urgent and major emerging issues that may be addressed in the course of the high-level meeting;

17. *Decides* that organizational modalities for the Commission should be reviewed in the context of the overall review and appraisal of Agenda 21 during the special session of the General Assembly and adjusted, as may be required, to improve its effectiveness;

Relationship with other United Nations intergovernmental bodies

18. *Recommends* that the Commission, in discharging its functions, submit its consolidated recommendations to the Economic and Social Council and, through it, to the General Assembly, to be considered by the Council and the Assembly in accordance with their respective responsibilities as defined in the Charter of the United Nations and the relevant provisions of paragraphs 38.9 and 38.10 of Agenda 21;

19. *Also recommends* that the Commission actively interact with other intergovernmental United Nations bodies dealing with matters related to environment and development;

20. *Emphasizes* that the ongoing restructuring and revitalization of the United Nations in the economic, social and related fields should take into account the organizational modalities for the Commission on Sustainable Development, with a view to optimizing the work of the Commission and other intergovernmental United Nations bodies dealing with matters related to environment and development;

Coordination within the United Nations system

21. *Requests* all United Nations specialized agencies and related organizations of the United Nations system to strengthen and adjust their activities, programmes and medium-term plans, as appropriate, in line with Agenda 21, in particular regarding projects for promoting sustainable development, in accordance with paragraph 38.28 of Agenda 21, and make their reports on steps they have taken to give effect to this recommendation available to the Commission on Sustainable Development and the Economic and Social Council in 1993 or, at the latest, in 1994, in accordance with Article 64 of the Charter of the United Nations;

22. *Invites* all relevant governing bodies to ensure that the tasks assigned to them are carried out effectively, including the elaboration and publication on a regular basis of reports on the activities of the organs, programmes and organizations for which they are responsible, and that continuous reviews are undertaken of their policies, programmes, budgets and activities;

23. *Invites* the World Bank and other international, regional and subregional financial and development institutions, including the Global Environment Facility, to submit regularly to the Commission on Sustainable Development reports containing information on their experience, activities and plans to implement Agenda 21;

24. *Requests* the Secretary-General to submit to the Commission on Sustainable Development, at its substantive session of 1993, recommendations and proposals for improving coordination of programmes related to development data that exist within the United Nations system, taking into account provisions of paragraph 40.13 of Agenda 21, *inter alia*, regarding 'Development Watch';

[PARAGRAPHS 25–34 OMITTED]

Instrument Establishing the Global Environmental Facility, Geneva, 16 March 1994

The Global Environmental Facility (GEF) was initially established in 1991 as a pilot programme of the World Bank, UNEP, and the UN Development Programme. Following decisions taken at the UN Conference on Environment and Development in 1992 to restructure the GEF in accordance with principles of universality, transparency, and democracy, a new instrument was adopted in March 1994. Its general function is to provide funding to help developing countries meet 'agreed incremental costs' of measures taken pursuant to UNCED Agenda 21 to achieve 'agreed global environmental benefits' with regard to climate change, biological diversity, international waters, and ozone layer depletion. It is also specifically designated for these purposes in the Ozone Layer Climate Change and Biological Diversity Conventions (q.v.). The GEF is thus an important instrument for promoting participation by developing countries in policies and conventions intended to protect the global environment, and for assisting their implementation. Its creation and remit reflect notions of 'common but differentiated responsibility' and 'additionality' in funding allocations which are core elements of the equitable treatment of developing countries in the Rio Declaration and the two Rio Conventions. Its governing body is a Council, and its policies are reviewed by an Assembly. The Council is composed of thirty-two members with a balance of developed and developing states. Decisions require a double majority of 60 per cent of all members plus a majority of 60 per cent (by contribution) of donors.

The 1994 Instrument is *repr.* 33 *ILM* (1994) 1273 with resolutions/decisions of UNEP, UNDP, and the World Bank (not reproduced here). Text of the original GEF is *repr.* 30 *ILM* (1991) 1735. Recommendations of the Rio Conference *repr.* UN, *Report of the UNCED* (June 1992), vol. 1, Ch. 33. See generally E. Helland-Hansen, 'The GEF', 3 *Int. Environmental Aff.* (1991) 137; D. Reed (ed.), *The GEF: Sharing Responsibility for the Biosphere* (Washington D.C., 1993); R. Ricupero, 'Chronicle of a Negotiation: The Financial Chapter of Agenda 21', 4 *Col. JIELP* (1993) 81; P. Sand, *Trusts for the Earth* (Hull, 1994).

TEXT

Preamble

Whereas:

(a) The Global Environment Facility (GEF or the Facility) was established in the International Bank for Reconstruction and Development (IBRD or World Bank) as a pilot programme in order to assist in the protection of the global environment and promote thereby environmentally sound and sustainable economic development, by resolution of the Executive Directors of the World Bank and related interagency arrangements between the United Nations Development Programme (UNDP), the United Nations Environment Programme (UNEP), and the World Bank;

(b) In April 1992, Participants in the GEF agreed that its structure and modalities should be modified. Agenda 21 (the action plan of the 1992 United Nations Conference on Environment and Development), the United Nations Framework Convention on Climate Change and the Convention on Biological Diversity subsequently called for the restructuring of the Facility;

(c) Representatives of the States participating at present in the Facility and of other States wishing to participate in it have requested that the Facility be restructured in order to take account of these developments, to establish the GEF as one of the principal mechanisms for global environment funding, to ensure a governance that is transparent and democratic in nature, to promote universality in its participation and to provide for full cooperation in its implementation among UNDP, UNEP and the World Bank (together referred to hereinafter as the Implementing Agencies), and to benefit from the evaluation of experience with the operation of the Facility since its establishment;

(d) It is necessary to replenish the resources for these purposes under a restructured Facility which includes a new GEF Trust Fund on the basis of this Instrument;

(e) It is desirable to terminate the existing Global Environment Trust Fund (GET) and to transfer any funds, receipts, assets and liabilities held in it upon termination to the new GEF Trust Fund;

(f) The Implementing Agencies have reached a common understanding of principles for cooperation as set forth in the present Instrument, subject to approval of their participation by their respective governing bodies;

It is resolved as follows:

I. Basic Provisions

Restructuring and Purpose of GEF

1. The restructured GEF shall be established in accordance with the present Instrument. This Instrument, having been accepted by representatives of the States participating in the GEF at their meeting in Geneva, Switzerland, from 14 to 16 March 1994, shall be adopted by the Implementing Agencies in accordance with their respective rules and procedural requirements.

2. The GEF shall operate, on the basis of collaboration and partnership among the Implementing Agencies, as a mechanism for international cooperation for the purpose of providing new and additional grant and concessional funding to meet the agreed incremental costs of meas-

ures to achieve agreed global environmental benefits in the following focal areas:

    (a) climate change,
    (b) biological diversity,
    (c) international waters, and
    (d) ozone layer depletion.

3. The agreed incremental costs of activities concerning land degradation, primarily desertification and deforestation, as they relate to the four focal areas shall be eligible for funding. The agreed incremental costs of other relevant activities under Agenda 21 that may be agreed by the Council shall also be eligible for funding insofar as they achieve global environmental benefits by protecting the global environment in the four focal areas.

4. The GEF shall ensure the cost-effectiveness of its activities in addressing the targeted global environmental issues, shall fund programmes and projects which are country-driven and based on national priorities designed to support sustainable development and shall maintain sufficient flexibility to respond to changing circumstances in order to achieve its purposes.

5. The GEF operational policies shall be determined by the Council in accordance with paragraph 20(f) and with respect to GEF-financed projects shall provide for full disclosure of all non-confidential information, and consultation with, and participation as appropriate of, major groups and local communities throughout the project cycle.

6. In partial fulfilment of its purposes, the GEF shall, on an interim basis, operate the financial mechanism for the implementation of the United Nations Framework Convention on Climate Change and shall be, on an interim basis, the institutional structure which carries out the operation of the financial mechanism for the implementation of the Convention on Biological Diversity, in accordance with such cooperative arrangements or agreements as may be made pursuant to paragraphs 27 and 31. The GEF shall be available to continue to serve for the purposes of the financial mechanisms for the implementation of those conventions if it is requested to do so by their Conferences of the Parties. In both respects, the GEF shall function under the guidance of, and be accountable to, the Conferences of the Parties which shall decide on policies, programme priorities and eligibility criteria for the purposes of the conventions. The GEF shall also be available to meet the agreed full costs of activities under Article 12, paragraph 1, of the United Nations Framework Convention on Climate Change.

Participation

7. Any State member of the United Nations or of any of its specialized agencies may become a Participant in the GEF by depositing with the Secretariat an instrument of participation substantially in the form set out

in Annex A. In the case of a State contributing to the GEF Trust Fund, an instrument of commitment shall be deemed to serve as an instrument of participation. Any Participant may withdraw from the GEF by depositing with the Secretariat an instrument of termination of participation substantially in the form set out in Annex A.

Establishment of GEF Trust Fund

8. The new GEF Trust Fund shall be established, and the World Bank shall be invited to serve as the Trustee of the Fund. The GEF Trust Fund shall consist of the contributions received in accordance with the present Instrument, the balance of funds transferred from the GET pursuant to paragraph 32, and any other assets and receipts of the Fund. In serving as the Trustee of the Fund, the World Bank shall serve in a fiduciary and administrative capacity, and shall be bound by its Articles of Agreement, By-Laws, rules and decisions, as specified in Annex B.

Eligibility

9. GEF funding shall be made available for activities within the focal areas defined in paragraphs 2 and 3 of this Instrument in accordance with the following eligibility criteria:

(a) GEF grants that are made available within the framework of the financial mechanisms of the conventions referred to in paragraph 6 shall be in conformity with the eligibility criteria decided by the Conference of the Parties of each convention, as provided under the arrangements or agreements referred to in paragraph 27.

(b) All other GEF grants shall be made available to eligible recipient countries and, where appropriate, for other activities promoting the purposes of the Facility in accordance with this paragraph and any additional eligibility criteria determined by the Council. A country shall be an eligible recipient of GEF grants if it is eligible to borrow from the World Bank (IBRD and/or IDA) or if it is an eligible recipient of UNDP technical assistance through its country Indicative Planning Figure (IPF). GEF grants for activities within a focal area addressed by a convention referred to in paragraph 6 but outside the framework of the financial mechanism of the convention, shall only be made available to eligible recipient countries that are party to the convention concerned.

(c) GEF concessional financing in a form other than grants that is made available within the framework of the financial mechanism of the conventions referred to in paragraph 6 shall be in conformity with eligibility criteria decided by the Conference of the Parties of each convention, as provided under the arrangements or agreements referred to in paragraph 27. GEF concessional financing in a form other than grants may also be made available outside those frameworks on terms to be determined by the Council.

II. Contributions and Other Financial Provisions for Replenishment

10. Contributions to the GEF Trust Fund for the first replenishment period shall be made to the Trustee by Contributing Participants in accordance with the financial provisions for replenishment as specified in Annex C. The Trustee's responsibility for mobilization of resources pursuant to paragraph 20(e) of this Instrument and paragraph 4(a) of Annex B shall be initiated for subsequent replenishments at the request of the Council.

III. Governance and Structure

11. The GEF shall have an Assembly, a Council and a Secretariat. In accordance with paragraph 24, a Scientific and Technical Advisory Panel (STAP) shall provide appropriate advice.

12. The Implementing Agencies shall establish a process for their collaboration in accordance with an interagency agreement to be concluded on the basis of the principles set forth in Annex D.

Assembly

13. The Assembly shall consist of Representatives of all Participants. The Assembly shall meet once every three years. Each Participant may appoint one Representative and one Alternate to the Assembly in such manner as it may determine. Each Representative and each Alternate shall serve until replaced. The Assembly shall elect its Chairperson from among the Representatives.

14. The Assembly shall:

 (a) review the general policies of the Facility;
 (b) review and evaluate the operation of the Facility on the basis of reports submitted by the Council;
 (c) keep under review the membership of the Facility; and
 (d) consider, for approval by consensus, amendments to the present Instrument on the basis of recommendations by the Council.

Council

15. The Council shall be responsible for developing, adopting and evaluating the operational policies and programmes for GEF-financed activities, in conformity with the present Instrument and fully taking into account

reviews carried out by the Assembly. Where the GEF serves for the purposes of the financial mechanisms of the conventions referred to in paragraph 6, the Council shall act in conformity with the policies, programme priorities and eligibility criteria decided by the Conference of the Parties for the purposes of the convention concerned.

16. The Council shall consist of 32 Members, representing constituency groupings formulated and distributed taking into account the need for balanced and equitable representation of all Participants and giving due weight to the funding efforts of all donors. There shall be 16 Members from developing countries, 14 Members from developed countries and 2 Members from the countries of central and eastern Europe and the former Soviet Union, in accordance with Annex E. There shall be an equal number of Alternate Members. The Member and Alternate representing a constituency shall be appointed by the Participants in each constituency. Unless the constituency decides otherwise, each Member of the Council and each Alternate shall serve for three years or until a new Member is appointed by the constituency, whichever comes first. A Member or Alternate may be reappointed by the constituency. Members and Alternates shall serve without compensation. The Alternate Member shall have full power to act for the absent Member.

17. The Council shall meet semi-annually or as frequently as necessary at the seat of the Secretariat to enable it to discharge its responsibilities. Two-thirds of the Members of the Council shall constitute a quorum.

18. At each meeting, the Council shall elect a Chairperson from among its Members for the duration of that meeting. The elected Chairperson shall conduct deliberations of the Council at that meeting on issues related to Council responsibilities listed in paragraphs 20(b), (g), (i), (j) and (k). The position of elected Chairperson shall alternate from one meeting to another between recipient and non-recipient Council Members. The Chief Executive Officer of the Facility (CEO) shall conduct deliberations of the Council on issues related to Council responsibilities listed in paragraphs 20(c), (e), (f) and (h). The elected Chairperson and the CEO shall jointly conduct deliberations of the Council on issues related to paragraph 20(a).

19. Costs of Council meetings, including travel and subsistence of Council Members from developing countries, in particular the Least Developed Countries, shall be disbursed from the administrative budget of the Secretariat as necessary.

20. The Council shall:

(a) keep under review the operation of the Facility with respect to its purposes, scope and objectives;

(b) ensure that GEF policies, programmes, operational strategies and projects are monitored and evaluated on a regular basis;

(c) review and approve the work programme referred to in paragraph

29, monitor and evaluate progress in the implementation of the work programme and provide related guidance to the Secretariat, the Implementing Agencies and the other bodies referred to in paragraph 28, recognizing that the Implementing Agencies will retain responsibility for the further preparation of individual projects approved in the work programme;

(d) arrange for Council Members to receive final project documents and within four weeks transmit to the CEO any concerns they may have prior to the CEO endorsing a project document for final approval by the Implementing Agency;

(e) direct the utilization of GEF funds, review the availability of resources from the GEF Trust Fund and cooperate with the Trustee to mobilize financial resources;

(f) approve and periodically review operational modalities for the Facility, including operational strategies and directives for project selection, means to facilitate arrangements for project preparation and execution by organizations and entities referred to in paragraph 28, additional eligibility and other financing criteria in accordance with paragraphs 9(b) and 9(c) respectively, procedural steps to be included in the project cycle, and the mandate, composition and role of STAP;

(g) act as the focal point for the purpose of relations with the Conferences of the Parties to the conventions referred to in paragraph 6, including consideration, approval and review of the arrangements or agreements with such Conferences, receipt of guidance and recommendations from them and compliance with requirements under these arrangements or agreements for reporting to them;

(h) in accordance with paragraphs 26 and 27, ensure that GEF-financed activities relating to the conventions referred to in paragraph 6 conform with the policies, programme priorities and eligibility criteria decided by the Conference of the Parties for the purposes of the convention concerned;

(i) appoint the CEO in accordance with paragraph 21, oversee the work of the Secretariat, and assign specific tasks and responsibilities to the Secretariat;

(j) review and approve the administrative budget of the GEF and arrange for periodic financial and performance audits of the Secretariat and the Implementing Agencies with regard to activities undertaken for the Facility;

(k) in accordance with paragraph 31, approve an annual report and keep the UN Commission on Sustainable Development apprised of its activities; and

(l) exercise such other operational functions as may be appropriate to fulfil the purposes of the Facility.

Secretariat

21. The GEF Secretariat shall service and report to the Assembly and the Council. The Secretariat, which shall be headed by the CEO/Chairperson of the Facility, shall be supported administratively by the World Bank and shall operate in a functionally independent and effective manner. The CEO shall be appointed to serve for three years on a full time basis by the Council on the joint recommendation of the Implementing Agencies. Such recommendation shall be made after consultation with the Council. The CEO may be reappointed by the Council. The CEO may be removed by the Council only for cause. The staff of the Secretariat shall include staff members seconded from the Implementing Agencies as well as individuals hired competitively on an as needed basis by one of the Implementing Agencies. The CEO shall be responsible for the organization, appointment and dismissal of Secretariat staff. The CEO shall be accountable for the performance of the Secretariat functions to the Council. The Secretariat shall, on behalf of the Council, exercise the following functions:

(a) implement effectively the decisions of the Assembly and the Council;

(b) coordinate the formulation and oversee the implementation of programme activities pursuant to the joint work programme, ensuring liaison with other bodies as required, particularly in the context of the cooperative arrangements or agreements referred to in paragraph 27;

(c) in consultation with the Implementing Agencies, ensure the implementation of the operational policies adopted by the Council through the preparation of common guidelines on the project cycle. Such guidelines shall address project identification and development, including the proper and adequate review of project and work programme proposals, consultation with and participation of local communities and other interested parties, monitoring of project implementation and evaluation of project results;

(d) review and report to the Council on the adequacy of arrangements made by the Implementing Agencies in accordance with the guidelines referred to in paragraph (c) above, and if warranted, recommend to the Council and the Implementing Agencies additional arrangements for project preparation and execution under paragraphs 20(f) and 28;

(e) chair interagency group meetings to ensure the effective execution of the Council's decisions and to facilitate coordination and collaboration among the Implementing Agencies;

(f) coordinate with the Secretariats of other relevant international bodies, in particular the Secretariats of the conventions referred to in paragraph 6 and the Secretariats of the Montreal Protocol on Substances that Deplete the Ozone Layer and its Multilateral Fund;

(g) report to the Assembly, the Council and other institutions as directed by the Council;

(h) provide the Trustee with all relevant information to enable it to carry out its responsibilities; and

(i) perform any other functions assigned to the Secretariat by the Council.

Implementing Agencies

22. The Implementing Agencies of the GEF shall be UNDP, UNEP, and the World Bank. The Implementing Agencies shall be accountable to the Council for their GEF-financed activities, including the preparation and cost-effectiveness of GEF projects, and for the implementation of the operational policies, strategies and decisions of the Council within their respective areas of competence and in accordance with an interagency agreement to be concluded on the basis of the principles of cooperation set forth in Annex D to the present Instrument. The Implementing Agencies shall cooperate with the Participants, the Secretariat, parties receiving assistance under the GEF, and other interested parties, including local communities and non-governmental organizations, to promote the purposes of the Facility.

23. The CEO shall periodically convene meetings with the heads of the Implementing Agencies to promote interagency collaboration and communication, and to review operational policy issues regarding the implementation of GEF-financed activities. The CEO shall transmit their conclusions and recommendations to the Council for its consideration.

Scientific and Technical Advisory Panel (STAP)

24. UNEP shall establish, in consultation with UNDP and the World Bank and on the basis of guidelines and criteria established by the Council, the Scientific and Technical Advisory Panel (STAP) as an advisory body to the Facility. UNEP shall provide the STAP's Secretariat and shall operate as the liaison between the Facility and the STAP.

IV. Principles of Decision-making

25. (a) Procedure

The Assembly and the Council shall each adopt by consensus regulations as may be necessary or appropriate to perform their respective functions transparently; in particular, they shall determine any aspect of their respective procedures, including the admission of observers and, in the case of the Council, provision for executive sessions.

(b) Consensus

Decisions of the Assembly and the Council shall be taken by consensus. In the case of the Council if, in the consideration of any matter of substance, all practicable efforts by the Council and its Chairperson have been made and no consensus appears attainable, any member of the Council may require a formal vote.

(c) Formal Vote

(i) Unless otherwise provided in this Instrument, decisions requiring a formal vote by the Council shall be taken by a double weighted majority, that is, an affirmative vote representing both a 60 per cent majority of the total number of Participants and a 60 per cent majority of the total contributions.

(ii) Each Member of the Council shall cast the votes of the Participant or Participants he/she represents. A Member of the Council appointed by a group of Participants may cast separately the votes of each Participant in the constituency he/she represents.

(iii) For the purpose of voting power, total contributions shall consist of the actual cumulative contributions made to the GEF Trust Fund as specified in Annex C (Attachment 1) and in subsequent replenishments of the GEF Trust Fund, contributions made to the GET, and the grant equivalent of co-financing and parallel financing made under the GEF pilot programme, or agreed with the Trustee, until the effective date of the GEF Trust Fund. Until the effective date of the GEF Trust Fund, advance contributions made under paragraph 7(c) of Annex C shall be deemed to be contributions to the GET.

V. Relationship and Cooperation with Conventions

26. The Council shall ensure the effective operation of the GEF as a source of funding activities under the conventions referred to in paragraph 6. The use of the GEF resources for purposes of such conventions shall be in conformity with the policies, programme priorities and eligibility criteria decided by the Conference of the Parties of each of those conventions.

27. The Council shall consider and approve cooperative arrangements or agreements with the Conferences of the Parties to the conventions referred to in paragraph 6, including reciprocal arrangements for representation in meetings. Such arrangements or agreements shall be in conformity with the relevant provisions of the convention concerned regarding its financial mechanism and shall include procedures for determining jointly the aggregate GEF funding requirements for the purpose of the convention. With regard to each convention referred to in paragraph 6, until the first meeting of its Conference of the Parties, the Council shall consult the convention's interim body.

VI. Cooperation with Other Bodies

28. The Secretariat and the Implementing Agencies under the guidance of the Council shall cooperate with other international organizations to promote achievement of the purposes of the GEF. The Implementing Agencies may make arrangements for GEF project preparation and execution by multilateral development banks, specialized agencies and programmes of the United Nations, other international organizations, bilateral development agencies, national institutions, non-governmental organizations, private sector entities and academic institutions, taking into account their comparative advantages in efficient and cost-effective project execution. Such arrangements shall be made in accordance with national priorities. Pursuant to paragraph 20(f), the Council may request the Secretariat to make similar arrangements in accordance with national priorities. In the event of disagreements among the Implementing Agencies or between an Implementing Agency and any entity concerning project preparation or execution, an Implementing Agency or any entity referred to in this paragraph may request the Secretariat to seek to resolve such disagreements.

VII. Operational Modalities

29. The Secretariat shall coordinate the preparation of and determine the content of a joint work programme for the GEF among the Implementing Agencies, including an indication of the financial resources required for the programme, for approval by the Council. The work programme shall be prepared in accordance with paragraph 4 and in cooperation with eligible recipients and any executing agency referred to in paragraph 28.

30. GEF projects shall be subject to endorsement by the CEO before final project approval. If at least four Council Members request that a project be reviewed at a Council meeting because in their view the project is not consistent with the Instrument or GEF policies and procedures, the CEO shall submit the project document to the next Council meeting, and shall only endorse the project for final approval by the Implementing Agency if the Council finds that the project is consistent with the Instrument and GEF policies and procedures.

VIII. Reporting

31. The Council shall approve an annual report on the activities of the GEF. The report shall be prepared by the Secretariat and circulated to all Participants. It shall contain information on the activities carried out under the GEF, including a list of project ideas submitted for consideration and a

review of the project activities funded by the Facility and their outcomes. The report shall contain all the information necessary to meet the principles of accountability and transparency that shall characterize the Facility as well as the requirements arising from the reporting arrangements agreed with each Conference of the Parties to the conventions referred to in paragraph 6. The report shall be conveyed to each of these Conferences of the Parties, the United Nations Commission on Sustainable Development and any other international organization deemed appropriate by the Council.

IX. Transitional and Final Provisions

Termination of the GET

32. The World Bank shall be invited to terminate the existing Global Environment Trust Fund (GET) on the effective date of the establishment of the new GEF Trust Fund, and any funds, receipts, assets and liabilities held in the GET upon termination, including the administration of any co-financing by the Trustee in accordance with the provisions of Resolution No. 91–5 of the Executive Directors of the World Bank, shall be transferred to the new GEF Trust Fund. Pending the termination of the GET under this provision, projects financed from the GET resources shall continue to be processed and approved subject to the rules and procedures applicable to the GET.

Interim Period

33. The Council may, pursuant to the provisions of this Instrument, be convened during the period from the adoption of this Instrument and its annexes by the Implementing Agencies until the effective date of the establishment of the new GEF Trust Fund (a) to appoint, by consensus, the CEO in order to enable him/her to assume the work of the Secretariat, and (b) to prepare the Council's rules of procedure and the operational modalities for the Facility. The first meeting of the Council shall be organized by the secretariat of the GEF pilot programme. Administrative expenses during this interim period shall be covered by the existing GET.

Amendment and Termination

34. Amendment or termination of the present Instrument may be approved by consensus by the Assembly upon the recommendation of the Council, after taking into account the views of the Implementing Agencies and the Trustee, and shall become effective after adoption by the Implementing Agencies and the Trustee in accordance with their respective rules and procedural requirements. This paragraph shall apply to the

amendment of any annex to this Instrument unless the annex concerned provides otherwise.

35. The Trustee may at any time terminate its role as trustee in accordance with paragraph 14 of Annex B, and an Implementing Agency may at any time terminate its role as implementing agency, after consultation with the other Implementing Agencies and after giving the Council six months' notice in writing.

[ANNEXES A–D OMITTED]

Annex E

Constituencies of the GEF Council

1. GEF Participants shall be grouped in 32 constituencies, with 18 constituencies composed of recipient countries (referred to as 'recipient constituencies'), and 14 constituencies composed principally of non-recipient countries (referred to as 'non-recipient constituencies').

2. The 18 recipient constituencies shall be distributed among the following geographic regions, bearing in mind the possibility of mixed constituencies:

Africa	6
Asia and Pacific	6
Latin America and Caribbean	4
Central, Eastern Europe and Former Soviet Union	2

3. For each geographic region referred to in paragraph 2, recipient constituencies shall be formed through a process of consultation among the GEF recipient country Participants in the region in accordance with their own criteria. It is expected that in this consultation process a number of criteria will be taken into account, including:

(a) Equitable and balanced representation from within the geographic region;
(b) Commonality of global, regional and subregional environmental concerns;
(c) Policies and efforts towards sustainable development;
(d) Natural resource endowment and environmental vulnerability;
(e) Contributions to the GEF as defined in paragraph 25(c)(iii) of the Instrument; and
(f) All other relevant and environment-related factors.

4. The non-recipient constituencies shall be formed through a process of consultation among interested Participants. It is expected that grouping of non-recipient countries will be primarily guided by total contributions as defined in paragraph 25(c)(iii) of the Instrument.

5. Consultations to form the constituencies shall take place following the acceptance of the Instrument by representatives of the States participating in the GEF. The GEF Secretariat will provide assistance to facilitate these consultations at the regional level. The Secretariat shall be informed of the initial composition of each constituency no later than 15 May 1994.

6. The grouping of constituencies as communicated to the Secretariat, including any adjustments pursuant to paragraph 8 of this Annex, shall be subject to confirmation by the Council after the effective date of the establishment of the GEF Trust Fund, taking into account the instruments deposited in accordance with Annex A to the Instrument.

7. The Participant or Participants in each constituency shall appoint a Member and an Alternate to represent the constituency in the Council. The names and addresses of the Members and Alternates for each constituency shall be communicated to the Secretariat no later than two weeks prior to the first meeting of the Council pursuant to paragraph 33 of the Instrument, and shall be subject to confirmation by the Participant or Participants in each constituency upon the confirmation of the constituencies by the Council under paragraph 6 above.

8. Any State that becomes a Participant in accordance with paragraph 7 of the Instrument after the formation of constituencies pursuant to paragraphs 3 to 6 above shall, after consultation with the Participants in the constituency concerned, notify the Secretariat as regards the constituency in which it wishes to be grouped and shall be grouped in that constituency subject to agreement by the Participants in the constituency and subsequent confirmation by the Council at its next meeting.

9. Each Council Member or Alternate shall represent the Participant or Participants in the constituency by which that Member or Alternate was appointed, subject to any adjustments pursuant to paragraph 8 above, and any termination of participation in accordance with paragraph 7 of the Instrument.

10. If the office of a Council Member or Alternate becomes vacant before the expiration of the term of office of the Member or Alternate, the Participant or Participants in the constituency concerned shall appoint a new Member or Alternate, whose name and address shall be communicated to the Secretariat no later than two weeks prior to the next meeting of the Council.

11. In accordance with paragraph 25(a) of the Instrument, the Council may adopt procedures to give effect to the provisions of this Annex.

11. SELECT BIBLIOGRAPHY

For those interested in further research the following compendia provide more extensive collections of treaties and other instruments:

BURHENNE, W. (ed.), *International Environmental Law: Multilateral Treaties*, FUST Projekt No. 51, IUCN Law Centre (looseleaf) (Berlin, 1994).

GURUSWAMY, L.D., PALMER, SIR. G. W. R., and WESTON, B. H., *Supplement of Basic Documents to International Environmental Law and World Order* (St. Paul, Minn., 1994).

HOHMANN, H. (ed.), *Basic Documents of International Environmental Law,* 3 vols. (London, 1992).

MARINE MAMMAL COMMISSION, *Compendium of Selected Treaties, International Agreements, and other Relevant Documents on Marine Resources, Wildlife, and the Environment,* 3 vols. (Washington, 1994).

RUSTER, B., and SIMMA, B., *International Protection of the Environment: Treaties and Related Documents,* 30 vols. (New York, 1982) with looseleaf continuation volumes (New York, 1990–).

UNEP, *Selected Multilateral Treaties in the Field of the Environment,* Vol. 1 (ed. A. C. Kiss) (Nairobi, 1983) and Vol. 2 (eds. I. Rummel-Bulska and S. Osafo) (Cambridge, 1991).

INDEX